ASAHEL NETTLETON: REVIVAL PREACHER

A BIOGRAPHY

BY

E. A. JOHNSTON

REVIVAL LITERATURE
PO BOX 6068
ASHEVILLE, NC 28816
828–681–0370
WWW.REVIVALLIT.ORG

First published 2012 by Revival Literature, www.revivallit.org

ISBN: 978-1-56632-154-9

Typeset in Bembo Standard 11 on 13 point by Quinta Press, www.quintapress.com

Printed in the United States of America

DEDICATION

With warm esteem the following chapters on the life and ministry of
Asahel Nettleton are dedicated to
Dr. J. I. Packer
Pauline in theology,
Whitefieldian in unity,
Christ-like in manner.

COMMENDATIONS

The momentous ministry of the Edwardsean evangelist Asahel Nettleton, a key figure in the Second Great Awakening, has been effectively forgotten during the past century and a half of less-than-Reformed revivalism. Dr. Johnston's masterful and thorough biography is a long-overdue tribute to this outstanding servant of God, and is priority reading for all who care about evangelism today.

J. I. PACKER

All Christians who long for revival and relish the study of it should feel greatly indebted to Dr. Johnston for his painstaking labor of love in amassing the most thorough biography ever written on Asahel Nettleton, whose ministry God greatly owned during the Second Great Awakening. This book's sections on revivals and Nettleton's personal letters are themselves more than worth its price. Oh, that the Spirit of God would stir us up in prayer for revival and would again thrust forth into the white, ready harvest men of such preachers who burn with passion for the salvation of the hell-bound!

JOEL R. BEEKE
President of Puritan Reformed Theological Seminary, Grand Rapids, Michigan

The current situation facing 21st century American evangelicals more closely resembles the situation in the Second Great Awakening than many realize. We are not in revival (oh that the Lord would grant us revival!). But evangelicals in general more closely resemble the doctrines and methods of Charles Finney than those of the more biblical Asahel Nettleton. We cannot guarantee a revival, but we should work for reformation along the lines of Nettleton. May the Lord bless this worthy study to many who cry for revival, so we may learn from the truths of the past and not repeat the errors of the past.

CURT DANIEL, PH.D.
Pastor, Faith Bible Church, Springfield, Il.

Asahel Nettleton lived in a time of transition between the old order of evangelism of the Puritans and Jonathan Edwards and the new evangelism and theology of Charles Finney and Nathaniel Taylor. Nettleton was a stalwart, standing firm in the line of Edwards and the Puritans, and against the New Measures introduced by Finney, warning of the consequences of adopting those New Measures. His warnings sadly went unheeded and we have reaped the consequences—a whirlwind of corrupt theology and false converts.

This biography brings to light anew the God-centered evangelism and methodology of Asahel Nettleton and details the decline of American theology which had already begun at the height of Nettleton's ministry. I highly recommend this new biography of Asahel Nettleton to all who desire to recapture the spirit and message of true biblical evangelism.

WILLIAM C. NICHOLS
International Outreach, Inc.

The life of the 19th century preacher, Asahel Nettleton, has never been appreciated or even known as it ought to have been. As Dr. E. A. Johnston has rightly said, "Nettleton is one of the most neglected figures in church history." There have really been only two works written about his life and ministry, the first being the 1844 *Memoir of the Life and Character of Asahel Nettleton,* by Bennet Tyler, and then a later biography, published in 1977, entitled *God Sent Revival* by John Thornbury. Other than these two published biographies, there remain only unpublished doctoral dissertations written on Nettleton.

As a result, the church in the 20th and 21st centuries has missed out on benefiting from this eminent servant of Christ, who labored as an evangelist, indeed, a true revivalist, in the eastern United States during the 19th century. It is, therefore, a special blessing for the church of Christ to once again have Nettleton's life brought before them in this new definitive biography, so well researched and written by Dr. E. A. Johnston.

Dr. Johnston has already written a number of books, including the authorized biography of J. Sidlow Baxter and a definitive two-volume biography on George Whitefield, the great British evangelist of the 18th century. But this large biography may well be his most important of all, from the standpoint of its bearing on the important ecclesiastical and doctrinal issues of the evangelical church today.

Dr. Johnston has made the evangelical church a debtor to him in providing a fresh and thorough look at the personal life, ministry, preaching, and theology of Nettleton, who was the leading evangelical itinerant evangelist in America during the years of the Second Great Awakening in the early 1800s. As a contemporary of Charles G. Finney, who was instrumental in bringing permanent damage upon American evangelicalism though his bad theology and humanistic methodology, Nettleton was the leading opponent of Finney's errors in his day. This volumes will give fresh and clear understanding to the Second Great Awakening and its issues at a time when both Nettleton and Finney preached for so many years.

Every pastor, preacher, evangelist, missionary, as well as anyone truly interested in revival and church history ought to read these two volumes closely. The issues clarified here are of the utmost importance for our present day need within American evangelicalism. Reading Nettleton's life from this newly researched and accurate perspective will be most beneficial.

MACK TOMLINSON
Elder and Itinerant Minister, Providence Baptist Chapel, Denton, Texas

George Whitefield we know, but who is Asahel Nettleton (1783–1844), the man with the unusual Bible name (Asahel meaning "made by God")? Read this new biography and you will discover that he was an outstanding American evangelist greatly used in revival. All burdened for revival in our time can learn from this God-made man—his personality, his preaching, and, above all, his passion for God. Nettleton's story will instruct, inspire and indeed impact you to be a servant of God, on fire for your Master's cause.

TED S. RENDALL
Minister & Lecturer, Olford Center for Biblical Preaching
Chancellor Emeritus of Prairie Bible Institute

Once again, author, biographer, Dr. E. A. Johnston, has given the Church a gift to be treasured. His scholarly work on the life and ministry of Asahel Nettleton is a must read for all who have an interest in the historical accounts of God's sovereign work in revival and the human instruments He used. I read the manuscript from a pastoral perspective and I was profoundly moved by the method and manner of Asahel Nettleton's ministry. Two specific areas of Nettleton's ministry especially captured my attention. First, unlike George Whitefield, who preached to thousands in the open air and who enjoyed great notoriety, Nettleton preached in the rural churches and only at the invitation of a pastor or of the church if there was no pastor. He saw himself as the pastor's assistant and worked with him, never against him. Secondly, Nettleton believed that revival was a sovereign act of God. He avoided emotionalism and focused on preaching sound biblical doctrine. His confidence was in the word of God and the Spirit of God. Yet, as you will see, Asahel Nettleton was one of God's key instruments during the Second Great Awakening.

My stroll through the pages of *Asahel Nettleton: Revival Preacher* gave me renewed appreciation for a man whom God used mightily in the Second Great Awakening. Nettleton was humble in his service to God, serious about the things of God, unwavering in his belief in the absolute sovereignty of God and devoted to the word of God. Herein is a much-needed message to the 21st century church.

DR. ROGER D. WILLMORE
Past President, Alabama Baptist State Convention

Dr. Johnston has produced a biography in which he embeds large elements of primary sources and pertinent secondary sources immediately within the text. This gives a haunting "You Were There" atmosphere to the text and heightens the importance of the theological underpinnings to revival that made Asahel Nettleton one of the bright gifts to the American church.

DR. THOMAS J. NETTLES
Professor of Historical Theology, Southern Baptist Theological Seminary Louisville, Kentucky

CONTENTS

INTRODUCTION

In the library of Hartford Seminary in Hartford, Connecticut hangs an oil portrait of a man forgotten by historians, his present obscurity standing in stark contrast to the times in which he lived. In nineteenth century America the name Asahel Nettleton, was a household word. In fact, a study of historical documents of 1810–1844 (the years of his public ministry) will reveal that Asahel Nettleton was the leading figure of the revival of religion known as The Second Great Awakening. He was friends with the leading religious figures of his day and he was one of the original founders of what is now Hartford Seminary; yet today he is practically unknown. Looking at his oil portrait one can see the haggard look in his blue eyes, a result of typhus fever and a life spent at full stretch for his Lord. In his day the name Asahel Nettleton, literally made strong men tremble at the news of his arrival in New England towns, for they knew that soon a revival of religion would occur and many would be face to face with their eternity and the God of that eternity. It was said of Nettleton, "that he knew human nature so thoroughly he could read a man's heart". He was the leading human instrument of God in over fifty revivals during the period known as The Second Great Awakening and his biographer Bennet Tyler stated that he was the means of bringing 30,000 souls into God's kingdom. His grave lies in a remote cemetery in East Windsor, Connecticut. The inscription on the brown mossy tombstone simply reads, "Rev. Asahel Nettleton D.D. Died May 16. 1844", yet he is among God's choicest servants.

A study of the life and ministry of the nineteenth century evangelist, Asahel Nettleton, is vastly important if we are to comprehend the reasons and circumstances of *why* the majority of our churches, in not only America but the world, hold to the theological views they have and conduct evangelism in the way they do. The preponderance of evangelism that is conducted today can trace its roots directly back to the "New Measures" movement of the nineteenth century and the personages of Charles Grandison Finney and Nathaniel William Taylor.

Concerning theology and the preaching of the Gospel, what is considered by the majority of the church today to be "orthodoxy" was considered by the orthodox New England ministers of the early nineteenth century to be "heresy" in their day. Why the grand shift in theological views? Did society play a part? Who were the primary religious leaders of America in the nineteenth century? What roles did they play in this giant theological seismic shift in American theology? These questions will be answered in this new biography on Asahel Nettleton.

Part of the reason why the name Asahel Nettleton is so obscure is that there has been scant biographical material published on his life. The first published memoir of his life was done by his good friend and colleague, Bennet Tyler, this work, *Memoir of the Life and Character of Asahel Nettleton* first appeared shortly after Nettleton's death in 1844. The second published biography of his life was a British edition of Tyler's work that was edited by the Scotsman Andrew Bonar (1854) and this book was identical to Tyler's except for some minor editorial changes by Bonar so not to offend British readers. It would be a century later, in 1977, that the only other published biography on Nettleton appeared—this was *God Sent Revival* by J. F. Thornbury. Also, two scholarly dissertations on Nettleton remain unpublished. These are: *Life and Letters of Asahel Nettleton, 1783–1844* by George Hugh Birney, Jr., 1943, Hartford Theological Seminary; and the more thorough *Asahel Nettleton: Nineteenth Century American Revivalist,* by Sherry Pierpont May, 1969, Drew University. The lack of existing material on Nettleton accounts for his relative obscurity today. Yet he is a man whose life needs to be studied! Especially if we are to impact our generation for Christ today.

No other man in history was so mightily used of God in revival as Asahel Nettleton. He labored amidst more revivals of religion than Jonathan Edwards and George Whitefield! One can learn much about how God moves in revival by studying Nettleton's life, therefore this book will be a useful tool for any serious student of revival. Secondly, the role that Nettleton played as a defender of the faith against the "New Measures" and the "New Haven Theology" reveals how theology in America shifted from its Puritan roots of Calvinism to a more Federalized man-centered theology. The roots of this Pelagian theology stemmed from Yale College, and specifically the teachings of N. W. Taylor, professor of theology at Yale. Asahel Nettleton fought almost the same battle as C. H. Spurgeon; Spurgeon had his "Downgrade

Controversy" which took a very real toll on his health and life; Nettleton fought "Taylorism" with its complete overhaul of New England Calvinism and this battle took a severe toll on Nettleton's health and quickened his early demise. One cannot study Nettleton without studying the central characters of importance in his day: Lyman Beecher, N. W. Taylor, and Charles G. Finney, each played a large role in the life of Nettleton. One must also get to the bottom of the so-called "New England Theology" as it doctrinally trickled down from Jonathan Edwards to Joseph Bellamy, to Samuel Hopkins, to Timothy Dwight, and to Jonathan Edwards, Jr. to N. W. Taylor and ending with Edwards Parks—the last of the so-called "New England Theologians". Without this understanding one is left wandering in the dark. Therefore, clarity and light has to be brought to our understanding of the theology of New England in the nineteenth century if we are to make any headway in comprehending where we stand today and how we arrived there—and amidst all this stood large the figure of Asahel Nettleton.

Nettleton wasn't perfect and he certainly had his flaws (which are discussed in a later chapter), however, few men in the history of the Church have been so magnificently used in times of revival! Even George Whitefield in his day never labored so long and so frequently amidst true revivals of religion as Asahel Nettleton. Yes, Whitefield reached more thousands than Nettleton, yet each man was the primary revival instrument in his time. A biography on an obscure figure as Asahel Nettleton will never reach the "bestseller list" but it is a book that needed to be written and published because we need to study men like Nettleton if we are to expect a God-sent revival in our day. For a study of his life is a textbook *on* revival. We place Asahel Nettleton on the same level as Jonathan Edwards in regard to *understanding* the true nature of revival; in fact, Nettleton had more experience laboring in revival than Edwards and much can be learned from him on this important subject.

Historical documents are an integral part of this work, the scarcity of Nettletonian material and the few biographical resources, demands that many of the historical materials presented will be provided in their *entirety*. These documents will be a rich and rewarding source of information for future Nettleton scholars. Two of these rare documents, *The Revival of 1820,* and *The New Measures Letters of Beecher and Nettleton* provide rich resources in themselves.

Asahel Nettleton neared the end of his life an invalid and in acute physical pain, his final words (heard by his good friend and biographer, Bennet Tyler) were reported to be: "While ye have the light, walk in the light;" in order to accomplish this, "cling to the cross of Christ." There are few men in the history of the Church who lie among the "mighty dead" as the great evangelist, Asahel Nettleton. To study his labors is to be amazed! It is my prayer that the reading of, *Asahel Nettleton: Revival Preacher*, will encourage you to do great things for God and that his life will inspire you to keep eternity and the judgment seat of Christ ever before you as you labor for Him who is worthy! All glory to His holy name!

E. A. JOHNSTON, PH.D., D.B.S.
Fellow of the Stephen Olford Center for Biblical Preaching

ACKNOWLEDGMENTS

Foremost, I must acknowledge the greatest help I received in performing this labor, for it was God who enabled me, equipped me, and assisted me to research and write the life and labors of His eminent servant, Asahel Nettleton. To God be all the glory forever and ever!

I want to express gratitude to my wife Carla and daughter Carly, for their acceptance of my many absences from them while researching and writing this lengthy work on Nettleton.

The germination of this project came from my dear friend, Richard Owen Roberts; it was his suggestion to me that a thorough and up-to-date work on Asahel Nettleton needed to be performed. His encouragement and support throughout this undertaking enabled me to persist in unraveling the multi-layered aspects of Nettleton and the Second Great Awakening.

I wish to express gratitude to Dr. Digby James of Quinta Press for his help in research, and talent in typesetting and faithful friendship although an ocean separates us. Also to Mrs Trudy Kinloch for her very thorough editing and proof-reading skills.

I wish to thank James Packer for his warm friendship and particularly his help with the complexities of the "New England Theology" and being a source of encouragement to me.

I am thankful to Iain Murray for his encouragement, friendship, and warm-hearted advice, as well as for the reliance I had upon his already thorough research from his book, *Revival and Revivalism*.

I am grateful to David Ford for his friendship and help in conducting research, particularly traveling to Hartford, Connecticut with me to labor over the "Nettleton Papers" at Hartford Seminary. Some of our greatest brainstorms for visiting "Nettleton sites" arose at Duncan Donut locations throughout New England!

I want to express thanks to Dr. John Thornbury for his friendship and wise Foreword. Also for all the pioneer work he performed on Nettleton some forty years ago with his wonderful biography, *God Sent Revival*. Without his book this one would be deficient.

I am grateful to Hartford Seminary in Hartford, Connecticut. Their warm hospitality and open access to the Nettleton Collection made this trip a pleasure rather than a task. I want to thank particularly Dr. Steven Blackburn, the Director of the Library for his friendship and aid in conducting archival research—he literally gave us free rein in the library and his help is greatly appreciated! Also gratitude is given to his Administrative Assistant, Marie Rovero, for her assistance and self-sacrificing help in conducting this research.

I wish to express gratitude to Ellen Fladger, Archivist/Head of Special Collections at Union College in Schenectady, New York, for her help in locating the Dr. McCauley house for us. I am grateful for her gift to me of the *Encyclopedia of Union College History*.

FOREWORD TO
ASAHEL NETTLETON: REVIVAL PREACHER

BY JOHN F. THORNBURY

A New England preacher mightily used of God and celebrated in his day as a great evangelist is, like the fabled phoenix, rising from the ashes in which for a variety of reasons a kind of cruel historical obscurity had buried him. I am glad that I have had a part of reviving interest in Asahel Nettleton through my book *God Sent Revival*, now in its second edition. All over the world, especially here in the United States where he labored so successfully, scholars, pastors, and lay people simply interested in the history of American revivalism are reading about Nettleton's life, studying his sermons and pondering what he did for the glory of God.

E. A. Johnston's book is a much more thorough study of this remarkable ministry, delving much deeper into the historical context of Nettleton's part in the Second Great Awakening and seeking not only to understand his genius as a herald of the gospel but also to explore the dynamics of his theology and the causes and consequences of the doctrinal disputes in which he was engaged. This is a much needed sequel to my book, which admittedly is only an introductory work designed to introduce Mr. Nettleton to modern Christians.

I will never forget visiting a few years ago the Billy Graham Center in Wheaton, Illinois and walking through the fascinating "History of American Evangelism" which, not surprisingly climaxed in the crusade ministries of Graham. There, early in the display was a cutout of Nettleton, acknowledged by the trustees of the Graham Center to be one of the pioneer evangelists of America. Not surprisingly the career of Charles Finney was alongside of Nettleton. Many, however, do not know that they, though contemporaries, differed drastically in not only evangelistic methodology but even in the very content of the gospel.

Nettleton was known, contrary to the vast majority of evangelists in the history of our Republic as a convinced Calvinist, an opponent of the "New Measures" which were sweeping the country in the twilight of his career, and a preacher whose approach to leading souls to Christ was vastly different than what is usually associated with mass evangelism. He did not give what is known as an "altar call", indeed he opposed the practice. And yet thousands were broken up with conviction under his preaching and turned to Christ. He was not part of anything like "area wide" types of crusades and confined his preaching to local churches, yet multitudes packed the meeting houses where he held forth.

And so given the fact that Asahel Nettleton's methods were so very, very different from what we call "modern evangelism", why suddenly all the interest in him? Why are so many students in seminaries writing papers and doctrinal dissertations on him? Why are preachers beating a path to the scenes of his labors and pouring over his sermons? What is going on?

The answer is not hard to find. A whole generation of young pastors and lay leaders are going forth into the service of Jesus Christ today with the firm conviction that something has gone drastically wrong with not only how evangelism has been conducted in recent years but with the whole spirit of modern Christianity. They have lived in a generation in America where approximately one third of the people have professed to be "born again" Christians. They have witnessed the explosion of mega churches with programs geared to appeal to every conceivable human interest. They have seen evangelical believers move energetically out of the churches into the cultural wars and wield, at least for a while, considerable influence in politics, public morality and the general social order.

And yet, in spite of all this feverish activity, in spite of the seemingly innumerable professions of faith, in spite of the astounding statistical success that evangelicals have logged, our country continues to spiral down deeper and deeper into moral and spiritual decay. The church seems not truly to be salt but like the material cast out into the street of which our Lord warned. We have witnessed numerous celebrated Christian leaders, some who are familiar faces on TV, perpetrating sins which make even worldly people blush. We hear that approximately one half of so-called Christian men watch pornography on the internet. People who profess the name of Christ are statistically about where society in general is when it comes to drug abuse, divorce, abortion and all the other social ills. Why is this?

The truth is that, as pessimistic as this sounds, in the minds of many these problems have arisen because multitudes have come into the visible church who have never had a true work of grace in their hearts. The standard of what conversion is has been so reduced that almost anything passes as a profession of faith. A counterfeit kind of Christianity has enveloped the churches and frankly it has come to a great extent because of flawed teaching and methodology in evangelism.

I give an illustration. I do not have the details here before me, but I know the case I cite is factual. An evangelist a few years ago known for his remarkable ability to get people roaring with laughter held a large series of mass meetings in an eastern city. Hundreds streamed down the aisles, coaxed by the persuasive preacher during the invitation. The usual "follow up" ensued as the Christian workers combed through the decision cards trying to find new members for their churches. To the chagrin of all, the "converts" could not be found. A worker went to the home of one who had gone forward and was rudely refused an entrance.

Nettleton saw the beginnings in his day of the cheapening of the gospel message and the disastrous tendency to "hawk" Jesus like some snake oil remedy for the ails of men. The last one hundred and fifty years have seen the development of a new theology, which has to a great extent, legitimized the worldly conduct of many professors of religion today by simply passing off their wickedness as the conduct of "carnal Christians." Although some of us believe that through his Pelagian theology and emphasis on the "anxious seat," Charles G. Finney helped propel this modern corruption; Finney himself would be appalled were he to return today and see how empty, vain and often frivolous is modern so-called evangelical worship.

We have today many noted Christian leaders claiming that a person can know Jesus as Savior and never really surrender to him as Lord. To such people Jesus is a kind of fire escape who has given them an insurance policy for heaven, which they tuck away and go on living as if Christ were just a notion. The great Alliance leader A. W. Tozer rightly denounced this "Christ as Savior but not as Lord" notion as *heresy*.

We need a new model for evangelism that is based on the New Testament teachings of Jesus of Nazareth who warned those who wished to come to him that they could not be his disciples unless they denied themselves and took up the cross. We need to revive the theology of Paul who preached both faith in Jesus and its essential accompaniment, repentance. In short, we need real conversions which come through the sovereign power of God, not through the well-meaning, but often ineffective persuasions of man.

Perhaps we even need an *old* model, an example of true revivalism which produced authentic, lasting converts. The integrity of Nettleton's evangelism was recorded over and over again in his day in numerous books, evangelical magazines, and of course in the two biographical studies that were published soon after he died. No man is perfect. Nettleton no doubt made mistakes. We could perhaps pick some flaws in his theological emphases. But he was a man mightily used of God. His devotion to the Lord and his gospel, his integrity as a faithful witness, and his incredible discernment of the human heart made him a powerful winner of souls. When he came to town people knew that almost certainly a revival would follow. When he left lives were truly changed and the social problems which modern Christians try to remove by legal action and strong-armed political tactics were amazingly improved.

It is time for a drastic change in the evangelical church. It is time for solid, searching, doctrinal preaching of the word of God. It is time for the true servants of God to lay aside the weak and truncated philosophies designed to attract, even amuse the wicked, and call on men to bow down before the sovereign Christ. Nettleton did. As far as he followed Christ, let us follow him. Although he did not have the natural talents of a Whitefield or a Spurgeon, his soul was so full of the red-hot fire of God's truth that his messages penetrated deeply into the hearts of those who heard him. Men with ordinary talents can take comfort as they study Nettleton's life, that they too can be mightily used of God.

Dr. Johnston's massive work is not just a biographical study, it is an encyclopedic resource on a very critical period in American history when changes took place which have shaped religion of our country permanently. He has provided massive direct quotations from some of the major historical sources of the events and issues of the early 19th century, thus making available to everyone materials long unavailable to the general public. Many will no doubt disagree with his analyses of the theological debates that shook the church, but none can deny that his perspective is one that was once widely held and is growing in influence in our day. The letters of Beecher and Nettleton on the New Measures, and excerpts from Dr. Sherry Pierpont May's doctoral dissertation on the great evangelist are here for all to peruse. This is in my opinion an important work, well written and thoroughly documented.

DR. JOHN F. THORNBURY

PREFACE

Without question, God Himself is the author of revival. The Lord God Omnipotent is the only one who can bring the church and the world out of the moral and spiritual abyss into which it has plunged. In every instance of true revival and awakening that has ever occurred, God alone has been the source. Even so, human instrumentality has played a vital part. Consequently the very language with which we describe revival movements recorded in biblical history include such phrases as "The Revival Under Moses", "The Revival Under Hezekiah", "The Revival Under Ezra", etc.

Not only are revivals usually led by "mere" men, there are the hidden springs of revivals which, while easily overlooked, are a vital part of the mighty acts of God.

Consider the great revival movement that occurred after the resurrection of Jesus Christ from the dead and first manifested itself in Jerusalem at the time of Pentecost. It was clearly divine in origin and yet the role of praying men and women is clearly evident.

Did not Simeon, a resident of Jerusalem and described as righteous and devout, have an important part? We are told that he was looking for the consolation of Israel and that the Holy Spirit was upon him. It had been revealed to him by the Holy Spirit that he should not see death before he had seen the Lord's Christ. He went regularly to the temple in prayerful expectation and, when Mary and Joseph brought in the child Jesus, he took Him into his arms and blessed God and said, "Now Lord, Thou dost let Thy bond-servant depart in peace, according to Thy word; for mine eyes have seen Thy salvation, which Thou has prepared in the presence of all peoples, *a light of revelation to the Gentiles, and the glory of Thy people Israel*" (Luke 2:25–32).

Was not the prophetess, Anna, another vital link? She was advanced in years, having lived with a husband seven years after her marriage, and then, as a widow to the age of eighty-four. She never left the temple, serving night and day with fastings and prayers. "And at the very moment she came up and began giving thanks to God, and continued to speak of Him (Jesus) to all those who were looking for the redemption of Jerusalem" (Luke 2:36–38).

In looking at hidden springs, how could we possibly overlook either our Lord's urgent words to His disciples, "And behold I am sending forth the promise of the Father upon you; but you are to stay in the city until you are clothed with power from on high" (Luke 24:49); and their response, "These all with one mind were continually devoting themselves to prayer, along with the women and Mary the mother of Jesus, and with His brothers" (Acts 1:14).

There can be no question but that the obedience and prayers of Simeon, Anna, and the disciples were a vital part of the Sovereign work of God that followed.

It is also urgent to recognize the role of hunger and thirst in these precious movements of divine grace.

Among the many expressions the church has used through the centuries to describe these periodic heaven-sent revival movements is the beautifully descriptive phrase, "*A Divine Visitation.*"

Very instructive is *the visitation* to which the angel Gabriel first made reference when he spoke to Zacharias the priest in the first chapter of the book of Luke: "Do not be afraid, Zacharias, for your petition has been heard, and your wife Elizabeth will bear you a son, and you will give him the name John. And you will have joy and gladness and many will rejoice at his birth. For he will be great in the sight of the Lord, and he will drink no wine or liquor; and he will be filled with the Holy Spirit, while yet in his mother's womb. And he will turn back many of the sons of Israel to the Lord their God. And it is he who will go as a forerunner before Him in the spirit and power of Elijah, to turn the hearts of the fathers back to the children, and the disobedient to the attitude of the righteous; so as to make a people prepared for the Lord" (1:13–17).

After the birth of John The Baptist, his father was filled with the Holy Spirit and prophesied saying: "Blessed be the Lord God of Israel, *for He has visited us* and accomplished redemption for His people, and has raised up a horn of salvation for us in the house of David his servant—As He spoke by the mouth of His holy prophets from of old—Salvation from our enemies, to show mercy toward our fathers, and to remember His holy covenant, the oath which He swore to Abraham our Father, to grant us that we, being delivered from the hand of our enemies, might serve Him without fear, in holiness and righteousness before Him all our days. And you child, will be called the prophet of the Most High; for you

will go before the Lord to prepare His ways; to give His people the
knowledge of salvation by the forgiveness of their sins, *because of the tender
mercy of our God, with which the Sunrise from on high shall visit us, to shine
upon those who sit in darkness and the shadow of death, to guide our feet into the
way of peace"* (Luke 1:67–79).

Think of what it would mean to have *the Sunrise from on high visit us!*
Then remember that when Christ approached the City of Jerusalem and
wept over it He said, "If you had known in this day, even you, the things
which make for peace! But now they have been hidden from your eyes,
for the days shall come upon you when your enemies will throw up a
bank before you, and surround you, and hem you in on every side; and
will level you to the ground and your children within you, and they will
not leave in you one stone upon another, *because you did not recognize the
time of your visitation"* (Luke 19:41–44).

O tragedy of tragedies! These scribes, Pharisees, and Sadducees were so
full of themselves they felt no need of Christ. The lack of hungering and
thirsting for righteousness which held them in its vice-grip, kept them
blinded. Thus *they not only missed the visitation from on high* but brought
about the complete destruction of all that they held dear.

At a time when revival is so desperately needed in the church, and
spiritual awakening in the world so urgent, wise men look in every
direction possible for encouragement and help.

Deeply aware of these things, E. A. Johnston, under the conviction that
he must do what he can, has carefully researched the life and ministry of
Asahel Nettleton. In this volume he has provided us a wonderful example
of the life style, the heart burden, and the preaching content of one of the
most blessed Gospel ministers in the history of the United States.

Asahel Nettleton is a largely forgotten revivalist. There is a reason!
Great controversy surrounded the ministry of Nettleton. He fought in a
powerful battle for the truth and lost. His noble struggle for the ancient
paths was lost to the novelties of the western evangelists. He often stood
alone and was like the voice crying in the wilderness. Unlike some of his
supposed friends, Nettleton, was a far-seeing man. He saw not only the
errors of his own day but their destructive influence in our day. He was
keenly alert to the pernicious influences of moving from a God-centered
to a man-centered Gospel. The error he stood against is the error we face
right now. Is God the agent of salvation or is man? Is revival nothing
other than the right use of the right means or a sovereign work of
Almighty God? Are men saved as a result of a decision they make or as
the result of the regenerating work of the Holy Spirit?

Nettleton believed both in revival and reformation. Had a thorough reformation occurred during his lifetime it would have greatly altered the subsequent history of Christianity in the world.

Now we are faced with a situation much worse than Nettleton faced. Through his Spirit empowered life and ministry a great many backsliders were reclaimed, thousands were brought into the kingdom of God, and many local churches were revived. But because of the short-sightedness of many who knew and applauded him, Christianity in America headed into a decline from which it has still to recover.

We are now positioned to continue in the self-destruct pattern Nettleton fought against until we are destroyed—like Jerusalem of old— or to return to the God-centered, doctrinally accurate, Holy Spirit-inspired ministry types of Theodorus Jacobus Frelinghuysen, Jonathan Dickinson, Jonathan Edwards, George Whitefield, William Tennent, John Blair, Samuel Davies, Timothy Dwight and Asahel Nettleton.

I beg of you, repent and return to the Lord!

We must do what we can with the conviction that God can and will do what we cannot. This book will help!

RICHARD OWEN ROBERTS

PART I:

REVIVAL PREACHER

Thus saith the LORD, Stand ye in the ways, and see, and ask for the old paths, where is the good way, and walk therein, and ye shall find rest for your souls. But they said, We will not walk therein

JEREMIAH 6:16

I

THE LEGEND OF THE KING'S SWORD

There was a legend about a magical sword used by an olde English king. It seems that whenever the king used this particular sword he experienced success and victory on the battlefield. His enemies learned to fear the king's sword.

Eventually the king grew old and feeble. An adversary of the king began to spread a rumor around the village that the king's sword no longer possessed supernatural powers, that it was now just an average, ordinary sword of little use to its owner. This story began to spread among the peasants until the entire village believed that the king's sword was now impotent. As the king's heir to the throne matured he too grew up believing the story about the sword's uselessness and ordered the royal blacksmith to forge him a *new* sword. A handsome, shiny engraved sword with jewels—much more beautiful to behold than his father's old sword. This was done.

One day an enemy force attacked the castle village and fell upon the inhabitants, killing and maiming many. The enemy then laid siege to the castle. The young prince grabbed his new bejeweled sword and went forth to defend his kingdom but to no avail ... rather than defeating his enemy he was captured. In fact, the entire village of the royal family was now under bondage to this evil enemy. Time passed and the villagers groaned beneath the oppressive bondage of the evil power. But there was nothing they could do but suffer. Eventually the old king died and his son the prince could not assume the throne because he was still a captive of this evil entity. The entire village groaned and lamented as they served their oppressive and evil new ruler.

During this time a nephew of the king grew to maturity and one day this lad called on the prince of the castle. The guards allowed the fair haired, harmless looking youth entry since he was royalty. The prince was held captive in a chamber with a guard at the door. When the lad was allowed to visit the prince he asked him where the old sword was that once belonged to the king. The prince pointed to a large cedar chest by the barred window—the chest was opened and there wrapped in an old blanket was the leather scabbard which held the king's sword. The lad asked if he could have the sword as a memento of his uncle the king. The prince nodded yes, telling the lad that it was just an old worthless sword of little use today.

The lad left the castle with the sword wrapped in the old blanket. Upon arriving at his part of the village he stopped by the barber's shop to get a haircut. The barber was one of the ancient men of the town. As the old barber cut the lad's locks he inquired about the bundle by the lad's feet. The lad told the barber about the sword. When the old man heard this his eyes lit up and his stooped shoulders straightened. He then proceeded to tell the lad about all the powers that the sword *formerly* possessed. The lad was curious and as he left the barber's shop he visited an old baker. He asked the elderly baker to verify the story of the magical sword. "Oh yes," said the baker, "I was an eyewitness to the king's victories with that sword, for I used to be the royal baker until the enemy captured the castle and placed us all in bondage." The baker turned away, his eyes were full of sadness. The lad left the baker and went home.

In his little hovel he unwrapped the blanket and pulled the old sword from the worn leather scabbard. Though it was large and double-edged the sword seemed just an ordinary sword. In fact, it was almost too heavy to wield properly. The lad lay down on a mat on the straw floor and fell asleep next to the sword. The lad dreamed of being a king! He dreamed he was king and fighting a battle with this sword. The enemy fled from the lad in fear! Was it the magical sword? He awoke to sunlight pouring in from a hole in his thatched roof. The lad grabbed the sword. Lifting it up with both hands he exclaimed, "It must be true!" With a new faith he rushed from his hovel and the first enemy soldier he encountered he brandished the sword and attacked! The enemy fell down dead. Soon another enemy was upon the lad, but brandishing the sword again he experienced victory! Finally, a troop of enemies fell upon the lad but the sword saved him once more. There were now *eyewitnesses* to these events and soon word spread among the villagers that the king's old sword was once again magical. Word got to the evil ruler at the castle and he personally led his largest band of soldiers to attack the lad. All the lad had to do was to brandish the sword and the enemy fell before him.

The lad was a hero! He and the sword set the captives free! The lad was made the new king. The prince was so bewildered and jealous that he killed himself by falling upon his bejeweled sword. From that day on there was peace in the valley of the king.

THE OLD PATHS

The Church has failed with its *new swords* and methodologies. It is time to seek the "old paths" once again. They have proved to be *mighty weapons* in battle with the evil and dark kingdom of this world. These weapons, the sword of the Spirit and the great doctrines of the Bible have been wielded by former mighty men who prevailed over the enemy and pushed back the darkness in their generations, men like George Whitefield and Asahel Nettleton. God smiled upon those faithful servants who relied upon His Holy Spirit and stood upon the great doctrines of His Word. Asahel Nettleton was such a man who preached the great doctrines of total depravity, God's sovereignty, the wickedness of the human heart, election, regeneration, the cost of discipleship, a hell for lost sinners, and a final judgment for all. He preached these doctrines unashamedly and with power and God used him as the primary human instrument of that marvelous move of grace in America known as "The Second Great Awakening".

It has been several generations since his death in 1844. The church has attempted to hold back the forces of darkness with its *new swords.* Unfortunately, these measures have largely failed. Is it not time that our generation of Christians should seek to learn the activities of those who in former times were mightily used of God? We will study in depth the life and labors of Asahel Nettleton, revival preacher, in the following chapters and through this exercise hopefully come away with far more knowledge in how to bring down the forces of evil and storm the gates of hell in our generation today—all for the glory of God! For there is much to learn from the life and ministry of Asahel Nettleton, a man mighty with the sword of the Lord.

The decline of Christian influence before a revival has sometimes been exaggerated in order to emphasize the scale of the subsequent transformation. The Second Great Awakening in America requires no such distortion of history in order to justify its title. By any assessment, an extraordinary period of Christian history began around the beginning of the new century. Voltaire is said to have claimed that by the early nineteenth century the Bible would have passed 'into the limbo of forgotten literature'. Instead, by 1816 many Americans considered themselves to be living in 'the age of Bibles and missionaries'.

IAIN MURRAY

2

THE LAND IN REVIVAL

The young country of America was in the midst of revival at the turn of the nineteenth century. The awakening had begun in 1792 and was spreading like a prairie blaze by 1812. It was in this spiritually awakened environment that Asahel Nettleton began to labor for God. The First Great Awakening had occurred in the colonies under the preaching of such men as George Whitefield, Jonathan Edwards, Gilbert Tennent, Jonathan Parsons, Samuel Davies, Joseph Bellamy, Thomas Prince, Jonathan Dickinson, and Samuel Blair. The leading preacher of that movement was Whitefield, and ironically the entire movement seemed to die out around the time of the death of Whitefield in 1770. But the tops of the mulberry trees began to stir again near the turn of the century. Here and there "the sound of marching" could be heard once again as God began to move once more among His people!

Such was the case in New England in the year 1792 when heavenly showers began to fall upon the countryside. We see from the following comments:

"About the year 1792 commenced three series of events of sufficient importance to constitute a new era ... There was a revival in North Yarmouth, Maine, in 1791. In the summer of 1792 one appeared in Lee, in the county of Berkshire. The following November, the first that I had the privilege of witnessing showed itself on the borders of East Haddam and Lyme, Conn., which apparently brought to Christ about a hundred souls. Since that time revivals have never ceased. I saw a continued succession of heavenly sprinklings at New Salem, Farmington, Middlebury, and New Hartford (all in Connecticut) until, in 1799, I could stand at my door in New Hartford, Litchfield County, and number fifty or sixty contiguous congregations laid down in one field of divine wonders, and as many more in different parts of New England. By 1802 revivals had spread themselves through most of the western and southern States; and since that time they have been familiar to the whole of American people."[1]

The comment by Griffin that the revivals had spread so far throughout the land that "they have been familiar to the whole of American people" is *startling!* Indeed this was the beginning of the revival in America known as "The Second Great Awakening". God raised up a host of godly men who labored amidst remarkable scenes of revival—most of whom are forgotten in history.

CAMPUS REVIVAL

One of the most stirring scenes of revival occurred on the Yale College campus in the winter of 1807 in New Haven, Connecticut. During this time Asahel Nettleton was a Yale undergraduate and he sat spellbound in the school's stain-glass chapel listening to the searching sermons that were preached by Yale's President, Timothy Dwight (grandson of Jonathan Edwards). Regarding this campus revival we have the following observations:

YALE

> "Dwight returned to Yale as President in 1795 and continued in that capacity until 1817. During this period there were no less than four distinct revivals of religion at the College. It is important to note that many of the students brought to surrender to Christ while at Yale were infected with the same spirit of revival that dominated their President. Some of these men filled pulpits in New England churches and were, under God, responsible for the many waves of revivals touching their local churches in the first half of the 19th century."[2]

These comments add support to the statement made earlier that there were many men whom God used in revival preaching during the Second Great Awakening, most of whom remain in obscurity but not in the annals of heaven. In the providence of the Almighty an obscure Yale graduate was raised up to become a mighty preacher during this time and soon the name, Asahel Nettleton, would become a household word in his generation. Asahel Nettleton was fourteen years of age when a mighty move of God swept over the New England countryside. To grasp fully the magnitude of these seasons of revival we turn to the eyewitness account provided by Edward D. Griffin, an eminent pastor in Portland, Maine whose predecessor was the great Edward Payson.

AN ACCOUNT OF THE REVIVAL IN CONNECTICUT

The year was 1798, Edward Griffin was then pastor of the church in New Hartford, Connecticut at the time of the revival. He was an eyewitness to God's power and his observations should be studied carefully by all students of revival. For if we are not familiar with how God has moved in former times how can we effectively recognize His effusions of grace when they appear? Therefore, we read Griffin's observations with interest:

> "Late in October, 1798, the people frequently hearing of the displays of divine grace in West Symsbury, (Canton,) were increasingly impressed with the

information. Our conferences soon became more crowded and solemn. Serious people began to break their minds to each other; and it was discovered that there had been for a considerable time in their minds special desires for the revival of religion; while each one, unapprised of his neighbor's feelings, had supposed his exercises peculiar to himself. It was soon agreed to institute a prayer meeting for the express purpose of praying for the effusions of the Spirit, which was the scene of such wrestlings as are not, it is presumed, commonly experienced. Several circumstances conspired to increase our anxiety. The glorious work had already begun in Torringford, and the cloud appeared to be going all around us. It seemed as though Providence, by avoiding us, designed to bring to remembrance our past abuses of his grace. Besides, having been so recently visited with distinguishing favors, we dared not allow ourselves to expect a repetition of them so soon; and we began to apprehend it was the purpose of Him whom we had lately grieved from among us, that we should, for penalty, stand alone parched up in the sight of surrounding showers. We considered what must be the probable fact of the risen generation, if we were to see no more of 'the days that were past' for a number of years, and the apprehension that we might not, caused sensations more easily felt than described.

"This was the state of the people, when, on a Sabbath in the month of November, it was the sovereign pleasure of a most merciful God very sensibly to manifest himself in the public assembly. Many abiding impressions were made on minds seemingly the least susceptible, and on several grown old in unbelief. From that memorable day, the flame which had been kindling in secret broke out. By desire of the people religious conferences were set up in different parts of the town, which continued to be attended by deeply affected crowds; and in which the divine presence and power were manifested to a degree which we had never before witnessed. It is not meant that they were marked with outcries, distortions of the body, or any symptoms of intemperate zeal; but only that the power of divine truth made deep impressions on the assemblies ... Little terror was preached, except what is implied in the doctrines of the entire depravity of the carnal heart—its enmity against God—its deceitful doubtings and attempts to avoid the soul-humbling terms of the gospel—the radical defects of the doings of the unregenerate, and the sovereignty of God in the dispensations of his grace. The more clearly these, and other kindred doctrines were displayed and understood, the more were convictions promoted.

"The order and progress of these convictions were pretty much as follows. The subjects of them were brought to feel that they were transgressors, yet not totally sinful. As their convictions increased, they were constrained to acknowledge their destitution of love to God; but yet they thought they had no enmity against him. At length, they would come to see that such enmity filled their hearts ... their hearts would recoil at the thought of being in God's hands, and would rise against him for having reserved it to himself to decide whether to sanctify and pardon them or not. Though the display of this doctrine had the most powerful tendency to strip them of all hopes from themselves, and to bring them to the feet of sovereign grace; yet as it thus sapped the foundation on which they rested, their feelings were excited against it ... Before conviction had become deep and powerful, many attempted to exculpate themselves with this plea of inability, and, like their ancestor, to cast blame upon God, by pleading, 'The *nature* which *he* gave me, beguiled me.' This was the enemy's stronghold. All who were a little more thoughtful than common, but not thoroughly convicted, would, upon the first attack, flee to this refuge. 'They would be glad to repent, but *could not*, their *nature* and *heart* were so bad;' as though their nature and heart were not they themselves. But the progress of conviction, in general, soon removed this refuge of lies, and filled them with a sense of utter inexcusableness. And in every case, as soon as their enmity was slain, this plea wholly vanished. Their language immediately became, 'I wonder I ever should ask the question, *How can I repent?* My only wonder now is, *that I could hold out so long.*' ... Some declared that if they could have their choice, either to live a life of religion and poverty, or revel in the pleasures of the world, unmolested by conscience or fear, and at last, be converted on a dying bed, and be as happy hereafter as if they had made the other choice, they should prefer the former; and *that* for the glory of God, and not merely for the happiness which the prospects of future glory would daily afford; for they believed their choice would be the same ... Their predominate desire still appears to be that God may be glorified, and that they may render him voluntary glory in a life of obedience, and may enjoy him in a life of communion with him ... some have been heard to say, 'I never had an idea what a heart I had till this week.' Each one seems to apprehend his own depravity to be the greatest. The church felt the shock. That same presence which at Sinai made all the church, and even Moses, 'exceedingly fear and quake,' rendered this now a time of trembling with professors in general. Nevertheless, it was with most of them a season of great quickening, and a remarkable day of prayer."[3]

This account of revival demonstrates that the revival preachers of the Second Great Awakening preached searching, doctrinal sermons to the consciences of their hearers and this was the hallmark of Asahel Nettleton's success in preaching. It is important to note that the subjects of the revival viewed their salvation as it was focused on *the glory of God* rather than their own *personal benefit* from salvation. This is critically important in our study of revival that the emphasis of the individuals wrought upon by the Holy Spirit was not on themselves or what they can get out of God but only on the glory of God and that His will be done. The entire salvation experience was God-centered.

Often, the very doctrines that these awakened sinners initially fought against became the very doctrines of the salvation of their souls. One common denominator was that every false hope of a self-righteous life was broken up under the great doctrines of the Bible and that the Law was the school-master that brought the lost sinner to see his rebellion against a holy God. There was no easy way to Christ afforded them except by way of the Cross.

THE PRE-EXISTING GROUNDS OF REVIVAL

An excellent explanation for the reasons why the "revival fires" of the First Great Awakening went out and the re-lit fires of the Second Great Awakening commenced, are found in some observations by Heman Humphrey. Dr. Heman Humphrey, President of Amherst College, had such an impact on his students that for the twenty three years of his tenure, of the 765 graduates over 400 entered the Gospel ministry! He was also good friends with Asahel Nettleton and often Nettleton preached in Humphrey's church in Pittsfield, Massachusetts. It was at Humphrey's church that a remarkable revival broke out under Nettleton's preaching. Therefore, his comments on revival are noteworthy and he details the reasons why God removed His Presence from the land and why God visited again in distinguishing periods of grace. His first observations conclude that the Great Awakening ended because it was a time of unsettling wars. Also, God-hating philosophy of the French Enlightenment gripped much of the nation at the turn of the century and much of this anti-God philosophy had infiltrated the colleges in New England. Dr. Humphrey elaborates on this by commenting:

"We are next to inquire, what were the causes of the alarming dearth and declension just mentioned, before we hail the dawn of a brighter day. In looking back upon that period, some of these causes are too obvious to be mistaken.

"First came what is familiarly called, the 'Old French war' [the Seven Years war]. While we slept, the enemy, ever awake and aggressive, had been skillfully drawing a line of circumvallation quite round the English colonies, to hem us in, by building a chain of forts from Louisburg and Quebec on the north, by the way of Detroit and St. Louis, down to the mouth of the Mississippi. And now it was, that France, aided by the warlike tribes of Indians whom she could enlist in the bloody enterprise, sought to bring all North America under the yoke of Rome. God interposed, and the attempt signally failed. But the danger, while it lasted, created universal alarm; and the necessary defense of the frontiers demanded all the force that could be raised, and absorbed the anxious minds of the whole population. In this state of things, it would have been strange indeed if the churches had been visited by revivals—if the cause of Christ had not declined, as it did.

"Scarcely was that danger over, when serious difficulties broke out between the colonists and the mother country, and continued to increase till they issued in the war of the Revolution. Here, again, it would have been very remarkable if, in the midst of all these agitations of the then infant settlements, revivals had sprung up. They did not. Humanly speaking, there was no room for them. And we know that God works by means, in favorable seasons, and orders events for building up his churches, as well as for accomplishing his other great purposes ...

"In such a state of things, when the American armies were wading through frost and blood to conquer national independence, and the anxious hopes and fears of the whole people were alternately swallowed up in the mighty struggle, how could religion prosper? The Spirit of God is a spirit of peace, and not of war. I know that God is able to build up his churches in the midst of wars and fightings, just as he is able to awaken and convert hardened sinners under the most unfavorable circumstances; but this is not his manner ...

"The minds of the people were too much agitated and engrossed by conflicting political interests, to have much room for more than the ordinary routine of religious observances. Revivals were hardly expected anywhere during those years of civil agitation, and they were not enjoyed. Zion languished. While the form of godliness remained in the churches, there was but little of the power.

"In the mean time, as might have been expected, *French Infidelity*, which our allies brought over with them, was sowed broadcast among our own officers and soldiers. Aided by Paine's 'Age of Reason,' Voltaire's assaults upon Christianity, Volney's 'Ruins,' and other blasphemous publications, it spread rapidly, especially among the upper classes. The Illuminati, so called, of France and Germany, who were secretly associated for the overthrow of all existing religious institutions had their affiliated societies in this country, enrolling not a few men of high social and political standing and influence. It became fashionable, in high places and low places, flippantly to prate against the Bible, and sneer at things sacred and divine. Instead of the Scriptures, French philosophy claimed to be the rule of faith and life, and ignoring all the 'rights of God,' was to usher in the glorious millennium of the 'rights of man.' … It seemed as if the floods of ungodliness must swallow up the church …

"But just then when it seemed to grow darker and darker, the night was far spent, and the day was at hand. A few years before the close of the century the light of a new revival epoch began to dawn. Here and there a church rose and shook herself from the dust. Sinners were awakened, and began to inquire what they must do to be saved. So that when the old century was departing, and the new century came in, many a field that had long been languishing began to rejoice under the reviving influence. Christ by his Spirit came down, here and there, like rain upon the mown grass, and like showers that water the earth."[4]

During this critical juncture in America's history, God raised up a host of powerful "revival preachers" to be the human instruments by whom the great Head of the Church could operate. Men, who in the Day of His power were mightily used and who now lie forgotten in history: Robbins, Backus, Mills, Gillett, Perkins, Strong, Porter, Hooker, Miller, Williams, Cooley, Hawley, Cowles, Hyde, Catlin, Stillman, Baldwin, Manning, Mason, Livingston, Furman and Marshall. Other men, whom God raised up would become more famous such as Timothy Dwight and Asahel Nettleton. But the main focus of the revival was the *preaching* by these eminent men. The Second Great Awakening was a *revival of preaching the great doctrines of Scripture*. We see this from Heman Humphrey's own personal observations during that time:

"Their preaching was not in man's wisdom, but in demonstration of the Spirit, and with power. It was eminently *scriptural*. The ministers of that day read and studied the Bible more than all other books. They had received it from their Master as their only commission, and in virtue of it, as ambassadors for Christ, they besought sinners in his stead to be reconciled to God. It was surprising to notice with what facility they would quote chapter and verse from all parts of both Testaments, without turning over a single leaf. Indeed, it sometimes seemed to me as if they knew all the Bible by heart; and it is no disparagement to say, that they did know much more of it than most preachers do now. They had a great deal more of it in their sermons. Almost all their illustrations, as well as their proofs, were drawn from its rich and inexhaustible treasures. 'Thus saith the Lord,' was enough for them, let who would criticize, cavil, or blaspheme. They did not shun, either from fear or favor, to declare all the counsel of God, as they understood it, whether men would hear, or whether they would forbear. They did not wreathe the sword around with flowers, but left the two edges bare and sharp, to cut where they would—the deeper the better; and they applied no emollients to heal the hurt slightly …

"Oh how we smarted under it. I remember it well in my own case, and how my heart rebelled against some of the doctrines which my Bible and my conscience told me were true, till, as I hope, I was brought to bow and submit at the foot of the cross. And as it was with me, so it was with multitudes of others. We complained of some of Paul's hard sayings, and wondered why our ministers dwelt so much upon them. We wanted to get to heaven in some easier way. But instead of abating one jot or tittle to relieve us, they pressed harder and harder, driving us from one refuge to another, till there was no hiding-place left. The law, which we had broken times without number, we were made to see was just; its fiery penalty hung over our heads, and we must submit or die. Under such preaching it was hard to get hopes; but when embraced, they were more to be relied upon, than if they had been gained in some easier way.

"Our spiritual guides and teachers never said to us, when under awakening, 'Don't be discouraged; wait God's time, and he will deliver you.' No, no, but, 'How long will you hold out in your rebellion against God?' They never asked us while in this state, 'Don't you feel better?' but, 'Why don't you submit to God, and cast yourselves upon his mercy, embracing the Lord Jesus Christ by faith, who came down from heaven on purpose to save the lost. Turn ye, turn ye, why will ye die?'

"I do not say that this law work, as it has been appropriately called, was alike marked and pungent in all cases. It was not. He who worketh all things according to the counsel of his own will, opened some hearts, as he seems to have opened that of Lydia, at once to receive the truth in the love of it. But I am quite sure, that in most cases the conversions in that revival were preceded by sharp conviction of sin and of deserved punishment. It was eminently a *law* revival, issuing in the more abundant and abiding consolations of the gospel. Those loved most, who felt that they had been forgiven most.

"As our pastors were careful not to encourage us that we had passed from death unto life without good scripture evidence of the change, they were very strict in their examinations for church membership. If they thought any of the candidates did not give satisfactory evidence of having been converted, they did not hesitate to tell them so."[5]

There is much "meat" in these accounts of revival, all we can do is *digest* it carefully and prayerfully, relying upon the mercies of God to move in His Sovereignty and rain righteousness upon His Church once again. Oh Lord, what You have done in former times, do again we plead!

Notes

1   Edward Griffin, Appendix in W. B. Sprague, *Lectures on Revivals* (Edinburgh: Banner of Truth Trust, 2007), pp. 402–403.

2   Richard Owen Roberts, *An Annotated Bibliography of Revival Literature* (Wheaton: Richard Owen Roberts Publishers, 1987), p. 141.

3   Bennet Tyler (revival account by Edward Griffin), *New England Revivals as They Existed at the Close of the Eighteenth, and the Beginning of the Nineteenth Centuries* (Wheaton: Richard Owen Roberts Publishers, 1980), pp. 63–82.

4   Heman Humphrey, *Revival Sketches and Manual in two parts* (New York: American Tract Society, 1859), pp. 96–99.
5   Ibid. pp. 104–106.

Although one of America's most significant evangelists, the name of Asahel Nettleton has long laid in the dust of oblivion. Having fallen into precious few of the errors of his predecessors, contemporaries or successors, it is tragic indeed that the evangelical public knows so little about this New England Congregationalist. A native of Connecticut and a graduate of Yale, the revivals which accompanied his ministry were among the deepest and most permanent on record. Although almost constantly hindered by poor health, much of New England, New York and the South as well as England were graciously benefitted by his mighty preaching.

RICHARD OWEN ROBERTS

Asahel Nettleton's house in East Windsor. Built in 1810 by cigar-maker Nathaniel Rockwell, Jr., he sold the house in 1835 to Nettleton. This is the house in which Nettleton died.

3

ASAHEL NETTLETON'S BIRTH

The New England hamlet of Killingworth would see the birth of two famous evangelists, who were cousins: Titus Coan, the great missionary and revivalist of the Hawaiian Islands, and Asahel Nettleton, the great evangelist and revivalist of the Second Great Awakening. Both men grew up together, played together, and even taught school together in the little green school house of Killingworth, Connecticut. Both Titus Coan and Asahel Nettleton's boyhood homes were rubble by the turn of the twentieth century, but their legacy lives on. It is a striking fact that God raised up two of His mighty servants from the same town and that they were cousins! On the life and ministry of Titus Coan we have the following:

"One of Killingworth's most notable citizens was Titus Coan who was missionary to the Hawaiian Islands from 1834–1882. His long course of service has few parallels in the annals of missionary life. Titus Coan was born 1801 in a house located on a now unused portion of Titus Coan Road. The house no longer stands but there is an inscription on a stone nearby noting his birthplace. As a boy he worked on his father's farm and received his early education in the Killingworth schools and from Rev. Asa King, the pastor of the Congregational Church. When a child, he was rescued from drowning by a friend and neighbor, Julius Stone. Later, he taught in the green school house on Roast Meat Hill Road and in neighboring towns. In 1829, he felt called by God and decided to become a minister. He entered the Auburn Theological Seminary in 1831. In 1834, he received instructions as missionary to the Sandwich Islands (Hawaiian Islands) from the American Board of Commissioners for Foreign Missions. He toured the islands preaching to the people and enduring great hardships fording rivers, climbing mountains, and facing tropical rains and sun. He was very popular with the people, and his church in Hilo grew until it numbered in the thousands, making it the largest Protestant Church in the world. He baptized over 14,000 persons and is sometimes called the 'Saint Peter of Hawaii.' Titus Coan died in 1882 and is buried in the Homeland Cemetery in Hilo."[1]

There is scant information in Bennet Tyler's biography on Nettleton regarding his birth and family relations, yet alone incidents of his childhood. Tyler even omits the names of Nettleton's parents!

However, from Tyler we have the following insights of Asahel's boyhood:

> "Asahel Nettleton was born in North Killingworth, Connecticut, April 21, 1783, the same day on which the birth of Samuel J. Mills occurred. He was the eldest son, and second child, of a family of six children, consisting of three sons, and three daughters. His parents, though but little known to the world, were esteemed and respected by their neighbors. His father was a farmer, in moderate, but comfortable circumstances; and in this employment Asahel was mostly engaged, until he entered college, in 1805. His childhood and youth, so far as is known to the writer, were characterized by nothing very peculiar. His early advantages of education were such only, as are furnished by the common district school. That he made a good use of these advantages, we may infer from the thirst for knowledge which he evinced at a later period, and from the fact, that while a young man, he was employed several winters in the capacity of a school-teacher.

> "His parents, according to the custom which prevailed at that period in some parts of New England, were professors of religion, on what was called the half way covenant plan;—that is, they were not admitted to full communion, but having publicly assented to the covenant of the church, they were permitted to offer their children in baptism. Asahel was of course baptized in his infancy, and while a child, received some religious instruction from his parents. He was, in particular, required to commit to memory the Assembly's Catechism, which, as he has often remarked, was of great use to him when his attention was awakened to the concerns of his soul … While a child, he was occasionally the subject of religious impressions. At one time in particular, while alone in the field, and looking at the setting sun, he was powerfully impressed with the thought that he and all men must die. He was so affected by this thought, that he stood for some time and wept aloud."[2]

Further light is cast upon Asahel Nettleton's family history by J. F. Thornbury, who writes:

> "Samuel Nettleton dutifully enlisted and became a member of the Continental Army, registering as a private on 9th May, 1775. Samuel's first stint in Mr. Washington's army was short and his company was disbanded in December of the same year … He no doubt returned to his farm at Killingworth. On 28th February, 1781 he married Amy Kelsey who came from one of the oldest Killingworth families. She was a descendent of John Kelsey who settled there in 1664. Amy was born on 9th July, 1750.

> "Samuel and Amy Nettleton had a family of six children. The oldest was a daughter named after her mother. There were three sons, Asahel, the eldest, Ambrose and David, and two other daughters, Lois and Polly, the last dying in infancy. David, the youngest of the three sons, died at the age of fourteen and only he and his father had headstones in the cemetery at Killingworth."[3]

Further information on Nettleton's roots and early life are found in the following comments:

> "Asahel Nettleton's New England roots go back about as far as they can go in New England. In 1638 some New Haven colonists bargained with the Indians for 'a small tract of land which lay between their colony and Guilford … to be used for additional colonization. Some men from Wethersfield, Connecticut, including Samuel Nettleton, approached the General Court of the colony and were sold a portion.' This land, called Totoket by the Indians, was renamed Branford and was

occupied by the new owners early in 1644 ... We know little of the above
mentioned Samuel Nettleton except that he immigrated from England, was
involved in the above cited settlement, and was a 'freeman, a member of the church,
and an active participant in the life of the colony.' We know that by the third
generation there were Nettletons in Killingworth, because John Nettleton,
grandson of Samuel, was born there in 1670. John's youngest children were twins,
Samuel and Abigail, born in 1713. The fifth child of Samuel's (out of eleven) was
Asahel's father. Most of Asahel's relatives, including his father, were Connecticut
farmers and most were Federalists. Asahel is the only minister in the entire family."[4]

Further information on Nettleton's early life is unknown, except that he
shared a one-room school house with his cousin, Titus Coan, they were
also both teachers there. That school house has been referred to as the
"blue school house" in a dissertation by George Hugh Birney, Jr., whose
unpublished thesis from Hartford Theological Seminary (1943) was
helpful in piecing together aspects of Nettleton's early life. This is the
one "goof" in Birney's research: it was not the "blue school house" but
rather, it was known as the "little green school house".[5]

Tragedy struck the Nettleton home with the early deaths of both his
mother and father, leaving young Asahel as head of the farm with the
burdens of care and responsibility for his siblings. He matured under
these hardships and it is a credit to him that he was able to work his way
into Yale with no family support behind him.

NETTLETON'S CONVERSION

A general revival broke out in 1801 in the town of Killingworth and a
product of that revival was a youthful Asahel Nettleton. Reverend Josiah
B. Andrews was the pastor of the church in Killingworth when the
revival commenced.[6] As is the case with most historic revivals, it began
with the young people in the community. We see this from the
following account:

"It seems, according to his report [Rev. Andrews], that two or three young
people came to him and requested that he preach a sermon to them on election day,
a day usually given over to 'feasting and merriment.' Reverend Andrews saw no
special reason for such a request and so refused them. When a larger number
repeated the request, however, he agreed to preach, 'tho upon a different day.' At
the appointed time, 'there was a full assembly of old as well as young,' and he added
that 'at this time the Spirit of the Lord was secretly working in them, tho there was
nothing further said, until the evening of the 10th of May following, when about
fifty persons desired a conference ... or a discourse upon the subject of religion.'
Finally recognizing 'that the Spirit of the Lord was in very deed in this place,'
Reverend Andrews not only spoke to them as they requested, but appointed a
weekly conference for prayer, lecture or sermon, and conversation about their
religious interest ... Thus, in mid-August he invited 'those who were under serious
impressions' to his house for 'Christian conversation.' More than 200 came; sixty of

whom were 'deeply affected with the plague of their own hearts' and the others were 'seriously alarmed.'"[7]

Of these "deeply affected" and "seriously alarmed" was a youthful Asahel Nettleton. As a convert of the revival, Nettleton was asked to give his testimony to the Connecticut Evangelical Magazine. This he did. The marvelous account of it is as follows:

"From my earliest age, I endeavored to lead a moral life, being often taught that God would punish sinners; but I did not believe that I should suffer for the few offences of which I had been guilty. Having avoided many sins which I saw in others, I imagined all was well with me, till I was about eighteen years old, when I heard a sermon preached on the necessity of regeneration, which put me upon thinking of the need of a change of heart in myself. I did not, however, well receive the discourse at the time, for I was sensible I knew nothing about such a change, neither did I wish to know, for I believed myself as good as others without it, and to be equal with them, I thought would be sufficient. However, the thought troubled me considerably from day to day, and caused me to think of praying, which I had never done, except repeating some form as a little child, and doing it to remove the stings of a guilty conscience, when I considered myself in imminent danger. Sometime after this, I heard another sermon that convinced me I had quenched the spirit, which occasioned me the most alarming fears that I should forever be left to eat the fruit of my own ways. Supposing I was alone in the thoughts of eternity, I separated myself from all company, and determined to seek an interest in Christ. I concluded something must be done to appease God's anger. I read and prayed, and strove in every possible way to prepare myself to go to God, that I might be saved from his wrath. The more I strove in this selfish way, the more anxious I was, and no hope was given. Soon I began to murmur and repine, and accused God of the greatest injustice in requiring me to return to him; and while I was striving with all my might, as I supposed, he appeared not to regard me. I considered God obligated to love me, because I had done so much for him, and finding no relief, I wished that he might not be, and began really to doubt the truths of his holy word, and to disbelieve his existence; for if there was a God, I perfectly hated him. I searched the scriptures daily, hoping to find inconsistencies in them, to condemn the Bible because it was against me; and while I was diligently pursuing my purpose, everything I read, and every sermon I heard, condemned me. Christian conversation gave me the most painful sensations. I tried to repent, but I could not feel the least sorrow for my innumerable sins. By endeavoring to repent, I saw my heart still remained impenitent. Although I knew I hated every thing serious, yet I determined to habituate myself to the duties which God required, and see if I could not by that means be made to love him, and I continued in this state some months. The fear of having committed the unpardonable sin, now began to rise in my mind, and I could find no rest day nor night. When my weary limbs demanded sleep, the fear of awaking in a miserable eternity prevented the closing of my eyes, and nothing gave me ease. No voice of mirth, or sound whatever was heard, but what reminded me of the awful day when God shall bring every work into judgment. All self-righteousness failed me; and having no confidence in God, I was left in deep despondency. After a while, a surprising tremor seized all my limbs, and death appeared to have taken hold upon me. Eternity, the word eternity, sounded louder than any voice I ever heard, and every moment of time seemed move valuable than all the wealth of the world. Not long after this, an unusual calmness pervaded my soul, which I thought little of at first, except that I was freed from my awful convictions, and this sometimes grieved me, fearing I had lost all conviction. Soon after, hearing the feelings of a christian described, I took courage, and thought I knew by experience what they were. The character of God, and the doctrines of the Bible which I could not meditate upon before without hatred, especially those of election and free grace, now appear delightful, and the only means by which, through grace, dead sinners can be made the living sons of God. My heart feels its sinfulness. To confess my sins to God, gives me that peace which before I knew nothing of. To sorrow for it, affords that joy which my tongue cannot express. Were I sensible that at death, my hope would perish, yet it seemeth to me now, that I could not willingly quit the service of God, nor the company of Christians; but my unfaithfulness often makes me fear my sincerity; and should I at last be raised to glory, all the praise will be to God for the exhibition of his sovereign grace."[8]

What is most remarkable about Asahel's salvation experience is that it was a *school* in which he learned how to discern the hearts of sinners in future revivals. One of his greatest gifts was the ability to discern in awakened sinners what *stage* of the salvation process a person was in. But he had to experience this himself! Notice there was no quick conversion here, but rather, for *months* he struggled between his own heart and the truths of the Bible. George Whitefield had a similar salvation experience. It is noteworthy that often the men whom God uses in times of revival first had to experience and see the wretchedness of their hearts, alongside the truths of the Bible and the Holy character of God.

Bennet Tyler comments that the "sermon on regeneration" was not the means which first alarmed Nettleton to his sinful condition, but rather, an annual Thanksgiving ball in the fall of 1800. In this account (related to Tyler by Nettleton later in life) we see God's Spirit already working in the heart of the teenage Asahel, drawing him to God and weaning him from the world. Tyler writes:

"On the night of the annual Thanksgiving, in the fall of 1800, he attended a ball. The next morning, while alone, and thinking with pleasure on the scenes of the preceding night, and of the manner in which he had proposed to spend the day, in company with some of his young companions, the thought suddenly rushed upon his mind, we must all die, and go to the judgment, and with what feelings shall we then reflect upon these scenes! This thought was, for the moment, overwhelming; and it left an impression on his mind, which he could not efface. His pleasing reflections on the past, and anticipations of the future, vanished at once, and gave place to feelings of a very different kind. These feelings he concealed; but he could not entirely banish them from his mind. The world had lost its charms. All those amusements in which he had taken delight, were overcast with gloom. His thoughts dwelt much on the scenes of death, judgment and eternity. He knew that he had an immortal soul that must be happy or miserable in the future world; and although he had consoled himself with the thought that he was as good as others around him, and that his condition was, of course, as safe as theirs; yet he now felt conscious that he was unprepared to meet his God. He at the same time perceived that he was liable every moment to be cut down by the stroke of death, and summoned to his last account. He had no peace of mind by day or by night. Although, at this time, he had no very just conceptions of the divine law, or of the depravity of his heart; yet he was sensible that he was a sinner, and that his sins must be pardoned, or he could not be saved. The duty of prayer was now forcibly impressed upon his mind, a duty which he had almost entirely neglected; and it was not without a great struggle in his feelings, that he was brought to bend the knee to Jehovah. At the same time, he gave himself much to the reading of the Scriptures and other religious books, and separated himself as much as possible from thoughtless companions. So far as he knew, and so far as is now known, there was at that time, no other person in the town under serious impressions [This was in the Autumn of 1800. The revival did not become visible till the following spring]. The young people with whom he had been most intimate, were exceedingly thoughtless, and given to vain and sinful amusements. They were, at this time, making arrangements for the establishment of a dancing school, and they expected his aid and co-operation in the measure. But to their astonishment, he utterly refused to have anything to do with it. He had made up his mind to quit forever such amusements, and to seek the salvation of his soul. But as he did not reveal his feelings to any of his associates, they knew not how to account for this sudden change in his appearance and conduct. Some, perhaps suspected the true cause; while others supposed that for some reason, unknown to them, his affections had become alienated from his former friends. Thus, for months, he mourned in secret, and did not communicate his feelings to a single individual. During this period, he had a strong desire that some of his young companions would set out with him in pursuit of religion: and although his proud heart would not permit him to make known to them the state of his mind, yet he occasionally ventured to expostulate with them on the folly and sinfulness of their conduct; and to some few individuals, he addressed short letters on the same subject. These warnings were treated by some, with ridicule and contempt. On the minds of others, they made an impression, which, as he afterwards learned, was never effaced. This was particularly the case with Philander Parmele, who was afterwards his classmate in college, and intimate friend through life [Mr. Parmele became pastor of the church in Bolton, Conn. At his house Mr. Nettleton was sick with the typhus fever in 1822. Mr. Parmele took the fever of him and died].

"When Mr. Nettleton first became anxious respecting salvation of his soul, he had not, as has been remarked, any very just conceptions of the depravity of his heart. He was sensible that he was not in a safe condition. He knew that he needed something which he did not possess, to prepare him for heaven. He had a general vague idea that he was a sinner, but he saw not the fountain of iniquity within him. As is common with persons when awakened to a sense of their danger, he went about to establish his own righteousness. He vainly presumed, that by diligent and persevering efforts, he should recommend himself to the favor of God. He was accordingly very abundant in his religious services. He not only abandoned those amusements in which he had delighted, and forsook in a great measure the society of those who took no interest in the subject of religion; but he spent much time in retirement, earnestly crying to God for mercy. He would often repair to the fields and forests for this purpose, and he sometimes spent a large part of the night in prayer. In this way, he expected to obtain the forgiveness of his sins, and the peace and consolation which God has promised to his people. But after laboring for some time in this manner, he became alarmed at his want of success. God seemed to pay no regard to his prayers; and how to account for this fact he knew not. At this crisis, he was assailed by infidel doubts. The question arose in his mind, whether he had not proved the Bible to be false. It is written, *Ask and ye shall receive, Seek and ye shall find.* He said to himself, I have asked, but I have not received—I have sought but I have not found. How then can these promises be true? And how can the book which contains them, be the word of God? He found himself disposed to cherish these doubts, and to seek for further proof that the Bible is not true. He searched the Scriptures on purpose to find contradictions in them, and he even went so far as to begin to doubt the existence of a God. Like the fool, he said in his heart there is no God; that is, he wished there were none; for he was sensible that if there was a God, he was not reconciled to his character; and he wished the Bible to be false, because he saw that it condemned him. But his efforts to satisfy himself that religion is not a reality, did not succeed. The thought would sometimes arise, what if the Bible should prove to be true? Then I am lost forever. This would fill him with inconceivable horror. These struggles in his mind, led him to a more just knowledge of his character and condition. He began to see the plague of his own heart. His doubts respecting the truth of the promises which God has made to those who ask, and seek, were dispelled by the painful conviction that he never had asked and sought as God requires. The commandment came, sin revived, and he died. He saw that God looks on the heart, and that he requires holy and spiritual service of his creatures; that *he seeketh such to worship him, as worship him in spirit and in truth.*

"He saw at the same time, that in all his religious services, he had been prompted by selfish motives. He saw that in all which he had done, he had no love to God, and no regard to his glory; but that he had been influenced solely by a desire to promote his own personal interest and happiness. He saw that in all the distress which he had experienced on account of his sin, there was no godly sorrow—no true contrition. He had not hated sin because it was committed against God, but had merely dreaded its consequences ...

"During this period he read President Edwards' narrative of the revival of religion in Northampton, and the memoir of Brainerd. These served very much to deepen the conviction of his utterly lost condition. The preaching which he heard from time to time, also greatly distressed him. As he says in his narrative, every sermon condemned him. Nothing gave him any relief. He seemed to be sinking daily deeper and deeper in guilt and wretchedness. One day, while alone in the field, engaged in prayer, his heart rose against God, because he did not hear and answer his prayers. Then the words of the Apostle, *the carnal mind is enmity against God,* came to his mind with such overwhelming power, as to deprive him of strength, and he fell prostrate on the earth. The doctrines of the Gospel, particularly the doctrines of divine sovereignty and election, were sources of great distress to him. There was much talk respecting these doctrines, at that time, in North Killingworth. Some disbelieved and openly opposed them. He searched the Scriptures with great diligence to ascertain whether they are there taught; and although his heart was unreconciled to them, he dared not deny them, for he was convinced that they were taught in the Bible. He would sometimes say to himself, if I am not elected, I shall not be saved, even if I do repent—then the thought would arise, if I am not elected, I shall never repent. This would cut him to the heart, and dash to the ground all his self-righteous hopes. For a long time he endured these conflicts in his mind. Meanwhile he became fully convinced, that the commands of God are perfectly just, that it was his immediate duty to repent, and that he had no excuse for continuing another moment a rebel against God. At the same time he saw that such was the wickedness of his heart, that he never should repent, unless God should subdue his heart by an act of sovereign grace. With these views of his condition, his distress was sometimes almost insupportable. At one time he really supposed himself to be dying, and sinking into hell. This was the time of which he speaks in his narrative, when he says, 'an unusual tremor seized all my limbs, and death appeared to have taken hold of me.' For several hours, his horror of mind was inexpressible. Not long after this, there was a change in his feelings. He felt a calmness for which he knew not how to account. He thought, at first, that he had lost his convictions, and was going back to stupidity. This alarmed him, but still he could not recall his former feelings. A sweet peace pervaded his soul. The objects which had given him so much distress, he now contemplated with delight …

"It was about ten months, as has been already intimated, from the time Mr. Nettleton's attention was first seriously turned to the subject of religion, before he obtained peace in believing. With him, what the old divines termed the *law-work*, was deep and thorough. This protracted season of conviction gave him a knowledge of the human heart which few possess; and which was doubtless intended by God to prepare him for that pre-eminent success which attended his labors as a minister of Christ."[9]

The observations of Nettleton by Tyler are important to our understanding of how Asahel Nettleton was used of God in times of revival. To better comprehend this, we must have a working knowledge of Calvinistic New England prior to Nettleton's time. For this was the backdrop from which he emerged, Nettleton's message of immediate repentance was *startling* to his hearers for many had not heard that preached before! They were told by the New England ministers to "wait God's time", with the emphasis placed upon "the necessity of God's act" in election. This is further explained by the following comments:

"We have already noted that after the excesses which occurred in the last days of the First Great Awakening, many of New England's clergy were chary of revivals. Although the New Divinity, under the guidance of Edwards, then of Bellamy and Hopkins, had provided a theological foundation for the revivals of the Second Awakening, there remained many in New England who were not ready to jump on the bandwagon in 1801. These reticent clergy were legacies from the Old or Moderate Calvinists of the First Awakening who tried to maintain a strict Calvinism and preached the total depravity of man and his dependence upon God to such an extent that moral agency and responsibility were often put in the background. They were never totally forgotten, but the minister's emphasis was upon the necessity of God's act rather than upon man's power and responsibility to repent. The inquiring sinners were told to use certain means (attend worship, study, read the scriptures, pray, etc.) and to 'wait God's time.' Josiah Andrews' description of the revival in Killingworth suggests that his theological leanings were with the Old Calvinists. The doctrines which he said he preached and his advice to the youth substantiate this. One of his converts, though, was to take a different stand. After Nettleton's conversion and study at Yale, he clearly became an advocate of the New Divinity position. The platform of the New Divinity and the basis of their revival preaching which urged man to immediate repentance, and not to wait God's time, was the correlation between man's dependence upon God and his free moral agency. Lest we be misunderstood, let us make it clear that the New Divinity preachers and theologians were not saying that man is able to save himself; rather they were urging man to accept his own guilt and responsibility and his *natural* ability to do something about it. They would go on to say that because of his *moral* inability he would not act until God gave him a new direction, or a new heart; but nonetheless man's responsibility and power were given a place of primary importance …

"As Nettleton told his experience to the readers of *Connecticut Evangelical Magazine* and to his lifelong friend and biographer years later, three main stages appear to emerge from the recognition of one's sin to the reception of a new will. Nettleton did not speak of steps, or stages, but they are evident in the narrative and they proved to be pedagogically informative in the way in which he was later to understand and guide those experiencing the same crisis.

"After the initial awareness of the inauthenticity of one's life, there was a time of 'self-righteousness,' during which the person attempts to make right his life through his own moral acts. When this does not work, the person moves into a second stage of doubt and despair, doubt first of himself and his abilities, then of the scriptures, then of the very existence of God, and finally a recognition of death itself. The movement out of this despair into the final stage is characterized by a freedom from the power of one's doubts and fears, a recognition that those inadequacies are one's own, and a desire to confess before God one's inadequacies. Nettleton's 'conversion' verified for him the validity of the Calvinistic doctrines of grace—human depravity, election, the sovereignty of God, etc. Thus whenever Nettleton saw meddling with these doctrines—whether by Charles Grandison Finney or Nathaniel William Taylor—he feared the resultant religious experience would be spurious."[10]

Thus the basis of Asahel Nettleton's conversion experience became the foundation for all his future labors in times of revival. He knew the windings of a lost sinner's heart better than most men of his generation, and this knowledge enabled him to be a "wise counselor" to many new converts in that awakening.

Notes

1   Thomas L. Lentz, *A Photographic History of Killingworth* (Killingworth Historical Society, 2004), p. 74.
2   Bennet Tyler, *Memoir of the Life and Character of Asahel Nettleton* (Boston: Doctrinal Tract and Book Society, 1853), pp. 11–13.
3   J. F. Thornbury, *God Sent Revival, The Story of Asahel Nettleton and the Second Great Awakening* (Welwyn, England: Evangelical Press, 1977), p. 26.
4   Sherry Pierpont May, *Asahel Nettleton: Nineteenth Century American Revivalist* (Unpublished dissertation, Drew University, 1969), pp. 31–32.
5   Thomas L. Lentz, *A Photographic History of Killingworth* (Killingworth Historical Society, 2004), p. 50.
6   "Connecticut Evangelical Magazine", 1804, contains the accounts of this revival in Volumes IV and V. It is interesting to note that during the revivals of religion in the 18th century, both in Great Britain and America, monthly periodicals surfaced which published reports of the revival. Similarly, in the Second Great Awakening, monthly periodicals provided details of events and testimonies related to the revival.
7   Sherry Pierpont May, *Asahel Nettleton: Nineteenth Century American Revivalist* (Drew University, 1969), pp. 18–19.
8   Bennet Tyler, *Memoir of the Life and Character of Asahel Nettleton* (Boston: Doctrinal Tract and Book Society, 1853), pp. 13–16.
9   Ibid. pp. 16–23.
10   Sherry Pierpont May, pp. 22, 23, 30.

We do not claim for Dr. Nettleton the rank of Whitefield; but yet he stands very high among those who have "converted sinners from the error of their ways, saved souls from death, and hidden a multitude of sins" (James v. 20).

ANDREW BONAR

The "Yard" at Yale College, New Haven, CT. Nettleton was a student at Yale.

4

HIS COLLEGE LIFE

Bennet Tyler grimly states in a single sentence: "In the year 1801, the father of Mr. Nettleton died." The magnitude of that statement in Asahel's life meant the following: he would now become the patriarch of the family, with its cares and burdens. The main source of income for his siblings was the family's farm, of which he was now the head. In short, the death of Samuel Nettleton would seemingly cut off all hopes of his eldest son, Asahel, to do anymore in life other than be a Connecticut farmer. But this was not God's purpose for the grieving Asahel. Teaching school in the "Little Green Schoolhouse" was money in the bank for him and this was his nest egg for a college education. It was a tremendous load upon him to run the farm, care for his siblings, and in addition to all these teach school. Four years after the death of his father we see that Asahel's perseverance was not for naught, for he enrolled in the freshman class of Yale College in the autumn of 1805.

Before we examine Nettleton's mediocre academic life, we must focus our attention on the President of Yale at this time, the eminent Timothy Dwight who was Jonathan Edwards' grandson. A brief biography is found in Sprauge's *Annals of the American Pulpit*:

> "Timothy Dwight, the son of Timothy and Mary Dwight, was born in Northampton, Mass., May 14, 1752 ... His mother was the third daughter of Jonathan Edwards, and inherited much of his intellectual superiority ... As an evidence of his great precocity, he is said to have mastered the alphabet at a single lesson; and at the age of four, he could read the Bible correctly and fluently ... In September, 1765, when he had just passed his thirteenth year, he was admitted a member of the Freshman class in Yale College."[1]

As President of Yale, Dwight was singularly responsible for driving out "French infidelity". The students of Yale were so caught up in the writings of Voltaire, Rousseau and other infidel philosophers, that the campus had become a hotbed of vice! One of the students, who would rise to prominence was Lyman Beecher. Beecher commented on his fellow classmates with the following:

> "Wine and liquors were kept in many rooms; intemperance, profanity, gambling, and licentiousness were common."[2]

President Dwight addressed these issues through the use of chapel lectures. It wasn't long before the searching preaching of Timothy Dwight pushed back atheism at Yale and in 1802 the campus was visited with a remarkable revival! Soon the entire focus of the campus had been altered with the reality of God and eternity. A student who witnessed these times commented:

> "Nothing very remarkable, however, took place, till the spring and summer of 1802, when the revival, in its triumphant progress on the right hand and the left, reached Yale college; and there it came with such power as had never been witnessed within those walls before. It was in the Freshman year of my own class. It was like a mighty rushing wind. The whole college was shaken. It seemed for a time as if the whole mass of the students would press into the kingdom. It was the Lord's doing, and marvellous in all eyes … It was indeed the bright dawn of a new Christian epoch, when the heavens were opened, and poured down righteousness upon Yale college, and upon scores of churches; and I may venture to say, that the influence of those revivals upon the cause of vital religion at home and abroad, has already surpassed the most sanguine hopes of those who witnessed and rejoiced in them.

> "At that time, when a student was converted in college, or before he entered, it was taken for granted by everybody, that he intended to devote his life to the service of Christ in the gospel. It was so at Yale, in the revival of 1802. I cannot call to mind a single convert who did not at once ask, 'Lord, what wilt thou have me to do?' and who did not set his heart upon becoming a preacher. Nearly all of them, as the catalogue shows, entered the ministry."[3]

When Asahel Nettleton arrived at Yale College in 1805 the college had acquired a prestige for academics. Although Asahel was not an intellectual and he did not excel in academics, he was an ordinary student who seemed more preoccupied with the Bible than he did his textbooks. However, he did stand out in the eyes of Timothy Dwight who saw great potential in Asahel. This is seen from the following:

> "Yale was the most prestigious school in Connecticut at the time and certainly many of the students came from the higher classes of society. To many of them probably Asahel seemed like a county bumpkin. His plain clothing and unpolished manners betrayed his rural background. He was quiet, shy, modest and psychologically an introvert. But one thing was evident to all, this young man was serious about his faith … The dedication and sincerity of Asahel did not escape the notice of the college president. Once he remarked of him, 'He will make one of the most useful men this country has ever seen.'"[4]

President Dwight's observation concerning Nettleton would turn out to be *prophetic*, for there was not a man in his generation who impacted the Church in such a positive manner as the soon-to-be revivalist. When

Asahel first arrived on campus his main purpose was to graduate to become a foreign missionary. He was good friends with Samuel Mills and together they had made a pact to go together to the foreign field with the gospel. But because of his poor health and the Providence of God, Nettleton never made it to the foreign mission field. His mission field was the *American church*.

Another revival broke upon Yale College in 1808 and Asahel Nettleton would be in the midst of those showers of grace, delighting in the presence of God and honing his craft in the counsel of the awakened. During the revival Nettleton remained at the bedside of an awakened sinner all night, reciting the invitations of the gospel. It was during these "revival times" that Asahel Nettleton gained the most useful knowledge which he would put into practical application while laboring in future revivals.

We will close this chapter with some personal observations of Nettleton from his college room-mate, the Rev. Jonathan Lee.

"I was classmate with Mr. Nettleton during the two last years of our college life, and roomed with him through the junior year ... My previous observations of him in his class, had left the impression that he was a modest and inoffensive youth, of unpolished manners ... and bearing the marks of a peculiar interest, solemnity and devotedness in the religious worship, and at the communion seasons in the chapel ... His best loved place was the chapel, listening with devout solemnity, to the prayers and preaching of the venerated Dwight. His best loved book was the Bible. His best loved day was the Sabbath—and his best loved friends, were those who knew the joys and sorrows of a pious heart ...

"In regard to his standing as a scholar, it is true, he was not, in this respect, distinguished, as he never rose above the ordinary rank in the common course of classical studies ... The state of his health through a part of the year, when he roomed with me, was much impaired, and in connection with this, he passed through a protracted season of deep mental anxiety and depression in the spring of 1808, in which he greatly questioned the genuineness of his Christian experience. So severe were his mental trials of this nature, as to unfit him for study, for some time, and he was excused and permitted to return home, on account of the state of his health. Before returning home, he was wont to repair to the President for instruction and counsel, and he directed him to the perusal of Edwards on Religious Affections, and loaned him also, his manuscript sermons on the Evidences of Regeneration. With them he went into the most intensely earnest and sifting self-examination that I ever witnessed, and in the course of it, he passed through such agony of spirit, as was suited to awaken the liveliest sympathy in those who could best understand and appreciate the nature of his distress ... Before the next term he gained peace, and enjoyed a better state of health; but it is evident that this interruption of his progress in regular study, had a retarding effect upon his scholarship.

"In the winter of 1807–8, a revival of religion began in New Haven, and in Yale College. The first subjects of it among the students were in the Freshman class. Nettleton was no indifferent spectator, but among the first to discover indications of

special religious impressions, and to seek out persons in a state of religious anxiety.
Then, contrary to what I had before witnessed of intimacy between the upper and
lower classes, often did I see him with one or two heart-burdened youth of the
youngest class, walking arm in arm in the college yard, before evening prayers,
conversing upon the great interests of the soul ... His feelings were most deeply
interested in the whole progress of the revival, and it seemed almost to absorb his
mind by day and by night."[5]

An interesting fact of Asahel Nettleton's college days was that of his
being a butler to pay off his debts. We see this in the following remarks
by Thornbury:

"Nettleton graduated from Yale in the spring of 1809, anxious to join Mills in his
rapidly developing missionary plans. But a problem had arisen to delay his own
participation in such endeavours. During his college studies he had accumulated
some debts which he felt should be dissolved before he attended to anything else.
Mills encouraged him to seek the assistance of some friends in this matter, but
Nettleton felt that he should take care of it himself. President Dwight offered the
position of Butler in the college to Nettleton ... The Butler acted as sort of
commissary for the students ... He held this post for a year ... The extra year at Yale,
though necessary, caused Asahel to miss missionary consultations at Andover ...
The circumstances of Asahel's absence probably changed the course of his life,
though as future events proved, it was providential."[6]

In this regard, he was similar to George Whitefield who, while at
Oxford, was a servitor to his fellow students because of similar financial
straits. It seems that God was using these humbling circumstances in His
choice servants to prepare them for greater things!

Notes

1   William B. Sprague, D.D., *Annals of the American Pulpit*, Vol. II (New York: Robert Carter &
Brothers, 1859), pp. 152, 153.
2   Charles Beecher, *Autobiography of Lyman Beecher, D.D.*, Vol. I (New York: 1864), p. 43.
3   Heman Humphrey, *Revival Sketches and Manual, in Two Parts* (New York: American Tract
Society, 1859), pp. 198–199.
4   J. F. Thornbury, *God Sent Revival* (Welwyn, England: Evangelical Press, 1977), p. 37.
5   Tyler, *Memoir of Nettleton*, pp. 28–33.
6   Thornbury, *God Sent Revival*, p. 41.

If there has been, since the days of the mighty elders in the Great Awakening, a preacher more successful in winning souls to Christ within the same number of years, than Nettleton, I have yet to learn his name ... Wherever he went, the Lord went with him, working mightily in turning men from darkness to light.

HEMAN HUMPHREY

5

CALL TO MINISTRY

Asahel Nettleton never made it to the foreign mission field as a missionary—God had other plans for him. Now that he had graduated from college he needed to be trained for the ministry which God was calling him to. Leaving Yale in 1810, (graduating in 1809) he experienced a personal tragedy—the death of his mother. His brother Ambrose agreed to assume the responsibilities of the farm and care of the family. It was not uncommon in his day that those entering the ministry first did some apprentice training under a more experienced clergyman. Jonathan Edwards practiced this by having young ministry students stay in his Northampton home; Joseph Bellamy was one of Edwards' first pupils. For these same purposes, Nettleton became an assistant to the Rev. Bezaleel Pinneo, of Milford, Connecticut and remained under the senior minister's tutelage until May of 1811. On the 28th of May, Asahel was licensed to preach by the New Haven West Association, "at the house of the Rev. Trumbull in North Haven. Later in the summer of 1811, he was ordained as an evangelist by the South Consociation of Litchfield county (Lyman Beecher's consociation)."[1]

The field in which Nettleton was to commence his labors was Eastern Connecticut. This part of Connecticut experienced spiritual "trauma" during the Great Awakening in the previous century under the wild preaching of James Davenport. Davenport was an odd man who had been both a pastor (in Southold, Long Island) and a friend of George Whitefield, often riding with Whitefield during the revival. Early in his public ministry God's hand was on Davenport and many were blessed by his labors, however, Davenport became emotionally unbalanced. Eventually he caused much damage to the revival and his wild antics were primarily focused on Eastern Connecticut where he caused division in the churches and consternation in public assemblies. Thus, when Asahel Nettleton began his own preaching ministry in Eastern

Connecticut he encountered many stories from the "aged saints" who
informed him of Davenport and the spiritual wreckage that lay in those
districts from the previous revival. Some observations on this are seen in
the following comments:

> "Rev. Joseph Fish, the pastor in Stonington, was still preaching about the
> disorders. The sermons were published in a pamphlet and Tyler suggests that
> Nettleton had access to them while in Eastern Connecticut.

> "When Nettleton was in that part of the state in 1811 and 1812, the unrest was still
> evident. Many of the churches were without pastors, and were left with the feeling
> that they had been in that condition for many years. The many divisions within the
> churches in the aftermath of the First Awakening had encouraged the growth of
> splinter groups; and evangelists, of various theological stripes, were still roaming the
> empty churches. Nettleton told this biographer that the older people still
> remembered Davenport and the unrest of the years and filled his ears with many
> stories."[2]

With this information before us, one can understand why Asahel
Nettleton placed such emphasis on *avoiding* emotional outbursts during a
revival. For the remainder of Nettleton's ministry he was careful to guard
against such wild excitement in revivals. The few instances where some
converts became physically overwrought, they were immediately
carried away from the meeting so not to further disrupt it. In this regard,
Nettleton wisely conducted revivals, monitoring any emotional excesses
and administering sound biblical advice to his distraught hearers. Thus
many years later those who were converted under his preaching could be
found faithful in the Lord, for they were birthed on "good ground".

Although Asahel Nettleton entered an itinerant ministry when
itinerancy was out of vogue in New England, he had prepared himself
for the ministry through the best means available to him at the time.
Earning a B.A. degree from Yale, becoming licensed as a minister in his
state of Connecticut, and submitting to training under a mature
mentor—the Rev. Bezaleel Pinneo. Thus equipped through the ways of
man, he then submitted to the ways of God through times of intense
Bible study and prayer. He had no uncertainties regarding his theological
beliefs, he was a solid New England Calvinist in the Edwardsean
position. Nettleton believed firmly that any revival was a sovereign act of
God and he attributed that same sovereignty to the act of regeneration—
man could not save himself. Yet, he also firmly believed that although
God was sovereign in the salvation process, it was man's duty to
recognize himself a sinner and repent immediately. This is where he
distanced himself from the New England Fathers, he did not tell sinners
to "wait God's time" but to "repent immediately". As the great message

of the First Great Awakening under George Whitefield was, "Ye must be born again"; the message of the Second Great Awakening under Nettleton was, "repent for the kingdom of God is at hand"(Matthew 3:2); and "unless you repent, you will all likewise perish"(Luke 13:3). Bennet Tyler produces evidence in support of this:

"The knowledge which he obtained while laboring in this region, led him to entertain great respect for the pastoral office. He was convinced that without a settled ministry, there could be no rational prospect of building up churches, or of enjoying genuine revivals of religion; that flocks scattered upon the mountains with no faithful shepherd to watch and feed them, would become the prey of 'ravening wolves.' He became also convinced that a tremendous responsibility rests upon those who labor as evangelists; and that it is their duty not to weaken the hands of settled pastors, but to do all in their power to strengthen them. This lesson was of immense importance to him, in preparing him for that course of labor to which he was destined; and it is doubtless one reason why he was enabled to shun those indiscretions into which most evangelists have fallen.

"About the close of the period which I attempted to describe in former letters, the Rev. Asahel Nettleton devoted himself to the work of an evangelist. With his eminent qualifications for this work, and usefulness in it I presume you are well acquainted. The fact, however, which it is especially to my present purpose to mention, and which probably many of you do not know, is, that this distinguished itinerant found no difficulty to labor with stated pastors without making himself their *rival*. If, in any instance, he could not conscientiously coincide in the views, or co-operate in the measures of a pastor, among whose charge he was invited to labor, he did not sow dissension in that church, nor seek to detach their affections from their minister, but quietly withdrew to another place. The consequence was, that the visits of this devoted servant of Christ, *were always sought*, and never dreaded, nor regretted by ministers or churches."[3]

It is interesting to note how God trains and equips His servants. With Whitefield, his early training was in the Holy Club at Oxford, England, it was there he visited prisons and widows' homes in obscurity before his rise to prominence. D. L. Moody spent years as an unknown evangelist to a rag-tag horde of Chicago street urchins whom he taught the basic truths of the gospel by gaslight in alleyways. For Nettleton, the training ground was obscure, rural churches in Eastern Connecticut that were waste places from Davenport's unwise excesses. Yet it is of supreme importance not to miss this aspect of his training, for few are the servants of the Lord who burst onto the public scene amidst wide acceptance and usefulness without first spending their due time, like the Apostle Paul, in Arabia. The fruit of this time for Nettleton was not in making converts but in making the preacher; this is brought out by the following observations of Thornbury:

"The importance of his ministry in south-eastern Connecticut was in the training that this unique period afforded him. As far as his preaching was concerned, there were few visible results. Though there were some conversions, he never saw anything close to a revival in this place. In fact, he was unable to do much to repair the damage which had been done in the previous century. But the education process for the future evangelist was going on. He had seen real revival at Killingworth and at New Haven, and he had cut out for himself the path he wanted to follow doctrinally. But one thing else was needed; the proper methods in evangelism must be determined. The wild-fire brand of evangelism of Davenport was a good example of what an evangelist was not to do. Thus, by a negative model, Asahel's concepts on how to promote a revival were being formed. This experience would stand him in good stead in his career as an itinerant evangelist, which was, unbeknown to him, just around the corner. Also it would give him the background to face the 'new measures' conflict which would burst upon him fifteen years later."[4]

Notes

1   Sherry Pierpont May, p. 50.
2   Ibid. p. 53.
3   Tyler, pp. 51–52.
4   Thornbury, p. 52.

As further evidence of the perfect impotency of all such rumors against Mr. Nettleton in Connecticut, I would state that about six years ago, on the failure of my health, I left my church and congregation in the care of Mr. Nettleton, under whose preaching, before my return, a revival of religion commenced, during which he secured eminently the confidence and affection of my people, which to this day remains undiminished. In short, there is not a minister in New England whose character for piety and purity stands higher than does that of Mr. Nettleton.

LYMAN BEECHER

6

NETTLETON'S PREACHING

In his biography of Nettleton, John Thornbury makes the case that Asahel Nettleton was the greatest evangelist since George Whitefield. It is true that Whitefield and Nettleton share many similarities. I would state that Whitefield preached to more people in a single afternoon on Kennington Common, upwards of thirty thousand, than Nettleton preached to most of his *life*. However I would also state that Asahel Nettleton actually labored in more revivals than Whitefield and was more familiar with them than any other man in *history*, including Jonathan Edwards. God used Whitefield uniquely for his day, and God used Nettleton uniquely for his day.

God will always raise up a man fitted perfectly for the task at hand in any generation, for God will advance His plans and purposes for mankind until the end of the age.

Thornbury comments on the two evangelists:

"Not since George Whitefield barnstormed the American colonies had New England seen the likes of Asahel Nettleton. In 1820, at the age of thirty-seven, he was the leading evangelist of the East, in demand everywhere as a speaker. Admiring young people swarmed about him, beleaguered pastors vied for his counsel, erudite college people sat at his feet and ordinary lay people revelled in his expositions of Scripture. More importantly, legions of new born souls all over New England rose in rank after rank to call him their spiritual father."[1]

The comparisons of Whitefield and Nettleton must cease here. Both men were mighty men whom God chose to impact their generations in a time of *His grace*. Whitefield's preaching, over 18,000 sermons, shook two continents and prepared the Colonies for the great changes which lay ahead through the Revolutionary War. George Whitefield preached in the largest cities existent at the time: Boston, Philadelphia, New York, Charleston, London, Edinburgh, and Glasgow. Nettleton, on the other hand, was hidden in rural parishes of Eastern New England and Eastern New York. Yet, although Whitefield's ministry was *wider in scope*,

Nettleton's was *deeper in lasting effect*. Both men made powerful use of Scriptural illustration and made the realities of the Gospel come to life! We see from the following:

> "In the accounts and descriptions of the great revivals in which Nettleton laboured, one thing comes across very powerfully, and that is that he was able to bring the awesome realities of the eternal world home to the souls of men. When he talked about the heinousness of sin, they felt its sting. When he portrayed the sufferings of Christ, they felt the trauma of Calvary. When he proclaimed the holy character of God, they trembled at the vision. When he thundered forth the judgements of hell, men were moved to escape that place."[2]

Whitefield was known for this ability as well. Apparently, both George Whitefield and Asahel Nettleton possessed the power to grip their hearers with the reality of heaven and hell and make the very scenes of the Bible come to *life*.

At this juncture we will turn to an eyewitness who heard Nettleton frequently and has provided an account of Nettleton's unique ministry. Heman Humphrey, President of Amherst College, when a pastor, frequently had the great evangelist in his church. Even Dr. Humphrey cannot help making comparisons between Nettleton and Whitefield:

> "And as he in a former age raised up George Whitefield to help the pastors wherever he went, and they received him, so I must here record the grace of God in raising up, and so eminently qualifying ASAHEL NETTLETON, to perform a similar service over a wide region where the revivals of which I am now to speak most remarkably prevailed. If there were others who were equally devoted, judicious, and helpful to pastors, I did not know them, and must leave if for those who did to name them. Mr. Nettleton's labors were so widely extended, so long continued, and so remarkably blessed, that it would be impossible for me, in my sketches of this period, not to refer to him often, as holding a high place among those whom God was pleased to honor in the conversion of souls. President Dwight, whose pupil he was and who knew him well, is reported to have said, 'Nettleton will make one of the most useful men this country has ever seen.' Of course, in the inspired sense of the term, this was not prophetic; but Dr. Dwight was justly celebrated for his remarkable penetration of young men's talents and character. His judgment seemed to be almost intuitive, and it seldom failed.

> "If there has been, since the days of the mighty elders in the Great Awakening, a preacher more successful in winning souls to Christ within the same number of years, than Nettleton, I have yet to learn his name, and what he did. I cannot refer to all the places where Mr. Nettleton labored, nor give the exact number, but it was very large—scores, I believe, where the revivals were very powerful, and most of which sprung up in immediate connection with his untiring labors. Wherever he went, as his Memoir and Remains by Dr. Tyler show, the Lord went with him, working mightily in turning men from darkness to light, and from the power of Satan unto God. His great experience in revivals, his deep penetration of the workings of the human heart in all the stages of awakening and conviction, and with all its conflicting exercises up to a comfortable hope in Christ, gave him an advantage, of which he availed himself to the full extent of his powers, which I am

persuaded has rarely if ever been surpassed, and seldom equalled in these modern times.

"I verily believe that no great warrior ever studied military tactics with more enthusiasm, or better understood the art of *killing* men with the sword of war, than Nettleton did how to wield the sword of the Spirit, to deliver them from captivity to sin and Satan, and save their souls. I am sure no warrior ever studied his art under so great a Teacher. No matter whether Nettleton had ever met an inquirer or caviller before or not, he seemed to see just where he stood, and how to address him at a glance. If all revivalists had the talent and wisdom and piety and meekness and deep Christian experience which he had, pastors with more work than they can do when God is pouring out his Spirit might safely receive them with open arms. But the ability to do what he did as a helper and do it so well, is granted to very few. It is one of the most difficult services in which an itinerant popular preacher ever engaged, to go in and labor with pastors of ordinary standing, in revivals. It requires wisdom, prudence, and self forgetfulness, which very few of that class possess, so as not to do quite as much harm as good, by throwing the ministers whom they came to assist into the background. Many a faithful pastor has been undermined and dismissed, unintentionally we must believe, to the great loss of the church, just in this way. Not so with Nettleton. Wherever he labored, he left the churches and their ministers stronger and more united than he found them. This was the universal testimony. I never knew or heard of an exception. Most manifest was it, that God had raised him up and kept him in this land for that very service, when he had set his heart upon a foreign mission. He labored with me three months in the most powerful revival that we ever enjoyed, and for whatever I know of the means which God has been wont especially to bless in reviving his work. I am more indebted to him than to any other man, more than to all others put together."[3]

We turn now to an account of Nettleton's *preaching style*. This narrative is provided by Asahel's main biographer, Bennet Tyler, who frequently heard Nettleton preach. Every student of preaching should study the following *carefully*—seldom is it taught in seminary:

"The preaching of Dr. Nettleton was, for the most part, extemporaneous. He rarely had any manuscript before him, unless it were a very brief outline of his discourse ... but notwithstanding these disadvantages, *he was an instructive preacher.* Although he preached principally without writing, he did not preach without study. He bestowed much thought on his sermons. They were rich in matter; and although they were so plain as to be easily understood by the most illiterate, they were interesting and instructive to persons of the most cultivated intellect. He investigated subjects thoroughly, and exhibited the result of his investigations with a clearness and force rarely, if ever, equaled. The remark of a plain man, after having listened to one of his discourses, will give some idea of the character of his preaching. 'While he was speaking,' said he, 'a stream of light went right through me.'

"*He was a doctrinal preacher.*——It was his opinion that a belief of the fundamental doctrines of the gospel, is the basis of all genuine religious experience. He was aware that there might be religious excitement, and much religious zeal, where these doctrines are discarded, and even opposed; but he had no confidence in such excitements. He had learned from his own observation and experience, that the preaching of these doctrines is suited to promote genuine revivals of religion; and that revivals, where they are not faithfully preached, are apt to run into the wildest fanaticism. He believed that faithful, judicious doctrinal preaching, is adapted to humble saints, and excite them to fervent prayer, and the diligent discharge of their various duties; and at the same time, to produce convictions in the consciences of sinners, to destroy their self-righteous hopes, and to bring them to the foot of the cross. He had no fears that the doctrines of grace, when clearly explained, and properly exhibited, would paralyze effort, and encourage sloth and spiritual apathy. He had abundant proof continually before his eyes, of a directly contrary effect. These doctrines, in his hands were the sword of the spirit, and the power of God unto salvation. But while he was pre-eminently a doctrinal preacher, he was at the same time,

"*A practical preacher.*—He preached the doctrines practically. While he explained them and rescued them from the misrepresentations of cavilers and errorists, and enforced them by irresistible arguments, he never preached them as matters of mere speculation; but always, as truths of everlasting moment. He applied them to the hearts and consciences of his hearers, as subjects in which they had a personal and infinite interest …

"*He was a wise preacher.*—Wise in the selection of his topics, and in his mode of discussing them; but especially in adapting his discourses to the state and circumstances of his hearers. In this respect, he was particularly distinguished. When he commenced laboring in a place, he very soon ascertained the state of the people, and what kind of instruction was suited to their condition. If they had previously had an undue proportion of doctrinal preaching, and were beginning to pervert the doctrines by contemplating them in such a light as to furnish them with an excuse for the neglect of duty; he found it necessary to press upon the consciences of sinners their obligations, and to urge the duty of immediate repentance. Where the previous instruction had been of an opposite character, he found it necessary to dwell much on the doctrine of regeneration, and other kindred topics. This is what, in familiar language he called 'cross-ploughing;' and he uniformly found it to produce the desired effect. During the progress of a revival he always seemed to know what was needed at every particular crisis, and all his discourses were admirably timed.

"*He was a plain preacher.*—By this I mean he exhibited the truth with remarkable clearness, so that everybody could understand it; and with such force of reasoning, that it could not be easily resisted. Although he possessed a strong and discriminating mind, and was somewhat fond of metaphysical discussion; yet he rarely introduced abstract and metaphysical reasoning into the pulpit. His reasoning was of the rhetorical kind, which, often at a stroke, carried overpowering conviction to the mind. It was said by one who was well acquainted with his mode of illustrating and enforcing divine truth, 'He is always unanswerable.' And it was even so. What he undertook to establish, seemed to be settled beyond controversy. And it was done in so simple and easy a manner, as to cause the hearer to wonder that he had never seen it thus before.

"*He was a solemn preacher.*—He carefully avoided in the pulpit, witticisms, ludicrous comparisons, and every thing suited to produce levity. He felt that he was standing in the presence of God, and addressing immortal beings on subjects of infinite moment. He had a higher object than to amuse his hearers, who were slumbering on the brink of eternal perdition. His heart yearned with compassion for them, and his object was to impress upon their minds a sense of their lost condition. The great realities of eternity were before his mind. He of course felt solemn. It was not affectation, but a reality. He had no sanctimonious tone. His manner was simple and unaffected. His articulation and emphasis were natural, and the deep bass tones of his voice were sometimes peculiarly solemn and impressive. Under his preaching, an awful solemnity usually pervaded the assembly. No one, unless it were some bold blasphemer, was disposed to trifle. Such were the manifest tokens of the presence of God, that the minds of the people were filled with awe, and the breathless silence was broken only by the occasional sighs and sobs of anxious souls.

"*He was a faithful preacher.*—Few men ever had a more vivid sense of the responsibility connected with the sacred office; or were enabled more successfully to resist the various temptations to unfaithfulness. He was, in an unusual degree, raised above the fear of man. He made it his object to please, not men, but God, who trieth our hearts; and no earthly consideration could induce him to keep back what he believed it to be his duty to preach. Still, he was never harsh and denunciatory; but always kind and affectionate. He never made it his object to give offence, but always to commend himself to every man's conscience in the sight of God. His heart glowed with love to souls, and it was his great desire to be instrumental in their salvation. And for this purpose, he set before them with great plainness their sin and danger, and solemnly and affectionately warned them to flee from the wrath to come.

"*He was an animated preacher.*—He felt deeply the truths which he uttered, and aimed to impress them strongly on the minds of his hearers. He was not boisterous or vehement; but there was an earnestness in his manner, which produced the conviction in all who heard him, that what he said came from the heart. He spake as a dying man to dying men. He felt that he stood on the verge of eternity, and that he was addressing immortal beings, to whom he must be a savor, either of life unto life, or death unto death.

"*He was an eloquent preacher.*—His, however, was not the eloquence which dazzles by splendid diction, and graceful delivery; and which fills the hearers with admiration of the brilliant talents of the preacher. It was the eloquence of thought and feeling—eloquence which made the hearers forget the preacher, in the all-absorbing interest which they felt in the subject of his discourse. 'If we were compelled,' say the Edinburgh Reviewers, 'to give a brief definition of eloquence, we should say, it was practical reasoning, animated by strong emotion.' It would be difficult to give a better description of Dr. Nettleton's preaching, than that contained in this definition.

"His sermons, being mostly extemporaneous, were not, of course, characterized by elegance of style. But they exhibited a clearness, and force, and vivacity, which are seldom found in the written discourses of the most celebrated preachers. He was, it is true, generally diffuse, and sometimes repetitious. He would frequently dwell upon a thought, and present it in different aspects, for the purpose of impressing it more deeply on the mind, and fixing it in the memory. But he was never tedious. He kept the attention of the audience riveted to the subject. Every eye was fastened upon him, and the whole assembly listened in breathless silence.

"His elocution, though not the most graceful, was natural and forcible. His voice was clear and melodious, and under complete command. His enunciation was distinct, and his emphasis, as I have already remarked, was natural, and sometimes remarkably impressive. He was rather moderate and slow in the commencement of his discourse; but as he advanced, he increased in fervor, till he reached, sometimes, the highest pitch of eloquence ... If power to arrest and chain the attention of large auditories for hours together, and to stir up the fountains of deep feeling in the soul, is proof of eloquence, then surely Dr. Nettleton was eloquent.

> "*He was a successful preacher.*—Soon after he began to preach, his labors were crowned with signal success, and for ten or eleven years he was almost constantly employed in guiding inquiring souls to Christ. Few men have ever been instrumental in the conversion of so many souls."[4]

It is important at this time to examine the *capacity* in which he preached, for Nettleton truly had a niche in the country parishes of Eastern Connecticut. Even though his labors were restricted mainly to rural areas, the physical size of the churches in which he labored were, at their time, some of the largest in their counties. An example of this is the church in Farmington, Connecticut, one of the largest churches of its day. One must not assume that Nettleton preached only to small gatherings, the crowds that heard him were *immense*. Often, people had to stand outside the church and listen to him through the open windows; some hearers even climbed trees to hear him preach! Everywhere he went there was a press to get in to hear Nettleton.

The following brief comments speak about Asahel's capacity and mode of preaching:

> "He still preached only on the invitation of the settled minister, or at the request of the church if there was no pastor. He still saw himself as the pastor's assistant, and worked with the local minister and never against him. His preaching was basically doctrinal, but it also tended closely to apply the doctrine being discussed, in such a way that the listener not only understood what was being said, but that he felt that the proclamation was for him. Nettleton believed that one must first have an understanding of the truths he thought were clearly in the Bible, and then he must be motivated to act upon them. His preaching was accentuated and made effective by his use of the inquiry meeting. In these meetings the questions and frustrations of those who were seeking direction were met by a short address by Nettleton and then by brief, but individual, conversation with each person."[5]

It was an interesting fact of Asahel Nettleton's ministry that the inquiry room played as an important role as did the pulpit! He excelled on a one-on-one basis with individuals, and he was an effective discerner of awakened souls and possessed an acute ability to communicate *exactly* what that person needed at that time.

One of the most accurate examples of Nettleton's theology is given by Heman Humphrey who had labored with him in revival. It is also a critical look at Asahel's abilities in the pulpit as well as his effectiveness with awakened sinners. The observations are an *unbiased* look at Nettleton and provide us with an honest appraisal of his preaching skills. Therefore, we read with interest Dr. Humphrey's observations:

> "In his theology, Dr. Nettleton was neither a 'high or a low' Calvinist. While he admired the illustrious Genevan Reformer, and subscribed, ex animo, to all the

leading doctrines of his immortal institutes, he called neither Calvin, nor any other man master. He was an Edwardean, rather than a high Calvinist; and yet profound as his veneration was for that 'greatest of theologians,' as Dr. Chalmers styles President Edwards, he thought it his duty to investigate every subject for himself. With his little duodecimo Bible, or his Greek Testament always in his hands, he was one of the most independent thinkers that I have ever known. He was, I might almost say, the last man to be captivated with visionary theories, or fanciful analogies and interpretations. Upon the 'foundation of the Apostles and Prophets, Jesus Christ himself being the chief corner stone,' he stood like a pillar upon the everlasting rock. Nothing could shake him. Whether he ever drew out his system on paper, I do not know; but if he did, it will be found eminently scriptural, lucid, and symmetrical—nothing more and nothing less, than sound, well digested and well guarded New England orthodoxy.

"As a preacher, Dr. Nettleton had many superiors, in what commonly goes under the name of pulpit eloquence. There was nothing particularly captivating in his voice, in his style, or his delivery—nothing to make you admire the man, or his writing, or his speaking; or in any way to divert your attention from the truths which he uttered. His prayers were generally short, and always fervent, scriptural and appropriate.

"When he rose to speak, there was a benignant solemnity in his countenance, which awed the most thoughtless into seriousness, while at the same time it exerted an unwonted desire to hear what he had to say. He had a voice of more than ordinary compass and power; and though there was nothing harsh or repulsive in its modulations, you sometimes regretted that he had not enjoyed better early advantages for training it. He always commenced on a low key, enunciating every word and syllable so distinctly, however, as to be heard without difficulty, in the remotest parts of the house. So simple were his sentences, so plain and unadorned was his style, and so calm was his delivery, that for a few moments, you might have thought him dull and sometimes even common place, but for the glance of his piercing eye, and an undefinable something in his whole manner, which insensibly gained and riveted your attention. As he advanced, and his heart grew warm, and his conceptions vivid, his voice caught the inspiration; his lips seemed to be 'touched with a live coal from off the altar;' his face shone; every muscle and feature spoke; his tones were deep and awfully solemn; his gestures, though he never flourished off a prettiness in his life were natural, and at times exceedingly forcible. But his eye, after all, was the master power in his delivery. Full and clear and sharp, its glances, in the most animated parts of his discourses were quick and penetrating, beyond almost anything I recollect ever to have witnessed. He seemed to look every hearer in the face, or rather to look into his soul, almost at one and the same moment. You felt that you were in the hands of a master, and never stopped to inquire whether he was a good or a bad pulpit orator. Whatever the critics might say, in one thing you could not be mistaken. He arrested your attention, and made you feel, for the time at least, that religion is indeed 'the one thing needful.'

"Dr. Nettleton's delivery was always solemn, always earnest, and not seldom even vehement. This was particularly the case in the height of those numerous and powerful revivals in the midst of which he labored for so many years. The action of his mind was intense. The yearnings of his soul over the impenitent were irrepressible. His countenance, his voice, everything showed it. And yet, incredible as it may seem, in his most impassioned appeals, there was not a particle of enthusiasm. By this I mean, that he was never hurried away into any extravagance of language, or emotion. He never, for one moment, lost the balance of his mind. He was always perfectly self-possessed. I have seen him in circumstances of overpowering interest, when the movements of the Spirit were 'like a mighty rushing wind,' and could never perceive any wavering in his judgment or his prudence. He was ever the same in the pulpit, in the lecture-room, and in the inquiry meeting—always earnest and solemn, but never carried away by his feelings, beyond the bounds of propriety.

"Dr. Nettleton's sermons were plain, solid, evangelical, instructive and directly to the purpose. He always knew what he aimed at, and he seldom, if ever, missed his mark. Dodging was of no avail. His style was perfectly unadorned. Tropes and metaphors he never sought for; and I am not aware that they ever obtruded themselves upon his imagination. What he aimed at was to present the truth, the whole truth, and nothing but the truth, to his hearers, in the plainest and most forcible language he could command.

"The great power of his preaching consisted in its perspicuity, its directness, its fearless exhibition of the most unwelcomed truths of the Bible, and its earnest, solemn, and often terrible appeals to the conscience. No preacher that I ever heard, could make the law thunder louder in the sinner's ear. The sword of the spirit was his only weapon; and he wielded it with extraordinary dexterity and effect. Few ministers, I believe, have ever studied the windings of the natural heart, with more diligence and success, than he did. Hence, those masterly analyses, which used so often to startle his hearers, as if all their thoughts had been suddenly laid open to the public gaze. In reviewing the history of Dr. Nettleton's life and labors, it is as clear to me that God raised him up to spend his best days in promoting revivals of religion, as that he raised up Whitefield for the same service on a wider theatre. They were unlike in many respects, as any two great revival preachers could be, but they had 'one Lord and one faith'—the same love for souls, and the same irrepressible desire to win as many of them as possible, to Christ. Each was fitted for the age in which he lived, and for the work to which he was called—Whitefield to blow the trumpet over the dead and buried formalism of the churches, both in Great Britain and America; Nettleton, to 'strengthen the things that remained and were ready to die' in destitute churches of Connecticut, Massachusetts, New York, and Virginia; and to help the brethren in gathering their spiritual harvests.

"Having no pastoral charge to confine him, and no family to provide for, and living, I may say for years, in the midst of these 'mighty works,' he was under better advantages for observing all the 'diversities of operations by the Spirit,' which are disclosed in 'times of refreshing,' than any of his immediate predecessors, or early contemporaries; and his Master had endowed him with the requisite gifts, both intellectual and moral, to make the most of these advantages. Shrewd, (pardon the epithet, as no other would so exactly express it,) observing, cautious, discriminating, and at the same time, 'fervent in spirit,' and mightily 'constrained by the love of Christ,' he was most happily guarded against feverish impulses on the one hand, and antinomian presumptions on the other. Enjoying, as he did, for so many years, the best possible opportunity for studying the theory of revivals, his benevolent, inquisitive and ardent mind would not allow him to rest satisfied, without putting it to the most rigid test of scripture, experience and observation. Herein he was in the truest sense a Christian philosopher, and his philosophy was strictly Baconian. It consisted in observing phenomena and recording facts. I have long thought, and it is still my deliberate conviction, that he understood the whole subject of revivals, better than any man with whom I ever conversed or labored. He had studied it more profoundly. Indeed no man could well be a more perfect master of his business or profession. Neither Caesar nor Napoleon ever studied the art of war with greater assiduity, than he did the heavenly art of wining souls to Christ. This may seem extravagant—I presume it will to some readers; but why should it? Had he not far higher motives for bending all the energies of his mind to learn how to save men, than they could have had for learning how to destroy them?

"But you wish me to say something of his *manner* of laboring in revivals, and of their *general character* under his preaching and management. This I am the more ready to do, from having had the best opportunities to observe and judge in one of them, which I have often since heard him speak of as among the most powerful he ever witnessed. He was with me three months, day and night, during which I saw and heard everything. I was anxious to learn all I could from one whose labors had been so eminently owned and blessed by the Divine Head of the church, and not being, if I may say it, of an enthusiastical temperament myself, I think I was enabled to form a pretty correct judgment of his preaching, of his daily intercourse with sinners in every stage of awakening and conversion, and of the effect of those measures which he had been testing in scores of other revivals.

"It has been said, that in such seasons, we ought to look to God continually in fervent believing prayer, just as if he was the sole agent in carrying on the work, and at the same time, to labor with all our might, just as if we had it all to do ourselves. This was Dr. Nettleton's view of the matter, and no man, perhaps, ever more fully carried it out in practice than he did. In his creed, the whole process of awakening, conviction and regeneration, was by the sovereign and special agency of the Holy Sprit. For this he prayed, and exhorted others to pray without ceasing, while at the same time, he labored with as much assiduity for the conversion of sinners, as if his Master had devolved the whole responsibility upon him. His theory was, that while 'the excellency of the power is all of God,' he works by means, no less in the moral than in the natural world. This led him to study the economy of grace in revivals, with the deepest interest; and as the result of it, to adopt the measures and use the means which seemed to him best adapted to the end.

"I do not say that his manner of conducting revivals, was in all respects the best that could have been adopted; much less that it would be best for every minister; but I have yet to learn, that a better and safer system of measures has been devised. Taken as a whole, it commends itself, to my judgment and observation, as eminently wise and guarded and scriptural. It was characterized by a deep and profound knowledge of human nature, as I think might easily be shown, did my limits permit. Let those who come after, improve upon it, or devise a better if they can. While I am far from believing that nothing remains to be learned in the heavenly art of winning souls to Christ, quite sure I am, that few if any of those professed revivalists who have succeeded Dr. Nettleton, and made the most noise in the churches, are the men to 'show us a more excellent way.' They have done what they could with strong lungs, startling appeals, new measures, and sweeping denunciations, and the blighting effects are truly mournful. In some wide districts which they have overrun, it is feared the churches will not recover from the desolating irruption for half a century. Most unwarrantable is the appeal which they sometimes make to Dr. Nettleton, as their fore-runner and exemplar. Nothing gave him so much concern, during the latter years of his life, as the manner in which revivals were corrupted and brought into discredit and run down, by noisy, rash and impetuous evangelists. It grieved him to the heart, that so many churches in the land were ready to countenance them, and he earnestly protested against their errors and extravagances, to the day of his death. Though he would not deny, that there might be some real conversions in the great excitements which attended their preaching, it was his solemn and painful conviction, that multitudes were deceived with false hopes, who, under different instruction and measures, might have been brought to a saving knowledge of the truth.

"In his own management in times of revivals, by preaching and personal intercourse, nothing was more deserving of being studied and imitated, that his *thoroughness, caution, and discrimination.* In these respects there was a heaven-wide difference between Dr. Nettleton and some of the most noted of his professed imitators. Being thoroughly 'rooted and grounded in the truth' himself, his presentations of it were clear, pungent and searching. His revival topics were systematically and admirably arranged. In his discourses he began at the beginning. A full believer in the total depravity of the human heart, he arraigned sinners, whether young or old, as rebels against God, and made the threatenings of the law thunder in their ears, as but few preachers have power to do. With him, acting as an ambassador of Christ, there was no such thing as compromise. The rebels must 'throw down their arms,' and submit unconditionally, or he would give them no hope of pardon. Hundreds, if not thousands, can witness, what a terrible dissector he was of the 'joints and the marrow.' At the same time that he showed the impenitent they were lost, he made them feel that they had 'destroyed themselves.'—It was difficult to say which he made plainest, their danger or their guilt; their immediate duty to repent, or the certainty that without being drawn and renewed by the Spirit of God, they never *would* repent. It was in vain for them to retreat from one refuge to another. He was sure to strip them of all their vain excuses, and deliver them over to their consciences, to be dealt with according to law and justice. He preached what are called the hard doctrines, such as divine sovereignty, election, and regeneration, with great plainness, discrimination and power. His grand aim was to instruct, convince and persuade; to this end, his appeals were constantly made to the understanding, the conscience and the heart. The passions he never addressed, nor were his discourses at all calculated to excite them. Any outbreak of mere animal feeling, he was always afraid of, as tending to warp the judgment, and beget false hopes. His grand aim was to instruct his hearers as thoroughly, and point out difference between true and spurious conversion so clearly, as to make it difficult for them to get hopes at all, without good spiritual evidence on which to found them. Knowing how apt persons are to cling to their hopes, whether good or bad, he depended much more upon holding them back, till they had good evidence, then upon shaking them from their false foundations.

"As might have been expected under such a course of instruction, the great majority of these who came out and professed religion, so far as I have had opportunity to observe, have 'worn well.' They have proved intelligent, stable and consistent Christians. The revivals under Dr. Nettleton's preaching, always strengthened the churches, and strengthened the pastors where they had them. I do not believe that an instance to the contrary can be adduced from the whole wide field of his labors, nor that a single church can be pointed out, which does not to this day feel their blessed influence. How different from the sad experience of hundreds of churches, congregations, and ministers, under the sway of bold, and reckless, and disorganizing revivalists. How many once united and flourishing churches, have been divided or broken up, and how many worthy pastors have been undermined and driven away by them. 'By their fruits ye shall know them.' 'The fire shall try every man's work, of what sort it is.' Brought to these tests, all the great revivals under Dr. Nettleton's labors, will stand on the records of the church, in striking contrast, as so many bright evidences of his wisdom, fidelity, and eminent usefulness."[6]

SERMON EXTRACT FROM NETTLETON

It is good at this time to provide an extract from one of Nettleton's sermons. Asahel Nettleton's sermon collection is housed at Hartford Seminary, in Hartford Connecticut, under the direction of Dr. Steven Blackburn, Director of the Library. The following sermon is a fair example of one of Nettleton's "revival sermons", as he is strongly calling for sinners to repent and come to Christ. It is also typical of Nettleton's theology which was Edwardsean. However, we pause here to present the following extract as an example of a revival sermon preached during the Second Great Awakening. Any student of revival can benefit from its careful study. Here now is that sermon:

INDECISION IN RELIGION

How long halt ye between two opinions? (1 Kings 18:21).

These are the words of the prophet Elijah. They were addressed to a large concourse of people assembled together on Mount Carmel. Displeased with the character and worship of the true God, they had generally departed from him. But to quiet conscience, they set up and worshiped false gods. Conscience, however, is not so easily pacified. At times it admonishes that all is not well. Whither art thou going and what will be the end of thy course? It led them to hesitate and halt between two opinions. The contest was not to be decided. At the direction of the prophet, the people were assembled. "And Elijah came unto all the people and said, How long halt ye between two opinions? If the Lord be God, follow him; but if Baal, follow him. And the people answered him not a word."

This sermon is addressed to all the impenitent. No sinner in this place intends to die without an interest in Christ. And yet many do not like to begin a life of religion now. Many hesitate—they halt between two opinions, whether to begin a life of religion now, or to defer the subject a little longer.

Our text calls upon all such to come to a decided choice, to go one way or the other without delay. "If the Lord be God, follow him, if Baal, then follow him." In the name of God, I come now to treat with you on this subject, "How long halt ye?"

Then let us inquire,

I. Why have you hitherto neglected to come to a decided choice?

II. How long do you purpose to halt?

I. Why have you hitherto neglected to come to a decided choice?

1. It is not for want of power to alter your disposition or make you willing to repent. You have all the faculties that Christians have. The true penitent has no more natural power than the impenitent. The natural power of the Christian before, and after repentance is precisely the same.

It is a clear point. God does not condemn sinners for being unable, but for being unwilling to repent. Let us appeal to facts on this subject. There are some sinners now in the prison of hell. Were they able to repent? Able or not able, the Lord punishes and will punish them to all eternity for not doing it. Is it for the want of power, or for the want of will that he punishes sinners? We had rather say it is for the want of will, inclination, or disposition to obey his commands.

It was not for the want of power that they did not repent. It is not for want of power that you have not yet repented. For you have all the power that you ever will have. You have all that is necessary—and if you had ten thousand times more than what you now have, it would not help the matter, nor make you willing to obey God. An increase of power would not help. Nor—

2. Is it because God requires any thing unreasonable. To repent, believe and obey God is most reasonable. What can be more reasonable than that you should be required to love God? If you were required to love a deformed character, that would be hard. But it is not so. You are required to love a perfect character. There is not a single spot or stain in all God's character. This is the character which you are required to love with all your hearts.

Again, God requires you to repent of sin. What can be more reasonable than this? Is it hard that you should be required to feel sorrow for sin? for that which is odious in itself? If you were required to feel sorrow for some good conduct of yours, that would be hard. But it is not so. You are required only to feel sorrow that you have done wrong.

So then, Why do you not love God? Why do you not feel sorrow for sin? Why do you not love to pray and praise and practice all the duties of religion? Why do you not come out from the world and be separate? Why not come forward and espouse the cause of Christ?

Why have you not done it already? Not because God requires any thing hard or unreasonable. It is more easy and more pleasant to walk in the path of duty, than in the path of sin. It is far more pleasant and delightful to obey the commands of God than to disobey them. Why then have you not done it? Surely not because God requires any thing unreasonable. Nor—

3. Is it because you have not been instructed in your duty. I trust no one can plead ignorance on this subject. You cannot say that you did not know that there was a heaven and a hell—that you did not know it was your duty to repent and become Christians—that you did not know that God required you to love him and to pray to him.

You cannot say that you have not been warned to flee from the wrath to come— that you have not been called upon over again and again to begin a life of religion. You cannot say that the Spirit of God has not been striving with you—that you have never been warned of the awful danger of resisting the strivings of his Spirit.

You cannot say that you have not been warned of the uncertainty of life. You cannot say that you did not know that you were here on trial for eternity—that you must die and go to the judgment seat of Christ—that unless you repent and believe you must lie down in hell to all eternity. You cannot plead ignorance—you have heard the gospel. Why then have you not complied with the terms of salvation? Why then have you not come to a decided choice? Surely it cannot be because you have not been warned. Where is the enemy? Nor—

4. Is it because you have not had time. For what time was given you but to prepare for eternity? Life and death have for a long time been set before you. Sabbath after Sabbath and year after year you have been called upon to make your choice. You have found time to sin; but why is it that you have found no time to repent and pray and become Christians? Suppose you had died yesterday, or the last year, you could not have said that you had not time to prepare for death. The reason then why you have not yet come to a decided choice is not because you have not had time. What can it be? Where is the enemy? Nor—

5. Is it because the subject is not important. The importance of the subject of religion is acknowledged by all. You may feel as though you had some important worldly business to transact. But after all it amounts to nothing. All is vanity. "The fashion of this world passeth away." After all their labor and sorrow, high and low, rich and poor, meet together and lie down in the grave at last. If you have not been "laying up treasure in heaven," you have been laboring in vain. Compared with the subject of religion, all other subjects dwindle into nothing.—The world itself will shortly have an end. "The end of all things is at hand. The earth also and the works that are therein shall be burned up."

But the soul is immortal. Of all that you possess, that alone will survive the ruins of time. "What shall it profit a man, if he shall gain the whole world, and lose his own soul?" Eternal life and eternal death are before you, and will you say that the subject is not important? If the sinner after suffering in hell could then be delivered, the subject would not be so important. Were you condemned to burn in the flames for only a thousand years, how would you feel? What horror would seize you? Would not your case be awful? Should you not be alarmed?

But this is nothing. If the sinner after suffering in hell thousands and thousands of years could then hear the sound of pardon, it would not be so alarming.—We would not be so anxious for him—we would not press him so hard to attend to the subject—we would let him alone. He might then go on. But it is not so; when the soul is once gone, it is gone forever. There is no coming back to enjoy a state of probation. He must suffer while God endures. The reason then why you have not come to a decided choice is not because the subject is not important. Nor—

6. Is it because salvation is not freely offered. Salvation is freely offered. "Ho every one that thirsteth, come ye to the waters; and he that hath no money, come ye, buy and eat; buy wine and milk without money and without price. The Spirit and the bride say, Come. And let him that heareth say, Come. And let him that is athirst, come. And whosoever will, let him take of the water of life freely. Come unto me, all ye that labor and are heavy laden, and I will give thee rest. All things are now ready." And you are invited, entreated, nay, commanded to accept. This always has been the case; salvation always has been freely offered to you.

The reason then why you have not yet come to a decided choice is not because salvation has not been freely offered. It is now freely offered, it has always been— and depend upon it, will never be more freely offered. Nor—

7. Is it because you intend to die without religion. Though you may labor to silence your fears and to soothe your consciences, yet you cannot always succeed. Though you cast off fear and restrain prayer, yet at times you cannot but reflect on the shortness of human life—that its pleasures, at longest, are quickly over and gone forever. Even in laughter the heart is sad, etc. The things of time are fast fading, and will soon forever retire from our sight.

You know that you must die and go to judgment—Yes, these blooming bodies on which you fondly dote, must fade and die. I well know that you intend to die the death of the righteous. So did wicked Balaam—So did all who are now in hell. Could you now be admitted to those unhappy regions, not one could be found who had made his calculations to come into that place of torment. And you are now treading in their steps.

We know that you do not intend to die without religion. For, were you assured that within a few days you must lie down in eternal sorrows; in the horrors of despair, you would now break out into the cries and shrieks of the damned. Your hearts would pine away in mournful complaint, "Who can dwell with the devouring fire? Who can dwell with everlasting burnings?" It is evident then that the reason you have not come to a decided choice is not because you intend to die without religion. What then can be the difficulty? You have all the power that you will ever have.—God's requirements are most reasonable.—The terms of salvation will never be altered.—You have had enough time.—The subject is of overwhelming importance.—Salvation is freely offered—it will never be more freely offered. What can be the difficulty? I will now tell you. Say as Esther of Haman, the adversary and the enemy is this wicked heart. You do not like the duties of religion. These hearts are so wicked that you *will not come to Christ.* This is the true reason.

1. The reason why we call on you to repent and believe is not because you cannot, but because you will not.

2. The reason why God will punish you for not obeying is not because you cannot, but because you will not.

3. The reason why the Almighty power of God is necessary to draw you is not because you cannot, but because you *will not come to Christ.*

The whole difficulty is to be explained by correcting the sinner's views of his own depravity. On the doctrines of grace all the difficulties meet in the same point—*wrong views of human depravity.* Only admit that the sinner never has and never will do what he can, and you will see why we *call*—why God *commands*—why he *will punish*—and why his power is necessary to subdue the human heart.

Man's heart is so wicked that it needs almighty power to make him do what he can—Not what he *cannot.* Many other methods of explaining the difficulty have been attempted, but all have failed—they have never been able to bring the monster to light. Indeed nothing else can hinder your loving God—Nothing else can hinder your sorrow for sin—Your praying and obeying all the commands of God. This is the reason which conscience assigns. This is the reason which God will assign when you stand at his bar. We have seen the reason why you have hitherto neglected to come to a decided choice. Let us inquire,

II. How long do you propose to halt? "How long halt ye?" My hearers, this is a question of infinite importance. I come now to treat with you on this subject. Here I would inquire, How long have you put off this subject? How many years have you *lived without God in the world?* How many warnings have you neglected? How long has the Spirit of God been striving with you? How many years have gone out of your own probation? So long God has been waiting to be gracious. What? and you have not repented?—Not yet begun to live a life of religion? Then so many years have gone out of your day of probation and nothing is done. So much of the precious day of salvation you have spent worse than in vain—All this while you have only been hardening your hearts in vain.

Once more we beseech you to make a solemn pause. All warnings hitherto have proved ineffectual. Sometimes, like Felix, you have begun to startle and look about you while the awful realities of eternity are sounding in your ears. For a moment you have been brought upon the point of deciding, but you go away and all is forgotten. "Go thy way for this time, when I have a convenient season, I will call for thee." The business has ended only in a vain and empty resolution; and the whole serves only to harden.

No decided choice is yet made. Now how long do you purpose to conduct in this manner? We entreat you, my hearers, to decide the business today. When will you take up the subject of religion in earnest? "How long halt ye?" Our text demands the time. I pause that you may fix the time now.—To help your decision I will suggest the thought that God sees you—Another, that God's Spirit will not always strive— Another, that death is certain and you have no security of life for a single moment.

My hearers, if there is nothing in religion, then renounce it—if the Bible is a farce, then fling it away. But if it be true, as we all profess, why hesitate to obey its precepts now? Being true—*it is tremendously true*—*the world will be in flames.* "How long halt ye?"

Ye parents, who never worship God in your families: Our text speaks to you. Your consciences have often been alarmed. At times you have been almost persuaded to adopt the resolution: "As for me and my house, we will serve the Lord." You have been upon the point of assembling your families and of carrying their wants to the throne of grace and of breaking through all difficulties at once. But hitherto your resolution has failed. Do you not see that you are likely to die as you are? Can you not look forward a little and see that you are going to the judgment seat without once have prayed to God in your families? Do you intend to die as you are? If not, will you decide the point? Go one way or the other. "If the Lord be God, then serve him. How long halt ye?"

Our subject speaks to you who are in the morning of life. The present is a season peculiarly interesting. Many of your companions are alarmed and anxious for their souls. A number we trust, have already come to a decided choice. They no longer halt between two opinions. "They have chosen the good part which shall not be taken away." They are now ready to *leave all.* No longer do they stand halting between two opinions, whether to pursue the vanities of the world, or to engage in all the duties of religion. They are now about to bid you a long and eternal farewell. At such a season, many anxious thoughts arise in your mind. While you see one and another of your companions leaving you, you cannot but reflect, that you too have a soul to be saved or lost.

Many seem now to be halting between two opinions. On the one hand you are unwilling to leave your sinful pleasures and companions. You are afraid of incurring the displeasure of God's enemies. You are ashamed to have it thought that you have any concern for your soul. You are ashamed to come out from the world, and openly espouse the cause of Christ. You are waiting for each other—You are ashamed of Christ, the Saviour of sinners—Nay, you are even ashamed of the God that made you. On the other, you know that the friendship of the world is enmity with God—that the companion of fools shall be destroyed. You know that the season of your life will soon be over and gone forever—that you must die and go to judgment. You know that the "Spirit of God will not always strive with men"—that your day of grace is limited—that soon you will have passed the bounds of divine mercy. At times these thoughts alarm you. Is it not so, my friends? Perhaps you are now upon the point of deciding. And so have you been before. Your situation is no better, but is this day worse than ever. How long will you trifle with your soul? How long will you dally with eternal realities? This indecision is what renders your situation so alarming. This is the high road to perdition—it is the path which all the wicked have trod who have gone down to hell before you. They went halting between two opinions and flattering themselves that they should certainly escape the torments of hell. And you are now heading in their steps.

My young friends, God will not be mocked. The business of religion above all others, requires decision. God requires the whole heart. He will have that, or he will have nothing. You are required to break off all your sins—to come out from the world and be separate. You are required to leave all—to take up every cross and to follow Christ *now*. If you halt at this, it will be of no use for you to think on the subject. You are required to endure shame and reproach for his sake. If you halt at this, Christ will have nothing to do with you. If you are ashamed of him, he will be ashamed of you.

You may think to obtain the favor of Christ by giving him a part of your services—by compromising with God. This is sometimes the case with those who feel some concern for their souls. Being ashamed of Christ, they have resolved to be religious in secret, and openly to serve the world. But you will not succeed in this attempt. "No man can serve two masters." You may in this way, obtain a false hope; but, you will not secure the favor of God. God will abhor all that you do. If you are not willing to engage in all the duties of religion and give yourselves wholly to God, you may stop where you are. The path to heaven is too straight. The righteous who take to themselves the whole armor of God will scarcely be saved.

Do you fear the reproach of your companions? Are you so weak, and so timid? Think: what is the breath of an enemy of God, to the blast of the soul by the breath of the Almighty? If you fear the frown of a fellow worm, how will you stand in judgment with an angry God? Be entreated to stand halting no longer. Go one way or the other, with all your hearts. Life and death are now set before you, and God is witness to the choice you make.

In view of all that God and religion require, "How long halt ye?" In view of all the scorn and contempt of wicked men, "How long halt ye?"

Finally: If the joys of heaven will not allure—if a bleeding Saviour has no charms for you—if the thunder of his vengeance does not strike terror through your guilty souls; then halt no longer—go on—"Rejoice, O young man in thy youth; and let thy heart cheer thee in the days of thy youth." Cast off fear and restrain prayer—Trample under-foot the Son of God—Resist the strivings of the Holy Spirit—Sport with eternal vengeance and defy the thunders of the Almighty.—But remember, that your fair morning will soon be turned into darkness. When your course is run, your bodies will fall into the grave, and your souls into the hands of the living God."[7]

Notes

1   Thornbury, p. 105.

2　Ibid. p. 107.
3　Heman Humphrey, *Revival Sketches*, pp. 210–212.
4　Bennet Tyler, pp. 326–333.
5　Sherry Pierpont May, p. 111.
6　Bennet Tyler, *Memoir of Asahel Nettleton*, pp. 357–365.
7　Nettleton Papers, Archives at Hartford Seminary, Hartford Connecticut.

The new gospel conspicuously fails to produce deep reverence, deep humility, a spirit of worship, a concern for the church. Why? We would suggest that the reason lies in its own character and content. It fails to make men God-centered in their thoughts and God-fearing in their hearts because this is not primarily what it is trying to do ... The old gospel ... was always and essentially a proclamation of Divine sovereignty in mercy and judgment, a summons to bow down and worship the mighty Lord on whom man depends for all good, both in nature and in grace. Its centre of reference was unambiguously God. But in the new gospel the centre of reference is man ... The subject of the old gospel was God and His ways with men; the subject of the new is man and the help God gives him. There is a world of difference.

J. I. PACKER

7

NEW ENGLAND THEOLOGY

The gospel of Jonathan Edwards, Joseph Bellamy, Bennet Tyler, and Asahel Nettleton was completely *God-centered*. The gospel message that these men preached was alive with the great doctrines of the Bible: ruin, redemption, election, regeneration, sin, the depravity of man, the cross of Christ, a literal and everlasting burning hell for lost sinners, and a future judgment for all mankind. This theology, which was central-specific to the revival preaching of both the First Great Awakening in America and the Second Great Awakening, had the smile of God upon it. For wherever it was preached by God-fearing men, the Spirit of God attended it with power! Such was the case with Jonathan Edwards in Northampton, MA and the seasons of revival there and such was the case for Asahel Nettleton and others who preached the same theology.

But the so-called "New England Theology" of Edwards soon became debased by his own followers, with each new interpretation it lost more of its power and influence. This began with Edwards' disciple, Samuel Hopkins who took these great truths and modified them into a system of doctrines which became known as "Hopkinsianism". Jonathan Edwards, Jr. modified his father's theology further than Hopkins by lowering divine sovereignty and raising human responsibility in the salvation process. Even Timothy Dwight, President of Yale College, who saw remarkable seasons of revival on the campus modified Edwards' theology further by giving even more ability to man. By the time Nathaniel William Taylor became the first professor of theology for the new Yale Divinity School, New England Theology was radically changed from the Edwardsean position until it no longer resembled itself. Each of the aforementioned men were good, well-meaning Christians who were the products of their day. During this time period both Universalism and Unitarianism were challenging the old orthodoxy of the Puritan fathers, and as each sincere man attempted to meet these heresies head-on they altered the theology of their fathers to make it *more appealing* to man's reason. This was unfortunate and a downgrade in theology was begun which ended up as "Taylorism". Taylorism stated that God is no longer sovereign in the regeneration of man, rather, man is the ruler of his own destiny and he can become a Christian *anytime he wishes by merely deciding to become one.* Also, Taylorism stated that there was no original sin or depravity of the human heart. This was also the theology of Charles Finney who so greatly influenced his generation and subsequent ones as well.

The basis of the theology of Jonathan Edwards, Bellamy and Nettleton (not the New Haven theology of Taylor and Finney) was centered on *man's ability* to respond to the great truths of the gospel message. Jonathan Edwards' concept of regeneration was that man has both the intellectual capacity (or ability) and natural capacity (or ability) to respond to the gospel by repenting and believing and loving God with his whole heart, soul, and mind. But man will not do so because man lacks the *moral capacity (ability)* and therefore refuses to turn to God in repentance and faith, because man loves his sins and refuses to make God his lord and master due to the evil disposition of his *heart*—which was inherited from his federal head: Adam. Therefore, God must make a man *willing.* And this is the meaning of grace and saving faith where God turns the heart of stone into a heart of flesh and gives sinful man the *ability* to see and understand the great truths of the gospel and respond to them in repentance toward God and faith in Jesus Christ. In other words, a lost sinner is born with all the capacity he needs to turn to God in repentance and faith (both intellectual and natural) but he will not, because his heart is evil and he loves his sins more than God. Therefore, he lacks the *moral ability or capacity* to turn to Christ unless God grants him this through grace which is saving faith. Man's heart must be regenerated (born again) before he can truly repent and believe the gospel message. This was the crux of Jonathan Edwards' theology which became the "New England Theology" of both his day and Asahel Nettleton's day. This is the way Asahel Nettleton preached: that man has no excuse not to turn to God and if he refuses to turn and repent it is rightly just of God to damn him for his rebellion and sin. Man is born with the capacity to turn to God, he is not a block of wood or a slab of stone which cannot respond to the gospel (High Calvinism states that man has *no capacity* to respond; because of total depravity he is a block of wood or stone until his heart is changed by God through grace—this was the Princeton Theology).

Edward's argued that man is not a block of wood or stone but is born with the necessary capacity to repent and believe, yet he refuses to do so because of his sinful heart. Whereas "New Haven Theology" (Taylorism) gave man even more ability to the point of being the master of his destiny. He can say "no" to God or "yes" to God anytime he wants to—it is entirely up to man. This was the theology of Charles Finney, man could choose to be saved anytime he wanted and man could choose to have revival anytime he wanted. This theology was man-centered. Whereas the theology of Princeton, Edwards and Nettleton was God-centered. God in His sovereignty elects those whom He has mercy upon and enables them to savingly believe the gospel by grace. In this chapter we will study the different *nuances* of the so-called "New England Theology"; for it began to move away from the Edwardsean position with Edwards' disciple, Joseph Bellamy. Bellamy held to the "Governmental Theory" of the Atonement, rather than the "Satisfaction Theory" of Edwards.

It is critically important to the study of the life and ministry of Asahel Nettleton to understand the theology he practiced, particularly the doctrines he preached. We must remind ourselves as we look back on the history of the nineteenth century, that Nettleton labored in incessant revivals for over ten years before Charles Grandison Finney appeared on the public scene. Nettleton and Finney disagreed on what the term revival meant and their theology was as different as night and day. If we wish to understand and come to grips with the problems of modern evangelism, we must comprehend the theology and evangelism which was exercised in the time of Nettleton and Finney. With these thoughts in mind, let us now turn to some observations on this topic from the pen of Iain Murray:

> "But there are aspects of biblical doctrine which are directly related to evangelism. These have to do with the real condition of human nature and the work of the Holy Spirit in regeneration. Here lies the difference between Arminian and Calvinistic teaching which has immediate consequences in practice. Arminianism treats believing and regeneration as amounting to the same thing. The gospel is to be preached to all men, the same light comes to all who hear it, and those that believe are born again. According to this view, the truth heard is the means of regeneration. But if this is so, why is it that among a congregation hearing the same gospel truth some respond and others do not? There are only two possible answers to that question: either man is not so 'dead in trespasses and sins' as Scripture represents and the difference can therefore be explained solely in terms of human choice, or there is a work of the Spirit *additional* to the outward hearing of the message–a work which lies behind the will, giving men a new nature. The latter, the Old School believed, is the biblical position. Men not only need the light of the truth, they need the capacity to *see* it; they need a removal of the enmity which causes them by nature to

'receive not the things of the Spirit of God' (1 Cor. 2.14); they need to be *made* willing. The voice of the preacher leads people to the exercise of faith, but the *ability* to believe comes only as 'the dead hear the voice of the Son of God' himself (John 5.25). This is a voice which the unsaved do not hear (John 10.16–27); it is the 'calling' which brings faith and justification (Rom. 8.30); and it is much more than the outward hearing of the words of the gospel. Regeneration is the putting forth of creative power in the implanting of a new nature. There can be no *exercise* of faith until men hear the gospel (Rom. 10.14) but it is the power of the Holy Spirit with the gospel which first gives men a believing nature. Salvation is through faith, not *because* of it. Men are not renewed because they believe, rather they 'see' and 'hear' because they are reborn (John 3.3; Acts 16.14; Eph. 2.4–9).

"All this was already clear in the teachings of Jonathan Edwards, 'The heart can have no tendency to make itself better, until it first has a better tendency'."[1]

JOSEPH BELLAMY

We must now take the time to study the theology of Edwards' disciple, Joseph Bellamy. Bellamy was mightily used of God as a revival preacher during the Great Awakening. His book, *True Religion Delineated* is a must-study for students of Asahel Nettleton. These two men typified Edwards' theology on man's moral inability and regeneration. We will look at what Bellamy taught on this important subject. Asahel Nettleton was such a close student of Joseph Bellamy that he collected the personal letters of Bellamy and at Hartford Seminary in the Nettleton Papers are handwritten letters of Bellamy to such men as John Erskine, James Davenport, Samuel Davies, David Brainerd, Jonathan Edwards and many more eminent men of their day. An extract from Bellamy's writings is now provided:

"Thus we see the law is exactly upon a level with our natural capacities; it only requires us to love God with all our hearts; and thus we see that the law is therefore perfectly reasonable, just, and equal. 'And now, Israel, what doth the Lord thy God require of thee, but to fear the Lord thy God, to walk in all his ways, and to love him, and to serve the Lord thy God with all thy heart, and with all thy soul?'

"Hence, as to a natural capacity, all mankind are capable of a perfect conformity to this law; for the law requires of no man any more than to love God with all his heart. The sinning angels have the same natural capacities now, as they had before they fell; they have the same faculties, called the understanding and will; they are still the same beings, as to their natural powers. Once they loved God with all their hearts; and now they hate him with all their hearts. Once they had a great degree of love; now they have as great a degree of hatred; so that they have the same natural capacities as ever. Their temper, indeed, is different; but their capacity is the same; and, therefore, as to a natural capacity, they are as capable of a perfect conformity to the law of their Creator as ever they were. So Adam, after his fall, had the same soul that he had before, as to its natural capacities, though of a very different temper; and, therefore, in that respect, was as capable of a perfect conformity to this law as ever. And it is plainly the case, that all mankind, as to their natural capacities, are capable of a perfect conformity to the law, from this, that when sinners are converted they have no new natural faculties, though they have a new temper; and when they come to love God with all their hearts in heaven, still they will have the same hearts, as to their natural faculties, and may, in this respect, be justly looked upon as the very same beings. In this sense, Paul was the same man when he hated and persecuted Christ, as when he loved him and died for him; and that same heart that was once so full of malice, is now as full of love. So that, as to his natural capacities, he was as capable of a perfect conformity to this law, when he was a persecutor, as he is now in heaven. When therefore, men cry out against the holy law of God, which requires us only to love him with all our hearts, and say, 'It is not just for God to require more than we can do, and then threaten to damn us for not doing,' they ought to stay a while, and consider what they say, and tell what they mean by their *can do*; for it is plain that the law is exactly upon a level with our natural capacities, and that, in this respect, we are fully capable of a perfect conformity thereof ...

"Why did not the Jews love their prophets, and love Christ and his apostles? What was owing to it? And where did the blame lie? They were acquainted with them; heard them talk and preach, and saw their conduct, and could not but plainly perceive their temper, and know what sort of disposition they were of, and what sort of men they were; and yet they did not like them; but they hated them; they belied them, slandered and reproached them, and put them to death. And now what was the matter? What was the cause of all this? Were not their prophets, and Christ and his apostles indeed lovely, and worthy of their hearty esteem? Did not all that they said and did manifest them to be so? Why, then, did they not love them? Was it not wholly owing to their not having a right temper of mind, and to their being of so bad a disposition? And were they not wholly to blame? They might say of Christ, that they could see no form nor comeliness in him, wherefore they should desire him; and where no beauty is seen, it is impossible there should be any love. But why did he not appear most amiable in their eyes? And why were their hearts not ravished with his beauty? His disciples loved him, and Martha, and Mary, and Lazarus loved him; and why did not the Scribes and Pharisees love him as much? Why, because his person and doctrines did not suit them, and were not agreeable to the temper of their hearts. The bad temper of their hearts made him appear odious in their eyes, and was the cause of all their ill-will towards him. And now, were they not to blame for this bad temper, and for all their bad feelings, and bad carriage towards Christ, thence arising? Yes, surely, if ever any men were to blame for any thing. And now, if God the Father had been in the same circumstances as God the Son was then in, he would not have been loved a jot more, or treated a whit better, than he was. Indeed, it was that image and resemblance of the infinitely glorious and blessed God, which was to be seen in their prophets, in Christ and his apostles, which was the very thing they hated him for. Therefore Christ says, 'He that hateth me hateth my Father also, but now have they both seen and hated both me and my Father.' And Christ attributes it entirely to their want of a right temper, and to the bad disposition of their hearts, that they did not love him, and love his doctrines. 'If God were your Father, you would love me.' 'He that is of God.'—of a godlike temper,—'heareth God's words: ye, therefore, hear them not, because ye are not of God.' In truth, the bottom of all our enmity is, that 'you are of your father, the devil,' that is, of just such a temper as he. And now, what think you, when Christ comes in flaming fire, to take vengeance on a ungodly world? Will he blame the Scribes and Pharisees for not loving him with all their hearts, or no? Or will he excuse the matter, and say, on their behalf, 'They could see no form nor comeliness in me. I appeared very odious to them; they could not but hate me, and no man is to blame for not doing more than he can?'

"From the whole, it is plain that mankind are to blame, wholly to blame, and perfectly inexcusable, for their not having right apprehensions of God, and for their not having a sense of his glory in being what he is, and for their not loving him with all their heart; because all is owing merely to their want of a right temper, and to the bad disposition of their hearts ...

"Thus we see, that, as to a natural capacity, all mankind are capable of a perfect conformity to God's law, which requires us only to love God with all our hearts; and that all our inability arises merely from the bad temper of our hearts, and our want of a good disposition; and that, therefore, we are wholly to blame and altogether inexcusable. Our impotency, in one word, is not natural, but moral, and, therefore, instead of extenuating, does magnify and enhance our fault. The more unable to love God we are, the more we are to blame. Even as it was with the Jews; the greater contrariety there was in their hearts to their prophets, to Christ and his apostles, the more vile and blameworthy were they. And in this light do the Scriptures constantly view the case. There is not one tittle in the Old Testament or in the New, in the law or in the gospel, that gives the least intimation of any deficiency in our natural faculties. The law requires not more than all our hearts, and never blames us for not having larger natural capacities. The gospel aims to recover us to love God only with all our hearts, but makes no provision for our having any new natural capacity; as to our natural capacities, all is well. It is in our temper, in the frame and disposition of our hearts, that the seat of all our sinfulness lies."[2]

The key to the "New England Theology" lay in the stress on man's *moral inability* to turn to Christ, having been born with all the *natural capacities* to love God with all one's heart. This is the distinguishing feature of Jonathan Edwards' theology which both Joseph Bellamy and Asahel Nettleton used so effectively in their preaching in time of revival.

ASAHEL NETTLETON'S THEOLOGICAL POSITION

We will now examine one of Asahel Nettleton's sermons to compare the same doctrine of "man's moral inability" with that of Edwards and Bellamy. God moved mightily through the preaching of Nettleton in the conviction of sin in his hearer's hearts. It is imperative to our study to closely examine the doctrines that Nettleton preached.

We are fortunate for the labors of William Nichols, who in the mid-1990s spent a great deal of time at Hartford Seminary copying and transcribing Nettleton's extant sermons. Today, many of these sermons are faded and difficult to read, so we are thankful for Nichol's collection of Nettleton's sermons in published form. The following sermon is a fair example of Nettleton's theology (the italicized words of the sermon were underlined in Nettleton's original hand).

GENUINE REPENTANCE DOES NOT PRECEDE REGENERATION

"Surely after that I was turned, I repented" (Jeremiah 31:19).

"Israel had departed from God. In this chapter his restoration is predicted, and the happy effects which would follow described. *They shall come and sing in the height of Zion, and shall flow together for the goodness of the Lord; and their soul shall be as a watered garden; and they shall not sorrow any more at all.*

"But this happy season was to be preceded by deep repentance. In the description of the Prophet we behold a vast company assembled, and commencing their journey up to Zion. *Thus saith the Lord; they shall come with weeping, and with supplications will I lead them.* The repentance of Ephraim, a name which here stands for the people at large is thus further described.—In the conviction and conversion of one, we see a specimen of the whole. *I have surely heard Ephraim bemoaning himself thus; Thou hast chastised me, and I was chastised as a bullock, unaccustomed to the yoke: turn thou me, and I shall be turned; for thou art the Lord my God. Surely after that I was turned, I repented; and after that I was instructed, I smote upon my thigh: I was ashamed, yea, even confounded, because I did bear the reproach of my youth.*

"In this account, we have, what is commonly called a state of conviction. God had taken him in hand. *Thou hast chastised me, and I was chastised.* But he would not yield, his heart was too proud, and too stubborn to bow. His conduct, he tells us was like that of a bullock unaccustomed to the yoke—wild, unmanageable, and determined not to yield to the hand of its master.

"His opposition is so great, he is convinced that he shall never overcome it. In this great work, he shall never assist in any other manner than as a rebel would help his antagonist to subdue himself. The conversion of a sinner like himself, he is convinced, could never be effected by the power of mere moral suasion. No finite power could do it. None but the God that made him, can manage the sinner.

"Under conviction of this truth, you hear him say: Turn thou me, and I shall be turned; for thou art the Lord my God. He then states what follows: Surely after that I was turned, I repented; and after that I was instructed, I smote upon my thigh: I was ashamed, yea, even confounded, because I did bear the reproach of my youth.

"His conversion was followed not only with a change of feeling, but with a change of sentiment.—*After that I was instructed.*——When he saw clearly his past conduct, his sins, his stubbornness, and where the difficulty lay, he was perfectly astonished. *I smote upon my thigh.* It is possible! How could I be so stubborn! *I was ashamed, yea, even confounded.* What is here said is true of every sinner who is brought to true repentance. From the words of our text we derive this doctrine, that Genuine repentance does not precede regeneration. *Surely after that I was turned, I repented.*

"Here it may be proper to state that there are two kinds of repentance. One arising from the fear of punishment, and dread of consequences; without either love to God or hatred to sin. Such was the repentance of Saul, of Judas, and others. Such is the repentance of awakened sinners, and all sinners in a greater or less degree. There may be great distress, many tears, and awful forebodings of a guilty conscience in the unregenerate. This may, and generally does precede regeneration. But this is not godly sorrow. *Godly sorrow worketh repentance unto salvation not to be repented of: but the sorrow of the world worketh death.*

"There is a kind of repentance which always precedes regeneration, but it is not the repentance which the gospel requires. That repentance which implies no love to God, and no hatred to sin, and nothing but terror and dismay is not commanded. But that repentance which God commands, and which ministers are bound to preach includes both.

"That this repentance does not precede regeneration is evident from the following considerations.

1. From the nature of true repentance. This repentance implies love to God. Sin is committed against God, and so the sinner is to exercise *repentance towards God*. This cannot be done without love. And before regeneration there is no love to God. For it is written, *Every one that loves is born of God. A crown of life is promised to them that love him.* But none can have this promise without regeneration; and therefore love to God cannot exist without regeneration. No one feels heartily sorry that he has offended a being whom he does not love. Much less does he sorrow that he has offended a being whom he hates. But all the unregenerate possess carnal minds; *And the carnal mind is enmity against God.*

"Genuine gospel repentance flows only from a heart melted into love to God.— *Against thee and thee only have I sinned.—Father, I have sinned against heaven, and in thy sight,* is the language of the true penitent.

"This repentance implies love to God's law. Sin is a transgression of the law. No one feels sorrow that he has broken a law which he does not love; much less a law which he hates. But the *carnal, or unrenewed mind is not subject to the law of God, neither indeed can be.* If then evangelical repentance implies love to God and love to his law, it is not an exercise of a *carnal,* unrenewed heart; for that is *enmity against God, not subject to his law, neither indeed can be.*

2. Repentance has the promise of salvation. *Blessed are they that mourn, for they shall be comforted. The Lord is nigh unto them that are of a broken heart, and saveth such as be of a contrite spirit* (Psalm 34:14). *But this cannot be said of any before regeneration. For except a man be born again, he cannot see the kingdom of God. The sacrifices of God are a broken spirit: a broken and contrite heart, O God, thou wilt not despise* (Psalm 51:17). *For thus saith the high and lofty one that inhabiteth eternity, whose name is Holy; I dwell in the high and holy place, with him also that is of contrite and humble spirit, to revive the spirit of the humble, and to revive the heart of the contrite ones* (Isaiah 57:15; also 66:1, 2).

"But this cannot be said of a natural man; *For they that are in the flesh cannot please God.* But repentance is pleasing to God, and has the promise of salvation. If the sinner does repent before he is regenerated, then, they that are in the flesh *can* please God. But the Apostle says they *cannot please him.* A promise of salvation is annexed to repentance; If then he can have the promise of salvation before regeneration, he can be actually saved without it; which our Saviour declares impossible. If the sinner can exercise repentance without a new heart, so he can every other Christian grace. He can love God, and believe in Christ without a new heart, as well as repent of sin. Regeneration is no more necessary to prepare the sinner to love God aright than it is to repent aright, for without love there is no true repentance.

"If he can repent without a new heart, he can exercise faith without a new heart. But that faith which does not imply love is not genuine. *For in Jesus Christ neither circumcision availeth any thing, nor uncircumcision; but faith which worketh by love.* It is no easier to repent aright than it is to exercise faith; for that repentance which is without faith cannot be accepted. *For without faith it is impossible to please him.* And then it will follow,

3. That regeneration would not be necessary. For if the sinner can love God and perform all the duties of religion without regeneration, this is all that is necessary to fit him for heaven. Now it is believed that sinners do not love God and the duties of religion, and therefore regeneration is necessary. But if the Christian graces may

take place without regeneration, then the ground of this necessity is entirely destroyed. There is no room for such a work. The power of God would not be necessary. For the work is done, and no change is necessary.

"That repentance does not precede regeneration will appear from the *nature of regeneration*. View it in connection with repentance. The change in regeneration is expressed by *taking away the heart of stone and giving an heart of flesh. I will take away the stony heart out of your flesh, and I will give you an heart of flesh*. From this it appears that regeneration is the act of taking away a *hard* and *stony heart*. Now, my hearers, this cannot be a penitent heart. If repentance does take place *before* regeneration than the heart of stone is not there. A penitent heart is not a *heart of stone; it is a broken, and a contrite heart*. And God never takes away such a heart. If repentance does precede regeneration it must be the repentance of a *hard and stony heart*. This, when compared with the idea of true repentance, would be a contradiction in terms, the repentance of a *heart of stone.—And I will give you an heart of flesh*. This is a broken and contrite heart, a heart susceptible of feeling. It is a penitent heart.

"When God takes away the heart of stone and gives an heart of flesh—that is regeneration. When God takes away the heart of stone and gives an heart of flesh— Then God grants repentance. A new heart is a penitent heart. Regeneration is necessary because sinners have hard, impenitent hearts. And this is the glorious effect of the power of God in the act of regeneration. It reduces the rebel into submission. It melts the stubborn heart into repentance. When God regenerates and grants repentance, he does it by one decisive act. Thus I consider the point established, that evangelical repentance does not precede regeneration.

"But, by the way, I would remark, that I have not asserted that the sinner is not under obligations to repent before regeneration. That it is not the *duty* of the sinner to repent before God changes his heart, that we have not asserted. It *is* his duty. The question has been 'what is duty?' But what is the fact?

"It is the duty of sinners to do many things which they never have done, and perhaps never will do. It is their duty to stop sinning, and to *love God with all the heart, soul, mind, and strength*. This is their duty. And so is it their duty to repent, without delay, but they have never done it, and some will never do it.

"By this time, my hearers will perceive a great difficulty in our subject. It is this: If sinners do not repent before regeneration, then you call upon them to do what needs almighty power to accomplish. This difficulty is not peculiar to this text, or to this subject alone. It is the same difficulty which runs through almost every subject which concerns our salvation.

"There are many who think they see a great inconsistency and absurdity running through almost every discourse which they hear. 'Ministers contradict themselves, they say, and unsay; they tell us to do, and then tell us that we cannot do.' This difficulty some of our hearers see and state for themselves; others think they see it, but cannot state it. This difficulty I am calculating to state in all its absurdity, 'You sometimes call upon sinners to believe and repent; and then tell them that faith and repentance are the gift of God. You call upon them to do what needs almighty power to effect.' My hearers, this is correct. We are guilty of all this absurdity; and the Bible talks just so too.

"But further; 'We sometimes hear ministers in one discourse inviting sinners and calling upon them to *come to Christ*; and then they will turn about and contradict the whole, by telling them that they *cannot come.*' And what think you of such absurdity, my hearers? What think ye of such preachers?

"That some have been guilty of this absurdity we do not, we cannot deny. Your charge is well founded. We dare not contradict it. I well recollect an instance of this kind. A celebrated preacher in one of his discourses once used these words: *Come unto me, all ye that labor and are heavy laden, and I will give you rest (Matthew 11:28)*. And then this same preacher in another discourse used this expression: *No man can come to me, except the Father which hath sent me draw him (John 6:44)*.

"Now what think you, my hearers, of such preaching and of such a preacher? What would you have said had you been present and heard it? Would you have charged him with contradicting himself? But so it was; this great preacher in one of his discourses did say, *Come unto me, all ye that labor and are heavy laden, and I will give you rest*, and in another, *No man can come to me, except the Father which sent me draw him*. And I have no doubt that others have since adopted the same expressions. This preacher, you will remember was none other than the Lord Jesus Christ. And I have no doubt that many ministers have since followed the same example of their divine master. And have therefore been guilty of the same absurdity, if such you would call it.

"Now my hearers, which will you do? Will you say that the difficulty can easily be explained, and that Christ is guilty of no absurdity? If you can explain the difficulty in Christ's preaching; then you can explain it with respect to all subsequent preachers. The same explanation which would relieve his preaching from all difficulty; with a little candor would do it in all similar cases. Will you adopt this course and say all is well? Or will you boldly assert that Christ is absurd, and that he contradicted himself? Then you turn infidel at once. You enter the lists with the Son of God, and boldly renounce divine revelation. Or will you say, I believe the Bible is the Word of God, and that Christ is consistent with himself, whether I can see *how* to reconcile this difficulty or not? I wish you to remember that this difficulty existed in our Saviour's preaching. Nor is it peculiar to a few texts only; the same difficulty runs through the Bible.

"This I will now state more at large: The Bible does call upon sinners to repent; and yet considers repentance as the gift of God. John, the harbinger of Christ, came preaching and saying, *Repent ye: for the kingdom of heaven is at hand (Matthew 3:2)*. *From that time Jesus began to preach and say, Repent: for the kingdom of heaven is at hand (Matthew 4:17)*. And the Apostles *went out and preached that men should repent (Mark 6:12)*. *God commendeth all men everywhere to repent (Acts 17:30)*.

"On the other hand repentance is the gift of God. Then Peter and the apostles answered and said—Him hath God exalted with his right hand to be a Prince and a Saviour, for to *give* repentance to Israel, and forgiveness of sins (Acts 5:31). The disciples with one voice glorified God, saying, Then hath God also to the Gentiles granted repentance unto life (Acts 11:18). In meekness instructing those that oppose themselves; if God peradventure will *give* them repentance to the acknowledging of the truth (II Timothy 2:25).

"Thus you see, John the Baptist, Christ, and his Apostles, and God himself urged the duty of immediate repentance. And on the other hand they ascribe it wholly to God. Again—The Bible calls upon sinners to believe in Christ; and yet, considers faith as the gift of God. *Repent ye, and believe the gospel (Mark 1:15)*. *Believe on the Lord*

Jesus Christ, and thou shalt be saved (Acts 16:31). And this is his commandment, That we should believe on the name of his Son Jesus Christ (1 John 3:23).

"On the other hand; faith is the gift of God. Unto you it is *given* in the behalf of Christ, not only to believe on him, but also to suffer for his sake (Philippians 1:29). For by grace are ye saved through faith; and not of yourselves: it is the *gift* of God (Ephesians 2:8); Jesus the Author and finisher of our faith (Hebrews 12:2). That ye may know what is the exceeding greatness of his power to usward who believe, according to the working of his mighty power, which he wrought in Christ, when he raised him from the dead (Ephesians 1:19). Here you see, sinners are commanded to believe, and threatened with eternal death if they do not do it. And faith is wrought only by the mighty power of God. Again: Sinners are represented as being dead in trespasses and sins (Ephesians 2:1). We know that we have passed from death unto life; because we love the brethren (1 John 3:14). I know thy works, that thou hast a name that thou livest, and art dead (Revelation 3:1). In this situation God commands them to live. For I have no pleasure in the death of him that dieth, saith the Lord God: wherefore turn yourselves, and live ye (Ezekiel 18:32). This is the command of God. Wherefore he saith, Awake thou that sleepest, and arise from the dead, and Christ shall give thee light (Ephesians 5:14).

"On the other hand, the effect is attributed wholly to God. You hath he quickened, who were dead in trespasses and sins. The Son quickeneth whom he will. The hour is coming, and now is when the dead shall hear the voice of the Son of God, and they that hear shall live. Again: A new heart also will I give you, and a new spirit will I put within you: and I will take away the stony heart out of your flesh, and I will give you an heart of flesh (Ezekiel 36:26). But on the other hand, God commands the sinner to make a new heart. Cast away from you all your transgressions, whereby you have transgressed; and make you a new heart and a new spirit: for why will ye die, O house of Israel? (Ezekiel 18:31).

"Again: Sinners are represented as departing from God. And thus God calls, Turn ye at my reproof (Proverbs 1:23). Turn ye; turn ye, for why will ye die. Thus saith the Lord, Repent and turn yourselves from all your transgressions; so iniquity shall not be your ruin (Ezekiel 18:30). Thus saith the Lord God; wherefore turn yourselves and live ye. On the other hand, the Bible ascribes this work wholly to God. Turn thou me, and I shall be turned, for thou art the Lord my God. And again, in our text, Surely after that I was turned, I repented.

"In all these passages you see that the Bible calls upon sinners to do what he needs almighty power to accomplish. Now whether I am able to explain this difficulty or not, it is the language of the Bible, I wish you to remember. You have seen that God does command sinners to repent, and believe, and make a new heart, and arise from the dead. And those ministers who do not, in his name, call upon them to do the same, do not preach as God has commanded them. You have seen that repentance, and faith, and a new heart are all the gifts of God. And whoever does not attribute them wholly to God robs him of his glory, and does not preach the Bible.

"Whoever preaches, and is not guilty of all this absurdity, does not declare all the counsel of God. Whether he can explain these difficulties or not, every minister is bound to preach in this manner. If he does not call upon sinners to do all these things; and when done, if he does not ascribe the whole to God, he does not preach the gospel. I wish my hearers to bear this continually in mind. That whether I am able to explain this difficulty or not, yet I am bound to preach it. I shall take it for granted that all my hearers believe the Bible to be the word of God. And if I should not succeed in explaining these passages to your satisfaction, the difficulty in reconciling these texts lies equally against all who believe the Bible.

"This then is the question before us: How can it be proper for the Bible to command sinners to do what needs Almighty power to do for them?——Many methods have been adopted to obviate this difficulty. One says: You must do as well as you can without a new heart, but you must try to repent—try to love God and the like. But I answer: The Bible says no such thing. God nowhere commands sinners to try to repent—to try to love him. But: God now commands all men everywhere to repent. Nowhere does it say, thou shalt try to love the Lord thy God, but it does say, Thou shalt love the Lord thy God with all thy heart. This is what God commands. And the sinner trying to repent and love God if he does not do it, amounts to nothing. He does not obey the command.—However hard the sinner may labor and toil; yet is he does not repent and love him, he does nothing in the sight of God. After all that he has done, he is still threatened with eternal death, as the consequence of his neglect.

"It is sometimes said, 'That faith is the gift of God, and you must do as well as you can without it.' But what says the Bible to one who does not ask in faith? Does it encourage him to ask without? The Bible answers: Let not that man think that he shall receive anything of the Lord (James 1:7). But faith and repentance and love to God are duties which the Bible enjoins; and which every minister is to urge on all his hearers. If he does not preach faith, and repentance, and love to God, he does not preach the gospel, nor urge them to do anything which God regards. Do as well as you can without faith? How will he ever exhort to these duties? Will he exhort the sinner to believe without faith—to repent without repentance, and to love God without loving Him?

"How, on this ground, would an exhortation exhort the sinner to do these duties as well as he can without doing them at all; or say nothing on the subject? In order to settle the difficulty it may be proper to inquire, Why is the power of God necessary to change the heart of the sinner? And to this question there are but two answers: Either because the sinner is unable, or because he is unwilling to do what God commands.

"Let us examine the first. By being unable, I mean just what the sinner means: 'That he would if he could, but he cannot.' Let us proceed on this ground, and what then? Is the sinner not to blame? If God is really such a being as to command the sinner to do what is in every sense impossible for him to do: Is there any ground for that ease which thousands feel when they plead this excuse? If God commands, and will punish the sinner for not obeying, what can be done? If this be the character of God, the sinner who is in his hand is in an awful condition indeed.

"Let us advance on the sinner's own supposition. Is this the character of God and are you in his hands, does it become you to oppose and quarrel with Omnipotence? Whatever his character may be, it becomes feeble worms to beware how they contend with God. Do you believe what you say, 'that you would if you could, but you cannot obey the commands of God?' Do you verily believe that you are in the hands of such a being; and can you remain at ease? My fellow sinner: Do you still plead that this is your inability? And will you still allow that God is just and righteous in commanding and punishing you for not doing what you cannot do?

"Let us try your own sentiment, for if indeed you cannot believe, or repent or make a new heart, I dare not deny the justice of God in your punishment. I acknowledge that God may be just though he has made it impossible for sinners to be saved. Grant that God has made no atonement for some sinners, and yet I frankly own that I can see no injustice here. He has made no atonement for the fallen angels; and yet they have no right to complain. God has made it impossible for them to be saved——he has reserved them in everlasting chains unto the judgment of the great day. And still they have no right to complain. Suppose he had done the same by all or any part of the human race, not one would have had any reason to complain. I dare not object even to a limited atonement on the ground of justice. Suppose God had made an atonement and made it sufficient only for one single soul, and all the rest had been consigned over to endless perdition, yet I can see no injustice in this.

"The sinner often pleads his inability as an excuse. Call upon him to attend the duties of religion, and he will tell you: faith, and repentance, and a new heart are the gift of God; and what can I do? This he intends for an excuse. Grant the sinner his own plea. Grant that God has made it absolutely impossible for him to repent, and believe, and be saved, and what then? What right have you to complain? Suppose a sinner has been guilty of a breach of the laws of this state, that he has been guilty of murder, and is committed to prison, bolted and barred. The criminal walks around by the walls, murmuring and complaining that he cannot get out, 'that he would if he could, but he cannot.' We ask, what then; what if he cannot make his escape?—— Why then he must suffer the penalty of a good law. He suffers no injustice——he has no right to complain; unless he can make it appear that he is innocent, he deserves death.

"Now suppose the sinner cannot repent, believe, and be pardoned and saved. What then? Why, then he must be lost; awful indeed! What is the sinner is forever lost? No injustice is done. He suffers the penalty of a good law, and that is all. The sinner has broken the divine law. Cursed is every one that continueth not in all things which are written in the book of the law to do them is the sentence of that law. And no reason can be given why this sentence should not be executed. Now unless the sinner can make it appear that he has never in all this lifetime committed one single sin, he has no reason to complain if God has made his pardon and salvation impossible.

"There is a strange disposition in the human heart to murmur and complain of God because he is just. The sinner thinks it hard and cruel if God will not allow him the privilege of sinning and rebelling against him. And in addition to this he feels as though God was bound to make him repent and love him. And not only so, but if he should stop sinning and begin to love God now; he feels as though God could not in justice ever punish him for one of his past sins. O, what a demand does the sinner make on God! And yet he will not allow that God, can in justice, make any claims upon him. If the sinner cannot repent and believe and love God, he is certainly in an awful condition.

"But though I do not allow that you are under any natural inability to repent and be saved, yet I confess I can see no injustice were you to be placed in this awful condition. And I wish you to remember that what you now complain of may very soon be real. Unless you do soon repent and believe, the very thing of which you now complain, you will be obliged to feel. Very shortly, my fellow sinner, you will be beyond the reach of hope. God will by and by make it impossible for you to come out of your prison. This is the case with all in the prison of hell. There they are fastened and they cannot get out. And it is a wonder of mercy that you are not now there. When you get there, you will have no reason to murmur and complain that you could if you would, but you cannot get out of the prison of hell. The great gulf will be fixed, so that, they which would pass from hence cannot. This is the condition in which all the finally impenitent will remain forever. And the sinner who is now out of Christ is every moment in awful danger of sinking into the same condition.

"But this instance of a criminal bolted and barred and surrounded by the massy walls of a prison I do not admit to be a correct illustration of the state of the sinner. Though the finally impenitent will be forever shut up in this prison, yet this is not the case with sinners on earth. Though I can see no injustice in God's making it impossible for sinners on earth to come out of their prison and be saved; yet there is one point in which this illustration will not hold.

"If the prisoner were to be invited and commanded to come out of his prison, while the doors were shut, and bolted, and barred; I confess I can see no propriety in such invitations and commands. The very fact that God does invite, and command sinners to come to Christ is, to me, a convincing proof that the difficulty lies only in the sinner's will. If the sinner were willing to do all in his power, that is the point where common sense would direct us to stop urging him.

"This single command, Turn ye to the strong hold, ye prisoners of hope is to me a convincing proof that all the bolts and bars of his prison are now removed. Christ has opened the doors of his prison and proclaimed liberty to the captives. God does not command the sinner to break through bolts and bars and massy walls. But this is the case with all who deny the distinction between natural and moral inability. They call upon the sinner to do what they themselves acknowledge absolutely impossible. This I do not admit.

"Again—If the prisoner were to be confined and punished without reprieve for all his past sins, that would be perfectly just, and right. Every friend to good government must heartily acquiesce. But if the prisoner were commanded to break through bolts, and bars, and massy walls, and then in addition to all his past crimes were to suffer tenfold punishment for not doing it; I confess I do not see the justice of it.

"But it is acknowledged on all hands that those who perish from under the light of the gospel will suffer an aggravated weight of condemnation. It shall be more tolerable for Sodom in the day of judgment than for such sinners. Of how much sore punishment shall he be thought worthy, who hath trodden under foot the Son of God. If I had not come and spoken unto them, they had not had sin. Now the reason why God invites sinners to come out of their prison is not because they cannot; but because they will not. The reason why he commands them to do it, is not because they cannot but because they will not. The reason why they are to be punished in such an awful manner for not doing it, is not because they cannot, but because they will not. Unwillingness always makes it proper to invite and command. The will and nothing else is the object of command. This and nothing else is the ground of punishment.

"Now God does certainly treat the sinner in all respects as though the difficulty was a criminal difficulty. He does treat them in all respects just as he would on the supposition that they were unwilling to do what they could. It is surprising with what little ceremony the Bible treats the inability, and all the excuses of sinners. I believe every one of my hearers must have been struck with this fact. The Bible commands and condemns without ceremony if he does not do it. The Bible speaks just as freely as though it was every whit unwillingness.

"I will now state what appears to me to be the real difficulty. The sinner will not do what he can. I know this is denied by many. They reason in this way—That because the Bible everywhere attributes this change to God; therefore the sinner cannot do it. It is said that if the sinner could produce this change himself, then the power of God would not be necessary.

"But this reasoning will not hold. Because the sinner has power to do what God commands, it does not follow of course that the sinner will exert that power. You will easily see that those who adopt this reasoning take it for granted that the sinner will certainly do the utmost in his power to obey God. But if the sinner will not do what he can, there is the same necessity of almighty power to make him willing to do what he can, as there would be to make him willing to do, or, rather, do for him what he could not.

"This point is illustrated as follows: Here is a child which has departed from his father; He calls upon him to return to him. He has power to run every way; but he will not return to his father. He invites; but no invitation is sufficient. He threatens; but no punishment is sufficient to make the child willing to do what he can.

"Now what is the duty of that child? Common sense declares that it is his duty to obey the command. But the child is unwilling. Now does this unwillingness make it improper for the parent to invite, entreat, and command the child to do what he can? If the child would, but could not obey the command, I could see no propriety in the parent's conduct. But if the child can, and will not; his unwillingness is no excuse. His unwillingness is the very thing which makes it proper to command. This unwillingness is the very thing for which he deserves punishment. This is plain common sense.

"But, says the parent, 'I will reveal one secret. You know not how dreadfully stubborn that child is. Though my commands are reasonable, and the child can if he would, yet he is so opposed to me that he never will do what he can. He never will come unless I go and bring him.' Here the child replies, 'How absurd you talk; You call upon me to do what you say I never will do unless you make me do it.' But because he is so wicked that he never will do what he can, he stands murmuring, 'What a cruel parent. Now I cannot come, how can I? What a cruel parent! He calls upon me to do what I never shall do: and how can I be blamed? My hearers, what answer would you make to that child?

"This, in my view, is exactly the state of the sinner. Whether we think it is a just comparison or not, God does. He says I have nourished and brought up children, but they have rebelled against me. All have departed from God and he invites, and entreats, and commands them to return. Turn ye at my reproof—Turn ye, Turn ye, for why will ye die? Now what is the duty of sinners? Why is it their duty to obey the command of God.

"Now suppose God to reveal this fact. That the sinner is so opposed to me that he never will do what I command him. I believe all will allow that this is the fact with all who have lost their souls. If so, then it may be with sinners now living, that they never will do what they can. When in hell all acknowledge it again. Does the unwillingness to do what he can make it improper for God to invite and command and punish? Unwillingness in the case of the child is the very reason why every parent would invite, command, and threaten, and punish. In that case, no one but the child would ever think of complaining. And has not God a right to deal with us in the same manner as we deal with others? Yes; you will say, provided I were equally stubborn with that child. *There lies the difficulty, my hearers, you cannot belive that you are so wicked that you will not do what you can.*

"But it is possible that stubbornness in the heart even of a little child might rise beyond the power of mere moral suasion. It is possible that it might rise to such a pitch that no invitations, commands, or threatenings of the parent would overcome it. *Unwillingness might arise to such a pitch in the heart even of a little child that it might be necessary for the parent to go and turn him by the strength of his arm.* If there may be such stubbornness in the heart of a little child; or rather, since there is such stubbornness in his heart, that he will not do what he can, though urged by his parent whom he loves with all his natural affection, then is it not possible that the sinner may be so stubborn in the sight of God? God does make the comparison. *And do you believe that you are less wicked than a little child?*

"If this is possible—then it may be possible for sinners to continue for years to hear the invitations, commands, and threatenings of the gospel and never do what they can. *Now the only reason why the parent's arm is necessary to turn the child is because it is so wicked that it will not do what it can.* If it were willing to do what it could, nothing *special* on the part of the parent would be necessary. *Just so I view the state of the sinner. They will never do what they can.* And that will always make it proper to call unto them to do it.

"On a dying bed confess it—why would one wish to recover if they are not conscious that they have not done what they could. Amidst this mountain of evidence we can summon the conscience of the dying sinner. If you hear any one find fault, you may take it for granted that he understands the subject. Ask him to explain these passages and to give a better interpretation.

1. Reasonableness of the command to make a new heart. Every time they are commanded to love God, repent, or believe, they are commanded to make a new heart.

2. Saved wholly by grace. If not repent certainly does nothing which influences God to give a new heart. So we read—*They that are in the flesh cannot please God.* It will take up a whole eternity to praise him for his grace.

3. A reason why Christians should pray for sinners. Sinners will never do what they could do. All hangs on the mere sovereign pleasure of God."[3]

What distinguished Asahel Nettleton from the older Puritan view of grace was that man is held accountable to God for not repenting and believing because he is born with all the natural ability to turn to God but does not, because *he will not, because of his wicked heart.* Man will not turn to God and love Him with all his heart, soul, and mind because man lacks the *moral capacity* to do it; and this is only given by the *mere sovereign pleasure of God.*

We must realize that God used Nettleton as a "revival preacher", in areas of intense spiritual alarm, where conviction of sin was found among the people as the Holy Spirit wrought on their hearts. Therefore, doctrines which were enumerated were the ones vitally necessary for the task at hand: the salvation of sinners and the need for repentance. The center of the controversy between the theological camp of N. W. Taylor and that of Nettleton, was man's freedom of the will and the involvement of God in the salvation process.

Andrew Bonar, who published a British version of Nettleton's *Memoirs*, had the following insightful comments concerning the doctrines which Asahel Nettleton preached. He takes notice that the same doctrines which Nettleton preached had been regularly preached in New England since the time of the Puritan fathers—but now the *power was gone from them*, because they had become intellectual doctrines preached to the head, rather than transforming doctrines preached to the conscience and heart!

ANDREW BONAR'S OBSERVATIONS

"We do not claim for *Dr. Nettleton* the rank of Whitefield; but yet he stands very high among those who have 'converted sinners from the error of their ways, saved souls from death, and hidden a multitude of sins,' (James v. 20). There was this difference between his preaching and Whitefield's, in its substance, that while the latter proclaimed, with amazing unction and effect, the plainest and simplest truths regarding sin and the Saviour, reiterating these, in every place, all his long career,— Dr. Nettleton, on the other hand, dealt very extensively, and very perseveringly, in full doctrinal statements opened up and pressed home on the conscience.

"There is a natural aversion to *authority*, even the *authority of God*, in the heart of man. And hence it has been that, both then and now, there have been zealous men who have loudly protested against those doctrines of grace usually called *Calvinistic doctrines*, pretending that the souls of men are by these doctrines lulled into sleep as far as regards their responsibility. Now, though such an abuse of these scriptural truths has often been manifested where men have grown lukewarm, yet the very opposite influence is that which they ought to exert; and whoever reads Dr. Nettleton's history, will see with what tremendous force they may be employed to awaken the conscience ... in regard to the special doctrines of grace,—the Calvinistic doctrines. They [referring to the New England Calvinist preachers of Nettleton's day, authors note] have so preached and prelected on them, so argued and defended them, that, in their hands, these truths have become little better than dry theses; and the preachers of those truths have dropt the tone of solemn, tender, conscience-rousing Boanerges, and become merely able defenders of favourite themes. In admirable contrast with such treatment of doctrine, Dr. Nettleton's preaching, avoiding this error altogether, set these high truths before his hearers, on all occasions, in a most thoroughly practical form. They saw in them the God of majesty, glory, grace, dealing with rebels, and were bowed down before Him."[4]

Asahel Nettleton wielded the doctrines of grace like a double edged claymore, cutting asunder all false hopes of security and placing before the lost sinner these great gospel truths in their bold clarity; and applying them to the marrow of the heart and conscience! Because these doctrines were so central to Nettleton's ministry it is important at this time to

examine the theology behind the institute in which he founded—
Hartford Seminary, in Hartford, Connecticut. Bennet Tyler was the
institution's first president, and Tyler's theology was Nettleton's
theology.

BENNET TYLER'S OBSERVATIONS

"I am now in the fiftieth year of my ministerial life; the first fourteen years of
which were spent in the pastoral office, in the western part of the state. Those were
days of great peace and quietness in the churches of Connecticut, and of great
harmony among the pastors of the churches. Scarcely any controversy existed
among them. Perhaps in no part of the Christian world, and at no period in the
history of the church since the days of the apostles, could there be found an equal
number of pastors of contiguous churches who were better united in sentiment.[5]

Most of them had received their theological training in the schools of
Backus, Smalley, Dwight, Hooker, and Porter. Their theological views
were such, substantially, as are set forth in the Westminster Confession
and Assembly's Catechism, and such as were maintained by Edwards,
Bellamy, Smalley, Dwight, Strong, and the conductors of the old
Connecticut Evangelical Magazine. There were shades of difference
among them, but none which affected the great cardinal doctrines of the
gospel, or which occasioned the least interruption of Christian or
ministerial fellowship. Those were days, too, in which God signally
blessed the labors of his servants by copious effusions of his Spirit. 'Then
had the churches rest, and were edified, and, walking in the fear of the
Lord and the comfort of the Holy Ghost, were multiplied.'

"But near the close of the period of which I am speaking, the harmony which had
prevailed began to be interrupted. New theological speculations were put forth,
which gave great dissatisfaction. The authors of these speculations did not avowedly
or formally deny any of the doctrines of grace; but they professed to explain certain
doctrines in a manner suited to relieve them of objections, and to render them less
repulsive to unrenewed men. But their explanations seemed to many to be a virtual
denial of the doctrines themselves, or at least to contain principles, which, when
carried out into their legitimate consequences, must utterly subvert them.

"These different views let to a protracted controversy, in which it was my lot to
bear a part. In looking back to that controversy, I wish to say, (and I say it for the
purpose of correcting a false impression which has been made upon some minds,)
that my views have undergone no change on any of the points which were then
brought under discussion."[6]

Bennet Tyler continues to relate the founding of the Theological
Institute of Connecticut, later to be Hartford Seminary. Central to New
England theology at this time, are the doctrines taught at this new
seminary which was first at East Windsor, Connecticut, and which were
the primary doctrines of New England at that time. The seminary,

founded by Tyler and Nettleton, was to become known for its tenacious stance against the New Haven Theology of Yale, under N. W. Taylor. We now return to Tyler's observations:

"If the time would permit, I would glance at the prominent points in that controversy, mention the theories which were maintained, and the errors which they were supposed to involve. Suffice it for the present to say, that principles were advanced, which, in the opinion of many, tended to subvert most of the distinctive doctrines of the Calvinistic system.

"As these theories had their origin in the only theological school in the state [Yale College], and were advanced by men whose talents, and learning, and official position gave them peculiar advantages for influencing the public mind, those who regarded them as dangerous errors, felt no small degree of solicitude. It seemed to them that a flood of error was coming in upon the churches, which threatened to sweep away the foundations laid by our fathers, and to make our beautiful heritage a moral desolation.

"In this state of things, the anxious inquiry arose in many minds, What can be done? Is there no remedy for the evils which we deplore, and the still greater evils which we anticipate? Must all who are trained for the sacred office in this state be imbued with these speculations? Must our churches be revolutionized? Can nothing be done to check the progress of these dangerous errors?

"These inquiries and apprehensions led to the calling of a convention of ministers, which met in this town, September 10, 1833. About forty attended, and spent two days in prayerful deliberation. That meeting has ever been spoken of, by those who attended it, as one of peculiar interest. Deeply impressed with a sense of the responsibility resting upon them, they looked to the great Head of the church for direction, and God seems to have poured out upon them a peculiar spirit of prayer. Nothing like a spirit of party was apparent in their deliberations, but great spirituality and harmony of feeling pervaded the meeting. The great and all-absorbing inquiry was, What do the honor of God and the interests of his kingdom require? They were unanimous in their result. Being convinced that they had discovered the path of duty, they went forward in the strength of the Lord. They resolved to establish a new theological seminary ... on the 13th of May, 1834, the corner stone of the seminary edifice was laid ...

"The object for which this institution was established, was not to maintain any new system of religious doctrine ... The doctrines which they intended should here be taught, were those which had been previously taught in the private schools of Connecticut, and which were maintained by the great body of Connecticut pastors at the beginning of the present century. The founders of the Institute were old school New England Calvinists. They repudiated the new speculations which had been recently put forth, and which claimed to be great improvements, but to be old errors put forth in a new dress;—errors which tended to subvert the fundamental doctrines of the gospel, to corrupt revivals, to promote spurious conversions, and to exert a disastrous influence on the cause of evangelical religion.

"They believed in the absolute supremacy of Jehovah, whose 'works of providence are his most holy, wise, and powerful, preserving and governing all his creatures and all their actions.' They believed that, 'God, according to the course of his own will, hath foreordained whatsoever comes to pass; and that all beings, actions, and events, both in the natural and moral world, are subject to his providential direction; and that God's purposes perfectly consist with human liberty, God's universal agency with the agency of man, and man's dependance with his accountability.' They also believed 'that it is the prerogative of God to bring good out of evil, and that he can cause the wrath of man to praise him, and that all the evil which has existed and will forever exist in the universe, will eventually be made to promote a most important purpose, under the wise and perfect administration of that almighty Being who will cause all things to work for his own glory, and thus fulfill his pleasure.'

"The theory that God prefers, all things considered a different system to the one which exists, a system from which all evil should be excluded, and that he is and ever has been, engaged in fruitless efforts to render all his moral creatures holy and happy, they repudiated as dishonorable to God, as virtually denying his omnipotence, and as representing him to be a disappointed and unhappy being, who is obliged to look with everlasting regret and sorrow upon the defeat of his designs.

"They believed that men, as free moral agents, are under perfect obligation to obey every divine command, and consequently that they posses those natural powers or faculties which constitute the basis of obligation. They adopted the distinction, which was made by Edwards and other New England divines, between natural and moral ability and inability, and they held 'that man has understanding and natural strength to do all that God requires of him, so that nothing but the sinner's aversion to holiness prevents his salvation.' By natural strength or ability, (for the words are synonymous) they meant nothing more than the possession of those faculties which are essential to moral agency. And this is all that sound New England Calvinists have ever meant by it. They had no sympathy with those who hold to a self-determining power in the will, or the power of contrary choice [Taylorism], nor with those who ascribe a right disposition, or a disposition to get a right disposition, or any thing which is inconsistent with the most absolute moral inability. They believed that sinners are dead in trespasses and sins, that they are morally helpless, and absolutely dependent on the grace of God for salvation. They believed, of course, all those doctrines of grace which this dependence implies—the doctrines of total depravity, of regeneration by the special agency of the Holy Spirit, of divine sovereignty, and of eternal and particular election. No men believed those doctrines more firmly, or insisted on them more strenuously, than they, notwithstanding they adopted the distinction between natural and moral ability and inability. And why should it be thought that the adopting of this distinction is inconsistent with the strictest orthodoxy, or that it has any 'proclivity to Pelagian and Arminian heresies'?

"To those who entertain this opinion, I would commend the following extract from an article in the Princeton Review for July, 1831. The orthodoxy of this work will not be questioned. The writer, after having shown that some preachers so exhibit this subject as to leave the impression that those laboring under this inability are not culpable for the omission of acts which they have no power to perform, and that others so present it as to lead sinners to feel that they have nothing to do but wait God's time in the use of means with an impenitent and unbelieving heart, goes on to remark,—

'The inconvenience and evils of these representations being perceived, many adopted, with readiness, the distinction of human ability into natural and moral. By the first, they understood merely the possession of physical powers and opportunities; by the latter, a mind rightly disposed. In accordance with this distinction it was taught that every man possessed a natural ability to do all that God required of him, but that every sinner labored under a moral inability to obey God, which, however, could not be pleaded to excuse disobedience, as it consisted in corrupt dispositions of the heart, for which every man was responsible. Now, this view of the subject is substantially correct; and the distinction has always been made by every person in his judgment of his own conduct, and that of others. It is recognized in all courts of justice, and in all family government, and is by no means a modern discovery. And yet it is remarkable that it is a distinction so seldom referred to, or brought directly into view, by old Calvinistic authors. The first writer among English theologians that we have observed using this distinction explicitly, is the celebrated Dr. Twiss, the prolocutor of the Westminster Assembly of Divines, and the able opposer of Arminianism, and advocate of the supralapsarian doctrine of divine decrees. It was also resorted to by the celebrated Mr. Howe, and long afterward used freely by Dr. Isaac Watts, the popularity of whose evangelical writings probably had much influence in giving it currency. It is also found in the theological writings of Dr. Witherspoon, and many others whose orthodoxy was never disputed. But in this country no man has had so great an influence in fixing the language of theology as Jonathan Edwards, president of New Jersey College. In his work on the Freedom of the Will, this distinction holds a prominent place, and is very important to the argument which this profound writer has so ably discussed in that treatise. The general use of the distinction between natural and moral ability, may, therefore, be ascribed to the writings of President Edwards, both in Europe and America. No distinguished writer on theology has made more use of it than Dr. Andrew Fuller, and it is well known that he imbibed nearly all his views from an acquaintance with the writings of Edwards. And it may be truly said that Jonathan Edwards has done more to give complexion to the theological system of Calvinists in America, than all other persons together. This is more especially true of New England; but it is also true; to a great extent, in regard to a large number of the present ministers of the Presbyterian church. Those, indeed, who were accustomed to the Scotch or Dutch writers, did not adopt this distinction, but were jealous of it as an innovation, and as tending to diminish, in their view, the miserable and sinful state of man, and as derogatory to the grace of God. But we have remarked, that in almost all cases, where the distinction has been opposed as false, or as tending to the introduction of false doctrine, it has been misrepresented. The true ground of the distinction has not been clearly apprehended, and those who have denied it, have been found making it in other words; for that an inability, depending on physical defect, should be distinguished from that which arises from a wicked disposition, or perverseness of will, is a thing which no one can deny, who attends to the clear dictates of his own mind, for it is self-evident truth, which even children recognize in all their apologies for their conduct.'"7

How did the theology of New England change if Edwards was the central-point? How did the Old School Calvinists come to differ from Edwards and his followers? This is what transpired: the "Old School" Calvinists' *reaction* to the excesses of Charles Finney's "New Measures" made them *retract too far back* from the Edwardsean position, regarding man's *ability* to come to Christ in relation to his *moral inability*. As this "unnamed" Princeton reviewer states, the Edwardsean position (of natural capacity and moral inability) was a *commonly accepted* doctrine by the *majority* of Calvinists extending back to Drs. Twiss and Watts! The question arises: Why do the majority of Calvinists today not hold to this Edwardsean position of the will? We believe it began at Princeton with the *retraction* away from Finney and Taylor which deviated *too much* from the Edwardsean position and the position of the revival preachers of that day. This may be a surprise to many, but nonetheless, the facts of history face us squarely and cannot be denied.

Unfortunately, the deep bog of the so-called "New England Theology" has simply mystified many who cannot get their heads around it. To better understand the historic position of "New England Theology" this is what transpired: Jonathan Edwards was the theological head of the "pure mountain stream" known as "New England Theology". It *evolved* into something quite different after his death by *new translations* of it from the pens of his disciples and followers (each one an avowed Calvinist). What ended up was a distortion of Edwards. We can follow this theological stream as it flows down the mountain by tracing the various interpretations of Edwards by his pupils. Each interpretation was a *move away* from Edwards by varying degrees. The first *move away* from the Edwardsean position occurs with his closest friends and disciples——namely, Joseph Bellamy and more particularly, Samuel Hopkins. Hopkins does more damage than Bellamy, with his system of theology which became known as "Hopkinsianism".

Joseph Bellamy, for the most part, moves away from Edwards on the doctrine of the atonement, by accepting the position of the "Governmental Theory" over Edwards' own position of the atonement which was "Anselmian"; that is, he held to the "Satisfaction Theory" of the atonement. Bellamy, however, took the position of Hugo Grotius (1583–1645) who taught the "Governmental Theory". Also, Edwards taught a "Limited Atonement", whereas, Bellamy believed in a "Universal Atonement". But the real *downgrade* occurs in Samuel Hopkins.[8] The theology of Samuel Hopkins is laid out with clarity in the "classic" book on New England Theology, *A Genetic History of the New England Theology*, by Frank Hugh Foster, who states:

> "Hopkins' system of theology was a growth in his own mind, and was formed by prolonged study, and in constant contact with other minds. It was presented in many partial views in a series of controversial writings beginning with the very unpopular tract, *Sin through the Divine Interposition an Advantage to the Universe* (1759). It was finally gathered up in one full presentation in his *System of Doctrines* (1793)."[9]

Basically, Samuel Hopkins theologically moved away from Jonathan

Edwards by *elevating* man's abilities and *lowering* God's sovereignty. We observe the following comments:

> "Samuel Hopkins (1721–1803) was another protégé of Edwards who modified things in a similar direction. His theology became known as Hopkinsianism. In his large *System Of Doctrines* and other works, Hopkins weakened original sin and allowed vestiges of moral ability to the will, for the will has to choose. Hopkins also taught that repentance precedes faith."[10]

The pure mountain stream of Edwards' thought became more and more diluted by each new interpretation of his theology by his followers. First Bellamy, then Hopkins, then Edwards' son, Jonathan Edwards Jr., (1745–1801), who moved away from his father's position by raising human responsibility and holding to a universal atonement. Then the grandson of Jonathan Edwards, Timothy Dwight (1752–1817), moved further away from the Edwardsean position by ascribing even more ability to fallen man than Jonathan Edwards, Jr. By the time Nathaniel William Taylor appeared on the public scene with his theological views, the Edwardsean position was so diluted it no longer resembled the former. N. W. Taylor was the first professor of theology at the newly-founded Yale Divinity School, and he propagated a theology which radically transformed the old "New England Theology" to the point of it no longer being Calvinistic but Arminian—and many argued that it was not merely Arminian but Pelagian. Oddly enough, each interpreter of Edwards claimed to be a follower of Edwards! Frank Hugh Foster aptly calls Taylorism the "Ripened Product"! N. W. Taylor delivered a famous lecture at the chapel at Yale College in New Haven, Connecticut in 1828. His theme was "moral depravity" and his sermon became the famous *Concio ad Clerum*. Foster brings clarity to Taylor's theology with the following comments:

> "The proposition maintained in this sermon [*Concio ad Clerum*] was 'that the entire moral depravity of mankind is by nature.' In it Taylor successively maintained, among others, the positions that moral depravity is sinfulness; that this is not created in man, nor does it consist in acting Adam's act; that it is not a disposition or tendency to sin which is the cause of all sin; that it is 'man's own act, consisting in a free choice of some object rather than God, as his chief good;—or a free preference of the world and of worldly good, to the will and glory of God.' ... He defines it ... Men's nature is not itself sinful, nor is it the physical or efficient cause of their sinning, but it is the occasion of their sinning. In the applicatory 'remarks' of the sermon he said again that 'guilt pertains exclusively to voluntary action.'"[11]

The "New Measures" methodology of revivals conducted by Charles Finney incorporated this philosophy of N. W. Taylor, that man was not born with original sin and therefore in the salvation process, man did not need a *new* heart (regeneration), because man did not possess a *bad* heart

to begin with. Salvation to Finney and Taylor was more *reformation* of
character, rather than *regeneration* of being "born again." Salvation to
Finney and Taylor lay more in the decision of the will to become a
Christian, rather than God transforming the heart and giving a new
nature through the act of regeneration. The mass population of 19th
century American churches unfortunately embraced this philosophy on
a wholesale scale and evangelism moved away from traditional New
England orthodoxy which had been for years, God-centered. Thus we
see in America at this time, the mid-1830s and forward, an acceptance of
the man-centered evangelism perpetuated by Finney and his followers,
as opposed to the God-centered evangelism of Asahel Nettleton and the
Puritan fathers.[12]

Notes

1 Iain Murray, *Revival & Revivalism* (Edinburgh: Banner of Truth Trust, 2002), pp. 363–364.

2 Joseph Bellamy, *True Religion Delineated; or Experimental Religion, as Distinguished from Formality on the One Hand, and Enthusiasm on the Other* (Boston: Congregational Board of Publication, 1750), pp. 93–101.

3 Asahel Nettleton, *Sermons from the Second Great Awakening*, editor, William C. Nichols (Ames, Iowa, International Outreach, Inc. 1995), pp. 60–73.

4 Andrew Bonar, *Asahel Nettleton Life and Labours* (Edinburgh: Banner of Truth Trust, reprint 1996), p. viii–ix.

5 Nahum Gale, D.D., *A Memoir of Rev. Bennet Tyler, D.D.* (Boston: J.E Tilton and Co., 1860), p. 67 (available on-line at www.quintapress.com/PDF_Books.html. Tyler is referring to the "Plan of Union" which allowed Congregational and Presbyterian churches to adopt measures which allowed both denominations full use of their churches. This harmony existed between Congregationalists and Presbyterians up to the great chasm caused by the followers of N. W. Taylor and the "New Divinity"; and Charles Finney and the "New Measures". [Author's note].

6 Ibid. p. 68. Some historians had stated during his life and after his death, that Bennet Tyler changed his theological position. Even Sherry Pierpont May, in her 1969 dissertation on Nettleton makes these same false assumptions, "Physical regeneration, held here so closely and tenaciously by Nettleton, was dismissed by the Taylorites, and finally perhaps by Bennet Tyler too", p. 141 of her dissertation (Drew University, 1969).

7 Rev. Nahum Gale, D.D., *Memoir of Rev. Bennet Tyler, D.D.* (Boston: J. E. Tilton and Company, 1860), pp. 68–76.

8 See the important volumes on Hopkins written by the brilliant Edward A. Park, *The Works of Samuel Hopkins* (Andover Theological Seminary, 1852).

9 Frank Hugh Foster, *A Genetic History of the New England Theology* (Chicago: The University of Chicago Press, 1907), pp. 129–130.

10 Curt Daniel, *The History and Theology of Calvinism* (Springfield: Good Books, 2003), p. 104.

11 Frank Hugh Foster, *A Genetic History of the New England Theology* (Chicago: The University of Chicago Press, 1907), p. 370.

12 For a more detailed analysis of New England Theology, see *New England Theology; With Comments on a Third Article in the Princeton Review, Relating to a Convention Sermon*, by Edwards A. Park (Andover: Warren F. Draper, 1852), pp. 1–53. This rare document is an apologetic for "New England Theology". Professor Park, of Andover Theological Seminary, carried on a public feud with Charles Hodge of Princeton, over doctrines of New England Theology. This treatise typifies both the misunderstandings of New England Theology and the trenchant battles over it during 19th century America. A version can be found on-line at www.quintapress.com/PDF_Books.

After studying theology under Rev. Bezaleel Pinneo of Milford, Connecticut, he was licensed to preach in 1811. The door for foreign service being then closed, Mr. Nettleton commenced his work as an itinerant evangelist in eastern Connecticut. Providentially, his work began in an area which was still badly affected by various excesses and divisions arising out of the Great Awakening. After careful study of the cause and effect of these numerous disorders, the young evangelist set a very sane course for himself and his future itinerant ministry. From the beginning of his labors, God crowned his preaching with glorious power, and revival after revival occurred.

RICHARD OWEN ROBERTS

8

EARLY LABORS

The first year of Asahel Nettleton's public ministry (1811) is obscure. Although a detailed record of the young evangelist's early labors is not available, we can conclude that God was teaching and honing His servant for wider service. Nettleton preached in what were known as the "waste places" of the Great Awakening; the scenes of James Davenport's destructive preaching, where the churches he had divided through controversy, now lay in ruins. It was here, in these "waste places", that initially proved to be "an unpromising field of labor". This in turn proved to be the best training ground that Nettleton could have engaged.

The fall of 1812 finds Nettleton in the midst of a glorious revival in South Britain, Connecticut. Bennet Tyler lived in South Britain at this time and it is here, during this revival, that their lifelong friendship began. Tyler provides us an account of this revival in South Britain from the standpoint of an eyewitness:

"There was at that time, a very interesting revival of religion in South Britain. This induced him to prolong his visit for one week. He preached on the Sabbath, and attended several other religious meetings, beside visiting with the pastor from house to house, and conversing with those who were anxious for their souls. His labors were very acceptable to the people, and there is reason to believe that they were blessed to the saving good of some souls.

"His manner at this time, was somewhat peculiar, but not so much so, as to injure his usefulness. His address at the first meeting which he attended, will not soon be forgotten by those who heard it. It was in a school-house, crowded with people, not a few of whom were under deep conviction of sin. As he arose, being an entire stranger, every eye was fixed upon him, and a breathless silence pervaded the assembly. With great solemnity he looked upon the congregation, and thus began, 'What is the murmur which I hear?—I wish I had a new heart. What shall I do? They tell me to repent—I can't repent—I wish they would give me some other direction.' He thus went on for a short time, personating the awakened sinner, and bringing out the feelings of his heart. He then changed the form of his address, and in a solemn and affectionate manner, appealed to the consciences of his hearers, and showed them that they must repent or perish, that it was their reasonable duty to repent immediately, and that ministers could not direct them to any thing short of repentance, without being unfaithful to their souls. The address produced a thrilling effect, and served greatly to deepen the convictions of those who were anxious.

"During the week that he remained in South Britain, he took a lively interest in the revival which was in progress, and he left the place with his heart glowing with love to souls, and with ardent desires that God would give him grace to be faithful to the people among whom he was going to labor. From that time, for ten years, it was his happy lot, to be employed almost constantly in revivals of religion.

"He went to South Salem. The church was destitute of a pastor, and was in a cold and backslidden state. Great spiritual apathy existed in the congregation. He preached on the Sabbath, and appointed one or two evening meetings in the course of the week. His preaching produced an immediate solemnity on the minds of the people; and in the course of a fortnight, there was a development of feeling, which made it apparent that the Spirit of God was operating on many minds. At the close of one of his evening meetings, several youths repaired to his lodgings in deep distress, to inquire what they must do to be saved. He pointed them to Christ, and with affectionate earnestness, urged them immediately to repent and believe the gospel. The next day, in visiting from house to house, he found others under deep religious impressions. The seriousness soon spread through the place, and the subject of religion became the engrossing topic of conversation. In the course of one or two weeks from this time, several were found rejoicing in hope. He was exceedingly anxious lest they should take up with a false and spurious hope. He warned them of the danger of self-deception, reminded them of the deceitfulness of the human heart, and pointed out the various ways in which persons are liable to deceive themselves. He also exhibited with great plainness the distinguishing marks of genuine conversion. The work became powerful, and increased with rapidity, and in the course of a few weeks, a large number gave pleasing evidence of having passed from death unto life."[1]

It is important to pause in our narrative to note just *how* Asahel Nettleton conducted a revival. It is obvious from the aforementioned that the church, before his arrival, was "backslidden" and in "spiritual apathy". By the means of his serious and searching sermons, aimed at the minds and consciences of his hearers, God began to stir hearts in conviction of sin. One distinguishing mark of Nettleton's ministry over that of Whitefield's was that he personally visited "from house to house" with those who were under "deep religious impressions." It is apparent from this that Nettleton's ministry was a *rifle approach* whereas Whitefield's was more of a *cannon!* Notice also that Asahel was mindful to counsel the newly awakened sinners as to their *spiritual state*, being careful to point out in very clear terms the "distinguishing marks of genuine conversions"; thereby diminishing the number of those resting on "false hopes". This is a valuable aspect of his ministry. It is evident that the stories Nettleton had heard concerning the spurious work of James Davenport (in the Great Awakening), had so alarmed and concerned him that he was overtly cautious for the rest of his life in regard to conducting revivals.

Although Nettleton had early success, he had to learn from his mistakes as we see from the following remarks:

"After about two months, he left the place. He did this, partly, because the people began to take measures to give him a call to settle with them as their pastor. Having devoted himself to a missionary life he was determined to listen to no such call. Another reason which induced him to leave, was, the presumption that the work after having made such progress, might be expected to continue, as well without his labors, as with them. In this respect, he committed an error, as he was afterwards convinced. In the early part of his ministry, he thought that he might accomplish the most good by laboring only a short time in a place—that when a revival had commenced, he might safely commit it to the care of others, and retire to a new field. But experience taught him that this was not the way to be most useful. He found it important to prolong his labors, when God was rendering them effectual to the salvation of souls.

"After he left South Salem, he preached a few Sabbaths in Danbury, a town in the western part of Connecticut. Here a work of grace immediately commenced, and several interesting cases of conversion occurred. Here, too, the people began to adopt measures to obtain him for their pastor, which induced him to leave sooner than he otherwise would have done. He afterwards expressed his regret that he did not remain longer in Danbury, as there was every appearance of the commencement of a great and glorious revival. The work made but little progress after his departure."[2]

For much of the first half of 1813 the evangelist's labors were confined to rural parishes of eastern Connecticut. But in the fall of 1813, Nettleton met a man who would figure prominently in his life, Lyman Beecher. It was Beecher who initially stood alongside Nettleton in the "fight" with Charles Finney at New Lebanon, New York; and it was Beecher who later in life appeared more sympathetic towards Finney. One thing was sure, Beecher often looked to Nettleton for advice and counsel regarding revivals and ministry. In regard to Beecher we have the following observations:

"Lyman Beecher, 1775–1863, celebrated clergyman and educator, spanned an age of national metamorphosis. His famous children pieced together a fascinating patchwork of letters and transcribed reminiscences of their father, which they published shortly after his death as an *Autobiography of Lyman Beecher*. ... the so-called autobiography provides a rich account of the man's career, but only an oblique indication that he was substantially related as both author and actor to a drama being played out in American religion. During his lifetime, and partly through his effort, the acknowledged authority of the established New England theocracy was being displaced in the national culture by the right of the individual to choose for himself, and the confidence that he could bring off the option. When not dismissed simply as the father of his children, Lyman Beecher has usually appeared in literature as a charming eccentric, or as the activist preacher who popularized the theology of Nathaniel Taylor."[3]

An example of Beecher relying on Nettleton's advice is found in the following letter. Beecher is writing to Nettleton to seek his guidance and help with the disestablishment of the Connecticut churches. Despite the *Faulkneresque* sentences of Beecher, we learn that he is greatly agitated over the possibility of breaches among the Connecticut churches and advocates unity throughout. He writes:

"My beloved brother,

The day before your letter came I was thinking to write and inquire whether you were angry with me that you neither came nor wrote. Your letter of course as coming from you as well as an account of the cheering information it contained was as cold water to a thirsty soul. I attempted in vain to send you a missionary but I hear you have gone into the village and are prospered. Before you leave there some one must be sent or if it can be done the subjects be united to Ashford Church and Society. Our legislature in past days have injured the cause by encouraging the multiplication of little societies. These are under the fostering care of the Domestic Missionary Society ... The policy of the present moment is to make as many strong societies as possible by uniting discreetly our scattered families and feeble societies. By little and little we must build up by the indefatigable industry of ministers and churches to raise up the foundations of many generations—We must be upon the alert to have families and even individuals. No one must be regarded as insignificant ... Our people must understand the signs of the times. And act accordingly. Episcopalians, Baptists and Methodists all act as one in favor of their respective denominations-are upon the alert to proselyte and also to preserve what they gain. If thus assailed the Presbyterians do not feel more as one body and do not act more unitedly as members of societies and as a denomination in the states they will gradually dwindle and be overthrown. Ministers cannot stand alone in this day. The churches must be made acquainted with the dangers that threaten them and with the pastors in the fear of God must act for the preservation of the inheritance of their fathers. I have from Brother Everest that the state of things in his Society is rather dark and that some of the ministers around him are beginning to admit the idea that Windham must be given up. Brother, Windham must not be given up. It will become a strong hold of Satan the gates of which will prevail against all the surrounding churches. It is a county town. And will by its central position and political influence be a center of Spiritual death. If the word of life and immortality be not maintained there——I know the town is in a dreadful condition. It inherits the obliquity of Sectarianism and the poison of infidelity and error from generation to generation. But God has a church there and is able to cause his church to stand. But not without means appropriate to the occasion are we to expect that he will do it. I have told Brother Everest that he must go home and get together all the spiritual members of his church——explain to them the situation is a case of life or death and set before them their hope as only in God and establish a stated prayer meeting it but. ... only can be united for revival that shall bow the oaks—and build the temple of God by materials torn from the ramparts of the enemy. That in the mean time he must select the most favorable spot to break up the fallow ground and establish there for winter an evening lecture and for summer a lecture at 5 o'clock with a humble determination to persevere amid every discouragement of hope defend for one year at least or until God shall grant the blessing of a district revival which may become perhaps universal and turn back the captivity of Zion. I have told him that I will make the situation of his church known to my church and that it must become a

subject of prayer extending from church to church that a light in Israel may not be
put out. I wish that you would go over to Windham yourself as soon as you can and
look at things with your own eyes and hear with your own ears and see what can be
and ought to be done and if there be a spot which you can take hold of and lend a
helping hand probably no greater or more important aid can be given to the cause by
you in that part of the state. At any rate go and see and advise and encourage Brother
Everest and write to me the state and prospect of Windham and the region round
about ...

"The effects of the New Constitution are not felt much by the churches as yet and
if appropriate exertions are made by the churches to stand—in other words if they
go to their duty as to make their existence a blessing to the kingdom of the redeemer
I believe they will be kept from falling. Why should he throw away his swelling
instruments of usefulness? He will not. Why should he maintain the form of
godliness without the power. It is not to be expected. The safety of the churches is to
be found in their active usefulness. In their activity to contend earnestly for the faith
in their vigilant and faithful administration of evangelical discipline. In their
attention to the catechetical instruction and religious education of children. In their
charitable efforts to propagate the table and to multiply pastors and missionaries for
our land and for the world—and in their associations for prayer—for the outpouring
of the Spirit and their exertions to obtain and extend revivals of religion. It is a
perilous time for formal covetous lukewarm churches. But those churches however
small that imbibe the spirit of the day whose pulse beats in unison with the strong
pulsation of the Christian world and who give to support among themselves and to
spread the gospel according to their ability have not in my opinion any thing to fear
... Nelson's last Telegrappie dispatch on entering the battle of Traffalgon was 'Old
England expects every man to do his duty.' And the order from heaven in the
present conflict is The Lord Jesus Christ expects the churches of Connecticut to do
their duty. In that case the result will be glorious. The state will be filled with
revivals ...

"Write to me your thoughts on the subject of conciliation between us and the
Baptists ... Write soon and write a longer letter than you commonly do—In short
give me your thoughts in return on the topics I have touched upon in this letter and
generally on the interests of the church in this state—I wish the sentiment which I
have expressed in the fore part of this letter as to the duty and safety of the churches
might obtain and pervade the state. You know what is discreet and if you think any
would be benefitted by it you may read such parts of the letter as you think
proper."[4]

Lyman Beecher would rise to prominence as one of America's most
influential religious leaders. Beecher and Nettleton would begin their
relationship in the midst of a revival at Beecher's church in Litchfield,
Connecticut, and end their relationship over controversy with the
"New Measures" of Charles G. Finney. However, it is necessary to state
that Asahel Nettleton did not end the relationship with Lyman Beecher.
It was Beecher who distanced himself from Nettleton as the public
acceptance of Finney's "New Measures" grew in popularity. When one
studies the life of Lyman Beecher it is discovered that he was more
politician than minister.

We now return to the narrative of Asahel Nettleton's first meeting with Lyman Beecher:

"In the autumn of 1813, he commenced his labors in Milton, a parish in the west part of the town of Litchfield. This was a waste place. The people were not only without a pastor, but had become so weakened by divisions and by the loss of their parish fund, that they almost despaired of ever enjoying again, the privilege of a preached gospel. Dr. Beecher, who was at that time pastor of the church in Litchfield, and another neighboring minister, agreed to solicit funds in their respective congregations, to support a preacher, for a season, in Milton. Having entered into this arrangement, they made application to Mr. Nettleton. In the mean time, the churches in the vicinity were requested to remember that people particularly in their prayers. In conformity with the arrangement, Mr. Nettleton came, and called on Dr. Beecher. It was the first time they had met. 'Thou hast well done,' said Dr. Beecher, 'that thou art come.' 'I ask,' said Mr. Nettleton, 'for what intent ye have sent for me?' 'To hear all things that are commanded thee of God,' said Dr. Beecher. On Friday, by the direction of Dr. Beecher, Mr. Nettleton took lodgings at the house of one of the members of his church, who lived on the borders of Milton ...

"The curiosity of the people was soon excited, and they flocked together to hear the stranger who had come so unexpectedly among them. At the close of one of his evening meetings, he informed them, that he had been requested to come and labor with them for a season, and he wished them to pray for a revival of religion, adding, 'whether you do or not, it is possible there may be one, for Christians in other places have agreed to pray for you.' This produced great solemnity. Several went from that meeting in deep distress. It was soon manifest, that God was in the place, of a truth. The work increased rapidly and became very powerful. It was characterized by remarkably clear and distressing convictions of sin. The subjects had a vivid sense of the opposition of their hearts to God, and in some instances, their distress was overwhelming. On one evening, two or three individuals were in such horror of mind, that it became necessary to remove them from the meeting, to a neighboring house. This, for the moment, created some confusion, but order was soon restored, when Mr. Nettleton addressed the people in the following manner, 'It may, perhaps, be new to some of you, that there should be such distress for sin. But there was great distress on the day of Pentecost, when thousands were pricked in the heart, and cried out, "men and brethren, what shall we do." Some of you may, perhaps, be ready to say, if this is religion, we wish to have nothing to do with it. My friends, this is not religion. Religion does not cause its subjects to feel and act thus. These individuals are thus distressed, not because they have religion, but because they have no religion, and have found it out. It was so on the day of Pentecost. The thousands who were pricked in their heart, had found that they had no religion, and were unprepared to meet their God. They had made the discovery that they were lost sinners, and that their souls were in jeopardy every hour.' These may not be the precise words, but such was the substance of his address. It produced a salutary effect. It served to check what would be the natural result of mere sympathy on such an occasion, and also to stop the mouths of those who might be disposed to cavil. I would here remark, that in most of the revivals under Mr. Nettleton's preaching, there were cases of overwhelming distress. But this distress was not the result of mere sympathy, but of clear conviction of sin; and in almost all cases, it soon terminated in a peaceful and joyful hope of salvation.

"Mr. Nettleton labored in Milton three or four months, during which time a

large number became hopefully subjects of renewing grace ... It has been
mentioned that Dr. Beecher and another neighboring minister, agreed to collect
funds for the support of Mr. Nettleton while preaching in Milton. Some money was
collected for this purpose, but he refused to receive it. The people had made him
some presents in clothing, and with this he was satisfied ... It may be proper to
remark, that during the ten years that Mr. Nettleton was laboring in revivals, he
received as a compensation for his services, barely sufficient to defray his expenses.
When he was taken sick in 1822, he was found to be entirely destitute, and money
was collected by his friends in different places, to defray the expenses of his
sickness."[5]

In Bennet Tyler's narrative he mentions a revival which occurred under
Nettleton's preaching in early 1814 in a place called South Farms. He
records some personal testimonies of some of the converts from that
revival; this record is found in his memoir (pages 62–67), which we will
now pass over, for we wish to pick up his labors in the spring of 1814 at
his hometown of Killingworth, Conn. It is interesting to note from the
following account of this revival that Asahel went home to *rest*—he was
fatigued and worn out.. The strain of constant preaching along with one-
on-one counseling had exhausted him. But as is a pattern of his career,
there is seldom rest for the great evangelist, soon he is engaged in yet
another revival. Even early on in his ministry, his reputation now
precedes him as he travels from town to town, throughout the New
England countryside.

We now resume the narrative of his ministry:

"Sometime in the spring of 1814, Mr. Nettleton left South Farms, and repaired to
North Killingworth, greatly exhausted by his labors, and intending to rest for a
season. At this time the people of Chester, a neighboring parish, were destitute of a
minister; their pastor, the Rev. Mr. Mills, having died a short time before. It being
known in Chester, that Mr. Nettleton was at home, application was made to him to
attend a funeral in that place. He at first declined, assigning as the reason, that he was
greatly exhausted by his labors and needed rest. The man who came after him, as he
turned to go away, burst into tears. This so affected Mr. Nettleton, that he
concluded to go. He attended the funeral, and at the close of it, he gave notice that
he would meet the young people in the evening, at the house of their late pastor. A
large number assembled, and the meeting was very solemn. Such were the
indications of the special presence of God among the people, that he was induced,
notwithstanding the state of his health, to continue with them a considerable time,
and had the satisfaction to witness a very interesting work of divine grace. In the
autumn of 1814, Mr. Nettleton commenced his labors in East Granby. This was a
waste place. The moral condition of the people was exceedingly deplorable. But
God saw fit to turn again the captivity of Zion. Under Mr. Nettleton's preaching,
there was a very interesting revival of religion. He preached here till some time in
the winter, when he was obliged to suspend his labors for several months, by
hemorrhage from the lungs."[6]

Since the death of his father, Asahel's health was poor at best. He never
fully recovered from the break in his health which occurred as an

undergraduate at Yale. Adding to his recurring bouts of sickness is the fact that he *seldom rested*, and in this regard he was very similar to George Whitefield—both evangelists simply wore out their bodies in constant battles for the Lord. His frail immune system and infrequent rest contribute to him contracting typhus fever in 1822 which nearly killed him. We now return to the narrative of his labors:

> "The Rev. J. B. Clark, the present pastor of the church in East Granby, in a letter dated Nov. 17, 1843, thus speaks of the effects of Mr. Nettleton's labors in that place. 'Most of these who were connected with the church, as the result of that revival, have worn remarkably well, so far as is or can be known. Many of them have been, and are still, bright and shining lights in the church of Christ. One of the subjects, Miss C Thrall, died as a missionary among the western Indians. The effect of that revival upon the church, and upon the community, was most happy and lasting.

> 'The interest of Christ's kingdom had suffered much from an erroneous ministry. The church lost all spirituality and fervency. The community were buried in sinful indifference. When Mr. Nettleton came among them, stupidity and slothfulness prevailed among all classes and all ages. The effect of his entrance to the place, was electric. The school house, and private rooms, were filled with trembling worshipers. A solemnity and seriousness pervaded the community, which had not been experienced for years before. There was no bustle—no *array* of means. All was orderly, quiet, and scriptural. There seems to have been an *increasing* solemnity, while the work continued.

> '… his sermons were in a high degree, practical. Doctrinal sermons were frequent, but these had a practical turn. They were eminently scriptural, and plain, and made men feel that *they* were the men addressed, and not their neighbors. He sometimes preached on the severer doctrines with great power and apparent good effect. At this day we can hardly imagine the effect which his visit had upon this waste place. This seems to have been Satan's chief seat. Infidelity had been infused into the very bosom of the church. Of course sin in every form abounded. There were no spiritual hymn-books in use, till Mr. Nettleton labored here; and then those hymns, in his hands, became solemn sermons.

> 'Mr. Nettleton is remembered with much interest, and peculiar affection by most of those advanced in life. When I have been speaking of him in my pastoral visits, the most intense interest is excited. From many expressions used as the old people speak of him, one may know that his labors are still remembered with affection.'"[7]

It must be noted that during historic revivals, hymns and worship played an integral part in the work. In the revivals under Asahel Nettleton, hymns were not only central to the revival, but aided it in quite a remarkable way. Nettleton carefully arranged hymns to reflect the different stages of a revival: the majesty of God; awakening and conviction of sin; repentance; praise and thanksgiving. Nettleton's famous book of hymns, *Village Hymns For Social Worship*, was birthed from the activities of revival.

Now back to the narrative, where we learn the evangelist is in better health:

"Early in the spring of 1815, Mr. Nettleton having so far recovered from his illness as to be able to preach, labored for a season in Bolton, with signal success. Here the people gave him a call to settle as their pastor, which he immediately declined, and recommended to them his friend and classmate, the Rev. Philander Parmele. Mr. Parmele was installed Nov. 8, 1815.

"From Bolton, he went to Manchester, to assist the Rev. Mr. Cook, whose people were enjoying a time of 'refreshing from the presence of the Lord.' By a divine blessing on his labors, the work was greatly promoted and extended.

"After this, he spent a few weeks in Granby, (west parish), where his preaching was crowned with very signal success. Peculiar circumstances prevented him from continuing long with this people; but there is reason to believe that many souls were savingly benefitted by his labors. There were but few places in which he labored, where so much apparent good was effected in so short a time.

"Of the revivals mentioned in this chapter, excepting the one in South Britain, no account was published at this time; and with the exception of that and the one in South Farms, so far as is now known, no particular account was ever written. As Mr. Nettleton kept no journal of his labors at that period, it is impossible at this late day, to give any more than a very general account of most of these revivals. Some of the facts which I have mentioned, fell under my own observation, and some of them were obtained in private conversation with Mr. Nettleton himself."[8]

The Second Great Awakening was spreading across New England at this time and God was again moving in the land that He had graciously blessed during the days of Edwards and Whitefield. Now the primary human instrument of the revival was Asahel Nettleton, and many of the "waste places" of the previous century were now transformed into watered gardens by the powerful preaching of Nettleton with God's Hand upon him in a remarkable way!

Nettleton had found his life-work, laboring in revivals of religion. He had learned from his mistakes and had become a more useful ambassador for Christ. With these thoughts in mind we have the following comments:

"There were two things during his stay at South Britain which contributed to the change in direction of his life-work. First, it was here that he himself was able to have a leadership role in a revival. He found that revivals were his native clime. Second, here the gifts for which he would become famous came to the surface. His preaching always featured the piercing eye, the analytical knowledge of human nature, the serious demeanor and the dramatic style. And then, the audience reaction: the solemn stillness, the hypnotic attention, and deep convictions which were manifested at the first service at South Britain, characterized his entire ministry."[9]

Notes

1   Tyler, pp. 55–57.
2   Ibid. pp. 57–58.

3   Stuart Henry, *Unvanquished Puritan, A Portrait of Lyman Beecher* (Grand Rapids: Eerdmans Publishing, 1973), p. 9.

4   Archival letter, Beecher to Nettleton, Hartford Seminary Collection. No date.

5   Tyler, pp. 59–61.

6   Ibid. p. 68.

7   Ibid. pp. 68–70.

8   Ibid. p. 70.

9   J. F. Thornbury, *God Sent Revival* (Welwyn, England: Evangelical Press second edition, 1988), p. 53.

There is a natural aversion to authority, *even the* authority of God, *in the heart of man. And hence, it has been that, both then and now, there have been zealous men who have loudly protested against those doctrines of grace usually called* Calvinistic doctrines, *pretending that the souls of men are by these doctrines lulled into sleep as far as regards their responsibility. Now, though such an abuse of these scriptural truths has often been manifested where men have grown lukewarm, yet the very opposite influence is that which they ought to exert; and whoever reads Dr. Nettleton's history, will see with what tremendous force they may be employed to awaken the conscience.*

ANDREW BONAR

9

THE DOCTRINES THAT HE PREACHED

I t is necessary to study exactly what Asahel Nettleton preached in regard to *doctrine*. He was indeed a doctrinal preacher, but there was more to this aspect of his ministry which needs to be carefully reviewed. He, like many "revival men" of former times, preached up the great doctrines of the Bible and these were:

1. The total depravity of man
2. The sovereignty of God in salvation
3. A future judgment for all mankind
4. The duty of immediate repentance
5. Election by grace
6. Regeneration *precedes* repentance and faith
7. The duty of a holy life unto God

When a study of historic revival is commenced it is noteworthy to learn that the *pre-revival* preaching and the preaching *during* revival has often centered around those aforementioned doctrines, which are the doctrines of grace. Go and study what George Whitefield preached and other "revival men" of the Great Awakening such as, Jonathan Edwards, Jonathan Parsons, Samuel Blair, Joseph Bellamy, Gilbert Tennent, Solomon Stoddard, Samuel Davies, Thomas Prince, Joseph Sewall, Theodorous Frelinghuysen, Jonathan Dickinson and others, and you will find a *common denominator* in all their preaching—it was *God-centered* and the focus was on the *glory of God* in both salvation and Christian service.

These aforementioned "revival preachers" centered their preaching ministry around God's sovereignty and the doctrines of grace; this was the theology of Asahel Nettleton. These doctrines are in five main points and are known as the Five Points of Calvinism. They form an acrostic of the word, TULIP. These five points are:

1. **TOTAL DEPRAVITY:** states that Adam's fall affected every member of the human race. Every man born is infected with "Original Sin" that is *imputed* to us from Adam, our Federal Head. Because man is "totally depraved" he cannot turn to God of his own free will. He is spiritually *dead*. Because of this "total depravity" man stands under God's wrath and condemnation for sin; both original sin and personal sin. Apart from grace, there is nothing in man that would make him desire or turn to God, therefore it is impossible for man to turn to God apart from God's unmerited grace.

2. **UNCONDITIONAL ELECTION:** states that God chose the elect solely on the basis of His free, unmerited grace. God in His sovereignty chooses the elect out of special love for them and He passes over the rest of mankind to be damned for their sins.

3. **LIMITED ATONEMENT:** states that Christ died especially for the elect. He paid a definite price for them, by His death and with His blood, that guaranteed their salvation.

4. **IRRESISTIBLE GRACE:** states that "saving grace" is irresistible. God sovereignly gives the new birth, faith and repentance to the elect. In eternity past, God decreed that the Father would choose the elect, the Son would go and redeem them, and the Holy Ghost would woo them and secure their salvation.

5. **PERSEVERANCE OF THE SAINTS:** states that God preserves all the elect and causes them to persevere in faith to the end. None of the elect can fall from grace and become finally lost.

These were the doctrines preached by Calvin, Knox, Whitefield, Spurgeon, Edwards, and Nettleton. C. H. Spurgeon remarked, "The old truth that Calvin preached, that Augustine preached, is the truth that I must preach today, or else be false to my conscience and my God. I cannot shape the truth; I know of no such thing as paring off the rough edges of a doctrine. John Knox's gospel is my gospel. That which thundered through Scotland must thunder through England again."

More on this with the following comments:

"It is worthy of notice, that it is *John*,—he who so fully opens up to view the love of God,—John who so expatiates on every proof of divine love, John who seems to feel the beating of the heart of God—more than any other,—he it is whose pen is so constantly guided by the Holy Ghost to refer to the doctrines of sovereign grace. It is he who records the words: "I know whom I have chosen," and, "I have chosen you," in xiii. 18; xv. 16; and it is he who speaks so often of those whom *"the Father hath given"* to Christ;—and is not all this *Election?* (John x. 11; vi. 37, 39; xvii 2, 6, 9, 11, 12). It is he who records the words of Jesus: "I lay down my life *for the sheep;"*—the method of salvation, *"one* for *all;"*—and is not this *particular Redemption?* (John vi. 44, 65). It is he who tells how Jesus said: "No man cometh unto me, except the Father, who hath sent me, *draw him;"* and "except it be given him of the Father,"—who relates the conversation John iii. 5; and who tells that a believer in Christ is born

not by natural descent, not by his own fleshly will, not by the persuasive power of
any of other man's reasoning, *"but of God;"*—and is not this *Special Grace?* (John i.
13). It is he who records, more than once, such declarations of Jesus as these: *"Every
man that* hath heard and *learned of the Father, cometh unto me"*—"all that the Father
giveth me *shall* come to me;"—and is not this *Irresistible Grace?* There is no free will
here (John vi. 45; vi. 37). It is he who has so fully given our Lord's words about His
sheep: "None shall pluck them out of my hand; they shall never perish; none shall
pluck them out of my Father's hand,"—"Of those whom thou hast given me, I have
lost none," (John x. 28, 29; xviii. 9).—and then, xiv. 16: "The Comforter shall abide
with you forever;"—and is this not the doctrine of the *Perseverance of the Saints?*
(John xiv. 16). We might add, it is he who, without attempting to reconcile the two
truths, states so broadly God's "blinding the eyes, and hardening the hearts" (xii. 40)
of the Jews; and yet their own sin being their ruin—"they believed not," (xii. 43)
"For they loved the praise of men more than the praise of God."

"Whitefield, and Edwards and Nettleton, never found themselves nor those they
addressed, hindered by these great truths; they were helped by them, not hindered.
No wonder; for do not each of these doctrines at once turn our eyes on *God himself,*
and cause us to hear His voice saying: "Come now, *let us reason together,* saith the
Lord?"[1]

The doctrine of regeneration was the grand, central theme of Asahel
Nettleton's messages. In the preceding century, George Whitefield's cry
was "Ye must be born again!" This same message was critically
important to Nettleton's usefulness during the Second Great
Awakening. While Whitefield's aim was to break up the formalistic false
security of his hearers with his passionate pleas of "Ye must be born
again!"; it was Nettleton's task to *explain in detail* what true regeneration
was as opposed to a spurious conversion. Nettleton would pick apart a
person's false hopes, little by little, driving home the great doctrines of
the Bible until his hearers were *undone* and crying out, "What must I do
to be saved?" He loved to elaborate on the Edwardsean theme of man's
natural capacity versus his moral inability. This is seen from the following
observations:

"Man is a free agent and therefore responsible for his own acts, but man is not
willing to change the bias or direction of his love. Only God, operating on the heart
of the man, can accomplish that. Nettleton follows the Edwardian distinction
between natural ability and moral inability. Man has the power, i.e. he *can* do but he
has not the desire, i.e., he *will* not do. As he says in another sermon: 'It is not for the
want of faculties which render you capable of doing your duty. [Your inability]
arises not from the want of faculties, but from the want of a disposition. They
[sinners] are said to be unable to do what they have no inclination to do. Only admit
that the sinner is so wicked, that he never will do what he can, you will see why we
call—why God commands—why he will punish—and why his power is necessary
to subdue the sinner's heart.'

"Nettleton's most explicit statement of the meaning of regeneration occurs in an
unpublished sermon on the text John 1:13,15: 'But as many as received him to them
gave he power to become the Sons of God, and which were born not of blood, nor

of the will of the flesh, nor of the will of man, but of God.' In his usual homiletical manner, he first considers the original meaning of the text as it applied to the Jews. He next moves to consider some false understandings of the doctrine. First he quickly dispenses with the notion that baptism is regeneration. 'Nothing is plainer, than that an external rite, cannot change the heart. Baptism,' he says, 'is only a *sign* or *token* of the saving influences of the Holy Spirit, it is not that work itself.' Secondly, he turns to the Pelagian and Arminian scheme. He treats them together, because 'they are in substance the same.' Pelagius' system, 'with a few modifications,' has been the scheme 'of the great body of all sectaries, who have dissented from orthodox-evangelical sentiments ...' according to Nettleton. Since Nettleton thought that Taylor is propagating a new Arminianism, it is well to quote at length from this portion of the sermon. 'The fundamental truths of the Pelagian and Arminian scheme ... are these. (1) That God not only proclaims the offers of grace and salvation to all men alike, but that the Holy Spirit is equally and sufficiently distributed to all men to insure their salvation, provided they duly improve the benefits bestowed upon them. (2) That the precepts and promises of the gospel are not only good and desirable in themselves, but so suited to the natural reason and interests of mankind, that they will of course be inclined to receive them, unless overpowered by prejudice, and an habitual course of sin. (3). That the *consideration* of the threatenings and promises of the gospel is sufficient to remove these prejudices, and reform that course. (4) That those who thus seriously reflect and amend their lives have the promise of the Holy Spirit and are entitled to the benefits of the new covenant.'

   "Nettleton comes out vehemently against such a view. To say that 'all men are regenerated alike, originally; all having an equal measure of the spirit; and the difference between one man and another, is ... ascribed wholly to himself; to the improvement he has made of the blessings vouchsafed' and that 'regeneration is a reformation of life, induced by moral suasion, or commenced in consequence of the understanding being enlightened and the affections moved by divine truth alone' is to deny the fundamental truths which he finds in the Bible and in his own human experience. This scheme undercuts his understanding of the total depravity of man as well as his belief in special grace. 'I admit,' he says, 'that the promises and threats of the gospel would be sufficient to persuade us to a holy life, *if* [italics mine] our understandings were neither darkened, nor our affections depraved.' But 'after all preparatory means——all the promises and threats of the gospel——all the operations of common grace, and all exertions of unregenerate sinners, they must be *born of God* to become his children. There must be a *new* creation,—a work accomplished by Almighty power—a sovereign,—special—supernatural act, like making a world, or raising the dead, as to the power exerted ... Persuasion is not sufficient to make men new creatures. If the Holy Spirit operates on the minds of men only by setting persuasive arguments, or motives before them, be the kinds never so diverse or well adapted to this purpose, yet after all, it depends on the will of man whether any shall be regenerate or not.'"[2]

Nettleton's theological positions on the new birth are pure Edwardsean. N. W. Taylor and Charles Finney stand in opposition to these truths. For them, salvation is a decision of the will, there is no need for new heart or inward change by the Holy Spirit. Asahel Nettleton wanted his hearers to understand that in salvation there was a "new creation ... a work accomplished by Almighty power ... a supernatural act like making a world, or raising the dead." Therefore his emphasis on the doctrine of regeneration was tenaciously proclaimed. Nettleton also made it clear that God is the author of salvation—not man, and that regeneration preceded repentance. We see from the following:

> "Repentance is not antecedent to regeneration. The new will which has been given in regeneration means that the person now loves God. From Nettleton's definition of depravity as lack of love to God, it quite naturally and logically follows that the sinner cannot love God. True repentance means love toward God, and this cannot be accomplished by a depraved heart. Only after the sinner's heart has been changed by God can he truly repent, i.e., 'no one can feel heartily sorry that he has offended a being whom he does not love.' To say that love to God and his law which would result in repentance is not possible prior to a change of heart effected by God is not to say that such is not the duty of the sinner. Again and again Nettleton presents the seeming contradictions: one must repent immediately, yet true repentance is possible only when the sinner receives the gift of a new heart. And again and again, Nettleton uses the Edwardian terminology, one has the power and the duty to repent, but he has not the will or inclination. In this sermon he puts it is way:
>
> 'It is unquestionably the duty of every sinner immediately to repent ... It is the duty of sinners to do many things which they never have done, and which some of them never will do. It is their duty to stop sinning, and to love God with all the heart, soul, mind, and strength. So it is their duty to repent without delay. But they have not done it, and some of them never will ... [There is] great difficulty on this subject,' Nettleton admits. 'If sinners do not repent previous to regeneration, then you call on them to do what it requires almighty power to influence them to do. This difficulty ... runs through the whole system of evangelical truth.'"[3]

In the next chapter, as we follow the narrative of Asahel Nettleton's labors, we will see how he *applied* these doctrines through his preaching in wonderful seasons of revival during the Second Great Awakening in America.

Notes

1   Andrew Bonar, *Asahel Nettleton Life And Labours* (Edinburgh: Banner of Truth Trust, reprint, 1975), pp. x, xi.
2   Sherry Pierpont May, pp. 137–140.
3   Ibid. pp. 141–142.

Such ideas as total depravity, the necessity of regeneration, justification through Christ alone, and the sovereignty of God in salvation, were not only believed but felt. Any notions of dependence on the merits of man's free will as a cause or ground of salvation were routed. The doctrines of grace were meat, bread, butter and milk to those who came to salvation under Nettleton's preaching.

J. F. THORNBURY

10

IN THE MIDST OF REVIVAL

In the spring of 1815, Asahel Nettleton accepted an invitation from some Congregational pastors in New Haven, Connecticut, to come and assist them in ministry. Nettleton began his labors at a school for young ladies, and as he related to them the revival accounts of South Britain and South Farms, he noticed that a deep seriousness settled upon the students. Many began to inquire about salvation. Soon a revival had broken out in New Haven among these female students and the plentiful effusions of divine grace spread to the campus at Yale College! Nettleton was once again in the midst of a revival which lasted for three months. But a larger movement of God would occur later in the year under the great evangelist's preaching at Salisbury, Connecticut, and during this revival a rumor was spread that Nettleton had *stopped* the revival which had begun! We see these unusual circumstances first from a letter written by Nettleton to Rev. John Frost, wherein he explains his behavior:

> "In 1815, in the town of Salisbury, Conn., after laboring awhile under great discouragement, there were some favorable appearances. A number were anxious, and a few in awful distress of soul, in one village. It was taken hold of by some ignorant, officious hands; and they were set to groaning and screaming, and alarmed all the village in my absence. Having heard the tidings, I hastened to the spot, and with kind, but decided severity called them to order. My attempts, by those who had given the work that turn, were considered as very obtrusive and daring. It was reported all over town, that a revival had begun in Salisbury, and that I had put a stop to it. They seemed to be very much grieved and shocked at my conduct. It took a number of days to restore order, but when it was done, the work of God advanced silently and powerfully, until all classes, old and young, were moved all over town. The language was, 'the fountains of the great deep are broken up.' Not far from three hundred were numbered as the hopeful subjects of divine grace in that revival."[1]

Bennet Tyler, who had first-hand knowledge of this revival, stated that it "was one of the most remarkable revivals which ever occurred under his preaching." The subjects of the revival had grown angry at Nettleton for

putting an end to the *emotional aspects* of it. By his not allowing the people
to groan and scream, many felt the revival had ended. Actually, the
revival was strengthened by the wise handling of these emotional
excesses, in a way which helped further the work. Some of Nettleton's
behavior during this revival is explained more fully by the Rev. Jonathan
Lee, who was a native of Salisbury and who witnessed this move of grace.
Rev. Lee comments:

"The first and greatest revival of religion which has taken place in Salisbury,
Conn., stood connected with the labors of Mr. Nettleton, and began in the summer
of 1815, and extended through the autumn and winter following. The church was
destitute of a pastor, and reduced to a small number, there being but seventeen male
members. Having been unsuccessful in their efforts to obtain a pastor, and seeing no
accessions, the few members remaining, felt a deep conviction of the necessity of the
effusions of the Spirit, to strengthen the things that were ready to die; and an unusual
spirit of prayer was felt, as they sought the blessing at the throne of grace. In those
circumstances, they applied to Mr. Nettleton, to come and labor among them. After
having waited with doubt and solicitude for sometime, he at length came, without
previously having sent any promise, or notice; and, as was ascertained, without
informing the friends with whom he had been, what was his place of destination. He
arrived at the house of one of the deacons of the church and lodged. He made such
inquiries, as were designed to ascertain whether his coming had been much looked
for and relied upon, in order to a revival of religion. For some cause his fears were
excited, perhaps from the fact, that deacon S. had that day been riding in
unsuccessful pursuit of him; and he at once declined staying or making any effort,
saying, 'I can do no good here.'[2]

"Endeavors were made to convince him, that he had not been the object of
reliance, and to persuade him to stay till the following Sabbath, and preach and take
opportunity to get acquainted with the state of Christian feeling. Yielding for the
present to the importunity, he prayed and conversed with the family, the laborers
being called in for the purpose from the field, and offered to meet at the same place,
at a particular hour, on the next day, any young people, who, when invited by the
deacon, should be disposed to come in. He next visited the other deacon and
pursued the same course and at his second visit, met with a company of young
persons at each place. He began talking to them in the most simple and solemn
manner, with the view to fix upon their minds some plain important truth, suited to
awaken and impress the conscience. There was no dilation of thought but one
weighty idea, such as the worth of the soul, or the necessity of true religion, dwelt
upon and reiterated, and left in its naked reality and solemnity on each individual's
mind. This noiseless commencement of his labors, was followed by visiting the
families of Christian professors, and by stated religious meetings in connection with
the labors of the Sabbath. A primary object was to find the state of feeling in
Christians, and to promote a humble, praying spirit. At an early date, after being
convinced of his duty to stay and labor, he called together the church, and with great
earnestness, besought them to lay aside all expectations from him, and pray with
humility and fervency, that the work of the Lord might be revived. At the same
time, he gave such counsels and cautions, particularly with regard to the instruction
and treatment of persons under conviction, as he judged necessary to guard against
unhappy results."[3]

We pause in this narrative for some comments regarding how Nettleton *prepared* the soil, so to speak, for a revival. His pre-revival work is of vast importance, as important as the work during and after a revival. From the aforementioned narrative, we notice that God is not yet moving among the people in any dramatic way. What Asahel is guarding against is any activity which may *hinder* the work of God once it is commenced. He is seen taking precautionary measures and counseling the Christians there to "guard against unhappy results", meaning false conversions and "wild fire". A study of his movements *before, during, and after* a revival are necessary to fully appreciate how God used this remarkable man in so many revivals during the Second Great Awakening. Nettleton understood every aspect of revival!

We now return to the narrative provided by Rev. Lee:

"This favored servant of Christ, came with no trumpet sounded before him, but in the meekness of his master, and the Lord was with him in very deed. Meetings became crowded and deeply solemn, and many obtained hope in Christ. He conversed individually with the anxious, and met at certain times at his boarding place, all who were disposed to be conversed with, on the state of the heart, and the salvation of the soul. In addressing meetings, he was wont to seize on some point of interest, bearing directly upon the state of mind in which his hearers were, and then press it with a rare degree of directness, plainness and force ...

"This revival was distinguished for its stillness and solemnity, for deep conviction of conscience, for discriminating views of divine truth, for humility and subsequent stability of Christian character. The subjects were of different ages, but generally youth. As fruits of the revival about two hundred were admitted into the Congregational church, besides several who united with other churches. Many of these young professors intermarried, and became heads of families, and have lived to train up many children for Christ. Not a few, in the twenty-seven years since elapsed, have died in the Lord. Those remaining, still constitute the strength of the church; for although some other favored seasons of ingathering have been enjoyed, none have borne comparison with this, for permanent influence upon the state of the community, for enlightened piety, and steadfastness of Christian principle and character. Many still look back to that date with the deepest interest, and liveliest gratitude, as the blest period of their espousal to Christ—as the memorable year of the right hand of the Lord. The name of Asahel Nettleton, the humble, skillful laborer in this field, at that season, employed in directing so many to Christ, is embalmed in many a heart ..."[4]

Bennet Tyler has some interesting observations regarding this revival in Salisbury. One unique feature of this revival is how God overthrew the most violent opposition and transformed opposing hearts to testimonies of His grace! Tyler comments:

"I will add a few facts, which were learned directly from Mr. Nettleton. In the commencement of this revival, much opposition was manifested on the part of the enemies of religion. But God overruled it to the furtherance of the gospel. As the people assembled one evening at a large school-house in which they had been accustomed to meet, it was found that all the seats had been removed from the house and concealed. A large congregation having assembled in and around the house, Mr. Nettleton observed to them, that he had believed that the Spirit of God was operating on the minds of the people, and that he was now confirmed in the belief. The people then repaired to the meeting-house, where the religious services were conducted with most evident tokens of the divine presence. The work, though still, was very deep and powerful, and it spread into every part of the town. It as first prevailed mostly among the youth, but it soon began to appear among heads of families, and some who were quite advanced in life, were numbered among the subjects. The conversion of a man from fifty to sixty years of age, who had been a violent opposer, seemed to be the means of arresting the attention of many. This individual was a man of considerable influence, and like Paul, before his conversion, was exceedingly mad against the church. But God, as there is reason to believe, subdued his heart, and he became as ardent in his attachment to the cause of Christ, as he had been violent in his opposition. 'What a glorious work of grace is this in Salisbury,' said he one morning, to Mr. Nettleton; 'I hope that all my family, and all the people of the town will become interested in it, even if I am cast off forever.' This was the first manifestation of a change in his feelings. The change in him was so striking, that many who had been skeptical were convinced that it must be the work of God. He took every opportunity to converse with his acquaintance, and to recommend to them the religion, which he had formerly despised, and God made him the instrument in awakening many to a sense of their lost condition as sinners.

"The interest became so intense in every part of the town, that whenever Mr. Nettleton was seen to enter a house, almost the whole neighborhood would immediately assemble to hear from his lips the word of life. Husbandmen would leave their fields, mechanics their shops, and females their domestic concerns, to inquire the way to eternal life. Religion was the great and all-absorbing theme in almost all companies, and on almost all occasions. Mr. Nettleton labored in Salisbury through the winter."[5]

During the Great Awakening under the preaching of George Whitefield, Benjamin Franklin commented that it "seemed all of Philadelphia was consumed with the subject of religion." Such is the case in national awakenings, and it was no different in the Second Great Awakening under the preaching of Asahel Nettleton.

In 1816 Asahel was thirty three years of age. His ministry was maturing into vast usefulness for God. In the spring of 1816 he visited Bridgewater, and labored particularly in the town of New Milford, which was in the southwestern part of Litchfield county, Connecticut. What is unique about Nettleton's ministry in Bridgewater is his disappearing act! We learn from the following:

"Here was a small church destitute of a pastor. The state of religion was very low. Unhappy dissensions existed in the church, and great stupidity prevailed among the people at large. Soon after he commenced his labors, there seemed to be a solemn attention to the word preached, but no cases of deep conviction of sin. He soon became convinced that there could be little hope of a revival of religion, until a better state of feeling prevailed in the church. He endeavored to impress upon the minds of the brethren, the importance of settling their difficulties, and of uniting their prayers and their efforts for the promotion of Christ's kingdom. But his exhortations seemed to have but little effect, and perceiving that they had no proper sense of their dependence on God, but were placing undue reliance on him, he thought it best to withdraw. Accordingly, without the knowledge of any but the family in which he boarded, he suddenly left the place.

"The next day was the annual State Fast. The people assembled, expecting to hear him preach; when to their astonishment, they found the pulpit vacant. The disappointment was great, but it produced the intended effect. The members of the church were deeply affected. They spent the day in prayer and mutual confession of sin. All their difficulties were healed, and brotherly love was restored. It was with them a day of deep repentance and humiliation before God. Numbers of the youth, whose minds had been somewhat impressed by Mr. Nettleton's preaching, when they found that he had left them, were brought into great distress of mind. Meanwhile he was spending the day, with a brother in the ministry in a neighboring town. On the Saturday following, he proposed to this brother, to go and spend the Sabbath in Bridgewater, and permit him to supply his pulpit. The arrangement was accordingly made. This brother found a most interesting state of things. A deep solemnity pervaded the congregation, and quite a number were found anxiously inquiring what they must do to be saved. When Mr. Nettleton learned the state of things, he returned to Bridgewater, and labored there with great success for several months."[6]

During this time in the revival, one of the worst opposer's of religion went to hear Nettleton preach in a school house. He would not enter the building because he was ashamed to be seen among the Christians, so he stood at the door listening to Asahel preach. As he stood in the doorway, the words of the sermon pierced his heart with conviction. Returning home later that evening the man had a sleepless night, but in the morning he had obtained peace and "seemed to be in a new world." Such was the effects of the revival in Bridgewater under Nettleton's preaching! Another account of this revival comes from the pen of Rev. Fosdic Harrison, who was the pastor in Roxbury, a town adjacent to Bridgewater. Rev. Harrison records:

"In the spring of 1816, when Mr. Nettleton was laboring at Bridgewater, he was frequently at my house. On one occasion, having been with me a day or two, I was expecting his assistance at an evening meeting; but a short time before the hour of meeting, he manifested his intention to return to Bridgewater. I urged him to stay and attend the meeting, but he still declined. We went together from the study into Mrs. Harrison's room. She was then in feeble health. On learning his determination to leave, she most earnestly entreated him to remain. Among other things she said, 'Do stay, Mr. Nettleton, I am unable to attend the meeting myself, but if you will stay, I will pray for you all the time.' We went out together, and he left, but her earnest entreaties went with him, and troubled him. Soon after this, he heard she was dangerously ill. He came directly over and said, 'Brother, learning that you were in deep affliction, I have come to pray with you.' We retired and bowed down together before God. Some of his earnest petitions I still remember, commencing this,—'Oh, Lord Jesus, she, whom thou lovest, is sick.' Soon after this, he came to attend her funeral. He remembered his refusal to yield to her importunate

solicitations to attend the meeting; and that he might comply with her entreaties as
far as he then could, he requested that a meeting might be appointed for that evening
at the house where she died. While the other brethren went from the funeral to a
monthly meeting of ministers in New Milford, and urged him to go with them, he
remained and attended the meeting in Roxbury. The last conversation he had with
Mrs. Harrison, the solicitude she manifested in the spiritual welfare of the people,
her promise to pray for him and them, were the theme of his discourse. He
reminded the people that her prayers for them were ended. His appeals were
powerful. Impressions were made, which, I trust, resulted in the saving conversion
of some souls. He remained with me a day or two, and his counsels and prayers were
truly refreshing."7

A more detailed look at the disappearance of Nettleton during the
revival at Bridgewater is found in Thornbury's biography on Nettleton,
God Sent Revival in a chapter, entitled, "The Case of the Missing
Preacher". Although Asahel Nettleton guarded against emotionalism
during his revivals, he demonstrated peculiar behavior on more than one
occasion which are inexplicable idiosyncrasies in his personality. On one
such occasion, while preaching in Charleston, South Carolina, in 1830,
his odd behavior drew sharp criticism from a fellow minister. This is seen
in the following observations:

"That Nettleton often was misunderstood and his motives and methods
misjudged is seen in an interesting reference to him in the diary of Basil Manly, Sr.
Manly, an influential Baptist preacher in the deep South, wrote his observations in
1830 during Nettleton's visit to Charleston. Because Manly was at least reticent
about the usefulness of the "New Measures" and at most one of their most piercing
critics in the South, his reactions to Nettleton deserve attention. The entire entry
into the diary says:

'The Rev. Asahel Nettleton, the respected promoter of revivals in the northern
states has been here for some time attempting to produce a religious excitement in
the community. His methods are peculiar: and it is said that tho' he takes a great deal
of pains to disclaim the idea of being able to do anything, there seems to be an
affectation of singularity for the sake of effect, and an air of self-sufficiency about
him. From what I have heard, I believe that an unbiased and discerning mind would
not fail to be impressed that those motives & sentiments lurk in his bosom, perhaps
unknown in some measure to himself. I was prevented from witnessing his
exhibitions for two reasons. As there was a revival in our church when he began and
the people were coming to our meetings in great numbers my attention was very
much taken up–& Mr. Nettleton's meetings were held on evenings, always I
believe, on the same evenings of our meetings. His other meetings I did not choose
to attend as they were more private, for this reason––As soon as he came here, I was
disposed to welcome him, at Mr. Thomas Fleming's in George St. But he sent word
that he was lying down, and declined seeing me. Supposing that he might have, at
the moment, some good reason for this, I sent up my name and character––under
the idea that if he wished to see me, I should afterward receive from him a visit, or a
request to call again. But nothing of this kind occurred––& I concluded that he
wished to have no intercourse with me. Yet this gentleman publicly complained ...
that he had received no attention in Charleston––publicly entreated the citizens,
again & again, to call on him at his lodgings, if it were only for *five minutes*. Said that

there was no religion in Charleston—intimated strongly that ministers & people were all in fault—and as I have understood from several has now left the city in disgust—**AMEN** say I. And so may all leave it who behave like him.'

"I cannot imagine a more regrettable misunderstanding than that entry suggests. Manly's preaching was of the same searching doctrinal character as Nettleton's and his concerns about the dangers of misguided professions of faith in the climate of 'revivalism' were just as profound."[8]

It appears from the above account that Basil Manly, Sr. had his feelings wounded by Nettleton's apparent rudeness. Since we do not have Asahel's side to the story, we can only assume he was weak from his bout with typhus fever and lay ill when Manly appeared at his place of boarding. But without knowing the exact details we can only speculate. It is true that Nettleton did exhibit odd behavior at times, and his judgment was not always sound. A major misjudgment on his part haunted him for the rest of his life: this was the infamous "Jesus Letter". It seems Nettleton grew concerned over some youth at a ball and he penned a letter to them and signed it, "Jesus Christ". This incident is covered in detail in the unpublished thesis on Nettleton, by George Hugh Birney, Jr., which was submitted to Hartford Theological Seminary in 1943 and is in their archives. The incident is recorded on pages 78–79 of that thesis. J. F. Thornbury comments on this embarrassing moment in Nettleton's life when the "Jesus Letter" was used against Asahel by his enemies. He writes:

"Such an opportunity came to Nettleton's enemies in the autumn of 1818. It was occasioned by an unorthodox and unwise method used by Asahel and Bennet Tyler in dealing with some young people at South Britain. Tyler was greatly concerned over the worldliness of some of the young people in his town, a concern he revealed to Asahel while he was visiting him in September. On the evening of 18th September, some of the young people were at a dance. The two ministers conceived a plan to startle the youths into a consciousness of the sinfulness and danger of their conduct. They proposed to write them a letter as if it had come from Jesus Christ. They knew this method was novel and dramatic, but felt that this should shock them into serious thought and make them think about their need of salvation.

"Accordingly the letter was put together by the two men at Tyler's house, addressed to the young people as a message from Christ. The letter contained a solemn warning in the words of Proverbs, in which God rebuked those who despised his counsels and reproof. They used such expressions as 'Because I have called and ye have refused, I have stretched out my hand and no man regarded', and 'Then shall they call me early but they shall not find me.' The letter was signed, 'I am, dear youth, Your much grieved friend, Jesus Christ.' At the bottom of the page a note was added: 'N. B. If the youth will agree to turn their meeting into a religious conference this evening please send back word and I will come and see you. If not, I will go into my closet and, with the help of God, will pray for you while you dance.' The postscript was signed 'Asahel Nettleton.'"[9]

This letter became a *disaster* for Nettleton and it caused him much anguish for the rest of his life. Enemies, on more than one occasion, dredged up this letter and used it against his ministry. Because of such attacks, friends such as Lyman Beecher, N. W. Taylor, and others had to rally to help defend Nettleton's character in the public eye. He regretted writing the letter, however the "Jesus Letter" reveals Nettleton's flair for the dramatic and this was part of his personality. Basil Manly's account of Nettleton's flair for the dramatic is quite *unflattering*. To say that Asahel Nettleton made no mistakes is hagiography. Nettleton could often be eccentric—but is this not part of the reason why crowds flocked to hear him? George Whitefield drew thousands to him because of his great oratory and drama in the pulpit. But these very characteristics of the two great evangelists, which made them so singular, was also fuel for their enemies.

Notes

1   Bennet Tyler, pp. 71–72.
2   Nettleton would often withdraw from a religious meeting if he felt that the people's eyes were on *him as a personality*, and not on God himself for the work of revival. Because of this behavior, he was often criticized and unfairly judged.
3   Ibid. pp. 72–74.
4   Ibid. pp. 74–75.
5   Ibid. pp. 75–76.
6   Ibid. pp. 76–78.
7   Ibid. pp. 78–79.
8   Tom Nettles, *Asahel Nettleton: Sermons From the Second Great Awakening,* edited by William Nichols (Ames: International Outreach, Inc.), pp. xii–xiii.
9   Thornbury, pp. 84–85.

By the turn of the century small pockets of genuine interest in religion had broken loose, and now, in the second decade, Nettleton's presence and preaching seemed to furnish the occasion of the release of religious interest. Wherever he went, below the surface of indifference, the people seemed waiting for his word.

SHERRY PIERPONT MAY

Administration Building at Union College, Schenectady, NY. Union College saw revival under Nettleton.

Inn at Saratoga Springs, NY. Nettleton often came to Saratoga Springs for the hot waters and relaxation. The original building has been torn down.

II

REVIVAL SCENES

Asahel Nettleton soon became an expert on the subject of revival. When he was laboring during the peak of the Second Great Awakening, there was no one in New England, or in the *entire nation* in his generation, who better understood the true characteristics of revivals of religion.

We resume the narrative of his labors while Nettleton was in Torrington, Connecticut in the summer of 1816. It was there in Torrington that a powerful revival broke out under his preaching and for three months the divine Presence permeated the community! The Rev. John A. McKinstry, pastor of the church in Torrington related the revival account as follows:

"How long the revival continued, I cannot definitely state. At the communion in November, the first fruits were gathered into the church; and in the January following, several more were added. The number that joined at these seasons, was about fifty. Others were added at subsequent seasons ...

"In regard to the revival, I may say, it extended through the parish, and was quite powerful. Even at this period, when first impressions have gone, the revival of 1816 is called *the revival at Torrington*, there having been none since of equal extent and power. The subjects of that work, with few exceptions, have adorned their profession, and some of them have been, and still are pillars in the church. The influence of this revival upon the church, and upon the community, was in a high degree salutary.

"The work was solemn, and the truths presented plain and searching. The true character and condition of the sinner was clearly set before him, and he was shown that his only hope was in the sovereign mercy of God through a crucified Saviour. The measures adopted, were such as were common in this region at that time; such as the ministry of the word on the Sabbath—frequent visitation, connected with personal conversation on the subject of religion; and more or less prayer meetings during the week. In personal conversation, Mr. Nettleton is said to have abounded, and many attributed their religious impressions to the truth presented at such times."[1]

At this time it is important to mention a magazine which was popular during the Second Great Awakening. This was, *The Religious Intelligencer*, which documented the revivals as they occurred throughout the country. In the second volume for the year 1816, we have the following comments regarding the doctrines which Nettleton preached: "The doctrines taught are those considered as the grand leading truths of the gospel; the strict spirituality of the moral law—the total depravity of the natural heart—its enmity to God—the necessity of regeneration by the spirit of his grace—an entire dependence on the merits of Jesus Christ for justification, pardon and acceptance—our obligations to own him before men, and to manifest our faith in him by a holy walk and conversation—the divine sovereignty—the electing love of God—and the final perseverance of the saints, as the only ground of the sinner's hope, and the anchor of the Christian's soul."

From Torrington Nettleton traveled to Waterbury, where a revival had already commenced before his arrival. In Waterbury Nettleton joined hands with Lyman Beecher in religious meetings and counseling individuals. After Beecher left Waterbury to return to his church in Litchfield, Nettleton remained in the midst of the revival for several months before traveling to Bolton, Connecticut to fill the pulpit for his ailing friend, the Rev. Parmele. Philander Parmele, it seems, was going through an emotional breakdown—"mental derangement". Nettleton remained in Bolton for some time until he was called away to assist another sick minister, the Rev. Williams of Middletown. It is interesting to follow his labors in Middletown, Connecticut, because it was here in 1740 that a youthful George Whitefield preached to four thousand near the river (as recorded in the journal of Nathan Cole). Asahel arrived in Middletown in the fall of 1817, he was thirty four years old at this time. A great spiritual apathy prevailed in Middletown before his arrival—but this was soon to change! As we see from the following comments:

"After he had preached in this place two or three Sabbaths, there were some cases of special seriousness; but understanding that the young people had appointed a ball on the day after the annual Thanksgiving, he expressed the purpose of leaving the place. The young people, hearing of his purpose, concluded to give up their ball, and sent a committee to invite him to preach to them on that evening. He very readily accepted the invitation. The meeting was appointed in the Academy. A large congregation of youth assembled. Some came from other towns. This meeting was one of thrilling interest. Some who had been previously awakened were brought to rejoice in hope, and great numbers were brought under deep and powerful conviction. God made the word 'quick and powerful, sharper than a two-edged sword ...' The scene of that evening will be remembered by not a few, while immortality endures. Several in deep distress followed Mr. Nettleton to his lodgings. He prayed with them, and with great difficulty persuaded them to retire to their homes. Many spent the night crying for mercy, and several found peace before morning. From this time, the work became powerful. Meetings of inquiry were held at the house of the pastor, but the place became too strait, and God provided one of greater convenience. A man who owned a large ball-room, and who had been a bitter enemy to religion, was awakened and hopefully brought to repentance. He opened his ball-room for meetings of inquiry.

"Mr. Nettleton labored in this place a number of months, and was made instrumental, as there is reason to believe, of the conversion of many souls. The Rev. Zebulon Crocker, the present pastor of the church, in a letter dated December 15th, 1843, speaking of the converts of this revival says, 'In the fall of 1817, the church was in a "cold state" as some have expressed it. Religion, I am inclined to think, was at a low ebb. The blessed work of the Spirit which immediately succeeded, it is to me evident, changed very much the aspect of affairs for the better, as a permanent result.'"[2]

The Second Great Awakening mirrored the First Great Awakening in this regard: the "revival fires" spread rather quickly after they were lit. This occurred under Whitefield and it was true under Nettleton. If one town was affected by the revival, it often spread like a prairie fire to the adjoining district. Even though Nettleton did not keep a detailed journal, we are thankful to the many pastors with whom he labored who did record the various aspects of those revivals. One such account is given in the following narrative of the revival at Middletown:

"During the revival in Upper Middletown, a few individuals from Rocky Hill, an adjoining parish, attended some of Mr. Nettleton's meetings, and became anxious for their souls. The seriousness spread, and at the earnest solicitation of the pastor, the Rev. Dr. Chapin, Mr. Nettleton visited that place. He arrived on Saturday, April 4th, 1818.

'When he arrived,' says Dr. Chapin, 'there was a meeting in the house of the pastor. At the same place, in the evening, there was another—which brother Nettleton attended. His acquaintance with the state of the public mind among us, began that evening. From that time, during the greater part of several months, he was indefatigable, laboring in season, and out of season, to the full extent of his health and strength. In connections with impressions and experience realized in 1818, eighty-four persons became members of Christ's visible church ... So far as man can judge, those eighty-four [twenty six years later] have adorned the doctrine of God our Saviour, in a manner equal, at least, to the fruits of those other revivals, which Christ has permitted us to enjoy.

'In an important sense, brother Nettleton's talent was *one*. In the cultivation and improvement of that *one*, he was unwearied. By the concentration of study, always directed to the most useful point, which is practical piety, that talent had rise to the first order. Hence the depth and exactness of his knowledge in true experience, and the things which are essential to salvation. Hence too, the quickness of discernment relative to the specific instruction, and the manner of imparting instruction, that every mind needed with which he came in contact.

'He had a quick and precise perception of the sources whence objectors and cavilers draw their difficulties. In replies, showing the true answer, and the only remedy, he was ready, appropriate, generally silencing, and convincing. In the whole of his intercourse, he was exemplary. He was remarkably cautious of appearances. He would not expose himself or his cause to reproach, by giving so much as the least occasion for the surmises of evil. If Satan's followers attempted the propagation of injurious reports, they were obliged to go far away from us for their foundation. The rumors thus procured, and put in motion, always, if investigated, proved to be false, and infernally malicious. Even the subtle vigilance of the evil Spirit, could find, in his conduct here, no foundation for its eagerly coveted slanders.'"[3]

Asahel Nettleton was known to remark that he could recognize a commencement of a revival by the way opposition mounted! In October of 1818, the great evangelist visited the town of Ashford in the eastern part of Connecticut. He remained there in the midst of revival for about two months before moving in the month of December to Eastford, Connecticut, where he labored in a church which had no pastor. A strong revival was birthed here to the extent that a year later, as the church records show, forty eight persons united with the church by profession!

Asahel Nettleton celebrated his thirty-sixth birthday in the month of April, 1819, in the town of Bolton, home to his close friend Philander Parmele. He labored in Bolton for two to three months amidst a vital revival, that had begun with prayer, prior to his arrival. Rev. Parmele published an account of this unusual revival:

"While Christians were thus daily wrestling in prayer, for the salvation of sinners, and were committing the cause of religion into the hands of God, their faith and patience were brought to the test. Satan, as though aware that his kingdom was soon to receive an attack, rallied his forces, and marshaled his bands to make resistance. Iniquity rushed in like a flood. The youth who, we expected, would be awakened, if our prayers were answered, were generally never more dissolute. Their minds were supremely occupied with scenes of mirth and parties of pleasure. If they received any impressions on the Sabbath, or at a religious meeting during the week, they were soon banished through the influence of worldly companions and vain amusements.

"To counteract the influence of these things, meetings were appointed for religious conversation with the youth, which were generally well attended, and soon became interesting. At one of these meetings, eight or ten of the youth were alarmed with a sense of their sins. Their convictions deepened, until they became overwhelming; and within a few days they were brought to rejoice in hope. This spread conviction like an electric shock through the society of young people ...

"May and June, with us, were interesting months. Most of the subjects of this revival, became reconciled to God, during this period. On the first Sabbath in July, thirty-five united with the church ... the youth, the middle aged, and the aged, composed this number. On the first Sabbath in September, twenty-one united with the church ... We would express our gratitude to those brethren in the ministry, who occasionally preached for us, during this revival; and especially to Mr. Nettleton, whose labors were signally blessed."[4]

In July of 1819, Nettleton traveled to Saratoga Springs, New York. It was his custom to visit "The Springs" to recover from his exhaustion from revivals. At Hartford Seminary, in their archives, is a handwritten record by Nettleton detailing an incredible revival which occurred at Union College, in Schenectady, New York. While resting at Saratoga Springs, in late 1819, he was requested by a local minister, Rev. Griswold, to take part in some local concerts of prayer. As usually was the case, Nettleton's time of rest was interrupted by new preaching invitations. God was moving in revival around the area of Saratoga Springs including, Malta, and Schenectady, New York. Soon, Nettleton became the main human instrument of these revivals. But it was the revival at Union College in Schenectady, which became the most powerful under Nettleton's preaching. Many of the converts of the Second Great Awakening were youths or college students. The revival at Union College was one of the most dramatic of his career. Today, one can visit the campus of Union College and actually see the house (scene of the revival surrounding the corpse of the deceased student) where this marvelous revival occurred in the home of Dr. McAuley, professor at Union College. The house is virtually the same today as it was in Nettleton's time, and where Nettleton composed much of the following account. The wide front porch, where he and Dr. McAuley used to sit evenings, still beckons with comfortable chairs. It is interesting to note that when Asahel Nettleton labored in revivals in the state of Connecticut, he was primarily in Congregational churches. However, when his labors moved to the state of New York, he was principally in Presbyterian churches or meeting houses. We turn now to Nettleton's record of these remarkable revivals:

"I can at present, give you nothing more than the outlines of what the Lord is doing for this section of the church. This region, and especially the county of Saratoga, has heretofore been as destitute of revivals of religion, as any part of this State. The commencement of this work was at Saratoga Springs last summer. At that place, about forty have made a profession of religion. These include some of the most respectable characters in the village. Directly south, is the town of Malta. For a number of years, there has been no Presbyterian church in that place. But the year past, there has been a very interesting revival among that people. Our meetings have been crowded, and solemn as the house of death. A church has been recently organized, which now consists of one hundred and five members. You can hardly imagine the interest which this revival excited in the surrounding region. Although the inhabitants are scattered over a large extent, yet I verily believe, I have seen more than fourteen hundred people assembled at once, to hear the gospel. On the east of Malta, is the town of Stillwater. Here, also, there has been a very powerful revival. Although there has been some excitement to serious things in this place in years past, yet this revival exceeds any they have ever before witnessed. On the 27th of February last, one hundred and three publicly presented themselves a living sacrifice unto the Lord; and about one hundred more are rejoicing in hope, and expect soon to follow in their example. The work is still advancing; numbers are under conviction. In Ballston, adjoining Malta on the west, the work has been very powerful. At their two last communions, they admitted one hundred and eighteen as the fruit of this revival, and the work is yet increasing.

"Directly north is the town of Milton. I visited that people Sabbath last, and preached three times to a crowded and solemn assembly. In this place, a revival has just commenced. Twelve are rejoicing in hope, and a number more are anxious for their souls. Eight miles to the northwest, adjoining Milton, is the town of Galway. Here the work is overwhelming. In less than two months past more than one hundred and fifty have been brought to rejoice in hope. Dr. Nott, from this college [Union College] visited them last Sabbath, and admitted ninety-five to the church, and the work is still progressing. On the south of this, is Amsterdam. Here fifty have recently been led to rejoice in hope. Adjoining this, is a place called Tripe's Hill. Here thirty are rejoicing, and the work in both these places is increasing. South from Malta, about twelve miles, is the city of Schenectady, and Union College, where I now reside with Dr. McAuley. He takes a lively interest in this good work. I first became acquainted with him last summer at the Springs, and more particularly at Malta, where he frequently visited us, and preached, and conversed, and attended the meetings appointed for those anxious for their souls. On a Sabbath, when a number were to be admitted to the church in Malta, he brought with him a number of students from the college. Some of them became anxious. About this time, one of the students was called into the eternal world. He was laid out in Dr. McAuley's study. The Dr. was anxious to improve this solemn providence to the best advantage. He assembled the students around the lifeless remains of their departed friend, and conversed and prayed with them in the most solemn manner. A number of them engaged to attend to the subject of religion in earnest. From that time, many of the students became deeply impressed with a sense of their lost condition. For them were appointed meetings of inquiry. And in this very room where they lately beheld the breathless corpse of their young companion, and where I am now writing, was witnessed a scene of deep and awful distress. About thirty of the students are brought to rejoice in hope.

"The revival is now very powerful in the city. Such a scene they never before witnessed. More than one hundred have been brought to rejoice in hope. Besides these, we had more than two hundred in our meeting of inquiry, anxious for their souls. We met in a large upper room called the Masonic Hall. The room was so crowded, that we were obliged to request all who had recently found relief, to retire below, and spend their time in prayer for those above. This evening will never be forgotten. The scene is beyond description. Did you ever witness two hundred sinners, with one accord in one place, weeping for their sins. Until you have seen this, you can have no adequate conceptions of the solemn scene. I felt as though I was standing on the verge of the eternal world; while the floor under my feet was shaken by the trembling of anxious souls in view of a judgment to come. This solemnity was still heightened, when every knee was bent at the throne of grace, and the intervening silence of the voice of prayer, was interrupted only by the sighs and sobs of anxious souls. I have not time to relate interesting particulars. I only add, that some of the most stout, hard-hearted, heaven-daring rebels have been in the most awful distress. Within a circle whose diameter would be twenty-four miles, not less than eight hundred souls have been hopefully born into the kingdom of Christ, since last September. The same glorious work is fast spreading into other towns and congregations. 'This is that which was spoken by the prophet Joel.'"[5]

Notes

1   Tyler, pp. 79–80.
2   Ibid. pp. 85–86.
3   Ibid. pp. 87–88.
4   *The Religious Intelligencer*, November 1820.
5   Archives, The Nettleton Papers, Hartford Seminary Library, Hartford Seminary, Hartford, Connecticut.

Not since George Whitefield barnstormed the American colonies had New England seen the likes of Asahel Nettleton. In 1820, at the age of thirty-seven, he was the leading evangelist of the East ... More importantly, legions of newborn souls all over New England rose in rank after rank to call him their spiritual father.

J. F. THORNBURY

12

THE LONG ISLAND REVIVAL

It is an odd coincidence that both George Whitefield and Asahel Nettleton were used as instruments of revival at Long Island, New York, in the town of Jamaica. In the archives of the First Presbyterian Church in Jamaica, Long Island, is an interesting story which connects Whitefield and Nettleton to the life of that church. Both preached in revivals at this church, though separated by a period of only fifty-eight years! The following historical document relates the connection between the two evangelists and the church in Jamaica, New York:

"The First Presbyterian Church of Jamaica was organized in 1662. Its membership for the most part had come from Halifax, Yorkshire, England. They had settled first in Hempstead, but moved to Jamaica in 1656. They brought with them the Town Meeting of New England, and centered everything in their lives and government in and around the church. In the church they held their town assemblies, their school, their courts, and in some cases the town prison. The Jamaica church served all these purposes at one time or another ... As early as 1666 Jamaica became a horse-racing center, and attracted crowds from far and near ... The vast throngs which followed the races attracted the attention of George Whitefield, called the greatest evangelist since the Reformation, by his admirers.

"Whitefield was invited to come to Jamaica by the church, and he accepted its invitation in 1740 and again in 1762. The crowds that came to hear him compelled him to preach in the open air. He stood under an apple tree on a spot which became the site of Union Hall Academy. Thousands hung upon his word. He swayed the multitudes with the magic of his eloquence ...

"The Rev. Seymour S. Finch, who was graduated from Columbia College in 1819, and had studied theology in the Seminary of the Reformed Dutch Church at New Brunswick, was the next minister, ordained on March 6, 1823. Upon his resignation in 1825, owing to dissatisfaction, the Rev. Dr. Asahel Nettleton was installed. He remained only a few months on account of ill health, and was succeeded by the Rev. Elias W. Crane in 1826."[1]

What is most remarkable from this document is the statement, "... in 1825 the Rev. Dr. Nettleton was installed ..." as *pastor* of the church. It has been "standard knowledge" in Nettleton biography, that the great evangelist was exclusively an *itinerant* preacher and never a pastor. But here we have a conflict with his history! Piecing this puzzle together, we offer the following theory: in 1822 it is a known fact that Nettleton suffered a near-fatal attack of typhus fever, which left him a semi-invalid for life. Three years later he is found laboring in the midst of a revival in Jamaica, New York, on Long Island, at the First Presbyterian Church, which was destitute of a pastor. Perhaps his frail health contributed to his decision to be installed as pastor of the First Presbyterian Church in 1825; this would have allowed him the use of the manse for living quarters and the convenience of the church next door. This way, he could "stay put" for a while and labor in the midst of revival and have his financial and material needs met. It seems that his health deteriorated even further at this time, and he had to step down as the church's pastor. This is merely conjecture, however, it makes sense, and we can add to the history of Nettleton's amazing life that he was an installed pastor, even if it was only for a few months!

Nettleton's biographer, J. F. Thornbury, mentions Nettleton's labors in Jamaica, New York in chapter 25 of *God Sent Revival*. Here are some of his observations:

"In February of 1826, he went to the town of Jamaica on Long Island, to preach in a church which was badly divided. As he frequently did, he went to this place unannounced. He made his first appearance on a communion Sunday. Accompanied by another preacher, he walked slowly up the aisle, taking his seat on the front pew. The bearing of the two gentlemen indicated that they were preachers, and great curiosity was excited as to their identity. Soon it was revealed that one of them was 'Rev. Mr. Nettleton, the great revival preacher'.

"One of the residents of Jamaica was an aged believer named Othniel Smith who had listened to George Whitefield preach in this community seventy years previously. He had heard of Nettleton and aroused considerable interest in him by telling one of the local residents, 'This Mr. Nettleton that is going to preach for us is a most wonderful man; he is said to be the greatest preacher that has been among us since the days of George Whitefield'. He went on to report of Nettleton's reputed ability to 'almost *read a man's heart*, so wonderful was his knowledge of human nature'.

"The church at Jamaica was without a pastor and the clergymen who had supplied the pulpit in preceding months had tried in vain to reconcile the warring factions in the congregation. They had expatiated over and over again on 'brotherly love', but the people shrugged off such preaching and continued their feuding. Nettleton's approach was entirely different. He ignored the surface problems and dealt with rock bottom issues such as 'the claims of God and the duty of sinners'. This policy was considered a tactical master stroke, and under such 'judicial management' the breach was healed and conversions started multiplying."[2]

Notes

1 Nassau County History: First Presbyterian Church of Jamaica, Henry Isham Hazelton, *The Boroughs of Brooklyn and Queens Counties of Nassau and Suffolk Long Island, New York* (1609–1924).
2 Thornbury, pp. 153–154.

This sketch was drawn up by Mr. Nettleton, a few months after he left Nassau, from brief memoranda which he kept at the time. It is, on the whole, a good specimen of the revivals which occurred under his preaching. In not less than forty or fifty places there were revivals in connexion with his labours, quite as interesting as this … the foregoing sketch will give the reader a very good view of his ordinary course of proceeding, and of the effects which accompanied his labours.

BENNET TYLER

Meeting House in Nassau, NY, a scene of revival. Nettleton wrote an account of this revival in his handwritten personal papers.

13

HIS JOURNAL ON REVIVAL

One of the most remarkable documents in the "Nettleton Papers" at Hartford Seminary, is his handwritten account of the revival at Nassau, New York. Nassau, was a village a few miles to the east of Albany, New York, and the scene of the most incredible revival of his career! A visit to Nassau today will reveal much how the town looked at the time of Nettleton's visit; in fact, the exact meeting house where the bulk of the revival occurred is still standing on the main street in town. What makes the account of this revival so unique is the way in which Nettleton recorded it. He first hurriedly scrawled the accounts of the revival on pieces of paper as he was in the midst of the it—he then rewrote these same accounts in a steadier hand that is more readable. Both of these documents exist at Hartford Seminary Library, and we now turn to it for the account of what God did in Nassau, New York in 1820 under Asahel Nettleton's searching preaching:

ASAHEL NETTLETON'S JOURNAL 1820

"The state of religion in this village and its vicinity, has for years been deplorable. The village contains a house for public worship, held in common by two denominations, the Dutch Reformed and the Presbyterians. The former, during the winter past, have had one sermon every other Sabbath, and the latter have had no settled minister, and no regular preaching for years. Indeed, their little church had become nearly extinct. The revival of religion in this place commenced as follows:

"In the month of February, a number of persons from this village visited Malta, during the revival there. One of this number was left at Malta, became a hopeful subject of divine grace, and shortly after returned to this village. The sacred flame began to kindle in the hearts of a few old professors. The news of distant revivals began to excite inquiry, and some few sinners became more solemn. One, after a season of distress, became joyful. For a moment, hope was cherished, that a glorious day had dawned; but the surrounding darkness prevailed, and hope at length expired. For a few weeks, I had been absent from Malta. On my return, I received repeated and pressing invitations to visit Nassau. Prompted by this state of things, instead of returning to Schenectady, as was expected, I concluded to defer it for one week, and visit Nassau.

"April 19. [all diary entries are for the year 1820, author's note]. Arrived at Nassau. Attended a meeting in the school-house. About fifty assembled, and nothing particular occurred.

"April 20. This evening attended a meeting in a large dining hall in a public house. The room was crowded. A number stood around the doors and windows, and listened with respectful silence and much solemnity. It afterwards appeared that not less than twelve or fifteen dated their first serious impressions from that meeting. A Mr. P——subsequently observed, 'I went to that meeting full of prejudice. You began to tell me the feelings of my heart and I began to be vexed and angry at one or two of my neighbors for informing you what I had said. I thought you was a man of great brass. On returning from meeting, I asked Mrs. P——how she liked it? She burst into tears, and we both wept.' Another whose mind was impressed at this meeting, was a young woman who had passed through a revival in the town of Salisbury, Conn., five years before. She had been somewhat anxious and lost her concern, and as I have since learned, had made light of the subject. She entered the room this evening in company with others, without suspecting that the preacher was a man whom she had ever seen before. She remarked afterwards, 'as soon as I saw the preacher, I felt distressed. I observed it was the same man that preached in Salisbury.' I was expecting a revival. From this time her former feelings returned; and in addition, she was overwhelmed with a sense of her guilt in having dropped the subject.

"April 21. This evening met those that were anxious, at D. M——'s. About thirty were present. As I commenced speaking to them in general, all were very still and solemn. Suddenly a youth sitting near the window, as if pricked in the heart, cried out in distress. This produced no diversion of attention, but increased the solemnity; for the cause was perfectly understood. After conversing with each one, we bowed the knee together at the throne of grace, and then in solemn stillness retired at an early hour. A number of these anxious souls belonged to one family. They reached home weeping. The father of the family had retired to rest. As the carriage came up to the door, he heard the cry of distress, and started from his bed to learn the cause. His daughter-in-law, on entering the house, threw her arms around his neck and exclaimed, 'My father, what shall I do? what shall I do?' She continued for some time in great distress, but before morning, was rejoicing in hope.

"April 22. Saturday——Was in some doubt what course to pursue, as the meeting house on the next Sabbath was engaged. Rode to Greenbush, and negotiated an exchange with the Rev. Mr. Marselus of the Dutch Reformed Church.

"April 23. Sabbath——Mr. Marselus preached at Nassau with power and effect, and at the close of the services, at my request, read a letter from Dr. McAuley, containing an account of the revival in Union College and Schenectady. This increased the solemnity. I preached at Greenbush in the forenoon, and at 3 o'clock, p.m., preached again in a ball-room at a public house, on the road about two miles from this village. When I arrived, I found the ball-room crowded to overflowing. At the close of the services, a number assembled around me. Some from curiosity, but many in deep distress, weeping aloud. I requested them to suppress their cries, and be as still as possible. At this meeting a number were awakened. This evening, preached in the meeting-house in this village for the first time, to a crowded and solemn audience.

"April 24. This evening met about sixty in a meeting for anxious inquirers. Among them were many in deep distress. This is expected would be my last meeting in this place. But I found so many in distress for their souls, and the number increasing, that I announced the appointment of one public meeting more in the meeting-house, on the following evening.

"April 25. Met in the meeting-house. More crowded than ever, and solemn as eternity. Preached on the *nature* and *reasonableness* of gospel repentance, and urged the duty of immediate compliance, and the danger of delay. Never more expecting to meet my anxious hearers in this world, I urged them by all the solemnities of the judgment, not to pass the threshold of the meeting-house that night, with impenitent hearts. They seemed to hear as for their lives. One from deep distress, found relief in the midst of the discourse, and lifted up a joyful countenance. No sooner had I closed and stepped from the stage, than she came near, and taking her husband by the hand, urged him to come to Christ. It was like a two edged sword. It pierced him to the heart. At this moment the anxious ones assembled around me, and took me some by the hand, some by the arm, and some by the coat, exclaiming, 'Don't leave us. What shall I do? What shall I do?' Nearly the whole congregation tarried. Those who could not come near, stood, some on the seats, and some on the sides of the pews, to hear and see. From the midst of this scene of distress, I addressed the whole congregation for about five minutes. Among other things I said, 'My hearers, I now no longer hesitate to tell you what I have hitherto been afraid to speak, that a revival of religion is begun in Nassau. Yes, from what I have seen, I can no longer doubt the fact. I believe you are about to witness a solemn and trying time in this place; and now you must prepare either to be taken or to be left.' I then told them, I would meet them in the morning at sunrise, in the school-house, and pray with them before I left, if they chose. I advised them to depart as still as possible, and to be retired through the night.

"April 26. Met them in the morning before sunrise. Two of those who went away in distress last night, came to me rejoicing this morning. They found relief before they slept. I prayed and conversed with them a few moments, and started for Schenectady before breakfast. Heard of one more rejoicing this morning. I called and found it so, and found others in distress. The distress in one house led me to another, and that to another, until I visited nine families before I left the place. It was truly affecting to witness these strangers crying for mercy. In this state I left them, and went to Schenectady. During my absence, I felt a deep interest for them in Nassau. The scenes that I had there witnessed, were continually before me. It rained, and I tarried two nights.

"April 28. Started from Schenectady for Nassau. Arrived at Mr. B———'s within three miles of the village, late in the evening. In this house, some whom I had left in great distress met me with joyful countenances. Here I was informed that the Baptists had a meeting at the meeting-house this evening. Wishing to embrace the opportunity to make an appointment, I drove on to the meeting-house, and found the house nearly full. All were standing, and about to retire, as the meeting had just closed. I made my way through the crowd, as I suppose, unobserved, stepped upon the stage, and announced an appointment for the next Sabbath. The effect of this little circumstance, was almost incredible. I could hardly say which was most prominent, the burst of joy or of grief. A number came to me with joyful countenances, while others were borne down with grief. It is this night just one week since the first instance of hopeful conversion occurred, and now about thirty appear to be subjects of grace. Many of these, it was afterwards found, obtained relief on the day, and some a few moments after I left them. This was a memorable day. For when they afterwards came together to give a relation of their Christian experience, we found that some on that day retired into the groves and fields, and some into their chambers and closets, to cry for mercy. I have since thought that the effects of my leaving them as I did, *in the advanced stages of their conviction*, was evidently beneficial. It drove them from all human dependence. Distressing as it is, and cruel as it may seem, it is necessary for them to feel that no arm but God's can help them. Similar effects from like circumstances, have heretofore been witnessed.

"April 30. Sabbath——The congregation was crowded and solemn. This day an event took place, unknown to me at the time, which was designed by the enemy to check and put a stop to the work, but which in the hand of God was made subservient to its advancement.

"May 1. Met about eighty-five in the meeting of inquiry.

"May 2. This evening held a meeting in the meeting-house, and took up the *common* sayings of Christians, which are calculated to check a revival by lessening the sinner's sense of obligation, and quieting him in his sins.

"May 4. At this date, we find about forty rejoicing in hope from this date to the 14th, preached nine times, and held one meeting for inquirers.

"May 15. This evening attended a meeting of inquiry, and found the number and distress of anxious souls, rapidly increasing. The distress of W. is greatly augmented. This is the person who had been a little anxious during the revival at Salisbury, and whose attention had again been excited, on entering our meeting the second evening in this village. From this time, her distress continued about three days and nights. Providentially she was in a family a number of whom were thoughtless and far from religion. This was loud preaching. So great was her distress, that she was unable to attend meetings, and was confined to the house. Many called to witness her distress. She had concluded that the day of grace was over; and she was now past the fear of mortals. She continued crying, *'Lord have mercy on my soul. I am lost——Oh, forever lost.'* In this situation, she sent for me to call and see her, that she might beg my pardon for what she had said, before she died. I called, and such was her agitation, that it was difficult to keep her in one position. Sometimes sitting and then kneeling, in a piteous tone she would cry out, *'young people, take warning from me! Young people, take warning from me!'* The house was constantly visited by curious spectators, often till late at night. Many thought that she could not live long. One physician asked my opinion, whether I thought she would die. From past facts, I have noticed that this *extreme* distress does not generally continue long, especially in seasons of revival—— sometimes but a few moments—*commonly* a few hours, and rarely over three days. And when this extreme distress exceeds this time, I begin to fear that it may subside, as it has sometimes done without a change of heart. On the third day, she was rejoicing in hope.

"The question is often asked, why is it that the convictions of some sinners are so much greater than those of others? I answer, I do not know. The sinner's distress does not always appear to be in exact proportion to his crimes. But one thing I have learned from observation, and that when persons of a particular description have been brought under conviction, they have been exercised with severe distress. Those who have once been anxious for their souls, and have been laughed out of it, and returned to the thoughtless world, if again awakened, are more distressed than ever. Those who once made it a business to retire and pray, and have long since dropped the subject, are usually if their attention is again excited, greatly distressed. Those who have labored hard to stifle and throw off their convictions, or those who have formerly resisted the strivings of God's Spirit, are usually the subjects of keen distress, if convinced of sin, a second time. Those who have scoffed at the subject of religion, and have mocked the messengers of Christ, and ridiculed the worship of God, are usually filled with great consternation and agony, when brought to a just sense of their character and state. Those who have made light of revivals of religion, by calling them enthusiasm, fanaticism, and the work of the devil—especially those who have taken an active part in ridiculing the conviction and conversion of sinners, in the season of a revival—those who have called revivals by the hardest names, who have expressed the greatest contempt of them, and who have done the most to bring them into disrepute—persons of this description, have been the most frightful monuments of distress, that I have ever witnessed. They despair of ever becoming the subjects of that work which they have treated with so much contempt. We have sometimes heard the champion of infidelity expressing his horror for fear of having committed the unpardonable sin. I am acquainted with the names of persons, who have become perfectly deranged in consequence of *their own opposition* to the progress of revivals. Conscience, without any other accuser, has driven the enemy of revivals out of his reason into a state of settled delirium. The confession and fate of Judas, show the power of conscience, and stand recorded as a warning to the opposers of religion to beware.

"May 17. This evening we met in the school-house. The room was crowded, and the meeting was exceedingly joyful. Every word that was spoken, seemed to find a place in some heart. Such a season of rejoicing is rarely witnessed. '*Old things are passed away, and all things are become new.*' It is not yet quite one month since the work commenced, and about sixty are supposed to be the subjects of grace.

"May 19. This evening we met in a private house, and at the close of the exercises, one of the young converts spoke to a stout-hearted sinner who had been struggling against his conscience, and he dropped upon his knees in distress of soul. Another followed me nearly home, inquiring *what must he do to be saved!* In this situation, I left him; but before we retired to rest, he came in with a new song in his mouth. The other went home in great distress, but found relief before morning.

"May 20. This was a solemn day throughout the village. Mr. L., a young lawyer, who had been anxious for a few days, and who had retired to rest in my chamber, came to my bedside early this morning in distress. He sat down to breakfast with us, and while at the table, heard the tidings that another of his mates had found the Saviour the last night. He instantly left the table and retired to my chamber. Sometime after, I entered the chamber and found him prostrate on the floor, crying for mercy. While he thus continued, waxing worse and worse, a number came up to see him; but he seemed to take no notice of them, and continued pleading for mercy. About 10 o'clock, a.m., whether with a new heart, I cannot say, I only record the fact, he came down stairs, expressing his joy that he had found the Saviour. At the same time, his fellow student M., in a house a few rods distant, lay prostrate in his chamber. I called and found a number assembled around him, while he lay crying for mercy. The burden of his prayer was, that God would pardon his self-righteousness. The fact was this. A few days previous, he and his brother lawyer, had shut themselves in a chamber, seeking, and striving and praying together for a long time, thinking without doubt, they should ere long succeed in becoming Christians. Here they continued, until both had become exceedingly self-righteous. They could see it in each other, and each was alarmed at it, and asked my opinion if they had not better separate. By all means, I told them. This sight of his heart was doubtless what most distressed him. About three o'clock p.m., he arose in like manner, rejoicing that he had found the Saviour.

"May 21. Sabbath——Held a meeting at a public house, (Mr. B's,) four or five miles from this village. When I arrived, the rooms were filled——doors and windows thronged. Those who seemed the most anxious, had placed themselves near the seat of the speaker. When I named the psalm, all was silence, except the sighs and sobs of anxious souls. The moment I began to speak, I felt that God was there. I addressed them from Gen. vii. 1. *'Come thou and all thy house into the Ark.'* I felt unusual freedom and satisfaction in speaking. The solemnity of the scene will long be remembered. When I had pronounced the benediction, I know not that a foot moved. All were standing, and still anxious to hear. I gave them an account of what I had witnessed from the surrounding regions of desolation, doubtless from motives of curiosity, having heard something of the wonderful movement in the village. While giving a relation of these wonderful things, every ear was attentive. Some were sighing, and some were gazing in wild amazement, the language of every look seemed to be, *we never heard such things before.* In one large room which was crowded entirely full, nearly all were in deep distress, besides many crowding round the doors and windows, all apparently equally anxious, except here and there a joyful convert. They were crowded so closely together, that I could not pass among them to converse. So I spoke to one and another here and there at a distance, as I could catch their eyes as they lifted them streaming with tears. All were utter strangers whom I addressed, and not a name could I call. My only method of designation was, by pointing and saying, I mean you, and you, or this sinner, and that sinner. Never did I feel a deeper compassion for sinners, than for these poor strangers. A number, I know not how many, were awakened this day.

"Preached in the village in the afternoon and evening. At this time, we concluded that the crisis of solemnity was past in the village.

"May 22. This evening attended the meeting for inquirers, and all things considered, it was the most distressing and painful scene hitherto witnessed in this revival. Unexpectedly, a number who had never before attended, came from the region of solemnity above described. Some came four or five miles, and crowded the meeting, and threw it into a scene of awful distress. The distress was so great, and the suppressed sighs and sobs became so loud, that I could scarcely hear my own voice. One or two found relief on the spot; and some lost their strength, so that we were obliged to help them out of the chamber. It was with the utmost difficulty that I could prevail on them to separate. Some would start to retire, but the cry of distress would call them back again, and in this state, we were long detained. After leaving the chamber, the distress was so great, it was almost impossible to prevail on them to retire. At length, all retired but one, who in great agony, tarried through the night. But many who came from a distance, remained over night in the neighborhood.

"May 24. This evening attended a meeting at Mr. G's. A number sobbed and wept.

"May 25. This evening met again at the same place. One who formerly thought he had obtained a hope and lost it, was again awakened, and at the close of the meeting cried aloud. He professes to have found relief, but I think without any good evidence of a change of heart. I fear he has again deceived himself.

"May 26. This evening met the young converts in a social meeting, and began to hear a relation of their Christian experience.

"May 27. This afternoon held a general meeting of the young converts, and of all others who chose to attend; the object of which was, to address the subjects of this work on the nature of a public profession of religion. Spoke of the duty——the qualifications requisite——and stated and answered objections. The duty; 1. To God. 2. To yourself. 3. To the church. 4. To the world, &c.

"May 28. Sabbath. Preached thrice to a crowded, attentive, solemn and yet joyful audience.

"May 29. This evening met nearly 200 in a meeting for inquirers. This meeting was anticipated by many with secret dread. Some Christians, doubtless, among the rest, who were present and witnessed the scene of distress at the last inquiry meeting were heard to say, that they dreaded to attend this evening. They could hardly endure the thought of passing through such a scene of distress a second time. And I can truly say, that for the first time, I felt the same reluctance. But to the astonishment of all, instead of an anxious, we had a joyful meeting. Most of those in such distress at our last meeting for inquirers, had found relief and were exceedingly joyful. What an astonishing change in one week! I felt that it could hardly be possible. We had lost our anxiety, and had little else to do, but to render united thanks to God for what he had done. But before we parted, I went round and collected into a circle, a number who were without hope, conversed with each one, addressed the whole and prayed with and for them, as those professing no hope. This was evidently the means of deepening their impressions.

"May 30. This evening met in the school-house. The room was crowded, and the audience were still, solemn, animated and joyful. The same was the general character of our meetings after this date. From this time, we spent a number of half days and evenings in hearing a relation of their Christian experience, preparatory to a public profession. These were interesting and animating seasons affording the best opportunity of learning the human heart in all its foldings of depravity and opposition; and the astonishing change wrought by the power of God's grace.

"June 25. Sabbath—This day sixty-eight made a public profession of religion, thirty-two of whom were baptized. At this time, more than a hundred had, to appearance, become the subjects of divine grace. A number more have since, publicly professed Christ; and of these, five young men are preparing for the gospel ministry."[1]

The astonishing fact from these journal entries of the revival at Nassau, New York, is the *calmness and orderly fashion* in which Asahel Nettleton conducted the revival. Amidst the drama of awakened souls crying out in agony, prostrate on the floor, even drowning out the evangelist's own voice to the degree that he could not hear himself preach; we witness a calm, experienced minister attend to the awakened souls as calmly as a field surgeon would attend the wounded in battle. Nettleton moved through the scene of distress attending to each person with the love of Jesus. Few are the laborers in the history of the Church who have ministered amidst such seasons of divine grace as Asahel Nettleton, and done so with such wisdom and discretion.

Note

1   Hartford Seminary Archives, "The Nettleton Papers", Hartford, Connecticut.

Asahel Nettleton was a thorough student of the human heart. He understood the windings and turnings of the depraved heart and knew how to expose its deceits to awaken the sinner to the desperateness of his lost condition.

WILLIAM C. NICHOLS

14

NETTLETON'S REVIVAL METHODS

To thoroughly appreciate Asahel Nettleton as a laborer in revivals, we must examine *how* he approached the meetings and how he *dealt* with the doctrines that he preached in those meetings with such force and effect. There was a certain pattern to his labors, that once established, was consistently executed with precision and dynamic force! Moreover, in this chapter we will examine the evangelist's intent behind his preaching, which had such dramatic effects upon his hearers. How Nettleton conducted a revival should be a matter of study for every revival student.

There have been few men who have understood the deceitfulness of the human heart as Asahel Nettleton. He became acquainted with his own heart's deceit in the trying period before his salvation. He knew all the excuses one could make to deny Christianity and the Bible. But what set Nettleton so apart from his peers, was his uncanny ability to recognize and distinguish the different stages of the salvation process. He knew full well that a lost sinner who was merely awakened to their lost condition did not yet posses salvation. He knew the process of conviction of sin by the Holy Spirit operating on a person's heart and conscience. Nettleton did not *rush* a person into a decision for Christ, rather, he was cautiously concerned about spurious conversions.

Nettleton knew how to apply the Law to sinners' consciences to awaken them to their rebellion against a holy God. He also knew that their salvation depended *entirely* upon God, and the evangelist was careful not to get in the way of the Holy Spirit's operations in the salvation process. He was a master at recognizing when God was at work in an individual's heart.

We see the effectiveness of Asahel Nettleton in the following revival account provided by the Rev. Joab Brace. Brace was the pastor of the church in Newington, Connecticut, when Nettleton labored there

amidst a glorious revival in the year 1821. It is interesting to note that the
revival in Newington, Conn. began in *prayer*. Here now is the account
by Rev. Brace:

"In the summer of 1820 an uncommon emotion was felt. There was a *sound in the
tops of the mulberry trees*, and although the indication was not distinctly understood at
the time; yet the result has proved that God had then actually gone forth. A number
of serious persons were under distressing apprehensions of ruin as coming on this
place, and they cried unto the Lord for help. Several women of the Church privately
instituted a weekly concert in the closet, to implore the outpouring of the Holy
Spirit. A few sinners were uneasy, and yet without very definite impressions; and
there was no awakening of a decisive character ...

"Above all other means, what raised the general attention, was the coming of
Rev. Asahel Nettleton on the last of December, 1820, as unexpectedly as a
messenger from heaven, apparently commissioned from the Almighty Head of the
Church, and accompanied by the Holy Spirit. Next morning he preached on being
ashamed of Christ. This fixed a listening ear. In the afternoon he dwelt upon the
causes of alarm to awakened sinners. In the evening the assembly was crowded, and
the attention profound. His text was—*Behold I stand at the door and knock*. The
discourse was closed with surprising effect by repeating the hymn; 'Behold a
stranger at the door.' When prayer was ended, while the people were standing, he
made a very close application of the subject to their hearts, in a short address which
was very silently and solemnly heard. He requested them to retire without making a
noise. 'I love to talk to you, you are so still. It looks as though the spirit of God was
here. Go away as still as possible. Do not talk by the way, lest you forget your own
hearts. Do not ask how you like the preacher; but retire to your closets, bow before
God; and give yourselves to him this night.' After the benediction, he inquired of
many persons individually, 'Have you made your peace with God? Do you calculate
to attend to this subject?' Many promised they would try to make their peace with
God immediately—that they would repent that night—and a permanent
impression was made. From this the flame spread over the parish; the current of
feeling was turned ... The people gathered around their minister with peculiar
attachment; meetings were crowded and solemn; the things of eternity filled the
people with awe. The work of God seemed to be in almost every house;—all the
people were ready to hear; sinners would bear the most pointed individual
application.

"... We have had almost every kind of meeting which are employed in such
seasons of religious attention—frequent meetings for preaching and exhortation—
district prayer meetings—an intermediate prayer meetings on the
Sabbath—meetings for enquirers—church meetings—morning meetings—
religious visits—and they have all been well attended. ... No meeting has been
found more powerful in promoting the revival than the meeting for enquirers,
which was attended by nearly all the awakened, from the man of seventy-five down
to children, and it was regarded as the seat of divine operations. They came as sinners
under condemnation, and just ready to sink into the abyss of perdition. Every
individual was spoken to on his own case; and appropriate prayers and addresses
were employed. ...

"The characteristic of the work may be thus stated. There were some instances of
deep distress; but none of that overwhelming kind, in which the subject faint, or fall
to the ground, or are unable to leave their seats. In some cases convictions were long

continued, in others the heart was speedily bowed. Some after long distress rose almost imperceptibly to a faint hope; in others the hope was bright and satisfying; no instances of extravagant joy occurred though several were much elevated. In convictions the subjects were much affected with their guiltiness before God, as well as with fears of everlasting destruction. When the sinner was humbled he acknowledged his great dependence on sovereign grace for acceptance in the sight of God; and was pleased with the idea of unconditional submission to the will and glory of God. One prominent feature in the converts was a fear of self-deception. Much was said on the danger of false hopes, which probably had an influence to check flights of joy. The effects of the revival are most pleasant. A spirit of prayer prevails, and particularly attention to family religion. With many persons the riches of this world have lost their charms. Great concern is manifested for the salvation of souls that are still careless ... On the whole, it has been a serious and delightful season. During Mr. N's stay with us, this place was a common center of divine entertainment, in comparison with which all the pleasures of this world are faint and feeble."[1]

In summary, we observe in Nettleton's manner of conducting revivals:

1. He understood the windings of the depraved human heart.

2. He preached doctrinally pointed sermons, aiming those truths at three key human levels: the head, the heart, and the conscience.

3. He took no credit for success, but gave God all the glory.

4. He recognized the need for the enabling of the Holy Spirit in preaching.

5. He was careful about spurious conversions and false hopes.

6. He used the "law" to be the "school-master" to bring lost sinners to Christ.

7. He strongly believed that an awakened sinner must be cast entirely upon God for their salvation.

8. He preached the duty of immediate repentance and faith in Jesus Christ.

9. He did not rely on preaching alone, but also placed emphasis on one-to-one counselling of anxious souls.

10. He guarded against any "wild fire" in revivals, and if emotionalism got out of hand he quickly checked it.

11. He emphasized the need to leave the church meeting *quietly*, not to talk about the preacher, but to reflect on the doctrines and truths taught.

12. He was a plain preacher whose primary concern was that his hearers *understood* with their minds, the doctrines he was preaching to them. Then, he relied on the Holy Spirit to apply those same doctrines to the hearts and consciences of his hearers.

13. He was not humorous in the pulpit, nor ever attempted to make his hearers laugh. His manner was always solemn, as if he had just left the presence of God before he ascended the pulpit stairs.

14. He was a master at making the Bible come alive. His illustrations were taken from Bible stories and characters—not from the newspaper's headlines.

15) He was not a boring preacher. Rather he was gripping. People flocked to hear him when they learned he was in town.

16. He was a humble man, never drawing attention to himself.

17. He was a holy man who sought holiness before the Lord throughout his life.

18. He was a plain man with no special outward gifts of oratory or personality.

19. He exercised a deep concern over the lost everywhere he went.

20. He knew that there was nothing special about him, but that it was God working through him, which gave the success and fruit of revival.

Note

1   *The Christian Spectator*, May, 1822 issue, pp. 273–277.

Good preaching is, after all, a form of mind control. Its goal is first to capture and then conquer the heart for the service of God. In this regard Nettleton was a master, and those who heard him usually felt carried along almost irresistibly by the power of his reasoning. Wayland said he, "would sway an audience as the trees of the forest are moved by a mighty wind."

J. F. THORNBURY

Church on the Hill, Lenox, MA

Congregational Church in Farmington, CT, where Noah Porter was pastor and scene of remarkable revivals under Nettleton in 1820–1821.

Lee Congregational Church, Lee. MA

15

AT THE HEIGHT OF HIS POWERS
1820–1822

Asahel Nettleton knew the power of God most mightily during the remarkable revivals which occurred between 1820 and 1822. What he did not know was the striking fact that these two years would be his last years of health and stamina. In the fall of 1822 he contracted typhus fever, which almost took his life. From 1822 onward Asahel Nettleton was a semi-invalid till his dying day.

We must mark carefully his labors of 1820–1822, for they reveal a man at the height of his powers and success. He would never labor so incessantly again. Although God will use him in future revivals, particularly in the South, in Virginia, the years of 1820–1822 are his most productive years as a laborer in the Second Great Awakening. This is seen in the following:

> "These revivals of 1821 and 1822 in many ways were the climax of Nettleton's career as an evangelist. He was still young and healthy and his body could stand the hours of riding from one place to another, as well as the exhausting demands made of the itinerant preacher, ministering to the needs of the congregations and clergy in the heightened excitement of a revival. For the most part the church was receptive to revivalism during these years. Those who opposed the revivals at the beginning of the century had for the most part come to accept them as a necessary and gracious means. There was great caution throughout New England that preaching be properly doctrinal and that undue enthusiasm be avoided, but since that was being followed, there was little tension among the clergy. The height of Nettleton's career as a revivalist is also the height of New England's acceptance of his type of revivalism."[1]

1820 to 1822, two years of robust activity for Asahel Nettleton, are followed by two years of *inactivity*, as he slowly recovers from the illness which almost killed him. The last half of the great evangelist's life is spent more in controversy than in revival, so it is of vast importance that we closely follow his labors before his bout of typhus fever.

We will first examine a revival which occurred under his preaching in

New Haven, Connecticut, in August of 1820. The revival spread from local churches to the campus of Yale College. We observe from the following comments:

> "The revival at New Haven continued for many months and eventually between fifteen hundred and two thousand were converted as a direct result of it. But the influence of Nettleton's visit was not confined to this city. Occasionally, during the summer and autumn, he preached in towns nearby with scarcely less effect than in the city of Yale. For some weeks he was in his home town of Killingworth where there were a hundred and sixty-two converts. In the latter part of December he was at Wethersfield, where the church was increased by two hundred through a revival. These spiritual awakenings were contagious and spread from one congregation to another."[2]

The following comments by Heman Humphrey confirm the same activity in New Haven:

> "In the same year, 1820, was a powerful revival in New Haven, and about three hundred were added to the churches. It extended to most of the neighboring towns. Out of thirty-one congregations in the county of New Haven, at least twenty-five were visited, during the winter and spring, with the special presence of the Lord, and it was estimated that within these limits between *fifteen hundred and two thousand* souls were called out of nature's darkness into marvellous light."[3]

On the 7th of September, 1820, Nettleton corresponded with friends by sending letters from New Haven, relating the revival accounts. As we read these letters, we cannot help but observe the *tenderness* and compassion of his heart toward the recent converts. Nettleton kept lists of the converts from the revivals and he would often pray for them individually through the years. At Hartford Seminary, a partial list of these converts are among his personal papers, listing their names, the town, and the date of their conversion. Since the itinerant never married, he considered new converts as members of his extended family in Christ and always maintained fond feelings towards them. We catch a glimpse of this from Nettleton's correspondence at this time:

> "*My dear friends:*
>
> The moment I take my pen to address you, I imagine myself seated in the midst of that same dear circle. Every name and every countenance appears familiar. The inquiry meeting, the crowded assembly, the heaving sigh, the solemn stillness, and the joyful countenance awaken all the tender sensibilities of my heart. My dear friends, no friendship, no attachment to this world, is equal to that created in a revival of religion. 'The fellowship of kindred minds is like to that above.'
>
> "What is felt at such a season, is in anticipation of the joys of the heavenly world. I doubt not your hearts retain the sweet recollection of what Paul hints to the Ephesian converts, 'Who hath raised us up together, and made us sit together in heavenly places in Christ Jesus.' But my dear friends, after all, *the milk and the honey lie beyond this wilderness world.* A voice from heaven is heard, 'Arise ye, and depart, for this is not your rest.'

"By this time some of you begin to learn, that you are on the field of battle. The world, the flesh and the devil, are potent enemies. You will have need to buckle on the whole armor of God. But whatever may betide, never, *no never* think of dropping the subject. True, the conflict may be sharp, and the pathway to heaven steep and difficult, but, brethren, *the time is short*. The conflict will soon be over. Think not much about present enjoyment, as about present duty.

"I must give you a short account of the revival at this place. Meetings are held every evening in the week, crowded, still, and solemn as eternity. Every Monday evening, we meet the anxious ones in a large ball-room. We have had from sixty to about three hundred assembled at these meetings, all solemn, and many in deep distress of soul. The cloud of divine influence, has gone rapidly over our heads, and covered us with awful solemnity. And there is the sound of abundance of rain.

"We visit by appointment, and make a number of visits in a day at a given hour. We sometimes meet ten or fifteen, and sometimes thirty at once. We converse a little with each one, speak a word to all in general, pray and pass on to another circle, and so we spend our time. Our visits are generally short, except one which will never be forgotten. This was August 25, at 2 o'clock, p.m., at the house of Mr. B. We entered the house at the time appointed, and found about twenty persons sitting around the room in pensive silence. All had been more or less anxious for a number of days, and one was in awful distress. This one I addressed more particularly, and urged the duty of immediate repentance, not without some hope that relief would be obtained on the spot; for I felt sure that this state of feeling, could not long be sustained. While pressing the conscience of sinner, I found that this distress had spread nearly throughout the circle. I detained them the usual time, and advised them all to retire home to their closets. Some started and went out the door, and others sat still with heavy hearts. Very soon, Emily returned, exclaiming, 'O, I cannot go home, I dare not go. I shall lose my concern. What shall I do?' and threw herself down in a chair, and her head on the table, in the deepest agony. All at once she became silent, and gently raised her head with a placid countenance, and was heard to say in a mild tone of voice, 'O, I can submit, I can love Christ. How easy it is; why did I not do it before?' We sat in silent amazement. Every word sunk deep into our hearts We felt the conviction that God was there. She seized her next companion by the hand, and with all the tenderness becoming a fellow sinner, began to press those very truths, which had so distressed her own heart, the duty of immediate repentance and submission to God. Every word became an arrow. I felt that the work was taken out of my hands, for I perceived that God had made her the most powerful preacher. All at once, A. become silent, and lifted her head with a countenance beaming with joy. 'The Saviour has come——O how happy.' This sent fresh alarm through every heart. And now A. and E. unite heart and hand, and begin with H. who had been in deep distress for some time. They urge with all the tenderness and firm decision of those who had felt the conviction, the necessity, and reasonableness of immediate repentance, and submission to God. The subject pressed harder and harder and harder still, when all at once, H. was brought out of darkness into marvelous light. These three now unite heart and hand, and with one voice bear testimony to the same heart-rending truth that God is right and the sinner wrong. The time would fail me to finish the story of this visit. We met at 2 o'clock, p.m., and were detained more than three hours. Suffice it to say, I never saw or heard of such an afternoon visit before, for the one half has not been told. At the close, we began to look about us to see, and inquire, *what hath God wrought!* We brought them into one circle. I said, is it possible! This is too much! Had I not seen it, I could not have believed it. For nine of those who entered the room in deep distress, were now rejoicing in hope. The anxious ones had retired, and we were left in a circle of young converts, if they are not deceived. *Not a hint had been given that one soul had experienced religion, or had any reason to hope.* This was the feeling, 'It is right I should love and serve God, and this I intend to do, whether saved or lost.' Oh, it was a delightful circle, humble, tender, affectionate and joyful. They appeared like children of the same great family.

"About eighty have been brought to rejoice in hope in this city during five weeks past. Besides these, about twenty-five students in Yale College, have become hopeful subjects of divine grace. But we much fear the bustle of commencement. It would be nothing strange, if all our prospects of a future harvest should be blighted, before another week shall end. Pray for us. My love to all my dear friends in Nassau, and tell them how I long to see them. *Live near to God. Live in peace, and the God of love and peace shall be with you.* In short, '*Only let your conversation be as it becometh the gospel of Christ, that whether I come and see you, or else be absent I may hear of your affairs, that ye stand fast in one spirit, with one mind, striving together for the faith of the gospel.*'

Yours as ever.[4]

It is a remarkable fact, that of the nine individuals—seemingly converted at the same time—in that little seated circle of youths, *five died shortly thereafter.* Two of these, sisters in their teens, Susan B. Marble and Adeline Marble, had memoirs of their lives published after their deaths which were used mightily as a gospel witness! Asahel Nettleton wrote to his dear friend, Mrs. Parmele, of Bolton, Conn., the following tender letter detailing the sad news. Nettleton is overcome with grief as he writes:

"May 15, 1822.

You recollect reading an account of the death of Susan B. Marble, in New Haven. She was one of the nine who were brought out rejoicing in an afternoon's visit. When I was in New Haven last, Betsey Bishop, another of that number died. She was an interesting youth. I had then so far recovered my health, that I went to the conference room, and addressed the people on the subject of her death, and alluded to that interesting afternoon. A number of that same circle called to see me one evening, and to talk over the interesting event. They used to meet frequently by themselves, and converse and pray together. It was a little band of love. Adeline Marble, Susan's sister, was one of this happy number. She was present at that evening visit—still clad in mourning. Last evening I saw from the paper, that she too has *gone to her long home.* I retired, and could not but weep—'Child of mortality.' Thus three of these blooming youth, have found an early grave. Had you seen them as I have, you too would weep, as well as rejoice."[5]

The years 1820–1822, in the life of Asahel Nettleton, are shining jewels in a glorious crown! Heaven had come down to visit man. There are few times in history where God has moved so mightily as these years. Revival after revival is felt under Nettleton's urgent preaching, and the dramatic scenes witnessed startle all who behold them. Conversions occur as quickly as lightning falling from the sky. God was calling in a harvest of souls during this phase of the Second Great Awakening and Asahel

Nettleton was his primary instrument of blessing. We continue with these glorious years of revival with the revival at Farmington, Connecticut.

REVIVAL AT FARMINGTON

In Farmington, Connecticut stands the huge wooden, white structure of the Farmington Church. The church is the same today as it was in Nettleton's day. The pastor of the church during Nettleton's visits, was Dr. Noah Porter, Yale graduate and eminent minister of that church for over forty years. The revivals which occurred inside that building were some of the most powerful of the Second Great Awakening! The wooden floor rumbled under Nettleton's deep voice as he preached eternity to his startled hearers. The church has a high, winding pulpit and one can picture Asahel in it, above the gathered crowd (the church seats over 1000), his arm raised with his Bible in hand, and his piercing eyes flashing across the assembly as he speaks of the flood in Noah's day and the judgment over that generation of antediluvians.

The revival at Farmington grew in power and influence early in 1821. Noah Porter, the pastor of the church at Farmington provides the following recollections of that mighty move of grace:

"The year 1821 was eminently, in Connecticut, a year of revivals. Between eighty and a hundred congregations were signally blessed. From the commencement of the year, a new state of feeling began to appear in this town. On the first Sabbath in February, I stated to the assembly the tokens of the gracious presence of God in several places of the vicinity, and urged the duties peculiarly incumbent on us at such a season. This I had often done before, but not with the same effect. Professors of religion now began evidently to awake. They had anxiety for themselves and for the people that would allow them no rest. In their communications with each other and with the world, they were led spontaneously to confess their unfaithfulness, and a few without the church, about the same time, were pungently convicted.

"In this state of things, Rev. Mr. Nettleton made us his first visit. His preaching on the evening of a Lord's Day, in this month, from Acts 2:37, was set home by the power of the Spirit upon the hearts of many; and his discourse on the Wednesday evening following, from Genesis 6:3, was blessed to the conviction of a still greater number. As many as fifty persons, it was afterwards ascertained, dated their first decided purpose of immediately seeking their salvation from that evening; and it is worthy of remark, that the same sermon was preached on the following week to two other large and solemn assemblies, in adjoining parishes, with no special effect that could afterwards be traced. The fact probably was that here it convinced numbers that the Spirit was already striving with them, and that then was their day. 'A word spoken in due season, how good is it!' At a meeting of the anxious on the evening of February 26, there were present about a hundred and seventy. Here were persons of almost every age and class, some who, a few weeks before, had put the subject of serious piety at scornful distance, and others who had drowned every thought of religion in giddy mirth, now bending their knees together in supplication, or waiting in silent reflection, for a minister of the gospel to pass along, and tell them, individually, what they must do. Twelve were found to have lately become peaceful in hope, and a great number to be powerfully convicted of sin. From this time, so rapid was the progress of the work, that at the next similar meeting, March 12th, there were present a hundred and eighty (the room would hold no more) of whom fifty supposed that, since the commencement of the revival, they had become reconciled to God; and, a week afterwards, I had the names of more than ninety who indulged the same persuasion concerning themselves.

"The state of feelings which, at this time, pervaded the town was interesting beyond description. There was no commotion; but a stillness, in our very streets; a serenity in the aspect of the pious; and solemnity apparent in almost all, which forcibly impressed us with the conviction that, in very deed, God was in this place. Public meetings, however, were not very frequent. They were so appointed as to afford the opportunity for the same individuals to hear preaching twice a week, beside on the Sabbath. Occasionally there were also meetings of an hour in the morning or at noon, at private dwellings, at which the serious in the neighborhood were convened, on short notice, for prayer and conference. The members of the church also met weekly, in convenient seasons for prayer, and commonly on the evenings selected for the meetings of the anxious. From these various meetings, the people were accustomed to retire directly, and with little communication together, to their respective homes. They were disposed to be much alone, and were spontaneously led to take the Word of God for their guide. The Bible was preferred to all other books, and was searched daily and with eager inquiry.

"Mr. Nettleton continued with us, except during a few short intervals, till about the middle of April. To his labours, so far as human instrumentality was directly concerned, the progress of the revival must chiefly be ascribed. The topics on which he principally dwelt were the unchangeable obligations of the divine law, the deceitful and entirely depraved character of the natural heart, the free and indiscriminate offers of the gospel; the reasonableness and necessity of immediate repentance; the variety of those refuges and excuses to which awakened sinners are accustomed to resort; and the manner, guilt, and danger of slighting, resisting and opposing the operations of the Holy Spirit. His addresses were not formal discussions, first of one and then of another of these subjects, but a free declaration of the truth of God concerning them all, just as they lie in the course of spiritual experience, and would best subserve the particular end which he was labouring at the time to gain. They were too plain to be misunderstood, too fervent to be unheeded, and too searching and convincing to be treated with indifference.

"It was a favorable circumstance that among the first subjects of the work there was a large proportion of the more wealthy and intelligent class. A considerable number of youths, belonging chiefly to this class, had just finished a course of biblical instruction, for which I had met them weekly for more than a year. These, with scarcely an exception, at the very commencement of the revival, embraced the gospel which they had learned; and by their experience of its power, commended it to the families where they belonged. Within three months, I suppose there were two hundred and fifty members of the congregation, who supposed that they had passed from death unto life. On the first Sabbath in June, a hundred and fourteen were added to the church; and at subsequent periods, a hundred and twenty besides. Of these a few have since been rejected, and others have declined from their first love. But I have not perceived that a greater proportion of hopeful conversions in this revival, than in others, previous or subsequent to it, have proved unsound. Many have died, and many have removed from our immediate connexion, but those who remain now constitute the chief strength of the church."[6]

From reading Noah Porter's account of the revival in Farmington, one can trace elements of Asahel Nettleton's "revival methods". These are not only noteworthy as a study in themselves, but they appeared in every single revival which Nettleton conducted. What God had revealed to him in those "early waste places" through trial and error, now formed a set pattern of ministry which he employed with maximum force!

THE REVIVAL AT PITTSFIELD, MASSACHUSETTS

In 1821, the 38 year old evangelist was yet again involved in another powerful revival. This revival occurred in the state of Massachusetts, in the town of Pittsfield at the church where Heman Humphrey was pastor. The towns of Lenox, Lee, and Pittsfield each became scenes of remarkable revivals. The church in Lenox, Massachusetts, Samuel Shepard's church, (which is now the "Church on the hill") can still be visited today; the ancient graveyard adjacent to the beautiful white church, contains the remains of Dr. Shepard and his family. Heman Humphrey's church in Pittsfield is no longer there, but we have the following record of that penetrating revival which occurred between 1820 through 1821.

The revival at Pittsfield was one of the most memorable revivals of Nettleton's ministry. For it was during a Fourth of July celebration, that the manifest Presence of God saturated the congregation and town to such a degree, that the enemies of the revival were immediately squashed! It is noteworthy to mention, that the people of Pittsfield had decided to celebrate their Nation's independence with an early morning prayer meeting, and a public religious meeting in the afternoon. In the early 1820s the churches in America still held a place of prominence and influence in their community. Here now is the following extract by Dr. Humphrey regarding the revival at Pittsfield, Massachusetts:

"Early in the month of May, the Rev. Asahel Nettleton, whose name is so familiar both to the friends and enemies of revivals, came to this town to 'rest awhile,' and to await the future calls of Providence. But he was not to remain long inactive; and the three or four weeks which he thought of spending in retirement here, were prolonged through as many months of unceasing labor. By the middle of May, there was some excitement; but whether it was the effect of mere curiosity, or of the Spirit beginning to move on the hearts of the people, it was at first impossible to determine. For a fortnight or more, nothing very decisive took place. Which way the scale would turn, was to us altogether uncertain. Every thing appeared to be hushed into silent and anxious expectation. It was the stillness that precedes an earthquake—though the subsequent shock was neither sudden nor violent.

"In the latter part of May, we ventured, though with considerable solicitude, to appoint a meeting for the inquiring, if there should be any such in the congregation. Nearly twenty attended, and some of them were found to be under very serious impressions. No professor of religion was invited or expected to attend. It was a meeting exclusively for those who were beginning to realize their exposure and their guilt. The next meeting was better attended, and it was found that a few were sinking in the deep waters of conviction.

"From this time, the work solemnly and steadily advanced, particularly in the heart of the town, where the strong man armed, had for a long time kept his palace. He lifted up his voice to summon the mighty to his standard, but it was in vain, for the God of Jacob was with us. So far was the enemy from making any impression upon the camp of the faithful, that his own ranks were thinned and disheartened, by the desertion of many on whom he had placed great reliance, and of whose unshaken allegiance, he had confidently boasted.

"During the whole month of June, the revival grew more interesting and decisive every day. Many were rejoicing in hope, and more were alarmed at their own stupidity and danger. The voice of prayer was heard for the first time in several of our principal families. Not less than five domestic altars were erected in one day. In this state of things, and when religion was the principal topic of conversation in all circles, whether large or small, it was natural for those who felt a new and deep interest in the subject, to wish for an appropriate celebration of the fourth of July, and arrangements were accordingly made for a prayer meeting at sunrise, and a public religious service in the afternoon. The prayer meeting was well attended. At two o'clock, our large house of worship was filled, and we had the pleasure of meeting there many of our Christian friends from different and even remote parts of the county. The audience was solemn, notwithstanding ... but here let me draw a veil over the painful interruptions which we experienced. Charity hopeth all things, *endureth all things*; and he is but a poor soldier, who can be frightened by mere powder. It is due to justice to state that all the respectable people in the town ... strongly disapproved of whatever tended to disturb us in our worship. But God meant it for good. Through the riches of his grace, an impulse was that day given to the revival, which was long and happily felt, and which we shall have reason to remember with no ordinary emotions of wonder and gratitude, for a great while to come. Instances of conviction and conversion became more frequent than they had been; and from this time, the work continued with little abatement, though never so rapid in its progress, as some revivals, till the month of October.

"The third Sabbath in September will not be forgotten by the present generation in Pittsfield; for 'that Sabbath day was an high day.'

"To see more than eighty persons, and one half of them heads of families, rising up to enter into covenant with God and his people—to look around and see who they were, and think where some of them had been—to behold them coming forward, high and low, rich and poor together, and kneeling to receive the baptismal seal—to hear their song—to witness their emotions, and to welcome them for the first time to the table of the Lord—Oh it was a scene which I shall not attempt to describe. We had our aged Simeons and Elizabeths there; and, we doubt not, there was joy in heaven. A solemn awe and stillness pervaded the great congregation, and some sinners were that day awakened by what they saw and heard in our sanctuary."[7]

We see from Dr. Humphrey's account the glorious *results* of the revival later that year. But we miss the sensational account of what occurred for he chooses to omit that information in his narrative out of modesty and humility. Fortunately, we have the details of what transpired on that Fourth of July meeting, and one cannot help but compare the scenes of that day to another revival which occurred a century earlier in London, England under the preaching of George Whitefield. Whitefield was in Moorfields, preaching to the masses, when he was attacked by the enemies of the revival; a sword was thrust near his head, rotten eggs and dead cats were thrown at him, and a soldiers' marching band tried to disrupt his preaching—all to no avail! So too, here in Pittsfield, Massachusetts in 1821, with Asahel Nettleton sitting in the congregation listening to Heman Humphrey preach, we see God move in his awesome splendor and power, quieting the noise of Satan's human instruments—all to His glory! A person who was in the congregation that day offers the following description of the events that transpired:

"The facts were these. The opposers of religion, finding that a *religious* celebration of our National Independence was agreed on, resolved to have a political celebration. They occupied the church in the morning.

"At 2 o'clock, they who loved the Lord, and respected his ordinances, began to assemble in the same place. The church was crowded. While the people were assembling, and as they passed near the rioters, crackers [firecrackers] were repeatedly exploded, in order to intimidate them. The service began. It went calmly and sweetly forward. The Rev. Mr. Humphrey, the pastor, took his text from John viii.36 *'If the Son, therefore, shall make you free, ye shall be free indeed.'*

"He had not proceeded far, when the word—*fire*—was given, and our ears were suddenly stunned, and the congregation startled, by the report of cannon. It was the attack of the adversary, and it was well kept up. But unfortunately for him and his agents, every shot preached louder than ten thousand thunders. Meanwhile the drum beat, and the fifes played, and the soldiers marched back and forth before the church door, animated moreover by the music of the cannon, and the prospect of a glorious triumph over the cause of God. But alas! They were laboring hard to defeat themselves. Some few Christians, indeed, of delicate frame, and quick sensibilities, were agitated and alarmed; and others, though not intimidated, dreaded the consequences of this violent attack; but generally, there were high hopes that this tumult would be overruled for good. And so it was. So skillfully did the preacher allude to, and apply his discourse to the conduct of the opposition out of doors; such advantage did he take of every blast of the cannon and every play of the drum, by some well pointed remark, that it all went like a two-edged sword to the hearts of listening sinners. Indeed, Mr. H. [Rev. Humphrey] afterwards informed me, that had he showed the heads of his sermon to his opposers previously, and earnestly requested them, when he had reached such a point in his sermon, to *fire*, and when he reached another point *fire*, they could not more effectively have subserved the purpose of his discourse, than they did. Those gentlemen who had walked in the opposers' procession, hung their heads, were disgusted, and in some instances were convicted deeply of sin. One gentleman, who had been previously somewhat serious, declared to me that every shot of the cannon pierced his soul, filled him with a kind of indescribable horror, and brought him, through the blessings of God, to such a hatred and detestation of sin in himself and others, as constrained him quickly to fly to Christ.

"I confess I trembled for the ark of God. Indeed I was so uneasy, that after the sermon was concluded, I went and expostulated with the ringleader, whose companion in wickedness I once had been, and over whom I thought I might have some influence. But I had reason to believe that in general the spirits of the children of God were perfectly unruffled. I sat near the Rev. Mr. Nettleton, and so delighted was he with the discourse, and so accurately *prescient* too was he of the result, that whenever an apt illusion dropped from the lips of the preacher, he would turn round with a holy smile, and whenever a shot from the cannon pierced our ears, he would say—it would involuntary escape from him—'*that is good—that is good.*' Speaking afterwards of the events of this day, he observed to me, '*Did you not feel calm. I thought there was a deep and majestic calmness overspreading the minds of Christians.*' I found that very many did indeed feel so. Nothing could be more appropriate, or more naturally arise out of his text, then Mr. H's description of the miserable bondage in which those out of doors were faithfully serving their master.

"The ministers looked forward with an alternation of hope and fear to the *meeting of inquiry*, as that meeting was generally esteemed a kind of spiritual thermometer, by which the degree of warmth and feeling in the society could be measured. This was held for an hour previous to the evening service. The time arrived. It was crowded—never so full before. The daring and outrageous attack in the day had driven many to the place in which he that appeared was always supposed to be asking, '*What must I do to be saved!*' This question was emphatically asked in the meeting. It was found that a most powerful impulse had been given to the revival. Nor was this impulse at all weakened by the evening service.

"The house was overflowing. You was there [referring to Bennet Tyler]. You marked the progress of things. Mr. Nettleton that evening put forth his mightiest efforts. His discourse was one continued flash of conviction. He spoke from that part of Genesis xix, which treats of the destruction of Sodom. '*Up, get ye out of this place.*' was closely and powerfully applied, and when he had given a full account of the nature and circumstances of Lot's expostulations with his sons-in-law, he came to speak of the awful stillness which remained over Sodom, while Lot was taking his leave. Oh, then, when all his warnings were despised, and they would not believe a word he said, then—then when Lot was safely out of Sodom—what a terrible storm of fire ensued! You remember, he turned the heads of the audience completely towards the windows. They involuntarily looked round to see the conflagration— to see Sodom in flames. It was quite overpowering."[8]

This last statement captures the essence of Asahel Nettleton's preaching ability: he literally made the Bible come to life for his hearers with precision and power! Evidently, Nettleton wisely applied the afternoon's proceedings, with the cannon-fire still ringing in their ears, to accentuate a town being destroyed by judgment from God, and this alarm was felt in the congregation as they could envision the encroaching flames beyond the windows of the Pittsfield church that dark evening.

An additional observation is provided for us from the pen of Samuel

Shepard, pastor of the church in nearby Lenox, Massachusetts, which experienced the revival of that year as well. Rev. Shepard provides some personal observations on Nettleton's preaching style, as well as the revival which touched the neighboring communities of Pittsfield, Lenox, and Lee, Massachusetts.

We turn now to Dr. Shepard's narrative where we learn that Asahel was experiencing poor health at the time of the revival:

"In the spring of 1821, Dr. Nettleton came to Pittsfield, in consequence of an invitation from Dr. Humphrey. Dr. Nettleton was in poor health, and Dr. Humphrey invited him to his house, with the hope, that by being relieved from pressing calls, he might recover his health. When Dr. Nettleton first came to Pittsfield, he took no part, I believe, in religious meetings. After a while, he preached once or twice in the course of a week. His preaching was soon attended with a divine blessing, and was undoubtedly instrumental of a revival of religion in Pittsfield, and several other towns in the vicinity. When I was from home on a journey, Dr. Nettleton preached in Lenox on the Sabbath, and two or three times in the course of the week after; and on my return, I found a revival begun, and progressing in the town. Many were awakened, and some were rejoicing in hope. He afterwards preached occasionally in my parish, as his engagements elsewhere permitted. The number of hopeful converts who were received into the church as the fruits of that revival, was ninety-one. Almost all of them continued to adorn the doctrine of God their Saviour, by the virtues of a sober, righteous, and godly life. 'These,' as I find stated in my church record, 'These are the fruits of a revival of religion in this town last summer. Rev. Asahel Nettleton, was apparently instrumental of great good in that season of refreshing from the presence of the Lord. May the Lord reward him for his labors of love; and may we as a church, be more humble and prayerful; and may God in his sovereign mercy continue to shed down his divine influence here.'

"You ask, 'what were the characteristics of his preaching, and in what did its chief excellencies consist?' I answer, He held no protracted meetings; nor did he adopt any new measures apparently for effect. His labors consisted principally in preaching the Word. He sometimes appointed what was called an inquiry meeting. At such meetings, he manifested an almost instinctive discernment of character; and his remarks, in accordance with it, were sometimes attended with a powerful effect. In his preaching, his humility was apparent to all. He was, I believe, eminently a man of prayer. That he entered the pulpit, or the inquiry meeting directly from the 'mount of communion' with his Maker, no one would readily doubt, who was witness of the holy calm, the indescribable, the almost unearthly solemnity and earnestness of his manner. His countenance was peculiarly expressive, his demeanor was dignified, and his voice was at times very melodious. The joy with which his heart seemed to be filled by a contemplation of the love of Jesus, in giving his life a ransom for sinners, marked his preaching, and imparted an unction and uncommon energy to his eloquence. When he spake of the glories of heaven, it was, almost, as if he had been there himself. When he made his appeals to the sinner, he made them with a directness, which placed before him, as in a mirror, his utterly lost state. It seemed at times, as if he was about to uncover the bottomless pit, and to invite the ungodly to come and listen to the groans of the damned; and then, drinking deeply of the spirit of his master when he wept over Jerusalem, to urge them to flee from the wrath to come, with an expression of countenance, which it is not in my power to describe. Many who came with a skeptical and caviling spirit to hear him, had their attention arrested at once to the great truths communicated by him, and at the close of the meeting, were anxiously inquiring what they should do to be saved. The success attending his preaching, seemed, in short, to be a plain and clear illustration of all the distinguishing doctrines of the gospel, by a humble, devout, praying, unpretending man, constrained to his duty by the love of Christ.

"The influence of the revival upon the interests of the church in this and other places, was very happy, and is plainly to be seen, especially in regard to the faith once delivered to the saints, up to this time. The tendency of Dr. Nettleton's preaching, and indeed of all his labors here and elsewhere, as far as I have learned in regard to them, has been to establish the churches in the faith and order of the gospel, and to strengthen the hands of every clergyman with whom he labored. I never heard that any minister, among whose people Dr. Nettleton labored, ever expressed any regret that he had been with them. On the contrary, when I at any time meet with a minister who formerly had assistance from Dr. Nettleton, especially in a season of revival, he never fails to express great respect for him, and unfeigned gratitude for the benefit derived to *him* and *his people* from his labors."9

THE REVIVAL IN LEE, MASSACHUSETTS

God was working wonders through the great evangelist in these last two years of full labor and strength! The "spiritual sparks" of the Fourth of July revival at Heman Humphrey's church in Pittsfield, blew over to neighboring towns. It was as if God was using Asahel Nettleton as His *firelighter* throughout eastern New England. Another mighty move of grace occurs immediately after the revival at Pittsfield; this revival, transpired in the town of Lee, Massachusetts, at the church of Rev. Dr. Alvan Hyde. The huge white wooden structure can still be visited today. Although the original building was destroyed by fire, it was rebuilt to the exact proportions as in Nettleton's day. The church in Lee faces the town's green square where community gatherings and festivals were held. It is a picturesque setting and one can easily imagine Nettleton at the doorway of the church, greeting visitors. Notice from the following story of the revival in Lee, how Rev. Hyde's congregation is wise in inviting the revival fires to blow by holding a day of *fasting and prayer*. Congregations and ministers of a different time, understood the God of the Bible and His movements among them and proportionately humbled themselves before the Almighty. It is to Dr. Hyde's account of the revival in Lee we now turn:

"In the summer of 1821, there was an evident increase of solemnity in the church and congregation, and some individuals were known to be anxious for their souls. This appearance continued for several weeks, under the same means of grace which the people had long enjoyed, but none were found who rejoiced in hope. The church often assembled together for prayer, and in the month of August we observed a day of fasting and prayer. The meeting-house was well filled, and deep solemnity pervaded the congregation. The hearts of many seemed to 'burn within them', and there were increasing indications from the rising cloud 'of abundance of rain'. We began to hear from one and another a new language, the language of submission to God.

"At this interesting crisis, the Rev. Asahel Nettleton spent a few days with us. He preached five sermons to overflowing assemblies, and his labours were remarkably blessed. The Spirit of God came down upon us, 'like a rushing mighty wind'. Conversions were frequent, sometimes several in a day, and the change in the feelings and views of the subjects was wonderful. At the suggestion of Mr. Nettleton, I now instructed what are called inquiring meetings, as I found them to be convenient, were continued through this revival; and I have ever since made use of them, as occasion required, sometimes weekly, for many months in succession ...

"The work of the Holy Spirit in 1821 was continued to us until the close of the year. Many young heads of families, and others in the midst of life were the happy subjects. The church received an accession of eighty-six persons as fruits of this revival."[10]

THE REVIVAL AT LITCHFIELD, MASSACHUSETTS

The great evangelist was to participate in yet *another revival* before the close of the year. In September of 1821, Nettleton's close friend, Lyman Beecher, invited him to take his pulpit for a few months while he traveled for his health (we find this amusing, since the exhausted Nettleton was the one who needed rest!). The revival fires were still burning at the close of 1821 as we see from the following details of Nettleton's movements in revival activity, as provided by his friend and biographer, Bennet Tyler:

"... then in the early part of September, repaired to Litchfield. He had labored much in Litchfield at different times previously, in connection with the Rev. Dr. Beecher; but as it was before he began to keep a journal, I am unable to fix the dates. His labors at these different periods were highly appreciated both by Dr. Beecher and his people, and were evidently blessed to the salvation of many souls. In the autumn of 1821, Dr. Beecher was obliged to suspend his labors, and travel for his health. At this time Mr. Nettleton supplied his pulpit from the beginning of September, till the middle of January, 1822. When he commenced his labors, he found things in a very unpromising state. A bad state of feeling existed in the church, and great spiritual apathy pervaded the congregation. But it was not long before things began to assume a new aspect. The church seemed to awake out of sleep, and to mourn over their backslidings. A spirit of prayer was poured out upon the people of God; and sinners began to inquire what they must do to be saved.

"Soon after the revival commenced, some events occurred which he feared would divert the attention of the people from the great concerns of the soul. One was a cattle show, and another a military review. But this unhappy result was prevented by the blessing of God on his prudent management. He particularly feared the effect of the military review on certain young men who were military officers, and whose minds were seriously impressed. He requested those individuals to meet him on the morning of that day, at the early dawn. They came. He told them that he was convinced that the Spirit of God was striving with them, but he feared that their impressions might be dissipated by the bustle of that day. He warned them to be on their guard—to refrain from all vain and trifling conversation, and especially to avoid tasting a drop of ardent spirits. He then affectionately and earnestly commended them to God in prayer. This timely warning had the desired effect.

"The following extract of a letter of his, dated Litchfield, Oct. 15, 1821, shows the state of the revival at that date.

'I have attended many meetings of late, and some of them crowded and awfully solemn. More attend meetings than can crowd into the lower part of the meeting house—more it is said, than usually meet on the Sabbath. I think I may say, there is great solemnity throughout the place. A number are in deep distress of soul—some of them men of influence. About fourteen are rejoicing in hope. I have ventured to appoint one meeting of inquiry. About one hundred attended, but they were not all under conviction. We are truly in an interesting state, trembling between hope and fear. I wish I had time to tell you a number of anecdotes about us in Litchfield.'

"In another letter, written by him at New Haven, in March, 1822, he thus speaks of the revival at Litchfield.

'The number of hopeful converts is about seventy, of whom thirty-eight have made a profession of religion. There is much Christian feeling in that place, and the work is gradually advancing, as a joint letter from a number of the young converts has recently informed me.'" [11]

It is as if God was allowing His choice servant to experience all the revival he could, for the day would soon turn night for the evangelist, for in a matter of months he would contract the deadly typhus fever which would alter the rest of his life and labors. Yet one cannot but marvel at the years of 1820–1822, the "years of the right hand of the Most High" (Psalm 77:10).

Notes

1   Sherry Pierpont May, p. 86.
2   J. F. Thornbury, p. 119.
3   Heman Humphrey, *Revival Sketches*, p. 261.
4   Tyler, pp. 113–116.
5   Ibid. p. 118.
6   Noah Porter quoted in W. B. Sprague, *Lectures on Revivals* (Edinburgh: Banner of Truth Trust, 2007), pp. 304–307.
7   Bennet Tyler, pp. 131–134.
8   Ibid. pp. 135–136.
9   Ibid. pp. 137–139.
10   Rev. Alvan Hyde in W. B. Sprague, *Lectures on Revivals* (Edinburgh: Banner of Truth Trust), pp. 281–282.
11   Bennet Tyler, pp. 165–167.

During the fall of 1822 Nettleton became ill with typhus fever. For almost two years his activities were strictly limited and he did almost no preaching. During his convalescence he compiled an evangelical hymnal.

SHERRY PIERPONT MAY

16

1822: REVIVAL FIRES AND TYPHUS FEVER

The year 1822 would bear significance for the rest of Asahel Nettleton's life. It would be a year of fantastic usefulness as God's servant in revivals and the year in which he contracted typhus fever which nearly killed him, and left him a semi-invalid for life. Up to the year 1822, Nettleton had been in incessant revivals for *eleven years*. In fact, it was this tremendous labor of constant ministry which had taken a toll on his physical health. Asahel's constitution, never hardy, had been tested to its limits by incessant activity and neglect of proper rest. It was in this already weakened state with an immune system on the verge of a breakdown, that the evangelist caught the deadly typhus fever.

The remarks of Nettleton's close friend, Bennet Tyler, sum up the shock of the sudden and disabling disease, and a net is thrown over the long and amazing career of his labors:

> "For ten or eleven years Mr. Nettleton had been laboring almost constantly in revivals of religion. During this time, he preached, generally, three sermons on the Sabbath, and several during the week, besides spending much time in visiting from house to house, and conversing with individuals on the concerns of their souls. How he could endure such accumulated labors, was a mystery to many. Undoubtedly his constitution was so impaired by these labors, as to render it impossible to recover from the shock of disease by which he was attacked in 1822. It pleased God in the fall of that year, to arrest his labors, and to lay him on a bed of sickness."[1]

However, in early 1822 the great evangelist was found laboring in *still-burning* revivals. In January of that year he returned to New Haven, Connecticut, after a year's absence. He preached in both the bustling city of New Haven, and at his Alma Mater, Yale College with great success. It seems he had a last burst of energy which thrust him into continuous labor, preaching more than twenty times in God-attended revivals! A letter of Asahel, dated March 20th, 1822 reveals he was at New Haven amidst remarkable scenes of revival. Little did he realize that his comet-like ministry was about to burn out, and rarely resemble former times, for his health would be permanently broken.

In this letter, Nettleton relates his immense preaching schedule:

> "After more than a year's absence, I have come again to New Haven. In the first place, I made an appointment exclusively for young converts, in a spacious ball-room, where we used to hold meetings of inquiry. Though the evening was dark and muddy, about three hundred assembled. Here we called to mind, the sighs, and sobs, and songs, and joys that are past—scenes never to be forgotten. And when I spoke of three of their number, who used to mingle their tears and joys with theirs on that floor but whose faces we should see no more, for they had gone triumphantly to rest, it was truly melting. We knelt, and wept, and prayed together.

> "I did not intend to tarry long in this place; but I have preached more than twenty times, and attended a number of inquiry meetings—at one, one hundred and sixty attended. There are seventeen recently rejoicing in hope, and five of them are students in college."[2]

This glimpse of the last outburst of robust activity in the evangelist's life is interesting, even more so, since it follows on the heels of the non-stop year of 1821! Asahel was no super-human and his frame is now *worn out*. We note from the following:

> "There seemed to be, however, little opportunity for rest. In the spring of 1822 he was active in building up the converts at New Haven, reminiscing with them about the 'never to be forgotten' revival days of recent memory. In May he began preaching in the northern part of the state, in the vicinity of Somers, Connecticut, just southeast of Springfield, Massachusetts. His ministry in this area was among the most fruitful of his entire life. A revival began at Somers, spreading in a generally southeasterly direction to other towns such as Tolland, North Coventry, Montville and Millington. All told, the conversions in this area numbered about thirteen hundred."[3]

Correspondence from Nettleton relates the revival activity in which he labored, and in it he details how God has been remarkably blessing the eastern part of the state of Connecticut:

> "The revival of religion in the eastern part of the State of Connecticut, has, perhaps, never been more interesting, than within a few weeks past. I propose to give you the outlines of this work, from the commencement, down to the present. It has heretofore been a common remark among Christians, that revivals have been much less frequent, and less powerful in the eastern, than in the western part of this state. Most of these churches, in years past, have been favored with seasons more or less reviving, but never with such a general and powerful refreshing from the presence of the Lord. This work commenced in Somers, June, 1822; and has continued increasing and spreading like fire, from house to house, and from heart to heart, with more or less power and rapidity, until the present moment. The following towns are contiguous, and have shared in one extensive revival.

> "In Somers, one hundred and fifty have hopefully been made the subjects of divine grace. In South Wilbraham, one hundred. In Tolland, one hundred and thirty. In North Coventry, one hundred and twenty. In South Coventry, North Mansfield, and South Mansfield, about one hundred in each. In Columbia, forty. In

Lebanon, ninety. In Goshen, thirty. In Bozah, between sixty and seventy. In Montville, ninety. In Chaplin, fifty.

"The work has recently commenced, and is advancing with power in Hampton, and within a few weeks, fifty or more are rejoicing in hope. Within a few weeks past, the Spirit of God had descended with overwhelming power in Millington, and Colchester. In the former place, about seventy, and in the latter, sixty are already rejoicing in hope. They have never before witnessed the like, in rapidity, power, and extent. In the above cluster of towns, all contiguous, more than thirteen hundred souls have hopefully experienced a saving change, in the Congregational churches, since the commencement of this revival; and of these more than eight-hundred have already made a profession of religion.

"In Chatham, also, the work is interesting; about seventy are rejoicing in hope, and fifty or more have made a public profession. In Hampton, Colchester and Millington, many are now anxious for their souls, and inquiring, *what must we do to be saved?*

"New instances of conviction, and of hopeful conversion, are daily occurring in these towns. The prospect of the continuance and spread of this work, is as favorable now, as at any period, if not more so. The Lord hath done great things for Zion, whereof we are glad, and let all her friends humbly rejoice, and bow and give thanks and exalt his name together."[4]

TYPHUS FEVER

Early October, 1822, was a dreadful time for New England—a widespread outbreak of typhus fever hit the land. Disease was a constant black cloud which drifted over New England in both the eighteenth and nineteenth centuries. In the eighteenth century the main disease to be feared was smallpox, Jonathan Edwards died from a smallpox vaccine. In the nineteenth century, the disease of typhus fever was rampant, striking unwary families and diminishing their households.

Asahel Nettleton was infected with typhus fever in October, 1822, as is seen from the following:

"October of 1822 arrived, a fateful month for Asahel Nettleton. It found him preaching, visiting, conducting inquiry meetings; his customary toil in the revival harvest fields for about ten years. That such activity put a tremendous strain upon his physical endurance cannot be doubted. The rewards he received during these incredible days of divine visitation far exceeded the heavy burdens he bore, but his schedule appeared herculean to others. As his biographer remarked, 'How he could endure such accumulated labors, was a mystery to many.' The stage was set for a breakdown, and that disaster come on 5th October.

"It was on this date that he visited a family in South Wilbraham, Massachusetts, where there was a case of typhus fever. Like yellow fever, which probably killed his father, typhus occasionally reached epidemic proportions in some communities in those days and was still an unsolved mystery. By the 16th of the month Asahel began to have the tell-tale symptoms, which included high fever, headache, and rash. Suspecting that he had contracted the disease, he went to the closest place to a home

he had, the parsonage at Bolton, residence of his life long friend Philander Parmele.
Here he was sure to find a welcome.

"He daily grew worse, and by 26th October he was completely confined to his
bed, complaining of 'head-ache, sore bones, difficulty in breathing, cold feet, heat
sweats, and a very great degree of dullness.' On the 27th, his friends sent for a doctor,
who diagnosed a case of typhus. The mortality rate of this disease for his age was in
the neighbourhood of thirty percent about this time, so understandably he and his
friends feared for his life. He was bedridden for about forty days, desperately ill much
of the time."[5]

At Hartford Seminary, in Hartford, Connecticut, is the hand-written
diary of Asahel Nettleton, detailing these dreadful days. It is in a little
blue folder and its brief entries are both poignant and terrifying. Most of
the entries were written with a trembling hand. The diary records his
terrible suffering during his sickness as well as the death of his best friend,
Philander Parmele, who contracted the disease from Nettleton and
quickly died. The diary also records the generous monetary gifts from
friends, as Nettleton was financially destitute at this time. Here now is
that diary in its entirety:

ASAHEL NETTLETON'S TYPHUS FEVER DIARY
Union August 5th 1818
Came to this place, Board at Mr Joseph Moor's
August 16. Came to Mr Eaton's
Sept 7. Came to Capt. Snell's.
18. Left Union & came to Rocky Hill
30. Left R. Hill, & came to Bolton——
Oct. 2. Came to Union. Capt Snell's
Oct 15th Left Capt Snell's
16. Came to Maj Lausons——
Oct 27th Left Union & came to Ashford
1819 Bolton
July 1. Started for Ballston. Tarried at Mr Barletts of Wintonbury.
2. Tarried at Sheffield
3. Arrived at Troy Mr Seymour
4. Sabb. Preached in 1 evening
5. Arrived at Saratoga Springs
Sickness in Bolton
October 5th 1822. This morning visited M S. in Wilbraham before
breakfast & took the typhus fever.
16th. This morning entered the hack in Th. & felt unwell—it was the

commencement of the typhus fever. Preached in Wethersfield in the evening.

26th. Grew more & more unwell up to this date—Head-ache Sore bones—Some difficulty in breathing—Cold feet—High swets & a great degree of dullness were the symptoms This day very sick & confined to the bed.

27th Sent for Dr. North—& for the first time it was ascertained that my complaint was the typhus fever—but it was concealed from me; tho' I suspected it.

Nov. 10th. This evening was the most trying time of my sickness.

Great difficulty in breathing—

Called the Physician. Took brandy freely.

14th This day Br Parmele wrote my will.

Was confined to my bed nearly 40 days. Unable to sit up or stand etc

Dec. 9th Was carried in my bed to Esqr Alvords.

27th Br Parmele died.

Presents received in my sickness

Somers	$52:20
New Haven	70:00
Tolland	26:42
Ellington	21:25
Litchfield	35:00
Mary Ann & Francis Devenport	50:00
Female Society in Andover Mar. 25	10:00
Coventry	9:53
Newington	10:62
Sarah Wetmore	5:00
Tolland (by Stearns)	13:00
Wilbraham Feb. 28th	8:00
Farmington May 6.	14:81
Mrs Grisvold Oxford	1:00
Pittsfield May 17th	$20:00
North Killingworth	2:00
Pittsfield	$20:00
Sept. 2. Sarah Wetmore	$10:00
Revival Society	15:00
	401:40

1823

June 3. Embarked at New Haven for Machias

7th Arrived at Machias in evening

8. Sabb. heard Rev. Abraham Jackson preach from 2 Chron. 12, 14. &
Tarried over night at the house of Rev. Marshfield Steele.

11. Rode to Lubec, 24 miles, & was much fatigued—Visited Rev.
Jonathan Bigelow—he & Mr Jackson & Steele the only Presbyterian
ministers within 70 miles of this place.

Machias—

13. Returned to Machias—

15. Preached P.M. No. 11.

16. Preached in the evening Acts 2.37. Christian Mirror—Ed. by Asa
Rand Portland Maine.

Machias is in the County of Washington.[6]

The brief diary entry which reads: "27th Br Parmele died." is stark and
foreboding. No one will ever know the personal trial and grief Asahel
Nettleton suffered on that date, realizing that his dear friend had
contracted the disease from him and *died*, leaving a widow behind. A
year later we see that Nettleton is out in itinerancy once again, preaching
occasionally and being able to ride a horse for twenty four miles! But
after the bout with the typhus fever, Asahel Nettleton would never again
enjoy the tremendous, incessant seasons of revival activity. He would
participate in revivals in future years, one particularly powerful in the
South, in Virginia, but his labors, from this time forward, were greatly
limited because of his poor health. We see from the following
comments:

"The diary entry for December 27th says simply: 'Brother Parmele died.'
Philander Parmele was Nettleton's closest friend. They were boys together in
Killingworth and were converted about the same time. They were at Yale together,
and we know from the letter which Nettleton wrote to him[7] about the use of
'means' by the unregenerate that they worked through many theological positions
together and sought each other's advice. They kept closely in touch with each other
during Nettleton's early travels and it was to Parmele's home in Bolton that
Nettleton usually retired when he needed a retreat. Thus we are not surprised that
when Nettleton became ill, he went to Bolton to convalesce. How difficult it must
have been then, when Parmele became ill—and finally, on December 27th, died
from the fever. Nettleton wrote to Miss Lydia Warren, in South Wilbraham,
Massachusetts, on March 4th, that he had gone through a great deal with his own
illness, 'But most trying of all,—was parting with our friend Mr. Parmele. Borne the
same year in the same town—anxious for his soul, and professed religion at the same
time with myself, he was my nearest friend ...'

"Nettleton never fully recovered from this illness. In later years there were cruel
references to his health, accusations that the fever had affected his mind, and that he
was never mentally himself. It is true that his health was never again robust, but the
positions he took on controversial subjects in later years were not the result of a
deranged mind—they were the same positions which he held prior to 1822.

"He preached only rarely for two years after his sickness. He went to Machias,

Maine, and Montreal during June, 1823, with his friend Dr. McAuley and some others. He hoped that such a trip would be relaxing and would hasten his recovery, but he was still too weak. He wrote to Mrs. Parmele in August from Greenwich, Connecticut, that the trip had been too much for him. 'It is more than 400 miles from New York,' he wrote. 'On our return we came to Saratoga Springs. I was quite sick, and by the advice of friends, I was persuaded to remain there a fortnight, during which time I recruited in some measure.'

"His biographer writes that even after the two years of near inactivity, he was only able to keep a limited schedule. Usually he preached only once a Sunday, occasionally twice, but 'without attending many extra meetings, or devoting much time to visiting from house to house,' yet he continued to travel widely and to be effective in revivals for another fifteen years."[8]

Notes

1   Tyler, p. 148.
2   Ibid. p. 142.
3   Thornbury, pp. 128–129.
4   Tyler, pp. 143–147.
5   Thornbury, p. 129.
6   Nettleton Papers, Hartford Seminary Library, Hartford, Connecticut.
7   See chapter entitled, "Nettleton's Letters", Letter #1.
8   Sherry Pierpont May, p. 91.

Come, Thou Fount of Every Blessing

Words: Robert Robinson, 1758; Adapted by Margaret Clarkson

Music: Asahel Nettleton, 1825.

So reads a hymn book entry. It is a remarkable fact that Asahel Nettleton was a music lover and frequently made music a prominent part of his revivals. So it is no wonder that we learn he is the composer of the music for one of the Church's greatest hymns!

E. A. JOHNSTON

Asahel Nettleton's own copy of "Village Hymns for Social Worship"

VILLAGE HYMNS FOR SOCIAL WORSHIP

Asahel Nettleton was never one for much inactivity! Therefore, we are not surprised to learn that during his two year period of convalescing he is busily occupied in compiling a hymn book for churches in New England. The hymn book, *Village Hymns for Social Worship* was published in 1825. Hymns were integral to the revivals which Nettleton held and played a prominent role in them. In the oil painting of Nettleton, he is seen holding this little volume of hymns, which had become vastly popular by the time of the portrait. At Hartford Seminary, this very volume of hymns, with his name on the flyleaf is among his personal papers. *Village Hymns* was his only published book, for Nettleton did not have a pen ministry; his labors were solely engaged in winning souls.

Asahel Nettleton grew wealthy with the popularity and success of *Village Hymns*, which outsold any other hymn book of his day. Its sales would only be eclipsed fifty years later by the Moody-Sankey hymn books of their day. The hymn book was unique in filling a void at that time, this was a desperate need for a selection of hymns for times of revivals of religion. To Nettleton's dismay, he was unable to compile (to his satisfaction) a collection of revival hymns which reflected the various stages of a revival: the majesty of God; awakening to sin, conviction of sin; repentance; regeneration; rejoicing in new-found religion. There were very few hymns of this nature in existence at this time period. Even though he was disappointed in the availability of such "revival hymns", he used what selections he could find and arranged them appropriately to reflect these stages of revival. Nettleton wrote the preface to the original edition and we quote from it now:

"With great satisfaction and pleasure have I often heard the friends of the Redeemer express their unqualified attachment to the sacred poetry of Dr. Watts.

Most cordially do I unite with them in hope, that no selection of hymns which has ever yet appeared may be suffered to take the place of his inimitable productions.

"Deficiencies, however, he unquestionably has. Numerous have been the attempts to supply them; but, hitherto, the judicious have been constrained to regret, that these attempts have succeeded only in part. Whether the book here published will add something to that supply, is submitted to the decision of the religious community.

"The compiler does not overlook the valuable labors of those who have preceded him in this department; while he concurs in the opinion, very generally adopted by his brethren in the ministry, that the various benevolent operations, and especially the prevalence of revivals, which are so characteristic of the present day, demand a New Selection of Hymns.

"In the year 1820, the General Association of Connecticut appointed a committee to devise measures for the prosperity of religion within their limits. I well remember, that at a meeting of this committee, the first item proposed was a New Selection of Hymns. Four years have nearly elapsed, and nothing has been done pursuant to their appointment.

"When, in the providence of God, I had the happiness of spending a short season, as a laborer for Christ, within the limits of the Albany Presbytery, the call for such a work in that region; and, as I learned from the most respectable sources, very extensively in the West and South, was not less imperious and pressing, than in districts where I had been more particularly conversant. In personal experience, and discoveries of this description, originated the resolution to undertake the work. The compilation here presented is the result. The task has occupied my attention much of the time for nearly two years. Especially has it cheered and comforted me, during the long continued retirement to which a severe sickness subjected me.

"The book, whatever may be its defects, is now most affectionately presented 'To Zion's friends and mine.' I anticipated difficulties, but am fully persuaded, that whoever undertakes a work of this kind will have to encounter many unforeseen embarrassments in the execution. I had hoped to find, in the style of genuine poetry, a greater number of hymns adapted to the various exigencies of a revival. Laborious research has, however, led me to conclude, that not many such compositions are in existence.

"This volume contains a number of original hymns, which I esteem a valuable accession.——To their authors, whose signatures are prefixed, or at their own request omitted, I tender my sincere thanks. I have obtained permission to insert a few of the originals from the Hartford Selection. These, though already familiar to many, will yet be consulted with feelings of new interest, when associated with the names of Strong and Steward. The reader will find, inserted in this volume, a few of the psalms and hymns to which it is designed as a supplement. But he is desired to recollect, that Dwight's edition of Watts is in extensive circulation. In his edition, some of Watts' psalms and hymns were omitted; and those which I have inserted are principally of this character.

"I have consulted all the authors and Collections of hymns to which I could gain access. I have availed myself of their labors; and have spent much time in attempts to remodel many of the materials thus collected. In all cases, excepting the hymns of established reputation, wherever abridgments or alterations were deemed conducive to the design of this volume, they have been made without hesitation.

"There is a numerous class of hymns which have been sung with much pleasure and profit in seasons of revival, and yet are entirely destitute of poetic merit. Some of my brethren, acquainted with this fact, will probably be disappointed when they find, that so many have been omitted. Others, unacquainted with their beneficial effects at such seasons, would exclude the whole of this class. I am satisfied from observation, as well as from the nature itself of such hymns, that they must be ephemeral. They should be confined to seasons of revival: and even here, they ought to be introduced with discretion; for on this, their principal utility must depend. A book, consisting chiefly of hymns for revivals, however important in its place, would be utterly unfit for the ordinary purposes of devotion—as prescriptions, salutary in sickness, are laid aside on the restoration of health.

"With respect to the hymns of a lower grade, I fully unite in the opinion of a much respected correspondent: 'That the safest course is to leave them generally out—that the warm heart of a young convert will take a strong hold, and that with pleasure and profit too, of many things, from which, in a more ripened state, he would derive neither.'

"After selecting a hymn, my first object has been to bring it into a form best adapted to be read or sung in meetings for religious purposes. With this view, some of them have been divided, and others reduced to a stricter unity of thought.

"With respect to the arrangement, it has cost me much labor. After all, I have not been able entirely to satisfy my own mind. I am aware that many of the hymns placed under different heads, might have been arranged under the same; and yet all these heads seemed indispensable. The Christian and the Convert, for example, might have been included under one head. But there are many things peculiar to the commencement of the Christian life, that it was deemed highly proper to collect a number suited to his case, and place them under the eye of the young convert.

"This part of my employment has been highly delightful; and I cannot but indulge the hope, that among the many thousands who have commenced their Christian course in the recent revivals, not a few of them will find this volume a pleasant and profitable companion on their way to the heavenly Zion. The character of some of the hymns is such, that with equal propriety they might have been differently arranged. I have, therefore, distributed them under the several heads where I thought them most needed—recollecting that the intrinsic value of the hymn was not at all affected by the page which it might occupy. Where the title of a hymn is omitted, it will be found in the next preceding, or in the running title. Tunes adapted to most of the particular metres will be found in Zion's Harp, a small collection of Music designed to accompany this volume.

"The compiler has only to add his grateful acknowledgments that this humble effort has met with such an extensive and welcome reception, and for the many tokens already received, that his labor has not been in vain."[1]

Asahel Nettleton makes reference, in his Preface, to 'the many thousands who have commenced their Christian course in the recent revivals'; this mass of people would become the primary audience who would purchase the hymn book. The churches of New England were anticipating such a collection and scrambled to get copies, it went through many reprints and initially sold thousands of volumes. We are thankful to the efforts of William C. Nichols and International Outreach, Inc. for again making this volume available, after it has so long been out of print. Regarding the reprinting of the hymn book we have the following:

> "The first edition of *Village Hymns for Social Worship* was published in Hartford, Connecticut in 1824. It was designed to be used as a supplement to the immensely popular psalms and hymns of Isaac Watts. Asahel Nettleton felt there was a great need for a new hymnal wherein hymns expressed the hearts of sinners under awakening influences, conviction of sin, and also reflected the heart of the new convert …

> "Hymnals in Nettleton's day were usually published in a text only format. Tune books containing collections of tunes for sacred music were published separately. Nettleton made use of these tune books in recommending at least two different tunes for each hymn in *Village Hymns*. Tune books such as *Templi Carmina* and *Musica Sacra* contain many of the tunes Nettleton selected. Nettleton also published a companion tune book to *Village Hymns* entitled *Zion's Harp*. It contained particular metre tunes which were generally not found as easily in the tune books of the time.

> "Nettleton drew his hymns from a variety of sources. Nearly 60 of the hymns of John Newton are included, largely, if not wholly taken from Newton's *Olney Hymns*. Close to 50 of the hymns of Isaac Watts are included along with hymns by William Cowper, Philip Doddridge, Samuel Davies, Timothy Dwight, Augustus Toplady, Charles Wesley, and Martin Luther. Some of the hymns were also written by friends of Nettleton like Abbie Hyde, the wife of a Congregational minister in Connecticut, and by others who preferred to remain anonymous."[2]

In *Village Hymns for Social Worship* the lives of George Whitefield and Asahel Nettleton again cross paths. This connection between Whitefield and Nettleton must not go unnoticed. The hymn, "Come Thou Fount Of Every Blessing" has a singular connection linking the two great evangelists. The author of the text for this hymn was Robert Robinson, of whom we have the following interesting story:

> "Robert Robinson had always been prone to wander. Apprenticed to a barber at fourteen, he spent more time reading and playing with friends than cutting hair. Then, still a teen, he went to a George Whitefield meeting, intending to ridicule it—and instead was converted. After his apprenticeship was over, Robinson went into the ministry. He wrote this hymn at the age of twenty-three as he served at the Calvinistic Methodist Church in Norfolk, England.

> "Late in life, Robinson did stray from the faith. Once in a stagecoach, he sat by a lady who was reading a hymnbook. She showed him "Come, Thou Fount," saying how wonderful it was. He tried to change the subject, but couldn't. Finally he said, 'Madam, I am the unhappy man who wrote that hymn many years ago, and I would give a thousand worlds to enjoy the feelings I had then.'"[3]

We must give Asahel Nettleton credit for his great labor on *Village Hymns* amidst his darkest days, as he convalesced from his bout of typhus fever. Evidently, his labors on the hymn book were therapy to his soul and the success of the book became one of his biggest joys in life. Sales from the book supported him for the rest of his life, allowing him to purchase a farm and large home, and contribute financially to the founding of the Theological Institute at East Windsor, Connecticut (later to become Hartford Seminary).

Notes

1   *Village Hymns for Social Worship*, compiled by Asahel Nettleton (Ames: International Outreach, Inc., reprint 1997), Preface.
2   Ibid. William C. Nichols, p. 1–2.
3   *The One Year Book of Hymns* (Wheaton: Tyndale House, Publishers, 1995), devotion for "September 19".

We must assert one other truth in connexion with these doctrines of grace. Most assuredly they are fitted to lead a man and a minister of Christ (witness Dr. Nettleton) to be zealous of good works, and zealous for souls,—bent upon God's glory, and bent upon the salvation of men.

ANDREW BONAR

18

RETURN TO SERVICE

Asahel Nettleton's heart thrilled within him when he realized, by God's good grace, he could again travel and preach. He re-entered the field slowly, exercising caution not to overwork himself. Rather than preaching several times a day as in former times, he preached once or twice a week. Alas, this was not to last. It is not long before we find the great evangelist pushing himself to the limit in a glorious revival in 1824. His labors are so intense that he once again becomes bedridden, an invalid who can "not visit, nor be visited." We catch up with his revival labors with the following narrative:

"In the autumn of 1824, an interesting revival commenced under his preaching in Bethlem. He continued in that place, assisting the pastor, the Rev. Mr. Langdon, who was sick, until his strength failed, and he was obliged to suspend his labors.

"In a letter to Mrs. Parmele, of Bolton, dated New York, April 18th, 1825 he says, 'The occasion of my first visit to Bethlem, was to see brother Langdon who was sick, and who had not preached for six months. He was thinking about asking a dismission when I arrived; but he postponed it. I preached for him two or three months. As many as eighty persons assembled at his house occasionally, at a meeting of inquiry, of whom about forty are rejoicing in hope. The burden of anxiety on my mind became so great that I could endure it no longer, and so I left them. Having some business which could be done in this city better than any where else, I accepted an invitation to spend the winter and spring here in retirement. I am so much retired, that my friends here say, I will not visit, nor be visited; and yet I have spent three-fourths of my time and strength in receiving visits.'

"In the spring of 1825, he preached considerably and with success, in Brooklyn, L. I. In the summer of 1825, he preached in Taunton. Here his labors were made effectual to the conviction and conversion of sinners. The parish in which he preached, was at that time destitute of a pastor.

"In the fall of the same year, he commenced laboring with the Rev. Mr. Cobb, in another parish in Taunton. In a letter to a friend, dated Taunton, Dec. 26th, 1825, he says: 'The state of things in this society has become quite interesting of late. Meetings are crowded and solemn as eternity. A number have called to see us in deep distress of soul. Some of them told us that they received their first impressions down at the green last summer. The fire was already kindled, and has recently burst into a flame in this part of the town. The number of inhabitants in this society, is comparatively small; and yet, last Saturday evening, we met about sixty in the meeting of inquiry. About thirty are rejoicing in hope. Of these, some are youth of the first respectability, and four or five men of influence. Old professors of religion tell us they never saw such a time before."[1]

It is important at this time to pause for comment. A rare document is included in his *Memoirs* which is provided by the Rev. Cobb. It so happened that Nettleton, after he wore himself out from too much preaching, became an inmate of Cobb's home. It is Cobb's personal observations of Nettleton which grip our attention, for they offer us a unique look at Ashael's ministry at this notable time, when he has just returned to service. What makes this account so unique is the picture of a semi-invalid absorbed in the midst of revival activity, and we catch a glimpse of Nettleton's labors, from the perspective of Rev. Cobb, and we are *amazed* that a sick man can accomplish so much. We can only imagine how *full* and *Herculean* were the great evangelist's labors *before* his bout with typhus fever! In this regard, Nettleton resembled Whitefield: both men labored for God with physically wrecked constitutions. These two Titans did more in poor health than healthy ministers performed their entire ministries! Rev. Cobb writes:

"Brother Nettleton came to Taunton in the summer of 1825, and the Trinitarian church in this town being destitute, by the decease of their beloved pastor, the Rev. Chester Isham, he labored two months and a half in that congregation. The prospect of a general and powerful revival of religion was very fair. About thirty converts were the fruit of his labors among that people. In this state of things, a candidate for settlement was procured, who subsequently became their pastor. Brother Nettleton retired, and came to live in my family for the first of October, and continued with me till the middle of January, 1826.

"There had for weeks previous been a solemn stillness in my congregation, and many had been specially awakened, though they had kept their impressions to themselves. When brother Nettleton commenced his labors, the revival immediately became manifest, and converts were multiplied almost daily during his stay.

"His sermons were clear, sound, able, full of thought, direct and simple, with unity of design. He seemed to be destined to be understood. He enlisted the hearts and hands of all the church, and especially the aged members—our fathers who were well informed, and who had borne the burden and the heat of the day. It was surprising to see what overpowering influence his kindness, devotion and faithfulness had upon all, old and young, saints and sinners. In this state of things, there seemed to be a very bright prospect of a glorious harvest. It was manifest that brother Nettleton had ready access to every conscience. As the revival progressed, he preached more and more closely and doctrinally. 'The great truths of the gospel,' were the weapons of his warfare, and were wielded with a spirit and an energy, which the people were unable to gainsay or resist. He was remarkably clear and forcible in his illustrations of the sinner's total depravity, and his utter inability to procure salvation by unregenerate works, or any *desperate efforts*. He showed the sinner that his unregenerate prayers for a new heart, his impenitent seeking, striving and knocking would be of no avail; and that absolute, unconditional submission to a sovereign God, was the first thing to be done. To this duty the sinner was urged immediately with great power and conclusiveness of argument.

"His visits among the people were frequent, but short and profitable. He entered immediately on the subject of the salvation of the soul, and the great importance of attending to it without delay. He did not customarily propound questions, and require answers, lest by this means he should turn the attention of sinners from their own wretched state, by leading them to think 'how they should reply to the minister.' He was so well acquainted with the human heart, that he seemed to have an intuitive perception of what was passing in the minds of those whom he was addressing. Thus he could so direct his conversation as to produce silence and self-condemnation, and confine their thoughts to their own lost and ruined state, sometimes remarking, 'You have no time to spend in conversation, before the salvation of the soul is secured.'

"When any indulged a hope which was not satisfactory, he would say, 'you had better give it up, and seek your salvation in earnest.' Well versed in all the doctrinal and experimental parts of the gospel; feeling deeply in his own heart the power of divine truth, he was qualified, beyond most, to judge of the character of other's experience; and though mild and conciliatory in his manner, he was faithful in his warnings against false hopes and spurious conversions. All selfish considerations in the concerns of the soul he discarded; and he never used any art or cunning to entrap, or produce commitment on the part of sinners. In the anxious circle he was short, direct in his remarks, concluding with a short and fervent prayer; directing his petitions solely to God, and not displaying eloquence, or seeking to fascinate the congregation. He seemed to lose sight of man, and to be absorbed in a sense of the divine presence.

"In his intercourse with people, he invariably produced favorable impressions on their minds in regard to their own pastor. He was not the *leader*, but only an *assistant* in the work. My people never before entertained and cherished so high, and so affectionate a regard for their pastor, as in this revival; and when he left us in the midst of it such was the effect of his course in this respect, there was scarcely a word of inquiry respecting brother Nettleton, and the work went on as though he were with us.

"In his daily habits in my family, he was constantly employed in searching the scriptures, or in conversation on religious topics—discussing doctrinal points, or matters relating to Christian experience. He was in this way very social, and an exceedingly agreeable companion.

"In his sermons, of which I heard sixty, he was, in manner, simple. He spoke with a clear voice—rather slow and hesitating at first, but gradually rising, till before the close, it was like a mighty torrent bearing down all before it. His eloquence was peculiar to himself, and consisted in conveying his own views and feelings to the minds of others. He never failed to impress his own ideas upon his hearers. As the revival became more interesting and powerful, he preached more doctrinally. He brought from his treasure the doctrines of total depravity, personal election, reprobation, the sovereignty of divine grace, and the universal government of God in working all things after the counsel of his own will. And these great doctrines did not *paralyze*, but greatly *promoted* the good work. Never had brother Nettleton such power over my congregation, as when he poured forth, in torrents, these awful truths. And at no time were converts multiplied so rapidly, and convictions and distress so deep, as when these doctrines were pressed home to the conscience. One evening, while our house of worship was filled to overflowing, he preached on the doctrine of election, and the people were so held by the power of truth, that when in the midst of the sermon, an intoxicated Universalist stepped within the door, and cried out with a stentorian voice, and with a horrid oath, 'that's a lie,' scarcely an eye was turned from the speaker towards the door.

"The above remarks will serve to give a general idea of the character of this revival. The work was still, and after the lapse of nineteen years, we are satisfied that the converts were generally, truly renewed in the spirit of their minds. They appear still to believe and love the doctrines of grace by which they were begotten to the hope of the gospel; and they have walked in newness of life.

"The influence which that precious revival exerted upon the church and society, has been good; and men who were not subjects of it, have been confirmed in their belief of the truth; and their convictions that revivals may be evidently the work of God, have been deep and lasting; and they speak of that season as a day of divine power and grace."[2]

Two letters exist which Asahel Nettleton wrote to the Rev. Cobb after that spectacular revival in Taunton, New York. The first letter is written from New York and dated, Feb. 6th, 1826, in it we learn how seriously ill the evangelist had become, at one juncture near death.

"My dear brother:—Yours of the 30th was received last Friday. It was truly refreshing to me, and to many of my friends. I cannot express the joy I felt on hearing the number and the names of some who entertained hope since you wrote last. The young converts and the anxious ones have scarcely been out of my mind since I left Taunton. Your letter contains more than I had reason to expect, but my mind will not rest satisfied without possessing the names of *all* who have found the Saviour. When I left you, brother Cobb, I did feel confident that the work would continue; but I did not think it would be so rapid. The family where I reside, have become so interested in the state of things with you, that they occasionally mention you and your people in their prayers. I think you will do well to note facts and dates as you pass along. You will find them useful hereafter. You will prepare an account for the Connecticut Observer, or some other paper, ere long. My heart has been with you ever since I left, and I was really in hopes of making you a short visit, at least. But I am sorry to say, I have been very sick with a fever, and for twelve hours, considered dangerous. I am surrounded with kind friends, and have every thing I could wish. I feel much better to-day, or I should not be able to write. The physician says, it will take some time for me to recover. I do hope you will give me some account from week to week of the state of things with you. I fear I shall not be able to labor any where during the two following months of inclement weather. If you cannot obtain help, and are unwell yourself, get together, if you only say *five words*, and pray five minutes. Meet the anxious once a week, if you can only pray with them. Give my love to all the young converts, and to all the anxious. Tell the latter, that I have not forgotten them——that they have scarcely been out of my mind since I saw them in the circle. They must never drop the subject. They will never have another such opportunity."

"On the 17th of March, a little more than a month after the date of the foregoing letter, he wrote again to Mr. Cobb, as follows:

'My dear brother—The lapse of time does by no means lessen the interest which I have felt in forming an acquaintance with yourself, and family, and the people of your charge. Not a day, or night has passed, since I parted with you, when those interesting scenes in which we mutually shared of *sorrows and joys that are past*, have not been fresh in my mind. Brother, these are scenes never to be forgotten. Other trifles may occupy our time and absorb the thought, and feelings of our heart for a season, and be forgotten, or remembered only with regret. But oh the scenes through which you are now passing, will follow you down through the track of time, and are forgotten *never*. I sympathize with you in all the sorrows and joys inseparable from the duties of a faithful pastor, at such a season. Now, more than ever, will be realized the weight of your responsibility.

> "Tis not a cause of small import,
>   The pastor's care demands;
> But what might fill an angel's heart,
>   It fill'd a Saviour's hands."

'I was pleased with the solemn stillness, the readiness to act, the apparent interest, and the decision of the members of your church. Were I present, I would affectionately say to them—be humble—be thankful for what God has already done—"keep the unity of the Spirit in the bond of peace"—pray *much* and *fervently* for the continued outpouring of the Spirit—do not feel satisfied with what has already been done. Brethren, pray for us—for your pastor, that the word of God may continue to have free course and be glorified.

'I cannot forget that interesting circle which used to meet to consult on the great concerns of the soul. Often have I fancied myself seated in the midst of that same circle—some weeping—and some rejoicing in hope. Their countenances are all familiar to my mind. With what feelings of affection and solemnity, and compassion, have I bowed together with you, my friends, around the throne of grace. While thus employed, often have I thought, shall we ever meet in heaven, around the throne of God and the Lamb? Shall we be companions forever, in that world of unclouded glory? The thoughts of such a meeting seem almost too much for such sinners as ourselves. But I know it is possible; and the vilest of sinners are *invited*. Some of the chief of sinners will repent, and be pardoned and saved; and why not such sinners as ourselves? Ah, none but sinners are saved, and some of the chief of sinners have already been saved. And I cannot but indulge the pleasing hope, that some—that many of your circle will meet in that world, where pilgrims meet to part no more. Let all those who indulge this heavenly hope themselves, come out from the world, and by their conduct and conversation, *declare plainly* that they seek a better country. You have yet to encounter the dangers of the wilderness, and you will need the whole armor of God. You who have long been companions in sin, will now become companions, helping one another on your way to the heavenly Zion.

> "Invite the strangers all around,
>   Your pious march to join;
> And spread the sentiments you feel,
>   Of faith and love divine."

'I cannot forget those anxious souls, who are still out of Christ. With joy have I heard the tidings of many, whom I left anxious for their souls. But I have the names of a number now before me, of whom no such tidings have been told. Where are they? Have they gone back to the world? My dear friends, if you have not already given your hearts to Christ, once more, from this far distant region, would I lift up my voice, and warn you by the worth of your souls, to flee from the wrath to come. I entreat you not to rest till you find rest in Christ. I have not forgotten you. I shall still remember you at the throne of grace, till the joyful tidings of your repentance have reached my ears; or the sorrowful tidings that you have dropped the subject of religion, and gone back to the world.

'Ever yours, in the best of bonds.'[3]

ANOTHER REVIVAL, IN JAMAICA, LONG ISLAND

In the winter of 1826 we find the 43 year-old evangelist amidst *yet* another revival. Asahel is in feeble health yet he drags his body around to labor for his beloved Savior. Nettleton visited Jamaica, Long Island, former scene of revival under Whitefield. A deep revival occurs under Nettleton's searching preaching, as we soon learn. Bennet Tyler records the event:

"In 1826, although in very feeble health, God made him the instrument of a great work of divine grace in Jamaica, L. I. He commenced his labors in that town, on the 24th of February, and continued to labor there until November. The people, when he first came among them, were very much divided; but under his judicious management, their divisions were healed. He preached on the Sabbath morning, and in the evening; omitting the usual afternoon exercise. And although he could not attend many extra meetings, or spend much time in visiting the people; yet there is reason to believe that God made him instrumental in the salvation of many souls.

"In his journal, under the date of May 8th, he speaks of fifty rejoicing in hope. In a letter to his friend, Mr. Cobb, of Taunton, dated July 13th, he says,

'My head, heart and hands are so full and health so feeble, that I have dispensed with every business, except what was absolutely indispensable. Since you left us, we have been much employed in listening to the relation of Christian experience by the young converts, preparatory to a public profession of religion. For a few weeks past, we have attended to little else. Had you been present, you would have been interested, if not delighted. On the 2nd of July, we held our communion, and seventy-two were added by profession, and three by letter. The assembly was full, and very solemn. Eighteen were baptized. Since that day, the revival has received a new impulse. Many were awakened, who have since come out joyful. It has often been observed, that it seemed like the judgment day. We have had but few meetings of inquiry since you left us. At our last, including young converts, there were about one hundred and forty. The work was never more interesting than at this time. A number of strangers from other towns have visited us, and have gone home rejoicing in hope, and others are in deep distress. If I continue long in this place, I think of appropriating one evening in the week to visiting a circle of strangers. You would be delighted with our assembly. We have long since been crowded out of our session house. Our meetings are now generally held in the church. Many professors, as well as young converts, say, we never knew what there was in religion before. "Old things are passed away, and all things are become new." Although a great proportion of this population are still strangers to the power of religion, yet there is little or no apparent opposition. Many who are left, are stuck with solemn awe, and for their own credit, are constrained to plead the cause of God. *"Then said they among the heathen, the Lord hath done great things for them."*

'I have by no means forgotten the young disciples in Taunton, nor those I left anxious for their souls. How I do long to see you, and all my friends in Taunton once more. I can only say, *Let your conversation be as becometh the gospel of Christ, that whether I come and see you, or else be absent, I may hear of your affairs, that ye stand fast in one spirit, with one mind, striving together for the faith of the gospel.*"

'Yours in the bonds of the Gospel.'"4

Notes

1   Tyler, pp. 153–155.
2   Ibid. pp. 155–158.
3   Ibid. p. 158–162.
4   Ibid. pp. 162–163.

In short, there is not a minister in New England whose character for piety and purity stands higher than does that of Mr. Nettleton.

LYMAN BEECHER

19

DEALING WITH SINNERS

One of the most peculiar aspects of Asahel Nettleton's ministry was *how* he dealt with sinners. His actions are completely opposite to modern-day evangelism and could even be called callous. However, his interactions with awakened sinners are a textbook for all serious students of evangelism! In the following account, we see how Nettleton dealt with an awakened sinner from the Jamaica revival previously mentioned. This account is given by a layman from the revival, and because of this fact and the uniqueness of the narration, we hold this account with the same importance as Nathan Cole's account of George Whitefield in Middletown, Connecticut in 1740.

The singularity of this account lies in the personal contact that this layman had with Nettleton: the man (a member of good standing in the Presbyterian Church of Jamaica) was awakened under Nettleton's powerful preaching, and became personally acquainted with the evangelist, even becoming his intimate friend. The great evangelist, a semi-invalid from typhus fever, was in need of frequent rides in a horse-drawn carriage for his health. This layman is the *driver* of that carriage which took frequent trips to the countryside from Jamaica, Long Island during this extraordinary revival of religion in 1826. Bennet Tyler included this account in his second printing of Nettleton's *Memoirs*, after this story appeared in the New York Observer, following the publication of the first edition of the *Memoirs*. Here now is that remarkable account, as related by the unidentified layman so magnificently impacted by Asahel's ministry:

"In perusing the life of Mr. Nettleton, I have had brought vividly to my recollections, scenes and circumstances connected with the revival of religion in Jamaica in 1826, of deep interest to me, and although more than eighteen years have passed, their interest is as deep as ever, and I think, strikingly illustrates the wisdom and the prudence of that truly wonderful man in dealing with awakened sinners.

"The first time I ever saw Mr. Nettleton was on a communion Sabbath in the early part of the winter of 1826. Two strangers entered the church, and, walking slowly up the aisle, seated themselves in the front pew. Many eyes were fastened upon them; and after service, as in common in the country, many inquiries were made as to who they were, for they were evidently clergymen. It was some time, before I learned that one of them was the 'Rev. Mr. *Nettleton*, the great revival preacher'. The church in Jamaica, as is mentioned in the memoir, had been greatly divided. We were literally two bands hostile to each other, and bitter in feeling. The Apostle might have said of us, we were hateful, and hating one another; and there seemed but little prospect of our ever being any better. It was but a sad spectacle on that day presented to this man of God.

"When, a few days after, I heard that Mr. Nettleton, the revival preacher, was soon going to preach for us, I never shall forget my feelings. I determined I would not hear him, and especially so, when an old disciple, long since in glory, Mr. Othniel Smith, who had listened with rapture to George Whitefield seventy years before, when he preached in Jamaica, said to me—'This Mr. Nettleton that is going to preach for us is a most wonderful man; he is said to be the greatest preacher that has been among us since the days of George Whitefield.' He said further, that, from what he had heard of him, he believed he could almost *read a man's heart*, so wonderful was his knowledge of human nature. I well remember I secretly said, 'He shall not see *my heart*, for I will not let him see me, so bitterly did I dread any thing like close, experimental preaching.

"I had long been a professor of religion, having united with the Rutgers Street Church in 1812, while Dr. Milledollar was the pastor, and notwithstanding I had always been outwardly consistent, (regularly observing secret and family prayer, constant in my attendance upon all the meetings of the church, as well as the public services of the Sabbath, as the weekly lecture, and the social circle for prayer, and active in all the benevolent operations of the day,) notwithstanding all this seemingly consistency of character, there was always a fearful whisper from the faithful monitor within, that all was not right. There was a secret dread of self-examination, an unwillingness to know the worst respecting my case, and the idea of coming in contact with a man who would be likely to expose my shallowness, if not hypocrisy, I could not endure. And accordingly I resolved that something should detain me from church when Mr. Nettleton preached. But although I sought diligently for any excuse, one even the least plausible, yet I could not find one; and, contrary to my secret determination, I went to church at the appropriate time with my family.

"After the Sabbath, numbers of the church members called upon Mr. Nettleton at his lodgings, to welcome him among us; and I was repeatedly requested to do so with the rest; but day after day I contrived to excuse myself, although I knew it was a civility that was expected of me. At length a brother, who had often urged me to go, called upon me to know if I would not take Mr. Nettleton a little ride in my gig, as he was in feeble health, having but just recovered from a protracted illness, adding that he found riding not only beneficial, but necessary, and he knew I could do it just as well as not.

"I never shall forget my feelings at this proposition. I at first refused outright, and was vexed that the proposition should have been made. I treated the brother rudely. He however continued to urge, and said he had gone so far as to tell Mr. Nettleton he knew I would do it cheerfully. But it was all to no purpose. I did not do it that day, but consented to call upon him the next morning, with my gig, at ten o'clock, if he would be ready. The next morning accordingly I called at the appointed time, and was introduced to him on the sidewalk; and never did culprit dread the face of his judge more than I dreaded to be brought face to face with a man, who it was said could almost *read the heart.*

"I received him politely, and we soon entered into a pleasing conversation, about almost any thing and every thing except personal religion. This I scrupulously avoided. I found he was in feeble health, and somewhat given to hypochondria; therefore I felt assured I could entertain him by talking about his own ailments. In less than one hour all my unpleasant feelings had vanished, and I felt as free and easy with him, as if I was riding with some long tried friend; and that which I so much dreaded became to me at once a source of great pleasure and of much profit.

"The first day he rode with me about six miles; and after that, for seven months, very few pleasant days passed, that we did not ride together from five to twenty-five miles. I became deeply interested in him as a man and as a preacher. Why I at first liked his preaching I cannot exactly say; but I was unwilling to be absent from a single meeting. The class of subjects he chose as his theme of discourse was new. The distracted state of the congregation led those clergymen who supplied our pulpit to select some subjects connected with Christian duty. Brotherly love, if I remember right, was the subject of discourse seven times in about three months. On the contrary, Mr. Nettleton presented the claims of God and the *duty of sinners,* and here I remember we had no opportunity of scrutinizing the sermon, to endeavor to ascertain on which side of the division the preacher was. This I considered a master stroke of policy.

"Thus smoothly and pleasantly, comparatively speaking, it passed along with me for about two weeks, when one evening he announced from the desk that he felt some encouragement to believe that the Lord was about to grant us a blessing. He said he had seen several individuals who were anxious for their souls, and two or three who indulged hope. How it would end with them he could not say, but he wanted the church to walk softly before the Lord, to be much in prayer, &c., &c. I felt then that my own case required looking into at once, or I was lost; and I resolved soon to attend to it, nor to let the present opportunity pass. Mr. Nettleton had never yet said one word to me on the subject of experimental religion, although I had been with him a great deal.

"The next day, as usual, I called for him to ride. I was obliged to go to Flushing that day, distant about five miles. Just as we were ascending the hill, a little out of the village, and before any subject of conversation had been introduced, and the horse on a slow walk, he gently placed his hand upon my knee and said—'Well, my dear friend, how is it with you? I hope it is all peace within.' I could not speak for some minutes. He said no more, and there was no occasion, for an arrow had pierced my inmost soul. My emotion was overwhelming. At length, after recovering a little of self-possession, I broke the silence by telling him frankly I was not happy—there was no peace within—all was war! war!! war!!! His manner was so kind, he instantly won my confidence, and I unburdened my soul to him. I told him how I had felt for years past, and how very unhappy at times I had been.

"He did not seem inclined to talk. All he said was occasionally 'Well—well—well' with his peculiar cadence. At length he said he did not feel very well, and he wanted to be still. This was a request he often made, and I though nothing of it. I have rode miles and miles with him, and not a word has passed between us after such a request.

"I continued to ride with him once and twice a day; but although I was anxious to converse, he said but little to me, except occasionally he would drop a remark calculated to make me feel worse instead of better—at times greatly deepening my distress. Some months afterwards, I spoke to him about this part of our intercourse. He said he did it intentionally, for he had reason to believe many an awakened sinner had his convictions all talked away, and he talked into a false hope.

"Two or three days after he first spoke to me on the subject of religion, he called at my house, and requested me to go and see a particular individual, whom he named and who was under distress of mind, and pray with her. I told him that I could not do such a thing as that, for I was not a Christian myself. He replied—'But you do not mean that your not being a Christian releases you from Christian obligations? If you do you are greatly in error. Good morning!' and he left me rather abruptly. In the afternoon, when I rode with him, he did not ask me if I attended to his request, for he knew I had not. He only made the request, as he afterwards told me, to thrust deeper the arrow of conviction; and it had the desired effect. My distress became very great, and I was unfitted for my ordinary duties. I felt as if there was but little hope for such a hardened sinner as I was.

"About this time he appointed a meeting of inquiry. I told him I should be there for one. He said I must not attend on any account—it was only intended for anxious sinners. I told him I certainly should be there, unless he absolutely forbade it. 'I do,' said he, with more than ordinary earnestness.

"Then, said I, you must promise me that you will appoint a meeting for anxious professors. He made no reply. This anxious meeting was the first he appointed in Jamaica. It was to be held at the house of a dear friend of mine, and one who knew something of the state of my mind. I went there in the afternoon, and made arrangements to be concealed in an adjoining bed-room, the door of which could not be shut, the bed being placed against it. I was on the ground an hour before the time appointed. Mr. Nettleton came soon after, to arrange the seats; about this he was very particular. He came into the bed-room where I was concealed two or three times; he wanted the door closed, but he found it could not be without disarranging the furniture, and he gave it up. He did not know I was there until some weeks afterwards. The temptation to be present at that meeting I could not resist. Some how I had received an impression that my salvation depended upon it. I had heard so often about persons being converted in an anxious meeting, that I thought if I could only be present at such a meeting, that was all that was necessary, and therefore I was willing not only to run the risk of offending Mr. Nettleton, but willing to submit to almost any humiliating circumstances, to accomplish my object. I thought it was altogether a piece of cruelty in Mr. Nettleton to forbid my being present, and I determined to carry my point privately, if I could not openly.

"Situated as I was, I could hear next to nothing as to what was transpiring in the anxious room. Mr. Nettleton addressed those present individually, and in a very low tone of voice, bordering upon a whisper. As he approached the open door, I could occasionally catch a sentence, and hear a deep and anxious sob—but these words, and broken sentences, and sobs, were loud and pointed sermons to me. I wanted to get out from my hiding place, that I might give vent to my pent up feelings; and my anxiety to be released, appeared to be greater than it was to be present. At times, it seemed as if I must cry out in bitterness of spirit, so agonizing were my feelings;

especially so as I heard him say to one individual, 'Is it possible? Well, I am afraid you will lose your impressions, and if you should what will become of you? If the Spirit is grieved to return no more, you *will* lose your soul.' After going around the room, and conversing with each individual, he made a few general remarks applicable to all respecting the danger of grieving God's Holy Spirit, and then dismissed the meeting after a short prayer.

"Instead of feeling any better after this meeting, as I expected to do, I felt worse and worse. Sleep was now taken from me, and I felt that death was better than life. Either that night or the next, I forget which, but remember it was the 27th April, I got out of bed about 12 o'clock, and went out into the woods. It was exceedingly dark. I fell down at the foot of a tree, and cried aloud for mercy in agony of soul. I felt that God was just in punishing me. I felt that the *longest* and the *severest* punishment he could inflict was no more than I deserved; my sins, my aggravated sins, appeared so great. I remained out of doors the most of the night. In the morning, early, before I went home, I called at Mr. Nettleton's lodgings. He sent word that he could not see me at that hour. I went away, and returned in an hour or so; he told the servant to request me to be seated, and he would be with me in a few minutes.

"Every minute now seemed an hour, and a long one too. For nearly thirty minutes he kept me in this state of horrible suspense, during which I was constantly pacing the floor with my watch in my hand. When at length he entered the room, I threw my arms round his neck, told him I was in perfect agony, and that I should die if he did not in some way comfort me. I told him it seemed as if I could not live another hour in such distress.

"'I can't help you, my dear friend, you must not look to me;' and he burst into a flood of tears.

"'What shall I do? what shall I do?'" I repeated over and over again, in a loud voice.

"'You must yield your heart to Christ, or you are lost!' said he; and adding, 'I do certainly think your situation a very alarming and dangerous one.'

"After a few minutes, he said, 'Come, let us kneel down.' This was contrary to his usual practice. He made a very short prayer, not more than a minute in length, rose from his knees, advised me to go home and remain in my room, and abruptly left me, almost overcome with emotion. Had there been any means of self-destruction within my reach, I believe I should have employed it, so agonizing were my feelings. He sent word to me by a young friend, that he did not wish to ride that day. I passed the most of the day in my room on my knees. Occasionally, I walked for a few minutes in my garden, and then returned to my room. It was the *just* and the *eternal* displeasure of an *angry* God that seemed to crush me to the earth. About the middle of the afternoon, one of the elders came to see me. He expressed surprise at my distress, said there was no necessity for my feeling so bad, he knew there was not. He tried to persuade me it would all be well with me *soon*. I told him that if he could satisfy me that it would be ever well with me, I would gladly and cheerfully endure my sufferings thousands of years. This feeling I distinctly remember. The *justice* of God and the *eternity* of his anger distressed me most. I sent for Mr. Nettleton, but he excused himself, and did not come.

> 'Thus every refuge failed me,
>   And all my hopes were cross'd.'

"It was past the middle of the afternoon, and approaching sundown, and I had not yet broken my fast. After a short walk in the garden, I again entered my room, locked the door, and threw myself prostrate on my settee, as near a state of hopeless despair as I can conceive a mortal to be on this side of the bottomless pit. I cried aloud, 'O my God! how long—how long, O my God, my God.' After repeating this and similar language several times, I seemed to sink away into a state of insensibility. When I came to myself I was upon my knees, praying not for myself but for others. I felt submission to the will of God, willing that he should do with me as should seem good in his sight. My concern for myself seemed all lost in concern for others. *Terror* seemed all exchanged for *love,* and *despair* for *hope.* God was glorious, and Christ unspeakably precious. I was an overwhelming wonder to myself. The cry of 'Blessed Jesus—blessed Jesus!' took the place of 'Lord have mercy.'

"After remaining in my room half an hour or thereabouts, I came down stairs, and met my dear wife, who had deeply sympathized with me in my distress. I exclaimed, 'I have found Him, I have found Him, and He is a precious Saviour!' She was very much overcome. She persuaded me to take some food, but I was so happy and so anxious to go to meeting, the bell having rung, that I could eat but little. I went over to the session house; it was crowded—benches in the aisle were filled. I obtained a seat near the door. Mr. Nettleton was reading the 211th hymn of the village collection—

'Of all the joys we mortals know,
Jesus, thy love exceeds the rest,' &c.

"I thought I never heard so sweet a hymn, nor so delightful music. I sung it at the top of my voice, of which however I was not aware, until I saw I had attracted the observation of all near me. My eyes were streaming with tears, while my countenance was beaming with delight, as a friend afterwards told me. I wanted to tell to all around what a Saviour I had found.

"After service, I walked home with Mr. Nettleton, and remained with him a few minutes.

'I knew this morning,' said he, 'that the turning point was not far off.' He cautioned me again and again, against giving way to my feelings, urged me to keep humble and prayerful, and not say much to any one. That night I could not sleep for joy. I do not think I closed my eyes. I found myself singing several times in the night. In the morning all nature seemed in a new dress, and vocal with the praises of a God all glorious. Every thing seemed changed, and I could scarcely realize that one, only yesterday so wretched, was now so happy. I felt it perfectly reasonable that he who had much forgiven should love much. I think I sincerely inquired, 'Lord, what wilt thou have me to do?' and though eighteen years have passed, God is still glorious, and Christ still precious to my soul; and unless I am greatly deceived, I still pray for a knowledge of my duty, and for grace to do it. I know that I still love to do good and make others happy; and of all anticipated delights which I can place before my mind, that of the enjoyment of sinless perfection in heaven is the greatest. But never was a sense of my unworthiness greater than it is at present.

'What was there in me that could merit esteem
    Or give the Creator delight?
'Twas even so, Father, I ever must sing,
Because it seem'd good in thy sight.
Then give all the glory to his holy name,

To him all the glory belongs,
Be mine the high joy still to sound forth his fame,
And crown him in each of my songs.'

T. W. B."[1]

Such were the "glory days" of the great evangelist and the numerous accounts of those individuals brought to Christ during seasons of remarkable revivals. Although feeble in health for the remainder of his days, Asahel Nettleton continued to labor in revivals, not in frequent outpourings of grace as in former days, but in intermittent showers of divine blessings which God was pleased to offer to the bruised evangelist's labors.

The horizon and spiritual landscape of those "glory days" would soon be altered by fellow evangelist, Charles Grandison Finney. Charles Finney was involved in revivals in western New York coincidently while Nettleton was immersed in the revival at Jamaica, Long Island in 1826. Finney was a newly ordained minister who was creating an immediate sensation wherever he labored. The sunny sky that followed Nettleton's labors would soon become darkened by controversy arising from the methodology used by Finney in revivals, called "The New Measures". A clash would soon occur between these two titans at the sleepy village of New Lebanon, New York, the outcome of which would alter the way evangelism would be conducted, not only in their lifetime, but in future generations to come.

Note

1   Tyler, pp. 163–173.

PART 2:
CONTROVERSY WITH NEW MEASURES
AND NEW DIVINITY

Connecticut-born Finney was raised in New York State. Although he desired to attend Yale, his actual education was gained under private tutorage. He was converted while practicing law and almost immediately launched into evangelistic work. Tragically, he began his ministry with a high view of man and an inadequate view of history. In Finney's mind the high view of God maintained by the New England preachers had created a dearth of revivals. Little did he know that even in western New York state there had not been a single year since 1798 in which revival had not gripped some church or community. Thus, while very successful in his itinerations, the excitement generated by his ministry alarmed many sober leaders of his day who knew that the new doctrines which he preached and the new methods he employed not only brought division and tension on every hand but would in time bring great harm upon the churches of the land. Some of Finney's contemporaries went so far as to say that if Finney's view prevailed it would mark the end of true revival in America. Undaunted by such criticism, Finney continued to follow his own convictions. Yet, just as predicted, the seasons of revival ended considerably before the death of Finney, and true revival has been scarce indeed in America since his day. While one must not question Finney's personal devotion to the Lord Jesus Christ, the blind acceptance of his position depletes the prospects of revival even in this hour. A return to a high and lofty God is the primary prerequisite to revival in any age.

RICHARD OWEN ROBERTS

Charles Grandison Finney

20

OMINOUS CLOUDS OF CHANGE

The traditionally Calvinistic, New England theological climate became clouded by encroaching Unitarianism and Universalism, both popular in large centers such as Boston and Philadelphia. Both Congregational and Presbyterian churches felt this increasing threat and did everything in their collective power to check it. However, theologically changing winds were blowing stronger over the New England countryside. A professor of theology at Yale Divinity School, by the name of Nathaniel William Taylor, would greatly alter the general acceptance of the "Old School Calvinism" in New England. N. W. Taylor's influential systematic theology, named "Taylorism" would make way for a more liberal breed of religion in America. The evangelist Charles G. Finney embraced "Taylorism" and by combining this philosophy with the "New Measures" that he employed in his revivals, helped to shape the direction of future evangelistic activity, not only in his generation, but for generations to come. An explanation of this is given by the following:

"The second great awakening, with all its intellectual, evangelistic, and humanitarian by-products and ramifications, was connected doctrinally with the type of theology which Asahel Nettleton proclaimed so boldly ... This type of God-centered theology, which had produced a successful generation of Christians and initiated many noble enterprises for the benefit of mankind, was now about to be repudiated ...

"The debate between the defenders of the old orthodoxy and the new liberalism is unquestionably one of the most significant in the history of American theology and evangelism. It signalled the beginning of a new and mighty force called usually by the name of 'modern evangelism' and spotlighted a theological cleavage which remains unresolved until this day." [1]

This "theological cleavage" soon became a *chasm*. The first indications that change was coming to the New England churches was seen in the battle between Unitarians and Universalists pitched against Calvinistic

Congregationalists and Presbyterians. The fear was that liberalism was
eroding the spiritual moorings of the New England founding fathers.
The gradual acceptance of liberalism is seen by the following remarks:

> "American Unitarianism, primarily a phenomenon of New England, grew
> equally from the sentiments of laymen no longer able to accept the harsher doctrines
> of Calvinism and the effort of ministers concerned to reinterpret orthodoxy for their
> own day. The liberal Christians (as they first styled themselves) did not withdraw
> from the church and, accordingly, became objects first of suspicion and then of
> attack. The liberals opposed revivals. They defined religion in rational and practical
> terms. Open and general strife was precipitated in 1805 by the election of the liberal
> Henry Ware to the Hollis chair of divinity at Harvard. Subsequently traditionalists
> founded their own seminary (Andover) and their own publication (the *Panoplist*).
> The manifesto of the Unitarians was a sermon of William E. Channing, delivered in
> Baltimore in 1819 at the ordination of Jared Sparks, in which the preacher appealed
> to reason and renounced traditional views of the Trinity and the person of Christ."[2]

Prior to this there had been harmony and unity among the
Congregational and Presbyterian churches of New England—but this
would soon change. To understand the background of this unity of
ministers, called the "Plan of Union of 1801" we turn to the following
comments:

> "While Asahel Nettleton was in Jamaica, Long Island, in 1826, he began to hear
> conflicting reports about the revivals in Rome and Utica and Auburn, New York.
> Over five hundred conversions were reported from Rome and a similar number
> from Utica. And over six hundred were added to the Cayuga Presbytery of which
> Auburn was a member. But there seemed to be some question about the propriety
> of some of the methods which were used in the revivals.

> "It was not at all unusual that a New Englander, like Nettleton, should take an
> active interest in the northeastern New York revivals. That part of New York state
> was New England frontier; it was a 'new' New England. Beginning in the early
> 1790s a flood of immigrants from Vermont, western Massachusetts and Connecticut
> settled in northeastern New York. Some settlers had come up from New Jersey and
> Pennsylvania, but most were from New England. The new settlers brought with
> them their educational and ecclesiastical institutions, and established common
> schools and churches along the New England pattern.

> "Coincident with the migration, as Nichols points out [Robert Hasting Nichols],
> 'was a lasting powerful religious quickening in the regions when it came.' The
> Second Great Awakening began in the 1790s and a heightened religious life spread
> throughout New England and the Middle States. Likewise in the new settlements in
> New York, the fervent revivalism of the Second Great Awakening surged
> periodically across the new frontier. Peaks were reached in 1800, again in 1807–
> 1808, in the years immediately following the War of 1812, and again in the mid-20s.

> "Before 1825 the Presbyterian and Congregational revivals on the frontier, with
> few exceptions, were like their New England counterparts. That is, they were
> 'conducted chiefly by settled pastors within the structure of parish activities, were
> accompanied by careful doctrinal instruction, and were generally restrained and
> orderly in manner.' They were revivals of which Nettleton approved. Philemon
> Fowler, in his excellent historical account of the Presbyterian church in the synod of

Central New York, takes great care to establish two points about religious life in the new era: First, the orthodoxy and regularity of the Presbyterians [and Congregational] churches in the area, and secondly the stillness and orderliness of the revivals, despite the noise and extravagancies of the Baptists and Methodists ...

"The importance of reports like Fowler's is that they show that neither layman nor clergy were uneducated or uncultured in frontier New York ... Under the Plan of Union of 1801 and the Accomodation Plan of 1808 the General Assembly of the Presbyterian Church and the General Association of Connecticut (and later of Vermont, New Hampshire, and Massachusetts) agreed to join forces in their missionary endeavors in the new settlements. Under the Plan of Union a Congregational church could settle a Presbyterian minister and still manage its affairs according to Congregational principles, or conversely a Presbyterian church could settle a Congregational minister ... They were called 'Presbygational' by some, i.e., Congregational churches under Presbyterian authority ...

"Because of the fraternal connection between eastern New York and New England, it is not strange, nor meddlesome, that an eminent evangelist like Nettleton should take a personal interest in the New York revivals."3

This "fraternal" unity of the Congregational and Presbyterian churches would now be threatened by both the "New Measures" of Charles Finney, and the opposing theology of N. W. Taylor. There would be other challenges to the "old orthodoxy" of New England, but these two central points would emerge as the largest threat to the traditional stability in both revivals, and in the pulpits.

The changes coming to orthodox New England were mainly in two forms:

1. A challenge to the doctrines of Calvinism.
2. A change in the "measures" used to conduct revivals and evangelism.

These changes had the potential to undermine *everything* Asahel Nettleton had labored for throughout his long career. The real threat of change to "old orthodoxy" did not appear from the twin evils of Unitarianism and Universalism, but in the two personages of Charles Grandison Finney and Nathaniel William Taylor!

CHARLES GRANDISON FINNEY

The *thunder* that Asahel Nettleton had heard come across the mainland to Long Island, was the emerging ministry of Charles Finney, a young itinerant evangelist from New York. The former lawyer was conducting revivals in Albany and creating a *sensation*. Nettleton had been receiving conflicting reports of Finney's activities and his curiosity and concern was roused to such levels, that he suddenly left the revival in Jamaica and traveled to Albany to see for himself what all the "noise" was about. We see the following comments concerning Finney:

"Finney was a very intense young man who reacted passionately and completely in whatever he did. His early experience of organized religion led him to the conclusion that most professional Christians were cold and indifferent concerning their faith and believed that they could do nothing about it. Finney often applied the popular jingle of the day,

> You can and you can't;
> You will and you won't;
> You're damned if you do,
> And you're damned if you don't,

to their brand of Calvinism. Because of his own personal experience before his conversion, he believed religion of the day had little to offer. Despite his negative attitude toward theology and formalized religion, he was a conscientious, moral man who continued a formal relationship with the church. His religious experience became the basis from which he drew his understanding of Christianity, and the means which he came to use were those which reinforced these views."[4]

Finney's initial success in public ministry came to him while preaching in Oneida County, in the western section of New York. It was there in Oneida County in 1825 that Finney filled the pulpit for his former pastor and friend, Rev. George Gale. Finney's preaching in Gale's church created a *sensation*. He was a dramatic actor in the pulpit, his hypnotic gaze and stentorian voice captivated his audiences. In addition to these abilities, Charles Finney was a tall handsome young man with a commanding personality which demanded attention. Soon Finney gained a following of local pastors while preaching in their churches. In Rome, he assisted Moses Gillet; he helped fill the pulpit at both Samuel Aiken and Samuel Brace's churches at Utica; and he befriends Noah Coe at New Hartford; and then John Frost in Whitesboro. Many of these local pastors were simply amazed at Finney's uncanny ability to make converts and create excitement within their churches. These "Finney revivals" soon attracted the attention of the synod in Albany, New York. Invitations came pouring in for Finney from all over the state of New York. The "Christian Spectator" magazine in their issue of November, 1826, reported that there had been *over 2500* new converts from the revivals conducted under Charles G. Finney!

The popularity of Finney grew to such degrees that soon bands of young itinerants became "Finney copycats" who employed his "new measures" in revivals and even mimicked his bold manner. It seemed that all of New York was on a *Finney craze* and wanted to jump on the bandwagon. However, not *everyone* was enamored with Charles Finney. Eminent ministers such as Edward D. Griffin, Bennet Tyler, Lyman Beecher, Heman Humphrey, William Weeks, and others grew concerned over what they witnessed in the Finney revivals, and they reported their concerns to Asahel Nettleton. More of this is seen in the following comments by Thornbury:

"It was while he was in Jamaica, during the summer months, that he began to receive reports of problems among the churches in the vicinity of Oneida County, New York. In former days he had often preached in the eastern sections of New York and he, of course, had many friends in that area. A considerable number of ministers wrote that the churches were being agitated by the introduction of 'new measures' in revival meetings. Some became so alarmed that they travelled to Jamaica and discussed these problems with Nettleton.

"At that time, great revivals were going on in this area of New York, as all acknowledged. But many of the pastors were dissatisfied with certain practices which attended these revivals. They felt that commonly accepted laws of propriety and wisdom were being violated by some of the visiting evangelists. One was that they were being exceedingly bold and harsh in their method of addressing the unconverted. Often individuals were specifically mentioned by name and called upon to change their method of living. This created a sensational atmosphere but grieved many of the Christians who felt that the unconverted should be dealt with in a more private and cautious way ...

"The most conspicuous innovation was the practice of calling upon people to make some kind of physical movement in public meetings to assist them in securing salvation. Sometimes they were told to 'rise up' from their seats. At other times an 'anxious seat' was arranged in the meetings, and sinners were urged to 'come forward' to the seat in order to become Christians. Such methods had been used for many years by the Methodists, but were discountenanced by most Presbygationalists ...

"These improprieties were, of course, objected to and resisted by many of the pastors and lay people, including some who had been actively involved in revivals themselves. But when they did not go along they were denounced with great harshness and were called 'dead', 'cold', and 'enemies to revivals.'"[5]

It is easy to see from these reports, how the revivals being conducted by Finney and his followers, would disturb the peace of Asahel Nettleton. Memories of the damage caused by James Davenport during the first Great Awakening made Nettleton cautious of the new methodology of the so-called "New Measures". If it were true that churches were being divided then the great alarm that arose in Nettleton's mind needed confirmation. And this is why Nettleton left a vibrant revival occurring in Jamaica to travel to Albany to witness for himself how Finney conducted revivals. To say that Nettleton and Finney were on opposite poles in regard to conducting revivals is an understatement. We see from the following observations by May:

"Finney's entire practical approach to revivalism was the opposite of Nettleton's ... Nettleton worked best with individuals—in their home or in the 'anxious' meeting. Finney made full use of the pulpit, and from it enjoined the masses to repent. He was a master of group psychology and played on their fears and anticipations. Finney appealed to the emotions and thereby hoped to reach the mind and the heart; Nettleton congenitally feared such an approach. For him the sinner must first understand. Finney disregarded the ecclesiastical and societal structures which Nettleton deemed essential for the continued success of revivalism and the health of the country: the relation of evangelist to settled pastors; the layman to the pastor; the young to the old; the woman to the man. Finney, despite political preferences, embodied what was soon known as the Jacksonian 'common man.' These were his people; this he understood. Nettleton was a Connecticut federalist, who had fought disestablishment; Finney was incomprehensible to him."[6]

Despite all the success Finney was enjoying, he soon would be forced to defend his actions against the accusations of clergy who strongly disagreed with his method of revivalism. Eventually sides would be drawn between ministers from the West, those who agreed with Finney, and those from the East such as Nettleton and his friends who *did not* agree with Finney. Sadly, these issues became trigger points for division between the once-happy Congregationalists and Presbyterians, who for so long, had shared common denominators. But now, division was ahead of them.

Notes

1   J. F. Thornbury, pp. 150–151.
2   Stuart C. Henry, *Unvanquished Puritan, A Portrait of Lyman Beecher* (Grand Rapids: Eerdmans, 1973), p. 115.
3   Sherry Pierpont May, pp. 167–171.
4   Ibid. pp. 178–179.
5   J. F. Thornbury, pp. 154–155.
6   Sherry Pierpont May, p. 181.

The presbytery of Columbia had a meeting somewhere within its bounds while I was at New Lebanon; and being informed that I was laboring in one of their churches, appointed a committee to visit the place and inquire into the state of things; for they had been led to believe from Troy and other places, and from the opposition of Mr. Nettleton and the letters of Dr. Beecher, that my method of conducting revivals was so very objectionable that it was the duty of presbytery to inquire into it.

CHARLES G. FINNEY

21

MEETING AT ALBANY, NEW YORK

W e wish we had been flies on the wall at the purported two meetings between the two greatest evangelists of the Second Great Awakening! Asahel Nettleton and Charles Finney met for the first time in Albany, New York. Unfortunately, the only account of what transpired in the meeting comes from the pen of Finney, far removed from that time, written by him as an old man in his seventies. The account is found in Finney's *Memoirs*, he comments:

"I had the greatest confidence in Mr. Nettleton, though I had never seen him. I had had the greatest *desire* to see him, so much so that I had frequently dreamed of visiting him and obtaining from him information in regard to the best means in regard to promoting a revival. I wanted exceedingly to see him, and felt like sitting at his feet, almost as I would at the feet of an apostle, from what I had heard of his success in promoting revivals. At that time my confidence in him was so great that I think he could have led me almost or quite at his discretion. Soon after my arrival at Troy I went down to Albany to see him. He was the guest of a family with which I was acquainted [*Note:* Finney went to Albany to see Nettleton in December 1826. Nettleton was staying with Rev. Henry R. Weed (1789–1870), a Princeton graduate who was minister of the First Presbyterian Church …]. I spent part of an afternoon with him, and conversed with him in regard to his doctrinal views on some subjects, especially those held by the Dutch and Presbyterian churches in regard to the voluntariness or involuntariness of moral depravity, and kindred topics. I found that he entirely agreed with me, so far as I had opportunity to converse with him, on all the points of theology upon which we conversed. Indeed there had been no complaint by Dr. Beecher or Mr. Nettleton of our *teaching* in those revivals. They did not complain at all that we did not teach what they regarded as the true Gospel. What they complained of was something that they supposed was highly objectionable in the *measures* that we used … Our conversation was brief upon every point upon which we touched. I observed that he avoided the subject of promoting revivals. When I told him that I intended to remain in Albany & hear him preach in the evening he manifested uneasiness & remarked that I must not be seen with him …

"Hence Judge Cushman who accompanied me from Troy & who was in college with Mr. N. & myself went to meeting & sat in the gallery. I saw enough to satisfy me that I could expect no advice or instruction from him, & that he was there to take a stand against me. I soon found out I was not mistaken. Since writing the last

237

paragraph my attention has been called to a statement in the biography of Mr. Nettleton to the effect that he tried in vain to change my views and practices in promoting revivals of religion. I can not think that Mr. Nettleton ever authorized such a statement for certainly he never attempted to do it. As I have said, at that time he could have moulded me at discretion but he said not a word to me about my manner of conducting revivals nor did he ever write a word to me upon the subject. He kept me at arm's length & although as I have said we conversed on some points of theology then much discussed, it was plain that he was unwilling to say anything regarding revivals & would not allow to accompany him to meeting. This was the only time I saw him until I met him in the convention at New Lebanon. At no time did Mr. N. ever try to correct my view in relation to revivals. After I heard more of his views & practices in promoting revivals I was thankful to God that he never did influence me upon that subject."[1]

We do not have Nettleton's side of this meeting and it is difficult to know what really transpired between these two giants of revival. It *appears* that Nettleton did not reach out to Finney to discuss the questionable "New Measures" at this meeting, thus avoiding a confrontation. It does appear that he did indeed, keep the youthful Finney at "arms length". It is sad that they could not be *brothers* promoting the kingdom of Christ in harmony. It is sadder still that these two men became opponents of each other to the bitter end. It is difficult to believe that Finney as a young man could have been "moulded" by anyone, he was too self-confident and too headstrong in his own opinions and path to be changed; he seldom took counsel of his pastor Rev. Gale, much less anyone else. However, we do blame Nettleton here for not reaching out to the younger evangelist and attempting an early reconciliation. We can try to make excuses for Nettleton's behavior, that he was worn out from preaching or ill from the typhus fever, but that being said, the blame still falls at his feet. The fact is Asahel Nettleton *did not* desire to aid Finney in revivals, quite the contrary, he viewed Finney as a *danger to revivals of religion* and as a force that had to be *stopped* and not enabled. When Asahel Nettleton looked into the piercing and hypnotic eyes of Charles G. Finney he saw only one man— the ghostly shadow of James Davenport, and it sent chills down his spine!

For some perspective on Nettleton's position on this encounter with Finney, it can be determined that much of his mind was already made up in respect to his views of Finney before they met in Albany. For these conclusions we look to Bennet Tyler who writes:

"Some young evangelists, in particular, attempting to imitate Mr. Finney, became much more extravagant than their leader. But a great excitement attended the preaching of Mr. Finney and his coadjutors, and multitudes were reported as the subjects of renewing grace. That very many of the reputed converts were like the stony ground hearers, who endured for only a time, few, I presume, will at this day be disposed to deny. Yet, it is believed, that some were truly converted to Christ.

"Connected with this excitement, various measures were introduced, similar to those which in former times had been the great instruments of marring the purity of revivals, and promoting fanaticism—such as praying for persons by name—using great familiarity in prayer—encouraging females to pray and exhort in promiscuous assemblies—calling upon persons to come to the anxious seat, or to rise up in the public assembly to signify that they had given their hearts to God, or had made up their mind to attend to religion. The result was, that where this spirit prevailed, and these measures were introduced, there was division in the churches. Those who adopted these measures, often appealed to the example of Dr. Nettleton, and made use of his name to sanction their proceedings. Those, however, who were acquainted with him and his labors in revivals, knew that these representations were not true. They knew that he never had introduced such measures, nor countenanced such a spirit as was connected with them.

"While these things were passing in the central and western parts of the State of New York, Dr. Nettleton, in very feeble health, was laboring in Jamaica, on Long Island. He was from time to time made acquainted with what was transpiring at the west, and was not without great solicitude as to the ultimate results. The lesson which he had learned while laboring on the borders of Rhode Island, in those places which had been made desolate by the operations of Davenport and his coadjutors a century ago, had prepared him to resist every thing which tended to corrupt revivals and promote fanaticism.

"He heard with inexpressible pain, that his own example was appealed to at the West, to sanction measures which he had always reprobated; still, although constantly urged by some of his friends to come out with a public testimony, he was very reluctant to do it, nor could he be persuaded to publish his views, till he was fully convinced that a regard to the interests of Christ's kingdom required it.

"In the winter of 1826–7, at the earnest request of some of his brethren, he visited Albany, while Mr. Finney was preaching at Troy. He had two interviews with Mr. Finney, hoping that by a free consultation, their views might be brought to harmonize, so far at least, that they might co-operate in promoting the interests of Christ's kingdom. But in this he was painfully disappointed. He found that Mr. Finney was unwilling to abandon certain measures which he had 'ever regarded as exceedingly calamitous to the cause of revivals,' and which, of course, he could not sanction. He perceived also that there could be no hope of convincing Mr. Finney of his errors, so long as he was upheld and encouraged by ministers of high respectability."[2]

If there was a *second meeting* as Tyler states, perhaps Nettleton was more proactive in that one to attempt to work out something agreeable with Finney, until he realized it was a futile cause, as Finney was apparently unwilling to change his ministry pattern in promoting revivals. Whatever transpired at this final meeting between the two evangelists will remain a mystery. We do know that Asahel Nettleton was prepared for a *fight*.

Notes

1   Garth M. Rosell & Richard A. G. Dupuis, Editors, *The Memoirs of Charles G. Finney, The Complete Restored Text* (Grand Rapids: Academie Books, 1989), pp. 204–206.
2   Tyler, pp. 236–238.

For Finney an appeal for a public action had become an essential part of evangelism. He believed that all that was needed for conversion was a resolution signified by standing, kneeling, or coming forward ... This was the main reason for the opposition to the innovations introduced into the Western revivals ... This was the heart of the issue, which Nettleton, in his letter to Aikin of Utica, described as a 'civil war in Zion'. But as we shall see, it was not as clear as this in 1827. It was 1835 before Finney openly denounced the orthodox side for their 'vast ignorance' ...

IAIN MURRAY

22

FIRST SHOT OVER THE BOW,
THE "CIVIL WAR IN ZION" LETTER

In a war there must be a "first shot"; this came in the form of an *open letter* from Asahel Nettleton to a Rev. Aikin. This letter was meant to be circulated among the ministers who supported Nettleton's views on the "New Measures" and this strategic letter eventually fell into the hands of Charles Finney, who realized he had a *war* on his hands. It was obvious that the veteran Nettleton was not "messing around" when it came to defending what he considered were vital revivals of religion. Nettleton firmly believed that Charles Finney embodied all the division-causing elements of James Davenport: emotionalism, fanaticism, and spurious conversions. Each of these led to church divisions and unrest, resulting in the "waste places" of the late 1700s. Thus, Nettleton moved to "nip this in the bud" and he fired the first shot over this contested issue which would ultimately divide the once-happy Congregational and Presbyterian churches. Asahel Nettleton saw this battle as a *civil war in Zion*. We turn now to the observations of Thornbury who writes:

"In January of 1827 Asahel Nettleton sat down, pen in hand, to give his personal, official assessment of the 'new measures' movement in New York. It came in the form of a letter to S. C. Aiken of Utica, New York, for whom Finney had preached in the summer of 1826, and who was becoming sympathetic with his evangelistic methods. The letter was designed for general circulation and specifically for the perusal of Finney and his friends. It was one of the most important letters that Asahel ever wrote and was a crucial development in the controversy at hand. It contains an exposé of the objectionable elements of the 'western revivals', suggestions for correcting these excesses, and a statement of his attitude toward Finney personally ...

"This lengthy epistle, along with other similar material, was printed in its entirety in a booklet entitled, *Letters on the New Measures in Conducting Revivals of Religion*, and thus preserved for posterity. It was published in New York in 1828 and is remarkably restrained in tone, utterly devoid of rancour and invective, and, in many respects, generous toward those with whom he was at issue ...

244 ASAHEL NETTLETON: REVIVAL PREACHER

> "Nettleton's letter was soon circulated among some of the pastors in New York and also reached Finney himself. He took it not only as a criticism of some of his followers but also as an attack upon himself which could not be ignored. He immediately jumped to his own defense by preaching a sermon in Beman's church from Amos 3:3 'How can two walk together except they be agreed?' ... Nettleton was, of course, stung by Finney's sermon."[1]

It will be helpful at this juncture to introduce a letter from Nettleton's personal papers at Hartford Seminary. This letter is written by a friend of Nettleton's, a Mr. C. E. Furman, who quite possibly may have been a disciple of Nettleton's. Furman had actually *attended* a Finney meeting and reported to Nettleton the following terrifying facts:

> "New York, October 19, 1826.

> ... At an inquiry meeting anxious sinners were weeping and groaning at a most bitter rate. Mr. Finney told them with the appearance of anger, that the only difference between them and the legions in Hell was, that the latter were weeping because they were there, the former because they were going there. Then he asked if any were willing to submit to Christ, if so, they would manifest it by rising. Two only arose, there said he, these are willing to submit, but you are hard, wicked, stubborn. After talking in the most threatening manner others and others arose and were I should think from the relation considerably flattered, but now said he, you have only manifested your willingness to submit—Have you submitted? If you have, then manifest it by kneeling: only one kneeled, there said he is one child of God who has absolutely submitted, all you are going to Hell but she to Heaven. He talked in this way till she visibly manifest the effects of flattery ... Mr. Finney met Mr. Frost of that place, a very good man who had before had a revival in his Church and because he would not acknowledge Mr. Finney a right in his manner, he called him Frost by name Frost by nature, and as cold as ice—Say you are these things right?"[2]

From these observations we may conclude that Asahel Nettleton had various "informants" who reported to him the apparent dangers of the western revivals. One of Nettleton's best sources was the Rev. William Weeks of Oneida County. Nettleton realized that before things grew to epic proportions it was now time for him to *act*. The result was the letter to Rev. Aiken. We now provide the infamous "Nettleton Letter" which caused such a panic in the "Finney camp".

> ALBANY, JANUARY 13, 1827

> "Seven years ago, about two thousand souls were hopefully born into the kingdom, in this vicinity, in our own denomination with comparative stillness. But the times have altered. The kingdom of God now cometh with great observation. Opposition from the world is always to be expected. It is idle for any minister to expect a revival without it. But when it enters the church of God, the friends of Zion cannot but take alarm.

> "There is doubtless a work of grace in Troy. Many sinners have hopefully been born into the kingdom; but it has been at an awful expense. Many of our first ministers have visited the place, to witness for themselves. Such men as Dr. Griffin,

Dr. Porter of Catskill, Dr. Nott, Mr. Tucker, Mr. Cornelius, and many more. Some of them have heard a number of sermons. After giving credit for preaching much truth, they uniformly say, 'I never heard the names of God used with such irreverence.' Dr. Griffin gave me a number of specimens. I do not wish to retain them. The church in Troy is greatly divided. Some have taken a dismission; others are consulting neighboring ministers about the path of duty; and others are beginning to attend worship by themselves.

"But the worst is not told. The spirit of denunciation which has grown out of the mode of conducting the revivals at the West, is truly alarming. We do not call in question the genuineness of those revivals, or the purity of the motives of those who have been the most active in them. You, doubtless, are reaping and rejoicing in their happy fruits. But the evils to which I allude, are felt by the churches abroad; members of which have gone out to catch the spirit, and have returned, some grieved, others soured, and denouncing ministers, colleges, theological seminaries, and have set whole churches by the ears, and kept them in turmoil for months together. Some students in divinity have done more mischief in this way than they can ever repair. I could mention names, but for exposing them. Some ministers and professors of religion have been to Troy, from the surrounding region, on purpose to catch the flame, and have returned home, saying, 'We do not want *such* a revival as they have in Troy.'

"The evil is running in all directions. A number of churches have experienced a revival of anger, wrath, malice, envy, and evil-speaking, without the knowledge of a single conversion—merely in consequence of a desperate attempt to introduce these new measures. Those ministers and Christians who have hitherto been most and longest acquainted with revivals, are most alarmed at the spirit which has grown out of the revivals of the West. This spirit has, no doubt, greatly deteriorated by transportation. As we now have it, the great contest is among professors of religion—a civil war in Zion—a domestic broil in the household of faith. The friends of brother Finney are certainly doing him and the cause of Christ great mischief. They seem more anxious to convert ministers and Christians to their peculiarities, than to convert souls to Christ.

"It is just such a contest as I have sometimes seen, in its incipient stages, in New England, between some young revival ministers on the one side, and whole associations of ministers on the other. The young revival ministers, wishing to extend the work into all the churches in their zeal would enter the limits of settled pastors, and commence their operations, and plead my own example for all their movements; and so the war would begin. And all those ministers who would not yield the reins and sanction their imprudences, would be sure to be proclaimed as enemies to revivals. Being thus defeated, these young ministers would come to me to make their complaints, and to work on my mind the conviction that all those ministers were enemies to myself; whereas the whole evil lay in a violation of all the rules of ministerial order, and Christian meekness, or in the inexperience, ignorance, and imprudence of these young ministers. I am sorry to speak thus of my best friends; but it is due to my brethren to say, that those very ministers, who had been thus slandered by my young brethren, have since come to me with tears, urging me to visit their flocks. There is not one of them but would bid me a welcome, and would rejoice in a revival; but they would not invite these young ministers to preach for them, who had been so rash in their proceedings, and guilty of slandering them as stupid, and dead, and enemies of revivals. In this manner, some of the most promising young revival ministers have run themselves out, and lost the confidence of settled pastors and Christians in general.

"The spirit of denunciation which has grown out of these western revivals, seems to be owing to the implicit confidence which has been placed in the proceedings of just such young ministers as leaders. They dared not attempt to correct any of their irregularities, for fear of doing mischief, or of being denounced as enemies to revivals. This I know to be the fact. Brother Finney himself has been scarcely three years in the ministry, and has had no time to look at consequences. He has gone, with all the zeal of a young convert, without a friend to check or guide him. And I have no doubt that he begins with astonishment to look at the evils which are running before him.

"The account which his particular friends give of his proceedings, is, in substance, as follows: He has got ministers to agree with him only by 'crushing,' or 'breaking them down.' The method by which he does it, is by creating a necessity, by getting a few individuals in a church to join him, and then all those who will not go all lengths with him, are denounced as enemies to revivals; and rather than have such a bad name, one and another falls in to defend him; and then they proclaim what ministers, elders, and men of influence have been 'crushed' or 'broken down.' This moral influence being increased, others are denounced, in a similar manner, as standing out, and leading sinners to hell. And to get rid of the noise, and save himself, another will 'break down.' And so they wax hotter and hotter, until the church is fairly split in twain. And now, as for those elders and Christians, who have thus been converted to these measures; some of them are sending out private word to their Christian friends abroad, as follows: 'I have been fairly *skinned* by the denunciations of these men, and have ceased to oppose them, to get rid of their noise. But I warn you not to introduce this spirit into your church and society.' And so, brother Finney's supposed friends, men of influence, are sending out word to warn others to beware of the evils which they have experienced. I heartily pity brother Finney, for I believe him to be a good man, and wishing to do good. But nobody dares tell him that a train of causes is set in operation, and urged on by his own friends, which is likely to ruin his usefulness.

"Whoever has made himself acquainted with the state of things in New England, near the close of the revival in the days of Whitefield and Edwards, cannot but weep over its likeness to the present. It is affecting, that the warm friends of Zion should unwittingly betray her best interests. But so was it then. The young itinerants, in their zeal to extend the work, began to denounce all those settled ministers who would not go all lengths with them. And then those members of churches who loved their pastors would assemble around to defend them; while those who favored the itinerants assembled around them, and imbibing their spirit, of course lost all confidence in a settled ministry: and so the churches were split in twain. The Spirit of God took its flight, and darkness and discord reigned for half a century. And those preachers who had taken the lead, having cultivated such a spirit, began to fall into awful darkness themselves, when they saw the ruin that followed their labors. Some of them made and published their recantations to the world, which are now extant. But it was too late. A retribution followed. Some few of the young converts were called to order by David Brainerd, who passed through Connecticut at that time, but after their recantations, these leaders were generally denounced by their own followers. Could Whitefield and Edwards, and Brainerd, and Davenport, now arise from the dead, I have no doubt they would exclaim, 'young men, beware! beware!'

"Some of brother Finney's younger brethren and friends may attempt to work on his mind the conviction that most of our ministers and churches are enemies to revivals, and unfriendly to himself. I feel it is my duty to speak in their behalf. I know it to be a mistake. The best friends of revivals, as they have heretofore witnessed them, are certainly the most afraid to invite him into their churches, and are the most alarmed at the evils that are rising. And, I must say, that his friends are certainly laboring to introduce those very measures, which I have ever regarded as ultimately working ruin to our churches; and against which I have always guarded as ruinous to the character of revivals, as well as to my own usefulness.

"For example: whoever introduces the practice of female praying in promiscuous assemblies, let the practice once become general, will ere long find, to his sorrow, that he has made an inlet to other denominations, and entailed an everlasting quarrel on those churches generally. If settled pastors choose to do it on their own responsibility, so be it. For one, I dare not assume so great a responsibility. In this way churches were once laid wasted. And it is by keeping out, and carefully avoiding every thing of this kind, that some of them have again been built, others kept orderly, and the character of revivals, for *thirty* years past, has been guarded. If the evil be not soon prevented, a generation will arise, inheriting all the obliquities of their leaders, not knowing that a revival ever did or can exist, without all those evils. And these evils are destined to be propagated from generation to generation, waxing worse and worse.

"The friends of brother Finney are afraid to interfere to correct any thing, lest they should do mischief, or be denounced as enemies of revivals. 'Brother Nettleton, do come into this region and help us; for many things are becoming current among us which I cannot approve. And I can do nothing to correct them, but I am immediately shamed out of it, by being denounced as an enemy to revivals.' Thus my ministerial brethren from the West, whose views accord with my own, have been calling to me, in their letters during the summer past. 'There is religion in it, and I dare not touch it. I see the evil and tremble at the consequences; but what can I do?' This is the language of many of his warmest friends. And so the bad must all be defended with the good. This sentiment adopted, *will certainly ruin revivals*. It is the language of a novice: it is just as the devil would have it. If the friends of revivals dare not correct their own faults, who will do it for them? I know no such policy. I would no more dare defend in the gross, than condemn in the gross. And those who adopt the former practice, will soon be compelled by prevailing corruptions, to take along with it the latter. The character of revivals is to be sustained on the same principles as that of the churches, or individual Christians. *If we would judge ourselves, we should not be judged.* It is not by *covering*, but by *confessing* and *forsaking*, that pure revivals are to prosper. In this manner their character has long been sustained. Things have not been left to run to such lengths in our day. A strong hand has been laid on young converts, old professors, and especially on zealous young ministers, as many of them now living can testify. I have been afraid to kindle fires where there was not some spiritual watchman near, to guard and watch against wildness, for which I might become responsible. Some students in divinity have caught and carried the flame into neighboring towns and villages, and no doubt have been the means of the salvation to some souls. But I am sorry to say, that some of them have run before me into the most populous places, and have carried their measures so far, and have become so dictatorial and assuming, that, in the opinion of the most judicious and influential ministers of my acquaintance, they have done far more mischief than good. They have pleaded my example for many measures, which, as to time and circumstances, I utterly condemn. Some of the means which I have never dared to employ except in the most interesting crisis of a powerful revival, they have caricatured in such a manner, and raised such prejudices against myself among strangers, that they have caused me much trouble. My plans have been laid to visit many towns and cities, and have been wholly defeated by these students in divinity thus running before me. I have been much grieved, and exceedingly perplexed on this subject. They assume an authority, unwittingly I allow, and adopt measures, which no ordained minister could do, without ruining his usefulness. Evils arising hence, have uniformly been arrested in their progress, by my taking the part of settled pastors among their flocks; at a great expense of feeling, on the part of my young friends, no doubt; but the cause of revivals evidently required it.

"I have been anxiously looking and waiting, all summer long, for such men as yourself and Mr. Lansing, and others most intimately acquainted with brother Finney, to take hold, with a kind severity, and restore order; but in vain. It is not expected that a powerful revival can exist among imperfect beings, without more or less irregularity and opposition; but it is expected that these things will generally subside, and leave the churches in a more peaceful, happy, and flourishing state than ever. This has been uniformly the case, where revivals have prevailed. But irregularities are prevailing so fast, and assuming such a character, in our churches, as infinitely to overbalance the good that is left. These evils, sooner or later, must be corrected. Somebody must speak, or silence will prove our ruin. Fire is an excellent thing in its place, and I am not afraid to see it blaze among briers and thorns; but when I see it kindling where it will ruin fences, and gardens, and houses, and burn up my friends, I cannot be silent.

"Had the evil been checked in the commencement, it would have been an act of kindness to brother Finney, and great gain to the cause of revivals. He would have found ministers every where bidding him welcome. His help is every where greatly needed. For a settled pastor, the entire confidence of other ministers would not be so important. But, whoever undertakes to promote revivals, by running through the world, in this age of revivals, must have the entire confidence of settled ministers generally; otherwise he will unsettle ministers, and desolate churches, wherever he goes. Without their hearty co-operation, he will certainly labor at great disadvantage: as if a mariner, steering his ship in storm at sea, in his zeal should quit the helm, and ply his strength at the mast.

"The practice of praying for people by name, in the closet, and the social circle, has no doubt had a beneficial effect. But, as it now exists in many places, it has become, in the eye of the Christian community at large, an engine of public slander in its worst form. I should not dare in this solemn manner, to arraign a fellow-sinner before a public assembly, without his own particular request, unless my expressions were of the most conciliatory kind. And no Christian minister, whatever his character may be, can adopt the practice without awakening the indignation of the world at large, and of Christians generally, against him. Much less can it be done by anybody, who takes it into his head positively to decide the question, and to tell God and the world, whatever may be the effect upon the individual thus named, that God will regard such a prayer in any other light than as that of a proud, self-righteous Pharisee.

"There is another interesting topic that lies near my heart; but the time would fail me to express my views and feelings on the subject. That holy, humble, meek, modest, retiring form, sometimes called the Spirit of Prayer, and which I have ever regarded as the unfailing precursor of a revival of religion, has been dragged from her closet, and so rudely handled by some of her professed friends, that she has not only lost all her wonted loveliness, but is now stalking the streets in some places stark mad.

"Some, in their zeal on the subject of the *prayer of faith*, are tormenting others with their peculiar sentiments, which, if correct, every body sees must equally condemn themselves; thus rendering themselves and their sentiments perfectly ridiculous.

"I have given you but an imperfect sketch of my own and the views of our brethren abroad on this subject; but I assure you, as a whole, it is not overdrawn. How to correct these growing evils I cannot tell. Our brethren, far and near, some of brother Finney's best friends at the West not excepted, by letter and otherwise, have long been urging me to lay the subject fully before him. The evils which have existed, abroad have certainly been very much concealed from him and his friends. It is certainly right that he should know something of the evils which have run from under him; and the feelings of the friends of Zion at large. I have nothing to say to him in the style of crimination or controversy. I have been too long on the field of battle to be frightened about little things, or to make a man an offender for a word. For Zion's sake, I wish to save brother Finney from a course which I am confident will greatly retard his usefulness before he knows it. It is no reflection on his talents or piety, that, in his zeal to save souls, he should adopt every measure which promises present success, regardless of consequences; nor, after a fair experiment in so noble a cause, to say, I have pushed some things beyond what they will bear. The most useful lessons are learned by experience.

"I wish I had health and strength to show brother Finney my whole heart on this subject. I have long been wishing to correct some of his peculiarities, that I might invite him into my own field and introduce him to my friends. Aside from feeble health, one consideration only has prevented me from making the attempt. Some of his particular friends are urging him on to the very things which I wish him to drop. I fear that their flattering representations will overrule all that I can say. And having dropped these peculiarities, his labors for a while might be less successful; and then he would resort again to the same experiment. But I can inform him, that the same measures which he had adopted, have been vigorously and obstinately pursued in New England, against the repeated advice of settled pastors, and that too, by one of the most powerful and successful ministers that I have ever known, until confident of his own strength, he quit them all, with this expression, 'We will see who will answer by fire'—a most unhappy expression, as he afterwards told me with tears. The result was, he lost his usefulness in our denomination. Some of his spiritual children, now excellent men in the ministry, have never dared to adopt his measures, but have uniformly opposed them. Others, ministers and laymen, who followed him, became disorganizers; and the leader himself turned Baptist, and soon after died.

"There is another method of conducting revivals, which may avoid these difficulties. Settled pastors occupy nearly the whole field of operation. They have, and ought to have, the entire management in their own congregation. Each one has a right to pursue his own measures within his own limits; and no itinerant has any business to interfere or dictate. It will ever be regarded as intermeddling in other men's matters. If they do not choose to invite me into their field, my business is meekly and silently to retire. And I have no right to complain. But many young men are continually violating the rules of ministerial order and Christian propriety in these respects. Impatient to see the temple rise, they are now doing that, which, appears to me, will tend ultimately, more than anything else, to defeat the end which they wish to accomplish. They are now pulling down, in many places, the very things which I have been helping ministers to build up; and for which I have often received their warmest thanks. It is a sentiment which I have had frequent occasion to repeat to my young brethren in the ministry, 'Better forego the prospect of much present good, in your own opinion, than to lose the confidence of settled ministers, without which you cannot be long and extensively useful.'

"There is, certainly, another and a lawful point of attack on the kingdom of darkness, which, when you have taken, and it is seen, possesses wonderful advantages. It will give no offence to the church of God. It will be sure to rally around you every faithful soldier of the cross. Though it may seem too slow and silent in its operations, yet, being the lawful method of conducting this warfare, it will secure the confidence of ministers and Christians, the consciences of the wicked, and a crown of glory.

"And now, brother, I have ventured to lay before you the subject of my prayers and tears, and I may add, the subject which brought me back to a region which I never expected to visit again. If you discover any thing in this communication unchristian or unkind, you will pardon it. If, in your opinion, it can do no mischief, or will do any possible good, you are at full liberty to show it to brother Finney, or any of the friends of Zion whom it may concern. We will lay the subject at the feet of our Divine Master, and there will we leave it.

Yours, in the best of bonds."[3]

Notes

1   Thornbury, pp. 169–173.
2   Manuscript letter, C. E. Furman to Asahel Nettleton, October 19, 1826, Hartford Seminary Collection.
3   Ms. letter, Asahel Nettleton to Rev. Aiken, Albany, New York, January 13th, 1827, Hartford Seminary Collection.

The letter, although addressed to Mr. Aikin, was intended for the perusal of Mr. Finney and his friends. Soon after it was received, Mr. Finney prepared and preached at Utica, a sermon on the text, "How can two walk together except they be agreed." This sermon was understood to be a vindication of the things complained of in Dr. Nettleton's letter. It was afterwards preached in Troy and published.

BENNET TYLER

23

FINNEY'S REBUTTAL:
"CAN TWO WALK TOGETHER?"

n infuriated Charles Finney entered the fray. He had been personally wounded by Asahel Nettleton's "circular epistle"; or "manifesto" as Lyman Beecher referred to it, and wasted no time in preparing and launching a counter-attack. This rebuttal came in the form of a sermon Finney preached in Utica, New York, entitled, "How Can Two Walk Together Unless They Be Agreed?", taken from the text of Amos 3:3. We must remember an important factor here: Charles Finney evangelist, was formerly Charles Finney the *lawyer*, and unfortunate was the person on the receiving end of Finney's verbal daggers! Finney's sermon, although not expository, serves its purpose well to respond to Asahel Nettleton's accusations. The sermon is *pure Finney*. He elucidates his points effectively, aiming his arrows at Nettleton and company with precision. It is obvious from the sermon, that Finney was prepared for an all-out *war* with Nettleton, Beecher, and anyone else who disagreed with him on how to conduct revivals. Finney had no intention of ceasing his "new measures" in revivals.

The "new measures" controversy was multi-layered. The main problem facing Asahel Nettleton in all of this was that the majority of the churches *wanted* Finney's "new measures". From 1827, in New England particularly, and in America generally, much of the religious populace was moving away from the stiff religious formalism that accompanied much of Calvinism in New England in that day. The masses, who were discovering their democratic freedom from Federalism, alongside a new found prosperity, simply desired to be the masters of their destiny—not a far away God they could not see. They did not want a God who was in control of their salvation or their lives. Rather, many wanted "control" of their destiny by the easiest means possible. Pelagianism was gladly accepted as the new theology in many churches, for those who embraced this philosophy saw no need to change their hearts toward God; there was no need for biblical *regeneration*, but merely outward *reformation*. This was a rejection of the God of the Bible by the people of America and God *removed the cloud and the pillar of fire* from the churches in the land, eventually bringing a close to the Second Great Awakening. And unfortunately for Asahel Nettleton, in many regards, he would end up *standing alone* fighting a losing battle; an Edwardsean who was going the way of the *dinosaur*.

The growing debate between the two mighty evangelists is seen in the following comments:

> "Nettleton was, of course, stung by Finney's sermon ... Thus began the debate over the new measures between Nettleton and Finney. Nettleton had referred to the uproar he found when he came to New York as a 'civil war in Zion ... a domestic broil in the household of faith.' By his letter to Aiken he joined the conflict, though he had hoped that his influence would have been great enough to put down the opposition. But such was not the case. Clearly the lines were being drawn between two opposing schools of thought on evangelism, each side headed by men of great ability and influence."[1]

For a more in-depth look at Finney's sermon we turn to Sherry Pierpont May who writes:

> "The text was Amos 3:3. 'Can two walk together except they be agreed?' According to Finney it is common in scripture to find 'a negative thrown into the form of an interrogation.' Thus, for him, Amos is really affirming in this passage that 'two cannot walk together except they be agreed.'
>
> "For two to be able to walk together they must be agreed in more than theory or understanding. Saints and sinners may assent to the same creed; and it is probable that holy angels and devils embrace the same truths. The agreement must be in terms of 'feeling' and 'practice' or in the 'affections.' As Finney says,
>
> '... the difference in the *effect consists in the different manner in which the person receives these truths, or feels and acts in view of them*. It is to be observed also, that the same things and truths will affect the same mind very differently at different times. This too is owing to the different state of the affections at these times ... All pleasure and pain— all happiness and misery—all sin and holiness—have their seat in, and belong to, the *heart* or affections. All the satisfaction or dissatisfaction, pain or pleasure, that we feel in view of any truth or thing presented to our minds, depends entirely upon the *state* of our affection at the time, and consists in these affections (Sermon *VIII*, Christian Affinity, Amos 3:3—"Can Two Walk Together Except They Be Agreed?" *Sermons on Important Subjects* by Charles G. Finney, New York: John S. Taylor, 1936, pp. 181–195).'
>
> "Finney believes that his theory of the affections is grounded in Jonathan Edwards' theology, but it is clear that the 'heart' or 'affections' is a much more comprehensive term for Edwards than for Finney.
>
> "Finney goes further, however, than merely saying that what is presented to one's understanding must correlate with one's affections in order to be effective. He adds

that it is necessary that what is presented agrees as to the 'depth,' tone, or level of one's affections. Thus,

'If any thing even upon the same subject (i.e., that which is already engaging the affections) that is far above or below our tone of feeling is presented, and if our affections remain the same, and we refuse to be enlisted and brought to that point, we *must* feel uninterested, and perhaps grieved and offended. If the subject be exhibited in a light that is below our present tone of feeling we cannot be interested until it come up to our feelings; and if the subject in this cooling and to us degraded point of view is held up before our mind, and we struggle to maintain these high affections, we feel displeased because our affections are not fed but opposed. If the subject be presented in a manner that strikes far above our tone of feeling, and our affections grovel and *refuse to rise*, it does not fall in with and feed our affections, therefore we cannot be interested; it is enthusiasm to us, we are displeased with the warmth in which we do not choose to participate, and the farther it is above our temperature and the more we are disgusted.'

"In this manner the indictment is extended beyond the impenitent sinner to include all 'lukewarm' professors of religion or 'cold' ministers whose feelings do not agree with Finney's. If a person's heart or affections are 'wrong' (the sinner) or 'low' (the lukewarm Christian), then he is offended and angered by one whose affections are 'high.'

"After his initial statement that the subject presented to a person must agree with the state and degree of his feelings, Finney spends the remainder of this fairly lengthy sermon illustrating his point:

'Suppose you hear a cold man *preach* or *pray*; while he remains cold and you are warm with feeling you are not interested, for your affections are not fed and cherished unless he comes up to your tone; if this does not happen you are distressed and perhaps disgusted with his coldness. Again: We see why lukewarm professors and impenitent sinners have *the same* difficulties with *means* in revivals of religion … The reason is that at that time their affections are nearly the same; it is the fire and the spirit that disturbs their frosty hearts. For the time being they walk together, for in *feeling* they are agreed.'

"Brother Finney used this principle to explain why Christians coming from an area in which there is no revival, rebel and raise objections about the means used in a place which is in the height of a successful revival. Simply, 'the praying, preaching, and conversation, are above their presenter temperature.' The greater the distance between the feelings of what is being presented and their own, the greater their displeasure. It is also on this principle that Finney shows that the impenitent sinners and cold Christians have little objection to dull or obtuse preaching. Such preaching is so close to their state of feeling that it is not offensive.

"Divisions and conflict within a church are easy to explain. There are often hypocrites or cold professors (including sometimes the pastor) in a church. 'When revivals are in a measure stripped of animal feeling, and become highly spiritual,' these people 'are disturbed by the fire and spirit of them, and inwardly and sometimes openly oppose them.' If it is the minister who is at fault, Finney suggests, 'let the church shake off their sleepy minister; they are better without him than with him.'

"Finney's concluding remarks stress the violent opposition which Christ and his apostles received from carnal professors of religion, as well as from sinners. With one finger clearly pointed at Nettleton and Beecher, Finney emphasizes the fact that it was the religious teachers and learned doctors, often the religious leaders of the day, who 'endeavored to prejudice the multitude against the Saviour, and to prevent their listening to his discourses' and finally crucified Him. The great amount of controversy, 'noise,' and opposition to the preaching and work of the apostles is explained solely by the fact that they

'were so much more holy in their lives and so much bolder, and more faithful in delivering their messages; that Christ was so much more searching, and plain, and pungent, and personal in his preaching, and so entirely 'separate from sinners' in his life; the apostles were so pungent and plain in their dealing with sinners and professed saints, and so self-denying and holy in their lives, that carnal professors and ungodly sinners could not *walk with them.*'

"And Finney cautioned his followers,

'Let us know if they [opposers of revivals] have less difficulty with *us,* and with our *lives,* and *preaching,* than they had with theirs [Christ and the apostles], it is because we are less holy, less heavenly, less like God than they were. If we walk with the lukewarm and ungodly, or they with *us,* it is because we are agreed. For two cannot walk together except they *be agreed.*'

"Finney's sermon, preached first at Utica and later in Troy, then published, was a declaration that the measures being used in the Western revivals were right; and that any opposition to them was from impenitent sinners, carnal professors (the Unitarians and Universalists), and lukewarm Christians (like Nettleton) who came in from out of the region and did not see what was going on. Finney, as was always the case, stressed the *choice* the opposer had; one could change his heart and subsequently be a part of the activity, or he could decide to remain as he was and oppose it. But the choice was his."[2]

One can see from Finney's "Papal Bull" that *anyone* who disagreed with him or the methodology he employed in revivals, was destined to be *denounced* by him and his followers as an *enemy* of revivals! We must remind ourselves that in the early to mid-nineteenth century a man's *honor* was primarily his highest asset. In an age of "dueling" over one's honor (Lyman Beecher wrote and published extensively against this public evil) no believer could be called *cold or carnal or lukewarm* without a fight on one's hands! If Asahel Nettleton was alarmed over Finney's behavior in conducting revivals, he was *startled* by the denunciatory slander aimed at his Christian character! His response to Finney's sermon, in the form of a published letter, was filled with *passion.*

For the most part, Nettleton's "answer" to Finney's sermon was well received by most ministers in the controversy. However a rumor arose that some prominent Congregational New England ministers were unhappy with Nettleton's "remarks". This rumor grew to such proportions it was necessary for some friends of Nettleton to take a public stand in his defense. This came in the printed form of a "public statement" from the following eminent clergymen:

"It having been represented to some of the subscribers, that we disapproved of the proceedings of the Rev. Mr. Nettleton, in reviewing a sermon preached at Troy, March 4, 1827, and in opposing the sentiments and practices which it seemed intended to vindicate and extend, we regard ourselves as called upon by a sense of duty to say, that the proceedings of Mr. Nettleton appear to us have been characterized by uncommon intellectual vigor, correct and comprehensive views of the interests of the church, and by distinguished wisdom, fidelity, firmness, and benevolence, well adapted to promote the interests of pure religion throughout the land.

Signed by, Lyman Beecher, A. S. Norton, William R. Weeks, H. R. Weed, Justin Edwards, Heman Humphrey, C. J. Tenney, J. Hawes."[3]

Battle lines were being drawn as to which ministers were siding with Nettleton, and who was on Finney's side (mainly the ministers of the West). For those readers who wish to see Asahel Nettleton's "letter" in response to Finney's sermon, we now include that letter in its entirety. Nettleton's letter was originally intended for Dr. Spring, of New York but was later published in the "New York Observer"; the letter was dated, Durham, N. Y., May 4th, 1827. This letter was also included in the collection of correspondence entitled, "Letters of Dr. Beecher and Dr. Nettleton on the 'New Measures'". Here now are extracts from Nettleton's lengthy epistle which dissects Finney's sermon point by point:

"My Dear Brother,

I have read brother Finney's sermon, from the words, 'How can two walk together except they be agreed?' The principle, on which it rests, is contained in the following sentences:

'If any thing, even upon the same subject, that is far above or below our tone of feeling, is presented; and if our affections remain the same, and refuse to be enlisted and brought to that point, we must feel uninterested, and perhaps grieved and offended. If the subject be exhibited in a light that is below our present tone of feelings, we cannot be interested until it come up to our feelings; if this does not take place, we necessarily remain uninterested. If the subject be presented in a manner that is far above our tone of feeling, and our affections grovel and refuse to rise, it does not fall in with and feed our affections: therefore we cannot be interested; it is enthusiasm to us, we are displeased with the warmth in which our affections refuse to participate; and the farther it is above our temperature, the more are we disgusted. These are truths to which the experience of every man will testify, as they hold good upon every subject, and under all circumstances, and are founded upon principles that are incorporated with the very nature of man.'

"Now all of this, so far as Christians and *true* religion are concerned, I take to be false in theory, contrary to fact, and dangerous in its consequences. Present to the mind of the Christian, whose holiness and flaming zeal shall equal that of Paul, the least degree of holiness in any saint, and he will not be offended, but interested. He would be greatly delighted with even 'babes in Christ.' And the higher the tone of his piety and holy feeling, the greater will be his delight, even 'upon the same subject.' Now, raise the tone of pious feeling up to that of the spirits of just men made perfect, and holy angels, and still they will not lose their interest, 'even upon the same subject.' They will rejoice even over one sinner that repenteth, far more than will those whose feelings fall to the level of the penitent himself.

"Nor is it true that Christians are always better pleased with those, whose tone of feelings is on a level with their own. The least saint on earth loves holiness in others, and rejoices in their growth in grace. And he loves those most, whose tone of holy feeling is raised farthest above him; and for the same reason, he loves the Saviour more than all. Every child of God, who reads his bible, is far better pleased with the high-toned piety of Job, and Daniel, and David, and Isaiah, and Paul, than he is with that of other saints, whose piety falls below theirs, or to the level of his own. What Christian can read the memoirs of Edwards and Brainerd, without deep interest? I know of no Christian that does not read them with far greater interest than he would have done, had they exhibited far less of the spirit of Christianity. And though Christians feel condemned, by their high-toned piety, yet for this very reason, they are not 'offended and grieved,' but love them the more. Though Christians are not up to the tone of piety exhibited by David and Paul, Edwards and Brainerd, yet they are highly delighted, and could walk together with them.

"Again: take the example of our Saviour. No Christian on earth is better pleased with any other. Though many of his friends have died and gone to heaven, whom he still loves, yet the Christian can say, 'whom have I in heaven but thee, and there is none upon earth that I desire beside thee.' The tone of the Saviour's pious and holy feeling is certainly raised far above that of all his followers. Hence, according to the sentiment of the sermon, he could have had no followers on earth, and can have none now. All his disciples must have been '*displeased* with his warmth.' And the higher it rose 'above their temperature, the more they must have been *disgusted*.'

"Present to the mind of the Christian the holy character of God. Is not this subject far above the tone of the feelings of any man? Now according to the sentiment of the sermon, if our affections are not brought to that point, we must feel 'uninterested, grieved and offended.' According to the principle of his own sermon, brother Finney and his friends cannot walk with God, for they are not agreed. It must be acknowledged, that God has an infinitely higher tone and degree of holy feeling than brother Finney. He is not 'up to it.' Consequently, on his own principles, they cannot be agreed. God is displeased with him, and he with God. Brother Finney must '*necessarily*' be displeased with high and holy zeal in his Maker, which so infinitely transcends his own; and the 'farther it is above his temperature, the more he will be *disgusted*.' 'These are truths,' he observes, 'to which the experience of every man will testify, as they hold good upon *every subject*, and under all circumstances, and are founded upon principles that are incorporated with the very nature of man.' ...

"The sermon in question entirely overlooks the nature of true religion. It says not one word by which we can distinguish between true and false zeal, true and false religion. ... If the tone of feeling can only be raised to a certain pitch, then all is well. The self-righteous, the hypocrite, and all who are inflated with pride, will certainly be flattered and pleased with such an exhibition; especially if they are very self-righteous and very proud. False affections often rise far higher than those that are genuine; and this every preacher, in seasons of revival, has had occasion to observe and correct. And the reason of their great height is obvious. There are no salutary checks of conscience, no holy, humble exercises to counteract them in their flight. And they court observation. 'A pharisee's trumpet shall be heard to the town's end, when simplicity walks through the town unseen.' If the preacher is not extremely careful to distinguish between true and false affections, the devil will certainly come in and overset and bring the work into disgrace. False zeal and overgrown spiritual pride will rise up and take the management, and condemn *meekness and humility*, and trample upon all the Christian graces, because they are not 'up to it.'

"Matters of fact which have passed under my own observation, might serve as illustration. I have often seen it; and the preacher who has not been tried with this subject, and learned to correct it, has not got his first lesson.

"Leaving out of the question the *nature of true* religion, as brother Finney has done out of his sermon, there is a sense in which his theory perfectly accords with experience and matters of fact. So far as false zeal and false affections are concerned, the principle of the sermon is correct. A and B are very zealous, and extremely self-righteous; and being equally so, they can walk together, for they are agreed. Both having come up to the same tone of feeling with brother Finney in his sermon;—now they are all agreed, and all pleased, having done all that the preacher required. Now the zeal of A 'strikes far above the tone of feeling' in his fellow, and both are 'displeased, grieved, and offended.' B does not come to the tone of A and 'therefore he cannot be interested; it is enthusiasm—he is displeased with the warmth in which his affections refuse to participate; and the farther it is above his temperature, the more he is disgusted.' The Christian and the hypocrite may come up to the *same tone of feeling;* and yet they cannot walk together, for *other* reasons. The character of their affections differs as widely as light and darkness. And the higher their affections rise, the wider the distance between them. And no tone or degree of feeling can possibly bring them together. Every effort of the preacher to unite them by raising the tone of feeling, will only increase the difficulty. This, too, accords with experience and matters of fact. Hence, those who adopt the same creed, and belong to the same communion, can have no fellowship. Though they are up to the same tone of feeling, and feel *deeply*, yet they cannot walk together, for they do not feel *alike*. Feelings which are not founded on *correct* theology cannot be *right*. They must *necessarily* be spurious, or merely animal.

"Without great care and close discrimination, the preacher will unwittingly justify all the quarrels and divisions in our churches. The church at Corinth valued themselves on their great spirituality, and high attainments in religion. Now on the principle of the sermon in question, their divisions and quarrels could be no evidence to the contrary, but much in their favor. Each one esteeming others worse than himself, would conclude that the whole difficulty lay in their not coming up to the tone of his own feelings. And this sermon would have confirmed them all in their good opinion of themselves. But *Paul* told them the very contrary was true. 'For whereas there is among you envying, and strife, and divisions, are ye not carnal, and walk as men.' Without the same care, the preacher will condemn others for keeping the unity of the spirit in the bond of peace; and for 'being of one accord and of one mind.' *That peace*, and harmony, and order, in which Paul so much rejoiced, will be disturbed, and broken, and trampled upon, by disorganizing spiritual pride, under a pretense that all are 'cold, and carnal, and stupid, and dead, and not up to the spirit of the times.' All who are thus inflated, will take the advantage of this sermon, and be sure to construe all opposition to their own disorganizing movements and measures, into an evidence of superior piety in themselves. And all false converts, and others inflated with spiritual pride, will join them, if great care be not taken to discriminate between true and false zeal, and to give the distinguishing marks of both. Spiritual pride will often court opposition, and glory in it, and sometimes adopt the sentiment, 'The more opposition the better.' ...

"All who are acquainted with the history of facts on the subject, know that it was on the principles of the sermon in question, that the revival was run out in the time of Edwards, and in Kentucky and Tennessee, rising of twenty years since. And all those ministers who do not discriminate between true and false zeal, true and false affections, in their preaching and conversation, and make that difference, and hold it up to the view of the world, if possible, clear as the sun, heartily approving of the one, and as heartily and publicly condemning the other, will turn out to be the greatest traitors to the cause of revivals. They become responsible not only for the sentiment in question, but also for all the corruptions which prevail in consequence of this neglect. The neglect of ministers to correct these evils for fear of doing mischief, or of being denounced as carnal and cold-hearted, or as enemies to revivals, is extremely puerile and wicked. On the same principle they must not attempt to correct intemperance and profane swearing in church members, lest they should be ranked among the wicked, as infidels and enemies to Christianity. The sentiment in question would, if carried out into all its consequences, defend every abomination in religion that could be named. It would soon come to this: that the only evidence that ministers are cold, and carnal, and stupid, and dead, is, that they cannot approve of every art, and trick, and abominable practice in laymen, women, and children, in their attempts to promote a revival. And their approbation of all these abominations would be taken as a good sign, and as an evidence that they are *awake*. Whereas none but carnal and cold-hearted ministers would be influenced by such mean motives. It is only a trick of the Devil, to frighten the watchmen of Israel from his post, that he may get possession of it himself; or, what he would like still better, by such base motives to entoil and enlist him in his service, by compelling him to adopt his own measures. So did not Paul. His two epistles to the Corinthians contain little else than an humbling disclosure of abominable practices and quarrels about men and measures in promoting a revival. So did not Edwards. Though he was denounced at first, he could not be frightened: but frightened his denouncers, some of them at least, into a public recantation. A denouncing spirit is that with which *real* Christians have no fellowship, and are bound to shun.

"Without regard to the admonition, 'take heed to thyself,' the preacher will be in danger of trampling upon the divine direction, 'In meekness, instructing those that oppose themselves.'

"'The servant of the Lord must not strive, but be gentle unto all men.' 'Be kindly affectioned, be pitiful, be courteous.' He will be in great danger of condemning the 'meekness and gentleness of Christ,' under the names of 'carnal policy' and 'hypocritical suavity of manner.' The preacher should be extremely cautious what he says against 'wisdom and prudence,' as a mark of 'puffing up' in his brethren; lest he trample upon the authority of his Divine Master, in the precept given him upon the same point:—'Behold I send you forth as sheep in the midst of wolves: be ye therefore wise as serpents and harmless as doves.' His precept is founded on the fact that wicked men may become more offended with what is wrong in manner, than with what is right in matter. Hence the preacher may lose their consciences, and the Devil has gained the victory. If the wicked *will* oppose, it becomes us to be careful how we furnish them with successful weapons against us. If we regard the direction of Christ, even though they rage, we may still keep our hold upon their consciences; and so long as we can do this, we need not despair of the victory. But when the preacher has lost the wisdom of the serpent and the harmlessness of the dove, the contest will end in a sham-fight, and the sooner he quits the field the better.

"Paul would allow none to be teachers but those of 'full age, who by reason of use have their senses exercised to *discern* both good and evil.' Hence he would not license young converts to preach. 'Not a novice, lest being lifted up with pride he fall into condemnation, reproach, and the snare of the devil.' So far as his *message* was concerned, the apostle himself went forth, 'saluting no man by the way'—'not as pleasing men.' Aside from the *simple truth* of that message, no man was ever more yielding and flexible in manner and measures. 'Give no offence, neither to the Jews, neither to the Gentiles, nor to the church of God.' 'Even as I *please all men in all things*—that they may be saved.' 'I am made all things to all men, that I might by all means save some.' Was this 'carnal policy?' and was Paul 'in a very *cold* state when he wrote that?'

"The wisdom of the measures adopted and recommended by Paul, appear from the fact that sinners may be more offended with what is *wrong* in manner than what is *right* in matter. If the preacher does not hold a balance between conscience and depravity he can do nothing. The very fact that the unrenewed heart is so opposed to God and the gospel, has by some been assigned as a reason for stirring up all its opposition. Whereas, aside from the simple exhibition of divine *truth*, Paul adopted a method directly the opposite. If the vigilance of human depravity should exceed the vigilance of the preacher in his manner and measures, by this very means he will quiet the consciences of his hearers. Regardless of his manner, Paul would have lost his hold on the consciences of sinners, and needlessly and wickedly have sent his hearers to a returnless distance from the gospel. This made him exceedingly careful 'lest he should hinder the gospel of Christ.' Since mankind *will* oppose, we should be careful not to put weapons of successful defense into their hands. While they oppose, we should be careful to keep their consciences on our side.

"A powerful religious excitement badly conducted, has ever been considered by the most experienced ministers and best friends of revivals, to be a great calamity. Without close discrimination, an attempt to raise the tone of religious feeling will do infinite mischief. This was the manner of false teachers. 'They zealously affect you, but not well.' It will be like that of Paul before his conversion, and like that of the Jews who were never converted, 'a zeal of God but not according to knowledge.' The driving will become like the driving of Jehu, 'Come, see my zeal for the Lord.' The storm, and earthquake, and fire, are dreadful: but God is not there.

"The design of these remarks is to show the infinite importance of distinguishing between true and false zeal,——true and false affections.

"On reading the sermon in question, I was reminded of the repeated complaints which for some time past I have heard from the most judicious, experienced and best revival ministers in the West; the substance of which is as follows: 'There are various errors in the mode of conducting revivals in this region, which ought to be distinctly pointed out. That on the prayer of faith. This talking to God as a man talks to his neighbor, is truly shocking—telling the Lord a long story about A or B, and apparently with no other intent than to produce a kind of stage effect upon the individual in question, or upon the audience generally. This mouthing of words; those deep and hollow tones, all indicative that the person is speaking into the ears of man, and not to God. I say nothing of the nature of the petitions often presented; but *the awful irreverence of the manner!* How strange that good men should go so far forget themselves, as evidently to play tricks in the presence of the great God.

"I have often been struck with this circumstance in the mode of preaching, that nothing was heard of the danger of a spurious conversion. For months together, the thought never seemed to be glanced at, that there was any such thing as a satanic influence in the form of religion, but only as openly waging war against all religion. Such a character as an enthusiastic hypocrite, or a self-deceived person, seemed never to be once dreamed of. The only danger in the way of salvation was *coldness, deadness and rank opposition.* On no occasion did the eye ever seem to be turned to another quarter in the heavens.

"The last paragraph contains the thought to which I allude. The sermon in question bears striking marks of the same character. It is an important part of a preacher's duty in a season of powerful revival, to discriminate between true and false conversion. Without this, every discerning Christian knows that the work will rapidly degenerate. The most flaming spiritual pride will be taken for the highest moral excellence, and will rise up and take the lead.

"Preachers who have not guarded well this avenue in seasons of powerful excitement, have always done more to arrest, and disgrace, and run out revivals, than all the cold-hearted professors and open enemies of religion together. It was this neglect in some zealous preachers, that run out the revival in the days of Edwards, and which led him to write his Treatise on the Religious Affections. ...

"It is of the highest importance that the preacher present to his hearers the distinguishing marks of true religion, the graces of the Spirit, in all their native loveliness; and at the same time, that he detect and expose every counterfeit. Having done this, he may labor with all his might to *bring them up to the highest possible tone.* He may exhort them to the exercise of 'Love, joy, peace, long-suffering, gentleness, goodness, faith, meekness, temperance; and to be kindly affectioned one to another, with brother love, in honor preferring one another. That they walk with all lowliness and meekness, with long-suffering, forbearing one another in love, endeavoring to keep the unity of the Spirit in the bond of peace. That they let nothing be done through strife, or vain glory, but in lowliness of mind let each esteem others better than themselves. Let all bitterness, and wraths, and anger, and clamor, and evil-speaking, be put away from you, with all malice. And be ye kind one to another, tender-hearted, forgiving one another, even as God for Christ's sake hath forgiven you. Likewise ye younger, submit yourselves unto the elder. Yes, all of you be subject one to another, and be clothed with humility.' He may exhort them 'to put on, as the elect of God,—and be covered all over with these shining graces,—bowels of mercies, kindness, humbleness of mind, meekness, long-suffering, forbearing one another; even as Christ forgave you, so also do ye. And above all things, put on charity, which is the bond of perfectness.' He may set their hearts all on fire with that heavenly Form—'so pure, so peaceable, so gentle and easy to be entreated, full of mercy and good fruits, without partiality and without hypocrisy:'—that is so 'long-suffering, so kind, envieth not, is not puffed up, doth not behave itself unseemly, seeketh not her own, is not easily provoked; thinketh no evil, rejoiceth not in iniquity, but rejoiceth in the truth; beareth all things, believeth all things, hopeth all things, and never faileth.' These are the prevailing characteristics of a revival of religion. Their absence cannot be compensated by flaming zeal.

"Nor is it sufficient that these and all other Christian graces be exhibited, and their counterfeit exposed in theory alone. For so hypocrites will claim them all as their own. Profession is not principle. 'By their fruits ye shall know them.' 'Who is a wise man? Let him show out of a good conversation his works with meekness of wisdom.'

> 'Easy indeed it were to reach
> A mansion in the courts above,
> If watery floods and fluent speech,
> Might serve instead of faith and love.'

"The most important part of the preacher's duty is, to exhibit the evidence of their existence in the heart, by corresponding actions in the life. And this, too, by being 'ensamples to the flock;' and by carefully copying the example of his Divine Master, 'beseeching them by the *meekness* and *gentleness* of Christ.'

"As the time would fail me to complete the subject, Edwards may, in part, supply this deficiency in brother Finney's sermon. I would therefore take this opportunity to recommend to all young converts a careful perusal of his account of the revival in New England, *fourth part*, and what he says on the marks of true humility and spiritual pride, of which the following is a brief abstract:

'Spiritual pride disposes one to speak much of the faults of others, and with bitterness, or with levity, and an air of contempt. Pure Christian humility rather disposes to be silent about them, or to speak of them with grief and pity. Spiritual pride is very apt to suspect others; an humble saint is most jealous of himself. The spiritually proud person is apt to find fault with others that are low in grace, and to be much in observing how cold and dead they be, and crying out of them and sharply reproving them for it. The humble Christian has so much to do at home, with his own heart, that he is not apt to be very busy with the hearts of others, and is apt to esteem others better than himself, and to take most notice of what is good in them, while he takes most notice of what is wrong in himself. In his clearest discoveries of God's glory, and in his most rapturous frames, he is most overwhelmed with a sense of his own vileness, and feels the deepest self-abasement.

'It is a mark of spiritual pride, when any are disposed to speak of what they see amiss in others, in the most harsh, severe, and terrible language; saying of their opinions, or conduct, or advice, of their coldness, their silence, their caution, their moderation, and their prudence, that they are from the *devil*, or from *hell*; that such a thing is devilish, or hellish, or cursed, and the like; so that the words *devil* and hell are almost continually in their mouths. And especially, when such language is used towards ministers of the gospel, and others whose age or station entitles them to particular respect. Humility leads the Christian to treat others that are in fault, with meekness and gentleness, as Christ did his disciples, and particularly Peter, when he had shamefully denied him.

'Spiritual pride disposes to affect singularity in manner and appearance, for the purpose of attracting observation. Humility disposes the Christian to avoid every thing which is likely to draw upon him the observations of others, and to be singular only where he cannot be otherwise without the neglect of a plain and positive duty. Spiritual pride commonly occasions a certain *stiffness* and inflexibility in persons, in their own judgment and their own ways. Humility inclines to a yielding, pliable disposition. The humble Christian is disposed to yield to others, and conform to them, and please them, in every thing but sin.

'Spiritual pride disposes persons to stand at a distance from others, as better than they. The humble Christian is ready to look upon himself as more unworthy than others, yet he does not love the appearance of an open separation from visible

Christians; and will carefully shun every thing that looks like distinguishing himself as more humble, or in any respect better than others.

'The eminently humble Christian is clothed with lowliness, mildness, meekness, gentleness of spirit and behavior, and with a soft, sweet, condescending, winning air and deportment. Humility has no such thing as roughness, or contempt, or fierceness, or bitterness, in its nature, which things are marks of spiritual pride; as are also invectives and censorious talk concerning particular persons for their opposition, hypocrisy, delusion, pharisaism, and the like.

'Spiritual pride takes great notice of opposition and injuries that are received, and is often speaking of them. Humility disposes a person rather to be, like his blessed Lord when reviled, dumb, not opening his mouth. The more clamorous and furious the world is against him, the more silent and still will he be.

'Spiritual pride leads those who are reproached, to be more bold and confident, and to go greater lengths in that for which they are blamed. Humility leads to improve the reproaches of enemies as an occasion of serious self-examination.

'Spiritual pride leads to a certain unsuitable and self-confident boldness before God and man. Humility leads to the opposite.

'*Assuming* is a mark of spiritual pride: putting on the airs of a master, to whom it belongs to dictate. Humility leads the Christian to take the place of a learner, to be "swift to hear, slow to speak." The eminently humble Christian thinks he wants help from every body, whereas he that is spiritually proud, thinks every body wants his help. Christian humility, under a sense of other's misery, entreats and beseeches; spiritual pride affects to command and warn with authority.

'If young ministers had great humility, it would dispose them especially to treat aged ministers with respect and reverence, as their fathers, notwithstanding that a sovereign God may have given them greater success than they have had.

'It is a mark of spiritual pride to refuse to enter into discourse or reasoning with such as are considered carnal men, when they make objections and inquiries. Humility would lead ministers to condescend to carnal men, as Christ has condescended to us, to bear with our unteachableness and stupidity, and still follow us with instructions, line upon line, precept upon precept, saying, "come, let us *reason* together;" it would lead to a compliance with the precept, "Be ready always to give an answer to every man that asketh you a *reason* of the hope that is in you with *meekness* and *fear*."'

"Such are some of the marks of spiritual pride and true humility pointed out by President Edwards. The abstract is given as much as possible in his own words. The whole of what he says on the subject deserves the most serious consideration.

"The friends of religion have been so much gratified with that beautiful hymn by Newton, that I shall venture to insert it in my letter:

TRUE AND FALSE ZEAL

"Zeal is that pure and heavenly flame
    The fire of love supplies;
While that which often bears the name,
    Is self in a disguise.
True zeal is merciful and mild,

Can pity and forbear;
The false is headstrong, fierce and wild,
    And breathes revenge and war.
While zeal for truth the Christian warms,
    He knows the worth of peace;
But self contends for names and forms,
    Its party to increase.
Zeal has attained its highest aim,
    Its end is satisfied,
If sinners love the Saviour's name,
    Nor seek it aught beside.
But self however well employed,
    Has its own ends in view;
And says, as boasting Jehu cried,
    'Come, see what I can do.'
Dear Lord, the idol self dethrone,
    And from our hearts remove;
And let no zeal by us be shown;
    But that which springs from love."

Your affectionate brother,
ASAHEL NETTLETON."[4]

Notes

1   Thornbury, p. 173.
2   Sherry Pierpont May, pp. 227–231.
3   *New York Observer*, issue dated November, 8th, 1827.
4   *The Letters of Dr. Beecher and Dr. Nettleton on the "New Measures"* (Quinta Press online reprint, www.quintapress.com, 2009), pp. 31–51.

It is not probable that any course of measures Mr. Finney could have adopted would have failed to jar more or less painfully on Mr. Nettleton's susceptibilities. Both were originals, both had their eccentricities, but their eccentricities were of the opposite kinds ... If we might presume to illustrate the difference of the two men in their styles of labor by a comparison, we should say that the latter set snares for sinners, the former rode them down in a calvary charge. The one, being crafty, took them with guile; the other, being violent took them by force.

CHARLES BEECHER

New Lebanon Congregational Church, New Lebanon, NY, the location of the New Lebanon Convention of 1827 which discussed Charles Finney's "New Measures".

24

THE NEW LEBANON CONVENTION

The brewing controversy between the ministers of the West (Finney), and those of the East (Nettleton) came to a head at the town of New Lebanon, New York. The meeting of these minsters took place in July of 1827 in the small village of New Lebanon, that was within a mile of the Massachusetts' border. The accessibility of this village was agreeable to all travelers from East and West. Today, it is easy to see why this site was chosen, as the church where they met still sits near the main highway which feeds both ways into New York and Massachusetts. The church used to be known as the "white church" and the building (rebuilt) is still a congregational church to this day.

The purpose of the "New Lebanon Convention" was to arrive at a *common ground* between the Finney/Nettleton camps. Accusations had been made prior to the convention, which had wounded both sides. Some of the most prominent ministers of their day attended this convention with the hopes of peaceful resolutions. The entire country had their eyes on New Lebanon and this meeting, and the eminent men involved felt that gaze of the nation upon them; they knew caution had to be exercised during these proceedings, so not to mar the name of religion in the eyes of her enemies.

The two main voices raised against Finney and his followers were those of Lyman Beecher and Asahel Nettleton. Both men were highly regarded and even feared in their day. Lyman Beecher was the most vocal opponent of Finney in organizing this convention, even to the point of threatening Finney with the following remarks:

> "Finney, I know your plan, and you know I do; you mean to come into Connecticut and carry a streak of fire to Boston. But if you attempt it, as the Lord liveth, I'll meet you at the State line, and call out all the artillery-men, and fight every inch of the way to Boston, and then I'll fight you there."[1]

Asahel Nettleton *did not* want to attend the convention. He saw no positive outcome from such a public arena, he felt these matters would be better addressed behind closed doors. Nettleton was also ill at the time and could not attend many of the sessions—this was mistakenly viewed as a weakness or "nervousness". Many of the ministers from Finney's side viewed this convention as a head to a "Nettletonian War".

The list of ministers attending the convention in the "Nettleton camp" were: Rev. Asahel Norton of Clinton; William Weeks from Paris Hill; Heman Humphrey, President of Amherst College; Joel Hawes of Hartford; Justin Edwards, (who would become President of Andover Seminary); Lyman Beecher of Boston, and Caleb Tenney from Wethersfield, Connecticut. Those ministers representing the "Finney camp" were: Nathan Beman; Moses Gillet of Rome; John Frost of Whitesboro; George Gale, (Finney's former pastor); Dirck C. Lansing from Auburn; Henry Smith from Camden; and Samuel Aikin of Utica (recipient of Nettleton's infamous letter). Heman Humphrey was chosen as moderator of the convention and other ministers came and went, according to their schedules. All in all about twenty men were there. The meetings were heated and the topics of the convention included the role of women praying in promiscuous assembles, irreverent familiarity with God, praying for sinners by name in assemblies, audible groaning in prayer and violent gestures, and other "new measure" concerns were vocalized.

The ministers of the West demanded the men of the East reveal the sources of the accusations made against them and there was resulting silence, which was viewed as a victory for the West. Also, Finney remarked in his *Memoirs* that Nettleton came in, "manifestly very much agitated"; desiring to read before the convention a "historical letter" which contained the grievances against the "new measures". Finney had a copy of the letter in his pocket, ready to produce it if Nettleton did not. Finney the lawyer came prepared and was cool as a cucumber throughout the proceedings. Very little of positive significance was completed during this nine-day "convention". No one was reconciled, nor were questionable "measures" agreed to be discontinued, other than some resolutions (with not all attending participating in the vote) on general behavior during meetings or revivals, mainly, women in public prayer with men. When Lyman Beecher, who had been so vocal against Finney before the convention, saw the popularity of Finney, he cooled down significantly. Reportedly, Beecher stated to an innkeeper on his return from the convention, "we came across the mountains expecting a fight with boys and instead met full grown men." After the convention,

Lyman Beecher forsook his close friendship with Asahel Nettleton to side with Finney and N. W. Taylor. In fact, two years after the convention Finney was preaching in Beecher's church at his invitation! Charles Beecher records in the "Autobiography" that after Lyman Beecher extended an invitation for Finney to come to Boston to preach at his church, Finney ran into Beecher's daughter Catherine stating to her, "Your father vowed solemnly at the New Lebanon Convention he would fight me if I came to Boston, and I shall never go there till he asks me." "So we wrote and invited him, and he came (August, 1831) and did very well."[2] But the "final blow" to Asahel Nettleton occurred prior to Finney preaching in Beecher's church in Boston. It came in an impersonal letter to Nettleton from his "old friend" who had gone over to the side of *popular opinion.* The letter informed Nettleton that "men of standing" had come to an agreement (without consulting Nettleton, and holding the meeting behind his back) that the public controversy over the "new measures" should end. It was obvious to many that the majority of churches in New England were on the "Finney bandwagon" and wanted the "new measures" in their churches. Thus, Lyman Beecher made the decision to end the "war" with Finney (because it was now *an unpopular* position to be against Finney) leaving Nettleton out in the cold as the last "Puritan" standing. We cannot imagine the *hurt and betrayal* Nettleton felt as he read the condescending letter, now presented:

"*Dr. Beecher to Mr. Nettleton.* Philadelphia, May 28, 1828.

"I could not answer your expectations in replying to the late publications, for want both of time and of documents, such as your letter just received contains. Besides, I could not feel so certain that it was best, as I wish always to do in any measure which is to affect deeply the Church of God. I concluded, at length, to come on to New York and to this place, and to confer with our friends, and with brethren on the other side, to see if we could find a stopping-place, and if not, to make all due preparation for publication.

"I have conferred with Dr. Porter, of Andover, our brethren Wisner, Greene, Skinner, and my son, with Brother Hawes, Mr. Holmes, of New Bedford, Dr. Richards, Mr. Eddy, of Canandaigua, with Mr. Peters, Dr. Rice, and many others and the opinion of every one is to forbear farther publication, if possible.

"1. Because, in respect to yourself, there is no need of it, no impression injurious to you having been made in New England, or to the west of Oneida county, and none in the Middle and Southern or Western States—none but among partisans on the other side.

"2. An attempt to rectify all their mistakes in your defense would injure you by keeping you before the public eye in a personal collision with Mr. Finney. We thought that your character and high standing in the Church is too important to be brought down into a protracted controversy of this kind.

"3. That controversy so much personal, and hinging so much on an individual, would help the wrong by giving notoriety, and enlisting public curiosity, and, if we press the subject beyond a certain time and point, public sympathy.

"4. It would tend to keep up a party in the Church, who, identified with their leader, might in self-defense be embodied to defend him, and might introduce a controversy into the Presbyterian Church, and by dividing ecclesiastical judicatures, involve and keep the whole Church in a blaze. We thought the best way to disarm our brethren of a dangerous power in the Church is to let them alone, and that every tub should be left to stand on its own bottom.

"5. We did deprecate the publication to the world of so many and such extravagant things as must come out should we enter on the work of proof; and there is no medium between immediate and entire silence and a thorough development, which, though it would justify us in our opposition, would, as much as it injured them, subtract from the cause, provided they will now stop. We wished to save them their character for the Church as well as ours.

"6. We could not but feel, from all that is past, that there can be no telling what sort of contrary testimony might on the other side be adduced to blast our own or their own character, to distract public sentiment, and to enable enemies to say that we are *all* liars. We thought that the general cause could not but be injured by such a contest. I do not say we anticipated willful falsehood, but we could not fail to apprehend that which would in reality be falsehood.

"7. We were inclined to believe that those brethren are tired of the controversy, and are now willing to get out of it if they can have a fair opportunity, and that not a few neutrals are urging them.

"8. We know that the public are becoming tired of the controversy, and that public sentiment is against publication.

"9. We considered it utterly impossible ever to come to a settlement by public discussion or private explanation, and that our own views on both sides being before the public, it was best to stop, and let the truth have its weight.

"10. They have denied so much in theory, and denied so many facts as being wrong and slanderous, that they stand bound before the public to good behavior in time to come, which must operate so far to restrain as to prevent the repetition, we hope, of any such excesses as will be as alarming as the past.

"11. There is such an amount of truth and power in the preaching of Mr. Finney, and so great an amount of good hopefully done, that if he can be so far restrained as that he shall do more good than evil, then it would be dangerous to oppose him, lest at length we might be found to fight against God; for, though some revivals may be so badly managed as to be worse than none, there may, to a certain extent, be great imperfections in them, and yet they be, on the whole, blessings to the Church.

"12. We thought that the publication of Dr. Richards and others, though it does not include your name, is, on the whole, about a fair offset to their late publications, and that this is the best time we can ever expect to have in which to stop. We therefore, who were present in the city, have, in accordance with the general opinion of our friends above named that farther publication should cease, signed with the brethren on the other side the document which you will see in the Philadelphian.

"You probably will feel as if they will take advantage of it; but I am fearless on that point, believing that the course is right in the sight of God, best for your own peace and health, and altogether better than to have you and Finney coupled together, as you would be by a public discussion.

"Rest assured that your reputation does not and will not suffer. I wish to suggest to you the propriety, since your health seems to deny much revival enterprise, that you should move round among the theological seminaries, spending time enough near one and another in succession to imbue the young men with correct views. Such a course would be invaluable in its influence, and enable you yet to do more good by imparting the result of your observations and experience, than you did in the revivals where you obtained them.

"I commend this thought earnestly to your attention; it will do more than ten years of controversy, without the possibility of an answer. Dear brother, be of good cheer; take care of your precious life, and live as long as you can, to bless, as you have done eminently, the Church and the world."[3]

Beecher's comment that Nettleton could do "more good. ... than you did in the revivals" by ceasing his itinerancy and feud with Finney, to lounge in a professor's chair at a seminary, is an *insult* to the profound work of grace which God performed for over eleven years in over fifty revivals with Asahel Nettleton as the human instrument. Unfair and untrue comments about Nettleton by his detractors surfaced over time. It began with Charles Beecher who made the following assessment of Nettleton's physical and mental state at the convention, "He himself was old and broken, Mr. Finney young and robust"[4]. Ashael was *only* 44 at the time! Historian, Whitney Cross makes the same erroneous statements, using Beecher as a primary source; and Cross's errors are more glaring:

"Asahel Nettleton, the famed evangelist of the Great Revival in 1800 ... But Nettleton too old to remember accurately his own earlier methods, and either touched by jealousy or already adrift in the conservative direction ... Nettleton soon parted company with Beecher ..."[5] We respond to these unfortunate mis-facts with the following:

1. Nettleton was not a famed evangelist in the Great Revival of 1800. In fact, he was not even *converted* at this time.

2. Nettleton was *not* "too old to remember accurately", again he was 44 and sharp as a tack!

3. Regarding the comment, "Nettleton soon parted company with Beecher" it was *the other way around*. Beecher became Nettleton's *Brutus*. Unfortunately, much Finney biography through the years has used both

Charles Beecher and Whitney Cross as *authorities* on Nettleton, which they were *not*.

The final result of the "New Lebanon Convention" was that the popular Charles Finney became more popular, while Asahel Nettleton, as an Edwardsean, fell into the shadows, like Edwards himself did for years to come until a resurgence in interest in Edwards' writings appeared in the last century. But the larger and more lasting impact of the "New Lebanon Convention" did not come down to personalities but to *theology*, and *methodology* in evangelism, which is felt *to this day*.

Notes

1   Charles Beecher, *Autobiography of Lyman Beecher, D.D.* Vol. II (New York: Harper & Brothers, 1865), p. 101.

2   Ibid. p. 108.

3   Ibid. pp. 104–107.

4   Ibid. p. 94.

5   Whitney R. Cross, *The Burned-over District* (Ithaca: Cornell University Press, 1950,) pp. 163–164.

Nettleton, Weeks, and others who were not willing to accept uncritically all that occurred during the Western revivals in Oneida County, have been often blamed for not providing more documented evidence against Finney. But the fact is that they were often unsure of who was primarily responsible for the various innovations that were being pressed on the churches by a large group of itinerants and their younger imitators who appeared in the wake of the revivals.

IAIN MURRAY

PILGRIM'S PROGRESS IN THE NINETEENTH CENTURY

T he aftermath of the New Lebanon Convention, especially after Lyman Beecher defected from him, made Asahel Nettleton a *political hot potato* whom few desired to stand alongside, fearful of their respective careers. Unpopular positions seem to thin the ranks of friends. Many dear friends remained at a distance in what had become a singular "Nettletonian War". Public opinion was shifting away from the theology of the Puritans, and many pastors embraced the new measures of Charles G. Finney, along with Pelagian theology. One friend who remained in the fight with Nettleton was William Weeks, of whom we have the following insights:

> "*The Pilgrim's Progress in the nineteenth century*, by William R. Weeks, D.D. ... An attempt at a Bunyan-like allegory, poorly executed, but yet loaded with revival information of the greatest possible consequence. A major portion of the book is devoted to a contrast between the lives, messages and methods of Mr. Bold (Charles G. Finney) and Mr. Meek (Asahel Nettleton) and the long range effect of their ministries. With prophetic insight, Weeks predicts the decline of true revival should the man-centered approach of Mr. Bold prevail in the American churches. Every serious student of revival should carefully read these extremely significant chapters."[1]

We now provide the sections from Week's allegory as it pertains to Finney and Nettleton and the New Lebanon Convention. A key to understanding *who* is speaking in the allegory is found in the pseudonyms used for those represented: **Mr. Meek** is Nettleton; **Mr. Bold** is Finney; **Mr. Scribus** is Rev. Aikin; **Mr. Fearless** is Rev. Beman; **Mr. Thoughtful** is Weeks. There is also dialogue between **Love-self** (who represents the "new measures") and **Thoughtful** (who represents the "Old Paths"). The section in Weeks' book pertaining to the "new measure" controversy is over two hundred pages long. Obviously, we cannot provide the entire document but will present key parts which represent the main controversy.

"One day, while Thoughtful and Ardent were walking out, it happened that they passed through a street a little to the west of Pilgrim street; and as they were walking along and observing the manner of the people, they saw a man, whom they afterwards found to be Mr. Bold, coming towards them with a hurried step, clothed partly in the habit which Evangelist wore, and partly in the dress of the people of the town. When he came up to them, he addressed them without any of the ordinary forms of salutation, as follows:

Bold. Are you true pilgrims, or only such by profession?

Thoughtful. We profess to be pilgrims; and if we are not deceived, we have some real regard for the Prince Immanuel.

Bold. Do you pray? Are you engaged in the cause of the Prince? Or are you no better than cold-hearted professors?

Th. We are not probably so ardent in his cause as we ought to be. Yet we think we take some delight in communion with our Lord.

Bold. Do you pray in faith? Or do you only mock the King, by asking things which you do not expect him to grant?

Th. We aim, in our petitions, to ask for such things as appear to us desirable; and then leave our petitions with the King, after the example of our Lord, saying, 'Not my will, but thine be done.'

Bold. Aye; I see that you have no faith. I do not want to hear any one pray so, more than once or twice, to be convinced that he is destitute of faith.

Th. We believe that true faith in the King consists in having confidence in his superior wisdom; and that leads us to make our judgment of what is best, subordinate to his.

Bold. Well, well: I see that you are as cold as ice. But if you wish to get your hearts warmed, come along with me. There is, in a neighboring street, a great and powerful work; and if you will but come and see, you will be filled with wonder and astonishment. Come along.

So Thoughtful and Ardent followed Mr. Bold into a street called Westerly street, [the Western revivals, author's note] where they soon perceived there was considerable excitement among the people, many of them being gathered in little groups, and talking earnestly among themselves; and from what they heard, it appeared that some were speaking of the great and glorious work which they said was going on, and others were contradicting and opposing. Mr. Bold, who led the way, often spoke to passers by, in the same abrupt manner in which he had addressed them, saying to one, 'You are an enemy to the King;' to another, 'You are going right to the pit' and the like, which seemed to be very offensive to those who were thus addressed; and some openly cursed him for his pains.

They soon went into a place of worship, and Mr. Bold commenced the exercises. In his prayer, there seemed to be several things quite unusual. There was a familiar, talking manner, as if the supplicant had forgotten his station, and was talking with an equal. There seemed also to be little or no confession of sin, in the prayer; but it seemed to be principally filled up with petitions for various individuals whose names were mentioned, and the opportunity seemed to be embraced, to tell all the bad things which the person officiating had known or imagined about them. He then preached a discourse, which contained much truth, but presented in a very singular way. The names and titles of the Divine Being were being used with such irreverence; and things were repeatedly said in such a way, as to make the blood of the pilgrims chill in their veins. He attempted to give force to his representation, by the machinery of the theatre. He acted out, in a manner which shocked the feelings of the pilgrims, the case of the sinner, sickening, languishing, dying without hope; going to judgment, and sentenced to the pit. He also represented the final judgment, assumed the chair of the judge, called up sinners of different characters, investigating their several pleas, and pronounced the sentence, *depart*. In addressing sinners, he used language which seemed stronger than is consistent with truth. 'O you wretches! you rebels, you desperadoes!' were expressions he used a number of times. And once he seemed to cap the climax, by saying, 'there is not a fiend in hell, nor out of hell, as bad as you are.'

The meeting was full, and the people seemed to listen with an expression of great curiosity in their countenances; but I observed at the same time, that there was very little of that appearance of deep and solemn feeling which I had seen under the preaching of Mr. Meek."[2]

It sounds like Finney was anything but boring in his preaching! William Weeks now draws attention to the distinguishing *differences* between the preaching of Mr. Bold and Mr. Meek. We read:

"*Thoughtful*. Does Mr. Meek use any measures for the purpose of producing an *effect*, any thing which may be called machinery?

Experience. No; unless what is called the *inquiry meeting* should be reckoned of that description. That is thought to be a measure of his introducing. It is simply the appointment of a meeting for those who are seriously impressed, at which he and the pastor may see them apart from others, and have personal conversation with each, and give them individually such instruction as their cases may severely require.

Th. Is Mr. Meek disposed to converse much with awakened sinners?

Exp. 'He has often remarked that a great deal of conversation has a tendency to confuse the mind, and to dissipate rather than to deepen religious impression. He would converse with them enough to keep the subject before their minds, and to correct any false notions which they might have imbibed. More than this he considers not only unnecessary, but prejudicial.'

Ardent. Does Mr. Meek use the *anxious seat*, or call upon sinners to rise in the public assembly, to signify their desire to be prayed for?

Exp. No, never; nor any of the kindred measures, such as calling upon Christians to rise by way of expressing a promise, or requesting sinners to promise to submit in a given time, or praying for persons by name, and the like.

Ard. Does he continue his meetings all night, sometimes, when there is a high state of feeling?

Exp. No. He never holds them to an unseasonable hour. He would think there was too much excitement, if there was a disposition to stay to a late hour. He would prefer to have all go home, and retire to their closets with their Bibles, and attend alone, each one to the state of his own heart. One pastor with whom he labored for a time, writes as follows: 'The state of feeling which at this time pervaded the congregation was interesting beyond description. There was no commotion, but a stillness in our very streets ...

Ard. What directions does he give to awakened sinners?

Exp. He directs them to repent and believe the Gospel. 'He urges upon sinners the duty of immediate repentance, and shows them that they can do nothing short of repentance, which will in the least degree, improve their condition. He endeavors to destroy all their dependence on their own works, to show them that all their religious services are selfish and sinful, and that God has made no promise of pardon to any thing short of faith and repentance.'

Ard. What does he think of telling awakened sinners to 'wait at the pool,' and hope to be healed?

Exp. He thinks the direction, as it would be likely to be understood by an awakened sinner, is entirely erroneous, and adapted to destroy his soul. I have heard him in his preaching, endeavor to correct this mistake, by placing in strong contrast with it some of the divine requirements, such as, 'Choose you this day, whom ye will serve,'—but *wait at the pool.* 'Behold, now is the accepted time; behold now is the day of salvation.'—but *'wait at the pool,'* 'God now commandeth all men everywhere to repent,'—but *wait at the pool.*

Ard. Of course he would not tell the awakened sinner to be 'patient and wait God's time.'

Exp. No. He says, 'to tell the anxious sinner to be patient, without a new heart, is the same as to tell him to dismiss his anxiety, and go back to a state of stupidity ...

Ard. How soon does Mr. Meek think it best that new converts should be received into the church?

Exp. 'He is cautious in admitting persons into the church. He does not encourage any to make a profession of religion till they give satisfactory evidence of a change of heart.'

Th. How came Mr. Meek to have such a deep sense of the importance of the pastoral office, having never been a pastor himself?

Exp. He learned it during his early labors in the ministry. He commenced in a part of Pilgrim street where there had once been flourishing churches, but which had been laid waste in the last century, 'by the measures which Davenport and other itinerants of that period had introduced. He became acquainted with some aged people, who gave him an account of the proceedings of that day, and of their results, as they had been developed in the course of half a century. He has often spoke with deep interest, of this period of his labors, and of the use which the information he at this time obtained was to him in after life. He learned that those who labor as itinerants, even if they have the best intentions, are in peculiar danger of mistaking false zeal for true; and of being betrayed into great indiscretions. He learned, also, that the imprudence of one itinerant may produce incalculable evils,—evils which will extend through many generations. While surveying these fields of moral desolation, he became deeply impressed with the importance of a settled ministry, the minds of the people become unsettled in regard to religious truth, and they are easily carried about by ever wind of doctrine; that errorists of every description come in and occupy the ground, and that when there is any religious excitement among them, it is peculiarly liable to run into the wildest fanaticism. In the midst of a people thus situated, religion and fanaticism become identified. They know of no other kind of religion; and, of course, they seek and expect no other. He found that the churches which had been made desolate by the labors of Davenport and his coadjutors half a century before, had remained desolate; that there still existed among the people the most violent prejudices against settled pastors, and all regular ecclesiastical organizations. He saw the same self-righteous and denunciatory spirit, which first rent and scattered the churches, was still prevalent, and that those measures which accompany and promote fanaticism, such as calling persons to the anxious seat, requesting them to rise to be prayed for, or to signify that they had given their hearts to God, encouraging females to exhort and pray in promiscuous assemblies &c. were still rife among them.

Th. Since you aver that the things complained of are but 'trifling mistakes,' and cannot be the true ground of objection to Mr. Bold and his proceedings, I will state some of them. We complain that those out of the church are treated in a harsh and uncivil manner, called by hard names and provoking epithets, and addressed with coarseness and vulgarity; which is manifestly wrong in itself, and adapted to harden them, and prevent their listening to the claims of the Gospel. We complain that children and youth have been treated in a manner adapted to frighten them unreasonably, by being threatened with immediate and inevitable damnation. And we complain of his, because we think it adapted to prevent their giving a proper attention to the real and sober threatenings of the Bible; especially when they find the threatenings which have been made prove untrue. We complain that children should be told things about their parents which are adapted to alienate their affections, and lead them to be disrespectful toward them. We complain of the personality of public preaching, by which the attention of the congregation is directed to particular individuals, as persons of an uncommonly odious character. We complain that persons should be prayed for by name, in a manner which implies strong censure of them, and which is often considered slanderous and abusive. We complain of the irreverent use of the divine name, and of the familiar use of the words, *devil, hell, cursed, damned,* and the like, in a manner which resembles the more vulgar sort of profane swearing. We are shocked with the affectation of boldness and familiarity with the Divine Being in prayer. And we are disgusted with the ostentation of those who pray so loud in their closets, as to be heard in the streets. We complain that the doctrines of the Gospel are not sufficiently preached; and those who do labor to instruct their people in them, are charged with hindering revivals by preaching them, and that particular pains appears to be taken, to render *orthodoxy* a term of reproach. We complain that the differences between true and false in religious experience is not sufficiently made known, and that the disposition to make a distinction between genuine and spurious revivals, if frowned upon as a mark of coldness and stupidity.

We complain that the most uniform and consistent Christians are pronounced cold, and stupid, and dead, because they do not alter as much as others, and that uniformity itself is denounced as a mark of lukewarmness. We complain of the unsparing denunciation of those who have been considered the best friends of revivals, as they have hitherto existed, because they do not approve of every new thing. We complain that those whose age and experience have given them opportunity to be most and longest acquainted with revivals, are put down by the converts of a few days old, as totally ignorant on the subject. We complain that aged ministers, of tried and approved piety, are publicly prayed for, by young men and boys, as old hypocrites or apostates, 'leading souls to hell.' We complain that females are urged forward to pray in promiscuous assemblies, contrary to the Scriptures, and in violation of that modesty which is so essential to their best influence. We complain of the confidence which some appear to place in impulses and impressions, especially as connected with the supposed prayer of faith, very erroneous views of which we think are promulgated. We complain that young converts and young persons, are put forward to their injury, and the older members of the churches, to whom it belongs to take the lead, are manifestly put in the background; and that old people in general are often treated with great disrespect, in direct violation of the divine injunction, 'thou shalt rise up before the hoary head, and honor the face of the old man.'

We complain of the disposition to crowd these new measures into every place, without regard to the divisions and contentions manifested by many to intermeddle with the concerns of churches to which they do not belong. We complain that so much stress should be laid upon the posture in prayer, as if *kneeling* was of course connected with humility, while little regard seems to be paid to that meek, humble, modest, retiring spirit, so essential to the right performance of the duty. We complain of the practice of loud groaning, in time of prayer, in a manner that has the appearance of being done to keep up excitement; and especially of falling down, and rolling about in a time of prayer, which has been practiced by some. We complain that distortions of the body, and other professed expressions of distress, should be practiced in public meetings. We complain that any should pray for others to be converted or removed out of the way, thereby turning their prayers into curses, under pretense of uncommon piety.

We complain that success should be considered an evidence of the divine approbation, as a principle which would lead to justify the falsehood of Jacob, by means of which he obtained the blessing. We complain that when evils are pointed out, they are not corrected, but are either denied to have existence, or are justified as good and right. We complain that the whole system of measures seems to be adapted to promote false religion; and thus, ultimately, not only destroy the souls of those who are deceived by it, but to bring revivals, and experimental religion itself, into discredit, and increase errorists and scoffers on every side. We complain that meetings are sometimes held all night, and for several days and nights in succession. We complain that in some meetings, anybody and everybody is at liberty to speak or pray, without being called upon by any responsible head. We complain that in some meetings, more than one speaks or prays at the same time. We complain of a want of truth in what is affirmed respecting men and things, in circumstances where there seems to be no room for mistake.

The real truth is what I wish to ascertain. Your friends have represented this as a new era in revivals. They have told of the measures of Mr. Bold and his friends as great improvements. They have urged them upon the ministers and churches in every direction, even against their wishes. And when objections have been made, it has been ascribed to coldness and carnality. The name of Mr. Meek has been used by many to sanction the measures of Mr. Bold …"[3]

This publication appeared after the deaths of Asahel Nettleton and William Weeks, and by that time the "new measure" controversy was all but forgotten; and this important warning of the "new measures" in evangelism has been neglected and covered in dust over the years as well.

Notes

1   Richard Owen Roberts, *An Annotated Bibliography of Revival Literature*, p. 486.
2   William R. Weeks, *The Pilgrim's Progress in the Nineteenth Century* (New York: M. W. Dodd, Brick Church Chapel. 1849). pp. 233–234.
3   Ibid. pp. 227–242.

Stone marking the site of the meeting house in Enfield where Jonathan Edwards preached his famous sermon "Sinners in the Hands of an Angry God" on July 8, 1741.

Here is abundant proof that the uncorrupted doctrines of Calvin, drawn from the scriptures of truth, are the weapons which the Holy Spirit chooses to employ in the conviction and conversion of sinners; and a complete practical refutation of all attempts to change or modify those doctrines, in order to render them palatable to the views of the carnal mind. And it must be a source of high satisfaction to you, sir, to witness in the ministerial career of Dr. Nettleton, such ample proof that the doctrines you have contended for, have been so conspicuously owned and acknowledged by the Holy Spirit.

H. SEWALL

26

FINAL REVIVALS

Asahel Nettleton was completely *exhausted* after the New Lebanon Convention. Physically he was at his lowest since the typhus fever attack in 1822. The emotional strain of the "New Measure" controversy had laid him low. So in the spring of 1827 the great evangelist limped to Durham, New York, and to the Catskill mountains, to retire for a season of rest. Asahel was feeling his mortality, and those sentiments are visible in the following letter he composed to the Rev. Williston, pastor of the church in Durham. The letter is dated, April 21st, 1827:

"Brother Williston—This day I am 44 years old. I feel thankful that a kind providence has led me to this place, and that I have had the satisfaction of a short acquaintance with you. I cannot express my feelings now. But in view of the uncertainty of life, I would say, that I am happy in the thought of laying my bones in your burying ground. I cannot tell how it may be in the solemn hour of death—and a willingness to die, I do not think, is, in itself, any evidence of grace. But the thought of leaving the world, appears rather pleasant; and above all, the thought of never sinning. I feel it to be a *great thing* to be a Christian. Such words as these appear sweet. 'I am now ready to be offered,' &c.

'O glorious hour!—O blest abode!
I shall be near and like my God;
And flesh and sin no more control
The sacred pleasures of the soul.'

"I feel a peculiar love to ministers—especially to those with whom I have labored in seasons of revival. Remember me affectionately to them all. They will find my feelings in the twentieth chapter of Acts. I feel a peculiar interest in theological students, and I have been wishing to leave something that would be useful— something which has been learned by experience. I would say to young men, it is a good symptom when they secure the confidence of aged and experienced ministers. The younger should submit themselves to the elder, and always speak kindly of them.

"My mind ranges over all the towns and places where I have labored in seasons of revival with peculiar delight. I have feelings of inexpressible tenderness and compassion, for all the young converts. They will find much of them in 1st and 2nd

Thessalonians. My affectionate regard to all my relatives in North Killingworth. Tell them to prepare to follow me. I die among kind friends. Tell your congregation, and especially the young people, to seek an interest in Christ without delay. When I am buried on yonder hill, tell them to remember the evening when I preached to them from these words, '*Seek first the kingdom of God.*' Whenever they pass my grave, tell them, they will each one remember, 'there lies the man who talked to me about my soul.' I die in peace with all mankind. In great weakness,

Your affectionate friend and brother,

A. N."[1]

Asahel Nettleton was not yet to die and it isn't long before we find him out of bed and preaching in another pulpit! Feeble as he was, he preached with power at Durham, where it was said, "God poured out his Spirit, and numbers were hopefully made the subjects of renewing grace." God delights in "broken things" and the great evangelist, broken in body, kept in the race and fought the good fight. A revival commenced under his preaching at Lexington Heights, New York on the Catskill mountains. Asahel had two favorite spots that he often repaired to for recuperation of his health, these were Saratoga Springs and the Catskill mountains, both in New York. He would visit the "Springs" and the mountain quietude both to repair his broken body and to renew his spirits—especially after a season of powerful revivals which drained him physically and emotionally. Often he recommended to itinerant preachers, the counsel of seeking rest in a quiet place of refreshing, "to review the past, and to attend to his own heart." Indeed this was the case while convalescing in the Catskills. After a brief season of rest he again is immersed in another revival, he relates this news to his friend, Charles E. Furman, pastor at Victor, New York. We read:

"My Dear Friend:——When I saw that the captivity of Zion was turned, I retired out of the region of news and noise, among these mountains. The bear and the panther, the wolf and the wild-cat, it is said, are occasionally seen or heard ranging the forests which surround the village and the mansion where I now reside. The deer I have seen leaping the fence and the mound, with a hound close to his heels. I have often been reminded of these words, 'And he was with the wild beasts; and the angels ministered unto him.' When the apostles returned to Christ, and gave an account of their mission, he said unto them, 'come ye yourselves apart into a desert place, and rest awhile.' Every itinerant preacher, especially if he has been engaged in a revival of religion, must feel the need of this last direction; or suffer greatly, if he long neglect it. I could not advise any one to be employed in a powerful revival more than three months, without retiring into solitude for a short time, to review the past, and to attend to his own heart. He will find much to lament, and much to correct; and it is by deep and solemn *reflection* upon the past, and by this only, that he can reap the advantages of past experience. It is not by passing through many revivals of religion, that we can gain any valuable experience on the subject. Many former, as well as some recent examples, prove the truth of this remark.

"The people where I reside, are destitute of a settled pastor. I have preached a number of times to a very crowded, silent, and solemn assembly. I have met a number in deep distress of soul: and recently some are rejoicing in hope, and begin to sing 'Redeeming Love.' We have a most excellent choir of youthful singers, some of whom are among the young converts. Last evening, I saw two of the most gay and thoughtless of them, who I feared were going to be left, and found them in awful distress. I had noticed that they did not sing in the choir on the Sabbath; thought they are favored with the sweetest voices. On my visit, I found the reason might be given in the following beautiful lines:

> 'How can my soul exult for joy,
> Which feels this load of sin;
> And how can praise my tongue employ,
> While darkness reigns within?
> My soul forgets to use her wings,
> My harp neglected lies,
> For sin has broken all its strings,
> And guilt shuts out my joys!'

"I have thought very seriously of requesting you to make us a visit, for I needed your help to write off tunes, and to aid in learning them. But my time here is so short that I could not request it. My health is feeble, though better than it was last summer. I have been advised by physicians to spend the winter at the South; and it is time to make my arrangements. I wish to hear from you soon. What is the state of things in Auburn? My best regards to Dr. Richards and to all my friends.

Yours truly."[2]

EXTRAORDINARY REVIVALS IN VIRGINIA

One of the most remarkable revivals in the career of Asahel Nettleton occurred while he was in Virginia. Recuperating from recent bouts of fainting spells, and under doctor's orders to go "South" for the winter he retired to the area of Hampden Sydney. While there, he preached for a new friend, Dr. John Rice, who was President of Union Seminary. The revival which soon appeared saturated Hampden Sydney with the presence of God in such power that even the most hardened sinners came to Christ! Dr. Rice, enthusiastic about the ongoing revival, wrote a letter to Archibald Alexander (of Princeton) detailing Nettleton's labors:

"When Mr. Nettleton had strength to labor, he soon was made instrumental in producing a considerable excitement. This has extended, and now the state of things is deeply interesting. Five lawyers, all of very considerable standing, have embraced religion. This had produced a mighty sensation in Charlotte, Mecklenburg, Nottaway, Cumberland, Powhattan, Buckinham, and Albemarle. The minds of men seem to stand a tiptoe, and they seem to be looking for some great thing. Mr. Nettleton is a remarkable man, and chiefly, I think, remarkable for his power of producing a great excitement, without much *appearance* of feeling. The people do not either weep or talk away their impressions. The preacher chiefly addresses *Bible truth* to their *consciences*. I have not heard him utter, as yet, a single sentiment opposed to what you and I call orthodoxy. He preaches the Bible, he derives his illustrations from the Bible."[3]

Some additional correspondence provides insight regarding this move of grace. The next letter, from Nettleton's own pen, is addressed to fellow minister, Rev. Cobb; it is written from New York, Feb. 17th, 1831:

"Many things have transpired in my own history since I saw you last, and some deeply interesting. My turns of faintness increased until 1827, when the physicians despaired of my life; and as the last resort, I was advised to go to a Southern climate. For three winters I have been in the Southern States, and my health has wonderfully improved, so that I have been able to labor almost incessantly. The scene of the deepest interest was in the county of Prince Edward, Virginia, in the vicinity of Union Theological Seminary, and Hampden Sydney College. Our first meeting of inquiry was at the house of Dr. Rice—the very mansion containing the theological students. More than a hundred were present, inquiring, 'What must we do to be saved?' Among the subjects of divine grace, were a number of lawyers, six or seven, and some of them among the leading advocates at the bar. Some were men of finished education, who are soon to become heralds of salvation.

"During my residence in Virginia, I took a tour across the Alleghany Mountains, about two hundred miles, to spend a short time during the warm season. On my way, I spent a few weeks at a place called Staunton, where I left a pleasant little circle of converts. On a certain Sabbath, as we were almost destitute of singers, I noticed a female voice, which from its fullness, and sweetness, and wildness, all combined, attracted my attention. On arriving at my lodgings I inquired of a young lady whose voice it could be, and whether we could not catch it, and tame it, and enlist it in our service? The name, I was informed, was S—— L. Will you not invite her to call and see us? 'O, she is a very gay and thoughtless young lady; was never at our house, and we have no acquaintance with her.' Tell her from me that I wish to see her—that I want the aid of her voice. N—— went out, and in a few moments returned with the interesting stranger, who sat down with a pleasing, pensive countenance, which seemed to say, now is my time to seek an interest in Christ. And so it was, that she and her sister, and fifteen or twenty others became deeply impressed, and soon became joyful in Christ. This little circle would call on me daily, linking hand in hand, and smiling through their tears, would sing, Redeeming Love. I bade them farewell—and now for the sequel. I have received a letter from Dr. Wardell, the worthy physician of that place, at whose house I resided, from which I will give an extract. 'We have had several instances of death from typhus fever since you left us. The only individual whom you know, included in this number, was one of your *little circle*—S—— L. It will be no less gratifying to you than it is to her friends here, to learn that she gave abundant evidence of the genuineness of the Christian profession. To go a little into detail. She had been complaining for several days, before she would consent to lie by; and did not call in medical aid for some days after her confinement. I first saw her six days from her first attack, when she was entirely prostrate. She said she believed she should not recover, nor had she any desire to live longer. So far from being dismayed at death, she seemed to view it as one of the most joyful events. I was in some perplexity to ascertain whether these were the feelings of a sound mind, and the vigorous exercise of faith; and closely watched for some *incoherences* which might settle the inquiry; but there was nothing of the kind. She was too weak to converse much, but had her friends summoned around her, to give them a word of exhortation; expressing a strong desire to be the means of leading one soul to heaven. She took great delight in gazing on those whom she had been accustomed to meet in your *little religious circle*, because she expected to meet them in heaven. She often spoke of you, and your little social meetings, prayed for you, and said she should meet you in a larger circle in heaven than she had ever done in Staunton. In order to test the correctness of her apprehension, I asked her if she would feel no diffidence in being admitted into the presence of a holy God, and the holy beings who surround his throne? She had strength only to reply—But I am washed—I am washed! She lived fourteen days after I saw her first. I have been thus particular, because she requested that some one would inform you of her death.'

"You will pardon me for sending you this little story. It cannot touch your feelings as it does my own. You may read it to your young people as a token of affectionate remembrance from

Their unworthy friend."4

We learn much of Asahel Nettleton's revival labors at this juncture from Jesse Armistead, an eminent minister who was an eyewitness to the revival in Virginia. In his account, Armistead relates the magnitude of the revival and its lasting effects. Prior to Nettleton's sojourn to Virginia, his labors had been restricted primarily to New England; eventually the evangelist will encompass the State of Virginia, traveling to Charleston as well. Traveling South in the winters for his health now became a formed habit till his death. What makes this revival account so valuable is the fact that it is the *last recorded account* of Asahel Nettleton's labors amidst great revival.

AN ACCOUNT OF THE SOUTHERN REVIVALS

"Cumberland Co. Va. July 17, 1844

"Rev. and Dear Sir—I am pleased to learn by a notice in the papers, that you are engaged in preparing a biographical sketch of the late Rev. Dr. Nettleton. I received, a few days ago, a request from our friend, Rev. Michael Osborne, that I would furnish you with such information as I could, in reference to Dr. Nettleton's labors in Virginia, and the estimation in which those labors were held by Christians here.

"It was my privilege while a young man in the ministry of the gospel, to share his confidence and his friendship, during his first visit to Virginia in 1828, and the beginning of '29, and I had on two occasions afterwards, an opportunity for intimate and most delightful intercourse with him. During the winter of 1828, he spent two weeks in my study at Buckingham C. H., to which place I had just been called as the pastor of the small Presbyterian church there, and which had enjoyed the privilege of his ministry for a few weeks during the summer of that year, with the manifest blessing of the Head of the church on his labors. He was then resting from the severe and exhausting labors which he had undergone during the summer and fall, at Hampden Sydney, Prince Edward Co., at Buckingham C. H., and in the valley of Virginia; and during those two weeks, I had the highly prized opportunity of full conversation with him about his views in theology, which the doctrinal history of which, he was uncommonly well acquainted; about the whole subject of revivals of religion; the proper manner of presenting divine truth to the understandings and consciences of men, in connection with a spirit of prayer, and a feeling and entire dependence on the Spirit and grace of God, to make the truth effectual; and plans for building up the kingdom of Christ. On all these subjects he was the most interesting and instructive individual with whom I have ever had intercourse; and on the subject of *revivals of religion*, incomparably the *wisest* man I ever saw. It was a subject which he had thoroughly studied in the light of revelation and ecclesiastical history, and on which he had an amount of experience and observation probably beyond any man living. You will render most important service to the cause of Christ, if you succeed, as I trust you may, in getting before the public mind, a full exhibition of his views on this subject.

"He was introduced into Virginia by the Rev. Dr. John H. Rice, then Professor of Christian Theology in Union Theological Seminary, Prince Edward Co., and very soon began his labors with the Presbyterian church in the immediate vicinity of the Seminary, and Hampden Sydney College. The Spirit of God accompanied his exhibitions of divine truth, and soon a most interesting and precious revival of religion was enjoyed with the church there. He was deeply interested in this revival of religion, and so were many others, because of the number of educated gentlemen, especially lawyers of high standing and extensive influence, who were hopefully converted during this blessed season of divine influence. Not many gentlemen of this profession, had, up to this time, been members of any church in this section of country. Those referred to, were from several adjoining counties; and this circumstance attracted no little attention, and sent out an extensive most salutary influence on the surrounding country; especially the county of Buckingham. This county, in execution of his ordinary plan of making the scene of a revival a center of influence for the surrounding country, he took an early opportunity to visit. He preached at the Court House for a few Sabbaths, to a small church which had been organized a few years before; and here his ministry excited great attention, and was accompanied with the special blessing of heaven. The revival at this place was not extensive, but it laid the foundation, as I had occasion to know, for building up quite a flourishing Presbyterian church in that region. I had on the ground an interesting opportunity to observe the practical effects of a genuine revival of religion, conducted on true scriptural principles, as I began to minister to that community in the beginning of the winter of that year. The views of religion which he presented, were so scriptural, and rational, commending themselves to every man's conscience; and the sympathies of the community, in the midst of deep interest and intense feeling, were so wisely managed, avoiding every thing like extravagance and fanaticism, that the sober and well-balanced minds of *those without*, could find no occasion to object to any thing that was said or done. When Dr. Nettleton went away, the consciences of the people were left on the side of rational and intelligent piety. The young people, too, grew up under the impression that revivals of religion are blessed seasons; so that when another revival came, the obstacles in the way seemed to be small. That church has been emphatically one of revivals every since, and has been mainly built up by them. The same impression, as I have had opportunity to know, was left on the public mind by the revival in Prince Edward Co., as indeed, it always will be, when a genuine revival of religion, properly conducted, is enjoyed.

"Towards the close of the summer of that year, Dr. Nettleton's health, which was quite feeble when he came to Virginia, rendered it proper as he thought, that he should visit the mountains, and the mineral springs located among them. He could not, however, during his excursion, debar himself the privilege of preaching the gospel. He labored for a few weeks, with the blessing of God, but not to the same

26. FINAL REVIVALS

extent as at Prince Edward, and Buckingham C. H., at Lewisburg, Greenbrier Co., and at Staunton, Augusta, Co.

"These trips gave him an opportunity for extending his acquaintance and his influence with the clergy of Virginia, by whom he was every where received with the utmost cordiality and Christian affection. The report of the blessing of God on his labors for Christ, which preceded him, opened the hearts of all our ministers and people towards him. You doubtless had an opportunity to know how the cordiality and Christian affection of his Virginia brethren affected him. On their part, I had many occasions to know, they regarded his visit to Virginia as a great blessing to our churches. I have always thought, that Dr. Nettleton's sojourn among us was worth more to the cause of Christ, from the influence which he exerted on the minds of ministers, than in any other point of view. He certainly exerted no little influence on the manner of preaching the gospel in this part of the state; but probably, yet greater good resulted from the interest which he excited on the subject of genuine revivals of religion. Our churches had been blessed with such seasons of refreshing before; but the subject had not been any thing like so well understood. The views which followed his visit, have powerfully influenced the minds of ministers and Christians generally ever since; and their hallowed influence, we may reasonably hope, will go down upon the church for many years to come. He felt great interest in the students of our seminary, who were soon to be in the field of ministerial labor, and cordially co-operated with good Dr. Rice, in efforts to imbue them with the right spirit for the great work of preaching the gospel. I well know how high a value Dr. Rice placed on his visit to the seminary, and on the opportunity which his young men enjoyed for witnessing his manner of presenting divine truth, and conducting things in a revival of religion. His interest on the subject of revivals was intense; and as he regarded them as the great means, in connection with the pastoral office, in building up the kingdom of Christ and saving a lost world, he was most deeply solicitous that correct views on the subject should prevail. He took great pains in explaining his views to those whom he regarded as being judicious and *trusty*; and guarded with extreme caution against every thing wild and fanatical.

"He had abundant reason to be deeply solicitous on this subject, as individuals at the North, and especially in western New York, had run revivals into extravagance, and then, as he said, attempted to plead the authority of his name and example for their ultra and extravagant proceedings. I never saw him so deeply excited on any subject, as in conversation about these abuses. His *measures*—if it be proper thus to characterize the means which he used in connection with revivals of religion, were new in this region, and excited great interest. The fact, however, was, that there was nothing new about his plans, except that he brought people together who were concerned about their soul and had made up their minds to attend at once to the subject of religion, into a general *inquiry meeting*, and sometimes into smaller meetings of the same kind in private homes, in the more distant parts of a congregation—for the purpose of personal conversation and instruction adapted to the peculiar cases of individuals. At these meetings, young converts were kept with those who were anxious. These plans were suggested by common sense and the necessity of the case, and were approved by the most judicious ministers amongst us. Some, however, were disposed, as had been done elsewhere, to try to improve on his simple plans, and as he knew that *imitations* were likely to rise up here, as in other places, and plead his authority for *measures* which he could not approve, he was reserved in communicating his views, unless to persons who he was convinced were opposed to running revivals into extravagance and contempt. This, in some instances, brought against him the charge of being reserved and *quere*—often because he would not sit down, when his time was directly needed for the Lord's work, to explain all his views and plans to every individual who chose to visit him— or because he could not go to preach at several places, as the same time, to which he was invited. It is enough to say, that he had the cordial approbation of the most judicious ministers and intelligent laymen in the region, and that his visit was regarded with special gratitude to the great Head of the church.

"It was not to be expected that the devil would be still when he saw so much done to make his strong holds in this part of the country *tremble from turret to foundation stone.* Accordingly one of his agents at Cartersville, in the lower part of this country, when I was there preaching as a licentiate, imported some stale slanders from Connecticut, about Mr. Nettleton. The name of this man was O. G. W——, from Connecticut, and he attempted to gain currency from his stories by the aid of a letter from R. S. H——, also of Connecticut. All these slanders were silenced by an overwhelming mass of testimony from a number of the first men in New England.

"Dr. Nettleton paid several other visits to Virginia in later years, but generally in such poor health, that he attempted very little in the way of preaching the gospel. To the last, he retained the confidence and affection of those who had known him in the days of his greater vigor to labor for Christ, and the salvation of souls.

"With Christian regard, Your brother in the gospel,

JESSE S. ARMISTEAD."[5]

HIS LAST NEW ENGLAND REVIVALS

Asahel was preaching in New England in the summer of 1829 when a powerful revival appeared while he was laboring in Monson, Massachusetts. This revival grew in intensity and influence, leaving lasting impressions upon the community of Monson. Years later, in 1844, Dr. Ely, pastor of the church in Monson, reflected on that revival in a letter to Bennet Tyler. It is important to our study of the great evangelist to note the remarks of Dr. Ely regarding Nettleton's ministry in his church. Dr. Ely viewed Nettleton as his *assistant*. This helps explain the warm feelings pastors had for Nettleton, he did not *replace* the pastors with whom he labored, rather, he was careful to maintain a secondary role, in order to build up the life of the church. Unlike, many of the itinerants in the western revivals, who disrupted the position of pastors and often divided the churches. Here now is Dr. Ely's account of the revival in Monson, Massachusetts:

"Dr. Nettleton was among the few whose memory will be long cherished by the churches, as an eminent instrument, in the hands of God, of reviving his work, and of bringing multitudes to embrace the Saviour for righteousness and life. He seems to have been raised up by the great Head of the church, to accomplish his purposes of mercy in the revival of pure religion, and in the conversion of sinners. His influence upon the ministry, and upon the churches where he labored, was peculiarly happy. He always left behind him a sweet savor of Christ. Harmony and Christian affection, between pastors and people, were the result of his labors, even where they had been most successful in the conversion of souls. His zeal and earnestness in preaching the gospel, where Christ was named, were so tempered with practical wisdom and singular prudence, that he was received, and loved, and remembered as a messenger from God, sent to bless the people.

"His labors among us in the year 1829, are recollected with affection and gratitude. The revival with which we were favored that year, commenced about the middle of July. It was unusually powerful and still, and rapid in its progress. There was less animal excitement—convictions of sin were more thorough, and conversions were more clear and decided, than in some other seasons of revival which we have enjoyed. We had but little to do, but to stand still and see the salvation of God. Mr. Nettleton, if I mistake not, was then preaching at Enfield, Mass. By my request, he came and spent a week with us the first of September, and preached frequently to the most solemn and attentive assemblies I ever witnessed. He then left us, and returned again in about ten days, and spent another week. He preached on one Sabbath only. On that day, I supplied his place at Enfield. He preached and held inquiry meetings in the evenings of the week, and visited the families with me in the day time. His labors were very acceptable, and eminently useful, and I bless God for his aid. Many were awakened under his preaching, and some hopefully converted; and those who entertained hope, were greatly enlightened and strengthened. He is remembered to this day with much affection.

"The chief excellence of his preaching, seemed to consist in great plainness, and simplicity, and discrimination—in much solemnity and affectionate earnestness of manner—in the application of the truth to the heart and conscience—in taking away the excuses of sinners, and leaving them without help and hope, except in the sovereign mercy of God. In short, it was conformed to the work for which the Spirit was sent into the world, viz., to reprove or convince the world of sin, of righteousness, and of judgment. This characteristic was most striking. His manner of dealing with awakened sinners, was peculiar. While it served to deepen their convictions, and lead them to Christ, it gained their confidence, and secured their belief of the truth. He knew, too, how to search those who expressed hope. And while he detected the hypocrite and encouraged the desponding, he was regarded by all with affection and reverence. A large number of the subjects of this revival, were young people, belonging to the first families in the place. Of about one hundred who expressed hope at that time, more than sixty belonged to the center district. Numbers of them have removed to other places, and others have died in the joyful hope of glory. Frequently have I heard them express their remembrance of Dr. Nettleton's labors, and of their obligations to him as the instrument of leading them to Christ. Some on examination for church fellowship, dated their awakening and conversion to his labors. Of the number admitted to the church that year, only four have apostatized. They have generally maintained the Christian character, and some of them are eminently useful in the church. His labors, though short with us, were *greatly* blessed; and I shall ever remember them with gratitude to the great Head of the Church, who disposed him to come and help us."[6]

Asahel Nettleton continued to follow the pattern of retiring to the South in the fall and winter months for health reasons. In the fall of 1829, he visited Charleston, South Carolina, mainly for rest, but occasionally preaching. In 1830, he traveled to North Carolina and preached in the Chapel Hill area. In the summer of 1830 Nettleton resumed his labors in

New England to the blessings of many. His health improved somewhat for he was able to labor in New York City and Newark, New Jersey for the months of November through February. God blessed again in revivals which occurred as he was assisting the pastors in those areas (Rev. Baxter Dickinson, Dr. Snodgrass and Dr. Spring).

REVIVAL AT ENFIELD, CONNECTICUT

The town of Enfield, Connecticut is known in revival history as the site of Jonathan Edwards' famous sermon, "Sinners in the Hands of an Angry God", which Edwards preached on July 8th, 1741. It was said as Edwards began his text from Deuteronomy 32:35, "Their foot shall slip in due time," that the presence of God was so startling that "there was a great moaning and crying out throughout the whole house. What shall I do to be saved. Oh I am going to hell. Oh what shall I do for Christ." Things grew to such intensity under Edwards' preaching that he had to cease preaching to ask for silence to be heard over the groans! A century later, Asahel Nettleton preached in Enfield and a deep move of grace commenced. The Congregational church in which Nettleton preached sits across the street from the stone marker which lies in a open field, marking the spot of the old meeting house where Edwards preached.

The leaves were beginning to turn as Nettleton arrived in Enfield that September of 1833. He was fifty years old and in poor health. The only record of that revival is from the Rev. Francis L. Robbins, pastor of the church in Enfield. Since this is the *last known* record of a revival of religion under Asahel Nettleton, we read it with great interest.

> "I have not known the man, who in my deliberate judgment, has been the honored instrument of heaven in turning so many sinners to the knowledge of the truth, and savings souls from death, as the Rev. Mr. Nettleton. As he was himself 'mighty in the scriptures,' and 'fervent in the spirit,' he spake and taught diligently the things of the Lord, and was not satisfied unless men exhibited scriptural evidence of true religion. When he went into a place, remembering what was said of his master, 'he shall not strive nor cry, neither shall any man hear his voice in the streets,' he labored as far as practicable without observation, striving to turn the eyes of his hearers upon themselves while they listened diligently to the word. His meetings, therefore, whether on the Sabbath, or at other seasons were singularly marked with stillness, order, fixed and solemn attention.

> "My people were sensibly struck with the correctness of this statement in relation to his labors here. For in this place he had 'seals of his ministry,' in a goodly number of hopeful converts who regarded him as their spiritual father, and remembered him with high respect and gratitude. I refer to the revival of religion here in 1833, when several of the choice, active and exemplary members of this flock, received deep impressions, and became, as we believe, in heart and spirit, the people of the living God.

"Mr. Nettleton came here in September of that year, at my solicitation, when my health was, and had been, for several months, in a very feeble and precarious state; and when some of our good people were fearful of the result, not only to myself, but to the interests of religion. When Mr. Nettleton came, it was like the coming of Titus, especially to myself. Many of God's professed people had left their first love, and were engaged in matters of 'doubtful disputation,' which tended more to alienate and distract their feelings, than to quicken them in the work of the Lord.

"Mr. Nettleton continued with us nearly three months. Under his lucid and frequent exhibitions of divine truth, and by solemn addresses to the church, together with instruction given in the inquiry meeting, and by direct personal conversation, deep impressions were made on the minds of a number, which resulted in a disposition to renounce themselves, and humbly accept the salvation of the gospel. As he labored to instruct the people in the things of the kingdom of God, and establish them in the faith and order of the gospel, he very generally secured their esteem and confidence, and left a salutary influence behind him.

"Not long after he left us, nearly twenty, mostly youth, who ascribed their conversion to the abounding grace of God, through his instrumentality, came forward, and made a public profession of religion. Several others, who entertained a hope at that time, clouded with many fears, have been revived and quickened, and prepared to profess Christ since that time; while others who were brought to serious consideration, under the religious exercises conducted by Mr. Nettleton, never, I believe, lost their impressions, until as objects of God's special remembrance, they were hopefully gathered in, in a subsequent revival. All of those who were brought hopefully from darkness to light as the fruits of that revival, so far as I have knowledge, (for a few have removed to other places,) have walked worthy of their vocation, bearing the fruits of righteousness unto the praise and glory of God."[7]

As Asahel Nettleton was mightily used of God during the Second Great Awakening, so too, was Satan active in opposing the revivals through various means. History has demonstrated that true revivals of religion face opposition from the prince of darkness. In fact, it can be accurately stated that no true work of grace in revivals of religion, will not face opposition from the enemy of our souls.

Notes

1   Tyler, pp. 174–175.
2   Ibid. pp. 175–177.
3   Ibid. p. 177.
4   Ibid. pp. 178–180.
5   Ibid. pp. 182–187.
6   Ibid. pp. 187–189.
7   Ibid. pp. 193–195.

His generally pleasant and profitable visit to Virginia was unfortunately marred by one circumstance. A man in Carterville, Virginia, who had opposed the revival, was in correspondence with a man in South Britain, Connecticut, who revived the stories about him which had originated in 1818 ... Thus were revived the old calumnies against Nettleton, and thus they were quenched.

J. F. THORNBURY

27

ATTACK ON HIS CHARACTER

When George Whitefield, the great British evangelist, was laboring in revivals that were shaking London in the mid-eighteenth century, he was publicly maligned as of object of reproach by the London stage; the play-actors dubbed him "Doctor Squintum" ridiculing the squint in his eye and accusing Whitefield of the most vile acts imaginable! When the American evangelist, D. L. Moody was laboring in hell-storming crusades in Edinburgh and Glasgow, Scotland in the late nineteenth century, some letters surfaced from enemies in Chicago which attempted to besmirch his character and end the work of God. So it is not surprising to learn that as Asahel Nettleton is fighting the kingdom of darkness in Virginia, amidst scenes of startling revivals during the mid-nineteenth century, that Satan *again* rises up in wrathful malice—through the use of human dupes who slander the character of the great evangelist, a character which was impeccable. One cannot imagine the dagger that penetrated his heart when these spurious reports began to surface in an attempt to undermine the present revival which was shaking the Virginian churches. To their credit, his old friends Lyman Beecher and Nathaniel William Taylor took his side and fought for him. Other respected ministers publicly came to his defense as well until the vicious rumors were revealed for what they were—rumors.

What made these accusations about Asahel Nettleton so alarming to the Virginia ministers were the *number* of accusations coming from supposedly "other reliable Presbyterians" from Connecticut. The rumors spread so quickly and so viciously that measures had to be undertaken to combat them or they would have greatly hindered the revivals which were spreading across the region of Virginia like freshly lit fires. We will first present the public rebuttal of these rumors and the reaffirmation of Asahel Nettleton's character by the ministers who rushed to his defense. Then, we will present the *details* of this public attack, which was only one instance of many attacks on Nettleton throughout his life. We now turn to the comments of Bennet Tyler:

"When Dr. Nettleton was in Virginia, in 1828, a man from Connecticut, who was residing there, put in circulation some slanderous reports, which induced the Rev. Dr. John H. Rice to write to several distinguished individuals at the North, for the purpose of ascertaining how Dr. Nettleton's character was regarded by those who had been well acquainted with his history. In reply to his letters, many testimonials were forwarded, among which were the following:

"YALE COLLEGE, Aug. 23, 1826.

"Rev. and Dear Sir:

"I have most cheerfully obtained the testimonials which you have requested in your letter of the 9th. Perhaps this is all which the occasion requires. The injurious reports to which you refer, I do not recollect to have heard of before. I am now told that they were some years since put in circulation here, examined into, and found to be groundless. That they were mere fabrications appears evident from this, that up to the present time, Mr. Nettleton's Christian character stands as fair as ever in the estimation of the people of Connecticut, to whom he has been so intimately known.

Most affectionately yours,

"Jeremiah Day.

"Rev. John H. Rice, D.D.

"The Rev. Asahel Nettleton has been long and extensively known and acknowledged in this State, as a faithful and devoted minister of Christ; as a man of exemplary piety, of rare self-denial, and of uncommon power and success, in his labors as an evangelist. Though occasionally assailed by calumny, his Christian character is above suspicion, in the view of the ministers and churches in this State, to whom he is intimately known, and who have cause for abundant gratitude that the blessing of heaven has descended in copious measures upon his public ministrations.

JEREMIAH DAY, President of Yale College;

LEONARD BACON, Pastor of the First Church in New Haven;

NATHANIEL W. TAYLOR, Prof. of Didatic Theology

CHAUNCEY A. GOODRICH, Prof. of Rhetoric;

ELEAZER T. FITCH, Prof. of Divinity;

SAMUEL MERWIN, Pastor of the United Society in the City of New Haven."

"Boston, Aug. 22, 1828.

"Dear Brother:

"It is, I should think, about ten years since those stories, imported into Virginia, by Mr. O. W., have been dead and buried in Connecticut, having served the generation of infidels and scoffers, and all haters of evangelical doctrine and of revivals, as long as they were able.

"Never, for a moment, were they believed by the ministers and churches of Connecticut, nor did they do him the least injury, only as they were sent after him, or sent *for* to the places where his preaching was blessed; nor even then only till the friends of religion had opportunity to obtain correct information on the subject. It would be difficult for a Virginian to conceive the virulence with which some persons in New England oppose revivals of religion, without understanding that in many places where the truth has been preached too faithfully to be endured in a state of disobedience, there is often a club of infidels or nothingarians, whose enmity is always made rampant by a revival of religion, and whose ridicule and misrepresentation are sure to be propagated by the irreligious and immoral. Such, in my opinion, is the origin of all the stories against brother Nettleton in Connecticut. His friends debated the question once, whether it might not be his duty to sue, not doubting that he possessed the entire power of bringing his accusers to punishment. But the conclusion was, with the religious and respectable part of the community, they do him no harm, and it will be better for the cause of religion that he hold his peace, and *live them down*. This he has done; and it is out of the power of such men as W. and R. S. H. to injure Mr. Nettleton in Connecticut. H., I suppose I know, W. I do not. But I know that in S. there was probably a larger club of infidels, or persons reputed such, than in almost any town in the State. The alleged dissatisfaction with Mr. Nettleton at New Haven is, in my opinion, utterly false. I have been often in that city, and am more familiarly acquainted there than in any other place in Connecticut, it being the place of my nativity, and of my father's sepulcher. I do know that Mr. Nettleton possesses eminently the affection and confidence of the ministers and churches, and most respectable laymen in the city.

"As further evidence of the perfect impotency of all such rumors against Mr. Nettleton in Connecticut, I would state that about six years ago, on the failure of my health, I left my church and congregation in the care of Mr. Nettleton, under whose preaching, before my return, a revival of religion commenced, during which he secured eminently the confidence and affection of my people, which to this day remains undiminished. In short, there is not a minister in New England whose character for piety and purity stands higher than does that of Mr. Nettleton.

"You will receive further communications in due time, for you may rest assured that we posses the means, and shall not fail to use them, of putting down such impudent falsehoods, and of vindicating the well-earned reputation of Mr. Nettleton.

Affectionately yours,

"Lyman Beecher."

To this letter is appended the following, from the Rev. Dr. Taylor:

"Dear Brother:

"Dr. Beecher has sent this to me unsealed, and I take the liberty to add a word. What he has said is as it should be——exactly my views of the matter. I should only object to further means of putting down these 'impudent falsehoods.' I think I know brother Nettleton too well to suppose he would wish it. If such testimonials as this of Dr. Beecher and others are not sufficient to give brother Nettleton a character in

Virginia, in defiance of the obloquy of his enemies and his Master's, he had better come back to Connecticut. The ministers and churches would be glad to receive him, and highly appreciate his labors. These slanders are simply the 'homage vice pays to virtue.' 'Wo unto you, when all men shall speak well of you.' Brother Nettleton is safe from this denunciation.

I am affectionately yours,

"N. W. TAYLOR."

"NEW HAVEN, Sept. 17, 1828.

"We, the undersigned, having been for many years acquainted with the character of the Rev. Asahel Nettleton, do hereby certify that we consider him as a man of unblemished purity of life; that we believe this to be the estimation in which he is universally held in this town, and in this State; and that no fact has ever come to our knowledge, which ought to impair the confidence of the public in his character as a Christian and a man.

DAVID DAGGETT,	BENJAMIN SILLIMAN,
SIMEON BALDWIN,	J. KNIGHT,
NOAH WEBSTER,	ELI IVES,
ELIZUR GOODRICH,	J.L. KINGSLEY."

"Similar testimonies were forwarded by other distinguished gentlemen, both in New England and New York; particularly by the Hon. John Cotton Smith, of Connecticut; and by the Rev. Drs. Spring, McAuley and Proudfit, and by the Hon. Jonas Platt, of New York."[1]

Asahel Nettleton was publicly attacked on several levels, each aiming to end his usefulness as a minister of the gospel. What were these slanderous and impudent rumors which aroused the indignation of such great and eminent men who rallied to Nettleton's defense? For these answers we turn to the research performed by Sherry Pierpont May; the following comments are those of Dr. May, including *all* the footnotes for the remainder of this chapter.

"Nettleton went into the South after his controversy with Finney and the new measure men of New York state, and yet, if we can piece together what we know about his work in Virginia from various letters, we can unhesitantly say that the New Lebanon convention had in no way changed his methods. The only noticeable effect was that it made him more cautious that his name not be used as authority to spread practices which he opposed. He still preached only on the invitation of the settled minister, or at the request of the church if there was no pastor. He still saw himself as the pastor's assistant, and worked with the local minister and never against him. His preaching was basically doctrinal, but it also tended closely to apply the doctrine being discussed, in such a way that the listener not only understood what was being said, but that he felt that the proclamation was for him. Nettleton believed that one must first have an understanding of the truths he thought were clearly in the Bible, and then he must be motivated to act upon them. His preaching was accentuated and made effective by his use of the inquiry meeting. In these meetings the questions and frustrations of those who were seeking direction were met by a short address by Nettleton and then by brief, but individual, conversation with each person.

"The Presbyterians in Virginia had not been touched by the extravagances of Methodists and Presbyterians as in some parts of the South. But they, as their northern brethren, feared from the external influence of the sects and the possible internal excesses of their own churchmen. There was also a sizeable group which opposed revivals altogether, fearing any revivals would lead to excess. From what we can gather from Nettleton's correspondence, we can say that he made an effective influence for controlled revivalism in the South. His following can be garnered from the large number of letters in later years, requesting that he come to preach for them.

ATTACK ON NETTLETON'S REPUTATION

"As Nettleton's views became well known and well received in many parts of the North, those whose opinions differed from his found that his views could not be bent. The same was true in the South. And as the use of measures which Nettleton opposed were more and more accepted in many churches, the opposition to Nettleton became pronounced. This reached a climax during his early months in Virginia.

"Within a few weeks after Nettleton arrived in Virginia he received a letter from his close friend and business adviser, George P. Shipman, from New York. Unfortunately parts of this letter are impossible to read. It has been water soaked and parts are torn and very faded. (Parts of other letters are stuck to the back and cannot be removed.) From the meager portions of the letter which I have been able to read, it seems that Shipman is acknowledging a letter from Nettleton, and then speaks of some abuses—perhaps some which have been published—of Nettleton. Shipman does not specify the abuses—or at least if they are there they are not readable. He does say that he called on [William A.] Hallock immediately and then wrote to Lyman Beecher and Dr. T. McAuly (of Union College, Schenectady, New York) to inform them of the abuses and to ask them to defend Nettleton. Shipman says that he now realizes that 'they' (perhaps the new measure opposers) feel that 'you [Nettleton] must be put down' and that it only remains to be seen whether or not Dr. Beecher and Edwards, and Rev. Weeks, etc. will come forward in defense of the truth.'[2] There is no mention of this incident in Tyler's biography of Nettleton.

"In another letter, equally impossible to read, dated February 27, from William R. Weeks, the writer says that there has been a letter (or article) about him (Weeks) by the Reverend Frost and Aiken (two of the ministers sympathetic to Finney) in the *New York Observer* of the 9th and 16th. He warns Nettleton to be guarded in what he says.[3] On March 17th, Weeks again writes to Nettleton saying that he has written 'a letter to Mr. Shipman in defense of you, which I give him the liberty to publish ...'[4]

"All three of these letters, all over 140 years old [as of 1968], are worn not from time, but from lack of care. They remained in a wet basement for many years, and as a result are water soaked and thus faded and very fragile. Their major value for us is to indicate that the truce that was made at New Lebanon between Nettleton and the moderate clergy on the one hand, and Finney and his new measure followers on the other, was an uneasy one. All of the other moderates were settled pastors, related to a local parish, or to a theological school or college. It was only Nettleton who traveled widely, preaching first in one church and then another. It was he who saw revival methods changing and was appalled when he found that his authority was sometimes used to sanction a method which he opposed. It was also he who, because of his stern and authoritative mien, his shy and retiring manner, his weak physical condition, his freedom to come and go as he pleased, was the various target for abuse. Thus he should not be too surprised at the gossip which was spread about him after the Convention.

"The specific nature of the talk in late 1827 and early 1828 we do not know. We do know, however, the nature of the stories which followed Nettleton into Virginia during the summer of 1828. On August 7th, 1828, the Reverend Jesse Armistead of Cartersville, Virginia, wrote the following letter to Nettleton, who was still a guest of Dr. Rice in Prince Edward. The letter begins, 'I feel bound to let you know that the enemies of religion in this place are doing all in their power to prejudice the public mind against you before you come.' It seems that Mr. Wheeler, a layman in the community, had received a letter from Mr. R. S. Hinman, a lawyer. The letter was postmarked at Salem Bridge. Several copies of the letter were being circulated to arouse opposition against Nettleton, and Armistead says that Mr. William F. Randolph, another lawyer who lived in the area, read a copy of the letter to him. He then gave the following abstract of the contents:

The first point is in reference to your celebrated letter to the young people assembled at the ball. He says that he has the original letter and is willing to furnish it for publication, should Mr. Wheeler wish to pursue the course. The account of the letter—of which he gives a transcript—is, that you said that you were present with the assembly, knowing their thoughts and giving an extract from the first chapter of Proverbs and then signing the name—*Jesus Christ*. Every thinking person understands this matter perfectly. But Wheeler and Company wish to torture—and, therefore, say that you were so completely infatuated, that you imagined you were yourself the Saviour, and signed *Jesus Christ* as your own name.

They speak of it as a forgery of damning character, as blasphemy. As to the note at the bottom of the tract with your own signature, they regard it as nothing, in opposition to their interpretation. He next mentions the affair of the young lady in Waterbury, and after detailing the circumstances, pretty much as I mentioned in my letter to Dr. Rice, he says that the story was not believed by him, and that he regarded it as a plan of the young woman, who disliked you, to get you away from the place. He mentions, however, that the people were tired of you, as he says they are every where that you stay any time,—and were glad to get you away.

He also speaks of another young woman, who was sent from some other town *to be converted by you*, and who herself reported that you were in the habit of calling her up very early in the *morning* for prayer, and that you sometimes went into her room before she was out of bed. Other persons were known, he remarks, to go to her room *for other purposes*. The last and most serious of his charges is, that when you were labouring in New Haven, before you left there, *the Presbyterians thought you a very unsuitable associate for their children*. This he heard from a lady, a member of the Presbyterian church in New Haven, two days before he wrote. I have given this abstract from memory, but think that it is strictly correct. What course you ought to pursue in reference to this letter, you know best. My judgment is, that you ought certainly to come here very soon ... Would it not be well to write to Waterbury and

Southbury, and get testimonials of your standing there? Dr. Tyler, the president of
Dartmouth, was formerly the minister of the congregation in which Wheeler lived.
His character of you would have weight here, as Wheeler speaks in high terms of
him. He says you *are no more* to be compared to Dr. Tyler, than gran [or grave] stones
are to be compared to diamonds ...

"In closing Armistead again urged Nettleton to come, saying that the opposition
is confined to the village, and the people in the outlying country are very eager for
his arrival.[5]

"We may smile at the nature of the charges, but the seriousness of the attack is not
to be laughed at. Men who opposed the kind of revivalism which Nettleton was
bringing into Virginia are striking where it would be most effective. Not theology,
but morality, would convince the people that Nettleton's tactics were suspect.

"An attempt by Armistead to get hold of the Hinman letter from Wheeler was
reproached, and the slander was circulated in the village.[6]

"Upon receipt of Armistead's first letter, Dr. Rice immediately wrote to New
England for certificates affirming Nettleton's good character. The response was
overwhelming and left little doubt as to Nettleton's integrity. Thirteen letters were
dispatched to the South, all bearing testimony to his Christian character and the high
regard with which he was held in Connecticut.[7]

"Individual letters were signed by Bennet Tyler, then the President of
Dartmouth; Jeremiah Day, President of Yale; Lyman Beecher, pastor in Boston at
the time; Nathaniel W. Taylor, Yale Professor, close friend and later antagonist of
Nettleton's; Dr. Gardiner Spring, pastor in Philadelphia at the time: the Honorable
John Cotton Smith, former governor of Connecticut; and Dr. David Porter, pastor
of the Catskill, New York, Presbyterian church where Nettleton had so recently
spent a great deal of time. A short testimony from New Haven was sent and signed
by Jeremiah Day, Yale's president; Leonard Bacon, the pastor of the First Church of
Christ in New Haven; Nathaniel W. Taylor, Chauncey A. Goodrich and Eleazer T.
Fitch, all Yale professors and later expositors of the New Haven theology; and
Samuel Merwin, the pastor of the United Society in New Haven. Perhaps most
interesting is a letter signed by a group of some of the most distinguished citizens of
Connecticut ... and Noah Webster, identified in the certificate as 'one of the oldest
inhabitants in this city, and well known to the public as author of the American
Dictionary of the English Language ...'!

"... The three specific charges—the ballroom letter at Southbury, the woman at
Waterbury, and the New Haven parents—were quickly put down. The fourth
could not be directly answered, because of the vague nature of the charge, so
Nettleton's good character could only be supported to refute it. These testaments—
by the leading clergy and distinguished men of Connecticut—were circulated
throughout Virginia, and so far as we know, nothing ever came of the attempt to
discredit Nettleton. He traveled extensively through Virginia, and his preaching
was successful. He received many requests to preach, many of which he had to reject
because of his health."[8]

This attack on Nettleton's character would pale in comparison with
future attacks from his enemies. One attack, the most vicious, occurred
in 1835, and what made it so trying for Nettleton was the fact that it came
from the hands of one of his former *friends*, Leonard Bacon. Bacon

publicly denounced Nettleton in cruel articles published in the *St. Louis Observer* and the *New York Evangelist*, which squarely placed all the blame for division in the churches upon his shoulders, claiming that before "Mr. Finney arose ... Nettleton introduced new measures" and that it was generally held that those ministers who labored with Nettleton were aghast at his "irregularities and imprudence ..." No crueler statements could have been made. The public attacks from Bacon became so strident and vicious that he became to Asahel Nettleton what Alexander Garden was to George Whitefield——his most bitter enemy. And the saddest thing from all of this was that Asahel had discipled Leonard Bacon years earlier, and had only shown him the greatest kindness and love. Documentation of this regrettable incident in the life of the great evangelist are found in his correspondence with friends such as Samuel Miller, of Princeton, in the "Nettleton Collection" at Hartford Seminary. The trashy letters and accusations from the bitter pen of Bacon need not surface here in a rehash of simply bad manners and jealousy. Suffice to say, the beleaguered Nettleton kept pressing forward in the service of his King, despite the reproach from his enemies, sharing in the "sufferings of Christ" who himself "bore reproach".

Notes

1   Ibid. pp. 347–350.

2   MS letter, from George Shipman, New York, February 14, 1828, to Asahel Nettleton, Prince Edwards Court House, Virginia.

3   MS letter from William R. Weeks, Paris, New York, February 27, 1828, to Asahel Nettleton, Prince Edward Court House, Virginia.

4   MS letter, from William R. Weeks, Paris, New York, March 17, 1828, to Asahel Nettleton, Prince Edward Court House, Virginia. Most of the letter is about himself and the abuse he has felt. He tells Nettleton that he wrote to defend himself against Frost, but decided not to publish it because he felt that Frost may have written to draw him out. In Weeks' words, the problem is as follows: "One story is that I am the origin of all the opposition to Mr. Finney's measures for which there is no ground; and that I have been influenced by disappointed ambition. That having failed some years ago in being able to rule the whole Presbytery of Oneida, I tried to get it divided, which not being accomplished, I got up the [Congregational] Association to have a body I could rule. And that the Presbytery being highly favored with revivals and the Association not, I and others were moved with envy, and therefore tried to depreciate the work and throw contempt upon it abroad." Cf. Finney's comments about Weeks in his *Autobiography*, p. 195.

5   MS letter, from Jesse Armistead, Cartersville, August 7, 1828, to Asahel Nettleton, Prince Edward.

6   MS letter, from J. Armistead, Cartersville, Virginia, August 21, 1828, to Asahel Nettleton, Staunton, Augusta County, Virginia, and forwarded to Lewisburg, Greenbrier County, Virginia.

7   MSS. All the testimonials are copied on four pages of legal size paper, and the following appears on the bottom of page 4: "The above are true copies from the originals, all of which are in my possession. Cartersville, November 4, 1828," signed by Jesse S. Armistead. These copies were sent to Nettleton, c/o Dr. A. Waddell, Staunton, Virginia, from Armistead on November 5th.

8   Sherry Pierpont May, *Asahel Nettleton: Nineteenth Century American Revivalist*, dissertation, 1969 (Drew University), pp. 110–121.

I had been in England long enough to feel the necessity of being very particular in giving them such instructions as would do away their idea of waiting God's time. London is, and long has been cursed with hyper-Calvinistic preaching.

CHARLES FINNEY

Hartford Seminary, Hartford, CT, the successor to the institution founded by Nettleton and Tyler (which houses the "Nettleton Collection")

Ellsworth School, East Windsor. The facade is all that remains of the Theological Institute of Connecticut founded by Nettleton and Tyler. Both men are buried in the cemetary behind the school.

President's House, East Windsor, opposite the Theological Institute, and home of Bennet Tyler.

28

TRIP ABROAD AND FOUNDING
OF THE THEOLOGICAL INSTITUTE

It is interesting to note that both Charles Finney and Asahel Nettleton visited Great Britain. Finney visited twice and preached in George Whitefield's chapels at Tottenham Court and Moorfields—Nettleton did not have that privilege. Finney's reputation preceded him and even though his audiences were large he did not care for London, as seen from his remarks:

> "Rain & smoke & dirt & the suffocating gases generated by millions of coal fires, & millions of human & of animal lungs, render the air quite unfit for respiration ... The utter & dangerous ignorance of men in *high places* of the laws of respiration & ventilation, of the nature & causes of atomospheric change, of the generation & effects of gases &c. &c. not only annoy me but absolutely endanger my life & waste my strength."[1]

While Charles Finney's visit to Great Britain drew many crowds to hear him, few were enamored of the visit of Asahel Nettleton. Asahel preached infrequently and seemingly without much success. Why this was the case we do not know. Apparently, Nettleton traveled across the pond for his health. Charles Finney, in his *Memoirs*, claimed Nettleton visited Great Britain to *offset* the public success of Finney's "Lectures on Revivals". Finney stated:

> "Mr. Nettleton amongst others visited England & Scotland it would seem for the purpose of counteracting the influence of those lectures."[2]

Yet this was *not* the reason for Nettleton's visit, Finney had not even *given* his lectures at this date. This is seen from the following footnotes of Finney's *Memoir*:

> "James had written to Finney:
>
> "The publication in this country, of your volume of sermons on Revivals produced on many minds at first a very strong excitement. It was extensively read by a certain class—and was on some accounts admired ... But it was by others, and even by some who first admired it, soon thought to be defective in evangelical unction,

and somewhat contradictory on the subject of divine spiritual influence ... Soon
after this Mr. Nettleton and others of that school of theology were in this kingdom
and your works were still more in disfavour (James to Finney, 29 January 1850,
Finney Papers, microfilm, roll 4).

"Nettleton had been in England from the spring of 1831 until August 1832,
before Finney had given his lectures. He had, however, sought to counteract the
prejudices that had arisen against American revivals by dissociating himself from the
practice of the 'anxious seat' and the excesses of the New Measures revivals, which
he had found had been widely reported."[3]

Apparently, a false view of American revivals had filtered into Great
Britain at this time. There was great concern among many British
clergymen that the "American Revivals" were nothing more than
enthusiasm and excitement, hence they were suspicious of them.
Although Asahel primarily visited Great Britain for his health, he was
soon thrust into public controversies and embroiled in debates over these
"American Revivals" of the New Measure stamp. Instead of having
preaching opportunities, he was forced into a position to defend and
define what true revivals of religion were in America and alter this false
conception produced by the western revivals.

The widely held British perception of American revivalism was that *all*
revivals used the "anxious seat" and that the majority of the American
churches approved of the New Measures of Finney. Asahel Nettleton
would spend a year and a half in England and Scotland without much
public success. Little is known of his time there, apart from a few letters
from British friends. His biographer, Bennet Tyler, merely mentions
three days of British activity in the *Memoirs*. We do know that Nettleton
had hoped for a British edition of his *Village Hymns* but it appears that this
hymnal was not as popular in Britain as in America. All in all the trip to
Great Britain was a vacation for the weary Nettleton and he returned to
America rested and reflective.

FOUNDING OF THE THEOLOGICAL INSTITUTE

East Windsor Hill, Connecticut was soon to be home to two eminent
men: Asahel Nettleton and Bennet Tyler. It was here in East Windsor
Hill, that Tyler and Nettleton would live, becoming neighbors on a tree-
lined country street. Nettleton would purchase a farm and build a large
house which he would remain in for the last ten years of his life. Tyler's
majestic home sat across the street from the seminary they had founded:
The Theological Institute. Its origins arose from the Taylor/Finney
controversy. They felt that a seminary was needed to train young men in
the tradition of Jonathan Edwards' theology, orthodox New England

Calvinism. Harvard had gone liberal, so had Yale; New Haven was a hot-bed of liberalism—only Princeton held to its traditional moorings.

On the tenth of September, 1833, at East Windsor Hill, a historic meeting took place. Fifty ministers from throughout the state of Connecticut converged upon the sleepy hamlet of East Windsor Hill, to gather their forces against "Taylorism" which was spreading a theological downgrade throughout New England. Asahel Nettleton was present at this important meeting of New England clergy. We see from the following observations how things transpired at this initial meeting:

> "At the first session, a committee of six was appointed to draw up the organization plans for the Pastoral Union. The committee produced a tentative constitution and Articles of Agreement, which were adopted, and the Union was legally formed for the purpose of promoting 'ministerial intercourse, fellowship and pastoral usefulness, the promotion of revivals of religion, the defense of evangelical truth against prevailing error.' Most importantly, the Union was established for the 'raising up of sound and faithful ministers for the supply of the churches.'

> "The last sentence reflected the seriousness of the situation in New England, as viewed by the participants in this conference. Most of these men were Yale graduates and their ties there were strong and tender. But Yale could no longer be counted on to produce the kind of ministers they believed the churches should have. Clearly, a new institution was needed."[4]

N. W. Taylor, of Yale, was influencing all of New England with his own brand of theology which denied original sin and the need for regeneration in salvation. But the theological downgrade was much broader than the "New Haven Theology" of N. W. Taylor; both the Congregational and Presbyterian churches of New England were in transformation by 1833. On the one hand was the rise of Unitarianism and Universalism, and on the other was liberalism on college campuses such as Harvard and Yale, which challenged "Old School Calvinism". In addition to these influences, "French philosophy" had taken root in the upper class of society, especially among well-to-do college students. Many began to doubt the validity of the Bible and religion or the necessity for either. Sadly, a spiritual decline ensued after the great revivals of the first part of the century, and many individuals (including some ministers) were turning their backs on the God of the Bible. Men like Bennet Tyler and Asahel Nettleton, whose theology was Edwardsean, soon became dinosaurs. Yet, amidst this spiritual decline Tyler and Nettleton felt a deep need to train up young ministers in the faith of the Fathers, to counteract those on the liberal side. Thus the Theological Institute was born amid such adverse spiritual conditions.

HARTFORD SEMINARY

Hartford Seminary, in Hartford, Connecticut, enjoys rich traditions tracing back to that institution's founders, Asahel Nettleton and Bennet Tyler. The original seminary was located in East Windsor Hill, Connecticut and the foundation stone was the "stepping stone" taken from the manse of Timothy Edwards, Jonathan Edwards' father. Thus, foundationally the theology of this new institution would reflect the Edwardsean position, and be firmly rooted in the Calvinism of the Puritan fathers of New England. Even today, as one visits Hartford Seminary and explores the history of that institution, one learns of the "missionary martyrs" that were graduates of Hartford Seminary during the nineteenth century. In the basement of the seminary library are plaques with the names of those graduates who gave their lives on the mission field for the sake of the gospel. We see this institution's early beginnings from the following comments:

"On 11th September, [1833] the Pastoral Union met and took up the most important business which lay before it, the matter of the founding of a seminary. The name and purpose of the institution ... would be the training of ministers and 'the teaching of sciences preparatory to, or connected with a collegiate course of study.' The management of the school was to be in the hands of a board of trustees consisting of twelve ministers and eight laymen. The trustees were to serve for one year, and they were subject to re-election. Asahel Nettleton was honored by being the first trustee to be elected ...

"The leaders of the movement began immediately to dig into their own pockets. Asahel Nettleton gave an outright donation of five hundred dollars, and pledged one hundred annually for the next five years. Two years later he gave five hundred dollars, and in 1839 an additional one thousand dollars. His total contributions of two thousand and five hundred dollars made him the greatest single donor to the seminary fund, with the exception of Erastus Ellsworth, a retired New York business man, who was also a member of the Board of Trustees. The original target of twenty thousand dollars for the school was very soon reached.

"Mr. Ellsworth, who had settled at East Windsor Hill, had recently purchased a tract of land in the town which was only a short distance from the 'corners'. The Board of Commissioners of the school, which had been elected to transact any business, decided to purchase this tract of land from Mr. Ellsworth as a suitable site for the seminary. They bought it from him at the price of two hundred and fifty dollars. East Windsor Hill was the birthplace of Jonathan Edwards and the site of the church of his father, Timothy Edwards. The plot for the future seminary was not far from where the old Edwards parsonage had stood.

"Having secured the pledge of sufficient funds for the school and decided on the location for its buildings, the Commissioners began the important task of selecting a head for the seminary. To many of the ministers, Asahel Nettleton seemed a logical choice. However, his health was still poor, and he would not allow his name to be considered for the post ... the thoughts of the Connecticut men turned more and more toward the Maine pastor, Bennet Tyler. He was himself a native of

Connecticut and knew intimately most of those involved in the Pastoral Union. Furthermore, he had had valuable experience in his years as president of Dartmouth College, at Hanover, New Hampshire. He was completely in sympathy with the theological sentiments of the Pastoral Union and had been one of the most outspoken opponents of New Haven theology. Since Tyler's writings had had no small part in the developments in Connecticut, it seemed fitting that he should be offered the position of president of the seminary which was being founded to expound his views.

"Tyler was Nettleton's choice; in fact he had never considered anyone else. Since the school house revival of 1812 they had been intimate friends and had stayed in close contact with each other. After the September conference at East Windsor Hill he had written to Tyler and asked him if he would accept the position of president of the seminary should the trustees offer the job to him. Tyler replied that he would have to receive more information about the school. He assured Asahel, however, that if he accepted the post he would want Nettleton to be associated with the school. Meanwhile, Nettleton asked him what provisions he would require for coming, particularly in the way of salary. Tyler replied that a thousand dollars per year, plus house rent and moving expenses would be adequate.

"On 16th October, 1833, at the first regular meeting of the Board of Trustees, Bennet Tyler was elected president of the Theological Institute of Connecticut. Nettleton was appointed to approach him about the matter. Tyler replied that he would like to come to East Windsor Hill to discuss the new school and his relationship to it. The week following his election, he came to Connecticut and acquainted himself with the situation. After talking with Nettleton and the others involved, he accepted the appointment. The Theological Institute of Connecticut had a president."[5]

Today the seminary in East Windsor Hill is gone. It was relocated to Hartford, Connecticut after the deaths of Nettleton and Tyler. There in East Windsor Hill, the former facade of the seminary still stands, as the Ellsworth School. The large white mansion across the street is Bennet Tyler's residence (now a private residence). Behind the Ellsworth school is a small ancient graveyard. There, side by side, lie the graves of Asahel Nettleton and Bennet Tyler. A serenity and solemnity accompany the graveyard, a reminder to the solemn work of God during the Second Great Awakening in young America. Down the street is Nettleton's home, a yellow two-storey private residence. Beside his home is the ancient cemetery where the remains of Timothy Edwards lie. And further down the street is a historical marker, showing the birthplace of Jonathan Edwards; each reminders of the fight for the faith and the grace of God in salvation during a movement of grace upon the land. Asahel Nettleton's brown mossy gravestone stands as a silent testimony to what God can do through a man entirely surrendered to Him.

Notes

1   Finney, *Memoirs*, p. 515.
2   Ibid. p. 496.
3   Ibid. p. 496.
4   J. F. Thornbury, p. 212.
5   Ibid. pp. 212–214.

The Old Burial Ground where Timothy Edwards, father of Jonathan, is buried (gravestone below). It is located near to the site of Jonathan Edwards' birthplace.

Being one day in very great pain, he said to me, "I ought not to complain; but all that I have ever suffered in the course of my life, is nothing in comparison with this. But it is nothing in comparison with what I deserve."

BENNET TYLER AT NETTLETON'S BEDSIDE

The gravestones of Asahel Nettleton (foreground) and Bennet Tyler (pillar) in the graveyard behind the Ellsworth School

REV. ASAHEL NETTLETON D.D., Died 1844, Aged 61 years
Text on Nettleton's gravestone in the graveyard behind Ellsworth School

29

DEATH OF NETTLETON

One will never know the extent of Asahel Nettleton's suffering toward the end of his life. The mental abuse suffered at the hands of his enemies took a severe toll on his already frail frame. The worst emotional trial came from former friend, Leonard Bacon, who, as we witnessed in a previous chapter, printed some of the most vile abuses against Nettleton; charging him with the worst possible accusations, which were the antithesis of the great evangelist's career. He was charged with introducing "strange fire" into revivals, injuring the people of God with his strange behavior, and being the instrument of bringing harm to churches rather than blessings. He was painted as another James Davenport, one who brought ruin to the cause of revivals. Ironically, the opposite was true. One would have to trace the history of the British evangelist George Whitefield to find such similar abuses.[1] Yet, Asahel Nettleton saw more revivals than even the great George Whitefield!

The yellow, two-story home of Asahel Nettleton sits on Main Street in East Windsor Hill, next to an old cemetery. Standing outside the home today one can imagine the pain-stricken invalid as he lay dying in his bedchamber. Among the circle of friends surrounding that bedside, was Bennet Tyler, who patiently nursed him in his final hours. While it is interesting to read about a Christian's active labors, it is also worthy to pay special attention to *how an eminent Christian dies.* Approaching the dark vale of death is a somber time, a reflective time, a sensitive time. How one prepares for death is a worthy study in itself. Although the great evangelist suffered intensely with chronic, excruciating pain which racked his feeble body, he *died well.* Therefore, it is with great care and interest that we turn to the surviving record of Asahel Nettleton's last days, as recorded by his trusted friend, Bennet Tyler. Tyler tenderly recorded these last moments:

"The sickness of Dr. Nettleton in 1822, gave a shock to his constitution from which it never recovered. For a considerable part of the time during the remainder of his life, he was exceedingly feeble; and at no time was he able to engage in arduous labor. Still he was not entirely laid aside. He preached, as we have seen, in many places, and in some with great success. Finding the climate of New England too severe for his enfeebled constitution during the winter months, he usually, for a number of years, spent them at the South; and by great care in avoiding excitement and excessive fatigue, he was able to enjoy a comfortable degree of health, for most of the time, until the summer of 1841, when he began to be afflicted with urinary calculi, which soon confined him to the house, and subjected him to great bodily suffering. Finding no relief from medical prescriptions, and being reduced to that state in which it was evident he could live but a short time, on the 14th of February, 1843, he submitted to the operation of lithotomy, by which he obtained partial relief, and hopes were entertained, for a season, of his entire recovery. But after a few months, it became manifest, that the disease was returning upon him. His sufferings again became exceedingly great, till on the 8th of December, 1843, he submitted to a second operation. For some time, he appeared to be doing well, and hopes were again entertained of his recovery. But these hopes were not realized. He continued in a feeble state until the 16th of May, 1844, when the powers of nature failed, and he resigned his spirit into the hand of God who gave it.

"During his protracted and severe sufferings, his piety was subjected to a new test. We have seen its efficacy in prompting him, while in health, to the most arduous and un-remitted labors in the cause of Christ; and it was no less efficacious in sustaining him in the day of trial. For many months together, his bodily pain was almost without intermission, and exceedingly great—at times, indeed, excruciating. But he was strengthened to endure it with patience and resignation. During the whole of his sickness, he was never heard to utter a murmuring word. He was often heard to say, "My sufferings are great, but they are nothing in comparison with what I deserve." A large part of the time during his sickness, his mind was vigorous and active. He read many books during this period, particularly D'Aubigne's History of the Reformation, with which he was much delighted, Gaussen on Inspiration, Tracy's History of the Great Awakening, the entire works of the younger Edwards, much of the works of Emmons, a large part of the works of Andrew Fuller, besides many smaller works. What he read, he read with great attention, and he would often make criticisms and comments of the things which he had read. But the Bible was the man of his counsel. He would often say, 'there are many good books, but after all, there is nothing like the Bible.' And it never was so precious to him as at this period. Although he had made it his study for more than forty years, and had acquired a knowledge of it to which few attain, yet he found it an inexhaustible fund of rich instruction. He could adopt the language of the Psalmist, "*How sweet are thy words unto my taste; yea, sweeter than honey to my mouth. Thy testimonies have I taken as a heritage forever; for they are the rejoicing of my heart. Thy Statutes have been my songs in the house of my pilgrimage.*"

"He not only read some portion of the scriptures every day, but he devoted much time, to a close and critical study of them. He usually kept his Greek Testament, and his Greek Concordance by him, and diligently compared different parts of scripture with each other in the original language, that he might be sure to get the precise meaning. I found him one morning with the Greek Testament in his hand. He said, 'you will perhaps wonder that I should be reading this. You may suppose that a person in my situation, would prefer to read the translation. But I seem to get nearer to the fountain when I read the original. It is like drinking water at the spring, rather than from a vessel in which it has been carried away. By reading the Greek, I get shades of meaning, which cannot be expressed in any translation.' It was common for him to entertain friends with comments and remarks on portions of scripture; and these comments were exceedingly interesting and instructive. Many an individual has gone away from his bed side, with a more lively sense of the worth of the Bible, than he ever felt before.

"He was not in the habit, during his sickness, of speaking very often of his own religious feelings; but it was manifest from the whole strain of his conversation, and particularly from the lively interest which he took in the truths of the Bible, that he generally enjoyed great peace of mind.

"On one occasion, having expressed to me his apprehension that his disease was incurable, I inquired of him the state of his mind. He expressed entire submission to the will of God—a willingness to be in his hands, and to be disposed of according to his pleasure. He spoke of the great deceitfulness of the human heart, and the danger of self-deception. He manifested an ardent attachment to the doctrines which he had preached, and seemed to derive from them great support in the near prospect of eternity; and he expressed a peculiar love for those of his brethren, who had been decided in their adherence to the truth, and in their opposition to prevailing errors.

"On another occasion, he conversed very freely concerning his own spiritual state. He gave me a more particular account of his conversion than he had ever done before. It brought to his recollection so many tender scenes, that he was greatly affected and wept abundantly. He spake of the doctrines of grace, and said with great emotion, 'I do not need any body to tell me that they are true. I am fully convinced of their truth, by my own experience.'

"One morning, as I entered the room, he said to me, that these words had been running in his mind.

'Death will invade us by the means appointed,
Nor am I anxious, if I am prepared,
What shape he comes in.'

"In the course of the conversation, he said, 'more of my life is written in Bunyan's Grace Abounding to the Chief of Sinners than any where else.' He was a great admirer of the writings of Bunyan, and often referred to them in illustration of his own opinions.

"On being asked whether he still entertained the same views of the errors, on account of which he had manifested so much solicitude—he spake with great emotion, saying, 'It is the bearing which these errors have upon the eternal interests of men, which gives them all their importance in my estimation. It is in view of death, judgment, and eternity, that I have looked at them. If I had not regarded them as dangerous to the souls of men, I should have felt no solicitude respecting them.'

"At another time, he wished me to read to him the following hymn, in Wardlaw's collection.

1. Come let us join our friends above
    That have obtained the prize,
And on the eagle's wings of love,
    To joy celestial rise.

2. Let saints below in concert sing,
    With those to glory gone;
For all the servants of our king,
    In heaven and earth are one.

3. One family, we dwell in him,
    One church, above, beneath,
Though now divided by the stream,
    The narrow stream of death.

4. One army of the living God,
    To his command we bow,
Part of the host have crossed the flood,
    And part are crossing now.

5. Each moment, to their endless home,
    Some parting spirits fly;
And we are to the margin come,
    And soon expect to die.

6. Dear Saviour, be our constant guide,
    Then, when the word is given,
Bid death's cold stream and flood divide,
    And land us safe in heaven.'

"He alluded to this hymn, several times, with great interest, during his sickness. On one occasion he spoke with great feeling of those who were hopefully converted in the revivals under his preaching, and said, the thought of meeting them in the future world, was often exceedingly interesting. 'But,' said he, 'I have never allowed myself to be very confident of arriving at heaven, lest the disappointment should be the greater. I know that the heart is exceedingly deceitful, and that many will be deceived. And why am I not as liable to be deceived as others?' He spoke of the opinion maintained by some, that none are ever actuated by any other principle than self-love, and said, 'I should have no hope of being saved, if I believed myself never to have been actuated by a higher principle.'

"He one day referred to the words of the apostle, "Despise not the chastening of the Lord, nor faint when thou art rebuked of him." He observed that there are two ways in which divine chastisements are improperly received. One is, *despising* them, that is, making light of them—disregarding them, as a stubborn, disobedient child sometimes sets at defiance and treats with contempt the chastisement of his father. The other is, *fainting* under them, that is, making too much of them, feeling as though they were too heavy to be borne, and greater than we deserve. 'We ought,' said he, 'to feel that all our sufferings, however great, are *light afflictions*, infinitely less than we deserve.'

"When asked one time, if he did not sometimes get weary of life, he said, 'It is wearisome. But I have sometimes heard persons express a desire to die, when it was painful to me. I desire to have no will on the subject.' He felt that it was as much our duty to be willing to live and suffer, if such be the will of God, as to be willing to die. Asking for the hymn-book, he read the following stanza:

"Be this my one great business here,
    With holy trembling fear,
        To make my calling sure;

Thine utmost counsel to fulfill,
And *suffer* all thy righteous will,
    And to the end endure."

"It was very common for him, when inquired of respecting the state of his mind, instead of giving a direct answer, to point to some hymn, or some passage of scripture as indicative of his feelings.

"On one occasion, finding him in very great pain, I said to him, 'I hope the Lord will give you patience.' He replied, 'I have need of patience.' I remarked that when suffering severe pain, it was profitable to think of the sufferings of Christ. he said that the words of the 228th Village Hymn had been running in his mind all night.

1. "Begone unbelief!
    My Saviour is near,
And for my relief
    Will surely appear.
By prayer let me wrestle,
    And he will perform,
With Christ in the vessel,
    I smile at the storm.

2. Determined to save,
    He watched o'er my path,
When, Satan's blind slave,
    I sported with death:
And can he have taught me
    To trust in his name,
And thus far have brought me,
    To put me to shame?

3. Why should I complain
    Of want or distress,
Temptations or pain?
    He told me no less;
The heirs of salvation
    I know from his word,
Through much tribulation,
    Must follow their Lord.

4. Though dark be my way,
    Since he is my guide,
'Tis mine to obey,
    'Tis his to provide;
His way was much rougher,
    And darker than mine;
Did Jesus thus suffer,
    And shall I repine?

5. His love in time past,
    Forbids me to think
He'll leave me at last
    In trouble to sink:
Though painful at present,
    'Twill cease before long,

And then, O how pleasant
The conqueror's song."

"Being one day in very great pain, he said to me, 'I ought not to complain; but all that I have ever suffered in the course of my life, is nothing in comparison with this. But it is nothing in comparison with what I deserve.' 'No,' said I, 'nor is it worthy to be compared with the glory that shall be revealed.' He requested me to take from the shelf and hand to him the Remains of Carlos Wilcox; and with great interest he read the following lines:

"But wherefore will not God
E'en now, from ills on others brought, exempt
The offspring of regenerating grace,
The children of his love? Imperfect yet,
They need the chastenings of eternal care,
To save them from the wily blandishments
Of error, and to win their hearts away
From the polluting, ruining joys of earth!"

"Speaking at one time of his disease, as that which for many years he had dreaded more than any other, he pointed me to the following passage in the Life of Samuel Pearce, as expressive of his own feelings.

"It was never, till to-day, that I got any personal instruction from our Lord's telling Peter by *what death* he should glorify God. Oh, what a satisfying thought, that God appoints those means of dissolution, whereby he gets most glory to himself. It was the very thing I needed; for, of all the ways of dying, that which I most dreaded as by consumption, in which it is now most probable my disorder will issue. But O, my dear Lord, *if* by *this death* I can most *glorify thee*, I prefer it to all others, and thank thee that by this means thou art hastening my fuller enjoyment of thee in a purer world."

"During his sickness, he greatly enjoyed the society of his brethren in the ministry, and other Christian friends; and was often heard to say that he never loved his friends so well before. Every little favor shown him seemed deeply to affect him and awaken emotions of gratitude. He would say, 'O, how kind this is.'

"On the first day of January, 1843, which was the Sabbath, he sent the following note to the Seminary church, with a request that it should be read at the communion.

'The Rev. Mr. Nettleton sends his very affectionate regards to the members of this church, requesting an interest in their prayers, that God would sanctify him wholly in spirit, in soul, and in body, and prepare him for the solemn hour of exchanging worlds, whenever it shall come.'

"The next morning I called to see him, and found him in an unusually happy frame of mind. After inquiring whether his note was received, he remarked with great animation, his eyes sparkling through the tears, that he loved the church more and more. He expressed a peculiar affection for the students of the Seminary, and an ardent desire that they might become faithful ministers of the gospel. He mentioned the great satisfaction which it had given him to hear of the prosperity and usefulness of those who had gone out from the Seminary. He then went on to expatiate on the importance of a high standard of ministerial character, an account of its great influence on the interests of the church. He deprecated particularly, in the ministers of Christ, every thing which savors of pride and self-sufficiency—every thing which looks like ostentation, or a desire to attract notice to themselves. He loved to see ministers humble, meek, unassuming, steadily devoted to their work, and more anxious to glorify God, and save the souls of men, than to acquire popularity.

"He often remarked that a time of health was the time to prepare for death, and the time to give evidence of an interest in Christ. He said he had seen persons who, when in health, were very much devoted to the world; but who, when brought upon a sick bed, were very religious; agreeably to the representation in Jer. xxii. 20,23. *"Go up to Lebanon and cry, and lift up thy voice in Bashan, and cry from the passages, for all thy lovers are destroyed.* I SPAKE UNTO THEE IN THY PROSPERITY, BUT THOU SAIDST, I WILL NOT HEAR. THIS HATH BEEN THY MANNER FROM THY YOUTH, THAT THOU OBEYEDST NOT MY VOICE. *The wind shall eat up all thy pastures, and thy lovers shall go into captivity; surely then shall thou be ashamed and confounded for all thy wickedness. O, inhabitant of Lebanon, that makest thy nest in the cedars* HOW GRACIOUS SHALT THOU BE WHEN THY PANGS COME UPON THEE."

"A short time before his death, when he was very ill, and when he thought it probable that he had but a short time to live, I said to him you are in good hands. 'Certainly,' he replied. Are you willing to be there? 'I am. I know not,' said he, 'that I have any advice to give my friends. My whole preaching expresses my views. If I could see the pilgrims, scattered abroad, who thought they experienced religion under my preaching, I should like to address them. I would tell them that the great truths of the gospel appear more precious than ever; and that they are the truths which now sustain my soul.' He said, 'you know I have never placed much dependence on the manner in which persons die.' He spake of a farewell sermon which he preached in Virginia, from these words: *While ye have the light, walk in the light.* He told the people, that he wished to say some things to them, that he should not be able to say to them on a dying bed. And he would now say to all his friends, "While ye have the light, walk in the light." While making these remarks, there was a peculiar luster on his countenance. I said to him, I trust you feel no solicitude respecting the issue of your present sickness. He replied with emphasis, 'No, none at all. I am glad that it is not for me to say. It is sweet to trust in the Lord.'

"During the last twenty-four hours of his life he said but little. In the evening of the day before his death, I informed him that we considered him near the close of life, and said to him, I hope you enjoy peace of mind. By the motion of his head, he gave me an affirmative answer. He continued to fail through the night, and at 8 o'clock in the morning, he calmly fell asleep, as we trust, in the arms of his Saviour. May all his friends remember his dying counsel,

"While ye have the light, walk in the light."[2]

Asahel Nettleton's remains were carried by the students of the seminary to the graveyard behind the institution which he founded, and he was laid to rest. While he was alive, two colleges conferred upon him honorary Doctor of Divinity degrees: Jefferson College (Pennsylvania) and Hampden Sydney College (Virginia). But his legacy is not found in academics or a professor's chair, but in the *lives which he touched* for the glory of God. The following observations by J. F. Thornbury sum up Nettleton's legacy:

"For the last few months of his life, he was an invalid. Henry Blake, one of the students, often sat with him at night and was like a nurse to him. He could not sleep much and talked often about the scenes of revival that seemed to come continually before his mind. The days and nights by Nettleton's bedside made a deep impression on Blake, especially the accounts he heard from him about the days when God was visiting the towns of New England in such a remarkable way. Blake later said, 'I have always cherished the impressions received from Dr. Nettleton during the months and years he lay dying in that hallowed chamber as among the most valued results of my theological course."[3]

Asahel Nettleton, age sixty one, left a bed of pain and suffering at eight o'clock in the morning, May 16th, 1844, to be escorted by angelic beings into the glories of heaven and into the very arms of Jesus Christ. While here on earth, Nettleton lived his life on the "full stretch" for his Lord in incessant revival labors that transformed the face of a nation. Slowly he withdrew from the changing religious scene he could no longer influence. Prophetically he declared to all who would hear him in his generation, that "new measures" and "new divinity" would weaken the church and cause spurious conversions. As the embers of true revivals of religion died out across America, something inside of him died as well. At his desk from his East Windsor home he penned the following concerned words to a friend:

"East Windsor, February 6, 1838.

"… I have but just returned from laboring a little in a place made waste by a series of protracted meetings and revivals of modern stamp. Many of the subjects of those revivals are now all unconverted, and some of them have come out joyful, and now do solemnly declare that they have never before been under conviction of sin or known any thing about regeneration … they now declare that the doctrines which they have been taught, they do know to be false from their own personal experience."[4]

Asahel Nettleton died long before May 16th, 1844. He died of a broken heart from seeing vital religion wane in America to such a sad degree that it no longer resembled the former. May his memory and labors revive in us today a true desire for vital religion and the salvation of souls—all to the glory of God!

Notes

1   See E. A. Johnston, *George Whitefield: A Definitive Biography* (Stoke-on-Trent, England: Tentmaker Publications, 2008) Vol. One, pp. 323, 327, 329, 332–338, 458.
2   Tyler, pp. 302–312.
3   Thornbury, p. 224.
4   Nettleton Papers, Hartford Seminary.

Dear Youth,

I have come into your assembly this evening on an important errand. I have heard every word you have spoken, and seen every thought in your hearts. I have come to inform you that my Spirit shall not always strive with you. Because I have called & ye refused, I have stretched out my hands & no man regarded, but ye have set at nought all my counsel, & would none of my reproof. I also will laugh at your calamity. I will mock when your fear cometh. When your fear cometh as desolation, & your destruction cometh as a whirlwind. When distress and anguish cometh upon you. Then shall they call upon me, but I will not answer; they shall seek me early, but they shall not find me.

I am, dear youth,

Your much grieved friend,

Jesus Christ.

**ASAHEL NETTLETON'S INFAMOUS
"JESUS LETTER" WHICH TROUBLED HIM
FOR THE REMAINDER OF HIS LIFE.**

The "McAuley House" at Union College, Schenectady, NY. Scene of the revival around the corpse and home where Nettleton stayed, preached, and wrote.

30

HIS LETTERS

We can learn much about a person by the study of their correspondence and eminent men of former days placed a great value upon retaining letters (and copies of letters) both to and from one another. Tragically, modern day emails will altogether eliminate this valuable resource for future historians.

The Nettleton Collection of Letters at Hartford Seminary in Hartford, Connecticut is a treasure trove of history both in the shaping of America as a world-wide force and a theological influence. Asahel Nettleton knew personally the value of collecting letters for he painstakingly collected letters by men who *influenced* him. In this collection are 18th century letters from eminent and famous men who impacted and shaped Nettleton's ministry and theology. There are two letters from Jonathan Edwards both written to his disciple Joseph Bellamy. One is written from Northampton 1748/9 detailing the recent sickness of his wife and family. The other is written after Edwards was forced from his Northampton pastorate, 1753, and is written from Stockbridge where he was a missionary to the Indians. Also in the collection are numerous letters by Joseph Bellamy to his friends (including rare letters from John Erskine in Scotland detailing recent visits to Glasgow by John Wesley and George Whitefield). There is a long letter from James Davenport (Nettleton's 18th century nemesis) revealing plans of Gilbert Tennent and Samuel Davies to visit Great Britain to raise funds for a new seminary—Princeton. But the pertinent letters for our study are those which contain the correspondence of Asahel Nettleton and his peers from the 19th century: eminent names such as N. W. Taylor, Lyman Beecher, Bennet Tyler, Heman Humphreys, Leonard Woods, Charles Hodge, and Charles Finney. To study these is to study history and the shaping of present day theology and evangelism.

I personally handled the following letters at Hartford Seminary.

Because of their frail quality I will use the resource provided by the following dissertation: *THE LIFE AND LETTERS OF ASAHEL NETTLETON 1783–1844. A THESIS Submitted to the Faculty of the HARTFORD THEOLOGICAL SEMINARY HARTFORD SEMINARY, FOUNDATION in candidacy for the degree of Doctor of Philosophy, Department of Church History. George Hugh Birney, Jr. May 22, 1943.*

When Birney handled these same letters it was sixty years ago and the collection was in better shape and more readable. Therefore, his valuable work has preserved the actual contents of these historic letters as many today are illegible and too frail to handle. To quote Birney's introduction:

> "To follow the story of his life is to follow the development of the Congregational churches of New England in the period in which he lived. His correspondence has a rightful place in the documentary material of that history. He is not better known, and his significance is not more widely recognized because, unlike many of his contemporaries, he never wrote for publication. His opinions, which were offered freely to many who are better known, are to be found only in his letters. Also, he did not live long enough in any community, and he was not closely enough connected with any church or institution to make the sort of impression that wins the attention of historians.
>
> "He was curiously uninterested in secular and political problems except where they touched on religion. However, he had a vital interest in all of the specific phases of the life of the church in his time. He was the outstanding evangelist in a revival age, and he was considered an expert on revivals. He was especially interested in the growing missionary enterprise, and it was only the working of circumstance that made him an evangelist instead of a missionary. He considered the temperance movement one of the most important of all of the reformatory programs of the church. He believed that the evils it sought to correct were among the gravest which threatened the continued success of the revival movement. In short, he was interested in practically everything which he felt affected the cause of Christianity and the winning of men to the Christian way of life." [1]

Here now are samples of Asahel Nettleton's correspondence[2] from the nineteenth century in a critical period for the formation of our modern society and church; they are both reflective of the man and the world in which he lived!

The following letters are given with only minor changes to punctuation, spelling, or grammar. The following "Letter Index" will be of help in locating these letters.

LETTER INDEX

#1.   To Philander Parmele, from A. Nettleton. 1809. (Parmele was Nettleton's best friend and in whose home Nettleton lay sick with the typhus fever—until Parmele himself caught the disease and died).

#2.   To Philander Parmele, from A. Nettleton. 1815.

#3.   To Philander Parmele, from A. Nettleton. 1815.

#4.   To Philander Parmele, from A. Nettleton. 1817.

#5.   To an Unidentified Correspondent. 1819.

#6.   To Philander Parmele, from A. Nettleton. 1819.

#7.   To Philander Parmele, from A. Nettleton. 1821.

#8.   To Miss Sarah Wetmore, from A. Nettleton. 1821.

#9.   To Miss Lydia Warren, from A. Nettleton. 1823.

#10.   To Mrs. Chester Isham, from A. Nettleton. 1825.

#11.   To Charles Furman, from A. Nettleton. 1826.

#12.   To Charles Furman from A. Nettleton. 1827.

#13.   To John Frost, from A. Nettleton. 1827.

#14.   To John Frost, from A. Nettleton. 1827.

#15.   To John Frost, from A. Nettleton. 1827.

#16.   To Seth Williston, from A. Nettleton. 1827.

#17.   To T. H. Skinner, from A. Nettleton. 1827.

#18.   To Joel Hawes, from A. Nettleton. 1829.

#19.   To Leonard Woods, from A. Nettleton. 1829.

#20.   To Leonard Woods, from A. Nettleton. 1829.

#21.   To Lyman Beecher, from A. Nettleton. 1829.

#22.   To Leonard Woods, from A. Nettleton. 1829.

#23.   To an unknown correspondent. 1830.

#24.   To Leonard Woods, from A. Nettleton. 1830.

#25.   To William B. Sprague, from A. Nettleton. 1833.

#26.   To Dr. Milo North, from A. Nettleton. 1833.

#27.   To John Smith, from A. Nettleton. 1834.

#28.   To Leonard Woods, from A. Nettleton. 1834.

#29.   To Leonard Woods, from A. Nettleton. 1835.

#30.   To George Shipman, from A. Nettleton. 1835.

#31.   To Bennet Tyler, from A. Nettleton. 1836. (Tyler was
      Nettleton's friend and biographer).

#32.   To Leonard Woods, from A. Nettleton. 1837.

#33.   To William Hallock, from A. Nettleton. 1837.

#34.   To Leonard Woods, from A. Nettleton. 1837.

#35.   To Eleazar Lord, from A. Nettleton. 1839.

#36.   To Charles Hodge, from A. Nettleton. 1839.

#37.   To Leonard Woods, from A. Nettleton. 1839.

#38.   To Leonard Woods, from A. Nettleton. 1839.

#39.   Receipt to Yale College. 1832.

#40.   To Samuel Miller, from A. Nettleton (no date)

There are more letters both to and from Nettleton but because of their poor quality (they literally fall apart when handled!) we have not included them. One of these is a rare letter to Nettleton from his cousin Titus Coan! Some letters still have their red wax seal upon them! Several letters are still in excellent condition—although many are so faded and broken they are impossible to read. It is interesting to note that although Asahel Nettleton was not considered a theologian, his correspondence was with the top theologians of America in his day! The letters themselves reveal much of Nettleton's itinerancy since he records the locations from which he composes the letters and often details the revival movements of the churches labored in. These letters, more conversational in tone, reveal much about the revivals in which he labored and the subjects of those revivals. These letters also introduce us to a more personal side of Nettleton revealing his warm-heartedness towards others and his deep concern over true religious conversion and defending the Church against the "New Measures" of his day. Letter #1 reveals a young Nettleton still in his mid-20s, still formulating his ministry philosophy.

LETTER #1

To Philander Parmele, E. Guilford,

Yale College 1809

Dear Friend,

It is now almost nine of the clock in the evening, & I shall scribble a line in the utmost hurry, & this shall be on one single subject. Stone has just gone from my room, he told me a little of your dispute at Mr Meigses & but a little. Write the very next opportunity & give me all the particulars. Stone guesses that Mr Eliott, through policy agreed with his parishioners on that subject. What the particulars of your dispute were I cannot tell, but if it was respecting the question "What shall I do to be saved"

Without any books by me I will give you the sentiments of a few celebrated authors. This I do from memory only—

"*When a sinner, does all that he can in an unrenewed state, it is no more than when a wind-mill does all it can*

(President Edwards on the Will)

"God promises salvation to sinners on condition of faith & repentance; *but he does not promise faith & repentance on any condition whatever.*" "The new heart as it respects the sinner to whom it is given, *is an unconditional gift*. For no covenant subsists between G. & impenitent sinners. (& then he goes on to explain the meaning of an important passage of scripture, one that is much pled in favour of the doings of the unregenerate) "There is a covenant between G. & *his people*, not only as it respects themselves, but as it respects *others;*" When, therefore, G. promises a *new heart to sinners;*" "He will be inquired of by *the house of Israel* to do it for them." (Mr Whitman of Goshen) This is in his own words, & he says much more. Query. Would it not be a contradiction to say that it was in consequence or on *conditions* of his doing something.

"Were some of our ministers present & heard the Apostles directions to the question "What shall I do to be saved" would they not say, No, you are wrong, the can't repent, tell them to pray for a new heart——wait God's time?" &c.

"To tell sinners that it is their *immediate duty to repent*, & at the same time to tell them that they are *required* to do something before they repent, is a plain contradiction." (Doctor West)

This he shows to be a flat contradiction.

"If the sinner is asking the question "What shall I *do* to be saved?" means what act of the body he shall perform; the answer is, *Nothing.*" (Mr Dutton of G.) This he said to me. The sentiments of Hopkins of Spring & of Wines on this subject, I suppose you know. Read Booth, particularly what he says on the conversion of St Paul——the Thief on the cross etc & let Mr Eliott read it, & then tell him, that Mr Mervin has it read in his conferences & it is very highly applauded, that Mr Stewert very highly recommends it. I suppose you have Mr Stewerts sermon on this subject, let him read that, I mean the one I copied. But why do I quote authors, let him read the bible.

My friend. You know that the question is asked "Are not sinners *more likely* to receive faith if they continue asking with their unbelieving hearts than if they did not? I have in mind one passage of scripture which, I apprehend, was designed to answer this very question, or *rather*, it anticipated this question, & therefore intended to prevent the *folly* of asking it. The question is plain and fairly stated "May the impenitent sinner, even "*think*" that he shall be more likely to *receive any thing of the Lord*," if he continue ever so long, asking without faith any more than if he had never asked at all?" The answer is (contained in the very question itself.) "Let not *that* man *think* that he shall receive any thing of the Lord." Now I would ask, can the Christian-can the sinner or any other intelligent being believe, that those who ask in this manner, are in any way fairer, or any more likely situation or circumstances to receive any thing now—tomorrow or next year or ever, than if they had never asked at all, without believing a lie? No one can deny the expression "Let not that man think" etc is a command for something, or some body; & it is a command in some way *respecting* one who might be inclined to think of asking without faith. If it is a command to christians not to let "*that* man even *that man* (not merely to practice in this manner of asking) but not even so much as *think* that he shall receive (not merely a new heart) but even *any thing* of the Lord. I say if this is a command to christians, & they brake it, they do it to their own hazard.

Again, if it be a command to the sinner not even to "*think*" that *he* shall receive etc. and yet, if christians or an Angel from heaven should persuade *that man, even that man,* that he should be more likely to receive any thing of the Lord, I say, in my humble opinion, should any one persuade him thus, he would not only oppose G. but would persuade *him* to break the command & believe a life.

You will look w( ) incoherent sentences etc for I write just as the thoughts come to my mind. You will please to give your ideas on this passage or the above passage "let not etc" I cannot excuse you without demanding of Mr Eliott an explanation of it, & ask him if it is not direct to the point; that is, if you think what I have said is correct. Ask him this plain question, that if you in any way or in any manner encourage the sinner to pray without faith, or even if you do not endeavor to correct his mistake if he himself *thinks* to receive any thing in this manner, if you should do this, ask him if you should not break a plain command of G. For certainly it is a command to some body.

He may, perhaps, say that the passage means that Christians must not think to receive without they ask in faith; but grant it; if so, then sinners who are acknowledged enemies to G. certainly cannot expect to receive before christians, granting that both were to ask without faith.

Tell Mr E. that he is *requested* to give his opinion on this text, though you need not tell by whom.

Write the first opportunity
Yours with esteem
A. Nettleton
To Philander Parmele
E. Guilford

LETTER #2

To Philander Parmele

Litchfield June 19th 1815

Brother Parmele

I left you at Hartford. My first business then was to bid them farewell at Granby. But previous to this informed you of my secret intentions to visit the other Society in G. Accordingly I went & spent one Sabbath & attended a number of conferences. I was astonished at the number that attended meeting. It is a very large congregation. There is every appearance of a great revival of religion there. A deep & general solemnity pervades the minds of that people. They informed me that they had never *so seen it in Israel*. Would time permit I could give you an interesting account. Their distress was so great that we had to stop & converse in meeting. How many anxious I cannot tell. Eight were rejoicing before I left them. One while I was talking & two or three on their way home were brought out rejoicing. What the end will be I know not, but there is every appearance of a great work. (I must charge you by all means to keep it to yourself at present, for I stand in some doubt, yet he sends his love to all, the Christians in N. H. Among those that were awfully distressed & crying out for mercy in one of our conferences, what was my surprise to find a young man by the name of Heman Towner.)—I then spent one Sabbath in T. Hills society & bade them farewell, & came on to Litchfield. Here I spent the next Sabbath with Mr. Beecher. According to a previous agreement we were expecting to set out immediately for L. Island. But we have been *wonderfully disappointed*. On the Sabbath (a fortnight yesterday) there were some indications of the presence of God. On Monday morning the great inquiry began; "*What must I do to be saved?*" You may possibly have heard of Miss Pierces school. Young ladies, strangers to us and to each other, lately assembled from every direction, have come on to Litchfield hill to inquire this way to the *Hill of Zion*. The greater part of that large school have suddenly *become deeply impressed*. Study has been principally suspended. They board at different places, 10, 15 or 20 in a house together. These places are as solemn as the house of death. On entering one house, the pious lady solemnly accosted Mr. Beecher. *The thrones are set and the books are opened.* She informed me that there was scarce a time when the voice of weeping or the voice of prayer was not heard in some part of the house.

It is indeed wonderful to see strangers from the east & from the west, from the north & from the south coming together to have a revival of religion in a strange land.

The distress of some has been very great. Joy now begins to beam in the countenances of some. It is now just a fortnight since the attention first began, & yet 12 are now rejoicing in hope. It is all new to them. And yet they all appear like children of the same great family. And the perfect strangers, I can assure you they have become the most intimate friends. *Is not my word like fire?* is a solemn query to those who have hitherto been hardening under its penetrating influence. The effect of divine truth on the hearts of sinners is wonderful! Hard hearts melt before it. Never did the doctrines of grace shine with such dazling luster. In one little circle composed of seven hopeful converts, by inquiry, I found one from New York, one from Massachusetts, one from New Jersey & one from Vermont & the others I cannot tell where, all of one heart' of one mind. There ends my narrative.

(Rest of letter torn off.)

LETTER #3

To Philander Parmele, Bolton, Connecticut.

New Haven August 4th 1815

Brother Parmele

I have received yours of the 14th ult, about 10 days after date. You have heard of the revival in this place. You requested me to give you a particular account of this work. I must beg to be excused. I cannot do it. It is so interesting & my health is so feeble that I shrink under the attempt.

A number have been alarmed. How many it is impossible to tell. It was just a week from the time I came to this place to the day on which the great inquiry openly and solemnly began. *What must I do to be saved?* For three days the distress of some was overwhelming. On the fourth day four were rejoicing. On the fifth day eleven more were rejoicing. From that time the work has been gradually spreading through the town. The prospect is still brightening. This morning I have found 2 more rejoicing in hope. Within about four weeks upwards of 50 have entertained hope (in) (t)his place. For the most part they appear to be perfectly aston(ished) at themselves. *Old things have passed away & behold all things are become new!* All appear like members of the same great family. Among those who have been awakened are a number of young lawyers. Among these Leonard Daggett & Sereno Dwight appear to be rejoicing in hope. Thus ends my narrative. Could I see you I might give you an interesting account. Have just heard from Litchfield. Since the late attention began, about 60 have entertained hope. This is within about 2 months.

The committee appointed by the General Association for the purpose of consulting on the subject of domestic missions have met in this place. They concluded to make application to you. Mr. McEwen will probably write you on this subject. I requested him to send my love & inform you that in case you did not conclude to settle soon, it was my opinion that you had better accept the appointment at least for a short time. But perhaps you are under engagements at Bolton. Where I shall be in future is altogether uncertain. No matter where we live no matter w(here) we die. In very great haste

Yours affectionately

A. Nettleton

P. S. My love to all my dear friends in Chester—particularly to those young persons, & tell them how I long to see them.

To Rev. Philander Parmele

Bolton

LETTER #4

To Philander Parmele, Bolton, Connecticut

Middletown Upper Houses, December 1, 1817

Brother Parmele,

A messenger is to pass your way this week, & I must write one line. I think I can say "the Lord is in very deed in this place." Mr. Williams is absent, attending his father, who is sick in Harwinton. There has been an increasing solemnity for some time past. Meetings crowded and solemn. We were all anxious to know how we should steer by Thanksgiving without losing our solemnity. As I was entering the meeting house door on Thanksgiving' day morning, a number of young men met me with a request that I would appoint a young peoples conference on Friday evening following. Instead of a ball, as usual, they would have a general conference. They assembled from all parts, and crowded a very large room in a kind of an academy. "It was like a rushing mighty wind, & it felled all the house where they were sitting." After meeting they came around in deep distress of soul. I found two who have been anxious for some time, now rejoicing in hope. (dear Banni Parmelee's oldest daughter was one.) One young man seized my hand exclaiming "I am a sinner." I am a sinner. What *shall* I do?" They left the house and went home sighing, & sobbing in every direction. I came home & found a number around the door of Mr. William's house, in the most awful distress. Some were standing, some sitting on the ground, & some on the door steps exclaiming "What shall I do." I shall die. I shall die. "I can't live." This alarmed the neighbors who called to witness the awful scene. With much ado I got them into the house, about eight or ten in number. The fact was, the young man afore mentioned, who left the meeting house in such distress, was walking in company with them, when all at once he found relief and exclaimed "*I have found the Saviour.*" He was now very joyful. *He* sat *clothed and in his right mind: and they were afraid.* My first business now was to warn them against a false hope. Prayed with them and enjoined it particularly on them not to go home together, but to *go* alone, & *be* alone, for the business must be settled between God and their souls. Maria (a young woman living in this family) was one of the number. She retired to her chamber, sighing and sobbing, and crying for mercy, and exclaiming "I shall die, I shall die." She came down and went out doors, and returned in the same awful distress to her chamber. And suddenly all was still and hushed to silence. I sat still below and said nothing. I soon heard the sound of her footsteps descending the chamber stairs. She opened the door and with a joyful countenance exclaimed *O, Sir, I have found the Saviour.* I continued to warn her of the danger of a false hope. She exclaimed "I love Christ. I do love him. O how sweet." In the morning, early, she called to see one of her anxious mates, who was so distressed the night before; and Lo! Barsheba exclaimed "*I have found the Sav.*" That was a happy meeting. The young aforementioned resided in the same family (this was John Towner's house). On Saturday evening about mid-night another, equally distressed, found relief. Within a few days 8 or 10 are rejoicing in hope. What will be the end, I know not. Do pray for us, and your friend.

A. Nettleton

P. S. My love to all my dear friends. Do write immediately, all the news you can, and do call and see us. I have no time to write, nor to look over what I have written. I know you will excuse my haste—people are now assembling.

Revd Philander Parmele

Bolton

LETTER #5

To an Unidentified Correspondent

July 7th 1819

My dear Friend,

With deep interest we have heard of the late wonderful displays of divine grace in many towns in Massachusetts. Tho' what we have witnessed in Connecticut the year passed is not to be compared with the account from some of those places, yet we can say, *The Lord hath done great things for us whereof we are glad.* We can still *speak of the glory of the Redeemer's kingdom and talk of his power.*

In the town of Ashford there is a very general revival of religion. It is extended over three societies: Ashford, Eastford, and Westford. This has been the place of my residence and the field of my labors during the winter passed. The work commenced in Ashford, the first society, where brother Judson is settled. The first instance of hopeful conversion was discovered at the close of the conference on the evening of November 4th. Within two days, five or six more were rejoicing in hope. It suddenly became very general through the Society. Conferences were crowded and awfully solemn. Two and three, and sometimes it was judged nearly four hundred assembled at an evening conference. Meetings were appointed exclusively for those anxious for their souls, at which 80 or a 100, and often more attended. Some who entered those meetings in deep distress have gone home rejoicing. Daily the glad news was heard that one or more had experienced deliverance.

About three miles from this is the Society called Eastford. It is a pleasant little village, but without preaching and literally a place of moral desolation. This we considered a favorable season to commence laboring in that village. But we deferred it entirely hoping to find some preacher to reside with them, and follow it up. We wrote to a number, and I made frequent and earnest application to the Dom. Missionary Society, but no preacher could be obtained. At length I made them a short visit, preached on the Sabb. and attended a conference and found them stupid. On leaving the place, I left this word, that if any were anxious for their souls let me know and I would call to see them. If but one only could be found anxious send word and I would come over and make one a visit. This excited their curiosity and the next Sabb. two thoughtless youths came over to attend meeting in brother Judson's Society and invited me to visit them in Eastford on Monday evening following. I gladly complied with their invitation—Went and found upwards of forty youths assembled at a private house. They seemed to be stranger to the object of the meeting, and came, I concluded, principally out of curiosity. Before we closed a number were affected. From this I took encouragement to appoint a general conference at a convenient schoolhouse on the following evening. This meeting was crowded and solemn as eternity. Here the enquiry was heard, *What must I do to be saved?* On Friday evening following our conference was thronged. At the close of the exercises, one was found rejoicing in hope. This was on new year's night. The revival commenced with the new year.

In that little place more than 40 became hopeful subjects of divine grace during the month of January.

LETTER #6

To Philander Parmele, Bolton, Connecticut

Saratoga Springs 12th July 1819

Brother Parmele,

I spent the next Sabbath after I left you in Troy, six miles above Albany. I arrived St. about sunset, & concluded to put up at a public house & attend meeting on the Sab. as an utter stranger. As I was entering the house with my trunk under my arm, I met Mary Seymour. I begged of her not to let me be known, but call me an old acquaintance, & let it pass at that; but the plan would not work, for I was now at the house of her brother, & the family must know me if nothing more, for we *must* become acquainted & enjoy the evening together. Eliza, you know, is married to a Mr Conant, & Emily Mills lives with him but just acrost the way & they too *must* know it, tho' they would not let their minister know me until after Sabbath, though he happened to be gone & Mr Hewet was preacher. Sabbath noon Mr Hewet came in & all beset me to preach, until I felt bad enough to go directly back to Bolton. And so to get rid of their noise I concluded to preach in the evening.—Arrived at the Springs on Monday, & found about a dozen ministers here—among them Mr Taylor of N. Haven, & Mr. Antel (?) Of Geneva, & Mr. Hawes of Hartford.—The waters are very powerful. How long I shall tarry I know not.—

Nothing special to write—Do write *immediately* all the news you can. How is the attention in Bolton, Coventy, & Andover in particular. And what was there in the letter from friend B. of N. H.?

I do want to see my friends in Bolton & Andover very much. I think of them & try to pray for them daily.

My regards to your family, & to all my dear friends in B. & tell them how I do long to see them. Write the first thing you do—direct to *Saratoga Springs*, County of Saratoga N. Y.

Yours affectionately

Asahel Nettleton

Rev. Philander Parmele

Bolton

Connecticut

LETTER #7

To Philander Parmele, Bolton, Connecticut

Tolland Aug 9th 1821

Brother Parmele

Last evening I arrived in this place & attended conference in the school-house—Another is Appointed in the same place this evening,—the appearances are favorable & the Methodist awake, & I fear a bad turn.

I did not come to tarry, for my health is unusually feeble since I saw you—But Br. Nash says I must tarry over Sabbath. Now Br. Parmele, will you not go to Somers for me next Sabbath & let Br. Nash supply your pulpit? I heard that you & Mrs. P. were both expecting to go & spend the next week there. C(an?) you not both go up tomorrow & spend the next week there? Will you not come this way, I wish to see you before you go to Somers to send them some word. If you cannot come this way, send Br Smith to Wilbraham, & tell him that instead of an anxious meeting on Monday evening, it might be well to meet all the young converts exclusively. The bearer is Mr Barnes of this place. Send back word, & go to Somers if possible—Love to your family

Yours in haste

A. Nettleton

Dear Brother

I feel it to be important that brother Nettleton should preach here next Sabbath, and you would think so too, did you know the circumstances. Don't fail.

Yours

A(?) Nash.

LETTER #8

To Miss Sarah Wetmore, Pittsfield, Massachusetts

Litchfield Oct 15th 1821

My dear Friend

I received your very acceptable letter of no date in season, I conclude from the postmark. It arrived in company than which none was more expected or welcome or read with greater interest. I should have written immediately, had I not been thronged by company from a distance, and now I have no time to arrange my thoughts if I have any. I have attended many meetings of late and some of them crowded and awfully solemn. More attend evening meeting than can crowd into the lower part of the meeting house, more, it is said, than usually meet on the Sabbath. I think I may say there is a great solemnity throughout this place, a number in deep distress of soul, some men of influence. About 14 in all rejoicing in hope. I have ventured to appoint one anxious meeting. About 100 attended, though not all under conviction. We expected Dr. Beecher home last Wednesday, but were sadly disappointed; and now when he will come we know not, tho we are expecting him daily. We are truly in an interesting state—trembling between hope and fear. I wish I had time to tell you a number of anecdotes about us in Litchfield.—I rejoice at the good things you state of Pitts, Lenox and Lee—names which are dear to my heart. I sometimes call to mind former days—days that have fled, but yet awaken the tenderest feelings of the heart. I often think how soon will the places which now know those dear friends know them no more. We are journeying. No situation, I have sometimes thought, is better calculated to impress the idea of the stranger and the pilgrim deep on the mind, than the writers. No person enjoys the society of his friends better and none feels greater pain at parting. What I constantly regret is that I know not how properly to express my gratitude for the ten thousand acts of kindness which I received from them. Can you not obtain the notes of that tune of which you speak, and make it a part of your next letter. Tell me what I must do in return for so many expressions of kindness? Funds you say "are raised for the support of a *third* child in India by name A. N." Do tell me, Sarah, *where* is the *first* and where is the *second* of that name supported; and *by whom*? You surprise me. I wish I had time to write more, but my time is come to prepare for meeting and I know you will excuse my haste. To tell you the truth, I set myself to write you a long letter the other day, after the manner of our usual plain familiar conversation on a topic suggested by your letter; and I liked it so bad that I burned it. You have sometimes given me hints which have been profitable; and which I have remembered. I esteem every thing of this kind as an act of friendship. And permit me to add that less fear of giving offense, and still greater plainess of speech might give still higher proof of Christian friendship.

Direct your next to Litchfield. My love to all my dear friends. Tell Brother Humphrey I have been thinking it would do good if he would visit Lenox and Lee *immediately*, if *possible* and hold anxious meetings in each of those places and let it be known before hand that he would be present.

Yours as ever A. Nettleton

Miss Sarah Wetmore

Pittsfield

Mass

LETTER #9

To Miss Lydia Warren, South Wilbraham, Massachusetts

Bolton Mar 4th 1823

My Very Dear Friends,

Some time in December last, I received a very affectionate letter signed by fourteen names never to be forgotten. It contained a friendly invitation to me to go to Wilbraham, as soon as able, & there receive the kind offices of christian friendship. As I read the letter, & dwelt with delight on each name, the interesting scenes, through which we had passed together, rushed full in my view. Had it been possible, most gladly would I have accepted of your invitation; & almost should I esteem it a privilege to be sick, if surrounded by such a circle of friends.——

A few days since, I received another token of friendship enclosed in a letter from one of the number of that same circle. You will please to accept my sincere thanks for this, & all your former acts of kindness. I need not inform you my dear Friends of trying scenes through which I have been called to pass since my last visit to Wilbraham. But our mercies are greater than our afflictions. Never did I experience so much kindness from friends as during my late sickness. I have often thought that their kindness has contributed much towards my restoration from that sickness. It certainly contributed much to the health of my mind by its cheering consolation. My spirits were better than they have formerly been while in usual health. I have some where seen an expression like this—"The sympathy of friends in affliction charms away half of the wo."

This I have found to be true by experience. But the most trying of all,—was my parting with our friend Mr Parmele. Borne the same year in the same town—anxious for his soul, & professed religion at the same time with myself, he was my nearest friend. Often have we met, & prayed, & wept & rejoiced together in revivals of religion—

I hope you will not forget the interesting scenes of last summer; I think I shall not. Revivals of religion appear the most important on a sick & dying bed. And thither we are rapidly hastening. I wish I had strength to tell you my views & feelings since I saw you last. During my deepest distress I was in the midst of revivals. The tune Loving kindness run sweetly through my mind over again & again thousands of times, connected with the two last verses of the eighth hymn. This I often mentioned to my friends, as also the 324 hymn. I do not recover my health as fast as my friends have been expecting. I have not strength to answer all the kind letter I receive from my friends. It is with difficulty that I have written this. My love to your Parents, & to all my dear friends, & tell them how much I do long to see them. Mr Smith is now preaching in Coventry. He calls frequently to see us & we talk over the scenes of last

ASAHEL NETTLETON: REVIVAL PREACHER

summer with peculiar delight. The revival which commenced in your region last summer is still spreading, & advancing with power in Coventry, both Societies. Let us not forget to pray that it may continue—And now I entreat you all to live near to God—Love one another—Live in peace, & the God of love & peace shall be with you.

I am ever yours in the best bond

Asahel Nettleton

Bolton March 4

Miss Lydia Warren

South-Wilbraham

Mass.

LETTER #10

To Mrs. Chester Isham, Taunton, Massachusetts

Taunton West Society Decr 25th 1825

Dear Madam,

Yours of the 11th inst. was duly & very thankfully recd. I had expected a communication from you before leaving this region; but, owing to its long delay had nearly given it up. Indeed,

I did not, as you know, expect to remain here so long—but the state of things in this Society has become quite interesting of late. Meetings are crowded & solemn as eternity. A number have called to see us in deep distress of soul—Some of them told us that they had been anxious for some time—that they received their first serious impressions down at the green last summer. The fire was already kindled & has recently burst into a flame in this part of the town. The number of inhabitants in this Society, you know, is comparitively small; & yet last Saturday evening we met about 60 in a meeting of inquiry—About 30 are rejoicing in hope. Of these, some are youth of the first respectability, & four or five, men of influence. Old professors of religion tell us that they never saw such a time before—But, owing to the small number of families in this society, this state of things cannot continue long. Mr & Mrs Cobb are all engaged, & say, "we have never seen our church feel so before." I told you in my letter, that I intended to linger around Taunton a while to see how the business terminated in the case of Mr Maltby—That business, you may have heard, was settled last week, when they recd his answer in the *affirmative*. The ordination is appointed on the 18th of Jan. Dr Porter of Andover is to preach on the occasion. The people are pretty well united—Judge Morton excepted. The subscription paper for Mr Maltby's sallary was presented to him, but he refused to do any thing.

What course the Judge will take, ultimately, is uncertain. When I reflect, how much he has done, both by his property & influence, for the establishment of that society—they all say more than any other man—& when I think of the controlling influence which he has held, & will still hold over the mass of population in this town, my mind is held in suspense. Ministers, in general, as I understand, have advised Mr Maltby to stay.

You would like to know the state of religion there. My fears have been fully realised. I preached once or twice in the *evening*, after Mr Maltby arrived. Since that, I have attended no meeting there of any kind. Now the trial is past, I will tell you in confidence, that all my private plans for doing them good have been frustrated. I never expected that any special exertions would be of any service while new ministers were making their appearance in the pulpit every Sabbath. I was only waiting for this state of things to pass by, in hopes I might have the control of the Sabbath. But the good people seemed impatient for the arrival of a candidate. I could not with a good grace tell them the dissipating influence it would have on the minds of the congregation—besides the impropriety of an interference with my own labors at such a season. A candidate should occupy the whole ground. And this ground is what I needed to forward my own plans, & without it I have never yet been able to do any thing to good purpose. I had made arrangements for extra help—such as I needed—provided no candidate made his appearance—had reconnoitred the whole field, preparing to bring the outskirts of the place into the Vestry & into a meeting of inquiry, as soon as they could well be attended to by closely following them up. My plans were unknown to any except Mr Judson. He arrived, but finding Mr Maltby on the ground, he left us without preaching, & continued his labor in Providence. I then tried for a while to bring Mr Maltby into my plan; by his refusing to preach as a candidate, that I might have an apology for preaching a part of the time on the Sabbath. And then if he & they were both satisfied, after such an effort to bring sinners into the kingdom, he would settle under additional advantages—& if not still all would be well. But either himself, or the committee or both chose a different course. The question has often been put & differently answered. Why I left Taunton, & why I do not preach for them? But to tell you the truth, tho' the committee have hired other ministers to preach in the absence of Mr Maltby, & tho' they have been destitute a number of Sabbaths, I have never yet had a chance to accept or reject an official invitation to do any thing for them. Could I see you I would tell you the particulars. There is a mystery hanging over the whole business. I suspect the good people have adopted the policy of having a revival in manner & form that will not offend the devil. And my skill will not do it.

Asahel Nettleton

Decr. 26th 1825

Mrs. Isham

LETTER #11

To Charles C. Furman, Auburn, New York

Jamaica 26th Oct. 1826

My Dear Friend,

Yours of the 20th inst. was duly recd. I thank you for every particular. It needs no apology for the relation of many things in *themselves* somewhat painful, when the motive is pure. The friends & the foes of religion may relate the same story, you know, with motives widely different. I have recd similar information by letter from respectable ministers in the west. Mr Fox whose name you mentioned is an acquaintance of mine. I think him a valuable man. It is very important to a young preacher that he avoid a censorious spirit—& always speak kindly of such as are held in reputation among Xns. And, if he labor among such—he had better forego the prospect of doing present *good* than to lose the confidence of these men. I can think of times in the commencement of my ministry when I had no doubt that a given course would be blessed to the conversion of many souls. I might have been mistaken. At any rate, acquiescence in the judgment of my brethren would secure their confidence—until I have been astonished to find them so generally willing to allow me to adopt my own course. The truth is, all Xns are imperfect. And all our exertions to do good are attended with more or less imperfection. Good measures will be often *innocently opposed*, for the want of experience *only*. The same measures may be very good, or very bad in different places, & under different circumstances.—

The question has often been proposed in publick print. "What is the best mode of treating anxious souls?" Much may be said & written to profit but, after all, we might as well ask & answer the question "What is the best method of treating all manner of sickness & all manner of disease among the people?" We may talk about the best means for doing good—but after all the greatest difficulty lies in doing it with a proper spirit. *Speaking the truth in love. In meekness instructing those who oppose. With the meekness & gentleness of X.* There lies the greatest difficulty. I have known anxious sinners drop the subject of religion in consequence of a preacher address'g them with an angry tone—Some have afterwards been awakened, & hopefully experienced religion, who have told me this fact—naming the preacher, & the words he used with a ... of *manner*—such as induced the feeling—"That is not a Xn spirit. I am not bound to mind what you say with such a spirit."—& do droped the subject. Mankind, it is true, will be sure to find fault with every thing that awakens their fears,—but we should endeavor so to conduct as to keep their consciences on our side in spite of all their opposition. Take care & not give them *just cause* to complain—Pardon my haste—Our family have nearly all had the intermittent fever—and bitter—Some deaths have occurred—Dr Shelton has lost a child—Dr Blatchford is very sick—Mr Crane is to be installed on Tuesday next—I have little time, or strength to write—but like to receive letter from you—Yours as ever

A. Nettleton

LETTER #12

To Charles E. Furman, Auburn, New York

Albany March 9th 1827

My Dear Brother

Since my communication to you I have written to Dr Richards a number of things concerning the present crisis, which with his consent I wish you to read to your friends and mine.

I wish to remind you that the remarks in my communication to you were not founded on *report* but, principally on facts which have fallen under my own eye in this city, and else where.

And facts to which the Watchmen of Israel have been eye and ear witnesses in *this* region. These facts I have generally withheld because the relation would be painful and almost endless. If the evils can be silently arrested we should certainly prefer it. But, otherwise, the cause of revivals will demand an exposure of facts and names, that all the friends of revivals, and especially students in divinity may take warning.

In further remarking on this subject, I may repeat something not exactly recollecting what I have sent to Dr R.

Much is said concerning the efficasy of these new measures. The united testimony of the watchmen of Israel being eye witnesses of their influence in the region of Utica and else where, will have due weight on the minds of all their Brethren at a distance. But no eye can be a competent judge of their ( )umate influence until years have passed away. For the greater the irregularities in the midst of excitement the greater will be the ? of spurious conversions and of unstable & lawless converts, as past experience has uniformly proved. But the number of conversions would, doubtless, have been equal or even far greater without these new measures. This I know to be the opinion of the ministers in the West whose age and experience ought to qualify them to be the most competent judges. But it is said that God has blessed these measures to the conversion of sinners. The same may be said of female preaching. And on this ground has the practice ever been adopted and defended. But where one is converted; thousands are probably hardened by this measure. And if any are disposed to admit the argument for female preaching, and ask—"How can that be wrong which God has blessed to the conversion of a soul"? I answer, that it is an acknowledged fact that profane swearing—opposition to revivals, mock conferences, sickness, and death and the plague, have all been over-ruled to the conviction and conversion of sinners. "And how can that be wrong which God has blessed to the conversion of a soul"? Shall we not multiply and defend these things? "Or *shall we be more squeamish than the Holy Spirit.*" The man who defends the principle in question appears bad in argument, but worse in practice.

There is no doubt a "cursed prudence" which has ruined her thousands forever. But the Preacher who condemns *Prudence* in toto will soon be forsaken by her *Inmate* Prov. 8th 12th. He may drive at the understanding and consciences of his hearers with all his might. But there is a point of prudence beyond which he cannot pass without losing his entire hold on both. Zeal, untempered with love and compassion for souls, will soon degenerate into harshness, and cruelty of manner and expression; which will have no other effect on an audience than ranting and scolding and even profane swearing—The result in morals will be, what men of business and the *children* of his world denominate "penny-wise" and "pound-foolish." It is like cutting off the heads of hundreds to save the life of one man. For where one is saved by mere violent efforts five hundred are hardened or sent at a return-less distance from the gospel——

I could name ? and places as interesting illustrations of these remarks. Even in this City, before, and since my residence here were it proper for me to say it I could tell you of many individuals who have been addressed by such preachers, in this abrupt manner "You are going right down to hell"—and were prayed for by name in the same harsh manner in the families where such preachers have lodged, until they have driven them entirely away from family worship, and from all intercourse with such preachers. I have heard of no good effects in any such instance in this city. But in our little social circles of different kinds we have found a blessing even in this wicked city—Some of the first class in Society and men of influence have ? but rejoicing. In all perhaps 70 or 80—and a number anxious for their souls. But few if any of this number have been addressed in the harsh manner above described. Had it been thus, I do believe that they would have been at a return-less ? from us, if not from the influence of the gospel—

In this manner you will ? my views of the "awful expence" of a few such revivals as that in Troy. It did not begin even there with the measures in question—The preacher under a mistaken idea of superior faithfulness, may lose the confidence of his hearers, and with it, his hold on their consciences, and there his usefulness must end—If he is a settled Pastor he must either alter his hand or quit the field—of usefulness at least. If an Itinerant, he will work himself out from every place and ultimately from the confidence of settled Pastors wherever he goes—To return—

But as to *this region* there is an utter mistake. Indeed of a blessing it is the prevailing opinion of the Watchmen that these new measures have been followed with a blight. In Canaan and Richmond and Stockbridge and Lenox, and Lee—in the last named place about 30 rejoicing during twenty four hours—and many other places where these new measures have not been introduced the work is silently solemnly, and powerfully advancing without divisions and quarrels in the church, commending itself to the confidence of christians and to the consciences of the wicked. In a number of places in this region where the work had begun and was going on well, it has evidently been checked by the introduction of these measures. While the work of God conducted by settled ministers was going on well, these new measures by some arch adversary have been foisted in as an admirable means of beginning and inovating a revival—

Alas! for the deceitful heart of man!

Even in Troy, it is well known that the work had begun and been gradually advancing for *more than six months*, under the conduct of the settled pastor, without any great division in the church, until some unconsecrated hands, male, and female, rudely grasped the art of God in the presence of the genuine ? of him—My own Dear Brethren whose business alone it was to bear that holy thing, shocked at the sight of such rudeness, kindly attempted to replace the ark. But it was too late. The usurpers began to thrust the Levites from them, saying "Don't you touch it" There is religion in it". The interest of souls are at stake "See how

God blessed these measures"—I should not dare put forth an adventourous hand to stay it. Your friends and mine are requested to read carefully and prayerfully 2 Sam. 6th Chapter. And so things have been left to run on, waxing worse and worse until any body and everybody, women, and children, have fairly trampled that holy thing into the dust in the presence and before the eyes of the Watchmen of Israel. Children have been heard to address their parents in the most insulting language. "You old grey headed sinners, you don't know how I have been praying for you. Why don't you repent" With the most assuming airs have they been heard, in the solemn act of prayer, to call their parents, "old, hardened, grey headed sinners going down to hell" in imitation of their leaders.

And all those christians whose judgment, and conscience, and *piety* revolt ? From the sight ? denounced as cold, and stupid, and dead, and "not up to the spirit of the times."

And if any one remonstrates, he is denounced as inter-meddling and as joining with cold hearted confessors (?) and with the wicked exactly in the style of Liberalism, Cumberlandism, and of N.R. in the Boston Recorder—who is trying to stop the mouths of all the Watchmen of Israel with this sweeping argument, that their testimony cannot be received. And why? Because it is a given principle, that every body must be more stupid and dead than himself, or, in other words, it must be taken for granted that N.R. has more "*primitive piety*" and zeal, and wisdom and humility, and meekness, and experience, than all the world beside some few "some where at a distance" only exci (?). But is christians must not tell their faults one to another because "it cherishes their own stupidity" what will he do with President Edwards who has undertaken to correct the errors of just such your ? sinner as himself? And has published them as christians and sinners all over the world.

Edwards on the revival of religion in New England is doing more, in this region to weaken the hands and destroy the influence of the men and the measures in question, than the observation of all other causes—especially his 4th part. It is a common saying among ministers and christians, who have been eye and ear witnesses, that if these men had set for the picture their likeness would not have been drawn more to the life. So completely have they fallen into the very manner and measure"—regains (?) which that man of God has warned them, that every body who has read it whether warm or cold hearted ministers and christians and even sinners themselves unite in pronouncing it a perfect likeness. It would be well for every zealous, young preacher, or student in divinity to read carefully his 4th part; if for no other purpose than to avoid this likeness, which may do him much evil before he knows it.

It is an old trick of the adversary to overset or disgrace a revival if possible. We are not ignorant of his devices. Thus was it in Malta & other places in the Albany Presby 7 years ago——

My greatest care & trouble & anxiety was to guard against & keep out the very things which have been fossiled in at Troy. A desperate effort was then made by some professors of religion to introduce the practice of female praying with males. I took a decided stand against it & with the aid of neighboring ministers prevented the practice & with it the consequences which would be sure to follow. As an expression of the feelings of the Alby Presby on the subject of revivals, 7 years ago I sent you the following:

"On motion of Dr McAuley resolved that a committee be appointed to express the sentiments of approbation which this Presby cherish towards the Rev Mr N. of the Litchfield Association, & his labors of love in Malta & elsewhere; & to request him when convenient to furnish this Presb. with a detailed memorial on the difficulties of ministers going to labor in destitute places; more especially in cases of revivals with as much detail as possible of the causes helping the increase or hastening the decline of revivals of religion——Dr McAuley & Mr Tucker were appointed the committee." Schenectady Jan 11th 1820" True extract from the Minutes of Pres. Jas. F. Henry Stated Clerk

The above extract may serve to correct a mistake recently circulating in the West that these ministers are unfriendly to revivals. The Lord will rebuke such a spirit, sooner or later. It is known to ministers & christians in all the regions that the character (?) of revivals was revised & sustained in the Albany Presby 7 years ago, by ? and wakefully guarding against & keeping out every interest (?) which has been transferred in Troy from the West; and which come from abroad and secretly belong to ? commend them to the public as an admirable means of commencing revivals. Hence revival ministers & christians have been trained in a conscientous understanding also from these men & ? measures as they can be in introducing them into the churches. They are driving ? back this banalism (?) under the delusion of a new era. The Presbytery of Troy is still in session & have not come to any important result. I understand that Br Beman & some others are making an effort to obtain Mr Fanning for the new church in Troy. Please to let me hear from you soon. My health is quite feeble & I can preach very seldom. My thanks to Dr. Richards for his kind remarks.

We have not yet concluded whether it is best to publish the letters to B. & F. Aikin. I have had a long interview with Br Frost & Coe—who feel as we do on the new measures—so far as I can judge. My opinion is that the young ministers have been kept in the dark on this subject by the concealment of the view of such men as Dr. R. Dr D.uois (?) etc etc. Ministers should not conceal their views from each other on so important subjects.

Affectionately

A. N.

To Charles E. Furman

Student Theolo Sem.

Auburn, N. Y. State

LETTER #13

[Letters to John Frost, Whitesborough, New York. In the course of the "New Methods" controversy Nettleton wrote three letters to send to John Frost. He sent only the second and the third. Though they are similar, they are all different in some details. All three are reproduced here].

Durham, 18th Mar. 1827

Mr Dear Brother,

You think that the "ministers in our region erred in not doing as you did," receive Br. F. with open arms." To tell you the truth, Br. the ministers & other Christians from this region & from N. England, who visited Oneida Co. last summer saw with their own eyes & heard with their own ears so many things, which they deplored, that it was the universal opinion, far & near, that irregularities were prevailing to such an alarming extent that the *character* of *revivals had gone back half a century*. And this I knew to be the sentiment of our best ministers, more than three months before I visited Albany. They were all deploring the introduction of these new measures into our churches:—knowing that they were the same which ran out the revivals in the days of Edwards, & the very same, too, which were every where employed by the Methodists and Smithites: & so they were guarding and watching against the introduction of them into their own churches, long before I came to Albany. It was the universal sentiment of ministers while I was laboring in Jamaica, last summer, that they could not, & should not dare to employ a preacher in their churches who adopted these measures. And this I knew to be the fact from personal conversation which scores of ministers & christians, who visited me in Jamaica, last summer. Even your own account of the Western revival, as you gave it, made an unfavorable impression on the minds of ministers in New York last summer. I repeat the idea for the sake of imprinting it on your memory—That ministers do not complain so much of irregularities existing in the West; for probably they are not a thousandth part so great within your own limits, as they are in the churches into which they have been transferred abroad. And even had these evils been a thousandfold greater at the West you would not have heard the mournful complaints of your Brethren at a distance, had it been in your power to confine the whole evil within the limits of your own churches & congregations. Your brethren know that you have the right, & are willing that you should exercise it of pursuing your own measures, when you can take all the responsibility. But when tidings came that these new measures had been introduced into Troy, Lansingburg, & Albany by the Brother from the West, & that all the ministers & christians in those places & all who visited in those places & could not approve of these measures were denounced as "cold and stupid, & dead, & enemies to revivals, & leading sinners down to hell,"—

which things, in this region were generally known to be facts, long before I came to Albany—the alarm was greatly increased. And now under these circumstances, how can you think it so strange that ministers did not "receive their Brethren from the West with open arms"?—Why, Br. this way the very evil which they dreaded, & against which they had been guarding for months.

For the moment one of these brethren was recd with open arms, the name of that minister who received him was made use of all over the country to sanction these men, & *all their calamitous measures.* It was this very thing, & nothing else, which placed Br. Beman in a situation where he must fall out, either with Br. Finney & his measures, or with all those ministers and Christians who could not be converted to these measures. There was no alternative. Br. Beman could not serve two masters, & so a shameful war was commenced in our Zion, merely in consequence of the introduction of these new measures into Troy, every minister of any value in all this region, & in all N. England, would have come up to the help of Br. Beman with all his heart, & soul, & mind, & strength. I know this to be the general sentiment, and you know it is mine. Now place yourself in the situation of settled ministers in this region, & then see whether you would be willing to receive "with open arms," the men whose measures had done so much mischief in the opinion of all your

Brethren, & so lend the influence of your respected name to give these measures your sanction?

And further, even in Albany Br. B & F. & N. & others had introduced these new measures against the wishes of all the settled ministers there, & so a war had already commenced in Doct. Chester's Chh. long before my arrival. Some of his most disorganizing members had begun to pray for him & others in public, by name, as cold and stupid, & dead, & unconverted. These disorganisers were using all their influence to weaken the hands, & destroy the influence of the settled ministers in Albany, & they felt greatly strengthened in their work by the example & presence of these brethren from the West. Now, under these circumstances would *you*, or any other minister in your Presby have "received these men with open arms?" I trow not.

Again: It was well known that there were ministers within your own limits, & those too, who had the confidence of the christian public, who would not receive Br. F. into their pulpits so long as they could avoid it without losing the confidence of their own people. And, it was further known that some who did receive him, did it with trembling anxiety for the consequences. *Brs Coe & Aikin themselves being judges*. And can you think it so strange that ministers who knew & had talked over all this, should not "receive them with open arms."?

And besides; Whether it be correct or not I will not venture an opinion. It is believed by many that even now your Presbytery would not care to employ Br F. within your own limits long in any one place. Now if this be the fact there must be something wrong somewhere, either in Br. F. or in the hearts of your Presbytery for the minister whose preaching on the whole exerts a healthful influence will establish himself not only in the affections but in the confidence of both minister & people; & in such a manner too as will render his return & his labors on the same field far more desirable than ever. The longer he stays the more will mutual confidence increase, as a general fact. If this be not the result of his labors, it will be known & told by ministers & christians & men of influence & will follow the preacher, & will certainly work mischief wherever he goes. This only by the *by*.

Turn the tables. Suppose the same scenes which you have witnessed in the Western revivals had transpired in Connecticut; & that certain young men had adopted & defended new measures which all our Western Brethren considered, as *innovations, antiscriptural,* & exceedingly *calamitous* in their *consequences*. And further, that Doct. Day & Taylor, & others in Con. whose reputation was established in the Western region, were known to agree with you, & all your Presy in their views of these measures; & that many of the best ministers in Con. would not employ these young ministers on any consideration so long as they could avoid it,—and that others who had employed them did it with "trembling anxiety for the consequences," & considered it a "bitter pill." Now suppose these young ministers should make their way into Oneida Co. where these things were known & the alarm had already been taken in consequence of disorganizing members who had arisen in our own Churches, & in conjunction with young converts from Con. had introduced all these irregularities into their private meetings against your own wishes, & had begun to denounce *you* & all your ministers who would not fall in with them in defending these men from Con. & their calamitous measures. Tell me, my Br. what wd you think of the ministers from Con. should they tell your Presby that "You erred in not receiving these missionaries from Con. as *we* did with open arms." And that if the "talents of these Evangelists were lost to the Chh. you must bear the blame?" Would it not appear to you to be a novel doctrine that your Presby were bound to receive such Evangelists from Con. on any terms?

But more especially when you knew that so many of the very body to which they belonged in Con. would not be strenuous in the adoption of any measures against the wishes of settled pastors." But how could they know this? They had always adopted them wherever they went. And it was too late for they had already succeeded in foisting them into Albany & Lansingburg against the wishes of the settled ministers. And besides I conversed with Br Beman & read to him the substance of my letter to Br. Aikin, weeks before it was sent; & labored with all my might to convince him of the calamitous tendency of these measures, until I lost all my strength, & in consequence spent the remainder of the night in faintness. I expected that Br. Beman would lay the subject fully before Br. F. as he told me he would. But al this did not avail.

I had also labored the same point with Mr. Hastings for hours together at different times, expecting that he would disclose my views to Br. F. & especially to your Presby before the publication of your Narrative. This conversation with Mr. Hastings I designed particularly to have some bearing on your forthcoming Narative, as he told me it was not then prepared.

Accordingly as soon as it arrived I perused it with great care to discover any traces of my conversation with Mr. H. But to my utter disappointment could find not one word except in the Remarks on the "Bunker-Hill Contest." I saw there a similarity of views. Nor was it until the return of Br. Cornelius, as I informed you, that I learned that my own & the views of my brethren had not been there communicated. Such was their concealment of my views that even in Troy & Lansingburg my name was used to vindicate these measures against those who opposed them, until an extract of my letter to Br Aikin was sent from Utica to Troy.——

Brother, is not all this concealment wrong? And now some of these very persons, who had thus carefully concealed my views up to the time of their disclosure in consequence of my letter to Br. Aikin, are trying to make the impression on the public mind that I acted a double part—— saying one thing to Br. F. & B. & Hastings and another to those who were disaffected in Troy. The same remarkable providential concurrence of circumstances to which you allude I had particularly noticed. And the whole evil is certainly to be attributed to the concealment to which I have alluded. Honesty is certainly the best policy I have witnessed a scene of proselytism on this subject which would have disgraced the age of politics, & which is utterly inconsistent with the spirit of Christianity. I have no right to conceal my sentiments on a subject of such everlasting importance. I am bound by all the solemnity attached to the ministerial office to declare my views of the dangers of these measures; and to clear my conscience from lending my name to sanction any of their calamitous consequences. And this I have endeavored to do by talking, as far as my health, & strength would admit. In the *first* place, To those who adopt the measures in question; & *Secondly* to every member of your Presby. Having witnessed a determination to conceal my views I wrote to Br. Aikin rather than to Br. Finney on purpose to prevent this concealment from your Presby.

After writing to Br Aikin I sent a line to Br Norton requesting him to call & see me at Albany.

I kept him two days & two nights, & spent nearly the whole time with him, laboring to convince him that no man could be an Evangelist in Revivals of religion in *our* denomination with these peculiarities & yet retain the confidence of settled ministers. That in process of time he would do more mischief than good, unless he continued in waste places, & churches, where these measures were already introduced; & even such could never be raised without excluding these measures. That I should not dare to recommend any young minister to labor in any of our established churches so long as I had no evidence that he did not out of principle exclude every thing of this kind, for I should be responsible for all the evils which he should introduce, & ultimately the blame would fall on me for recommending him.

I further told him that if the time should ever come when he should be convinced of the truth of my remarks, & should *ex animo*, renounce these things, that, *paribus*, I would recommend him to my friends, & give him all the support of my power. Of the result of my two days of hard labor I know nothing.

As to the talents & piety of Br. F. of which you speak, I wish you ever to remember, that the evils of which ministers so much complain have nothing to do with the subject. It would be impossible for any man, give him the powers of Edwards, the eloquence of Whitfield & the piety of Paul to *be* an itinerant preacher in *our* denomination, & not do infinitely more mischief than good, adopting the measures in question. Paul himself would have frustrated & hindered the success of his own ministry had he committed half of the outrages on the consciences & piety of many of our best christians which I know these young men have done in this region by attempting to introduce their new measures. Paul, I need not tell you, was exceedingly careful "lest he should hinder the gospel of Christ."

As for giving "Br. F. the benefit of my own experience"; it seems just like requiring of me an impossibility. Especially when I knew that my whole Course of experience would condemn the very measures which himself & some of our Brethren in the West have strenuously defended—knowing as I did that all the ministers who had opposed these measures were denounced. I knew too, that he & his friends were extremely solicitous that I should sanction the very things which I wished him to drop—and know too, that so long as a single minister of your Presbytery defended him in these measures it would be a hopeless task for *me* to attempt to correct him, without showing him another mode of conducting Revivals, which could not be done by talking, only by having strength to take him into the field where the Spirit of God was operating, & so talking about facts as they should arise in the progress of a revival.

Where a man's practice may be *seen* and the *results* known, when years have passed away—

then, & not till then his experience will be known to be either good or bad. But where a man has had no time to look at consequences, such as, what will made sound, or rotten, stable or periodical religion; what will build up or weaken society; What will secure the confidence of settled ministers and intelligent Christians *when years have passed away*?—What will leave a powerful & healthful moral influence on the consciences of the wicked, & especially on the most intelligent part of community,—& will make them see that revivals are not confined to the lower classes of society, & that without a revival, they will probably be lost etc. etc. I say, where a man has had no time to look at these & such like consequences, you can not talk to good advantage. You will be misunderstood, or your motives misconstrued.

Whether I have mistaken the character of Br F. or not, I tell you, that I do not believe that he will give up these peculiarities, while Br. Beman, or Lansing, or *one settled minister* in your Presby can be found to uphold & defend him. "Their flattering representations", as I informed you in my letter to Mr Aiken, "will over rule all that I can say." And I should betray a shameful confidence in my own strength, as well as ignorance of mankind to think otherwise. Br. F. will need a prodigious moral influence to bring him back; for he must give up much of his own, for the sake of adopting the experience of another; which is no easy matter; unless his own is first *proved* to be so bad that he must abandon it at any rate.

With some additional extravagancies on the prayer of faith, the measures in question are the same which were pursued by James Davis, & other itinerants in N. England at the time when I first entered the ministry. Settled "pastors received them with open arms,"—thinking to correct them, until they found themselves involved in endless quarrels and divisions among themselves and their own people. Ministers then wrote to the Associations which licensed them, to call them to order. But it was too late. They had more light & wisdom than all the settled Pastors. And I know not whether a single one of them was ever convinced of his errors in any other way than by becoming a settled pastor himself, & then he would be sure to swing as far over on the other side. I have since labored with some of the latter class of ministers in their own parishes. They had become greatly prejudiced against the man, & the very measures by which themselves were converted, as well as against myself, supposing that a religious excitement could not exist without all these irregularities, until an actual experiment *by another mode* of conducting revivals corrected the mistake.

Now I am ashamed to tell what belongs not to me, but to such men as Drs Mcauley, Taylor, Tyler, Humphrey & Beecher, & many obscure & excellent ministers in N. Eng. with whom I have labored, & Who know the facts to which I allude. And besides, there is something extremely forbidding in a man's talking much about his own experience & wisdom etc. especially with strangers on your first acquaintance.

On other subjects mankind & even ministers exercise far more wisdom & common sense than on the subject of religion. No body ever thought of making a skilful physician, politician, or warrior *at once*; but most of our young men, warm-hearted, Christian, & even old ministers, themselves, do take it for granted that a "skilful" minister can be made out of a "novice" *at once*. And ministers of influence must be to blame if they do not accomplish the task. "The children of this world, are in their generation wiser than the children of light."

In estimating the talents requisite for an Itinerant preacher other considerations are no less important than intellect, or piety itself. And these qualifications cannot be known *a priori*.

Nothing but an actual experiment can develop the powers of a man to do good in revivals; & at the same time to secure the confidence of Christians & ministers wherever he goes. I could tell you of facts to illustrate my remark, I could tell you of some excellent young men who could not fail to do good, where they were well known, & under the eye of settled minister to control their movements, who, on going into different parts of N. Eng. & elsewhere would do some good for a while, but ultimately far more mischief, & would certainly have lost their own character had they not been privately called away from that field. In this way I think I have saved some of our young ministers from losing all their influence, & so from leaving our own denomination. When they have fallen out with settled pastors, I never thought of disputing the point who was to blame. If any evils have been running, or even suspected to exist, I have always been the very first to inquire into them, & to take hold with a strong hand to correct them, not sparing in the least my best friends. Evangelists have no more right to intermeddle with ministers & their flocks, than they have with their families, wives, children, & domestic concerns; & any murmuring complaints on this point go on the supposition that an Evangelist may "lord it over" all the pastors, & their flocks. If my young friends or myself have ever been injured by settled pastors, silence is better than self defence. I need not add infinitely better than denunciation.

You say that Br. F. has, or had confidence in my opinion, & I ought to have told him my views. I have told him in as gentle a manner on paper as I knew how to do it. And I leave it to you what has been the effect? And whether I could have chosen a better method. When he called to visit me I was already worn out with conversation, & once I had a meeting to attend & to preach in the Evg. And notwithstanding, I did tell him that I feared his talents & efforts could not be kept within the channel where they were greatly needed; & assigned some reasons, as far as time & strength would permit.

You regret that "walls of adamant should separate such men." By whom do you suppose these walls were erected? And whose business is it to clamber over? I leave it to you & to settled pastors whose business alone it is to decide the question whether these innovating measures shall be adopted or not. I am willing to submit the question to our own conscience, whether I shall *adopt* or Br. F. *drop* the measures in question. I know you do not wish me to sanction them. For no man can be an Itinerant, in our denomination with these measures, & not create endless quarrels in our churches. When I entered the ministry there was no man I wished more to see, & hear & converse with than James Davis or some of the preachers of his stamp. But I found I could not be connected with him or any who adopted his peculiarities without losing the confidence of settled pastors. And hence I have spent much of my time, since, in helping settled ministers to build up what they with him had pulled down.

You complain of the extravagance of Br. Beecher's letter to Br. B. & F. as calculated to do any thing rather than correct errors in them. Now you know the plain & pointed style of preaching adopted by Br. B. & F. and from your knowledge of mankind what method should you think best calculated to correct them? Mild & gentle, or more severe measures? I should like your opinion. For one, I fear it will need the same strength of moral influence to bring them back which they have exerted to bring others over to their measures.—

N. B. Brother F. This is a part of what I wrote immediately on receiving your letter, & which I refused to send for want of time to write out illustrations. Show it to none but friends. If may contain useful hints.

Your affectionate brother
A. N.

LETTER #14

To John Frost, Whitesborough, New York

Durham Mar. 28th 1827

My Dear Brother,

I retired to this place for a short respite, my health being feeble. I have just recd from Albany a bundle of letters, & yours of the 13th inst. for which you will accept my best thanks. I am sorry that my health will not

permit me to tell you all my heart. I was glad that you & Br Coe came to
Albany, but was sorry that you could not tarry longer, & see more of the
ministers in our region. Your Presby I find, have been kept in ignorance
of the state of things in N. Eng. & in the Presbn church generally—so far
as certain measures are concerned & I may add, you do not now know a
hundreth part of the *facts* on which our *best ministers,* in whom I know
you place implicit confidence, have formed their opinions. And I may
say—I think there is not *one* settled minister in your Presb. had he been in
the place of these ministers & known the same facts but would have
formed the same views, & had the same feelings. You think that the
ministers in our region erred in not doing as you did "receive Br F. to
their arms." To tell you the truth, my Br., the ministers & other Xns
from this region, New York & all N. Eng. who visited Oneida Co. last
summer saw with their own eyes and heard with their own ears so many
things that they deplored that it was the *universal opinion,* far & near, that
the *character of revivals had gone back fifty years*—& this I knew to be the
general sentiment of our best ministers more than *3 months before I visited
Albany.* The ministers were universally deploring the introduction of
these new measures & were guarding & watching against them for
months before I came to Albany. It was the universal sentiment of
ministers while I was laboring in Jamaica last summer that they could not
& should not dare to employ a preacher in their own churches who
adopted these peculiarities. This I knew to be the fact from personal
conversation with scores of ministers while I was in Jamaica last summer.
I respect the idea so that you may remember & never forget that
ministers are not complaining so much of irregularities existing in the
West. They know that you have the right, & are willing you should
exercise it of persuing your own measures within your own limits where
you can take all the responsibility. But when tidings came that these new
measures had been introduced into Troy & Lansingburg & Albany, by Br
Beman, Nash, Finney, Foot & Norton—that all the ministers & Xns in
those places & all who visited those places were denounced as "cold &
stupid & dead & enemies to revivals & leading sinners down to hell"—
which things every body in this region knew to be facts long before I
came to Albany the alarm was greatly increased. And now under these
circumstances how can you think it so strange that ministers did not
receive their Brethren from the West "with open arms!" Why, my Dear
Brother, this was the very evil which they dreaded & against which they
had been guarding for months. For the moment *one* of these Brethren
was recd "with open arms"—the name of that man who recd him was

made use of all over the country to sanction these men & *all their calamitious measures*. It was this very thing & nothing else that placed Br Beman in a situation where he must face out with Br Finney & his measures, or with all those ministers & Xns that could not be converted to these new measures. Br Beman could not serve two masters & so a war has commenced in Zion—merely in consequence of a revolution in the introduction of these new measures into Troy. Had it not been for the introduction of these new measures into Troy, every minister of any value in all this region & in all N. Eng. would have come up to his help with all his heart & soul & mind & strength. I know that is the general sentiment & you know it is mine. Place yourself in the situation of settled ministers in this region & then see whether you would be willing to receive "with open arms," the men whose peculiar measures had done so much mischief in the opinion of all your brethren—& so lend your respected name to give these measures your sanction. Even in Albany, Br Beman & F. & N. had introduced these new measures against the wishes of all the settled ministers there, before my arrival—& a war had already commenced in Dr Chesters church. The most disorganising members of his church were opposing him, & felt strengthened in their opposition by the names of these Brethren from the West. How under these circumstances would *you*, or any other man in your Presb. have recd these men "with open arms"? I trow not.

Besides: It was well known that these were ministers within your own limits & those too, who had the confidence of the christian publick, who would not receive Br F. into their pulpits so long as they could avoid it without losing the confidence of their own people. And, it was further known, that some who did receive him, did it with trembling anxiety for the consequences—Br Coe & *Aikin himself* being judges. And can you think it so strange that ministers who knew, & had talked over all this, should not "receive them with open arms"? And besides whether it be correct or not I will not venture an opinion. It is believed by many, that even now your Presby would not care to employ Br F. within your own limits long in any one place. Now, if this be the fact there must be some thing wrong some where—either in Br F. or in the hearts of your own Presby. For the minister whose preaching exerts on the whole a healthful influence will *establish* himself in the affections & confidence of both minster & people—which will render his return & stay in that place *far more desirable than ever*. The longer he stays the more will mutual confidence encrease as a general fact. If this be not the result of his labors it will be known, & told & will follow the preacher & will certainly work mischief wherever he goes. This only by the bye.—

As to the character & talents & piety of Br F. which you & our Brethren at the West think I have mistaken I wish your never to name it again. I assure you, once for all, that *I believe every word that you say to be the sober truth*, & a great deal more might be said. I have never had any other opinion on that subject. And his enemies have all helped to confirm it. And yet, all that I have ever said and am now saying would be true of the evils of which we complain. It has nothing to do with the character or talents or piety of Br F. It would be impossible for any man—give him the powers of Edwards, the eloquence of Whitfield & the piety of Paul, to be an Itinerant preacher in *our* denomination & not do infinitely more mischief than good *if he adopted the measures in question*. Paul himself would have "hindered" & "frustrated" & rendered his own ministry of "no-effect" had he committed half of the imprudences & outrages on the consciences (of weak Brethren if you please) & piety of many of our best Xns—which I know these young men have done in *this region* by attempting to introduce their new measures. Paul, I need not tell you was exceedingly careful "lest he should hinder the gospel of C."

As for giving "Br F. the benefit of my own experience"—it seems to me just like requesting of me an impossibility. Especially when I knew that my whole course of experience would condemn the *very measures* which himself & some of our brethren in the West have strenuously defended & that all others who would not approve of them Br F. & his friends had denounced. I knew too that he & his friends were extremely solicitous that I should sanction the very things which I wished him to drop—& I knew that so long as *one* minister in our Pres. defended him in these measures, it would be a hopeless task for me to attempt to correct him—without showing him another mode of conducting revivals which could not be done by talking only by having strength to take him into the field where the Sp. of God was operating, & so talking about facts as they should arise in the progress of a revival. Where a man's practice can be *seen* & the results known when years have passed away— his experience will be known to be either good or bad. But where a man has had no time to look at consequences—such as what will make sound, or rotten—stable, or lawless converts—what will build up or weaken society—what will secure the confidence of settled ministers & intelligent Xns when years have passed away—what will leave a powerful & healthful moral influence on the wicked & especially on the most intelligent part of community—& will make them feel that revivals are not confined to the lower classes of society, & that, without a revival, they will probably be lost etc etc I say where a man has had no time to look at such & suchlike consequences, you cannot talk to good advantage. You will be misunderstood or your motives misconstrued. Br. F. will need a prodigious moral influence to bring him back, for he must give up much of his *own* for the sake of adopting the experiences of another—which is not so easy a matter—unless his own is first *proved* to be so bad that he must drop it at any rate. Brother, I have full confidence in you, & in every settled minister in your Presb. There is no loss of confidence—entire confidence in your Presb.—Some things in my letters to you & Br Aikin need illustration—I love to talk with you & Br Coe—& I only regret that you did not tarry longer. Your visit will not fail of doing good. By the way, I had forgotten to tell you that there has been a fight in this town about 5 months since, headed by raw recruits from Camden Oneida Co. A young convert from that place appeared here Saying that "He knew all about how to conduct revivals"— Pointing to the meeting house he told of "the abominations which were portrayed on those walls." Speaking of Br Williston he says "Are you afraid of him

are you afraid of him?" All his movements were in the attitude of war. It seems that he meant to show his own heroism by an attack upon him. And so in the evening he broke out denouncing him & prayed for him as a "liar" etc etc. And another told the people that "Mr. W. was the head Achan in the camp & that his character was as *black as hell*" & much more to the same purpose—

Br W. told the people at the close that he considered the man as crazy & that that was the most charitable construction of his conduct. One church member joined him & is now under process of discipline. Now such things would never come from revivals if not borrowed from the leaders. Errors adopted & defended by an Itinerant will be the first things which young converts will try to imitate & they will in this way be conscientious in doing what every body knows to be a great sin. Br Williston you know. He thinks it his duty to require a publick confession of the crime, & all the church & even the world think the same. You know but little of the awful consequences which are growing out of these new measures. Many revivals have been overset & disgraced & destroyed in the same manner. The minister in Hunter has a council occasioned by a similar outrage on himself & will doubtless be dismissed. And you cannot think it strange that when the cause is known to all the world that ministers should be alarmed. Now your advice is to(ld). I expect to return to Albany shortly, & never expect to visit this region again.

You say that Br F. has, or had confidence in my opinions. And I ought to have told him my views. I have told them in as gentle a manner on paper as I knew how to do it. And I leave it to you what has been the effect; & whether I could have chosen a better method. When he called to visit me I was already worn out with conversation & once had a meeting to attend & to preach in the evening. And notwithstanding I did tell him that I feared his talents & efforts could not be kept within our denomination & told him some reasons as far as time & strength would permit. And I leave it to you & your Presbytery & to the christian community which will appear the most unaccountable for him to hold fast these new measures & require me to adopt them or for me to retain my views of these measures & require him to drop them. I know that you do not wish me to sanction them. For no man can be an Itinerant in our denomination with these measures & not create endless quarrels & division in our churches.

I do not intend to publish without the cooperation of my Brethren at the West unless compelled by necessity. The sentiment of many at the West that "the reason why ministers do not approve of certain measures is because they are cold & stupid & dead," has prevailed to such an alarming degree that no body is willing to tell certain young men their faults which they see will ruin them if not corrected—for fear of being slandered by them. Brothers; this will turn out to be true. "Reprove not a scorner lest he hate thee." "He that rebuketh a wicked man getteth himself a blot."

You know the plain & pointed method of preaching adopted by Br Beman & F. to awaken & arouse cold hearted ministers & christians to a sense of duty. Now, from your knowledge of mankind, what, in your opinion would be the most likely method to convince these men of an error—soft & gentle, or violent measures. I should like your opinion on this subject.

I will try to make a good use of your letter & of the kindness of feeling manifested by your Presbytery. I feel no loss of confidence in any one. Tho' I have understood that "*There is now an attempt made very extensively to injure my credit with the christian* publick, by those who feel themselves condemned by my opinions." This I knew to be true, for I am not without an extensive acquaintance even at the West. I am now sharing in the denunciations of My Brethren at the west. But, as I said I feel no concern on that subject. I have no credit to gain or lose in this world.

Your affectionate
brother A. N.
Rev. John Frost
Whitesboro
Oneida Co
N.Y.
Copy of a letter to Br Frost
Imperfect

LETTER #15
(THIRD SIMILAR LETTER TO REV. FROST;
MORE OF A FINAL COPY. AUTHOR'S NOTE)

Copy of a letter to Revd J. Frost

Durham April 18th 1827

My health being feeble I retired to this place for a little respite. A few days since I recd from Albany a bundle of letters and yours of the 13h inst. for which you will accept my best thanks. I immediately sat down and wrote 3 or 4 sheets which I intended to communicate for your own private use. But on reading it over I found that time & strength did not allow me to be sufficiently explicit—& that much of what I had written would require illustration by a detail of matters of fact which would fill a volume. I therefore concluded not to send it at least for the present. I was glad that you & Br Coe came to Albany, but regret that you could not tarry longer, & see more of the ministers in our region. Your Presbytery, I find, have been kept in ignorance of the state of things in N. Eng. & in the Prebyn. church generally, so far as certain measures are concerned. And I may add, you do not know a hundredth part of the *facts* on which our *best* ministers, in whom I know you place implicit confidence, have formed their opinions. And I may say, I do think there is not *one settled* minister in your Presb. had he been in the place of these ministers, and known the same facts, but would have formed the same views and had the same feelings.

You think that the ministers in our region *erred* in not doing as you did "receive Br F. with open arms." I thank you for an expression of your views on this subject. A detail of facts in this region would doubtless fully satisfy your own mind on this subject. All these, however, I omit in my present communication. I assure, you, my Br, that there is no loss of ministerial confidence between settled ministers in N. Eng. and settled ministers in Oneida Co. Nothing is wanting but a perfect understanding on the subject of certain *new measures*. And these facts, nobody can fairly

communicate to your Presby. without writing a volume. I found it
perfectly easy to converse with yourself & Br Coe whose minds & hearts
were open—and whose experience as settled pastors rendered it
perfectly easy to make ourselves understood. I only regret that you did
not stay longer & see more of our ministers in all this region. Br Gale too,
is a man of an excellent spirit. I have thought much of him since our short
interview. As he is not a settled minister why can he not visit us again. If
my health were sufficient, I have thought, Deo volente, I should like him
as a fellow labourer in a revival of religion. Short as it was your visit to
Albany will not fail of doing good & be assured it is only a want of a
correct knowledge of facts that can prevent any settled minister in your
Presb. of a similar spirit from heartily sympathizing with ministers in this
region in the troubles which have been transferred into their churches
from the West. By the way, I would just mention to you that there has
been a sham fight in this town about 5 months since, headed by a raw
recruit from Camden, Oneida Co. A young convert from that place
appeared here as "full" (1. Cor. 4.8) as he could hold; saying that "He
knew all about how to conduct revivals." And pointing to the meeting
house told of "the abominations that were portrayed on those walls." He
told Br Williston he wished to see him & talk with him, all in the style of
insolence & war. Speaking to others of Br Williston he says "Are you
afraid of him." "Are you afraid of him." All his movements were in the
attitude of defiance. It seems that he meant to show his own heroism by
another attack upon him. And so at an evening meeting at which Br
Williston preached, he fell upon his knees at the close, & told the Lord a
long story about Br Williston—How he had talked with him, & what he
had said in his sermon that was false, & so tried to convince the people &
the Lord that Br Williston was a liar & going down to hell if he did not
repent. The people by this time were all in a ferment of indignation. Br
Williston then spoke to the people telling them that he thought the man
was crazy—& that that was the most charitable construction on his
conduct. At this, his brother arose & told the people that "Mr Williston
was the head Achan in the camp"—& that his character was as *black as
hell*" etc. etc. (Borrowed expressions. See my letter to Br A.—Dr.
Griffin) All the people now were filled with such indignation to hear
their beloved Pastor so slandered in a religious meeting that some went
to these men & tried to still them—while others with Br Williston began
to retire.—Br Williston says that he has no doubt, that when the
congregation began to retire that these men were thinking that he & all
the congregation were on the point of conviction & just ready to "break

down." One church member only caught the spirit. He says that "His brother made more prayer while he was in this town than all its inhabitants both *learned* & unlearned." Among other things he told the Lord that "Old professors had better be sent to hell than to stand in the way as they did." And prayed that the "Lord would remove the tall oaks of Basham & make room for the young saplings."—By the way, the Deacon with whom I reside is a man of great *moral* as well as uncommon *corporeal excellence*. This man is under process of discipline for his conduct that evening. Br Williston you know. He thinks it his duty to require of the man a publick confession of his offence, & all the church & even the world think the same. When the Deacons went to talk with him to convince him of his error—he said that he had nothing against Br Williston—but "he did it to have a revival etc. etc." A female from Camden was present & heard the conversation, & calls it "persecution." What the end of this thing will be I cannot tell. The people here all think that if Br Williston had not been a man of singular piety & prudence that he must have been dismissed before his time.

A similar outrage has been committed on a minister in a neighboring town in this vicinity. An Elder in that church, who spent a night with me in this place (and wishes me to visit them) gave me particulars. He thinks it will end in the dismission of the Pastor at the next meeting of Presby. now such things as I have related would never have come from the Western revivals if they were not borrowed from their leaders. Errors adopted and defended by a popular Itinerant preacher will be the first things which young converts as well as many others, will try to imitate. And if these errors become topics of publick discussion, and especially if they hear that other respectable ministers uphold & defend their favourite preacher in these things, they will be conscientious in imitating even their *sins*—thinking them to be their greatest excellencies. And if other preachers do not adopt them they will be denounced. You know but little of the awful consequences of upholding a young Itinerant *revival* minister in such errors, I may add, of refusing decidedly & publickly to correct them. Br. F. has not been to Camden, but Br. N. has.

When I began to tell Br F. something about my manner of proceeding; he observed that he did not think that young men could adopt it—And I have no doubt he thought it would require too much time & care to secure the confidence of settled ministers that he & other young men could not have patience or skill to attempt it—And I believe that your young ministers, and I fear some older ones have so concluded. And that the shortest & best method of getting along with settled ministers is to "break them down" or denounce them at once as cold & stupid & dead if they do not fall in to defend all their innovating measures. And I am mistaken if the former *connivance* of some & the *silence* of others in your Presb. has not confirmed the young men in this course. This is certainly the leading feature in the character of all the young converts who have run out from under these young men into all this region. And I fear that the good spirit of some older ministers has not been improved by the tincture received from the younger. When I first arrived in this region I was thunderstruck to observe with what little ceremony ministers & christians were denounced. It was so perfectly novel to me, and, as I had ever been accustomed to regard it as a great sin, I thought that a gentle hint to the offenders would be sufficient to distress their consciences. But judge of my astonishment when I found no conscience there. "This was the way to arouse them." "All those ministers who could not bear to be treated in this manner manifested a bad spirit." And so I have found that reason & argument & even scripture itself has little or no weight with those who make feeling their standard & are so confident that they are right that all who differ from them must be wrong. So was it not with Br Frost & Coe.

By what has transpired, the aged people in this town, have been reminded of the age of Separatism. They think that the same Spirit has again revived. They have told me a number of anecdotes concerning Davenport of which, they say, these things have reminded them. The lady of the house where I now reside mentioned one concerning her grand father Jones of Saybrook Connecticut, who was a professor of religion & considered a pious man. Driving his team in the hurry of summer on passing the house where Davenport was preaching he halted a moment & heard Davenport cry out "Lord convert that sinner or strike him dead."

Br Williston has no doubt that satan has transformed himself into an angel of light to overset genuine revivals, & to substitute false conversions in their stead. He took the alarm last fall & give his people a warning in a sermon from these words. "Lest satan get an advantage of us; for we are not ignorant of his devices."

I have given you but a very imperfect sketch of what has transpired in this town where the Pastor & people are more established in Doctrine & prepossessed in favour of revivals than in almost any other in all this region. Now, multiply these sham fights in every village & town all over the land & I leave it to your judgement & conscience to determine the result. And I tell you that they have been multiplied & are still multiplying & will certainly increase in all & every one of our churches all over the land where the Watchmen do not take the alarm & make a decided stand by forestalling the opinion of the people over whom they are set to watch. And now let me add that so far as I am acquainted; all those watchmen who are awake & have taken the alarm, are the very men in whom you & I place the greatest confidence. And these too are the men whose judgements & consciences & piety are trampled upon by being denounced as "cold & stupid & dead & enemies to revivals" by the Insurgents. I would ask you to read over my letter to Br Aikin in connection with the scene which has transpired in this town. I assure you once more that the picture I sent you is not "overdrawn."

The views of Br Williston on this subject have been formed entirely on facts which have passed under his own observation. They are the same with those of the ministers named in that letter, & I may add, of all in this region in whose opinion you would place any confidence. Now where all the ministers & pious people have taken the alarm by such sham fights conducted by these raw recruits, what kind of contest, think ye, would ensue, were they to be re-enforced by their admired leaders?

In their attempt to correct the evils which have been transferred into their churches, I wish to remind you, that ministers are acting only in *self defence*. They feel it to be their duty to guard against a revolution in their own churches both as to *measures* and to *what real religion is*. And this cannot be done without forestalling the opinion of their own people as to the expediency of such a revolution. If this can be done & yet the popularity of the few missionaries who have adopted & defended the measures in question be saved, they will certainly rejoice. Otherwise their unpopularity is not to be compared with the universal calamity which they wish to avert from their own churches.

I have tried to view this subject on all sides—& to ascertain what the general interest of religion requires & how it will appear when the present generation of ministers are sleeping in their graves. Had your Presbytery been as conscientious in introducing the new measures into your own churches, as the great body of our best ministers are in guarding against & keeping them out of theirs, I do think that I should not be offended with a resolution from your Presbytery not to employ me or any other man as an Evangelist in your own churches until we should renounce our own & adopt your views of the measures in question. Such a resolution would, indeed, affect my usefulness among your own people; but not among the ministers whose views should accord with my own. On the contrary, it would tend rather to establish my influence with such Pastors wherever my views were known. And, vice versa, such a resolution on the part of settled Pastors not to employ any Evangelists who have adopted & defended the measures in question without renouncing them would greatly affect their usefulness were they to enter the field of such Pastors. But it would tend only to establish the character of such missionaries with all the settled Pastors whose views might accord with their own, e.g. in Oneida Co.

Again, the ministers who act in self defence in this matter have all the burden on their own shoulders. It requires neither wisdom, nor piety, nor prudence, nor Evangelist, to introduce these new measures into our churches. Any settled Pastor can do it among his own people with perfect ease—without an Evangelist—& even against the united counsels of all the ministers in the American churches. Indeed, there is not one minister in 20 who can *prevent* this revolution in his own church where a few disorganizing members unite against him unaided by an Evangelist, who, to turn the current in his favour must be an acknowledged revival man. And when these measures are fairly & fully introduced under the sanction of revival men there is not one settled Pastor in a hundred who has prudence & weight of character sufficient to roll back the current without being swept from the field. It is no difficult thing to set "hay wood, & stubble" on fire. These materials are in every church & it wants only a tar-match to set them agoing. Now if it be thought best & if one half of your Presbyt. will join me in the enterprise I have no doubt that in 6 months from this time we will work a revolution all over the Western country, which all the settled Pastors who may oppose us shall not be able to bring back in their generation. Feeble as my health is the task may easily be done & I need not take the trouble of visiting the West. Only let me write & set students in Divinity & lay men & females & young converts & everything else all at work, & then sanction all their imprudences by denouncing all that should dare to oppose them as "cold & stupid & dead & enemies to revivals"—"as not up to the spirit of the times," & the work is done. And how perfectly easy it would be to answer every argument of the most experienced ministers & silence every objection whether pious or impious by asserting "Revivals are different now & must be promoted by different means"— "Our fathers have not understood the subject; they did not know how to *pray*; nor did they know how to preach nor to promote revivals"—"We live in a new era"—"God blesses these means; & for us to find fault is to be more *nice* than God" "It is the Lord's work, & if he does not do it *right* we are not responsible."

I know you do not wish me to sanction this course. I do not believe that Br Beman, & Aikin, & Lansing wish it. And what I have said is only in vindication of the resolutions adopted by your Presbytery. I rejoice in their adoption as well as in the consciousness of a perfect unison of my own views & feelings with those of the settled Pastors in your Presbytery. Our object is one. We wish to promote the general cause by helping settled Pastors in N. Eng. & this region & at the same time to do it in such a manner as not to destroy the influence of settled Pastors at the West.

The remedy against the prevalence of the evils in question, lies more within the power of your Presbytery than in any other body. The combined wisdom of a whole neighbourhood, town, or kingdom could not correct the disorders or prevent the mischiefs of a lawless, ungoverned *child*—without the decided co-operation of his parents— The more noise he makes & the greater the alarm raised among the neighbours, the better it will suit him. The same is true with the young convert who is taught by precept & example this lesson—"The more opposition the better."

I am happy to say that the tidings that your Presbytery to not approve of some measures, for which many lawless members of churches in this region in conjunction with some from the West have pleaded your sanction, have already operated as a powerful check upon many. None but the Head can restore order in the household of faith. Every parent, you know, must govern his own children. And how important that they be taken in season! I fear that some ministers cannot say with Paul—"Ye know how we exhorted—and charged every one of you, as a father doth his children"—to cultivate humility, meekness, gentleness & all the graces of the Spirit, & to observe all the rules of christian propriety. Union of effort among ministers is of the highest importance. Let us therefore adopt no measures in which all settled Pastors & evangelists cannot unite. Let Br Beman & Lansing & the settled Pastors in the Oneida Presbytery adopt any measures by which the cause of revivals may be promoted; & I will cheerfully do any thing to assist so far as my feeble health will permit.

Ministers, you know, claim the privilege of corresponding, & of freely communicating their views on the great interests of the Redeemers kingdom. And in times of danger they are bound by their profession to speak freely & fully their own minds. The *silence* of the Watchmen of Israel is criminal in proportion to the magnitude of the danger he descries. And now permit me to suggest whether there has not been a criminal *silence* on the part of settled Pastors & experienced Ministers at the West in suffering their own "scruples" & counsels to be overruled by the counsel of the young men?

LETTER #16

To Seth Williston, Durham, New York

Durham, Ap. 21 1827

Br Williston,

This day I am 44 years of age—I feel thankful that a kind providence has led me to this place & that I have had the satisfaction of a short acquaintance with you. I cannot express my feelings now. But in view of the uncertainty of life would say that I am rather happy in the thought of laying my bones in your burying ground. I cannot tell how it may be in that solemn hour & a willingness to die I do not think is any evidence of grace—but the thought of leaving the world appears rather pleasant & above all, the thought of never sinning—I feel it to be a *great thing* to be a christian—Such words as these appear sweet "I am now ready to be offered etc."

> "O glorious hour, O blest abode
> I shall be neare & like my God
> And flesh and sin no more control
> The sacred pleasures of the soul."

I feel a peculiar love to ministers especially to those with whom I have labored in seasons of revival—Remember me affectionately to them all—They will find my feelings in the 20th chap. of acts.—I feel a peculiar interest in Theol. Students & have been wishing to leave something which might be useful—Things which have been learned by experience. I can only say that it is a good symptom when they secure the confidence of aged & experienced Ministers—The younger should submit themselves to the elder & always speak kindly of them. My mind ranges over all the towns & places where I have labored in seasons of revival with peculiar delight—I have feelings of inexpressible tenderness & compassion for all the young converts—They will find much of.—

My affectionate regards to all my relations in N. Killingworth & tell them to prepare to follow—I die among kind friends—Tell your congregation & especially the young people to seek an interest in Christ without delay—When I am buried on yonder hill, tell them to remember the evening when I preached to them from these words, "Seek first the kingdom of God" When ever they pass my grave tell them they will remember "Here lies the man who talked to me about my soul."—I die in peace with all mankind.

In great weakness Your affectionate friend
& brother A. N.
Rev. Seth Williston
Durham

LETTER #17

To T. H. Skinner, Philadelphia, Pennsylvania

Durham N. Y. Ap. 25th 1827

My Dear Brother

Your joint letter of the 14th together with one from Esq Evarts urging the same request was duly received. Most gladly would I comply were it in my power. You cannot be more willing to receive me than I should be to come—and so I had been thinking for some time past. But my health is too feeble to allow me to labour at all.

I am extremely anxious that things may be conducted well among your people at this interesting crisis. The eyes of our Br Watchmen at a distance, especially in N. Eng. are turned towards Phil. with a kind of trembling anxiety. I know it from personal conversation as well as from repeated communications. At this eventful, critical & in some respects alarming crisis in the history of revivals the enquiry has often been made "Has Br Skinner received the watchword"

Never did the character of revivals stand so high & never were they in greater danger of being overset & disgraced in our day. Never were revivals more pure & powerful in some places & never more corrupt & disgraceful in others. In some places the most hopeful beginnings have suddenly vanished & the whole ended in a disgraceful & shameful sham fight by suffering it to be conducted by ignorant & officious hands.

The greatest danger arises from the indiscreet conduct of the professed friends of revivals. And now at this distance & with my feeble health you cannot expect me to give many important hints. I can only say, from the natural ardour of your own feelings & the complexion of your letter you are in great danger of oversetting before you know it. Many a revival of religion has been run out by holding meetings too frequent & too long—— not allowing sufficient time for retirement, reflection & secret devotion.

Professors of religion as well as sinners anxious for their souls *must seek solitude* & *"mourn apart."* It is best therefore not to hold meetings every night in the week—but give all a chance & enjoin it upon them to be much alone. Beware of a great deal of loud & noisy conversation—a religious gossiping. There should be little or no talking after meetings are closed—all had better retire in perfect silence. Do not allow anybody & every body to take an active part in religious meetings; for so things will run into wild disorder. You & your Session must all be united & take the entire control. Do not use harsh, boisterous & incorrect expressions in preaching or praying—which, commonly evince an utter absence of the fear of God as well as the christian graces.

> "The Spirit like a peaceful dove
> "Flies from the realms of noise & strife."

Zeal often rise high & even becomes furious where there is not one spark of grace. Be careful not to run before your own hearts. Do not *talk* much about the appearances. You had better drive slow—very slow than to overset. It is easy to kindle false fire but it is next to impossible to quench it. A powerful religious excitement badly conducted is a great calamity, infinitely worse than nothing. And what a calamity must such an excitement be in your city! Should it not turn out well, you will remember what I now tell you. You will wish that you had said little or nothing about a revival & will regret that you had ever raised the publick expectation. The impatience of many zealous professors for a revival of religion, & their imprudent zeal to hasten & proclaim it is the principal engine which the great adversary is using to overset & disgrace the cause of revivals. These are only brotherly hints. You have the good wishes & prayers of the friends of Zion at this interesting crisis. Do, if possible, consult Dr Spring & Mr McAuley. They will be safe counsellors. I can say no more at present. Let me hear from you direct to Albany—It is doubtful whether I ever leave this place. I am reduced to a skeleton & can sit up but little. I am in good hands—& among kind friends. And tho I do not expect it—nor can you expect it; yet if the Lord will I should like much to dwell a little under your roof. Never did I receive an invitation with which I would more gladly comply. My best regards to Mrs S. & believe me your in the best of bonds

Asahel Nettleton

P. S. About 120 have already made a public profession as the fruits of the recent revival in that wicked City of Albany. But we have been careful to keep all still as possible. The revival in Pittsfield & all over Berkshire is wonderful—By far the most so of any in our land—All orderly.

Rev T. H. Skinner D.D.

Philadelphia

LETTER #18

To Joel Hawes, Hartford, Connecticut

[In March, 1829, Nettleton received a letter from a "gentleman in New York," probably G. P. Shipman, concerning the division in the Bowery church over "New Measures." He thought Joel Hawes would be interested in the information it contained so he had an extract copied for him. The following note is added to the manuscript in Nettleton's own handwriting. Birney].

Staunton Va Mar. 7th 1829

My Dear Brother,

The above extract was drawn off, as you see by another hand to send to Drs Beecher & Edwards; but your letter having arrived I concluded to send it to you & Br. Hawes. I have no doubt of a settled determination to send the new measures over our land. But I do not intend to lift a finger to prevent it ; until I can first be sure of the cooperation of settled pastors.—I have long been absent from Prince Edward about 200 miles over the mountains in the interior of Virginia. I took a journey to the Springs last summer & did not return as soon as was expected. Having witnessed some excitement on the subject of religion in this region I tarried until I got winter-bound & could not well journey. But expect to start, Deo volente, early week for Pr. Edward. Your letter was retained in Pr. Ed. until it was evident that I would not return before the op(en)ing of Spring. So many th(ings) (have) transpired since I saw your last (it had been) vain for me to think of writing (more than an) outline— My health has been three months then at any time my sickness—I thank you for & for your interest in Yale College—I have no definite course but I hope to return to the North Spring. You will pardon the br letter for the sake of the extract—My regards to your family—You mentioned a revival in Bolton which led me to send a line to Br Hyde—My love to Br Hawes & to all my old friends

Yours affectionately

Asahel Nettleton

P. S. Dr Alexander, in a letter to Dr Rice, attributes the "dismission of Rev. John Smith of Trenton to his employing Mr Norton, a friend of the new measures, contrary to the wishes of many of that people." Mr Danforth, lately dismissed from his church in New Castle Del. states in the rs, the reason to be "the prospect of greater as an Evangelist." I tarried with him on my way South & Finney was laboring from what I then saw & have since heard doubt that the people were tired of both.

Since the death of Dr Chester, his church in Albany has split & the minority are building a new house. From a knowledge of the state of things when I was there I have no doubt that the dividing line runs with Finny-ism. Two members of that church while I was there established opposition meetings in their own houses, where they could & did call on females to pray in presence of males. One of them declared to me that this practice would certainly prevail & that *Deacon Stillman of Wethersfield was in favor of it.* The man's name. He was never considered remarkable for his piety but was flaming on the subject. I did not ask Mr Mills how he came by his information. I only know that he was quite intimate with Mr & Mrs Norton. Deacon Stillman I know took correct ground with Sally Stoors in Mansfield. I say nothing about these subjects in this place. I am surrounded by an interesting circle of young converts, & am about to bid them a last farewell.

LETTER #19

To Leonard Woods, Andover, Massachusetts

New York May 6, 1829

My Dear Brother,

You have doubtless read Erskine on the "Unconditional freeness of the Gospel." The writer, no doubt wishes to promote the cause of religion. But the tendency of that work I do think, is directly to defeat the object.

In the early part of my ministry, the sentiments of Hervey & Marshall I found in many places meeting & checking the progress of conviction in some sinners & giving false peace to others. I have found some poring over Marshall's "Gospel mystery of sanctification," *trying* to believe it; but conscience *awakend by the Spirit of God,* would not suffer them to rest in a belief that their sins were pardoned while they had no evidence of a change of heart. I was invited to a house to converse with an interesting young lady who had been long anxious for her soul. Many efforts had been made to give her consolation but in vain. "What do you think of this book," said she, "it is Marshall on sanctification & was recommended to me by such an one—& if, I *dare* believe it I should think that I was a christian"? "There is one part of it which you ought not to believe" was my answer. I perceived that her conscience was more orthodox than the author. She gave it up, & her convictions increased but soon terminated in hopeful conversion. The faith which Marshall required did not commend itself to her conscience. Believing that her sins were pardoned against the dictates of conscience & the bible, seemed to her like believing a lie to make it true. How to reconcile this I suppose

Marshall found to be a "mystery." Hence the title of the book. Hence too, the more conscience is awakened to perform its office the more difficult divines of this sentiment find it to deal with sinners. The great object they think is to give sinners peace. And all their efforts are directed to this single object. When the sinner begins to see his character & condition in some measure as it really is—when the word of God begins to take its effect & conscience to perform its office, now every effort is made to counteract the very means which the Spirit of God employs to bring the sinner to a reconciliation. Erskine agrees substantially with Marshall in his views of faith. It consists in believing that your sins are pardoned. The former built his system upon Hervey & Marshall with this wonderful improvement that you are not required to believe a lie in order to make it true; for *the sins of all mankind are pardoned whether they believe it or not. Pardon is universal & unconditional—The atonement is itself the pardon & is unaffected by man's belief or unbelief.* While in all their rebellion & infidelity *it is lavished upon the mass of the guilty without any discrimination. The use of faith is not to remove the penalty or to make the pardon better—for the penalty is removed & the pardon is proclaimed whether we believe it or not—but to give the pardon a moral influence, by which it may heal the spiritual disease of the soul. Mankind are sanctified by the belief of the pardon.*

I cannot but notice how one error grows out of another. The definition of "*atonement is the actual removal of sin.*" If so then it must include pardon *irrespective of character,* antecedent to faith or repentance or conversion—& of course limited to the elect. And faith consists in believing that your sins are pardoned, or that you are one of the elect. But to avoid this difficulty limited atonement becomes unlimited; & so the atonement is made for all mankind, therefore, *pardon is lavished upon all mankind.* This is the most plausible universalism that I have ever seen. If mankind can only be made to believe that their sins are pardoned this will make them *love God—restore the keystone of the arch—sanctify them—give peace of conscience*—& justify them. Now all of this in being taken for granted without one text to prove it, & with the whole bible against him—"He that believeth not is condemned already, & the wrath of God abideth on him." "Cursed is every one that continueth not in all things"—"Except ye repent ye shall all perish." "Repent & be converted that your sins may be blotted out" Etc Etc he adopts every method in his power to make all his (readers) believe that their sins are pardoned. To doubt this must be a great crime—unbelief is the greatest sin—& the more conscience awakes to perform its office of conviction the more guilty & criminal is the sinner for listening to its admonitions. When the

Spirit of God is convincing of sin—the *commandment comes & sin revives,* &
the sinner sees & feels that he is lost & needs pardon, the more he tries to
take it off by convincing him that it is all a false alarm. If he does not
believe that his sins are pardoned before *he has one thought of repentance,* or
of asking it the poor man makes God a liar. "He that believeth not"—that
his sins are pardoned, "hath made him a liar." He tries to wield the whole
moral influence of the gospel against the conscience of an awakened
sinner to overcome his convictions. see page 162–5

My dear Brother, the evil which such a book from the pen of one who
has already acquired a reputation as a writer & a christian cannot be
calculated in this world. Here are false views of faith, of the atonement,
of pardon, of justification, which he makes to consist in a *sense of pardon!*
There is no such thing as evidence of a change of heart. But believing
that your sins are pardoned will produce that change—make you *love
God* & thus *give peace,* & *confidence* & *restore the keystone of the arch.*

I cannot but express to you my full conviction that the sentiments
contained in that book are more directly calculated to prevent
conviction of sin, & put a stop to genuine revivals than any thing that has
ever been published. (And I am surprised that it should be published by
Crocker & Brewster of Boston.) It is recommended by many & by some
of our brethren of whom we might hold better things. I found it in
Virginia. Some who had recommended it were utterly astonished when
I stated my views of it. And the moment they saw it felt just as I did about
its tendency.

I have just heard that you intend to review it. I know not what you
think of it—but pardon me for expressing my views of it so freely. I think
you cannot do a better service to the church, & I hope you will give the
book-sellers a hint.

(In a letter to Dr Rice we were glad to learn that you were
corresponding with Brother Taylor on the subject of his speculations. I
wish I had time to give you an account of my interviews &
correspondence with Br Taylor ever since your controversy with Ware
on total depravity. These speculations are working mischief wherever
his pupils go—all over the country. Nine tenths of our best ministers &
christians are grieved, & can see no possible good that can result from his
enterprise—but mischief & nothing else. His sermon shows more
metaphysical darkness & weakness than I could imagine would ever
come from his pen.) By admitting that infants are redeemed by X & need
regeneration he is at war with himself. Regeneration & redemption by
Christ without sin or a moral character needs explanation. He will not

admit a *physical change*—but what other change do they need if they be not sinners? Pardon my incoherence & haste in writing on subjects of such everlasting importance to ourselves & our fellow sinners, & believe me very sincerely & affectionately yours in the fellowship of the gospel.

  Asahel Nettleton

Rev. Leonard Woods D.D.

Andover

Massachusetts

LETTER #20

To Leonard Woods, Andover, Massachusetts

                       North Killingworth. July 13, 1829

My Dear Brother,

  You kind letter was recd by the hand of our friend Dr Rice, for wh. accept my best thanks. I met him on his way at New Haven, where I spent more than a week, in conversation with Brs Taylor, Fitch, Bacon & Merwin on the subject of their peculiarities—first with each one singly—then in co.—I cannot tell you on paper. I gave them distinctly to understand what I believed to be the opinion of ministers & christians generally, all over the country, with the exception of his own pupils & some few of his own personal friends. I told Br T. that he was greatly *deceived* in thinking that he had convinced many of his brethren of the correctness of his views. That I was convinced that the review of T. & Hervey in the last 2 C. S. [Christian Spectator] contained many things more palpably heterodox than any thing that they had ever published— & that instead of laying fears it would encite still greater alarm. It goes abroad as Dr Porter's of Farmington—but he never wrote more than 8 pages of it—& that had nothing to do with Hervey, only with the note in T's sermon. I told them that I recognized in it some of the very expressions which I saw in a lecture delivered in Y. College, 1822, by Prof. Goodrich—& sent to Dr Breech (Beecher?) at Litchfield. I was then laboring at L. & when I read that lecture I told Dr B. that I could not go with them. I immediately sat down & wrote to Br Taylor—that I was sorry to dissent from Brethren whom I loved, & whose opinion I so highly valued—but frankly told them "Neither my judgment nor conscience, nor heart can acquiesce in the views in question"—After stating my objections at large, I closed, as nearly as I can recollect, in these words: "Cui bono? I fear it is a trick of the adversary to send Br T. on a wild goose chase after what he will never find, &, if found, would not be worth one straw." You will pardon me for telling you what is of no consequence in itself. My only object, you will understand, is to let you know that my fears have been awake on this subject ever since 1820. And I have all along from that time to this disputed him on these subjects.

Our Brethren in N. Haven are, ostensibly, together; but if I am not mistaken, Br Fitch & Bacon would be glad to trace back their steps; tho' they have not so fully committed themselves to the world—only to Br T., *perhaps*.

The object of Br T——s note seems to be to vindicate the character of God in the sincerity of the calls & offers of the gospel; which I nothing doubt. But, if I see the bottom of the thing, he will gain nothing to the sincerity & goodness of God, unless he can prove that God *did not* convert those who have been converted. In short, the *holiness* of mankind must be an effect as much out of Gods power, & as really independent of him, as the same thing in his sons would be out of the power & independent of their father. God would rejoice if the sinner by his self determining power would become holy. But then what would become of others whose holiness might be depending on the motive derived from his punishment had he not converted himself? Other beings might fall, or could not be converted without all this amount of misery as a motive. The answer to this I suppose would be——They have power to do their duty without this motive, but *will not*, & God could not make them, without destroying their moral agency. So that sin & punishment are as really necessary to produce & preserve the greatest amount of good on this plan as on any other. Hence we may conclude that if all would continue holy without the sin and consequent punishment of any part of God's kingdom he would rejoice—but he foresaw that this was impossible. etc etc. I am beginning to regret that I have entered on this note as I find I have not time to express my views of it, if I understand it. But if I do not & others do not understand it, I think surely nothing is gained. The general impression, however, is, I think, a bad one—that the government of the Universe of moral agents depends primarily, if not wholly, on themselves. Whatever sentiment necessarily implies that infants are not sinners from their birth, do not need redemption by Xst, regeneration by the H. Sp. & that death in their case is not *by sin*, I frankly confess I do not believe. And all these & much more, if I mistake not, lies at the bottom of the Theology at N. Haven. They account for the death of infants on the principle of *general laws*. The wheels of his providence are so erratick that God cannot prevent their crushing thousands of infants who are perfectly innocent. He would be glad to do it, but he cannot take them out of the path or prevent their being crushed. "Who ever perished being innocent?" Ans. thousands of infants. "If God spared not the angels that sinned" etc. I thought was proof that "the Lord *knoweth how* to deliver the godly" etc. but it seems that he *does not know* how to do it. But I must stop. I wish very much to see you & the other brethren at Andover, so as to satisfy my own mind on some points, as to what is the best course to be pursued. I am alarmed at the confidence which Br T. seems to feel that he can convince others of the correctness of his views. Pardon my great haste on subjects so vast.

I hope to spend a few days in Hartford this week. Br (Hawes?) wishes to get out or keep out of this controversy.

So far as I am acquainted, I do not believe that ministers & Xns generally will follow Br T.

Will you be so good as to request Br Hooker to send one of his papers, of Humanity to North Killingworth to Ambrose Nettleton, for the first year only. Please to remind Br Hooker that I have paid for it, without intending to call for it. But it is greatly needed here.

I have not yet seen your review of Erskine, & do not know where to find it. Please to direct it to me at Hartford.

Yours affectionately Asahel Nettleton
P. S. Will it be possible for Br Hewitt to come into the County of Middlesex & spend a little time. We all wish it. Will he not name the time?
N Killingworth July 11 1829
Rev. Leonard Woods D.D.
Andover
Mass.

LETTER # 21

To Lyman Beecher, Boston, Massachusetts
Extract of a letter to Dr. Beecher dated Enfield, Mass.

Sept. 18. 1829

While at Amherst I read through Dr. John Taylor of Norwich & much of Edwards in answer. And I must say that so far as I understand the subject the sentiments of our N. Haven brethren are more in accordance with the former than with those of the latter. And so far as the *interpretation of the bible* is concerned, Br. Taylor's students, some of them at least, whether conscious of it or not, I cannot say, in every important particular are fully with Dr. T. of Norwich & at war with Edwards. The reviewer of Taylor & Harvey does not give us the meaning of the texts which seem to cross his path; but he had adopted principles which are at war with all that Edwards has written on *original sin* & *the nature of regeneration*. If the sentiments contained in that review be correct, then Edwards was wrong in his interpretation of every text in his piece on *original sin*.

Br Taylor has not come to the most important part of his work—to give us the meaning of the bible. After abandoning imputation what he calls physical depravity, we shall be compelled to adopt the sentiments of Dr Taylor of Norwich & genuine Arminianism, or actual sin, from the commencement of the soul, or deny that infants need redemption by Xst & regeneration by the H. Spirit; or if they do need redemption, it must be a redemption from something which is not sinful in any sense, & if do need regeneration, it must be a change of something which is not sinful in any sense. If the soul be innocent, it can be redeemed from nothing, & could never join in the song of the redeemed "Unto him that loved us & washed us from our sins in his own blood." If the soul be innocent, it could not be regenerated, only for the worse. Then, if you *doubt*, as some are beginning to do, whether the soul commences at birth, would it not be idle to reason about the *nature* of that which has no existence. To admit the necessity of "redemption by the blood of Xst" & "regeneration by the supernatural influence of the H. Spirit," of something of whose *nature* we know nothing, & of whose existence we doubt, is bad Philosophy as well as bad Theology. I say these things to show that Br T. cannot stand where he is. His students do not take the ground *assumed* in his printed sermon, that "infants need redemption" & "regeneration by the H. Spirit." When interogated by Ecclesiastical bodies, "Have infants souls" They answer, "I don't know." "Do they need redemption?" "I don't know." "Regeneration?"

"I don't know." "Is it proper to pray for them?" "I don't know." "What is the meaning of such, & such texts?" "I don't know." Now I do not wonder that ministers are alarmed at N. H. Theology. Interrogations like those above will always be put to his students whenever examined by Ecclesiastical bodies. And since the alarm occasioned by the recent publications, I anticipate that ministers will be better prepared, more critical and sensitive than ever on all these points. And if Br T. cannot furnish his pupils with plain answers; & answers to that shall comport with his printed sermon, I think that they will be in a worse predicament than ever.

Have just recd the last no. of the Spectator & Hervey's & Taylor's pamphlets issued on commencement day. I have read them through, but have not time or room to give you my thoughts on paper. Hervey has adopted *nearly* my views, & Taylor in some places admits, and then again rejects them. Now he admits "infants are sinners from their birth" pa. 30th & this is in perfect accordance with his admission that they *have souls,* "need redemption by Christ," "regeneration by the Holy Spirit." & now why hesitate to admit that death in their case is "by sin!" But this he will not admit, but tries to evade it, & to prove their innocence refers to Deut. 1.39 These "little ones & children" were all from 20 years old & under. See numb. 32.11. They were not summoned to the field of battle to go up & take possession of Canaan & hence it is said they "had no knowledge between good & evil." quoad hoc. If that proves any thing to Br. Ts, purpose, it proves that all mankind under 20 years of age "have no knowledge between good & evil." He quotes also, & so does Stuart, Jonah 4.11. I have formerly heard these same texts quoted for the same purpose by Meth. & Arminians—& I feel disposed to give the old Answer. 1. It wants proof that there were infants. 2. "Cannot discern between their right hand & their left."is a proverbial expression of great ignorance in adults, & no when applied to infants. 3. It is incredible that Nineveh should contain 120,000 infants. 4. It would better accord with the book of Jonah & with our Lord's account of their ignorance & repentance to admit that 120,000 embraced the entire population who repented at the preaching of Jonah, & that the city was spared on account of their *repentance,* & not for the sake of infants—thus making void their repentance.

As to Taylor's last piece on the means of regeneration, it seems to me that he has turned the thing bottom upwards. In his description of the means of regeneration, he (includes the exercised or) of a new heart. "The (carnal) mind, which is enmity against God" suspends all its enmity & selfishness & sin for a time, & then goes to work on the principle of self-love—How long the sinner continues in this state of neutrality he does not inform us. But no matter; the sinner does not use the means of a new heart until the old heart is gone, & he is in a state favorably disposed like the prodigal son after "he came to himself."

No sinner ever did what Br. T. considers as using the means of regeneration until God had first regenerated him. The distinction between supreme selfishness & self-love in the impenitent exist only in Theory—never in matter of fact. e.g. The sinner goes to Br. T. & tells him as follows "I have always been with the old doctrine of the entire sinfulness of the doings of the unregenerate & therefore have done nothing to make a new heart. But when I saw your views I was pleased— I found that I was right, that "sin could never be the means of holiness," but that the "exercise of self-love" might. Accordingly, I have suspended my selfishness, & have not committed a single sin for some time past, & have been to work on your plan, the desire for happiness or principle of self-love & so I have "made a new heart." I have put off the old man" & I thank you for your discovery." How would Dr. Taylor like such an account? It sounds like the talk of a Pharisee. No sinner ever suspended his selfishness until subdued by divine grace. "The carnal mind"—"The enmity against God." "The heart of stone" remains until "slain"— "subdued", or "taken away" by the act of the Spirit—

A. Nettleton

Mr. Nettleton to Dr. Beecher

LETTER # 22

To Leonard Woods, Andover, Massachusetts

Worcester Oct. 26, 1829

My Dear Brother;

I recd your friendly note, together with one from Brother Tyler, just as I was entering the stage at Boston. The hint at the close has sunk deep in my heart, & I have been trying to hush all my fears—

I give you a short extract from Br Tyler's. "Since you left us I have made some progress with the review. I have advanced to my 8th sheet, & have yet worked up but a small part of my rough materials. Where this matter will end I am utterly unable to predict. There is one point which has struck me with force since you was here—that is the practical tendency of these views when exhibited in the preaching of the gospel— their tendency to destroy conviction & produce spurious conversions etc. This part of the review ought to be executed much better than I can do it."

I hope you will have a good understanding with Br Tyler, & in case they should refuse to insert his piece in the Sp. of Pilg. [Spirit of the Pilgrims, publication] that you will advise him what to do with it—I ask, would it not be well to print it, with your remarks on the note in Br Taylor's sermon? Or would it be better to publish them separate? But I have resigned the whole & pray to God to grant wisdom to guide—

In haste Yours affectionately

A. Nettleton

Rev. Leonard Woods D.D.

Andover

Mass.

LETTER #23

To an unknown correspondent. [to a faculty member at Princeton College]

Schenectady Jan 11th 1830

On motion of Dr McAuley, Resolved: That a Committee be appointed to express the sentiments of approbation which the Presbytery cherish towards the Rev. Mr. Nettleton of the Litchfield Association, & his labors of love in Malta & else where; and to request him, when convenient, to furnish this Presbytery with a detailed Memorial on the difficulties of ministers going to labor in destitute places; more particularly in cases of revivals: with as much detail as possible, of the cause helping the increase or hastening the decline of revivals of religion. Dr McAuley & Mr Tucker were appointed the Committee."

True extract from the Minutes of the Presbytery of Albany.

James V. Henry

Stated Clerk

The above ministers in 1827, were individually & as a body, denounced by the friends & followers of Mr Finney, as enemies to revivals, because they (did not) adopt they *new measures.*

The above Extract was sent to me at that time to publish, as a contradiction of the slanderous report fabricated & circulated by the *New measuremen.* It has never been published,—as it did not belong to me, Prov. XXVII. 2.

Malta in 1819, was a waste place; & what are now called *new measures* were rank among the Methodists & others, in all that region. I took a decided stand against them, which drew upon me all the power of their vengeance. We succeeded in organizing a chh. there of more than a hundred members; which for a number of years enjoyed the labors of a settled pastor. Thus, by guarding against & excluding what are now called new measures, churches have been organized, pastors settled, & the character of revivals has been elevated & the confidence of ministers & christians & the consciences of sinners more & more secured for a number of years.—But since the desperate attempt to revolutionize our churches by introducing the old, stale desolating "new measures," they have again become waste. Whether the church in Malta has shared the same fate & from the same cause, I know not. Mr Olmsted of your seminary, a native of that place will inform you. I wish you to converse with him very particularly on this subject.—By the way, will he not inform me, by mail, forthwith, whether the *anxious seats* have ever been introduced in that church, or in any of the Presbyterian meetings, or any meetings held in common with other denominations. If so I am sure they cannot retain a settled pastor long in that state of things.

In regard to the Evangelists who were on the field before me, & pushing what are now called new measures wherever they went, I observe that *one* excitement under their measures would make more noise, than 50 of far greater purity & power, conducted without them. All Evangelists who have adopted these measures in New Eng. so far as I am acquainted, have lost the confidence of settled Pastors; & for a number of years had quit the field or entered some other And, during the most powerful & intensive revivals in New Eng. for many years together I never heard of any division among ministers & churches about measures for promoting revivals of religion among us. They went on with more & more purity & power & with less & less difficulty in management, until 1826, when a desperate effort was made by Mr. F. & others from the Oneida Presb. to introduce his measures, the consequences of which are now becoming obvious to all the world. As to *settled Pastors*, who admitted the reality of revivals, & labored to promote them in *our* denomination, I say, there was no dispute & no division among them on the subject of measures, for more than 30 years previous to 1826. In proof, I appeal to *all* the religious magazines & newspapers & challenge Mr. F to point out one practice or measure that was made the subject of serious dispute or division among the friends of revivals, until—1826. The first thing I ever saw or heard on this subject was in the Western Recorder in 1827, & afterwards in the N. Y. Evangelist. These facts will be known when we are *dead*. *Prior* to this, all the ministers of *our* denomination, who admitted the glorious reality of the sacred name, which is now used with such irreverent, & frequent flippancy, so far as I know, were of *one heart & one soul* on this subject.

I do hope that Mr F's *"voice* will be heard by the Theol. Students at Princeton." That a committee will be appointed to respond to what he says on the mode of making revivals by his views of the nature of regeneration & of the anxious seat.——My kind regards to all your family & your colleagues.

Very affectionately
A. Nettleton

LETTER #24
Added to the Notes on the Christian Spectator
Sent to Rev. Leonard Woods, Andover, Massachusetts.

New York 16 Dec 1830

My dear Sir

I commenced taking some very hasty notes on the Spectator but have not time to attend to the subject—& hearing that you were intending to publish a second edition of your letters the thought occurred that I would send them to you, tho' they are of little value—

In stead of an appendix would it not be well to add another letter, directed to the Editor of the Spectator. That will give you opportunity to say some things to better advantage such as you could not otherwise— their treatment of Edwards, Dwight & Bellamy etc etc They do explain scripture to make it accord with their philosophy in relation to the character of infancy—the nature of sin, & the nature of divine influence. All these questions are determined first by philosophy & then they bend the tenets to suit it. And so is it with T's students [N. W. Taylor].

In his attempt to demolish orthodoxy I do think Dr. T. has resorted to principles & modes of reasoning which, if turned against himself would prevent him from adopting any system. His views of free-agency are such that God could not promise to "keep Xns by his power thro faith unto salvation", or to confirm saints & angels in heaven without destroying their free agency—Because a free agent *may* sin—God cannot make it impossible without performing a contradiction. He overlooks the distinction between *natural* & *moral* impossibility. Hence he cannot prove that infants *will sin* with absolute certainty without falling into the same absurdity which he charges on you. Instead of finding strong consolation in the promise of G. confirmed by two immutable things in which it is *impossible* for him to lie"—Dr T. must say that God can make no such promise without either destroying free agency or, in case he should fulfil it, he would perform a contradiction.—I was asked by one of our good brethren who was inclining to Taylor's theory on the introduction of sin "Would not your mind be relieved on the subject of God's *sincerity if it were true.*" Ans. Yes. And for the same reason that a weak man had done the best in his power. But Paul never thought of this theory in his reply to the caviler "Nay but man" "What if God willing to show his wrath & make his power etc." But when my friend had found relief on the theory that God had made free agents that he could not prevent from sinning, I should be most awfully alarmed on the subject of my own future holiness in heaven. Taylor's theory requires me to give up my confidence in God's power to prevent holy beings from sinning, & to *trust* entirely in *my own free agency* for time & for eternity, directly the reverse of some part of its influence as stated pa. 568,9. All my feelings revolt—"How can we pray" Thy will be done on earth as in heaven."

His *preceptive* will when God does all he can to make them obey? This prayer ought rather to be directed to sinners.

My notes are so eliptical that I am sure you can hardly decipher them. If you have one spare moment, do drop me a line informing when your second edition will be out. Direct to this city-tho' I may be absent it will be forwarded. Yours as ever

A. Nettleton

LETTER #25

To William B. Sprague, Albany, New York

Philadelphia Mar. 16th 1833

Mr Dear Br.

Your very acceptable letter was forwarded from New York & is just recd. It contained much in which I feel a deep interest; & tho' I cannot express on paper the thousandeth part of my thoughts, I must scribble a letter at random. I thank you for the information you give concerning the conduct of the Ed. on the Spec. & your determination in future. As to the influence which the Evangelist has had in destroying the high character which Am. revivals had acquired in Eng. & Scotland, if I can find time I will give you some account hereafter. You may have seen the letter published in a late No. of the Evangelist from Wm. Wardlaw of Glasgow. I think it is excellent & only wonder that the Ed. of that paper should consent to do it—vanity apart.

The Ed. you will observe, attempts to neutralize its effect by saying that Mr. W.'s views must have been modified by the medium thro' which they were recd—insinuating that they were recd from myself. The fact is, Mr. W. recd his views entirely through the medium of the New York Evangelist, as the letter itself has intimated—if you will narrowly observe. When Br. Dickinson and myself arrived in Edinborough, we were soon informed by some of the ministers there that doctor Wardlaw and Ewing had written to them to put them on their guard against American revivals—which fact we did not know how to understand until we arrived at Glasgow. Here I put up at the house of Wm. W. a nephew of Dr. W. and there I saw a number of the New York Evangelists.—but made not a single remark on the character of that paper as I recollect. In the course of my first visit in a large company of the Evangelical ministers and laymen, the subject of American revivals was first introduced by a gentleman with an inquiry about the effect and propriety of "anxious seats." I informed then that I had never adopted the practice & that it was never approved of in New Eng. unless they had commenced the practice since I had left America.

They all spoke with astonishment, saying that they thought the practice had been approved & adopted all over the U. States & that it was regarded as a powerful means of promoting revivals of religion. This practice, they observed had long been adopted in Eng. and Scotland— but only among a certain class of Methodists and the Ranters. The Ranters, by the way, are a denomination older than that of the Methodists, and arose about the year 1641. When the company learned my views and feelings on this subject they seemed all to be astonished— They had, what they called a "Revival Society in Glasgow" and had published a number of Narratives on Am. Revivals, and had become greatly interested; until one of their number had written to someone in N. York to send them all the information they could on the subject and the means of promoting such a work. In answer to this call they had recd a number of the N. Y. Evangelists, and had read themselves into an utter dislike both of the doctrines and measures employed in the Am. Revivals, and had become quite discouraged. And now they urged me to consent to meet the members of their Society and to disabuse them on the subject of the objectionable measures.

But as I had contended with these measures so long on one side of the Atlantic I did not wish to do it on the other. And so I held no meeting whatever on the subject. The Ed. of the Evan. or whoever he was who furnished these papers must thank himself for the effects produced by that paper. I am sure it has done more to destroy the confidence of the good people in that kingdom, in the genuineness of the Am. revivals than all the opposition ever made by their avowed enemies.

As to Beeman's preaching as you have described, I cannot say I am at all surprised. I have been aware of his movements ever since I was in Albany. I spend one afternoon and evening and a part of the next day with him at Br. Weed's house, and read him my letter to Aiken before it was sent and explained my views and told him that the measures he was then pushing would as certainly ruin the character of revivals as that the sun would continue to travel in the heavens. I also informed him that if he continued his course and was himself a Xian he would be plunged into awful darkness—as Davenport was. He knows what I think. But I have told no one of that interview except the members of the N. Lebanon convention—and there I did it in the presence of Beeman.

You have doubtless seen that the Vill. Hymns are undergoing a tedious revision by Norton in three or four of the recent No's of the N. Y. Evan.

There is much that I could reply to with success, but I do not like the attitude of self defense. I have almost been persuaded to invite someone to do it, but I do not like, even to do that. Watts, Dwight, Newton and Cooper all come under condemnation by the great critick, H. Norton of N. York. Perhaps you might say that in your paper. One of the hymns that comes under his ban, has no author's name attached to it 346 of V. H. but it is Newton's. As these hymns are used all over Engl ask Norton if he had not better send his criticisms to Eng. I have not access to these No's of the Evan. now, but I recollect that Beeman in his preface, complains of Hymns arranged under Conviction as calculated to quiet sinners in their sins; but he gets rid of the difficulty by giving him to understand that *he is a Christian* even with an "unrelenting," "stubborn" heart. 105 (106?) altered in Beeman. And Norton complained that the original represents the sinner waiting for God to "move" him. But Beeman has retained the same word in the last verse. Does he mean to tell the hard hearted sinner that he is an Xn, by placing that hymn under that head? Or does he adopt the sentiment that if an impenitent sinner will call himself a Xn. that he may then be sincere in mourning over a hard heart and may wait for God to "move" him in Beeman's book but not in Vill. Hymns. Norton has also misquoted and misrepresented the first verse of 371 Vill. H. for *Had* waited he has got it *Has*. Beeman's contains only 330 Hymns and of these I have counted more than 40 that are taken from Watts Ps. and Hymns—which of course, are not the supply. But they are determined to write it into practice by running down others. Could you not publish some parts of B.'s sermon at this meeting, and inform the public that B. has a book of his own?

A copy of a letter from "A. Nettleton to Dr Sprague"

LETTER #26

To Dr. Milo L. North, Hartford, Connecticut

Enfield Nov. 13th 1833—

My Dear Brother,

I was in Hart. a few days since & called at your former place of residence, hoping to see you; but found you had removed; & my time being limited, was obliged to return without accomplishing my wishes.—I understood that you had a letter from Hon. G. Smith, which I should like to see. Can you not favor me with a copy or an extract?

In regard to the new Theol. Sem. Br. Spring has no doubt given you a true account. But in as much as misrepresentations have gone abroad, it may be well to furnish our friends with the means of correction.

ASAHEL NETTLETON: REVIVAL PREACHER

Some of our neutral brethren effect to be grieved that they were not invited to attend the convention at E. W. [East Windsor, CT]. But neither was I invited, as was the case with many others who heard of it, & came & saw & heard & approved. Was ever a convention heard of in which all the ministers of a State were invited? Could they all be accommodated? Was this done when the N. Haven Sem. was founded? It has been falsely reported that a certain anonymous pamphlet which was distributed among the members of that convention formed the basis of their proceedings. It is true, that pamphlet was distributed at the close of the convention, as it was since at the close of the meeting of the Consociation of Hart. North. But its contents had nothing more to do with the proceedings of the one than of the other. I doubt very much whether many of the members of that convention knew a single word of its contents until after they had returned to their homes. That pampht had nothing more to do in the founding of our new Sem. [The Theological Institute] than it had in the founding of Yale College.

Whatever may be the private opinion of individual members of that body, the ground which they took is simply this—that ministers whose views are expressed in the confession of faith published by the Pastoral Union of the State of Con. have the same right to educate young men for the ministry & to publish their sentiments to the world, as the founders of the N. H. Sem. have to do what they have done. Nothing more. Nothing less. Having heard the name of Dr Humphrey used against us, I wrote him on the subject & recd an answer, from which I made extracts, & put them into the hands of Br Vanarsdalen (?) which you can see; &, if you think proper send to your correspondent, Hon. C. Smith. I would like you to do it, as you are so well acquainted with him. As most of our Trustees have accepted of their appointment, perhaps, if the subject were explained to him, he would be willing to do it still. I wish you would ascertain this point for us. At any rate, I wish him to know the ground we have taken, & the feelings of Dr Humphrey on this subject.

I have recd a letter from Dr Griffin, in which he says. "I rejoice exceedingly at the firm stand which the brethren of Connecticut have taken against the New Haven school, by establishing another *in the same State*. All whose *hearts* are on that side, though their *feet* professedly stand on fence, are alarmed, & deplore such a division among brethren. But if we love the Saviour & his truth more than our erring brethren, we must maintain his truth & his honor tho' it separates between us & them. If the errors be cardinal, there can be no doubt on this subject. And that they are cardinal in the present case, will soon be believed by all who do not embrace them. I vote for the new school with all my heart."

"I had a letter from brother Tyler the other day, asking my advice. I spoke decidedly in favor of his acceptance of his appointment."—"I am willing & even desirous that this letter should be shown where it can do any good." etc. etc.

Dr. Church, one of the leading ministers in the State of N. Hampshire, hearing of the appointment of Dr Tyler, as President of our Sem. wrote him a letter, from which Dr. T. sent me the following extracts.

"You are," says he, "devoted to Christ & his cause, & he may employ you as he sees good. Thus he has done. Your removals have hitherto been for the advancement of knowledge & holiness. And for similar purposes you may be advantageously removed again. And if the proposed Sem. is found for Christ & goes into successful operation for him, your usefulness to the church may be much increased by being placed at the head of it. An institution of the kind proposed, I think is much needed in Connecticut at this time, & may be more needed hereafter. In such a Sem. by the grace of God, you may exert a very good & extensive influence; & I think you are bound on christian principles to listen to overtures on the subject, & hold yourself in readiness to take charge of it, if the Lord so direct in his providence. And the united voice of men of faith & prayer whose business it is to select a presiding officer, you may & ought to regard as an intimation of your duty. This should be considered fully by your people. They should regard the greater good which you may do to the cause which they so much love, by your removal, & cheerfully acquiesce in it."

You will pardon me for sending you these extracts—but they will tell you how many of our best ministers feel on this subject. Since his appointment Br. Tyler has been on to see us, & to survey the ground. He feels very much as we do. He read to us a number of letters which he had recd on this subject from ministers of the first standing for piety & influence from different parts of New Eng. all very much in the same strain—like that of Br Humphrey, expressing freely & decidedly their solemn conviction of the alarming tendency of the N. H. divinity.

Please send by Br Robbins, if time will permit, otherwise by mail.

Yours affectionately

A. Nettleton

P. S. Make just what you please of this letter—My regards to Mrs North & other friends.

LETTER #27

To the honorable John C. Smith, Sharon, Connecticut

                   Alexandria D. Ce. March 4th 1834

Hon J. C. Smith

Dear Sir,

I have just seen your disavowal, which is copied from the N. Haven Rel. Intel., [Religious Intelligencer] & is now going the rounds in the public papers.—As I was instrumental in securing that appointment, I must apologize for the offence. We had some previous intimations of your views & feelings in regard to the N. H. theology, which seemed to be very much in accordance with our own. In a letter to Dr North, as you will recollect, was a sentiment of yours in language, nearly as follows: "I have been reading & chafing over the last no. of the Ch. Spectator & if I understand the writers, there is brewing at N. Haven a heresy of fearful dimensions." Had we been wholly ignorant of your views on a subject of such vital importance to the interests of religion, we certainly should not have made the appointment—& so have been guilty of such a gross impropriety as we now stand charged with before the public—of using your "name unauthorized" for a purpose which never entered my heart. The writer of that notice accompanies it with a remark which does great injustice to the friends of the new Seminary. He adds: "Gov. Smith is a friend to Yale College, & it is not right his name should be made use of unauthorized to strengthen the hands of those who are striving to injure its prosperity." Did Gov. Smith "authorize" any one thus publicly to impeach our motives in making that appointment? Tho' others may, & doubtless will continue to impute our conduct to such unworthy motives—"is it right that the name of Gov. Smith should be made use of unauthorized" to fasten this public stigma upon us?— Besides—Is The N. Haven theology so identified with the "interests of Yale College" that you cannot withdraw your hand from the former without "injuring the interests" of the latter?—That all her power & influence must be wielded in favor of what neither the judgment, nor conscience, nor piety of our best ministers cannot approve? So this matter now stands before the public. And so let it be. Of the two evils we feel happy in the consciousness that we have chosen the least. As ministers & as christians, we do greatly prefer to bear the imputation of "striving to injure the interests" of our Alma Mater than to lend the sanction of our names any longer in aiding on a "heresy of fearful dimensions." And the latter, it seems, is the attitude in which your name now stands forth before the public. Nor do I believe—judging from the difficulties with which myself & others have had to encounter in a similar struggle—it will be in your power to rescue it again from that perversion without another public disavowal. It is generally believed that a crisis is coming in the providence of God when neutrality will be impossible. The evil we deplore has been let alone too long already—It is known to be of such a nature that it will never cure itself. The admission of such a thought would be an impeachment of the character of the wisest & best sons of the church in every age. Those ministers whose knowledge & experience & piety ought to qualify them to be the most competent judges do very generally unite in the opinion that an undermining process has long been working ruin in our churches—& that silence & inaction cannot longer be observed without, virtually abandoning the whole field to the adversary. Much as you may know on most subjects, you cannot understand this matter as well as those watchmen of Zion who have entered into its arcana, & have been intimately acquainted with its origin & progress in spite of argument & friendship & counsel & entreaty & warning & lamentation. I am certain—for I have tried it for more than *thirteen years, faithfully*, as my correspondence, if ever collected will show—that no kindness or magnanimity on our part will be appreciated or regarded, but as it ceases to oppose the N. Haven theology & falls in with it. Silence is construed into acquiescence. And every thing which has been done, or can be done, short of *open* & *decided resistance* is despised & ridiculed & trampled upon as timidity & tameness. Those ministers who have examined this matter the most thoroughly, do solemnly believe that God in his providence is now designing to try the strength of moral principle. The tendency of the N. Haven theology is developing itself more & more in spurious conversions—in lowering, & lowering exceedingly the character of piety in our churches—& is fast running out genuine revivals of religion; & is bringing up in their place a religion with which our best ministers & christians have no fellowship. And what is not a little mortifying to the sons of the Pilgrims who travel thro' England & Scotland & the U. States, this disasterous influence is every where diffusing itself & is known to originate in the once peaceful & happy state of Con. And not a redeeming consideration is left—not a light or a signal appears to the gazing millions to inform them that her glory has not departed. My love to Brother Perry. Most affectionately yours

A. Nettleton
Hon. J. C. Smith
Sharon, Connecticut

LETTER #28

To Leonard Woods, Andover, Massachusetts

Portland June 18th 1834

Rev. & Dear Sir,

Yours of the 6th was recd just as I was on the point of starting for Boston—on a visit to N. Bridgewater to lay the subject of our Sem. once more before Mr Thompson in behalf of the Trustees. We are not willing to give him up without making one more effort. My impression is that he would have accepted the appointment had it not been for the influence of his ministerial brethren who accord with us in sentiment, but do not feel the importance of doing any thing to prevent the spread of the evil we deplore. And now my belief is that he only wants counsel from his brethren in whom he feels confidence. Without some such aid I do not see how he can well ask for a dismission without seeming too desirous to leave. Can you not write him on the subject of accepting his appointment as it is continued by the Trustees—& write in such a manner that he may read your letter to his people. Also, request your son to do the same, as (I) know Mr T. feels great confidence in your family; & could he be fully *assured* that you both felt full confidence in his qualifications for the office & a sincere desire that he would accept it, I am persuaded that he would be inclined to do it—perhaps in September. Can you not give the hint to Dr Codman, or some minister in Mr Thompson's Association to become his advocate in this matter? In so doing I think you will render essential service to the cause of Christ. Verbum sat——

I was misinformed about Dr Porter's letter to Dr Beecher——that it was just before his death. I should be pleased to receive a copy of it if convenient & proper. Dr B read it to me shortly after he recd it, & desired it come to aid him in writing an answer. I informed him that I agreed with Dr P in what he had written.

Your pieces in the Lit. & Theol. Review are read with uncommon interest, & universal approbation by *our* ministers so far as I can learn. The work too is quite popular, & we think will do much good. I have read your pieces with deep interest—because they are so intimately connected with the subject of experimental religion.

You desired me to send you my remarks on the article in the Spec. which I have done without one word of alteration. I fear it will not answer your expectation. It was only the spontaneous effusions of my heart in a letter to a brother minister, or which I had preserved the copy which I herewith send you. It does not contain a fourth part of my serious objections to that article. I do not consider its professed admissions as a fair statement of the real doctrines of that school. I have read it to a no. of ministers of that school who positively deny that there is any such "infallible tendency or propensity to sin in that constitution or nature of that soul." At the same time there is continual perversion of the orthodox views, which, in unrenewed men, we have been wont to regard as a mark of enmity. I wish I had time to state all my objections, even to that piece, with long quotations, but I cannot do it on paper.—

I am by no means certain that you will approve of my remarks & I have written may need explanation. These subjects are so familiar to your own mind that, I confess I feel great reluctance in sending this sheet. And I should not consent to do it but for the benefit which I hope to receive from your faithful remarks on what you may think is out of the way.—If you approve on the whole, & are prepared to defend my remarks, I wish you to read them to Br. Skinner, but not without. As I am expecting to make some stay in & about this place—perhaps for two or three weeks— please drop me a line soon. Yours very truly & affectionately

A. Nettleton

P. S. Query 1st. The N. H. divines in that article admit the difficulty & ? apologize for it, just as all sinners do. Is not this worse than an absolute denial of its existence?—Suppose I should boldly assert from the sacred desk, "My hearers, I admit that you all have an "infallible tendency or propensity to sin"—but this is not sinful—Some have a strong, infallible propensity to lie, cheat, & steal, but this is not "sinful"—it is neither *bad, vile, vicious nor pernicious* as you have all formerly been taught by orthodox divines, in every sermon of their both from the pulpit & the press. etc. etc. If I were to come out in this style would they not revolt at once? Query 2. Did any sinner ever make a holy choice, or give his heart to God—as the N. H. divines insinuate—without a previous change in this *tendency* or *propensity* to sin? Again. They assume that any definition of regeneration which does not advance it to be an act of the sinner is wrong.

Query 3. If God works *in the sinner to will* in regeneration is not God's agency *prior to* or *back* of action as really and absolutely as on the scheme which they oppose? Admitting that the affections* are under the entire control of the will as the muscles of the body are, & that whenever the sinner wills it, all his affections obey,—still the sinner may plead how can I *will* to change my affections unless God first works in me to *will* etc. And the N. H. divines, to be consistent, must deny that God does in any way move the will. I have not room to explain. The testers & exercisers are united in making God the author & sole mover in securing the effect—regeneration.

Both equally abhor an attempt to make the sinner feel his independence for the sake of pressing his obligation. Pardon my haste.

★ (or suppose the sinner) has no affections—nothing but a (? &) that he loves God with his will (his) tendency has to sin notwithstanding—as then philosophy (courage) to assume—yet if they allow that God works in him to *will*, they gain nothing—but lose all advantage in pressing his obligation—unless you go a step farther & deny that God does work in him to *will*. The sinner might ask this N. H. divine what can I do to deserve or command that influence?

LETTER #29

To Rev. L. Woods, Andover, Massachusetts
Copy of a letter to Dr. Taylor

E. Windsor July 14th 1835

My dear Sir

Yours of the 2d ins. arrived in my absence. Hence this delay. You say: "I did not approve of our conducting such a correspondence *by proxy.*" I thought you did; for so it had been conducted on your part by Mr Swift, who in his letter to Dr Tyler says: "The responsibility of investigation rests mainly upon myself, and if God spares my life a little longer, I am determined in his help it shall be known whether the report is true or false." I approve of the "determination" of Mr Swift in this matter & why should you attempt to take it out of his hands?

You say: "I consider a *personal interview* between us, as altogether a preferable mode of attempting the explanation which the case deemed to demand." This "personal interview" you have had, *first* at N. Haven &, *then*, at E. Windsor. The only interview I have had with you since my return from Europe were on this and no other subject, so far as I can recollect.

You say: "I had preferred *no charge* against you, as you represent." (In a) letter which I recd last Spring, the writer says: "An Episcopal minister told me three or four weeks since—as he was informed by a disciple of Dr Taylor—that a scheme was in progress to convict you of *falsehood*, & to expose you to the world. I thought it incredible & paid no attention to it. Now, however, I believe there is a "desparate effort" making to cover Dr Taylor with the skin flayed (?) From your back."—I have since been waiting & wondering what the good brother who sent me the above could possible (allude?) to. Your letters are expounding the matter. You say: "I had preferred *no charge* against you as you represent." Indeed! You have certainly expressed your belief that I am the author of a false & slanderous report. And if this does not amount to a charge I know not what does. You have further said: "In my own view I should now be fully authorized to believe you to be the *original author of the reports specified.*" Were I to inform you that there was a report in circulation that you had been guilty of some scandalous sin, & that "from certificates which I have obtained from different individuals, it appears, as the case at present stands, that the report is true."——And suppose you & your friends had in vain requested me to inform you *what* the sin is & *who* the persons are who have certified the same, in what terms would you speak of my conduct? Should you not feel that I was bound to give you the information, & that I acted a very unchristian part in refusing to do it?—— And especially if I should be calling on you to bring some accusation against it yourself either on this, or, on some other subject? You say: "That you may have no pretext for withholding the explanation required on the ground that I refuse to specify the *reports* alluded to, I would refer you to the *questions* in my letter of June 1834, as specifying the *points* on which I wish you to answer." "The report," it seems, is growing into *reports & questions & points* which have nothing to do with the subject.

"You refer me to the *questions.* I am not thus to be diverted from one thing to another. See Luke 23:9. I regard this only as "a pretext for withholding the information required." You have charged me with being the *criminal author* of a *false* report—& you tell me too that it is *certified* by different individuals; & yet "you pertinaciously refuse to tell me what it is. Instead of flying off to *report & question & point* you will please to stick *to the point.* "A report" you say "which I deem? false & highly injurious to me has been circulated; & accordingly certificates which I have obtained from different individuals appears, as the case at present stands to be traced to you as the author. "The report," to which I did suppose you & Mr Swift have "according to certificates, obtained by Dr Tyler from different individuals, appears, as the case at present stands, to be traced to yourself & Mr Finney as the authors." If you allude to something else I cannot divine what it is. You are urging me to tell both your dream & the interpretation thereof.-

But as *you have obtained certificates from different individuals concerning one report* without much aid from any statements of my own, I prefer that you should go on as you have begun. And tho you seem to be shy of the names, yet one thing is certain, you cannot in conscience under any defence whatever, withhold from me the charges or things certified.

You say: "As to informing you *who* the persons were (who) have certified; this was at my option; nor a matter ? claim by you." So I now say, as to answering your questions—"this was at my option; not a matter of just claim by you."

There is, however, nothing in your questions wh(ich I am) unwilling to answer either publicly or privately, but, I wish to remind you that in urging your claims upon me, you have adopted a principle which has fastened all those charges & insinuations on yourself. Why have you so long neglected to answer the questions specified in "Dr Woods' Letters to Dr Taylor?" They are identically the same which you put to me in your letter of June 1834. On reading Dr Woods' 8th letter to you published 1830, one would think you had selected your questions from the list which he specified, & then & there called on you to answer in behalf of his brethren. "The difficulty," says Dr Woods, "lies not at all between you & me personally but between you & the Christian community. And if you will in any way satisfy them etc etc. I, & others shall have nothing to do, but to testify our joy that our mistake has been corrected, & our entire confidence in your restored; & so the whole matter may come at once to a happy termination." "But," he continues, "in order to bring about this happy result, there is evidently some thing for you to do." This you have not done. Hence, he might now adopt your own language & say: "That you might have no pretext for withholding the explanation required, on the ground that I refused to specify the points alluded to, I would refer you to the *question* in my 8th letter of July 1830, as specifying the points on which I wish you to answer, beginning with"—page 102, "In the *first* place etc onward to the end. Dr Woods, as I understand has rather recently been pushing you for an answer. The years have nearly elapsed & no reply to "Dr Woods Letters to Dr Taylor" has yet appeared to my knowledge, unless *by proxy*, a measure which "you do not approve" in others.

When a champion has thus appeared in presence of all the armies of the living God—if the figure suits you—& he has stood calling on you, so long & so loud as to be heard & seconded across the Atlantic,; I cannot but ask, Why do you attempt to divert public attention by turning aside in search of one among the crowd or in one cave. See 1 Sam 24:14—

And now on the principles assumed in your letters to me, all the ministers who differ from you on the points specified, & in whose name Dr Woods addressed his letters to you, I say all these ministers as a body,

or each & every one singly may adopt your own language to me, & say:
"I had hoped that the letters which Dr Woods wrote you July 1830,
would have secured a satisfactory explanation from you, long before this,
at least that you would have deemed them worthy of notice. In this I
have been disappointed. And not only so. Such was the (?) in which the
subject was presented in those letters, that in my view I should now, on
account of your long (refusal?) to reply, be fully authorized to believe
you to be the *advocate* (of the ?) doctrines, & hence, the responsible
author of the reports certified." Nor shall I feel under any obligation to
either as a Christian or "a gentleman" to answer yours of June 1834, until
I have publically answered the call of Dr Woods in 1830. It (will?) be
obtrusively taking the matter out of his & your own hands. (How?) can
you as "a christian" or "a gentleman," ask me to do it; until you have first
put in practice your own lesson. "Brother, deal frankly." Come out &
"Show Thyself a man."—

You profess to be "*utterly unable to say on what point of Christian faith we
differ.*" And yet I have disputed you face to face, day after day & night
after night whenever I met you ever since 1821, with feelings of deep
concern, as God knows, & as your own conscience will, sooner or later,
testify. But, I need not be surprised at this; as I have heard of your saying
the same in regard to Dr Woods, Dr Tyler & others with whom you
have been publicly contending for several years past. To your
controversy with them I refer you to learn the points of difference
between us; & if you have not all this time been "beating the air" your
mind may be satisfied—

You say: "There is now, I am sorry to say, too much reason for
believing that you intend to avoid a personal interview with me on this
subject. And especially from what Mr Bacon informed me. He put the
question to you, as he answers me several times *where you might be found*;
& you pertinaciously declined giving an answer."

The case was this. I met Mr Bacon, passing the door of the house of Dr
Tyler, on his return fro Enfield Gen. Assn. He asked me if I was ever
coming to N. Haven. To wh. I replied; I may, perhaps, in case you have
business for me. I then invited him into the house. Among other things, I
informed him what I had heard Mrs Dunning, Mr & Mrs Donnaghe say,
in the winter of 1833, when I was *last* in N. Haven, viz; that "Mr
Nettleton has exposed himself to ecclesiastical censure." This was all
news to me. I desired them to state to me the ground of his complaint
that Mr Bacon should be trumpeting such a report in the city of N.
Haven; but they could not inform me. I then concluded to call on Dr

Taylor & ascertain from him; but was given to understand that "Mrs Taylor was very bitter against Mr Nettleton." I then repaired to the study of Dr Taylor in college. I knocked at his door; but hearing no voice, I called & spent the evening with President Day, & left for N. York in the morning. On meeting Br. Bacon at E. Windsor I invited him into a room alone for the express purpose of ascertaining from him what he alluded to when he reported in N. Haven that "Mr Nettleton had exposed himself to ecclesiastical censure." I put the question to him seven times: "On what ground did you make such a report?" But he "perniciously declined giving any answer"——except a difficulty in his memory. Nor do I yet ever surmise what it can be.——

I would thank you to ask Brother Bacon, whether he did not say, at the house of Esquire Dixon in Enfield, that "Mr Nettleton (has) done nothing but mischief for ten years past." & whether Mrs Bacon did not attempt to apologize for what he said on the ground that Mr N. had been, & was still partially insane——

Now it so happens that the eldest daughter of Esquire Dixon professes to be one of an interesting circle of young converts under my recent labors at Enfield——also, another member of the same family. I bring no charge against Br. Bacon. He doubtless thinks he is doing great good & sincerely desires to bring about a reconciliation, where alienation has never been expressed only on one side.——As to my refusing an interview with you on *this* or any other subject, it is not correct. But as Brs. Taylor & Bacon & Swift & other ministers had been so long talking & writing & obtaining certificates against me, & that too in such a public manner all over the world without saying one word to me on the subject; & this matter was known at Princeton & Andover. I did inform Br. Bacon that I had been *advised* not to consent to a private settlement. But whether I had concluded to follow that advice I did not (?) On this subject I have never sought nor Claimed (?) an interview. Mr Swift says: "I told him Mr Punderson——that this was a charge so definite that it could be scratched out, & the truth or falsity of it ascertained, I would pledge myself to him that it should be done." I shall do nothing to interfere with the fulfilment of this pledge. But shall do all in my power to help him to redeem it.

But, after I shall have seen Mr Swift, & learned from him how the matter stands, *then*, since you have requested an interview in your own name; I now inform you that whenever you are ready, & shall give due notice, I will, with pleasure, meet you & all my accusers face to face at E. Windsor.

Yours as ever
A. Nettleton
To Rev. L. Woods, D.D. Andover Mass
East Windsor, Ct
July 24th

LETTER #30

To George P. Shipman, New York, New York

Sag Habor Sept 21st 1835

My Dear Br,

As Br. Pillsbury is going West on business, of which no doubt you have been informed, I should like to put into his hands $2.000 if it can be obtained in season.

Sands informed me that he thought he could pay me $500 shortly—If the $500 of which you spoke in your last can be obtained without much trouble, you may hand it to Br. Pillsbury. If I can obtain the other 1000 I shall sent it to him, but I fear I shall not be in season, as I am under the necessity of going to Hartford. If you can borrow the remainder for a few days or weeks I think I shall be able to replace it punctually. At any rate I must request you to send me a line to Hartford immediately informing me what sum you & sands shall be able to make out, so that I may send a check for the remainder. Please to put a letter in the office on Wednesday as I am hoping to be in Hartford on Thursday.

Yours very affectionately
A. Nettleton

P. S. Should you find it difficult to make out the $2000 perhaps you & sands may make out $1,600. Please inform by mail as soon as possible. Direct to Hartford.

Mr. Geo. P. Shipman
N. York

LETTER #31

To Bennet Tyler, East Windsor, Connecticut

Petersburg Feb 4th 1836

My Dear Br,

Yours of the 27th is just recd & all its statements, as I understand them are correct. The meeting of the orthodox ministers in Dr. Beecher's study at Boston on Oct. 1829, I wish you to understand, was at my particular request & for the express purpose of disclaiming any fellowship with the speculations of Dr Taylor & to make the impression that if he continued to push them upon our churches, he & their authors must alone share all the responsibility of the mischief wh. they would certainly produce. My fears had become greatly increased by the following brief history of facts. In 1827 in feeble health I was ordered south—& by Dr Rice was conducted to Prince Edward in Virginia. The same prejudices against the N. England ministers which are said to prevail in other parts of the Presbyterian church, I do suppose were equally strong in Virginia. But in process of time, as my health encreased I began to preach & visit in little circles—which Bacon now ridicules—a deep solemn, silent & almost universal seriousness prevailed all the region. And some of the first lawyers, & persons in the higher classes of society became deeply interested, & joyful in hope in a manner "unexampled in Virginia,"—as it would seem from a letter to Dr Alexander in the Memoirs of Dr Rice, pa. 343. This was in the Spring & Summer of 1828. The time would fail me to give you an account of the character & extent of this revival in a number of Counties in all the surrounding region. Some I have known to come more than 20, 30, or even 40 miles in their covered carriages— & generally, they were persons who regarded themselves as unconverted, & would even solicit the privilege of attending the meeting of inquiry & other circles for religious conversation. In this manner the work spread into the adjoining counties & distant part of the State. Dr Rice would often say that the work has gone among a class hitherto uninfluenced by the subject of religion—You never had such a hold on any population in your life as you now have on that class in Virginia. Pardon me for saying this. In writing this little sketch I have done violence to my sense of propriety, & crossed every fibre of my heart.—In this state of things I was about to return to the North to avoid the excessive heat of summer. But lest I should not return, was prevailed on by Dr Rice to cross the Mountains, & spend the season near the Springs & so return in the fall, which I did not do until the early part of 1829. Meanwhile certain disciples of Dr Taylor had visited Prince Edward, &, during my absence, had set the whole Seminary agog on the wonderful discoveries which had recently been made by Dr Taylor of N. Haven. As the story was going he had discovered the *essence of sin*— which was likely to make as great a revolution in the systems of theology, as was in the science of chemistry on the discovery of the *basis of potash* by Sir Humphrey Davy. But they were regarded by Dr Rice & others as the rankest Pelagianism. At this time Dr Taylor's concio ad clerum & the first number of the Quarterly Ch. Spec. had found their way into Virginia. With the first no. Dr Rice recd a letter from Prof. Goodrich, informing

him that the first Article on the means of regeneration was from the pen
of Dr Taylor—"an attempt," he remarked, "to explain the reason why
Nettleton's preaching has been so much blessed." "I want you to read
that article" said Dr R. "& give me your opinion." I told him I had read
it, & do not & never did agree with Dr Taylor on that, & many other
subjects, connected with it.—

   Hitherto all jealousies & suspicions about the N. Eng. ministers &
theology had, so far as I could learn, been entirely discipated in the great
revival of religion which was still advancing in all the region; & there was
never such a call for ministers in the State of Virginia. And the cause of
Presbyterianism was never to prosperous, & many whose predilections
had heretofore been only Episcopal, were seeking entrance into the
Presbyterian church, as is well known in all Virginia. No ministers were
more popular or welcome now than congregational ministers from N.
Eng.—All would have recd them with open arms. As Dr Beecher was
well known to be a particular friend & favorite of mine—&coworker in
stemming the current & fury of new measures, his name stood first on the
list. Wherever I went his name went, & vice versa. But now the scene
was beginning to change. What do you think of the N. Haven divinity?
& what do ministers generally think in N. Eng? was the enquiry
everywhere. And I could not be silent on these forthcoming
speculations, without raising the suspicion against all N. Eng. &, the
frankness of the Virginian would not allow me to be silent for the sake of
dividing the tremendous responsibility with Goodrich & Taylor in a
matter of such infinite moment to the souls of men. I spent a number of
days with Dr R. & his pupils in explaining my views on these
speculations & in disabusing myself & N. Eng.—& ventured to
exonerate Dr Beecher from any share in that responsibility which, it
seems, he is determined to take on himself. Dr Rice was the first person
who I ever heard call the New Haven speculations Pelagianism, & his
views had been derived entirely from their published writings & their
disciples. On my return to N. E. in the summer of 1829 I spent 10 days
with Dr Taylor at N. H. informing him of the mischief he and his pupils
were doing at the South, & laboured to bring him to take ground on
these doctrines in which we could all unite. Of the result of this
interview, & the topics discussed I may give you some account hereafter.
I then went to Hartford, where I met Dr Beecher who read me a letter he
had recd from Dr Porter, complaining of his declining orthodoxy. He
read it again in a circle of ministers in Dr study. I afterwards met the
ministers in the memorable conference with Dr Taylor in Dr Porter's

study at Andover, which terminated in a determination expressed by Dr Woods to publish, as he did, his 8 letters to Dr Taylor. Having determined to visit the South with Dr Porter, I thought it best to foreclose the possibility of being claimed in future by Dr Taylor or his pupils, as was the case in the South & else where, I forwarded a note from Andover to Dr Beecher, desiring him to assemble the orthodox ministers in his study in the morning of a specific day which was done. I then declared to them the (unrest) that was rising in Virginia & else where the consequence of the speculations of Dr Taylor & his pupils, wherever I met them, & the jealousies wh. had been laid but which would inevitably be raised against myself, & all N. E.—I told them, I knew it was a matter of little consequence in itself whether I agreed with Dr Taylor or not; but to prevent any future misunderstanding, I desired them distinctly to understand that such were my views of the tendency of his doctrines in running out genuine revivals of religion. That if all N. Eg. went over to them I should prefer to stand alone.

And I desired the ministers present to announce that fact to others. The ministers retired, & I went into the woodhouse with Dr B. as you have been informed.—But, in the evening of the same day Dr B. read me a piece of his on infant depravity with wh. I was pleased. And I understood Dr B. to say that as he was writing that piece, in taking aim, he thought he saw the head of Dr Taylor in his way; & if he did not get out of his way, he shouts fire & knock him over. I understood him to say that he told this to Dr. T. All this satisfied my mind that he did not after all his threats agree with Dr T. & that he did really wish me so to understand him. Accordingly I left him & on my way South called at N. Haven & Bacon asked my opinion whether Dr B. agreed with Dr T.—I informed him that he did not. But one year after in 1830, at the anniversary at Andover, I met Dr Beecher in the street with Bacon at his side, & Dr Beecher called me to account for what I had said to Bacon. "Why did you report that I did not agree with Dr Ta.?" "Indeed, said I, but what did you read to me? It is easily contradicted. I will now report that you do agree with him." "No you shall not." What then shall I say? what are you if you are not a Taylorite? What shall I say when others ask me what you are? "*Tell them Taylor is me,*" was his reply. From that time to the present I have not felt at liberty to say yes or no to the question which has hundreds of times been asked by ministers, "Where does Dr. Beecher stand?" Does he agree with Dr. Taylor? My answer is, you must ask him.—I have sent copies of your long letter to Stowe in answer to his inquiries; to Dr. Miller, and H. S. Pratt, omitting only the following sentence: "I have heard him express his disapprobation of the course pursued by S Phila"—This is all correct; but tchinson & myself thought it not put it into the hands of any ex & Beecher. In regard to the letter of Dr Rice in his Memoirs pa. 243 can you not send it to the Watchman with the name of Dr Alexander to whom it was directed—omitting the first paragraph & the names of Shirk & Young?

Yours truly A. N.

Rev. B. Tyler D.D.

E. Windsor

Connecticut

LETTER #32

To Leonard Woods, Andover, Massachusetts

E. Windsor Mar. 8th 1837

Rev. & Dear Sir,

You will pardon me in sending you another hasty line, on the subject of my last. You will observe that they have published it in the N. Haven Intelligence as the result of the meeting with Dr Taylor in Dr Porter's study in 1829. Just as I had anticipated. They have since published it in the Con. Obs. & N. Y. Evangelist. In the two last no's of the Evangelist, Finney & Leavett have virtually both come out Perfectionists, & justify the modern Perfectionists in claiming to be perfect. But what is most remarkable of all is that Leavitt should publish in these nos of his paper a remarkable *prediction, & its exact fulfilment on the same sheet.* In your letter to Mr Plumer you say: "Dr Porter, Mr Everts & Dr Cornelius were most deeply alarmed & distressed with the loose speculations which have come from the N. Haven school & from Mr Finney & others of that stamp. I know how they all felt, & what a full conviction they had that the notions wh. were peculiar to Dr Taylor & Mr Finney, would, if they prevailed undermine the fair fabric of our evangelical churches & spread a system far more unscriptural & pernicious then Wesleyan Methodism." Now what could be more in point. Their fears were well founded, as the two last nos of the Evangelist fully demonstrate. Finney in those nos, recommends Wesley on perfection, etc etc. I do not wonder that Leavetts imagination was frightened with the witch of Endor, or rather with the ghost of Samuel. But I must not enlarge. We are all waiting your movements in this matter. As the time for the mail has nearly expired I must stop my scribbling hoping to hear from your soon. In great haste

Yours truly

A. Nettleton

The above facts are too good not to be published to the world in juxtaposition.

Rev. L. Woods D.D.

Andover

Mass

Letter #33

To William A. Hallock

E. Windsor July 29th 1837

My Dear Brother

In answer to yours of the 27th I beg leave to say that I am personally acquainted with the Rev. J. A. James, & regard him as an excellent man & minister of Christ. Most of his published works I regard as purely evangelical & adapted to do great good. But I cannot say the same in regard to his "Anxious Inquirer directed & *encouraged.*" The title will indicate my objection. He confounds the anxious sinner with the young convert—says *You* whose religion is so feeble—*your tender piety*—*pious feeling* etc. & speaks of them as *newborn babes*, & as *lambs of the flock*. This, I know is common in England. But were I to enumerate the probable causes operating to prevent deep conviction of sin & powerful revivals of religion in that country I should name this mode of treating awakened sinners as among the most prominent. "The great good alleged as having been done, by such works I fear will not bear examination. Many have been *comforted* but not *converted*. So did not Pres. Edwards (Vol. 3pp 34, 195 6)

Indeed your letter has expressed my mind fully on this subject. In this opinion, I doubt not, the leading minds in N. Eng. will unite.

Yours truly

Asahel Nettleton

Rev. Wm A. Hallock

N. York

LETTER #34

To Leonard Woods, Andover, Massachusetts

E. Windsor Hill Aug 28th 1837

Rev. & Dear Sir,

I wrote you some time since a letter which I desired you to read to Rev. Baxter (?) Dickinson, should he call on you at Andover. In case you recd that letter, will you be so good as to return it by mail informing, in it, whether you read it to Mr Dickinson. Perhaps he has taken it with him or you may have forwarded it to Lane Sem.—if so please inform me as soon as convenient. My object is to ascertain *whether*, & if so *when* he recd it. Also, as I kept no copy, I wish to obtain one.

I have just seen & read with pleasure your letter to Br. Tyler. As you say, I have no doubt that "Taylorism is going to be let out at the tale of the cart." My reflection on that remark is this: "If Drs. Woods & Tyler have done the church a good service in demonstrating its contents to be bad, have not the Gen. Assembly done nobly in taking a lift at the cart to let it out?"

Yours affectionately
A. Nettleton
Rev. L. Woods D.D.
Andover
Mass

LETTER #35

To an unidentified correspondent

E. Windsor Feb. 6th 1838.

My Dear Brother,

Yours of the 24th ult is just recd, as I have but just returned from laboring a little in a place made waste by a series of protracted meetings & revivals of modern stamp! Many of the subjects of those revivals are now all *unconverted*, & some of them have come out joyful, & now do solemnly declare that they have never before been under conviction of sin or known any thing about regeneration.

I cannot give you particulars only that they now declare that the doctrines wh. they have been taught they do know to be false from their own personal experience. I should be exceedingly glad to labor as I did before I had the typhus fever in 1822, were it not that the Gen. Association of this State have adopted resolutions against all Evangelists as injurious to the cause of religion, as you doubtless have heard and I have never been in the habit of obtr any labors (of) settled Pastors as you know—especially would it now be improper even would my health permit.

In regard to the business on which you wrote—the land in Illinois, I have nothing to say—I leave it wholly with them & you to direct.

In great haste
Yours as ever
A. Nettleton

Letter #36

To Eleazar Lord, Tappan, New York

Elizabethtown Feb. 5th 1839

My Dear Friend,

Yours of the 2d inst. is just recd. As I have not been to New Brunswick the one directed to that place has not been recd. On my way there I called here, expecting to take the next car. But Br Murray informed me that he had engaged to take an agency in behalf of the salaries of Princeton Professors during the month of Jan. & that I must, if possible, supply his pulpit interim.

To this I consented. Br M. visited N. York & Phila. & succeeded far beyond his expectations. I have preached several times—but held no extra meetings except *one* for the youth, one evening only. Last week, was confined to the house, & mostly to my bed with sick headache & bilious complaint. As I began to recover Br Murray was taken down & confined in like manner;- is better, but not able to preach. Meetings have been more crowded & solemn than usual. A number are enquiring—& some recently rejoicing in hope. Of the latter, 4 in one house. I rejoice to hear that you have organized a church, & have a Lecture room. I am hardly able to labor, & the travelling is becoming bad on the braking up of Spring. I think you will do well to continue to obtain supplies as usual for the present. In case I find it convenient to visit you, I will come on without any ceremony—& preach if able & the way be open. If not, will be silent & have the pleasure of a visit, if nothing more.

Love to all your family.

Yours very affectionately

Asahel Nettleton

Eleazar Lord Esq

Tappan

York State

Letter #37

To Charles Hodge, Princeton, New Jersey

E. Windsor Sept. 10th 1839

My Dear Brother,

This note will introduce to your acquaintance the Rev. Wm Thompson, Prof. Bib. Lit. in our Seminary, an esteemed & valued friend of mine—unobtrusive, & somewhat retiring,—you will find him a man very much after your own heart. He has long been desirous of becoming acquainted with the officers of your Seminary & especially with yourself.

He is on a short visit at a sister's in the vicinity of N. York. I desired him to improve this opportunity & visit Princeton. His brother, Augustus, a graduate of this Sem. I have desired to accompany him. He has recently returned from Germany, where he has spent some time.—Besides your Colleagues, I must desire you to introduce them to my friends James Alexander & Prof. Dod, & Dr Breckinridge.

Accept my thanks for your letter, & the Pamphlets, all which came safe to hand. Did you ever read any thing more vexatious, absurd & inconsistent, than Stuart's article in the last Repository? I intended to send you my remarks upon it; but it is too bad. Have you seen Dr Dana's answer to it? There is trouble enough in that camp. By the way, Prof. Dickinson has an appointment at Auburn. They were hoping that Prof. Briggs would leave & make more room for——but, we have heard that he intends to remain in the ship. Was this by advice from Princeton? And will that Sem. be manned with old-school men? We are not in the habit of inviting students to our Sem.; but in case any from your region wish to spend a little season in New Eng. I think they will find E. W. a pleasant place. One of our students has spent one term at Andover & one in the Sem. in New York. He thinks the elements are at war in both——but rather worse in the latter.

My love to your family——your friends & mine

Yours in the best

of bonds

Asahel Nettleton

P. S. I have broken the seal to say that after all, my two friends may not find it convenient to visit you at this time, as Prof Thompson is under the necessity of returning sooner than he had anticipated; in which case I ordered this note to be put in the Pt. office at N. York.

A. N.

Rev: C. Hodge D.D.

Princeton

N. J——

LETTER #38

To Leonard Woods, Andover, Massachusetts

E. Windsor Sept. 30th 1839

Rev. & Dear Sir,

I write at the particular request of Dr. Tyler. In your letter to him, about 2 years since, giving an account of the two meetings during the anniversaries at Andover in 1829 & 1830, you state the resolution brought forward by Rev. L. Bacon, "that all controversy by books, pamphlets etc, pertaining to N. Haven theol. cease on both sides." You add, that "you could give the names of those who voted for it, & of those who retired." As this is likely to be a matter of some importance in the history of this controversy, Dr Tyler wishes you to send him the names of those who voted for & against,—or rather refused to vote at all for Bacon's resolution. If Mr Bacon's statement, in the Record, be true, that no one can possibly understand Dr Taylor's Theology until he has understood & embraced his system of philosophy, how very important that Dr Taylor's book be forthcoming, in obedience to the call of Dr W. in his 8th letter to him in 1830. And who must bear the blame of this long delay & darkness but Mr Bacon & Co. As I expect to be absent from this place for some time, I would thank you to send directly to Dr Tyler, at E. Windsor Hill.

We should be exceedingly gratified with a visit from you—So many things of importance have transpired of late that I cannot write them. Be so good as to reply immediately.

Yours in the best of hands

A. Nettleton

Rev. Leonard Woods D.D.

Andover

Mass

Letter #39

Received of the Revd Asahel Nettleton Fifty Dollars being one half of his contribution of One Hundred Dollars towards the fund of One Hundred Thousand Dollars in aid of the funds of Yale College—New Haven October 2—1832.

Tilliman

This subscription was made with the understanding that there was no connexion between the College & the Theological Department. But subsequent events have shown that I was misinformed. The Theological Professors claim this connexion. Hence, in strict justice I do not feel bound to keep it. Again. Professor Fitch, since the $100,000 fund has been secured, has come out in the chapel of Y. Coll. in defence of the obnoxious theology of New Haven; & on this ground I object to the payment of this subscription. "For if I build again the things which I destroyed, I make myself a transgressor." Gal. 2:18

A. Nettleton

LETTER #40

An undated letter to Rev. Samuel Miller, Princeton, N. J.

My dear Brother,

Before reading Mr F's sermon in the N. Y. evan. of the 7th inst. I fancied myself possessed of the power of taciternity on the subject of "new measures." "But *who can* withhold himself from speaking?" That, surely must cap the climax. His argument in favor of *anxious seats* from white wigs, shortbreeches, pitchpipes & other new measures for promoting revivals of religion in past years must be very convincing to all who admit his premises. And who will deny that these measures were the means of conversion of many souls & of elevating the character of American revivals in their day? And yet, what persecution did the new measure men endure who had the heroism to introduce them into our churches? These wigs, breeches, etc—important links in the "Succession of New Measures," have had their day—thanks to their much abused authors—& are now succeeded by *anxious seats*. Whether they were ever regarded as the *test* of piety, or put *in the place* of baptism, as "anxious seats, now are," we are not informed. Dr. Ely it seems adopts either, at pleasure, & without any previous examination of the candidate, as at Newcastle.

When last at Princeton I did not address the students on the subject of revivals for reasons which I need not repeat. See also, the last two pages of the pamphlet on new measures. Long have I waited in silence, expecting a crisis when the friends of pure revivals would make a simultaneous & decided stand against doctrines & measures which are rapidly changing the *character* of piety in our land. Is not this the crisis? Princeton is now attacked by name. If you speak, fail not to make free used of the above named pamphlet. Reading it will suggest trains of thought & illustrations of the spirit of Mr F.'s lectures. See Dr Beecher's preface to his letter to Beman. F's last shot on fanaticism is aimed at what Dr B there says about him & his measures, & ought to be published.

A word in regard to what the Editor of the N. Y. Evan. says about myself page 1 Col. 4th "Before Mr Finney arose—Mr. Nettleton was much blamed for his irregularities & imprudence." That Methodists, Episcopalians, Unitarian, & Universalist preachers, together with the whole host of infidels, were opposed to my entire course, was a fact well known to the world. But, that any *settled* ministers in New England, in *our* denomination who were not avowed enemies to all revivals, "blamed me for irregularities & imprudence," I never heard of until I saw it in the Evangelist. And for this information the Editor is indebted to the St. Louis Observer—away in the "far West" on the banks of the Mississippi. I wish Dr Miller would write the Editor of that paper & state your own views & those of your Colleagues of this matter & ask him to send you his authority for his statements *forthwith*. Had you not better send him a short piece to publish on this subject. Read & erase this note. Why Leavitt should go such a distance for information which every man, woman, & child, who has known my manner of life from my youth up, knows to be false, I can easily conjecture. The truth is, I never set foot seventy miles out of New England before 1827. If Leavitt feels *quite sure* that these *new measures* have done so much

good, & that they are destined to elevate the character of American revivals in their progress through our churches, & down through succeeding generations, why take so much pains to load one poor sinner with all this honor? The advocates of these measures are beginning to apprehend danger ahead and, that *they* have set in motion & sanctioned measures which they cannot, and dare not attempt to control. Measures which identify them with man whom they are ashamed to own, and whom they cannot & dare not attempt to "shake off", lest they should meet a retribution—measures which every minister who has any knowledge of the operation of moral causes know certainly will run the very name of a revival into utter disgrace. Anticipating this result they are now darkly laboring to throw the tremendous responsibility upon others—to clear the guilty & condemn the innocent.

What measures do I now "oppose which I used to adopt, & which", they assent, "I introduced"? I can think of none. As for the *anxious seat*, I declare before all the world, that I cannot claim the honor of "introducing" that measure; for it was practiced both in this country and among the Ranters in England long before I was born. Never yet in a single instance have I adopted it. And what is more, I never was pressed to witness the scene when adopted by others in my life. And this fact I desire my friends would publish to the world. My reasons for not adopting this practice I would publish to the world but for one consideration:- I fear that the evils attending this measure have not yet been sufficiently *felt* to appreciate my testimony on this subject, and that ministers and Churches will be obliged to feel them yet more, before they will be convinced of their *ultimate consequences*.

I have never opposed what are called *New Measures*, because they are *new*; for they are older than any man living. I know not of a single measure adopted by Mr. Finney and his followers, that was not adopted by other denominations in all the waste places, which I visited, when I commenced preaching in New England. These measures have been pushed to their utmost, & have done their best. I had become stale in many places before I entered the field. They were rank in nearly all the waste places, I have ever visited; and I knew them to be the very measures by which they were made waste.

It is true that some Evangelists of *our* denomination, who called themselves *revival men* had gone into these waste places before me, & were laboring in powerful religious excitements, & were practicing what are now called *new measures*, which they had borrowed from other denominations. I had a great curiosity to go and see how these evangelists managed matters. But I soon learned that they were at war with all the settled pastors in their immediate vicinity on the subject of these measures. Some settled pastors had already received one of these evangelists who had succeeded in introducing his borrowed *improvements* into our Churches which had divided and distracted them, precisely as they are now doing in many parts of our land. And all these pastors were watching and guarding against the intrusion of these evangelists and their measures in New England, with the same vigilance, that they were guarding against the intrusions of other denominations. For it was found that these measures, once introduced, had made an inlet & prepared the way for the success of other denominations. I had not been on the ground one month before I felt, in regard to these evangelists & their measures, precisely as Mr. Finney says "young men" *act* when they come out of your Theological Seminary.

"They look about, and watch and start, as if the devil was there." Knowing that I could not be associated with these evangelists & their measures without losing the confidence of settled pastors, I quit that field, & took another, where I could manage in my own way. Nothing has been more common in revivals where I have labored from the beginning than these *anxious seats* among other denominations. And nothing has ever given me more trouble & perplexity in guarding anxious sinners against spurious conversions. For hundreds of sinners, awakened under my labors, have gone to the altar & anxious seat to be prayed for by others, & have returned rejoicing that their sins were pardoned. But, I have generally found that they gave no evidence of regeneration; & the event has proved that they were like the Stony ground hearers.

In this opinion all the ministers with whom I have ever labored in revivals of religion, I have no doubt are united. In process of time it will appear that the *character* of the religion which multiplies under these measures is entirely different from that which prevails where they are utterly excluded. And I have no more doubt that the bustle and trepidation attending the call to anxious sinners to come out before a public assembly is calculated to efface conviction of sin & induce false conversions that I have of my own existence. And so I have ever regarded this, with all that are now called new measures; & I do not think any better of them since they have been introduced into our own denomination.

I speak from matters of fact as they have fallen under my own observation. Hence I found it expedient to appoint meetings of inquiry, not as a "*test*" of piety, nor even as a "*test*" of conviction; but to guard against this, as well as every other danger of falling short of regeneration. In this manner I labored, excluding what are now called *new measures* wherever I went, until settled pastors, often, very reluctantly on my part, drew me into their own field of labor. And, I can assure *you*, that if any one thing, more than all others, secured to me the entire confidence of settled pastors, & opened their churches & the hearts of all the most intelligent Christians, it was my willingness to assume the responsibility, and endure the odium of excluding what are now called *new measures*.

Thus I continued my labors until 1819, when I visited Saratoga Co. in the State of N. Y. where the name of *Revival* was less popular, as you know, than in many sections of the Presbyterian Church. In less than one year, more than two thousand became hopeful subjects of divine grace, according to the Narrative published by the Presbytery of Albany: of which thousands of copies were reprinted in Glasgow, Scotland: and I think was the occasion of forming the Revival which flourished in Glasgow, until the N. Y. Evangelist found its way there; the doctrines & measures & spirit of which turned the current against *all* our revivals ...[3]

A. Nettleton

NETTLETON'S DIARY

At the Hartford Seminary, in the Nettleton Collection, is a diary reflective of his typhus fever attack. The condition of the diary is good and it is legible in its entirety. The following are the contents of this important diary at a critical juncture in the evangelist's life.

Union August 5th 1818
Came to this place, Board at Mr Joseph Moor's
August 16. Came to Mr Eaton's
Sept 7. Came to Capt. Snell's.
18. Left Union & came to Rocky Hill

30. Left R. Hill, & came to Bolton—

Oct. 2. Came to Union. Capt Snell's

Octr 15th Left Capt. Snell's

16. Came to Maj Lausons—

Oct. 27th Left Union & came to Ashford

1819 Bolton

July 1. Started for Ballston. tarried at Mr Bartletts of Wintonbury.

2. Tarried at Sheffield

3. Arrived at Troy Mr Seymour

4. Sabb. preached in 1 evening

5. Arrived at Saratoga Springs

Sickness in Bolton

October 5th 1822. This morning visited M S. in Wilbraham before breakfast & took the typhus fever.

16th. This morning entered the hack in Th. & felt unwell—it was the commencement of the typhus fever. Preached in Wethersfield in the evening.

26th. Grew more & more unwell up to this date—Head-ache Sore bones—Some difficulty in breathing—Cold feet—High swets & a great degree of dullness were the symptoms This day very sick & confined to the bed.

27th Sent for Dr. North—& for the first time it was ascertained that my complaint was the typhus fever—but it was concealed from me; tho' I suspected it.

Nov. 10th. This evening was the most trying time of my sickness. Great difficulty in breathing—

Called the Physician. Took brandy freely.

14th This day Br Parmele wrote my will.

Was confined to my bed nearly 40 days. Unable to sit up or stand etc

Dec. 9th Was carried in my bed to Esqr Alvords.

27th Br Parmele died.

Presents received in my sickness

Somers	$52:20
New Haven	70:00
Tolland	26:42
Ellington	21:25
Litchfield	35:00
Mary Ann & Frances Devenport	50:00
Female Society in Andover Mar. 25	10:00
Coventry	9:53

Newington	10:62 _
Sarah Wetmore	5:00
Tolland (by Stearns)	13:00
Wilbraham Feb. 28th	8:00
Farmington May 6.	14:81
Mrs Grisvold Oxford	1:00
Pittsfield May 17th	$20:00
North Killingworth	2:00
Pittsfield	$20:00
Sept. 2. Sarah Wetmore	$10:00
Revival Society	15:00
	401:40

1823

June 3. Embarked at New Haven for Machias

7th Arrived at Machias in evening

8. Sabb. heard Rev. Abraham Jackson preach from 2 Chron. 12, 14. & Tarried over night at the house of Rev. Marshfield Steele.

11. Rode to Lubec, 24 miles, & was much fatigued—Visited Rev. Jonathan Bigelow—he & Mr Jackson & Steele the only Presbyterian ministers within 70 miles of this place.

Machias—

13. Returned to Machias—

15. Preached P.M. No. 11.

16. Preached in the evening Acts 2. 37. Christian Mirror—Ed. by Asa Rand Portland Maine.

Machias is in the County of Washington.

Notes

1   George Hugh Birney, Hartford Seminary Foundation, 1943, pp. 3, 4.

2   Hartford Seminary is in need of financial aid to preserve the Nettleton material. Any contributions to help are to be made out to the "Nettleton Library Preservation Fund", 77 Sherman Street, Hartford, CT 06105–2260.

3   George Hugh Birney, Jr. *The Life and Letters of Asahel Nettleton, 1783–1844* (Thesis, Hartford Theological Seminary, 1943) pp. 236–415.

APPENDIX I

REVIVAL OF 1820

We are happy to provide the following rare document, *Recollections of Nettleton and the Great Revival of 1820*, by Rev. R. Smith, published in 1848, four years after Nettleton's death. A careful study of this remarkable account of the "1820 Revival" will immensely reward the student of revival. It is only by studying the movements of God in revivals of former times that we today can possess discernment to recognize true revivals of religion when they graciously appear. In times of spiritual declension, pagan society influences the sleeping Church and acts as both its compass and barometer. Conversely, in times of revivals of religion, the Church's compass is the Bible and her barometer is the Spirit of God, and it is the Church which influences an ungodly society, checking its immorality and pushing back darkness in the land. Therefore the study of true revivals is of vast importance. *Recollections of Nettleton and the Great Revival of 1820* is of immense value and it is for this reason we happily provide it in its entirety.

RECOLLECTIONS

CHAPTER I.
INTRODUCTORY

It was the opinion of a great man, who had much to do with Revivals of Religion in this country, that the last great series commenced about the beginning of the present century. "They have never for a moment since ceased," said he, and it was his expectation that they were to continue, until the opening of the millenial state of the world.

Whether these bright anticipations of *Dr. Griffin* are to be realized or not, all will agree, it is believed, in the desirableness of such a dispensation; and must allow, that in many of these movements, some of the greatest and most happy displays of the Divine benevolence, have been witnessed. At present, the special and simultaneous effusions of the Spirit seem measurably suspended, that, among other sins which have brought this dearth upon the churches, is to be reckoned the abuse of these special mercies.

In these circumstances it seems desirable that there should be authentic collections of the most remarkable phenomena connected with those Revivals, while some remain who were privileged to witness them, but when the principal actors are passed away.

Of the former class is the writer of these Recollections; and while he has not quite reached that period of life, when we are apt to suppose that "the former age" must necessarily be "better than the present," (*laudator temporis acti,*) he is strongly and abidingly impressed with the belief, nevertheless, that for power and purity, we have had no *such* Revivals since, as those now contemplated. Perhaps it is not to be expected that we should. That would be a narrow view of Providence, which should confine it to one mode of operation, even in so great a blessing as that of the gift of the Holy Spirit. But one mode surely may be less mixed with human imperfection than another, and hence the benefit of *comparison.* We are to "try the spirits," even in this matter; and we feel, therefore, that we may be doing some service to the coming generation, as well as recording due acknowledgments to the goodness of God, by preserving these memorials while we can. We have witnessed and participated in other Revivals since: we hope yet to see many more; but for those of purity, power and permanency, we can never cease to look to the past, and with something like longing misgivings. While we would not undervalue any of God's acknowledged servants, living or dead, we are often ready to say of those who have passed away from the scenes now to be reviewed,

> "Those suns are set! O, rise
> Some other such, or all to come is empty boast
> Of old achievement, and despair of new."

CHAPTER II.
THE FIELD.

The *locality* which we propose to contemplate in these Recollections, is that of *Saratoga County* and its vicinity, in the State of New York. The principal actor in these scenes had indeed been already engaged in similar labors for some eight years in Connecticut [Asahel Nettleton]; great and happy results had followed his labors there, of which detailed accounts are given in his interesting *Memoir*. That Memoir has also glanced at the movement in Saratoga County. It was felt by the writer himself, however, to be but a meagre sketch which was given; and to more than one individual has it appeared, that something further extended, as well as more in detail, is due to this part of the wondrous work of God.

To the writer of these notices—whose residence was then in the county, and has been with a brief exception, for the twenty-seven years that have since passed—this locality has seemed to have been the *focus* of that great cloud of mercy; and he loves to contemplate the shower at first heard in the distance——then nearing us; here gathering its most copious and benignant outpourings, and then passing off to water other fields, until only the bright and beautiful *rainbow* appeared, to tell where the blessing had been.

This region comprises most of the towns in the southern part of *Saratoga county: Schaghticoke, Pittstown, and Nassau,* in *Rensselaer* county, together with *Schenectady, Princetown, Amsterdam,* and some minor places on the *Mohawk river.* Most of these places, particularly those in Saratoga county, were settled by an intelligent, and to a considerable extent, a New England population. They were principally Presbyterians or Congregationalists; but many, particularly those on the Mohawk river, were of Dutch origin; and all, in general, attached to the order, and other benefits of religious institutions. As long since, as before the revolutionary war, a Presbyterian congregation had been gathered at *Ballston*, which took its name from their first pastor. A Congregational church emigrated to *Stillwater*, from some part of Connecticut, bringing the materials of their meeting house with them. A flourishing college had already existed for some thirty years at Schenectady, [Union College] and which, it will be seen, shared largely in this religious movement. Many excellent men had lived and died, supplying these churches; and some of them were no strangers to Revivals of Religion. Some of the pulpits were now vacant; one congregation (afterwards greatly favored,) had been organized recently; and in another place, great desolations had supervened a former church organization. Thus, while a good degree of religious order existed, it was, in general, what might be called a low and barren state in the churches of this region.

It was in this locality then, and in such a state of things, that the visitation of mercy, of which we are to speak, reached us. It was, indeed, a timely visitation. Long did we rejoice in it; and "if a drought has since succeeded," or other characteristics have attached to some partial movements which have been experienced, we will still rejoice in whatever good any of them have yielded, and labor in our measure to promote a return of these heavenly blessings.

It is proper to add here, that as most of these churches were ecclesiastically connected with the Presbytery of Albany, that body published an official *narrative* of the work, to which we shall frequently have occasion to refer in these chapters. But that narrative was necessarily brief, and often formal and statistical. Our object is something more than this. It is to give facts indeed, and such as are reliable; but we aim to awaken popular interest also. We shall therefore give incidents and their aspects, principles and inferences from them, specimens and examples, and sometimes also our own passing impressions: and we have ventured to hope from all this, such a retrospect of God's ways, as may be profitable to read, as it certainly has been to the writer to record.

CHAPTER III.
THE COMMENCEMENT OF THE WORK.

The commencement of the Revival we are noticing, may be said to have been in the latter part of the summer of 1819. But even here we speak of development, rather than of origin. Believing as we do, that here, as in the Spirit's work of Regeneration, the beginning of a true Revival is secret, or but seldom traced. Indeed, it will be found characteristic of *this* Revival, and one of its best marks, that when God's servants were awakened to the use of special means for promoting it, they often found that the Spirit had already "gone out before them."

This seems to have been the case in the earliest encouragements which were noticed *in Pittstown*, on the eastern side of the Hudson river. A beloved brother, then stationed at Stillwater, had his attention directed to this place, as early as *August*, 1819, and bestowed his labors of love, with much success. Crowded assemblies were every where seen, whether in school rooms or in the sanctuary, at week services, or on the Sabbath. It was evident the Spirit of the Lord was already "poured out." "Many pricked in their hearts," says the Presbyterian narrative, "were enquiring what they must do to be saved? and fleeing to the only hope of the wretched, were finding in Him, everlasting security, joy and peace."

These results greatly quickened the spirit of this faithful brother, enlarged his efforts, and ultimately led to the commencement of the still greater work among his own people. In a review of this part of the field, it is the opinion of this brother, that "four hundred conversions took place in the circle of Stillwater, Schaghticoke, Saratoga, Easton, and Pittstown." Churches were formed, and several ministers settled as the sequel of that work.

"When these things were noised abroad," and reported at ecclesiastical meetings, they were as life to the dead, in many minds, and the brethren returned from these convocations, to make like efforts, and find to their surprise, the work *already begun* among their own people.

We have deemed it important to dwell thus distinctly upon this first state of the Revival, for reasons already mentioned. The work was *found*, not *produced* by man's efforts. The *cloud* was first seen hanging over these places, and thence extended itself in the use of appropriate means, as we shall see, to many others.

CHAPTER IV.
THE PRINCIPAL INSTRUMENT.

B ut before proceeding further in the history of these movements, it seems proper to give some account of the *Principal Instrument*. And here, no one conversant with this Revival, will hesitate to name the *Rev. Asahel Nettleton*, of Connecticut, whose Memoir, by Dr. Tyler, is now before the public. Most of the other actors in these scenes, were young and inexperienced men. That individual is now dead, and cannot be affected by any opinions which may be formed concerning him, favorable or unfavorable. We are free to say, therefore, that we look upon Mr. Nettleton as specially raised up by Providence, for conducting a great and pure Revival of Religion, and that taking him altogether, he was at the time we speak of, the best qualified of any man we have known, for such a service. His theological education had not been extensive, but his theology, formed as it was on his own attentive study of the Bible, and his *special observation of the work of the Spirit*, was as safe, perhaps, as any which could now be found.

His system was that which has technically been called old fashioned New England orthodoxy, to which, in all its relations, he strenuously adhered through life.

But it is not so much as a theologian we wish now to speak of Mr. Nettleton, as of his practical piety, and as an eminent promoter of Revivals of Religion. For this last he was evidently raised up and qualified. His mind was discriminating and wonderfully self-possessed. Nothing uncentered him: he seemed never taken by surprise; but to perceive and to do just what you afterwards saw to be required, was as it were, intuitive, or rather "given him in that hour."

An example may be given. Mr. Nettleton, while faithful and zealous for the doctrines of grace, and preaching them plainly on proper occasions, was opposed to being drawn into public controversy. It was sometimes attempted to do this, and it happened on one occasion, that two individuals came to his meeting expressly to entrap him. So they introduced themselves to him after service, as anxious inquirers. They said they had heard him that evening with much interest, and must acknowledge the subject he had recommended to them, to be important, very important; indeed they felt anxious to know more about it. But there were *certain difficulties of doctrine*, which yet embarrassed their minds, and they trusted that he, as a religious teacher could enlighten them. They hoped he would pardon the intrusion; but they were truly anxious to know his views of—of—; in short the great subject of inquiry was the doctrine of *predestination and election!* From their peculiar manner, Mr. Nettleton had long since perceived that their object was to get some remarks from him, which they could report, in their own way to others, while being alone, it would be impracticable to correct their statements. But he was not to be thus entangled; so he answered, calmly, as they drew along into the vestibule, "It is true, gentlemen, religion is an important subject, and particularly to you. If, as you say, you are anxious, it is a critical and infinitely important time in your lives. The subject of the doctrines of which you enquire; is also serious—very serious; and if you are to study it, it is highly important that you should study by the use of the best helps. Permit me, gentlemen, to recommend for this purpose, a certain book. It is a book I have read some, and I have great confidence in its views of these subjects. It is a very good book—very able and entirely to be relied on, in my view; I advise you to get it, perhaps it may relieve your minds. Gentlemen," said he, drawing near to them, in an emphatic whisper, "that book is *the Bible!* that book is *the Bible!* Good night, gentlemen!" It is believed they never troubled him again.

Mr. Nettleton, at the time of visiting us, might be about thirty-five years of age. He was in poor health, and not of prepossessing personal appearance or manners. Though courteous, he was reserved, and so entirely controlled by judgment rather than emotion, that some would have pronounced him austere. Yet he had evidently much natural emotion, and when it was awakened by appropriate and worthy occasions it could almost carry him away. We remember hearing an instance, when reading in his room, there was reported to him the joyful conversion of a man on whom he had much set his affections. Mr. Nettleton rose from his chair, and hurled his book across the room in unutterable intensity of feeling.

His talent, as a preacher, being rather of the reasoning and discriminating character, the almost uniform first report was, that *he was not eloquent*. So in the usual acceptation of the word, perhaps he was not. But if eloquence consists in the power of holding attention, and deeply impressing human minds, then was Mr. Nettleton eloquent, and at times, beyond almost any man we have ever known. His slowness, his repetitions, and his careful discrimination, all had reference to an *object*, and that he seldom failed to reach, sometimes in irresistible and overwhelming results.

The great secret of the power in this extraordinary man, has seemed to us to have consisted in these following things. *His own deep religious experience:* his *clear conception of divine truth,* as taught by the Bible, and his own observation of the Spirit's work: *his knowledge of human nature: his self-command,* and *quick perception of right expedients,* according to the occasion.

So manifest was his holy sincerity at the time we knew this man, as to impress the beholder at first with a sort of awe. His prayers, for the same reason, were short and hesitating, as if afraid of saying too much before God; and so humble was his hope, that we have heard it related, as among his last sayings, that he considered it barely possible that such as he should be saved.

Mr. Nettleton's views of divine truth, and its applications, were, as we have said, very clear. Yet did they not resolve themselves into abstract or exclusive propositions. No man was further from what has been called the *one idea* propensity. We remember a young clergyman once to have asked instructions of him, as to the best manner of visiting and conversing with sinners? "The great difficulty is," said he, "*in feeling right yourself;*" and he had no *rule* to give him. Similar to this was the result of an interview that a company of us contrived to have with him one afternoon, the great object of which was to get the results of his own experience on these subjects. He came indeed, but we could get him to say but very little. "Few general propositions," he said, "could be laid down on such a subject." *Principles* were indeed of importance, and *facts* were to be observed, but these every one must study and attend to for himself."

When he did speak or advise, however, it was always in wisdom; it was open and honest, and no uninspired man, it is believed, has made fewer mistakes. Let this his be judged of by a few examples. Mr. Nettleton considered it not profitable *to have many preachers* in a Revival. If he were not well acquainted, or had not entire confidence in the fitness of a man, he would suffer himself to appear almost rude, rather than invite him to preach. "Now," said he, in the presence of a good father who had been introduced to him one evening just before going to the church; "here is another good brother, and I suppose he thinks I must invite him to preach." So anxious was he to have the most entire *stillness* in an audience, that we have known him to spend a full half hour in getting them seated, and then, in some cases, to request them not to attempt to rise during the offering up of prayer. He was so far from relying on *mere sympathy* in religious awakening, that he seemed rather to be afraid of it, and he once separated two bosom friends who had taken their room together under convictions, let they should too much operate upon each other.

He watched his opportunities, and seldom attempted to speak to a person on the subject of personal religion, when surrounded with noise, or distracted with the cares of a family; but meeting a poor woman of these circumstances one day *on the road*, he said a few solemn words to her, pointed to a grove she was about to enter, and went on. She took the hint, and there alone, and in solemn prayer, committed her soul to God, and found a hope of salvation.

One of the peculiarities of Mr. Nettleton's dealings with sinners, was in his almost uniformly aiming to *destroy false confidence*, to pluck away their *props*, as he would call it, and bring them to *immediate submission*. A woman in an anxious meeting, was in a great conflict and such was her distress, that she actually sunk upon the floor. "Madam," said Mr. Nettleton, "it is evident the spirit is striving with you, and you *must submit*." "O, I cannot—I dare not," and she uttered a shriek that brought into the room another clergyman, to whom she made the same application. "O, Mr. G——," said the poor creature, "what shall I do? *Must* I submit?" Mr. G—— had been instructed in the same school; he saw instantly how the case stood, and answered tenderly, but firmly and solemnly, "*Yes*, madam, you *must*." She was utterly overcome, fell into spasms, was carried by her female friends into another room, and laid upon a bed. In a few minutes she was rejoicing, and the first exhortation she gave was, as she flung herself upon the neck of her husband—an unconverted man—"O, my dear husband, you *must submit*, you must submit." Can there be any doubt that in this case *submission* was the proper direction, and that to have given any other would perhaps have been fatal.

Mr. Nettleton seemed to rely entirely on the work of the Spirit. So jealous, so fearful was he when he discovered that a people or individual were trusting to human instruments, that he would seem at times to be actually rude in disappointing them. He tore himself away from a place on one occasion, when there were more than a hundred supposed to be under convictions. A distressed woman who heard of his departure, exclaimed that "he was as bad as Satan, for he had come there only to torment them, and then left them to do as they could." Poor woman; she soon learned to her joy, to resort to a better helper. For similar reasons he would never *urge* an attendance on the *anxious* meetings, (as they were called,) but if any were found to be truly serious, and manifested a desire for such a privilege, it was managed in an unostentatious manner to have them invited.

His manner of conducting these meetings, was to go round and speak to each individual present, in a tone so low as not to be heard by others, to give a word of pointed exhortation, and close all by solemn prayer. There was seldom *singing* in these meetings, all was solemn, still, and reflective, and if an improper person was found to have intruded himself, Mr. Nettleton knew how to dispose of him.

A young man of infidel principles had crept into one of these meetings, avowdly for the purpose of making diversion, or to see what he could find to report. Mr. Nettleton had the good fortune to be informed of this, but took no notice of it, until having opened the meeting with prayer; he proceeded in the usual manner, till he came to this young man, when the following or similar conversation ensued.

"Well, my young friend, do *you* feel as if you wanted religion?"

"No, sir; I did not come here to be catechized, sir!"

"Well, you don't want religion you say, but you believe you have a soul, do you not?"

"I don't know how that may be. Yes! Every body believes as much as that, I suppose; but I say, sir, I didn't come here to be catechized."

"Well, you have a soul then, and you sin sometimes, I suppose. There is such a thing as sinning, is there not?"

"I don't know how that is; but, I say, sir—"

Mr. N. interrupting him. "Don't know whether there is any such thing as sin or not! You believe there is a God?"

"Yes, I suppose so; any body may admit that; but I tell you what it is sir, I didn't come here to be questioned in this way. I—I—(and he began to look as if he would gladly have been any where else,) I expect to be treated—like—a gentleman!" But even this could not save him.

"You say then you believe there is a God, and He rules the world I suppose, and is just and good, and yet there is suffering in the world; and you don't know whether there is any such thing as sin or not! Young man!" said Mr. N. turning terribly upon him, and laying a heavy hand upon his knee, "young man, I understand you perfectly, and I knew your business here from the beginning. *You are an infidel!* And now I tell you what you have before you to do. You have to prove that Jesus Christ was an imposter, or you will be damned! Jesus says, 'He that believeth not, shall be damned!' You do not believe, and you must prove that Jesus Christ was an imposter, or you will be damned." The young gentleman took his hat and left: and Mr. Nettleton had only to calm the agitated meeting, by remarking, "You see how weak poor infidelity is."

We will exhibit a few more items of Mr. Nettleton's views on particular subjects.

He did not approve of much or promiscuous speaking in religious meetings. Although glad to avail himself of approved gifts in others, he did not encourage much speaking by young converts, unless it was to relate their experience, and that after a previous interview with them.

He was very careful *to guard against contradictory instructions to anxious sinners,* by those who undertook to direct them. "Suppose a parent should be correcting a child, and exhorting it to submit, but the other parent should come into the room and seem to take the child's part, how fatal would such a course be to the object had in view in correcting him."

He did not encourage very frequent meetings. Generally he preached twice or thrice on the Sabbath, and once more in the course of the week. The remainder was devoted to the inquiry meeting, and visiting from house to house. More private prayer-meetings were also encouraged; the aid of females in this way, was highly valued by him.

Mr. Nettleton *never countenanced the early admission of young converts to church membership,* but thought much of training them and watching over them for a season, as candidates for this privilege.

Mr. Nettleton, *never interfered with, but always encouraged and strengthened the bonds of the regular pastors of the churches.* We believe it may be said safely, that of the many whom he visited and labored for in this region, *not one lost influence, or was dismissed in consequence of such visit.* We may add, that we cannot remember a single instance where *a division* was left in the churches.

He never approved of special efforts, to *produce a religious excitement;* on the contrary, he aimed only to *follow* where the Lord led the way, enjoining of course, the discharge of duty at all times. So jealous was he in this respect, that he would not visit a place where he feared they were relying upon him. Indeed we have heard him say, that *he* could not labor where there was not already some religious feeling. Yet he did, on urgent solicitation, sometimes visit a place on a sort of trial. We remember one such, where he preached, and preached earnestly, for a few times. They *heard* him, but that was all, and he left them saying, it was of no use to stay, since it was evident that Christians there could not be brought up to their duty.

It only remains that we add a few things of Mr. Nettleton, *as a preacher,* and here we shall gladly avail ourselves of what is so well said in his *Memoir,* as to leave but little for enlargement or alteration.

"He was not what is usually called a popular speaker. There was nothing particularly captivating in his voice, his style, or his delivery— nothing to make you admire the man or his writing, or in any way divert your attention from the truths he uttered." Never indeed has it been our privilege to hear the truth, *the truth itself,* without any reference to a thought of the man, to commend itself, as at his hand. And this was evidently his great aim. With him apparently Christ was every thing, and himself nothing. You almost forgot that there was any such being as man in the pulpit, while naked truth in all its unadorned majesty and sweetness came flowing down from the place.

"When he began to speak, there was a benignant solemnity in his countenance, which awed the most thoughtless, while at the same time it excited an unwonted desire to hear what he had to say. He always commenced on a low key, enunciating every word and syllable distinctly, and frequently repeating a leading sentence to make it better remembered. So simple were his sentences, so plain and unadorned his style, and so calm his delivery, that for a few moments you might have thought him dull, and sometimes common place. As he advanced, and his heart grew warm, and his conceptions vivid, his voice caught the inspiration, his face shone, his whole physical frame seemed to dilate," and there were times when he was awfully overwhelming. Men held their breath, and the audience moved slowly away, not to talk of the preacher, but to meditate, to read, and to pray. His sermon on the *Flight of Lot out of Sodom,* has probably seldom been excelled for solemn impressiveness and lasting effect.

He preached the whole truth, yet not the whole on any one occasion, or without regard to times and seasons. On the great subjects of *Man's duty and God's sovereignty,* for instance, he was wont to exhibit the first, very strongly in his early addresses to sinners, "and now," said he, "if they become awakened, I can tell them their dependence, and hold them up to the doctrine of God's sovereignty, as long as I please."

So of choosing his other subjects. He frequently selected precisely those that were *the opposite of what he supposed would be expected;* and this for the purpose undoubtedly of making a more profitable impression. In fine, Mr. Nettleton was evidently a peculiar man, a wise master-builder, and unusually furnished to that post of his Lord's service, to which he was called. He was deeply pious; he loved the truth; he loved the souls of men; he prayed, read his Bible, and reflected much on what he saw, and he was divinely directed, beyond all doubt, to his great and eminent success. We are by no means disposed to claim for him an exemption from human imperfection; he was as far as any one from claiming this for himself. But taking him all in all, and for the times in which he lived, we do believe that no light has since arisen, of equal splendor, and that no principles or measures essentially differing from his, can be expected to succeed as well.

Such as he was, approved or disapproved, we have now exhibited him, and as far as possible from his own sayings and acts. Other leaders, and other eminent helpers there were in the same great work. Some of them are still living, but it is believed they will be disposed to regard themselves as disciples, at that time; and however, they may have been prospered since—agree in regarding our deceased evangelist, as *the great instrument of the Revival of* 1819–20.

CHAPTER V.
THE PROGRESS OF THE WORK.

We propose now to follow the progress of this great movement, and its order of advancement, so far as it can be traced from place to place, and

AT SARATOGA SPRINGS. Mr. Nettleton came to this place for his health, in July or August of 1819, evidently intending to remain in obscurity, as he was much worn down by his recent labors in Connecticut. He was induced, however, to visit Malta, eight miles to the south, where it would seem that some tokens of the Spirit's presence had been manifested already, and here, at a private house, were his first labors, in a town so greatly favored afterwards, as we shall see.

From thence he returned to the Springs, but all was apparently yet dead or dying in the spiritualities of this place. "Those who are acquainted with the character of this village, as a watering place," says an esteemed correspondent, to whom we are indebted for much of this account, "are not prepared to expect any seriousness here during the gay and fashionable season." The Presbyterian church here, had commenced with nine members, only two years before, and was now under the care of the late Rev. D. O. Griswold. In 1819 it had increased to twenty-two members; most of this number, however, had been received by letter, and no special out-pouring of the Holy Spirit had thus far been experienced. In the midst of this coldness and gaiety, Mr. Nettleton came amongst us like any other stranger, though in a very unobtrusive manner. He commenced preaching in a school-house, in the latter part of August, and did not officiate in the church until some weeks afterwards. I well recollect the impression which this produced on me at the time. I had not then heard or seen him. But understanding that a stranger had selected a *school-house* instead of the church, for evening lectures, I inferred that he considered himself too inferior in talents to be placed in contact with several popular preachers who were then in the village. Still I had been urged by a pious old lady to hear him, in company with her son, who was my personal friend. This we resisted for a time, but at length, to gratify her, more than for any thing else, we attended an evening lecture. I was surprised to find the house so much crowded, but there was nothing in the appearance or manner of the preacher, which was calculated at first to arrest my attention. His text was at *Heb.*, xi. 16—"or profane person, as Esau, who for one morsel of meat, sold his birth-right." His method of introducing it, was somewhat startling. But I sunk down into a state of indifference, for the time being. I thought the preacher had too many repetitions—that his language was not of that high order which I had oftentimes heard and admired, and that he was far from being an eloquent man. Soon, however, I lost sight of all this, and found *that he was depicting my own case!* and that, like Esau, I had sold my birth-right! I felt the full force of his reasoning, and for the first time in some years, was greatly alarmed.

At the close of his sermon, and before dismissing his audience, he cited a case which had come under his own observation, where one who had evidently despised her birth-right, by slighting the warnings of the gospel, had suddenly sickened, and died, without hope. The solemn manner in which this was related, produced an overwhelming effect. There was not a dry eye in the house; and I doubt whether there was one present, not already a believer, who did not resolved from that time to seek an interest in Christ. Certain it is that many dated their first serious impressions from that evening.

My friend and myself walked silently from the place for some distance, before speaking, each being afraid to address the other, (as it was afterwards ascertained,) lest a serious remark should excite ridicule. At length an encouraging word from one, broke the silence of both. We walked, arm in arm, for two hours, and before separating, had solemnly pledged ourselves to each other, that we would, from that moment, earnestly seek an interest in Christ. The next morning I called on Mr. Nettleton, expecting from him words of comfort, and that direction which I so much needed. But he scarcely replied to me, except to say that I must repent. This, at the time, seemed unkind; but I afterwards learned that it was the course he frequently adopted with the awakened sinner. He took away, if possible, every earthly prop, and merely pointed "*to the Lamb of God, who taketh away the sin of the world.*"[1]

From that time forward, all the meetings were crowded and solemn. There was no tumult, no noise. Every thing was still, though every mind seemed filled with the magnitude of the work, which was going forward. There were a few opposers; but their opposition seemed rather to increase than diminish the convictions of others.

"*Behold how great a matter a little fire kindleth!*" The work thus commencing, continued, and principally under Mr. Nettleton's preaching, for some months. The whole number who dated their conversion from this Revival, was about eighty. In general they have continued steadfast, intelligent Christians. A large number of Evangelical churches have grown up with the growth of that important place, and all of them, it is believed, more or less, taking character from this early and powerful work of grace.

AT MALTA. Incipient developments had occurred here, as we have seen, on Mr. Nettleton's first visit. Encouraged by these indications, these few faithful brethren had sustained their meetings, and "in October a licentiate from the Presbytery of New York came among them, whose preaching and other labors were greatly blessed. Two students from the Theological Seminary at Princeton, also labored among them, so that on the 26th of October, there was a little church collected, consisting of twenty-four members, most of them recent converts of the faith of Christ." (*See Presbyterial Narrative.*)

From this time Mr. Nettleton labored here stately for about eight months, with occasional visits to other places, and no where else perhaps, in this whole field, were more demonstrations given of the mighty power of God. "It was but a little while, until weeping and anxious distress were found in almost every house. The habitations of sin, the haunts of intemperance, the strong holds of error, the retreats of Pharisaic pride, and the entrenchments of self-righteousness, were equally penetrated by the power of the Holy Ghost." "Often and anxiously was the inquiry now made; *what shall we do to be saved?* During three weeks the awakening spread over different parts of the town, and became almost universal. Every house exhibited the solemnity of a continued Sabbath. So profound was the stillness, that a recent death could have added nothing to it, in many families. Common conversation was rarely engaged in, and every ear was open to hear the gospel." Within the year, about one hundred were added to the Presbyterian church in this place; how many to the other churches, we have not yet the means of knowing; but it was quite considerable. These converts have in general remained steadfast, and grown in grace. The church has since experienced changes, it is true, but it is remarkable that amidst all their trials and mutations, and while individuals have in a few instances "made shipwreck of faith," there has ever appeared something which could not be removed; much of which was evidently acquired during this visitation.

It was also from Malta, more than from any other point, that the tidings of this grace were "sounded out" to adjoining places. Christians came to admire and to participate, and then returned to carry back the sacred influence to their homes. The sacred flame thus ran from town to town, and sometimes to distant places. The Revival at Nassau, fourteen miles east of Albany, had a connection of this sort, which was truly remarkable, but which cannot here be related.

It is in remembering this part of the happy work of 1820, that we feel disposed to exclaim often: "O scenes surpassing fable, and yet true!" They come before us in the recollection of crowded school-rooms, animated with up-turned human faces, and hushed as the silence of death; in the figure of a grave and humble preacher, exhorting us "to be as still as possible;" while awful and soul-piercing truths were moving us as the trees of the forest are moved by mighty winds. Here we remember the forest-girdled church also, whose packed and half-finished walls seemed ready to burst from the pressure within; or here, the busy and anxious sleigh loads, hurrying from, far and near; or here, the private prayer-meeting, with anxious souls refusing to be torn away when the exercises were over; or there we follow home the solemn rejoicing group, and witness congratulations, such as may not be described, "such as Heaven looked down to see."

We do not mean to intimate that these scenes were uniform, or altogether unmixed. Trials and difficulties would intervene of course, and shades come, at times, over our brightest prospects. But we mean to say, that fewer occasions of sorrow and regret occurred in connection with this Revival, than any other we have known; that it was long continued and powerful, and in many of its scenes it was most touching and God-glorifying, like what may be expected in that great day hereafter, when a revolted world shall return with weeping and rejoicing unto the Lord.

We may mention as illustrating the spirit of zeal in this work, that a distinguished fellow laborer, whose other duties confined him during the week at Union College, has been known to gather his sleigh load of pious students, on Sabbath morning, ride eighteen miles, preach three times, and return before he slept.

AT STILLWATER. The commencement of the work here has been intimated already. When the beloved brother told his people of the wonders which he had witnessed at Pittstown, a deep impression was made, and ministers and people gave themselves to prayer, publicly and privately. Nor did they seek the Lord in vain. "A deep solemnity spread over the whole community, (in the words of the Presbyterian Narrative,) and every where meetings were crowded. Some were deeply impressed with a sense of sin, and fully convinced of their need of an interest in Christ. Sinners from a distance came to hear the gospel, and hung on the lips of the preacher as though they heard for their lives. Such was the state of things down to the beginning of October (1819), when their pastor having attended the annual meeting of the Synod of Albany, which held its session at Cherry Valley, returned home, and with a heart overflowing, recounted to his people the wonders of grace, which God was doing in Cooperstown, New Hartford, Utica, &c., and noticing God's mercy to their neighbors in Malta, warned and admonished them of their danger and their duty. His exhortation was brought home by the Holy Spirit, in demonstration and power. It was sealed upon every heart, it seized upon every conscience.

"The Bible class and the Sunday schools were deeply affected. They felt the first influences of God's spirit. Many of them soon became reconciled unto God; meetings became more frequent, full, crowded! In the course of a few days, the Spirit was poured out on several neighborhoods, on families of every habit. The benign influence spread over into Schaghticoke, where at a single lecture, preached by the pastor of Stillwater, between thirty and forty were awakened! And so did it flourish there, that in a little while almost the whole number were rejoicing in hope.

"In the north part of Stillwater, where the means of grace were seldom enjoyed, the work of the Lord commenced, and became very powerful. Scarcely one family was passed over. In a large district, though harassed by sectarian contentions, where praying families were very rarely found, there was soon scarcely one house where prayer was not wont to be made; where sacrifice and a pure offering were not daily offered up to God! Many whole families, young and old, every soul, were hopefully converted to Christ. But, in *the village*, God's power was most conspicuous. Many of the inhabitants were of the most hopeless kind—boatmen, tipplers, tavern-haunters, gamblers, gain-sayers, infidels, and atheists—were mingled and mixed with the unholy multitude. The ways of Zion languished because few came to her solemn feasts. There were many who lived in the village, who scarcely ever attended in the house of God, or in any other visible way acknowledged his supremacy. They were literally stout-hearted, and far from righteousness, without God and without hope in the world; and yet (we cannot refrain from ascribing glory to God in the highest,) this multitude, bad and unblessed as it was, felt the power of the Holy Ghost, and yielded to His influence, and received the gospel of His grace gladly, and submitted themselves to Him, whose right it is to reign, and in whom all the families of the earth are blessed. We dare not descend to particulars here. The narrative would fill a volume. Our limits will not suffer us to do more than simply state, that whether the Lord moved among the most pure in morals and manners, or among the most polluted in heart and life; as soon as the eye saw that it *was God,* the heart felt its own pollutions, and abhorred itself in dust and ashes, and trembled at the Lord's word. Fearfulness seized upon the hypocrite; the careless, the scoffer, and sceptic alike, were brought down to the lowest dust. You might have heard them inquiring with all the apprehensive anxiety of the jailer, 'men and brethren, what must we do to be saved?'; and in all the humility of the publican praying, 'God be merciful to us miserable sinners.'

"In the upper congregation, where there had been a great work of grace in 1815, there were little appearances of any awakening, until late in the winter of 1820; but the Lord's mercies were not clean gone, for he appeared there also in His great glory. And so universally did His grace abound, that there remained not one family in all that congregation, where there was not one or more witnessing souls. The awakening was not confined to any one age or sex, or class of character; it was general! And to the glory of God's grace be it spoken, the most profligate, generally, were the most prompt in their submission to God. The converts were of all ages, from seventy-five years down to twelve years; and in the short space of six months, one hundred and ninety-four were added to the church, of whom *one hundred and three* were added in one day, and there were twenty-three added afterwards, making the whole number two hundred and seventeen. The whole number who cherished hope of forgiven sin, was considerably over three-hundred, with the township."

AT BALLSTON. The Revival commenced here in the order of the geographical relation of the place to Malta, where some of our people had attended a communion season, and were much stirred up. It happened also, that on the 12th day of December, four or five church members being together after one of our evening meetings, felt in an unusual degree the necessity of a Revival of Religion, both in their own hearts, and through the congregation; in consequence of this, they solemnly covenanted with each other to observe a special concert of secret prayer for this object, at a particular hour of the day.

This was the first visible movement among Christians; but it ought to be told, for the encouragement of others, that there had existed for several years in this church, a small female praying society, who had made it one article in their constitution, that they would never cease, while the organization lasted, to pray for a Revival of Religion!

The session of the church were awakened next. On the day appointed for our state thanksgiving, after attending the public services, they held a special conference among themselves. They inquired into each other's official faithfulness——examined their own hearts, and compared views with regard to the state of religion in the church. Much tenderness of feeling was manifested on this occasion, and it was agreed, before they separated, to call a meeting of all the members of the church, for a similar object. This meeting was held on the first Monday in January, and was indeed a solemn and melting season. After prayer, several exhortations were given, and we then began a free conversation with individual members, on the state of their religious experience, as well as their views and feelings in regard to our spiritual condition as a church. Almost all were either found prayerful and strong in the belief that God was about to pour out his spirit upon us, or they were mourning their coldness, backslidings, and neglect of duty. Some of our most exemplary professors were almost wholly in darkness, but they were panting for the light of God's countenance, "as the heart panteth after the waterbrooks."

The awakening among God's people was now general. Our hopes in his design of mercy for others, rose in proportion; nor did we wait long, ere our expectations began to be realized. At a Saturday evening prayer meeting, held the same week, the first decided impressions appeared to be made on the minds of impenitent sinners. Five or six young persons were unusually affected during the meeting, and on conversing with them after its close, discovered a vivid apprehension of their sinfulness and danger, and a strong determination to seek after God. Most of these subjects ultimately gave evidence of having "passed from death to life."

Our first *anxious* meeting was appointed within a few days afterwards, and though it was distinctly made known that none but those under concern were expected at this meeting, we found, to our surprise, that about sixty were assembled. Here was a scene, novel to most of us, and interesting beyond description. We saw one whole company of sinners bowed down, apparently with the same sentiment of awful condemnation, and some to such a degree as not to be able to rise from their seats, while they bewailed their case with bitter weeping, and besought the prayers and instructions of Christians on their behalf.

After this, new instances of conviction became numerous; we heard of them daily, and in almost every part of the town. The first cases of hopeful conversion, occurred this week also, in two precious youths, who found relief and great joy. Almost every one was now convinced that a work of divine grace was indeed begun. The church were fired, and the session, dividing themselves two and two, resolved to visit forthwith every family in the congregation. This important work they were enabled to carry into effect, and with great benefit both to themselves and others. The Lord was before us, and it was found that many families and individuals not before known to be affected, and who might have remained so, but for this movement, were already convicted, *or predisposed* to be so upon the first appeals of divine truth!

All the means usually employed to promote Revivals of Religion, were now diligently used. Besides the exercises of the Sabbath, we had weekly lectures by the pastor and others, who came occasionally to his assistance, in different parts of the town. We had anxious meetings also, and conferences and prayer meetings, and frequently several on the same evening, at different places. The people seemed never weary of attending, and the difficulty was rather to satisfy them without appointing more meetings than we thought to be best. They would flock together during all the inclemencies of the season, and listen, when met, with so deep and profound an attention, that in a room crowded to overflowing, it would almost seem you might hear a pin drop or the beating of a watch. The stillness, at times, seemed to have something like mystery about it; it was sublime, it was awful; you almost seemed to be in eternity. Strangers who have come into these meetings have expressed themselves as feeling like Eliphaz the Temanite, when a spirit passed before his face, and the voice of the eternal was heard challenging him, "Shall mortal man be more just than God? Shall a man be more pure than his Maker?" Some of the most signal convictions seem to have been wrought by the Spirit in these circumstances, and apparently in many instances, several at the same moment. These things, notwithstanding it would be a mistake to suppose that there was any thing like enthusiasm manifested in this movement. No dreams, no visions, or supernatural impressions (except a single instance,) were pretended or relied on. No efforts were made to excite the passions or imagination. Noise was repressed, and convictions were, in general, rational and deliberative Plain doctrinal and conscience-exciting truths were principally presented in preaching, and these sermons were those most frequently blessed. Much was urged as to the obstinacy of the sinner's will, his entire responsibility, great guilt and entire dependence on God, to save him from destruction.

These have been the main instrumentalities relied on; but instances of conviction have occurred in modes and circumstances altogether aside from human calculation. More than once indeed have human wisdom and foresight been entirely set aside, and the church has thus been taught to believe that the best way to carry on a work of God in Revivals, *is just to lie in the dust of humility, doing duty as it arises, and suffering God to carry on the work himself.* The principal duties are those of prayer, patience, Christian intercourse, and continual waiting on the ordinary means of grace.

On the 21st of February, we had our *first* communion season, since the commencement of the work. It was preceded by a day of fasting and prayer, and proved indeed a season of great interest. *Fifty-nine* new communicants then sat down to the table of the Lord, in the presence of an immense assembly of spectators, not less, it was supposed, than two thousand—the whole number of communicants being about five hundred.

The week following, it was found that the Revival had received a new impulse. Here a husband, and there a wife, who had been separated at the late communion season, was found trembling and seeking the way of salvation. Our evening meetings were still more thronged, and in the coldest evenings of an unusually severe winter, many assembled who were not able to obtain admittance to our school-houses, and have been seen to raise the windows and stand without in devout attention to the word of God. Often on these occasions has the scriptural expression occurred to our minds, "These, whence come they? and who are these that fly as clouds and doves to their windows?" The house of God on the sabbath was equally thronged, even the intermission season was usually spent in religious exercises, and we were obliged to enlarge our accommodations by supplying movable seats. At this time the Revival might be considered at its height, and it was observed that for three or four weeks there was not one day in which we did not hear of one or more persons who were made to rejoice in hope. All our usual means of promoting the work were continued, and at the end of six weeks from our last communion, *fifty-seven* more were added to the church at a season of great solemnity.

Two additional circumstances may be mentioned, as remarked in this Revival. It prevailed to an unusual extent among persons of advanced age, and it was singularly destructive, for the time being, of doctrinal error. Socinianism was not attacked, except as included in teaching the opposite doctrines; and Universalism was not *attacked* at all. It seemed as if the presence of the Spirit had of itself blighted it. Several persons once professing to believe in this doctrine, were hopefully converted, and few, very few remained, it is believed who would have been willing then to admit their attachment to such a system.

The particular excitement might be considered as continuing until the *second sabbath of May*, the season of our *third communion*. At this time twenty-six were added to the church, making the whole number received on examination in about three months, *to be one hundred and forty-two*. The opening of the spring brought the busy season of the year; the more unfavorable state of the roads, and the shorter evenings, made a difference in our outward attention to the means of grace; and yet good influences continued, and other additions to the church were made in consequence of this Revival, throughout the year.

On the whole, no church or people, perhaps, in all this wonderful movement, had greater occasion for gratitude to Almighty God, or were laid under higher obligations to exhibit its lasting memorials, than those of Ballston. And for a long and happy season, these memorials remained. The church was greatly enlarged; our bounds extended; our strength increased; and the moral and intellectual state of our whole population evidently improved The generation of the young were specially favored. They now loved the things that were "lovely and of good report;" and it would not have been easy at that time, to find an intemperate or licentious person among them, or to get up and sustain any merely worldly amusement.

Mr. *Nettleton* was amongst us only on two occasions during this winter; but our people saw a good deal of him in other places, and we were favored besides with the occasional visits of other eminent helpers. The good *Dr. Yates* of Union College, (of whom it was said, *he was always in a Revival spirit,*) was several times with us, as was also another zealous and gifted professor in that institution, then just commencing his ministerial career. An excellent *Brother Williams*, since dead, also visited us, and with an anecdote connected with his name, and one other calculated to show the simple power of God's instrumentalities in converting souls, we will bring this narrative to a close. Mr. Williams had preached an excellent sermon at one of our school-house meetings, on the *Parable of the Sower*. In specifying with great fidelity the different classes of hearers of the word, one would have supposed him sufficiently particular, and that it was not easy to escape an individual self-application. "But," said an ingenuous young female, who gave this account of her conversion afterwards, "I heard Mr. Williams, but that did not touch me. After sermon our pastor addressed us, and made the subject still more particular. Still I remained uninterested, for I never thought it could mean *me*. Then we were dismissed, and as we were getting out of the room, the singers began one of their hymns, '*Stop* poor sinners, stop and think before you further go.' This was, indeed, very solemn, somehow. I felt strongly, though I did not yet think any thing in particular of *myself*; but when our minister came right up to me in that awful crowd, and said, 'Well, *Eliza*, what do *you* think of these things? Has not the *Sower* sowed any thing for you this evening? Don't *you* need religion? O, Eliza, you know you do.' Then to be sure, I thought it did mean *me*, and I couldn't stand it any longer."

On another occasion the pastor was to be absent for the sabbath, on an exchange with a brother minister of Albany. On his way downward, he called to see a young female of his flock, who was understood to be under conviction. He found her exceedingly distressed, so much so indeed, that her otherwise beautiful features had become dark with anguish, and truly dreadful to look upon. He understood that at a female prayer meeting held the day before, she had been entirely overcome, and carried out of the room. The pastor felt distressed to leave her in such circumstances; but he instructed and prayed with her as well as he could, and her case was not much out of his mind during his absence. On Monday, as he returned, he called on her again, and the first thing he observed on her entering the room, was the entire change in her countenance. "Well, Jane," said he, "I need not ask you, you feel better, I see it in your looks." "O, yes, O yes, tongue can't express it, how happy I am." "But what did it, Jane? how came you to feel so differently?" "O, sir, He said, '*Ho, every one that thirsteth, come ye to the waters.*'" Dear child! she referred to the preacher whom she heard the day before quote this passage. But it was not his text; he only referred to it in a very usual way; but God was working with his word, and Jane *believed* to the rejoicing of her soul.

The writer of these Recollections will be pardoned for the length of the narrative of *Ballston*, and these details of incidents, if they have not much intrinsic value. He was the pastor of this people at that time: in the strange providence of God he is now, after an absence of twenty-two years, their pastor again. It is natural he should feel an interest for this people. He has hoped to do them good by these reminiscences; he is sure the giving of them has afforded him pleasure, for if there has been any thing useful in his now somewhat protracted life, aught which was pleasant in passing, or the fruits of which he hopes to meet in Heaven, it was connected with the Great Revival of 1820.

AT CHARLTON. Here, too, a refreshing from the Lord was experienced during this remarkable season. Charlton was one of the oldest Presbyterian congregations in Saratoga county. Among an intelligent, orderly, and well indoctrinated people, the work did not commence suddenly, or progress rapidly, but it finally assumed the form "of a slow and progressive opening of the heart to receive Divine truth." Added to the stated means of grace, the ususal means of promoting Revivals at that time, were used. Conferences, prayer meetings, meetings for inquiries, and special visitations of families, were put in operation; God's people were earnest in prayer, and the results which followed in other places, were to a good degree attained here. There were eighty-four members added to communion in the course of the year.

AT EAST GALWAY. This place seems to have been next visited, and in a way to show another variety in the sovereign dispensations of grace. They were at the time without a pastor, although a faithful licentiate preacher had been with them the preceding autumn, who after the Revival, became their minister. In the Presbyterial Narrative, the church is described as "greatly diminished in numbers, cold, stupid, and discouraged." Symptoms of a Revival first began to appear among them about the end of February. Its principal care and labors devolved, for a considerable time, upon the eldership.—There appeared first, an unusual seriousness in one of the district schools. On the first sabbath in March, the president of Union College visited them, for the administration of the Lord's supper. *Seven* were added to the church on that occasion; the ordinances were very impressive, and several, it was believed, were then awakened.

The week following, the solemnity was evidently increased, and on Tuesday evening, at a conference, some twenty to thirty persons were so deeply impressed, as to be either unable, or entirely unwilling to leave their seats after the services were closed. Some stout-hearted young men were found wringing their hands in great agony, and asking, "What must we do to be saved?" School rooms became too small for these conferences; the church was resorted to, and soon filled to overflowing. The faithful eldership redoubled their exertions. They visited all the families by districts, conversed with individuals, and attended numerous religious meetings. They also succeeded in securing the stated services, for a season, of the preacher before mentioned; and it is remembered, and will long be remembered by this people, with what disinterested and affectionate zeal, he devoted himself to this work. For not less than seven or eight sabbaths in succession, was he with them, proclaiming the gospel of reconciliation, faithfully, plainly, and with great apparent effect.

Many whole families were hopefully converted to God, and in the course of a few weeks, more than two hundred and fifty, of every age, were rejoicing in hope. *One hundred and sixty* were added to the Presbyterian church; the Baptist and Methodist churches were also enlarged. The special means were continued by the eldership for some time longer. They were then relieved, in some measure, by the settlement of a pastor. Bible classes, sabbath schools, and catechetical instructions, were for a long time well sustained; and this congregation was distinguished for its liberality in the support of benevolent institutions.

IN WEST GALWAY, the Revival commenced about the same time, and apparently with great promise; but as the excellent brother laboring there was in a feeble state of health, and soon afterwards entered into his rest—little is known of the particular progress of the work. About one hundred, however, are said to have been added to the church, in consequence of this movement, and a good degree of its influence still remains among that people.

AMSTERDAM, Montgomery county, is contiguous to the last named place; and here the work assumed a decided and most interesting character about the 1st of March. "Several neighborhoods in the township were awakened at once." Cries for help came from every quarter; and minister and session soon found themselves in the very midst of God's wonderful workings. Their meetings of every name were full—were crowded. The whole of any day in the week, and as much of the sabbath as remained after the public services in God's house were over, was employed in visiting from house to house. The evenings were spent in conference, or prayer, or anxious meetings. And although many who attended these meetings, were often heard, when at home in their families, in their fields, and in their secret retirements, to groan out in agony, or to cry aloud in anguish of heart; yet in these meetings there was no noise, no confusion, no disorder. Sometimes indeed the prayer for mercy was forced from the broken heart in a heavy whisper, or in a stifled groan. Sometimes too the dreadful struggle within was rendered visible in the palsied frame or writhing hands, or other symptoms of spiritual distress, deeply affecting all around; but nothing like rant or confusion, or enthusiasm! Instead of this, an awe, a stillness, an oppressive silence, which cannot be described, pervaded the whole, and often rendered it difficult to breathe. It was the sinking of the wounded heart, the fainting which precedes the last agony of life. The hearts of rebellion had received their mortal wound, and were yielding beneath the power of God. Many who visited these meetings from motives of curiosity, totally careless! beholding the mighty power of God, were terrified at their own hard and impenitent hearts, convicted of sin, awakened to a sense of the misery of their state, and forced to enquire also, 'What they must do to be saved?' On one evening, set apart for a lecture and personal conversation, fifteen were powerfully awakened.

There was no difficulty in assembling the people, but often very great difficulty in separating and getting them to return home. Sometimes sleigh loads of these, after leaving the meeting, and riding half a mile or a mile homewards, would turn back again to the place of prayer, to hear still more about the salvation of Jesus. And they often did this, through lanes and ways and snows, that would have been deemed impossible by persons of any other state of mind.

The awakening in Amsterdam had one prominent feature somewhat peculiar. Sinners were generally very suddenly and alarmingly aroused; their convictions rapidly aroused to the highest pitch, were extremely painful in their operations, and yet protracted beyond any thing witnessed in other places. The truths which bore most heavily on the minds of sinners in this awakening, were the awful depravity of the heart, so manifest in its unreasonable and continued rebellion against God. Their own personal guilt and pollution; their evident danger of eternal death. Every one thought his own heart the worst, and his own case peculiarly aggravated.

Generally the first dawning of comfort in the soul, has been through the application of precious truth, while reading the Bible, or hearing it explained; or while in the act of secret prayer. The reality of the change which so many professed, became every day more visible by the love and unity, and growing holiness, and increasing light and gospel knowledge of those who named the name of Christ." (*Presbyterial Narrative*, pp. 25–27.)

The immediate result of this work at Amsterdam, was the addition of one hundred and sixty-two members to the church; but this is far from expressing the whole of the benefit. The place has been distinguished since as before, by a succession of good and faithful pastors, and several pure Revivals of Religion. The providence of God has remarkably taught them indeed, that his servants "do not continue by reason of death." But one has been removed only to be supplied by another of a similar spirit, and we cannot deny ourselves the mournful pleasure of recording here the name of a brother, whose first and final excellence on earth shone forth in this Revival. *Rev. Halsey A. Wood*, was at the time pastor of this people, and recently entered upon the field of his public ministry. Amiable and unpretending, but a man of great clearness of mind, warm piety, sound judgment, and great firmness of purpose and pursuit. With what devotedness, with what zeal and real love for the work did he now lay himself out for early usefulness! By night and by day, in his own congregation and in others, in the ecclesiastical meetings, and in all appointments of the church, whoever else might be, we were sure this brother would not be wanting. *Nunquam non paratus!*

A lovely friend, an able helper, a successful laborer. Having a fine constitution, enjoying almost uninterrupted health, and so well acknowledged by the master, we fondly trusted he was to last long, and with still increasing acceptance. But God's ways are not as our ways, nor his thoughts as our thoughts! Brother *Wood* was suddenly cut off by a fever, in the autumn of 1825, and his dust has since been occupying a rural burying ground, overlooking the village, which he loved, and where his first and early labors were bestowed.

Why the church must lose such men, and why the feebler often survive to record their memories, are questions not for us to answer. It is a consolation to know, however, that such characters do not cease to be useful when they die. The Revival of 1820, will always be identified by the church of Amsterdam, with the memory of this beloved pastor.

SCHENECTADY AND UNION COLLEGE. *In the week of January,* 1820, there was a very sudden death in one of the students of Union College. The alarm was great, and the professors and pious students availed themselves of the opportunity to make a suitable impression of the dispensation. A prayer meeting was held in the room where the corpse had been laid out, and many resorted to it, either from sympathy, or for those higher ends which the occasion seemed to demand. Solemn exhortations were given, and many fervent prayers were there offered, for two succeeding days. The effect was soon visible, and many of the Lord's servants believed that a work of special grace was already begun. The praying was now increased in fervency and in frequency. Inquiry meetings were held, where the sinner's obligation to immediate submission was much urged, and some at length began to rejoice in hope. That which was at first regarded by many, as only *a nine day's wonder,* and was opposed by some, eventually become a general concernment, and continued for about three months, with great power and interest.

By the 1st of April between thirty and forty of these students were found rejoicing in hope, most of whom connected with Evangelical churches, and several afterwards devoted themselves to the gospel ministry. What a mercy! not only for individual salvation, but for Zion and the world! "From the college an awakening spread down into the city, (of Schenectady,) and in February became very interesting there.

Its first appearance was among the few praying people, the females especially, who met weekly to pray. Their hearts were drawn out to God, most entirely and ardently. A few lectures at private houses were blessed greatly. Many date their convictions from these meetings. The numbers began rapidly to increase. A private house would not hold the people. The academy room sufficed only for a few weeks, and before it was yet believed that the Spirit of the Lord was moving on the hearts of sinners, *the Presbyterian church* was scarcely large enough to accommodate the Wednesday evening lecture!

The church was destitute of a stated pastor, and help was obtained as it was found most practicable. The Lord was their great help. Lectures were very much crowded; conference meetings, meetings for prayer, and meetings for anxious sinners were full and solemn, and greatly blessed. Young and old, moral and profane, felt the benign influence. It was not confined to any one denomination; and be it remembered, to the glory of God's grace, that *a great unity* of action and of feeling, pervaded the whole. There was scarcely any sectarian or divided views manifested until the close of the whole work. It was a very silent, solemn, heartfelt operation; slow in progress, but blessed in result. Nearly three hundred, we trust, were converted to God."

Mr. Nettleton was a good deal in this place. The other labors, so far as preaching was concerned, devolved principally on the clerical members of the college faculty. But the Lord showed here, as in other places, that he has many other helpers, besides his official servants.

From Schenectady the work spread, and with happy effect, into the immediate vicinity, generally by the instrumentality of pious students from the college, and such occasional labors as the professors were able to bestow. The churches of *Princeton, Duanesburgh* and *Carlisle,* were also visited at this time; but the strength of the mercy shower seemed evidently abated with the opening of spring, or rather was passing eastward, and was at length gone. Still we *heard* of its wonders, in *Greenbush* and *Nassau,* and thence in Massachusetts and Connecticut, and more or less in connection with the labors of that remarkable man, who was so greatly useful amongst us.

But here we follow it not. Our object has been, thus far, to trace the work in a particular district, to gather its incidents, and to mark its instrumentalities, as calculated to instruct us, and illustrate the mighty and more indispensable power of God.

We have been aware of performing a difficult task. In a narrative of a Revival of Religion, embracing so large a field, and implicating so many individuals, it were probably impossible to do entire justice, and we should not be surprised (should this publication be noticed at all,) if places and persons should deem themselves neglected, or unfairly represented.

For the correctness of the statements, as far as they go, we think we can vouch; but a more correct or fuller account, we shall be quite willing to see. In the opinions or deductions which we have to offer, we of course are alone responsible.

Note

1   Was this a proof of want of emotion, as has been sometimes charged upon Mr. Nettleton? It may be told in answer, that this writer is the individual on hearing of whose conversion, Mr. N. *threw the book across the room!*

CHAPTER VI.
RESULTS, AND A COMPARATIVE VIEW OF THE WHOLE WORK.

This part of the subject demands our candid and most conscientious regards. For the great end of these reminiscences would be lost, and our agency in giving them, be unworthy, if not criminal, did we not make such deductions as the facts shall be found to warrant, and which shall prove to be for the benefit of those who will read and observe them.

We *first* remark, therefore, that if by *results*, is to be understood here the *immediate* effects of this Revival, the facts now exhibited leave us no room for disquisition. In the number of souls hopefully converted; in the enlargement of the churches; strengthening of believers and building up the various institutions of benevolence and religion, and in further favoring the cause of order, morals and truth in every department, it was universally acknowledged, that the Revival had been a blessing, distinct and manifest.

The deportment and spirit of the subjects also, was such as to bear the best tests of examination on this subject. Reviewing the ground after more than one year had elapsed, the testimony of the Albany Presbytery, is as follows: The converts "have been uncommonly united together in Christian love, and out of a number not less than two thousand, who have been hopefully converted, and of whom fourteen hundred have united themselves to the Presbyterian church not more than four or five are known to have shown signs of apostacy." *(Presbyterial Narrative.)*

Still our conclusions cannot be final, until we have examined *the degree of permanency of these results*, and something of *the general state of these churches in after years.* And here it cannot be denied, that while many of these *churches have continued to advance, and never abandoned the high ground then taken, either as to doctrine, spirit, or practice, there has been declension among others*, and in some few cases an actual diminution in numbers and graces at least for a season.

Truth compels us to state, that ministerial changes have been frequent in one or two of these congregations, and divisions and unhappy differences on points of church order; but in no instance, we believed, could these evils be traced to the Revival, nor have they amounted to essential heresies, or been of long duration.

The result of a trial of more than twenty years, therefore, is thus far this; that while there have been deliquencies and declensions in some of the churches which are now reviewed, there has *not* been a falling off, as a whole; but on the contrary, an increase in numbers, strength and efficiency, as compared with their preceding state.

For the evils which have now been referred to, we believe that *adequate causes* may be assigned, and as it is our duty to deal fairly with this whole subject, some of these *causes* must now be assigned.

One of these causes undoubtedly was (for we have known no Revival in which it did not obtain to some extent,) *the too hasty admission of candidates to the communion of the church.* The hearts of sessions and all others, at such seasons, are open to hope and charity. Young converts, sincere and warm, but with little experience, desire the privileges of full communion. We do not pretend to know the heart; we follow our most favorable feelings, and the candidates are admitted, even in doubtful cases, and without further trial. Sometimes these wear well, but in other instances (and they are *very many* in more modern Revivals,) you have every reason to fear, afterwards, that they had no true religious experience. No doubt that some such cases occurred in the work, which we have reviewed, and these, so far as they extended, have been among the causes of trial and evil.

Another cause is to be assigned probably, in *the want of proper religious instruction of young converts, after the Revival was past.* Decided attention indeed was paid to this subject in many places, and with the happiest results. But others either had no pastors to take hold of this particular duty, or it came to be felt unhappily that didactic and doctrinal preaching was scarcely required or agreeable, after so much of higher emotions; and more loose views of truth have in consequence obtained. We do by no means believe this error has been as common here, as in some other Revivals; but wherever it has obtained, declensions and divisions, and the other evils mentioned have been more apparent. But on the other hand, in proportion as sound and stated preaching, Bible class, catechetical and sabbath school instruction have been enjoyed—these evils have been avoided, and young professors, as well as others, have appeared *to grow in grace.*

But finally, it is well known, and may not be omitted to be *mentioned here, that a class of Revivals, in many respects different from those we have reviewed, have since been experienced by the churches,* and we do not think a just appreciation of the whole present state of things can be made, without adverting to these, and making a fair comparison.

It is well known that about the year 1824 or '25, what have usually been styled NEW MEASURES, began to be adopted for promoting Revivals, such as *protracted meetings,* the *anxious seat,* the more *vehement excitement of natural sympathies,* and corresponding instructions, as to *human ability* and the *ease of obtaining Religion.*

It is known that Mr. Nettleton never approved of these measures, or the doctrinal views with which they were connected. He prophesied that 'they would *run out* true Revivals," and finding he could not resist them successfully, retired from that time into comparative obscurity.

Now it is a fact, that these Revivals have not, in general, borne substantial fruits. They have been of short duration, and followed in many instances, (we might say in most instances,) with more or less of evil to the churches, even where stated exertions have afterwards been made to give them a right direction. They have often been connected with divisions, strifes, unsettling of ministers, heresies, and a multitude of developments of spurious experiences in professors, such as give infinite trouble to churches, and for which no remedy seems to exist.

We do by no means affirm or believe, that these have been the only fruits of these more modern Revivals; but that they exist, and to a far greater extent, than was common in older movements of this sort, is what all observe, and few we think will be disposed to deny.

These Revivals have *followed,* at least, upon those former Revivals, and were in some sense connected with them; and now *what is the conclusion,* to which an enlightened friend of true religion would feel compelled to come in relation to this whole subject? Will he conclude that the whole doctrine of special influences of the Spirit, is a delusion, and belongs practically only to the religion of fanatics? Certainly he cannot, if a believer in the Bible—for numerous Scriptures, as well as observed cases in church history, are clearly against this decision; or will he come to think, as some at present seem inclined, that the influences, though real and most desirable, are so varied in their forms as not to be expected again to be seen in our churches; but that the same blessings are to be enjoyed if enjoyed at all, only in the more ordinary movements of stated ordinances. To this, we answer, that if it shall so appear in the result, and without involving the guilt of neglect on our part, and conversions and sanctification and church life, can truly be secured in the wisdom of God

to the extent needed, without *special and observable movements*, we shall
not only be reconciled to it, but consider it on some accounts, as a more
desirable dispensation. But as this has not yet been, at least, in our
country, and until it is so, we have many reasons for expecting and still
laboring for what are called Revivals of Religion. That they should be
special, is no more to be wondered at, than that regeneration is so—
while the very *diversity* that is now contended for, leaves room to expect
it, as one of the modes of the Spirit's operations.

Nor does the tendency to degeneration of Revivals at all prove the
falsity of the doctrine of Revivals; every good thing tends to degeneracy
in human hands. Thus was the Great Revival of New England followed
by the aberrations of *Davenport*, and other and purer Revivals must
succeed, before this injurious influence could be wholly removed. True
Revivals are of God; then they have been of signal service to the church;
and if in any instances they have been followed by those less pure, and
evils have ensued, the fault has been in their management, not in the
thing itself.

Nor are we yet warranted to doubt that Revivals may be again
enjoyed. We should labor and pray for their return, for we do not see
how the churches in this country can, at present, dispense with their
influence, and hope to live.

Now our believing all this, has been one reason for giving this history,
and we shall conclude therefore, by presenting in summary, *those principal
things in which the Great Revival of Saratoga county* SEEMS TO HAVE DIFFERED
FROM MOST OF THOSE WHICH HAVE RECENTLY FOLLOWED.

1. And one great difference undoubtedly was, *in the peculiar
qualifications of the principal actor*. Taking him all in all, we believe, and we
think it will appear from these pages that Mr. Nettleton was peculiarly
adapted to this vocation, and that none like him, in this respect, have
since been raised up. God indeed is not confined to one class of agencies,
and we are quite willing he should send by whom he will send; but still, if
among his instruments one is clearly less wise, less holy, or less self-
governed than another, we should expect it would appear in the greater
imperfection of their work.

2. *A second* and important difference in favor of our older Revivals has
been, as we believe, that *more of doctrinal truth was then preached and insisted
on as entering into religious experience.* The subjects of entire *moral and
original depravity, human dependence and God's sovereignty,* as well as
atonement, regeneration, and the *whole work of the Spirit,* were more
frequently insisted on, and it was not sought so much to *explain* them on

principles of human philosophy, as to urge them on the authority of God's word. There was more of "thus saith the Lord!" and leaving it there for the sinner to dispose of as he might.

3. Moreover, *the effort was almost never made then, to convince the sinner how able he was to repent,* (though his *excuses* were taken away of course, by showing that his inability *was moral,*) but far more was it insisted that it was *not* so easy and *sure* a thing to obtain religion in the manner usually attempted; and when the awakened were found, as they always are found at first, to rely on self-sustained efforts; the object then, always was to *take away* their expectations! "Knock out their props," said Mr. Nettleton, "and let them fall."

4. One of the most marked of all the differences was, *that in the measures which were then used to promote Revivals, men did not seem to go before the Spirit, but always rather to follow it.* This appears most clearly in what has now been recorded, both of Mr. Nettleton's efforts and those made by the churches. A protracted meeting got up in a cold and unprepared state of things; the getting Christians to rise and pledge themselves, without any evidence of the Spirit leading them thereunto, or urging a sinner to the anxious seat against his will, and with almost physical violence, were things unheard of, and would have been wholly disapproved: yet *very great exertions* were used where the Spirit prepared the way; and "Up, for the Lord *has* gone out before thee," was often found in appropriate exhortation.

5. *There was less noise and less "observation,"* as well as *less attempt to move upon curiosity and other human sympathies,* than has usually been in more modern Revivals.

6. There was more care given *to secure correct advice and instruction for sinners under conviction.* Great pains were taken to have no *contradictory* instructions. Sinners were advised to be a good deal alone, to attend to their Bibles, pray much, and rightly, and *submit* at once to the teachings of the Holy Spirit.

7. *It was attempted to have, as far as possible, only discreet and judicious persons to exhort in religious meetings.* Not many were called on even to pray, and *females* never, in promiscuous assemblies, although in prayer-meetings by themselves, and in other appropriate departments they were always encouraged, and were found to be among our most efficient helpers.

8. *Mr. Nettleton never encouraged speedy admission to church communion.* Great pains were taken by sessions, that as far as possible thorough examinations should be had, especially with the young. And yet they

probably proceeded too fastly in some instances, as has been already suggested.

Finally, more pains than are now common, seem then to have been taken for the instruction and establishment in the truth of young church members. This practice was somewhat varied of course, under different pastors; but it was constantly recommended, and more or less aimed at by all. For this purpose, *Bible classes* and *other associations* were formed. *Sermons and series of sermons were preached to the young, and books of a didactic character were prepared,* all having in view a more doctrinal education of those who had thus happily come into the church in early life.

In short it was never permitted to these young disciples to suppose that their work was done, or that the care of others for them had ceased when they had become professors of religion; and this we cannot but regard as one of the reasons of the greater general steadfastness in this class of church members, as then witnessed, beyond that which has since been seen.

There were other devices of a minor kind, the object of which was to *bind Christian hearts together,* and with the mention of one scene of this sort, which he well remembers, the writer of these Recollections will at length close.

It was on occasion when the Revival had nearly closed, and a company of some one hundred dear young converts were met by themselves to receive appropriate instructions. The place was an old academy building—since gone down to the dust, as have many who were then assembled within its walls. The text selected by the preacher was *John's IIId epistle, the 4th verse*—"*I have no greater joy than to hear that my children walk in the truth.*" And never was the unworthy pastor more conscious of entering into the full sentiment of the text, than on that occasion. A little sea of upturned youthful faces was before him, and every mind seemed easy to be moulded as the plastic clay. We sympathized; we ran together at once, in our assent to the truth, in views, in holy feelings, in love itself, chaste, elevated, and heavenly, and yet without any thing to destroy reverence, for it was "*love like unto the angels.*"

When the preacher had finished his more formal instructions, and urged the sanctions by all the force of the occasion, he dismissed this meeting, and told these young disciples *they might rejoice together now, in a somewhat freer manner.*

And they did rejoice exceedingly. The scene cannot be described. They sung, they conversed, they congratulated, they strengthened each other, and *hearts* were then bound together, we have no doubt, by ties which have since sweetened earth's toils, beautified Zion, taken off death's bitterness, and are enduring still where toil and death are no more.

"When shall we all meet again?" Never in this world certainly. But should this sketch ever meet, in earth's wide waste, any of the dear *"children"* then assembled, and now, like the writer, "passed into the sear and yellow leaf," it may inform them that their then youthful pastor still lives, and has often been cheered in his pilgrimage, by learning that one and another of them was *walking in the truth*, or has finished his course in peace.

In the hope of yet aiding others in the same course of duty and blessedness, he has undertaken, and now finished, this history of the GREAT REVIVAL OF RELIGION IN EIGHTEEN HUNDRED AND TWENTY.

APPENDIX.

SPECIMENS OF NETTLETON'S PREACHING
(First published in the New York Observer).

They said he was *not eloquent;* and in the usual acceptation of the word, he was not. He generally chose the plainest subjects, preached doctrinally, as well as experimentally: and his object being only to do good, he urged his positions with great force, not withholding *repetitions,* in many instances, for the sake of greater effect.

But they said, "he was not eloquent," and this was the impression under which I sat down to hear him for the first time.

It was a season of great interest, in the memorable winter of 1820–1, when a Revival was being experienced—and it did appear as if the mind of a whole population was moved by an unseen and awful influence from above. A company of young ministers had come together, hoping to learn something from this veteran evangelist, in relation to their professional duties. But he scarcely *told* us any thing! He was nervous and exhausted, and seemed really ill. Well, I remember his appearance. He sat by the open fire, got off his shoes and roasted his feet, took some pearl ash and cider, and finally went to bed. After tea, however, he seemed more revived, and we went to the evening meeting together. It was known that Mr. Nettleton was expected to preach, and almost the entire population were seen assembling. Sleigh load after sleigh load arrived, some of them to my knowledge from a distance of not less than eight miles—and not the most busy fair or parade day, ever exhibited more zeal—tempered however with solemnity and the strictest regard to order. Mr. Nettleton was remarkable for the pains he always took to "keep his audience as still as possible." I have seen him spend half an hour in packing them away in a closely crowded school-house, for this purpose. But to proceed. I watched for the effect of this appearance of things upon our friend, and found he was not insensible to it, more than any of us. As he walked up the middle aisle to his little temporary desk under the pulpit, and saw the waiting masses on either side, I could observe his nerves to strengthen at every step.

He took his place, gave out the 39th of the Village Hymns, and made his prayer. It was short, hesitating, and very solemn. It seemed as if he was weighing every word, and seeking to express exactly "what *he felt* he needed from the great God," and nothing else. Then he took his text— Gen. xix, 17—and it was as it seemed to me, admirably appropriate. Many had been already awakened in our congregation, and some were rejoicing in hope. But there was a *lingering* with others, a sort of pause in the work, and we feared it was about to decline.

The preacher probably knew this, and his object appeared to be to start these lingerers anew, and by the grace of God to carry the work further. It could be surmised how he would treat this subject in view of such a state of things. He first run over the whole history. I remember his introductory remark. "God," said the speaker very slowly, "God does not always speak *by words.*" And soon coming round to the same idea again, "God, I say, does not always speak *in words!*" It was the more impressive language of *God's acts*, to which he was about to direct us; and he then went on to describe the terrible fate of the cities of the plain. He gave us their character, the forbearance of God towards them, the visit of the angels and their treatment by the sons of Belial, the scoffing of the sons-in-law, (all spiritualized and applied as he went along,) and approached his more immediate object. After infinite trouble, and strangely overcome reluctance, "the Lord being merciful unto them," the family of Lot are at length without the walls of the city.

"And now," said the speaker, turning to sinners, "now, ye who are determined to remain behind, I have no more to say to you;" and he waved his arms with an abandoning gesture backwards, until it did seem they felt themselves given up, and almost hopeless. "I say, I have no more to do with you, my concern is with those who are out of the city, and on the plains." And then with a look and voice and manner, indicating the deepest feeling, he repeated his text— *"Escape for thy life, look not behind thee, neither stay thou in all the plain; escape to the mountain, lest thou be consumed."* It may now be imagined, perhaps, the effect of this announcement, and his further prosecution of it!

His object evidently was to show to awakened sinners the danger of delay, or any pause, or looking back even for a moment. I remember one remarkable expression. "The sinner that looks back, in such circumstances," said he, "don't know what he does. *He rocks an infant giant.*" And then he described Lot's wife, until it was an absolute reality before our minds. "She began to run as well as others. But she began to hesitate; she began to doubt perhaps whether it could all be true; she should like to see how the city looked now; she would just look over her shoulder, and run still; she tried; when suddenly she was struck, stock and stiff, by a bolt from heaven:" and we seemed to see a cold, straight pillar of salt standing before us!

These are not imaginings of my own, nor did it on that occasion seem at all extravagant in the speaker. The fact was, it was dramatic, we were all in for it, and the master spirit carried us on at pleasure.

Thus he drove the trembling fugitives across the plain; the "little hill" was reached at length, and then rejoicing in deliverance, all this happy experience was made to body forth a like rejoicing in the recently converted sinner.

The preacher had said he would have nothing more to do with those who remained in the city. But he did have a word more to say concerning them, and it was on this wise. Abraham is made to get up to the place where he had stood before the Lord; and he *sees* that burning, "*when all the smoke of the city went up as a furnace.*" A hundred times have I heard this scene described, or attempted to be described. But only now had I seen it made a reality. We saw the beautiful sunlight falling for the last time on those doomed towers, the overdrawing noon cloud, the arrest, the consternation of the godless inhabitants, the heavens riding over their heads, the savage lightnings, the bursting earth, and the sheets "of fire and brimstone descending from God out of heaven," all these were made to pass in awful vividness, and when the speaker said that "all this was so, and we might see the evidence of it at any time, if visiting the scorched shores of the Dead sea," I found myself actually looking out into the night as if expecting to see the conflagration!

Many, I doubt not, in that awestruck congregation, turned in the same direction. At all events, the object of the sermon was evidently attained.

Some, on that memorable night, we have reason to believe, "*fled for refuge* to the hope set before them." The work received a new impulse, and the next day we found several new cases of anxious inquiry.

In consequence of what I saw this evening, *I changed my mind with regard to his being eloquent;* for what *is* eloquence but that which has the effect of eloquence?

Specimen II.

His object this time was, evidently, to *indoctrinate* certain converts who had recently obtained a hope. It was at an advanced stage of the Revival;

indeed the season was nearly passed; and the place of preaching was a school-house. Well do I remember the rushing, solemn zeal with which we gathered. It was winter; the winds blew boisterously, and deep massy snows obstructed the ways that led to the place of that humble meeting. Yet they came, men, women, and children, from far and near, and the house was filled to overflowing long before the appointed hour.

Mr. Nettleton spent the best part of half an hour in *packing* that rushing crowd. He would beckon one here, and another there; put this one on the end of a box, this other on the stairs; clear a plank, clap a boy in a corner, and make one more seat for some old lady on his own chair, until all were fastened in some way, and there was no more moving without or within. He finally told them they were so crowded, he thought they had better not attempt to rise in prayer; and then, after the usual preliminary services, began his discourse.

His text was *the second chapter of Ephesians, the first seven verses.* His division of the subject, somewhat formal was, as nearly as I can recollect, as follows:

1. The condition of man by nature.
2. The nature of that mercy by which he is saved.
3. The manner of his change and the privileges of it; and
4. The ultimate object of this grace.

On the subject of man's state by nature, he insisted much, and carefully. Besides showing that he "walked according to the course of this world," he insisted that we are "by nature, children of wrath;" and dwelt much on the entireness of our moral corruption, by repeating the figure here used. "He is dead—'dead in trespass and sins.' Not sick merely, or likely to die; but dead, really dead; entirely destitute of moral life or holiness, and exhibiting only corruption and deformity in the sight of God." This was asserted, proved, illustrated, and repeated until it was understood, reflected on and felt, and then the speaker proceeded.

II. "But God, who is rich in mercy, for his great love, wherewith he loved us, even when we were dead in sins." *When* did God begin to love us? where and at what time did mercy move? Was it after we began to be holy and to love God? Ah, had he waited until then, this mercy had never been! But when did God begin to love us? "even when we were dead in sins." Yes, dead! dead to law, dead to moral loveliness, dead to strength, dead to all hope, and morally loathsome in his sight. Here, you perceive, was another fundamental doctrine taught, and the hearers did not know the name of it. But they saw it must be so, and drank it in with eagerness, wonder and delight.

III. Next comes the change; or our being quickened or raised up. This was "together with Christ." It was by Christ, and after the manner of his resurrection. "Thus were ye regenerated by the influence of the Holy Spirit, and for the sake of your Almighty Saviour" And all this, be it remembered, you being "dead in trespass and sins." ("By grace are ye saved;") you see Paul throws it into a parenthesis here, as if he felt crowded for room, to express so great a truth; but he must utter it again and again, "By grace are ye saved!" and then a double gesture of the speaker seemed to express the feeling of enclosing, embracing, and hanging upon this great and glorious truth!

Then he dwelt upon some of the privileges of this happy state, under the representation of "sitting together in heavenly places." He did not critically explain the expression. He just took the common sense view of its expressing Christian fellowship. "Sitting together in heavenly places." Perhaps Paul was reminding them of some happy Revival season at Ephesus. O, do *you* not remember such seasons? and was it not a blessing indeed, thus to rejoice together in Christ Jesus! Indeed it was a happy season—a happy place: "'twas heaven below." And you must, you do desire to live always in such a frame as this. Well, hearer, watch, pray, and obey always, and then you may, "for by grace are ye saved!"

Thus he accomplished two leading objects—the binding of hearts, as he would sometimes call it, and the magnifying, in all things, the honor of sovereign grace. And therefore, behold—

IV. The ultimate object of this mighty work of God. The ultimate, the great object is now intended. He did not wish to have concealed the interest they had in it. This was great, very great; but Christians, this is not the great end of your being thus saved! No; but it is to illustrate the honor and glory of God hereafter. "That in the ages to come, He might show the exceeding riches of his grace, in his kindness towards us in Christ Jesus." Thus he says in another place, "For this cause I obtained mercy, that in me first Jesus Christ might show forth all long suffering, for a pattern to them that should hereafter believe." And here is the great, the worthy end, for which all this wondrous grace of God has been! In eternity past—in all its after developement—now, and as it will be "in the ages to come"—the object is to illustrate, as it could never have been seen without this, what Deity is—in all his wondrous perfections, worthy of our adoration, wonder and love! Christians, you are to be held up hereafter for showing this. Should you not rejoice in the thought? To stand as mirrors in a future world; to reflect the exceeding grace of God!

to be pointed to by adoring intelligences, when they exclaim, "Behold what the exceeding grace of God can do!"

Thus happily, as it seemed to us, were these young disciples brought forward to take large and comprehensive views of the ends for which they were to live, and to feel the whole nature of their hope and their true condition. They could not be self-trusting, who thus understood the plan of salvation; they could not be narrow in their views of social privileges in religion; they could not want for appropriate motives to zeal and holy love. Having thus urged these views, the speaker's main objects for that occasion were evidently accomplished.

A man was present who had recently obtained a hope, after a season of great distress. Having previously communicated with the preacher, he was now called upon to state his experience, which he did in a few words, and then the meeting was brought to a close. That man still lives, as do many others who attended this remarkable meeting. Should this sketch meet their eyes, may it strengthen their faith![1]

Note

1   Rev. R. Smith, *Recollections of Nettleton and the Great Revival of 1820* (Albany, E. H. Pease & Co., 1848), pp. 1–150.

APPENDIX 2

FRANCIS WAYLAND'S OBSERVATIONS OF ASAHEL NETTLETON

Eyewitness accounts of the preaching of Asahel Nettleton are worthy of inclusion in any biography of him; if those observations are from an eminent Christian in his own right, then more notice needs to be taken of them. This is the case of Francis Wayland, pastor, educator, and President of Brown College, whose life in ministry is worthy of careful study. He encountered Dr. Nettleton in the midst of revival at Union College, Schenectady, New York when the great evangelist was at his height of physical powers and popularity as a revival preacher. The record of Dr. Wayland's recollections is unique and we include it as a stand-alone entry in this biography of Nettleton. This record recounts the great revival at Union College from the summer of 1819. The eyewitness testimony of Francis Wayland bears weight. His comment on Nettleton in regard to the evangelist's preeminence as the leader of the Second Great Awakening is worthy of record: "I suppose no minister of his time was the means of so many conversions." And the comment that, "It as generally admitted that his appearance in a town was the precursor of a revival;" is a strong endorsement indeed.

It is with great pleasure and gratefulness to God for providing us with this *inside recollection* of Asahel Nettleton! Wayland was a tutor at Union College when he met Nettleton. He writes:

FRANCIS WAYLAND ON ASAHEL NETTLETON

"About this time all that region was overspread by a revival of religion, especially through the labors of the Rev. Asahel Nettleton. It extended to Schenectady, and entered the college. There was a powerful impression made upon the students, and many of them were converted. The occasion was blessed to me in awakening my conscience and recalling me to my duty. I labored as well as I knew how in the promotion of the work, and saw with delight a great change in the moral character of the young men. In the portion of the college which was under my care, a prayer meeting was established, which continued, I think, until I resigned my office. At nine o'clock every evening, all who chose met at my room for reading the Scriptures and prayer. For some time almost every student in my division attended, each one in turn conducting the meeting."

In the following letter Mr. Nettleton gives a graphic account of the scenes which so deeply deeply affected the character of the subject of our memoir:—

"South from Malta about twelve miles is the city of Schenectady, and Union College, where I now reside with Dr. McAuley. He takes a lively interest in this good work. I first became acquainted with him last summer at the Springs, and more particularly at Malta, where he frequently visited us, and preached and conversed, and attended the meetings appointed for those anxious for their souls. On a Sabbath, when a number were to be admitted to the church in Malta, he brought with him several students from the college. Some of them became anxious. About this time one of the students was called into the eternal world. He was laid out in Dr. McAuley's study. The doctor was anxious to improve this solemn providence to the best advantage. He assembled the students around the lifeless remains of their departed friend, and conversed and prayed with them in the most solemn manner. A number of them engaged to attend to the subject of religion in earnest. From that time many of the students became deeply impressed with a sense of their lost condition. For them were appointed meetings of inquiry. And in this very room, where they lately beheld the breathless corpse of their young companion, and where I am now writing, was witnessed a scene of deep and awful distress. About thirty of the students are brought to rejoice in hope. The revival is now very powerful in the city. Such a scene they never before witnessed. More than one hundred have been converted. Besides these, we had more than two hundred in our meeting of inquiry, anxious for their souls. We met in a large upper room, called the Masonic Hall. The room was so crowded that we were obliged to request all, who had recently found relief, to retire below, and spend their time in prayer for those above. That evening will never be forgotten. The scene is beyond description. Did you ever witness two hundred sinners, with one accord in one place, weeping for their sins? Until you have seen this, you can have no adequate conceptions of the solemn scene. I felt as though I was standing on the verge of the eternal world, while the floor under my feet was shaken by the trembling of anxious souls, in view of a judgment to come. The solemnity was heightened when every knee was bent at the throne of grace, and the intervening silence of the voice of prayer was interrupted only by the sighs and sobs of anxious souls. Some of the most stout, hard-hearted, Heaven-daring rebels have been in the most awful distress. Within a circle whose diameter is twenty-four miles, not less than eight hundred souls have been hopefully borne into the kingdom of Christ since last September. The same glorious work is fast spreading in other towns and congregations. 'This is which was spoken by the prophet Joel.'"

Mr. Wayland writes to Mr. Wisner,—

"Your very welcome letter was received a few days since. I could not till this evening steal time to answer it. I entered my hall this evening, saying, 'Now for a long letter to brother Wisner.' As I walked up stairs, I heard the voice of praise and thanksgiving. I entered the next room to mine, and found about twenty-three, many of them new converts, engaged in a prayer meeting. I joined with them; and this had delayed me, till now my watch points to ten o'clock.

"The Lord hath done great things for us, my brother, whereof I hope we are glad. But we are not half glad enough. There are now about twenty happy converts, and nearly that number more, under serious conviction. As yet the work has been most powerful among the most moral and religiously educated. You may readily conceive that the aspect of college is somewhat altered. It is no difficult thing to collect a prayer meeting at a moment's warning. In fact, if two or three meet together, prayer seems to be almost the necessary consequence. About a week ago I mentioned to one of the converts, who rooms next to me, the expediency of instituting a section prayer meeting, or more properly a family meeting, at morning and evening. It was joyfully acceded to. They chose to meet in my room. And since that time, at the ringing of the first bell in the morning, and between nine and ten o'clock at night, we offer up our devotions at the domestic altar. This incident expresses, I think, the general feeling about college. I have said that the work was generally confined to those who had been religiously educated. This is not, however, universal. The name of Bob———used to be proverbial for everything that was lying or mischievous. He is now calling on all who come in his way to repent and believe the gospel."

Of the remarkable man already alluded to, Asahel Nettleton, Dr. Wayland writes,—

"He was among the most effective preachers I have ever known. I never heard logic assume so attractive a form, or produce so decisive an effect. When reasoning on any of the great doctrines in Romans, for instance, election, the utter depravity of man, the necessity of regeneration, or the necessity of atonement, his manner was often Socratic. He would commence with what must be conceded by every one present; then, by a series of questions, each deliberately considered, and not suffered to pass away until the speaker and hearer gave the same answer, his opponents would find themselves face to face with an absurdity so glaring, that notwithstanding the solemnity of the scene, the hearer could hardly escape the disposition to laugh at himself, for holding a belief that appeared so utterly untenable.

"In other styles of address he was equally successful. The doom of the sinner, the danger of delay, the condition of the thoughtless, the vicious, and the blasphemer; the exercises of the soul from the first moments of conviction, the subterfuges of the human heart, and the final act of submission to God, were portrayed by him with a power of eloquence that I have rarely heard. I suppose no minister of his time was the means of so many conversions.

"He was in an unusual degree obedient to impressions received in answer to prayer. I believe he never went to a place, unless he had received an intimation that he had a duty to discharge there; and he rarely visited a place where a revival did not follow him. In conversing with persons under conviction, he exhibited a knowledge of human nature almost intuitive. Nor was it merely with awakened sinners that his preaching was remarkably successful. It was his habit (when he could stay long enough in a neighborhood) to collect the converts and explain to them the doctrines of the gospel, point out to them their danger, and then to build them up in the faith, before he left them.

"In preaching, his countenance beamed with a holy earnestness, such as befitted one sent directly from God as an ambassador to men. At this time he very rarely entered the pulpit, or preached in the daytime. He preferred a vestry or a school-house; and if he spoke in the body of the church, he addressed the audience from the deacons' seat, or the platform in front of the pulpit. His manner was quiet, especially at the commencement; his voice grave and deep-toned; his whole aspect was that of a man who had just come from intimate communion with God. He never used notes (although I believe he sometimes wrote out some of his sermons), and rarely employed ornament of any kind. He would stand up, throwing a red bandanna handkerchief over his left arm, and in tones varying but little from those of earnest conversation, would sway an audience as the trees of the forest are moved by a mighty wind.

"His manner of life was consistent with his appearance in the pulpit. His residence was generally with the minister of the parish in which he was laboring. The time not employed in preaching or conversation with inquirers, was devoted to secret prayer and the reading of the Scriptures. He was never seen in what is called general society. His whole time seemed devoted to labor for souls. He was unmarried, and, to avoid remark, he never rode or walked with a lady alone. He was wholly insensible to the influence of money. His dress was plain, and well worn. When money was offered him, he would either return it all, or would accept only what was wanted for his present necessity.

"Notwithstanding all this, I have rarely known a man who was, for a great part of the time, more thoroughly abused. It was generally admitted that his appearance in a town was the precursor of a revival. This fact aroused all the virulence of men at enmity with God. His mode of conducting meetings was somewhat peculiar, and his preaching singularly bold and uncompromising. Thus he greatly excited against him those professors of religion who did not like anything new in the mode of preaching. Hence, at first, good men would frequently turn aside from him, and too readily give heed to the slanders of wicked men. I knew very well a physician of eminence, a pleasant, kind man, though utterly destitute of religion, residing in a village where Mr. N. was laboring, who circulated a falsehood about him, retailing a conversation, which, he said, Mr. N. had had with him in his office, when the fact was, that Mr. N. had never been in his office; and it subsequently appeared that the doctor was wholly ignorant of his person. To such attacks, Mr. N. never deigned to make a word of reply, nor did he ever intimate that he knew of their existence. He considered that a man's character is the best defence of his reputation, and he left it to time and to the providence of God to refute the slanders.

"A man so unique and so successful was of course blessed with many imitators. But they could much more easily imitate his peculiarities, than the spirit with which he spoke. Some of them preached a very different doctrine from that in which he gloried. Others failed entirely in moral character. The spirit of revivals declined, and this sort of preaching was made, I fear, a thing of gain. He became involved in controversy with some of the most eminent men in the Congregational church. These differences led to painful results, and it may, I fear, be said that the peculiar type of revival preaching which I remember at this time, rose and declined with this excellent man. I write this in part from general recollection, at the distance of a long intervening period. In some of the facts I may unintentionally have erred."

We need not fear to believe that Providence had wise and gracious designs in so ordering his circumstances that Mr. Wayland should be mingled with the scenes of this revival, and especially that he should form the acquaintance and enjoy the counsels of Mr. Nettleton. "I became intimately acquainted with Mr. Nettleton, and my conversations with him were of great use to me."[1]

Note

1   Francis Wayland and H. L. Wayland, *A Memoir of the Life and Labors of Francis Wayland, D.D., LL.D.* (New York: Sheldon and Company, 1867) pp. 106–111.

APPENDIX 3

RECOLLECTIONS OF NETTLETON

This chapter is a collection of descriptions of Asahel Nettleton's preaching by eyewitnesses. We will begin with a sketch of Nettleton's ministry written in 1864, just twenty years after his death. It is authored by a college chum who knew him well. The author relates the "stages" of how Nettleton conducted a revival—this being the only account of this nature recorded! Thus it is a rare and valuable account of the great evangelist's preaching ministry.

"The writer knew him well, and was oft refreshed under his ministry in the great revivals of 1820–21, while a student in Yale college. The whole city was overshadowed with the cloud of mercy, and the renovating influences kept falling, more or less, for the space of two years.

"Originally Dr. Nettleton's intention was to embark on some foreign mission; but by the force of circumstances this intention was defeated, and he found himself in the work of home evangelization, to which thenceforward his life and labors were consecrated. He put himself on the current of events, and was borne along as by a divine impulse. He went nowhere without having, as he supposed a call of Providence. He left when the same mysterious index finger pointed him away. From every quarter invitations flowed in upon him; but only those were responded to which seemed to him to contain in them the voice of God. If the cry, "Come over and help us," came from a church which was paralyzed by inaction or corrupted by worldliness, he gave it usually no heed. The supposition was that they were looking less to the Almighty than to an arm of flesh. Nothing grieved him more than the idea, implied or expressed, that *he* could breathe life into dry bones. He regarded it both as an insult to heaven and to his own understanding. He! Why, there was never a more consciously impotent human instrument. Never was there a preacher more oblivious of self, nor one that entered more into the spirit of the sentiment, "Our sufficiency is of God." On one occasion, having arrived in a town with a view to labor for the upbuilding of Zion, he overheard certain prominent members of the church saying in an exultant strain, "Mr. Nettleton has come, and we shall have a revival of religion." The words pierced him to the heart. He went to his closet and wept. He ordered his horse at once, saying as he took leave, "I can't stay here any longer. The people are in a wrong state of mind." His absence created inquiry. Christians began to study into the matter. They saw their error in looking to man instead of God. They repented and put their faces in the dust; and soon the indications of the Spirit's presence were manifest. Hearing of this, Mr. Nettleton returned and preached to them with great zeal and success.

"There was at first view nothing in his appearance that was striking or calculated to arrest the attention. Of medium height, with a somewhat haggard look, large blue eyes, prominent Roman nose, high oval forehead, with light and slightly gray hair brought up from each side to cover its baldness, and an air of abstraction, as if conversing either with his own thoughts or with the great Invisible, he seemed always bent on some object, near of remote, connected with the salvation of men. His whole energies appeared to be working in this direction. His prayers all breathed of this. If he was seen conversing with an individual, you might be sure that he was trying to get into the sympathies of that heart, so as to reach it with the truth of God. This he did, not by direct and blunt assailment, but gradually and gently, as the sunbeam steals into the crevice. His knowledge of men went deeper than any minister's I have known; and it was the more marvellous, as he was never known to have mingled much in promiscuous society. There was a sweet and attractive gentleness in his manners. He seemed to have conquered all the proud, sensual, or irritable feelings. An air of vestal purity surrounded him. You felt as if you were in presence of not only an amiable, but a holy man. These traits, by disarming prejudice, made his ministry potent for good. In many respects he resembled the apostle Paul. The self-denial, the absolute self-renunciation, the absorption of his whole soul in his work, the heavenly mindedness, the simplicity and singleness of his aim, all reminded one of that apostle. What was said of Paul by the Corinthians, that his presence was weak and his speech contemptible, might in some degree be applied, especially by those who judge of eloquence by shining qualities, to Mr. Nettleton. He lacked the grandeur of person and of intellect which some of the great pulpit orators have possessed. His voice was sharp rather than full or melodious, and his gestures, though emphatic, were ordinarily not graceful. His power as a preacher lay in intense earnestness. His whole being was concentrated in efforts to save the soul from death. Out of the pulpit as well as in it, this was evident. No man ever dreamed of attributing to him any selfish ends. It was manifest that the highest motives only swayed him. To this noble, disinterested spirit, more than to any graces of oratory, did he owe his influence and his success.

"There was, however, at times an eloquence that rose above all rhetorical rules, and though it dazzled not the fancy, stormed and carried the conscience and the heart. True, the Spirit of God was present to evoke it and give it power; so that every word told with terrible emphasis, and every sentence fell like the hailstones in Revelation, each one weighing a talent, causing men to cry out in audible accents, What shall we do? Still, none who listened on such occasions could deny that for clearness, force, and pungency, his sermons were unequaled. It was the highest style of pulpit eloquence, for it carried souls on its pure, impetuous current into the divinely appointed ark of safety. There was in it a spiritual elevation, as if God himself was speaking—as if the lips were all aglow with a coal from heaven's altar.

"The preaching of this distinguished evangelist, to be appreciated, had to be heard continuously, and under circumstances of more than ordinary interest. His first efforts were modest, his manner calm but clear, and his aim was rather to awaken interest than to excite the passions. Usually he began with the church, hoping to bring them to a higher tone of consecration. If successful in this, he turned his thoughts upon the careless and the impenitent, believing that a very intimate relation subsisted between a revival in the church and a resurrection of the dead in sin. His preaching had a strict adaptation to these varying circumstances. It rose as the current of feeling rose. It kept on, growing deeper and more impetuous as the revival influence augmented. It was like an electrical atmosphere, showing on the distant clouds some faint corruscations. But as they rolled up and came nearer, sharp flashes might be seen. By and by the whole concave was trembling with awful detonations. Such was Nettleton's preaching as the revival atmosphere deepened in breadth and volume. We have known him to preach in one of the largest churches in New Haven, every foot of the floor and aisles filled with dense masses, all wearing such a look as can be depicted only by the Spirit of God. Hundreds under conviction turned their tearful eyes in the direction of the pulpit, their sighs almost audible, repressed only by the proprieties of the place. How still—how intensely, awfully still! Truly, this is the house of God; yes, to many the gate of heaven. The preacher is himself oppressed, sustained only by the thought that God can and will do his own work. He has gone on and up with the advancing tide of feeling, until now his whole soul is elevated to its utmost power and energy. Talk of eloquence! Never before had I a just impression of what pulpit oratory is. Here is a humble preacher, uttering words so simple that a child can comprehend their meaning, with a manner earnest and solemn, and a heart deeply touched with emotion; and as he goes on, by illustrations so striking, reasoning so convincing, and appeals so tender, the audience can scarce refrain from an outburst of agony. Tears rained silently in those pews, and convictions went deeper and deeper, while many an eye was turned anxiously towards the cross, the only hope set before them. To appreciate Mr. Nettleton, one should have heard him as the writer heard him under the culminating power of a great revival. Never shall I forget the sermon on 'Dives and Lazarus,' delivered in the very height of the religious excitement. Rich men were there. It seemed as if everybody was there, so great was the crowd. The preacher was in his best frame. He gave full scope to his ardent soul. He had great power of description. It was not imagination so much as vivid conception. He could set religious truth in strong lights. On this occasion he carried us forward to the awful and glorious future. He took us into heaven, and even into hell. He gave us a glimpse of the glorified Lazarus, and startled us by a vision of the rich sensualist wrapped in sheeted flame. Towards the close the excitement became almost unbearable. He summoned the lost Dives back to this world. He bade the audience make way for him, pointing along the central aisle. The preacher gazed fearfully in the same direction. The audience instinctively half turned their heads. Now the flame-tormented soul ascends the pulpit. Starting aside, the preacher says, 'Listen to one risen from the dead—risen even from hell;' when in deep despairing tones the imagined Dives begins to address them. He warns them as only a returned emissary from hell could warn men. It was a scene of intense interest. Never could it have been carried through but for the wave of feeling which had been gathering for weeks, and was not at its flood. This sanctioned it, saved it, made it a success. Many were awakened by it to a sense of their sins.

"The sermons of Dr. Nettleton were usually constructed in a clear, methodical manner. The language was of the simplest kind. The point soon began to appear, and grew sharper and more prominent as he proceeded. Towards the conclusion he would make some sentences cut as with a two-edged sword. He used much repetition. A strong, pungent truth would be echoed once, and twice, and even thrice, each reverberation louder and more solemn, as if he hoped by repeated blows to drive it through the most obdurate conscience. I never knew a preacher who could repeat a sentence so often without diminishing its power. He aimed at direct impression; and no minister perhaps in this country has been more successful in turning many to righteousness, nor will any, as we think, shine more illustriously among the stars of the celestial firmament."[1]

The second account of Asahel Nettleton was published in 1864 as well. It seems there was a concerted effort by ministers of his day to keep his memory green. The following extract is from a brief sketch of Nettleton's extraordinary ministry and the impact it left upon the church and society. We include the author's wise observations on revival and that of what makes an orator effective.

THE REV. ASAHEL NETTLETON, D.D., THE AMERICAN EVANGELIST

"When it pleases God to send a time of unusual refreshing upon any portion of his Church, and to pour out in great measure his Holy Spirit upon the souls of men, it is highly becoming and indispensably necessary that his ministers and people should evidence the highest wisdom in all their dealings with the souls of the awakened, the recently converted, and the revived. A time of revival is a season when the mighty power, the unbounded love and the unsearchable wisdom of God, are strikingly displayed. But on this very account is it necessary that the greatest wisdom, prudence, charity, and order of men of God, should be exhibited in their highest degree. There is a tendency in the *world* to revile the work of God; in the formal to discredit it; and in the cold professor to doubt it; while there is a tendency in the *awakened* and the converted, and sometimes even in the spiritual director, to be extravagant, to mix faith and sense, and to set up visions and fancies for the oracles of God. We may learn a lesson from those who have gone before, and who were the honoured instruments, in the hand of God, of a saving blessing to thousands. Sketches of the revival work of such men as Nettleton, M'Cheyne, Burns, and others of recent times; of Edwards and Tennent, Robe and M'Culloch, Whitefield and Wesley, Berridge and Grimshaw, and others of a past epoch, cannot fail to be full of suggestions of great practical value.

"Ere proceeding to the subject of this sketch, let us make another remark. In the commencement of the dispensation of the Spirit, awakenings and conversions on a large scale were the experience of the Church. In a very short period after the outpouring of the Spirit, *eight thousand* converts were added to the Church in Jerusalem. In the last epoch of this dispensation, as pictured by the pen of prophecy, conversions on a large scale are evidently to gladden the Church. The question, then, may be fairly asked, Are these the normal effects of the gospel? The history of revivals proves that at every period of spiritual awakening, conversions were numerous. Has the Church, then, lost at times the art of prayer and faith, in relation to the awakening of souls? Have its formal prayer and feeble faith made the heavens decline their showers and the hearts of men their furrows? It is to be feared that we have not been rightly aroused ourselves, and have not laboured in faith and with prayer for large blessing. May the tide of awakening which has been in our day rising on every side, bear all God's people, as well as many careless sinners who are high and dry upon the strand, out into the ocean of unbounded blessing...

"'Though he was often surpassingly eloquent,' says Dr. Sprague, [of Nettleton] 'and would hold his audience as by a spell, yet his power was exerted in turning their views upon themselves and their Saviour, and in sending them away, not to extol his eloquence, but to weep for their own sins.' This is the height of pulpit, as of all eloquence. Fenelon has characterized the two styles of oratory as exemplified by Cicero and Demosthenes thus: that at the end of the speech of the one the cry would be, 'Oh, what an orator!' at the end of the speech of the other it would be, 'Up, let us march against Philip!'. The latter is the preacher's only valid aim. His end is the saving of souls: his very calling has that as its object. The style and manner of address are to be subservient to the saving of souls."[2]

This typifies the preaching of Asahel Nettleton—when he finished preaching the audience was stirred and challenged to *act*. *"Up, let us march against Philip!"*

Notes

1   Rev. J. B. Waterbury, D.D., *Sketches of Eloquent Preachers* (New York: American Tract Society, 1864), pp. 43–51.
2   Rev. Robert Steel, M. A., Ph. D., *Burning and Shining Lights* (New York: T. Nelson and Sons, 1864), pp. 125, 126, 136.

APPENDIX 4

The attached rare document on the revival of religion of 1820 is important on several levels: it provides an unbiased look at Asahel Nettleton's ministry as seen through the eyes of his peers; it documents the effects of the Second Great Awakening as it occurred in the state of New York, which at this early time period, was still a sparsely populated frontier; it makes comparisons between this revival of religion and the one which occurred in Northampton, MA in 1734 under the ministry of Jonathan Edwards; it provides eyewitness reports of the revival and lists the great benefits and several hindrances to a revival of religion. Therefore this document should be required reading for any true student of revivals. It is with great pleasure we provide the following narrative.

A NARRATIVE OF THE REVIVAL OF RELIGION, WITHIN THE BOUNDS OF THE PRESBYTERY OF ALBANY, IN THE YEAR 1820

BY THOMAS MCAULEY, HALSEY A. WOOD, MARK TUCKER, ELISHA YALE, WALTER MONTEITH, AND ELIPHALET NOTT

PRINTED BY ISAAC RIGGS, 1821, SCHENECTADY

At a meeting of the Presbytery of Albany, held in Schenectady, on the 8th June, 1820:

"*Resolved,* That the Rev. Dr. McAuley, the Rev. Mark Tucker, and the Rev. Halsey A. Wood, be a committee to receive statements from the members of Presbytery, of the origin, progress, and present state, &c. &c. of the great work of God's grace within their congregations, and to embody them in the form of a *narrative*, together with whatever may appear to have helped the progress, or hastened the decline of the revival."

At a meeting of the Presbytery, in Amsterdam, held on the 9th January, 1821:

"*Resolved*, That the Rev. Elisha Yale and the Rev. Walter Monteith, be a committee to *prepare a report* of the state of religion within our bounds; and that said committee be added to the committee appointed on the 8th June, 1820, for the purpose of drawing up a narrative of the origin, &c. &c. of the awakening; and that their report be incorporated with the narrative of the aforesaid committee, and that the whole be presented to the Presbytery at its adjoined meeting to be held in Malta, on the 6th February next."

At a meeting of the Presbytery, Malta, 6th February, 1821:

"The joint committee appointed at the two last stated meetings, to draw up a *narrative* of the great work of God's grace, including a report of the present state of religion within the bounds of the presbytery, presented the following narrative, which was accepted.

"And on motion, the said narrative was re-committed to the joint committee aforesaid, with the addition of the Rev. Dr. Nott, for revisal, and *ordered to be printed*.

Attest,

WALTER MONTEITH,
Stated Clerk."

NARRATIVE

TO THE REV'D. PRESBYTERY OF ALBANY.

THE committee, appointed "to receive written statements from the members of presbytery, detailing the *Origin and Extent, Progress and Present State* of the great work of God's grace within your bounds; together with *the causes helping its progress* or *hastening its decline*, and to embody them in the form of a regular narrative," beg leave to report, that they have attended to that duty, and that from such *written statements* as were forwarded to them; and also from *the statements made by the ministers and elders in presbytery,* at *Stillwater and Amsterdam;* and also from their *own knowledge of God's wonderful workings*, within the prescribed bounds, they have drawn up the following narrative, with the accompanying observations, which they most respectfully submit to the presbytery:

1ST. THE ORIGIN AND EXTENT.

As to the origin of this great work, your committee feel constrained to speak with great diffidence; almost every congregation traces it to a cause, originating in and operative only upon itself. Sometimes it seems to have commenced in two very distant places at the same time; and again in two very contiguous places, at very different times. At one place in a Sabbath school; at another, in a prayer meeting; in another, at a conference or an evening lecture, and still at another, in the secret exercise of prayer among God's children.

The *sensible cause* too, was not uniform; sometimes it was recounting God's wonders among other sinners; sometimes urging God's children to their duty, or warning sinners of their danger. In one place, a sudden death; in another place a plain unpolished sermon. In one place, an unaccountable impression that God was about to pour out his spirit; exciting Christians to self-examination and prayer, and to double diligence in the discharge of their duties; and in another still, visiting from house to house, and warning every man of his duty and danger, and pressing everyone to attend to the great concern of salvation. But as to the great, invisible, all-pervading and operative cause, there is no diversity, 'TWAS GOD THE HOLY SPIRIT, operating by the gospel. There were indeed a very great diversity of operations, but the same spirit wrought all things in all.

In August and September of 1819, there was some attention to religion in and around the village of Saratoga Springs: subsequent to this, the township of Malta was visited with the refreshing influences of God's grace. About the same time there were very encouraging symptoms of an awakening in Stillwater, which had been preceded by a very powerful, although a very short work in Pittstown-Hollow: throughout all that region, every meeting was crowded, every means and every effort blessed. God's people were unusually animated in their prayers, and encouraged and comforted in their approaches to God. For some months, the special influences of God's spirit, seemed to rest only upon the region just described; nor were they felt beyond, until in January and February of 1820, when the eye of faith and the heart of affection, hailed their approach and felt their influence throughout Amsterdam, West-Galway, East-Galway, Ballston and Schenectady; not all at once indeed, nor in regular succession, as to local situation, but in very rapid succession as to time. Union College too, was neither the last nor the least sharer in the influences of God's sovereign grace. In February, the first, second and fourth wards of the city of Schenectady, the town of Charlton and other places, were benignly visited. In March and April, Milton, Greenbush and Nassau, and in May the third ward of Schenectady, were visited with overwhelming power.

In May it began to decline, everywhere almost; or rather, it was found to have declined, excepting in the third ward, where it had just commenced, and from which it spread into Princetown in June, and where it is still slowly operative, as it is in several other places within the bounds of your presbytery.

Since that period the church has enjoyed much of God's presence, and the light and consolations of his holy spirit. The multitudes who have been gathered into Christ's fold, are walking together in love, growing in grace, in knowledge and in humility; are progressing in holiness, free from contention, from error, from schism, and adorning the doctrines of God their Saviour by a gospel faith and practice.

With this outline of the *origin and extent* of this great work before you, your committee have no doubt of your feeling a deep interest in the progress of it, which they are about to present to you in detail.

2D HEAD—PROGRESS AND PRESENT
SARATOGA.

In July or August, 1819, the Rev. Mr. Nettleton, visited Saratoga Springs, for the benefit of his health. Shortly after that time he visited at a house in Malta, where a few people were assembled together. And if we might express our opinion we would say, this little providential meeting was the blessed means of commencing the great work of God in Malta. From thence Mr. N. passed on to the Springs; but all was dead or dying there; the gospel had been long preached there, but with very little apparent effect. The circumstances of that place, so peculiarly unfavorable to gospel holiness, are well known to the presbytery; and those circumstances were never more unfavorable or influential, than at that time. This messenger of God had come to prove the healing influence of the Saratoga waters; but having had long experience of the life-giving influence of the *waters of salvation*, he could not rest day or night, until he had endeavored *by all means* to bring dying sinners to prove *their* efficacy: and God was with him, and God's anointed servant placed there, was with him in sentiment, in love and in labour. At first, there were some found mocking, and others saying, "what will this babbler say now?" but God honored his own cause. An invisible agency was operative on many an heart; pride and prejudice, hatred and hardness, ignorance and enmity, guilt and pollution yielded to its influence. The views and feelings, hopes and fears and affections of many were almost instantly changed. And with the exception of a few *high-toned blasphemers*, evidently left as a beacon on some hidden shoal, to be seen and known of all men, to warn them back from certain destruction; all the scoffers and sceptics, infidels and unbelievers of the place were soon found mingling in humble undistinguished company with sinners of every other name, inquiring what they must do to be saved? In September and October the work was progressive, every day was fully employed by the people of God. The pastor of the village, and his helping brother, publicly and privately, and from house to house were engaged warning every man, and persuading every man, in season and out of season, exhorting, rebuking and entreating; and the Lord was found everywhere present! Many were pricked in their hearts and forced to cry out, men and brethren what shall we do! More than *fifty* were brought to rejoice in the hope of eternal life through Jesus Christ our Lord. And although this number may appear but small when compared with the numbers that flocked to Jesus elsewhere; yet, let it be remembered, that the numbers from which they were gathered were very small. The permanent residents in the village are few, and the surrounding country is circumscribed and very thinly inhabited. There have been fifty-five added to the church; eighteen adults baptized. The awakening continued until the commencement of the watering season in 1820, when it seemed to cease all at once. Some doctrinal disputation in the north part of the settlement had a very injurious effect. Sabbath schools are flourishing and very beneficial; monthly concert well attended; *some few instances of recent conversion*; children are catechised weekly; and as a fruit of holiness in the lives of those who have named the name of Christ, we would mention a female charitable society, which, amongst the acts of its benevolence, has sent down twenty-three dollars in aid of the funds of your presbytery for the education of the poor, pious youth for the gospel ministry! One of their number has departed this life triumphantly.

MALTA.

Your committee would next turn your attention to Malta, literally a moral wild. With the exception of a very small Methodist church in one corner of the town, and two or three of God's children in another corner, there was neither piety nor prayer, no mean of grace nor desire of salvation. There had been indeed, many years before, been a small church there, but it was broken down and in ruins; not a single member remained who had any claim to right or privilege in it. The pride and prejudice and ambition of rule, that broke it down, were still in existence indeed, brooding over the ruins of their own producing, endeavoring sedulously to raise them as a bulwark between sinners and salvation, and rejoicing in their long continued success. There had been several attempts made to introduce the stated ministration of the gospel, but without any encouraging effect. Such was the state of things in the fall of the year 1819, when Mr. Nettleton first preached among them. There had been one or two hopeful conversions in August; and in September and October, there were a few awakened. About the beginning of October, Mr. Hunter, a licentiate from the presbytery of New-York, visited the place, and his preaching and other labours of love were greatly blessed among them. Mr. Waterbury and Mr. Olmsted, from the theological seminary of Princeton and Mr. Armstrong of Moreau, were all providentially led to the place, and continued for some time to labour in their several spheres of action, with very encouraging success, so much so, that on the 26th of October, there was a little church collected and organized consisting of twenty-four members, mostly recent converts to the faith of Christ. Other ministers had preached occasionally in the place; but from the time when the church was formed, Mr. Nettleton preached for seven or eight months almost constantly among them, and his labour of love was highly rewarded by the great head of the church. From the very commencement of his labours, the work of the Lord's spirit became more powerful, and rapidly progressive. It was but a little while until weeping and anxious distress were found in almost every house; the habitations of sin; the families of discord; the haunts of intemperance; the strong holds of error; the retreats of pharisaic pride; the entrenchments of self-righteousness, were all equally penetrated by the power of the Holy Ghost. Foundations of sand sunk out of the reach of feeling and deceived confidence! Refuges of lies fled from the eye, and fancied security from the heart of the unregenerate.

In some cases sorrow was soon turned into joy, but in other cases anxious distress continued long; it was deep, heart-felt and awfully pungent; and brought the distressed almost down to the gates of death.—— Under its influence, error lost all its alluring importance; and violated obligation, forfeited happiness, a long rejected Saviour, and approaching wrath, death and judgment, with the retributions of eternity, filled every heart, occupied every thought, and agitated every feeling. Often and anxiously was the inquiry made, "What shall we do?" During several weeks, the awakening spread over different parts of the town until it became almost universal. Nor were the attempts so often and so offensively made to draw the attention to doctrinal disputation, every influential in stopping its progress. Every house exhibited the solemnity and silence of a continued Sabbath; so profound was this stillness and solemnity, that a recent death could have added nothing to it in many families. Common conversation was rarely engaged in, while every ear was open to hear the gospel, every heart prepared to receive the tidings of salvation. There were some melancholy exceptions indeed, but we shall not name them. The breath of the Lord rested on their unholy influence, and it was wilted and withered and gone forever. The holy one paralyzed their efforts against his anointed, and scorned their opposition to the spread of Messiah's kingdom. Within the year there were added to the church more than one hundred, and there were perhaps fifty others who cherished a hope of forgiven sin. Some of those who joined the church have been severely tried; but the trial of their faith has eventuated in the confirming of their hope and confidence in God. All who have named the name of Christ, are giving good reason to believe, that they have rested on the sure foundation, and gained a dwelling in the ark of safety. There is no tendency to error amongst them, but a great and growing attention to the pure and simple doctrines of the bible. There were fifty adults baptized.

There were some special cases, clearly manifesting the sovereignty of God's grace and the freeness of his salvation.

STILLWATER.

Your committee would invite your attention, in the next place, to Stillwater, where the Lord hath displayed the wonderful riches of his grace. Verily "the Lord's ways are not our ways, nor his thoughts our thoughts." If he smiles on the wilderness, it is in a moment like the garden of God. The most obdurate heart is "willing," in the day of his power.

Late in the summer of 1819, the spirit of the Lord was poured out upon Pittstown-Hollow. Many, pricked in their hearts, were inquiring what they must do to be saved? And many were fleeing to the only hope of the wretched, and finding in him everlasting security, and receiving with him joy and peace. We mention Pittstown in connection with Stillwater, because it was principally through the voluntary labours of Love of the *minister of Stillwater*, that God's gospel became the ministration of life unto so many in that very destitute region, where a little church was soon gathered and a good many added to the disciples of Christ. The glad tidings of God's grace to the sinners of Pittstown-Hollow, had a very awakening influence on God's people in Stillwater! Where minister and people gave themselves to prayer, publicly, privately and secretly. A concert for secret prayer was held at sunrise on Sabbath mornings, and very generally observed. They cried unto the Lord, and he hearkened and heard them, and granted, in his own time, their whole desire. A deep solemnity spread over the whole community; every meeting was crowded; some were deeply impressed with a sense of sin, and fully convinced of their need of an interest in Christ. Sinners from a distance came to hear the gospel, and hung on the lips of the preacher, as though they heard for their lives. And again did they return to listen, with increased attention, to the glad tidings of great joy; peace on earth, good will towards men!

Such was the state of things down to the beginning of October, when their pastor, having attended the annual meeting of the Synod of Albany, which held its session at Cherry-Valley, returned home, and with an heart overflowing, recounted to his people the wonders of grace which God was doing in Cooperstown, New-Hartford, Utica, &c.; and noticing God's mercy to their neighbours in Malta, warned and admonished them of their danger and their duty. His exhortation was brought home by the holy spirit, in demonstration and power. It was sealed upon every heart, it seized upon every conscience.

The bible class, and the Sunday schools, were deeply affected. They felt the first influences of God's spirit. The great work commenced with them! Many of them soon became reconciled unto God; meetings became more frequent, full, crowded! In the course of a few days, the spirit was poured out on several neighbourhoods, on families of every habit. The benign influence spread over into Schaghticoke, where at a single lecture, preached by the Pastor of Stillwater, between thirty and forty were awakened! And so did it flourish there, that in a little while almost that whole number were rejoicing in hope!

In the north part of Stillwater, where the means of grace were seldom enjoyed, the work of the Lord commenced and became very powerful. Scarcely one family has been passed over. In a large district, though harassed by sectarian contentions, where praying families were very rarely found, there is now scarcely one house where prayer is not wont to be made; where sacrifice, and a pure offering, is not daily offered up to God! Many whole families, young and old, every soul, were hopefully converted to Christ. But, in *the village*, God's power was most conspicuous. Many of the inhabitants were of the most hopeless kind. Boatmen, tipplers, tavern-hunters, gamblers, gain-sayers, infidels and atheists, were mingled and mixed with the unholy multitude. The ways of Zion languished and mourned because few came to her solemn feasts. There were many who lived in the village who scarcely ever attended the house of God, or in any other visible way acknowledged his supremacy. They were literally stout-hearted and far from righteousness, without God and without hope in the world; and yet, (we cannot refrain from ascribing glory to God in the highest,) this multitude, bad and unblessed as it was, felt the power of the Holy Ghost, and yielded to his influence, and received the gospel of his grace gladly, and submitted themselves to him whose right it is to reign, and in whom all the families of the earth are blessed.

We dare not descend to particulars here. The narrative would fill a volume. Our limits will not suffer us do more than simply state, that whether the Lord moved among the most pure in morals and manners, or among the most polluted in heart and life; as soon as the eye saw that it *was God*, the heart felt its own pollutions and abhorred itself in dust and ashes, and trembled at the Lord's word. Fearfulness seized upon the hypocrite; the careless, the scoffer and skeptic alike were brought down to the lowest dust. You might have heard them inquiring with all the apprehensive anxiety of the jailer, "men and brethren, what must we do to be saved!" and in all the humility of the publican, praying, "God be merciful to us" miserable "sinners."

In the upper congregation, where there had been a great work of grace in 1815, there were little appearances of any awakening until late in the winter of 1820; but the Lord's mercies were not clean gone, for he appeared there also in his great glory. And so universally did his grace abound, that there remains not one family, in all that congregation, where there is not one or more witnessing souls. The awakening was not confined to any one age, or sex, or class of character; it was general! And to the glory of God's grace be it spoken, the most profligate, generally, were the most prompt in their submission to God. The language of fact corresponds with the words of Christ, publicans and harlots are first in entering the kingdom of God. The converts were of all ages, from seventy-five years down to twelve years; and in the short space of six months, one hundred and ninety-four were added to the church, of whom one hundred and three were added in one day, and there have been twenty-three added since, making the whole number two hundred and seventeen. There were ninety-four adults baptized. The whole number who cherish a hope of forgiven sin, is considerably over three hundred, within the township; some of whom have joined other churches, and some have not gained strength enough to confess Christ before men in any church.

The attention began to decline, as the spring opened with all its engaging and perplexing cares. Three weeks suspension of the means of grace, too, had a very deadening influence. Those who have named the name of Christ, are walking worthy of their high vocation. There has appeared only one or two cases of hopeless declension. At the present appearances are becoming more favorable. The monthly concert is well attended, and the church offers its alms with its prayers. At every concert they make a collection for the benefit of foreign missions. They have a *bible society*, and have recently formed a *female cent society*, consisting of nearly three hundred members, who charge themselves with the entire education of one poor, pious young man for the gospel ministry. The *bible class* and *Sabbath schools* are well attended.

There is no tendency among the young converts to error, but a remarkable progress in bible knowledge and practical piety.

MILTON.

In Milton there was some attention in the spring of the past year; but the world gained the ascendancy. Their minister was obliged to leave them, a little while previous to the appearance of the religious attention, for want of subsistence. How far this operated unfavorably, the Lord knoweth. Your committee would only notice, that Milton, although almost surrounded by the awakening, from its origin until its end, scarcely counts twenty converts; and it is believed few of these were awakened there. At present all is cold and lifeless there.

BALLSTON.

Of Ballston, your committee need say but little, as there has been a report published, which has put you in possession of all the important facts relating to the origin, progress and present state of the awakening in that place. Nor would they deem it expedient to make any report at all, were it not for the sake of connection.

The work of grace does not appear to have commenced in Ballston, until after it had begun to decline in Saratoga, and had nearly gained its height in Malta and Stillwater. At that time the people were very generally cold and careless, and were not free from serious apprehensions that they would be unable to retain their minister. But the Lord had mercy in store for them. The good news from Malta, Saratoga and Stillwater, seemed to arouse some among them. Minister and Session, in free conversation, candidly confessed to each other their consciousness of many defects in the discharge of their several duties. They confessed and mourned over these in the presence of God, and entered into new engagements to be more faithful in future. They districted the congregation, and resolved to visit every house. They called together the church members, and conversed freely with them on the state of their hearts. They agreed to avoid all doctrinal disputation and to attend to their own hearts, and so to let their light shine, that others seeing it, might be led to glorify their heavenly father. This was about the beginning of January, 1820. Just about this time or a little previous to this, several of the session and others, attended the communion in Malta, and various other meetings in succession. Their hearts were greatly refreshed. They caught the holy flame of divine love, and returned home making the solemn inquiry, **What do we have all the day idle?** They commenced the work of domestic visits and personal conversation; and to their utter surprise, found the spirit of the Lord working everywhere before them. They urged sinners to pray, and sinners complied! And while they were yet praying, the Lord heard them, and many an heart of hardness was broken and melted and removed! The heart of rebellious stoutness submitted! The heart of unbelief yielded! And while repentance melted down the most obstinate, they were led by the right hand of God's righteousness, to trust in the mercy of God and rest for acceptance and salvation on the righteousness of Jesus Christ. Some entire house-holds were converted to God. Five children out of one family were born again. Convictions were deep, powerful and pungent, generally of short continuance when compared with those in other places. In eight months one hundred and sixty were added to the church; perhaps forty others cherished a hope in Christ. Sectarian folly, was evidently injurious to the awakening. We "know that offences must come," "but wo to" every one "by whom they come." Those who have been admitted to the fellowship of the church, are dwelling together in unity, cherishing a spirit of gospel peace. There has only one case of hopeless backsliding occurred. No tendency to error visible amongst them. Sabbath schools are greatly blessed; monthly concerts well attended; bible class making a very encouraging progress; the young converts evidently learn faster than before they became pious. There were seventy-six adults baptized.

Of the happy results of this awakening, we have to notice, that a female member of this church was led, in the dispensation of Divine Providence, to take charge of a female academy in South-Carolina. The young ladies under her care were of all ages, from eight to eighteen. On the Sabbath day she confined their attention to the *Bible* and *Baxter's Saints Rest*, and has had the unspeakable satisfaction of seeing twelve of her pupils brought to rejoice in Jesus, as their only Redeemer, and that too in one single week.

CHARLTON.

Your committee would further report, that there appears to have been a very general attention to religion in Charlton; especially among the young.—The work seems to have been a slow, progressive opening of the heart, to receive divine truth; and a powerful influencing of conscience to obey the truth. And although the work was not so rapid in its progress, nor powerful in its operations, at any time, as to entitle it to the name of an awakening; yet it was sufficiently so, to denominate it *a time of refreshing from the presence of the Lord*. It was encumbered with many embarrassments; but the Lord did not suddenly take away his holy spirit. Conference and prayer-meetings were instituted and continued, generally well attended and greatly blessed. Anxious meetings too, were productive of very extensive blessings. There were eighty-four members added to the church during the past year; and God has granted a pastor to that people, and everything is now very encouraging among them. No schism, no error, no cases of backsliding. The hopes of God's people are greatly elevated. The Lord's name be for ever praised. There were eighteen adults baptized during the year.

EAST-GALWAY.

Your committee would next present East-Galway to the notice of presbytery; a place this, highly favored of the Lord! Visited once and again, with an outpouring of his spirit. Your committee feel themselves again met, and relieved from the labor of a lengthy report, by a very excellent statement, published some time ago, by a member of the session of that church. But still, for the sake of connection, they will take a cursory view of the awakening there. The church had been destitute of a pastor for three years; its members were greatly diminished in number, cold, stupid and discouraged. They were in this state in the fall of 1819, when Mr. Chester, a licentiate under your care, commenced his labours among them. His labours were greatly blessed, in establishing Sabbath schools and reviving the attention of professing Christians. But his health failing, he was obliged to intermit his labours, until the beginning of May, after which he became their *stated pastor*. The session districted the congregation and visited every member. On the first Sabbath in March, 1820, the Rev. Dr. Nott administered the communion of the Lord's supper. About a week previous to which, there appeared an unusual attention to bible reading, in a school, near the center of the town, particularly among the female scholars. On the Friday of that week, several of the scholars were borne down with a sense of their sin. The school was visited; and on one side where the females sat, many were weeping for their sin, while on the other side, some were disposed to mock; but in a little while they also gave up their opposition, and were melted down. This was not noised abroad, lest opposers should say, that *the children were frightened!* On the Sabbath, seven came forward and confessed their faith in Christ Jesus before the world; and on that day many were deeply convicted of sin. On Monday the attention in the school was increased, and the monthly concert in the evening was crowded. At the regular conference on Tuesday evening, from twenty to thirty were so distressed, that they could not leave their seats. Some stout-hearted young men were found wringing their hands, in the greatest agony, and asking what they should do to be saved? The next day more than forty were found to be under deep and powerful convictions! Conference rooms soon became too small. The church was soon crowded to overflowing. And although the number was so great, there was an awful silence, a stillness in which *the breath of a child* might have been heard. The mouths of gainsayers were soon stopped; and even infidels were constrained to acknowledge the power of God. There was no settled minister there, nor even a transient one; and with the exception of seven or eight Sabbaths, in which the Rev. Dr. Nott preached, there was no means used, excepting the little that the session and some students from the college at Schenectady, were able to do, in visiting and in meeting with the anxious. The preaching alluded to, was greatly blessed; it was accompanied with the demonstration of the holy spirit and with power. And the church in that place will long remember, this labour of love, this ministration of grace; so seasonable, so salutary, so saving! Many whole families were converted to God. From some families seven, from others six, and from others five, were brought to rejoice in hope of forgiven sin. In all the wonderful work of God's spirit, through this community, we have witnessed nothing equal to His work in this place; either in the pungency of convictions, or shortness of their duration. In a few weeks, more than two hundred and fifty of every age, from eighty-two down to ten years, were rejoicing in hope; of whom one hundred and sixty were added to the church. Several others to the highly respectable Baptist churches in the town, and some to the Methodist church; but your committee are not able to state the precise number. It was altogether the Lord's doings, and marvelous in our eyes!

There are none who seem to have apostatized.—They are all, holding on their way, very lively in their affections, animated in their hopes, consistent in their Christian walk, growing in gospel grace, steadfast in doctrine, and abounding in deeds of charity. They charge themselves with the entire expense of the education of *one young man*, and half the expense of the education of *another* for the gospel ministry.

There are two bible classes, well attended; and several Sabbath schools, in a very flourishing condition. Catechetical exercises are well attended and greatly blessed. The elders visit frequently from house to house, and talk freely with every professor, on the subject of personal religion and growth in grace. There have been fifty-seven adults baptized.

WEST-GALWAY.

Your committee have not been put in possession of the history of the awakening in West-Galway. Mr. Farrer, the minister of that congregation, was in ill-health, during the latter part of that glorious display of God's power to save. *He now sleeps in Jesus!*

All that your committee can state, with confidence, is, that the awakening commenced and progressed in a manner very similar to that in East-Galway; or rather, was identified with it. There were ninety-five added to the church. Several others are cherishing a hope of eternal life. Sabbath schools and monthly concerts are well attended. Only one instance of backsliding. No doctrinal difficulties. They have received the gospel of God, without any doubtful disputations. There were twenty-eight adults baptized.

EDINBURGH.

There has been no special attention at Edinburgh, during the last year, and there were only two added to the church.

PALATINE.

In this newly formed church, there has been no revival, but there are two Sabbath schools. The monthly concert is observed. The church is very small and weak.

JOHNSTOWN.

From Johnstown, that old and very respectable corner of God's vineyard, your committee have no heart cheering intelligence to communicate. A little dew from heaven above, seems to descend upon it. Just enough to keep it from total sterility! But the early and latter rains are withheld; no refreshing shower, causes it to bud and blossom and bring forth fruit. There have been only twelve added during the past year, to the communion of the church. There is much of the exterior of godliness among the people; and we trust a good deal of its power among old professors; but very few are enquiring the way to Zion. The means of grace are well attended. Love and harmony prevail in the church. There are bible classes in *seven* different districts, attended weekly, with evident good effect. Ministerial visitations, catechetical exercises, monthly concerts, are all punctually and well attended. Surely they are a people preparing for the Lord. O! for a time of refreshing from his presence among them!

AMSTERDAM.

The church in Amsterdam dates the commencement of its revival, from the first of March, 1820; but there were very interesting symptoms of it, previous to that date. Christians had been awakened; had trimmed their lamps; a spirit of prayer had been poured out upon them; vice of every kind had become more bold and openly daring; profligates more than usually hardened in sin, and working iniquity with uncommon greediness, putting heaven's power and God's abounding grace to the proof! And in addition to all this, a few had been brought to Jesus, by means which seemed very inadequate. These were sure indications, that God was, in very deed, in that place.

But from the first of March, the work assumed a very decided character. Several neighbourhoods, in the township, were awakened at once. Cries for help, came from every quarter; and minister and session, soon found themselves in the very midst of God's wonderful workings! Their meetings, of every name, were full, were crowded. The whole of every day in the week, and as much of the Sabbath as remained after the public services in God's house were over, was employed, in visiting from house to house. The evenings were spent in conference, or prayer or anxious meetings. And although many who attended these meetings, were often heard, when at home, in their families, in their fields and in their secret retirements, to groan out in agony, or to cry out aloud in the anguish of heart! When pierced with the sword, or broken down under the influence of the spirit; yet, in these meetings, there was no noise, no confusion, no disorder! Sometimes, indeed, the prayer for mercy was forced from the broken heart in a heavy whisper; or in a stifled, agonizing groan. Sometimes too, the dreadful struggle within was rendered visible, in the palsied frame, or writhing hands, or other symptoms of spiritual distress, deeply affecting all around; but nothing like rant, or confusion, or enthusiasm! Instead of this, an awe! A stillness! An oppressive silence, which cannot be described, pervaded the whole, and often rendered it difficult to breathe. It was the sinking of the wounded heart! The fainting which precedes the last agony of life. The hearts of rebellion had received their mortal wounds, and were yielding beneath the power of God! Many who visited these meetings from motives of curiosity, totally careless! beholding the mighty power of God, were terrified at their own hard and impenitent hearts; convicted of sin; awakened to a sense of the misery of their state, the madness and folly of their present course, and forced to inquire also, what they must do to be saved. On one evening, set apart for lecture, and personal conversation, fifteen were powerfully awakened.

There was no difficulty in assembling the people, but often, very great difficulty in separating and getting them to return home. Sometimes, sleigh loads of convinced sinners, after leaving the meeting, and riding half a mile, or a mile, homewards, would turn back again to the place of prayer, to hear still more about the salvation of Jesus! And they often did this too, through lanes and ways and snows, that would have been deemed by persons in any other state of mind, to have been impassible. The awakening in Amsterdam had one very prominent feature, somewhat peculiar to itself, and which we deem worthy of notice: sinners were generally, very suddenly and alarmingly aroused; their convictions suddenly raised to the highest; extremely painful in their operations, and yet protracted beyond any thing witnessed in other places. Your committee would not dare to decide, whether this was owing to the constitutional habits of the subjects of the work, or whether it was exclusively owing to the sovereign working of the great God, who works as he pleases, and baffles the feebleness of human reason.

The truths which bore most heavily on the minds of sinners, in this awakening, were the awful depravity of the heart, so manifest in its unreasonable and continued rebellion against God. Their own personal guilt, and pollution; their evident danger of eternal death. Every one thought his own heart the worst, and his own case peculiarly aggravated.

Generally the first dawning of comfort, in the soul, has been through the application of precious bible truth, while reading the bible, or hearing it explained, or while in the act of secret prayer. The reality of the change, which so many profess to have experienced, becomes every day more visible, by the love and unity, and growing holiness, and increasing light, and gospel knowledge of those who have named the name of Christ.

Thus far, there have been no instances of backsliding, or apostasy. Every one who has turned toward Zion, is still progressing. In this, your committee recognize a clear evidence that the work is the Lord's! wrought by the power of the Holy Ghost! In this there is a proof of the out-pouring of God's spirit, which neither the enemies of God, or of revivals, can refute. Persons of every shade of color, and character, have become subjects of this great work, and are made one in Christ Jesus.

One hundred and sixty-three have professed the name of Christ, and been added to the church; forty-two of whom were baptized. A few have been connected with other churches, and there are, perhaps nearly fifty, who cherish a hope that they are new creatures; yet, have not ventured to make a public profession, but are still praying, and looking, and waiting, for more satisfactory evidence of the certainty of their change.

The general excitement has subsided; but still there are frequent cases of conviction occurring. God is yet in that place; they feel his influence! They acknowledge his power! They look and pray for another glorious display of his powerful working. Meetings are well attended; monthly concerts, and bible classes, signally useful. Liberality increasing; their faith is productive of gospel good works.

PRINCETOWN & DUANESBURGH.

The Lord has visited, in his mercy, this neighbourhood, and poured out his spirit upon it. Many are deeply convicted of sin; some are rejoicing in hope. About thirty have been added to the church. Gainsayers are closing their lips of folly, and sitting down in silence. God's dear people are encouraged to say: "This is our God! We have waited for him, and he will save us! This is the Lord, we have waited for him, we will be glad and rejoice in his salvation; for in this mountain, shall the hand of the Lord rest."

NEW-SCOTLAND.

Your committee have nothing to report from New-Scotland; but much to mourn over, because there is so little of the spirit or power of religion there.

ESPERANCE, BOWMAN'S CREEK, BERN, HAMILTON-UNION & WESTERLO.

In these five churches there is little to claim your notice, except coldness and deadness. In Bowman's creek, there is a little excitement, and some favorable symptoms in Westerlo; but no general attention. O that the Lord would no longer leave these parts of his vineyard, to receive his grace in vain! There have been a few added to some of these churches during the year, and to others of them, none at all!

CARLISLE.

In the church of Carlisle, every thing seems well. The pastor of that little flock returned, last September, from the meeting of the Synod at Brownville. His heart animated and enlarged; and fully resolved to give himself wholly to the labour of the Lord's vineyard; and the Lord has blessed his labours already. Very recently he has beheld ten in one family connection awakened; and two of them cherishing an hope of forgiven sin. The attention is becoming more general; prayer meetings more numerous; bible classes well attended; Sabbath schools very useful. He has admitted seventeen to the church, during the past year.

1ST. & 2D. CHURCH—ALBANY

In this ancient corner of the Lord's vineyard, there have been much care and culture. It has been pruned, and hedged, and watched, and watered with much praiseworthy pains; but alas it brings forth very little fruit; "a cluster or two on the tops of the youngest boughs." There have been thirty-seven added to the first church, and twenty-eight to the second church, during the last year.

There is no part of the church committed to your care, that needs so much your prayers, or should so much excite your sympathies, as the two churches in Albany! Let it be a distinct and never to be forgotten article in every prayer, that the Lord would return and visit that place, and make it a praise in the earth!

SCHENECTADY & UNION COLLEGE

Your committee would invite your attention, in the last place, to the city of Schenectady, and Union College, situated there. In the third week of January, 1820, there was a very sudden death in the College. A member of the Senior class, in the full vigor of life, was suddenly removed. The alarm was very great; the call was loud, and sensibly heard and felt. There were prayer-meetings held around the *bier*, which was placed in an officer's room. There, for two days, did the students resort, from feelings of sorrowing sympathy; and there, was the question often proposed, "Suppose this call of God had been directed to you, were you ready to obey it?" The *negative answer,* was often carried back to the heart, by the holy spirit, and rendered productive of genuine convictions. Many, indeed, thought it was all fright! and would soon pass over. But the Lord's ways are not the ways of man, no, not of the most sanctified of men! *A nine days wonder!* was the common name given to the student's anxious distress. But nine days only augmented their misery, multiplied their convictions, and deepened their distress. The fright! *if such must be called,* became more general. There was indeed a fright, a fear of death! But, be it remembered, it was fear of death eternal! There was a strong desire of life, but it was life eternal! There were many on the Lord's side, who believing that the spirit of the Lord was among us in his mighty operations, held prayer-meetings, and meetings for conference and personal address. Anxious meetings too, were often held. The sinner's danger and the sinner's duty, were often and closely pressed; and some, at last, began to rejoice, not that they had escaped an early grave, no! but that they had obtained an interest in him, who is the resurrection and the life; that they had received the Lord's Christ, and became the sons of God, through faith in his name. So powerful and rapid was this great work of God's grace, that in the third week of February, *eleven,* and in the first week of April *between thirty and forty* were rejoicing in hope of forgiven sin! During the time of the awakening, it was discovered, that a few of those under exercises of mind, had been so for a long time, but had concealed it, in their own hearts, until it became a common subject. Of all these, there is but *one* who seems to have been a self-deceiver, and to have deceived others. The rest are giving good reason to believe, that their change was a real change. Seventeen joined themselves to the Presbyterian church, six or seven to the Dutch church, and six or seven to the Episcopal church; and there are a few who have not yet joined themselves to any church. Several, who have been admitted to the first degree in the arts, have devoted themselves to the gospel ministry. The effect on college was visible and salutary. There seldom was a session of so much order, tranquility and industry. The subjects of the work, generally, acted on the principle, that they could not be fervent in spirit unless they were diligent in their business.

From the *college,* the *awakening* spread down into the city. And in February became very interesting. Its first appearances were among the few praying people, the females especially, who met weekly to pray.

Their hearts were drawn out to God, most entirely and ardently. A few evening lectures, at private houses, were blessed greatly. Many date their convictions from those meetings. The numbers began rapidly to increase. A private house would not hold the people. The academy room sufficed only for a few weeks; and, before it was yet believed that the spirit of the Lord was moving on the hearts of sinners, the *Presbyterian church* was scarcely large enough to accommodate the Wednesday evening lecture. The church was destitute of a stated pastor, and help was obtained as it was found most practicable. The Lord was their great help! Lectures were very much crowded; conference meetings, and meetings for prayer, and meetings for anxious sinners, were full, and solemn, and greatly blessed. Young and old, moral and profane, felt the benign influence. It was not confined to any one denomination; and be it remembered, to the glory of God's grace, that a *great unity* of feeling and action, pervaded the whole. There were scarcely any sectarian feelings, or divided views manifested, until the close of the whole work. It was a very silent, solemn, heart-felt operation; slow in progress, but blessed in result. Nearly three hundred, we trust, were hopefully converted to God. Of these, one hundred and forty-six were added to the Presbyterian church, about eleven or twelve to the Episcopalian, about one hundred and fifteen to the Dutch, and a considerable number to the Methodist church, who are generally holding on their way rejoicing. **There has not one caused of *hopeless declension* occurred in** the Presbyterian church. Three of the young converts have died! One very *tranquil*, and two very *triumphant*. The awakening had to encounter great opposition, obstinacy and prejudice, slander and ignorance, suspicions and formality! Yet, still, the Lord's work prospered; and many were added every week to those who rejoiced in God, and had hope in Christ. There were twenty-nine adults baptized.

From Schenectady, as a center, the work spread into the adjoining country. In a little region, about three miles west of the compact part of the city, the awakening broke out in May; and out of a population not exceeding one hundred and fifty, there were thirty-two hopefully converted to God in four weeks; but a little proselyte feeling killed the whole in a few days. The cotton factory too, about one mile south of the city, was blessed with a divine influence; twelve or fifteen were brought to rejoice in God there. In Watervliet too, from twenty to thirty rejoice in hope, and many others were deeply impressed; but a vital opposition to the work of grace there, was permitted to quench the spirit, and the work ceased in a single week. There are many, who, putting profession for piety, and sanctification for regeneration; the word and ordinances, for the power of God's holy spirit; *virtually deny* the doctrine of the new birth, and oppose, with all the obstinacy of ignorance, the gracious operations of the Holy Ghost; not knowing what they do.

In the city there are some who are still seeking the way to Zion, sorrowing; and some who cherish a recent hope. A few recent convictions, but no general excitement.

Your committee would observe, as one of the good effects of this awakening, that the news of God's wonderful workings in Schenectady, was made a very powerful means in promoting the awakening in Greenbush; where, they understand that about one hundred have been brought savingly to Christ. There have also, under the ministry of Mr. Nettleton, been a great work in Nassau, where about one hundred have been hopefully brought to repentance in a few weeks.

Such has been the progress, and such is the present state of the awakening within your bounds, and such is the state of all the churches under your care; so far as your committee have been able to ascertain, from the sources to which they have had access.

There are *twenty-four churches* under your care; and the spirit of the Lord has been poured out upon *twelve* of these, and upon the *College*. The additions to the churches, during the year 1820, as reported to Presbytery, amount to nearly *one thousand four hundred!* Of these there have been three hundred and twenty-four adults baptized! Surely "the Lord hath done great things for us, whereof we are glad."

3D HEAD—THE CAUSES HELPING THE PROGRESS OF THE AWAKENING.

Your committee feel disposed to detain you only a very little while, on this part of their report. But still, any tolerable degree of fidelity, will necessarily lead them into considerable detail. The first of the helping causes they would present to your notice, was *family visitation*. By this they mean, visiting a family for the express purpose of religious inquiry; in order to ascertain the religious state of the heads of the family, and the religious attainments of every member; the amount of their bible knowledge, and the manner in which they perform their religious duties: whether or not they are seeking God, and by all means pressing them to the right performance of their acknowledged duties. Another mode of visiting, which was found very advantageous among the different sections of a family, or of several *contiguous families*, was, at an appointed hour, to have a company of as many as could conveniently be gotten together, of one sex, absent from the observation of others, from the noise of their families, and the perplexities of the world: not admitting professors of religion; entering into no worldly conversation; no perplexing inquiries; no doctrinal disputes, but only into the great concern of salvation, in a manner adapted to the *capacities* and *attainments* of those present. And when every heart became solemn, and every attention fixed, then falling prostrate before God, the hearer of prayer, and praying to the point; nor afterwards entering into any worldly chat, but going thence, thinking and praying. These visits were sometimes made to male heads of families; sometimes to the female heads; sometimes to young men, or young women; sometimes to people of color, which gave an unembarrassed opportunity of *suiting an address* to the persons present. This mode had many great advantages, and was found eminently useful.

The *second cause*, was, *personal application* to every one; pressing the sinner's conscience and encouraging his speedy return, to him from whom he had revolted. And repeatedly pressing this subject, by all the motives of time and eternity.

The *third cause* was, *religious intelligence*. Telling them what God was doing for sinners in other places. Telling them what he had done for our own souls, having had compassion on us.

The *fourth cause* was, *frequent meetings* for conference, or lecture, or prayer. And through all this awakening, so far as we know anything of the matter, either from our own experience and observation, or from the account given by the subjects of the awakening, there have been a great many awakened at these extra meetings.

The *fifth cause* was, *anxious meetings*. These were meetings which sprung up out of the circumstances of the case. It was found, in many places, impossible to visit for confidential conversation, so many and so often as circumstances required. Nor was it possible to devote as much time, to serious inquirers, who might call on their minister, as they should wish, or really needed. And besides all this, it became so uncertain when ministers could be found at home, they were so often sent for to visit distressed persons, that it was on the whole thought best, to appoint a special hour, in some retired place, where no eye but God's could see them, and no ear but his could hear; and devote that time to prayer, suited to the occasion and the cases of those present; and to hold conversation with each individual on the state of their hearts. This was generally done in a *low whisper*, with each individual, while the others were left to their silent and solemn reflections. After holding conversation with the whole, individually; the meeting was closed by addressing some suitable exhortation to the whole, and again joining in prayer. Sometimes these meetings have been called conversation meetings; sometimes meetings of anxious inquiry; but generally the name of *anxious meeting* has prevailed, because the sole object and design was, to direct the anxious inquirer in the way to Zion; to resolve the doubts, to strengthen the resolutions, to remove the ignorance or the error, to point out the dangers and difficulties of the anxious soul. And above all, the helping causes of the awakening, your committee would place these meetings, when rightly conducted, in the first place; nor is there any means used, against which the grand adversary strives, with such unwearied effort. Strong proof this, that he fears their influence. Your committee have known many, who went to these meetings, merely from a motive of curiosity, and who left them burdened with a sense of sin, weeping as they went.

The *sixth cause* was, *avoiding all controversy—absolutely refusing to touch it.* From a full conviction, that the first duties of a returning sinner were repentance towards God, and faith in our Lord Jesus Christ. And in close connection with this, keeping all, as much as possible, clear of sectarian feeling; of party spirit; of proselyting conduct, endeavoring to make all feel and understand, that the *shibboleth* of any party, would prove a poor substitute for a *change of heart!* That an admission to any church, could not procure a dispensation from the necessity of the *new-birth*, or an *interest in Christ*.

The *seventh cause* was, *plain gospel preaching*. By which we mean to be understood, an exhibition of the gospel, in its plain, obvious, unsophisticated meaning. Neither veiling its glories under the covering of metaphysics, nor concealing its common sense, under scholastic dogmas. Neither polishing down its honest bluntness of expression, nor softening the rigors of its precepts or threatening; nor holding back its encouragements, invitations and promises; but honestly and always declaring the whole council of God, as we find it in the scriptures; as the power of God unto salvation, to every one that believeth. Thus preaching it in season and out of season, publicly and privately and from house to house, and from heart to heart; exhorting, persuading and entreating, by every motive influential on man. Giving to this preaching all the force of the preacher's head and heart, affections and conscience; all the moral and muscular manhood of his nature; in the church, the lecture room, the conference and prayer meeting; the domestic visit and confidential interview, under the full impression, that every hour souls are sinking down into hell, for whom the messengers of God's mercy have to render an awful account. Your committee have often witnessed the practical profit too, of giving that strength to the preaching of *four* sermons, which is often consumed on the *polish*, the *finish* of *one*.—And been fully convinced, that nothing more or less than *God's gospel*, under the influences of *God's spirit*, can convert the soul, can save the sinner; and that he who brings this gospel home to the heart and conscience in the plainest, purest form, preaches salvation best; preaching the gospel too in the order of the gospel, and in the words of the gospel; in its sweetness and its severity too, and in all the decision and conclusiveness of its logic; putting its blessing and its curse side by side, and bringing them honestly home to the sinner's heart. However unpalatable to the unregenerate, however contrary to carnal policy, it was the manner constantly pursued. Doctrine was never separated from duty, nor the sinner encouraged until he had submitted to Christ.

The *eighth cause* was, *singing of Hymns and Psalms,* storing the memory and heart with them.

And *lastly*, BIBLE READING, and PRAYER above all things. God's word gives light, makes the simple wise and converts the soul. God hears and answers prayer.

Your committee would not be understood to say, that God cannot work without means; but, that he does greatly bless his own means, for the conviction and conversion of sinners; and they are willing to be understood as saying, that he did bless the means employed during this awakening, beyond any thing they ever witnessed before.

4TH HEAD—THE CAUSES HASTENING ITS DECLINE.

1st. *Interrupting the stated means.* Your committee have known a few weeks suspension of the preached word, have such a bad effect, that months of hard labor, were not sufficient to bring things back to their former situation.

2d. *Ceasing to press sinners on the great doctrines of faith and repentance.* Sinners in a state of excitement must be followed up, the begetting sin at such a time is, endeavoring to get clear of their convictions. They must not be let alone!

3d. *Doctrinal disputation,* or theoretical discussion; any thing that had a tendency to turn the sinner's attention from the state of his heart, was exceedingly injurious. And the more important the thing was in its nature, and the nearer allied to religion, the greater influence did it have, and the greater advantage did the adversary take of it.

4th. *Badly conducted meetings*, have been found to discourage many, and to originate another cause of great injury.

5th. *Reporting that the awakening was at an end!* Christians then intermitted all their exertions, because they thought them useless; anxious sinners felt that it was then too late, and they either sunk down in a desponding state, or gave up all thoughts of the subject.

6th. *Calming the fears of awakened sinners*, by telling them that all would now be well with them, if they only held on! And O how weak and wicked was this delusion! And for that very reason how influential was it! They who told them so, were not aware how wide the distance and difference between *conviction* and *conversion* is; or they would never have told a soul, confessedly in a state of nature, not yet reconciled to God; in open, though remorseful rebellion against him; whose guilt was increasing, and whose pollution was deepening every hour; that all would now be well, if it only holds on so.

7th. *Encouraging the sinner to linger, by advising him "to wait God's time."* This takes for granted that the convicted sinner has done all his duty; has become reconciled; has submitted to God; and that God is now in fault, for not having granted acceptance and relief. This is plainly laying all the blame on God, of the sinner's obstinacy. And the unregenerate, catches at this bait of destruction, and feels that it now rests on God's delinquency; and it rests satisfied because it rests in its sins, and revels in its pollutions on God's account. These two last mentioned causes have had awfully bad effects.

8th. *Turning the attention of awakened sinners to any book besides the bible.* We have known the reading of Edwards on the Affections, though of unqualified excellence, totally discourage young Christians, and drive back again to the world, some who were under convictions. Some people can see no difference between a *babe* in Christ, and one *full grown, strong in the faith*.

9th. *Proselyting views of conversation*. In more instances than one, have we known an attempt to proselyte, put an entire stop to the awakening. Your committee would notice this, as a very influential cause, in order that it may be carefully attended to. Some good men, and many that are not good, are nevertheless, so attached to some particular sect or party, that they would rather have no awakening, than have it in a community to which they do not belong; which is a very emphatically mode of expressing a sentiment, which they would indignantly disavow when put into words; that is, that they would rather sinners should go down to hell undisturbed, than that they should go to heaven any other way, than through the door of their party! And it is somewhat strange too, to what shifts such sectarian feeling will drive men, for the justification of their own unholy views. One will ridicule the doctrine of a new birth, as a new doctrine. Another, will ridicule all Christian feeling and experience. Another, will affirm that, no man can ever know whether he is born again or not. Another, will deny the possibility of being born again at once; of any sudden change being produced on the heart. Another, will ridicule the idea, that the hope of an interest in Christ, is at all necessary to the communion of the church; and will urge sinners to come to the communion table, because that is the only place to get religion. They will laugh at *extra meetings*; speak of them with trembling tenderness, as an awful worm and canker, at the root of God's vineyard; and affirm, that if God does not permit them to ruin it, yet, still they are, at the very least, altogether useless! And some have been afraid to have their children attend them, for fear of immoral effects, who have not feared to send them to dancing schools. Nor are the meetings themselves, only spoken against, but they who hold them, are considered as fools or enthusiasts, &c. &c. These objectors have gotten a system of saint making, and they who are not sainted according to its worm-eaten forms, are sinners still; no matter how they manifest faith and holiness; no matter how they love God, or Christ, or his people. The evil influence of al this, arises from this circumstance, that sinners, who do not know the difference, will listen most readily to such men, professedly pious, as speak to them in the smoothest terms. It falls directly in, with the carnalities of their hearts, to think that sinners have got nothing to do; that they are *not much in danger*, and that those, who think differently, are fools. Your committee have had reason to weep over the baneful effects of this weak and wicked conduct.

10th. *Breaking up anxious meetings while there are any anxious souls who wish to attend them.* We have known some instances, where anxious meetings were broken up, when there were still some anxious souls; and now, at the distance of several months, we know of only very few of these that have gained relief, and the most of the others have become very cold and careless; and Christians too, were very much discouraged. In short, it evidently killed the awakenings wherever this course was pursued.

11th. *Giving anxious souls a false ground to rest upon. A speculation;* an *inference; a notion;* or anything besides *Jesus Christ, the sure, the only foundation.*

12th. *Untimely preaching.* By this, your committee mean, pressing the *deep* and *difficult doctrines* of the bible, on the attention of sinners who had scarcely realized the elementary truth, of their own alienation from God. Forcing babes in Christ, to receive strong meat, when they can scarcely bear the pure milk of the word! Your committee have known some mournful results of this folly, both among young converts and awakened sinners.

13th. *Cooling preaching.* Your committee are not sure, that they give the right name to this kind of preaching; but they will explain their meaning. They mean *speculative discussions*, at a time, when the hearts of the hearers are deeply distressed. An endeavor to persuade convicted sinners, that they ought to be very suspicious of any indications of feeling, as savoring of enthusiasm, &c. That true convictions are never accompanied with feeling, &c. Your committee, mention this kind of preaching, *emphatically,* because some good men were led to it, no doubt, from an idea that the church was in great danger of becoming enthusiastic! That those who felt it a primary duty, to press faith and repentance, almost exclusively, were too evidently zealots! That errors of every hateful name would flow in and spoil the beauty of God's husbandry; and that it now devolved on them to set all things right! The heat was too great, and needed cooling. Now, this would all be well! All right, if the head was the seat of religion; if an *enlightened understanding alone* would answer, as a substitute for a renovated heart. It would not be so very bad either, if doctrines, separated from duty, would ever lead to vital holiness of heart. Your committee feel that you are fishers of men, and, that man can never be caught by the head alone; he must be caught by the heart also, if ever caught. God's requirements are on the heart; God's residence is there, the influence of exhortation, persuasion, and entreaty is there; the motives exciting fear, love, gratitude, are operative there; the exercise of faith, repentance, submission, is there; and your committee have known more injury done in one half hour, by such an effort of misjudged benevolence, than could be repaired in a month. Your committee do not undervalue speculative discussion, nor calmness, nor caution, but let everything be done in its season, and in its due measure. A man may weep, and pray, and repent in agony, and yet, be neither *zealot* nor *enthusiast.*

14th. Your committee might mention many other things: such as, visiting, or receiving visits of ceremony, or friendship, while under conviction. Engaging in worldly conversations, or pursuits. The *ungodly lives of professors.* THE LEVITY OF THE CLERGY. And their INDOLENCE too. Their WELL-MEANT BUT MISTAKEN ZEAL against *sects and parties*; thus turning their feelings from the perishing state of those souls committed to their care; but they refrain.

And in conclusion, beg leave to notice the general character of the whole work. It was a deep heart work; free from delusions, from dreams, from visions, from new revelations. Sinners were brought to see themselves awfully ruined! Going down to hell, unable to help or extricate themselves from their miseries! Sinking under the penalty, and far from the purity of God's law; and thus shut out from every other hope, they were shut up to the faith of the gospel. They were led to see *Jesus* as the *only way* to God the father; as an able Saviour; as a very willing Saviour; as a Saviour just at hand, promising "whosoever cometh unto me, I will in no ways cast out." And they have come, renouncing all reliance on themselves and trusting wholly on the finished righteousness of Jesus the redeemer, as the only ground of acceptance with God the father. Taking him for wisdom, righteousness, sanctification and complete redemption; and resting on him, have obtained joy and peace in believing; have cherished a hope of forgiven sin; a good hope through grace. And those who cherish this hope, have generally been humbled and diffident; oppressed with a sense of unworthiness; excited by a strong desire to have others partake of the same blessings with themselves. They have uncommonly united together in Christian love. And out of a number, not much less than two thousand, who have been hopefully converted to God, of whom near *fourteen hundred,* have united themselves to the communion of your church, not more than *four* or *five,* are known to have shown conclusive signs of apostasy, now at the distance of almost a year.

> "And when God makes his jewels up,
>   And sets his starry crown;
> When all his sparkling gems shall shine,
> Proclaim'd by him, his own:
>   May they, a little band of love,
>   Be sinners, sav'd by grace;
>   From glory unto glory chang'd,
>   Beholding face to face!"

Your committee would also beg leave to notice, that from documents before them, in which they have the most implicit confidence, it appears that there has been a work of God's grace carried on in Orange county; nearly, if not altogether as extensive, as that detailed in their report; and would express their regret, that their limits will not allow, even an abridged account of it. They would, however, notice that in all its features, it is exactly like your own. That the means employed; the causes helping or hindering its progress, and the glorious results, do not differ perceptibly. In one place, *Deer-Park*, where Mr. Blain is placed, there were over sixty brought to God in three weeks; and the work was stopped in a single day, by a dispute about baptism! And they would also state, that in the counties of Otsego, Chenango, Cortland, Madison and Ontario, there has been a similar out-pouring of the spirit within the same year, and the fall of the year preceding; bringing into the family of God, more than two thousand children.

In Columbia too, and Rensselaer counties, and in many other places, the Lord's glory has been seen and his saving health experienced.

At present there is a glorious work of God's grace going on in Cherry-Valley, where nearly two hundred are rejoicing in hope. It is spreading into Springfield and Middlefield, Cooperstown, Auburn, Camillus, Onondaga, Brutus, Salt-Point, and other places. We hear too from New-Haven, from Weathersfield, North-Killingworth, city of Hartford, Newington, Farmington and several other towns in Connecticut; from Dr. Spring's church in New-York, and from Coxsackie, Catskill, Hudson, Kinderhook, Athens, Claverack and the Boght, where the Lord's Christ is conquering gloriously. Surely every heart is ready, in angelic strains, to say, "glory to God in the highest, there is peace upon earth and good will to men."

All which is most respectfully submitted.

THOMAS McAULEY,
HALSEY A. WOOD,
MARK TUCKER,
ELISHA YALE,
WALTER MONTEITH,
ELIPHALET NOTT,
Committee.

POSTSCRIPT

Your committee cannot help noticing the surprising resemblance between this work of God, and that work of his in Northampton, in 1734, under the ministry of President Edwards, whose praise is in all the churches. The history of which, we have in the 3rd vol. of his works; which history, changing names and dates, would be a tolerably good history of the late revival; and the committee would most earnestly recommend the perusal of that book to everyone. And they would beg leave, to refer to passages where the strongest points of resemblance are found. They have used the Worcester edition of 1808.

In page 15.   It will be found that worldly conversation was very rarely admitted.

——17.   The subjects were elevated in singing, and greatly devoted to that exercise.

——18.   Some people mocked; called the awakening a distemper!

——21.   Some ministers came to see! Went home; told their people all they saw; which was the occasion of an awakening with them.

——22.   All ages and sexes were subjects of the work; communions were frequent; *eighty admitted in one day.*

——24.   Several whole families were savingly converted.

——25.   Great diversity of operations on the sinner's hearts.

In page 27. Convictions increased, as the penitents drew near relief.

——29.   The enmity of the heart, unusually excited in some.

——30.   Awakened sinners, first exercised most about outward sins, afterwards, most exercised about heart sins.

——33.   Some, only a few days under conviction, some, a great while.

——38.   Some obtained comfort in reading or hearing some text of scripture, others, without any particular text occurring.

——42.   Some had great joy, some laughed, some wept for joy.

——43.   The judgment and practice of some ministers were severely blamed.

——44.   Telling of conversions, was a great mean of carrying on the work.

——50.   The renewed heart was full of *Christ,* his *grace,* his *love,* his *suitableness,* his *excellency.*

——53.   The converts made astonishing progress in doctrinal knowledge.

——55.   They were greatly afraid of a false hope; of being hypocrites; of being deceived, &c.

——57.   Often refreshed, by telling experiences to each other.

——59.   The causes of stopping the work.

In all these, there was no difference between the work in 1734, in Northampton, and in 1820 *in your* vicinity; nor was there any difference, in the *mode,* and *kind of opposition,* in the two great and wonderful works.

Page 190.   Ministers were blamed for addressing the *affections.*

——195. For preaching terror.

——200. For frightening children!

——201. Converts were blamed for talking and rejoicing.

——213. For singing so much.

——215. And children for holding meetings, &c. &c. &c.

Robert Fleming too, that *celebrated Scotch divine,* in his *book* on the *fulfilling* of the *scriptures,* as quoted by Mr. *Willison, of Dundee,* by Dr. *Owen,* by *president Edwards,* and others, as worthy of highest credit, shows us, that awakenings in Germany, in Holland, in Ireland, and in Scotland, had been very general and powerful. And we find, that those which he describes, especially in the *West of Scotland*, were exactly like those of our own day. Page 302, Art. 3, he speaks of that wonderful work of God's grace in the year 1625, every feature of which, and of the opposition it met with, and of the slanders it was assailed with, and of the effects which followed, were similar to the work before us. And again, in page 303, Article 4, he gives the account of the remarkable outpouring of God's Spirit, on the 21st June, 1630, at the *Kirk of Shots*; where, under *one Sermon*, nearly five hundred were hopefully converted to God, and they mostly continued lively and solid Christians. And he tells us too, that the preceding night, had been mostly spent in prayer, by the Christians of that place! And that the awakenings in Ireland in 1628, were very similar.

From the Evangelical Magazine of October, 1816, there has been copied into the Religious Intelligencer, vol. 2, page 469, an account of a most glorious revival in Glenlyon, in the *Highlands of Scotland*, in that year; which, in all its leading features, corresponds exactly with the awakening in Saratoga county and elsewhere.

BIBLIOGRAPHY

PRIMARY

Archives of Hartford Theological Seminary, Hartford, Connecticut

Lyman Beecher and Asahel Nettleton, *Letters of, The "New Measures" in Conducting Revivals Of Religion* (New York: G. & C. Carvill, 1828, online reprint by Quinta Press, 2008).

Lyman Beecher and Charles Beecher, *Autobiography, Correspondence, etc. of Lyman Beecher, D.D., Vol. 1 &2* (New York: Harper & Brothers, 1864).

Joseph Bellamy, *True Religion Delineated* (Ames, Iowa: International Outreach, Inc., 1997, reprint from 1750).

George Hugh Birney, Jr., *The Life and Letters of Asahel Nettleton, 1783–1844* (Thesis, Hartford Theological Seminary, 1943).

Andrew Bonar & Bennet Tyler, *Asahel Nettleton Life and Labours* (Edinburgh: Banner of Truth Trust, 1996, reprint from 1854).

Connecticut Historical Society, Hartford, Connecticut

Whitney R. Cross, *The Burned-Over District* (Ithaca: Cornell University Press, 1982).

Charles G. Finney, *The Memoirs of Charles G. Finney, The Complete Restored Text* by Garth M. Rosell & Richard A. G. Dupuis, Editors (Grand Rapids: Academie Books, 1989).

Charles G. Finney, *Lectures on Revival* (Minneapolis: Bethany House Publishers, 1988).

Frank Hugh Foster, *A Genetic History of the New England Theology* (Chicago: The University of Chicago Press, 1907).

Nahum Gale, D.D., *A Memoir of Rev. Bennet Tyler, D.D.* (Boston: J. E. Tilton and Company, 1860).

Edward D. Griffin, *The Life and Sermons of Edward D. Griffin*, Volumes 1 & 2 (Edinburgh: Banner of Truth Trust, 1987, reprint from 1839).

Charles E. Hambrick-Stowe, *Charles G. Finney and the Spirit of American Evangelicalism* (Grand Rapids: William B. Eerdmans Publishing, 1996).

Keith J. Hardman, *Charles Grandison Finney, Revivalist and Reformer* (Grand Rapids: Baker Books, 1990).

Stuart C. Henry, *Unvanquished Puritan, A Portrait of Lyman Beecher* (Grand Rapids: William B. Eerdmans, 1973).

Samuel Hopkins, *The Works of Samuel Hopkins, Volumes 1–4* (Boston: 1852, from reprint; Kessinger Publishing).

Heman Humphrey, D.D., *Revival Sketches and Manual in Two Parts* (New York: American Tract Society, 1859).

D. M. Lloyd-Jones, *The Puritans* (Edinburgh, Banner of Truth Trust, 2002).

E. A. Johnston, *George Whitefield A Definitive Biography, Volumes One and Two* (Stoke-on-Trent, England: Tentmaker Publications, 2008)

Thomas L. Lentz, *A Photographic History of Killingworth* (Killingworth, Connecticut: Killingworth Historical Society, 2004).

Sherry Pierpont May, *Asahel Nettleton: Nineteenth Century American Revivalist* (Dissertation for Drew University, Madison, New Jersey, 1969).

Iain H. Murray, *Revival & Revivalism, The Making and Marring of American Evangelicalism 1750–1858* (Edinburgh: Banner of Truth Trust, 2002).

Iain H. Murray, *The Old Evangelicalism* (Edinburgh: The Banner of Truth Trust, 2005).

Iain H. Murray, *The Invitation System* (Edinburgh: The Banner of Truth Trust, 1973).

Asahel Nettleton, *Sermons from the Second Great Awakening* (Ames, Iowa: International Outreach Inc. edited by William C. Nichols, 1995).

Asahel Nettleton, *Village Hymns for Social Worship* (Ames, Iowa: International Outreach Inc. William C. Nichols, 1997).

Edwards A. Park, *New England Theology; With Comments on a Third Article in the Princeton Review* (Andover: Warren F. Draper, 1852).

Edward Payson, *The Complete Works of Edward Payson*, Vol. 1 (Harrisonburg, VA: Sprinkle Publications, 1987).

J. Paul Reno, *Daniel Nash: Prevailing Prince of Prayer* (Asheville: Revival Literature, 1989).

Richard Owen Roberts, *An Annotated Bibliography of Revival Literature* (Wheaton: Richard Owen Roberts, Publishers, 1987).

Rev. R. Smith, *Recollections of Nettleton and the Great Revival of 1820* (Albany: E. H. Pease & Co., 1848).

Wayne Somers, *Encyclopedia of Union College History* (Schenectady: Union College Press, 2003).

William B. Sprague, D.D., *Annals of the American Pulpit*, Volume II (New York: Robert Carter & Brothers, 1859).

William B. Sprague, *Lectures on Revivals* (Edinburgh: The Banner of Truth Trust, 2007, from reprint of 1832).

Augustus Hopkins Strong, *Systematic Theology: A Compendium and Commonplace Book Designed for the Use of Theological Students 1886* (Rochester, NY: E. B. Andrews, 1886).

J. F. Thornbury, *God Sent Revival, The Story of Asahel Nettleton and the Second Great Awakening* (Welwyn, England: Evangelical Press, 1977).

Bennet Tyler, *Memoir of the Life and Character of Asahel Nettleton* (Boston: Doctrinal Tract and Book Society, 1858).

Bennet Tyler, *Remains of the late Asahel Nettleton, D.D.* (Weston Rhyn: online reprint by Quinta Press, 2008).

Bennet Tyler, *New England Revivals* (Wheaton: Richard Owen Roberts Publishers, 1980, from reprint of 1846).

Francis Wayland and H. L. Wayland, *A Memoir of the Life and Labors of Francis Wayland, D.D., LL.D.*, Volumes I & II (New York: Sheldon and Company, 1867).

William R. Weeks, D.D., *The Pilgrim's Progress in the Nineteenth Century* (New York: M. W. Dodd, Brick Church Chapel, 1849).

SECONDARY

Curt Daniel, *The History and Theology of Calvinism* (Springfield: Good Books, 2003).

Timothy Dwight, *Theology Explained & Defended*, Volumes 1–4 (Birmingham: Solid Ground Christian Books, 2005, reprint from 1850).

Lewis A. Drummond, *The Life and Ministry of Charles G. Finney* (Minneapolis: Bethany House Publishers, 1985).

Charles G. Finney, *Finney's Systematic Theology* (Minneapolis: Bethany House Publishers, 1976).

Charles G. Finney, *How to Experience Revival* (Springdale: Whitaker House, 1984).

Charles G. Finney, *So Great Salvation* (Grand Rapids: Kregel Publications, 1965).

Charles G. Finney, *The Guilt of Sin* (Grand Rapids: Kregel Publications, 1965).

Charles G. Finney, *True Submission* (Grand Rapids: Kregel Publications, 1965).

Charles G. Finney, *Victory Over the World* (Grand Rapids: Kregel Publications, 1965).

John H. Gerstner, *Jonathan Edwards: A Mini-Theology* (Wheaton: Tyndale House Publishers, 1987).

John L. Gresham, Jr., *Charles G. Finney's Doctrine of the Baptism of the Holy Spirit* (Peabody: Hendrickson Publishers, 1987).

Donald M. Lewis, Editor, *Dictionary of Evangelical Biography 1730–1860, Volumes One and Two* (Peabody: Hendrickson Publishers, 2004).

Michael McClymond, *Encyclopedia of Religious Revivals in America, Vol. One* (Westport, Connecticut: Greenwood Press, 2007).

Basil Miller, *Charles Finney, The evangelist who sparked one of America's greatest revivals!* (Minneapolis: Bethany House Publishers, 1942).

Samuel H. Miller, *The Dilemma of Modern Belief, The Lyman Beecher Lectures* (New York: Harper & Row, 1963).

Iain H. Murray, *Jonathan Edwards A New Biography* (Edinburgh: The Banner of Truth Trust, 2000).

Iain H. Murray, *D. Martyn Lloyd-Jones Authorised Biography, Vol. 2* (Edinburgh: The Banner of Truth Trust, 1990).

Timothy L. Smith, *Revivalism and Social Reform in Mid-19th-Century America* (New York: Abingdon Press, 1955).

William B. Sprague, D.D., *Annals of the American Pulpit, Volume I* (New York: Robert Carter & Brothers, 1859).

Robert Steel, *Burning and Shining Lights* (New York: T. Nelson and Sons, 1864).

J. B. Waterbury, *Sketches of Eloquent Preachers* (New York: American Tract Society, 1864).

INDEX OF NAMES

INDEX OF PLACES

INDEX OF SUBJECTS

CPSIA information can be obtained at www.ICGtesting.com
Printed in the USA
BVOW071040121112

304983BV00002B/1/P